THE PRESS AND THE PRESIDENCY

Books by John Tebbel in the Field of Communications

The Press and the Presidency (with Sarah Miles Watts)

The Media in America

A History of Book Publishing in the United States (Vols. I-IV)

The American Magazine: A Compact History

A Compact History of the American Newspaper

Makers of Modern Journalism (with Kenneth N. Stewart)

The Life and Good Times of William Randolph Hearst

George Horace Lorimer and The Saturday Evening Post

An American Dynasty

The Marshall Fields

Paperback Books: A Pocket History

Open Letter to Newspaper Readers

THE PRESS and THE PRESIDENCY

From George Washington to Ronald Reagan

John William, 1912- Tebbel

Sarah Miles Watts

New York   Oxford
OXFORD UNIVERSITY PRESS
1985

Oxford University Press

Oxford   New York   Toronto
Delhi   Bombay   Calcutta   Madras   Karachi
Kuala Lumpur   Singapore   Hong Kong   Tokyo
Nairobi   Dar es Salaam   Cape Town
Melbourne   Auckland

and associated companies in
Beirut   Berlin   Ibadan   Mexico City   Nicosia

Copyright © 1985 by John Tebbel and Sarah Miles Watts

Published by Oxford University Press, Inc.,
200 Madison Avenue, New York, New York 10016

Library of Congress Cataloging in Publication Data
Tebbel, John William.
   The press and the presidency.
   Bibliography: p.
   Includes index.
   1. Presidents—United States—History.
2. Press and politics—United States—History.
3. United States—politics and government.
I. Watts, Sarah Miles.   II. Title.
E176.1.T37   1985   353.03′5   85-4887
ISBN 0-19-503628-X

Printing (last digit): 9 8 7 6 5 4 3 2 1

Printed in the United States of America

Preface

One of the paradoxes of these paradoxical times is the fact that while "the media" and "the press" are perennial subjects of controversy and daily comment by the population at large, there is little written about them for the general reader. With a handful of exceptions, the literature consists of the highly partisan views of columnists and politicians and the scholarly work of political scientists, sociologists, and others engaged in media studies.

What is lacking in most of what has been written is the historical viewpoint. Until this volume, for instance, there has been only one full-length study of the presidents and the press, beginning with George Washington. That was James Pollard's *The Presidents and the Press,* first issued in 1947, which carried the story through Franklin Roosevelt (a paperback supplement ended with Truman). Everyone who works in this field must be grateful to Pollard for his pioneering study, and we acknowledge our debt to him.

In this volume, however, we have intended to go considerably beyond what Pollard did and write a history that would explore in depth the shifting relationship between press and government from the beginning to the present. While Pollard's work was divided into discrete chapters, this book is written as narrative history, a form long unfashionable but now reviving somewhat as a legitimate approach.

While the book is intended for a general audience, we have appended a list of sources for those requiring it. We have not neglected the immense body of scholarly work that has been done on the presidents, including the most recent studies. But in addition we have explored contemporary letters and diaries and the non-scholarly books about events written by reporters and editors who were on the scene. The latter have been used with due regard for possible bias and faulty recollection.

If we define historical writing as "critical thinking about the past," as some have done, interpretation and a point of view become inevitable. Thus, in this volume, we have treated the history of president-press relationships as a continuing narrative, in which both institutions have changed considerably, yet in many respects have remained the same. We have attempted to show the vital importance of the First Amendment foundation upon which the whole structure rests and how it has fared from Washington's day to our own. The book is consequently both a study of the presidency itself, including the personalities of the presidents, and a study of the changing character of the press.

The viewpoint of the book, reduced to its simplest terms, is that the presidency has evolved into an imperialistic institution which is now capable of manipulating and controlling the media, and through them the public, in ways beyond the vision of the Founding Fathers. Government is now, consequently, in a position to exert the controls that the architects of the Bill of Rights, and particularly the First Amendment, expressly sought to prevent. Moreover, it may well be able to nullify the First, in a relatively short time and with public support. In the terms of Presidents Nixon and Reagan, we have already felt the first effects of that power.

By providing a view of the past which tells us how we have come to that point, we hope we will give some readers, at least, an understanding of what we may expect in the future and equip them with the kind of information which, as James Madison believed, is the way to make democracy work—that is, information pointing the way toward controlling the power of government and thus preserving the freedom of the governed.

John Tebbel
Sarah Miles Watts

Southbury, Conn.
Brockport, N.Y.
June 1985

Contents

THE PRESS AND THE PRESIDENCY

PART ONE

Foundations

Washington and the Federal Presidency

In the shifting relationship between the press and the presidency over nearly two centuries, there has remained one primary constant—the dissatisfaction of one with the other. No president has escaped press criticism, and no president has considered himself fairly treated. The record of every administration has been the same, beginning with mutual protestations of good will, ending with recriminations and mistrust.

This is the the best proof we could have that the American concept of a free press in a free society is a viable idea, whatever defects the media may have. While the Founding Fathers and their constituencies did not always agree on the role the press should play, there was a basic consensus that the newspaper (the only medium of consequence at the time) should be the buffer state between the rulers and the ruled. The press could be expected to behave like a watchdog, and government at every level, dependent for its existence on the opinions of those it governed, could expect to resent being watched and having its shortcomings, real or imaginary, exposed to the public view.

Reduced to such simple terms, the relationship of the presidents to the press since George Washington's first term is understandable only as an underlying principle. But this basic concept has been increasingly complicated by the changing nature of the presidency, by the individual nature of presidents, by the rise of other media, especially television, and by the growing complexity of beliefs about the function of both press and government.

In surveying nearly two centuries of this relationship, it is wise to keep in mind an axiom of professional historians—that we should be careful not to view the past in terms of our own times, and make judgments accordingly. Certain parallels often become obvious, to be sure, but to assert what an individual president should or should not have done, by present standards, is to violate historical context. Historians occasionally castigate each other for this failing, and in the case of press and government, the danger becomes particularly great because the

3

words themselves—"press" and "government," even "presidency"—have changed in meaning so much during the past two hundred years.

Recent scholarship, for example, has emphasized that colonial Americans believed in a free press, but not at all in the sense that we understand it today. Basic to their belief was the understanding, which had prevailed since the invention of the printing press in the fifteenth century, that whoever controlled the printing press was in the best position to control the minds of men. The press was seen at once as an unprecedented instrument of power, and the struggle to control it began almost as soon as the Gutenberg (or Mazarin) Bible appeared at Mainz in 1456, an event which meant that, for the first time, books could be reproduced exactly and, more important, that they could be printed in quantity.

Two primary centers of social and political power—the state and the church—stood to benefit most from the invention of the printing press. In the beginning it was mutually advantageous for them to work together; consequently it was no accident that the first printing press on the North American continent was set up in Mexico City in 1539 by Fray Juan Zumárraga, first Catholic bishop of that country. It gave the church an unprecedented means of advancing conversion, along with the possibility of consolidating and extending its power, thus providing Catholic Spain with the same territorial advantages that would soon be extended elsewhere in the Americas.

When British colonies were established in North America during the early part of the seventeenth century, it was once again a religious faith, this time Protestant, that brought the first printing press to what is now the United States. But while colonial printing in Central and South America remained the province of the Catholics for some time and was used primarily for religious purposes, in North America secular publishing became an adjunct of a church-dominated press almost at once and was soon dominant.

It is part of American mythology that the nation was "cradled in liberty" and that the colonists, seeking religious freedom, immediately established a free society, but the facts are quite different. The danger of an uncontrolled press to those in power was well expressed by Sir William Berkeley, governor of Virginia, when he wrote home to his superiors in 1671: "I thank God there are no free schools nor printing, and I hope we shall not have these hundred years; for learning has brought disobedience, and heresy, and sects into the world, and printing has divulged them, and libels against the best government, God keep us from both." There are those in twentieth-century America who would say "Amen" to Berkeley's view of printing and "libels against the best government."

At home in England the danger was also well understood by those who controlled the colonies. After he ascended the throne in 1685, King James II sent these instructions to his governor in the colony of New York, Thomas Dongan: "And for as much a great inconvenience may arise by the liberty of printing within our province of New York, you are to provide by all necessary orders that noe person keep any press for printing, nor that any book, pamphlet or other matters whatsoever bee printed without your special leave & license first obtained.'' This paragraph was retained in instructions to royal governors for the next forty years.

There was no conception of a ''free press'' in the mind of the Reverend Jose Glover, the man who was first charged with bringing a press to America in 1638. He was merely a pious instrument in the hands of pious men, English Puritans who were struggling against the censorship imposed by the Crown. In his relentless drive in England to purge the Anglican faith of all nonconformist elements, Archbishop William Laud not only had succeeded in dissolving some of the Puritan churches in Holland, where the English Puritan ministers were getting their works printed, but he had made life so difficult for Dutch printers that their Bible exports to England virtually stopped. As a consequence, those who had already fled from High Church oppression to the Massachusetts Bay Colony were in a position to form a new center for producing Puritan tracts, which would then be smuggled into England as they had been from the Netherlands. The church was also well aware that in the New World a printing press would be a most useful tool for propagation of the faith, as it had been for the Catholics in Mexico.

In the colonies control of the press eventually passed from church to state, as it did elsewhere, but when the inhabitants began to urge its freedom early in the eighteenth century, they did not understand ''freedom'' as we do today—or at least as it is understood by American libertarians. When John Adams declared in 1765, in his *Dissertation on the Canon and Feudal Law,* that he knew of no ''means of information . . . more sacred . . . than . . . [a free] press,'' he did not mean it in twentieth-century terms. Adams and others of his time saw press freedom as the essential weapon required in their power struggle against the Crown.

So well was this lesson learned before the Revolution that ten of the first thirteen states included a free press provision in their constitutions, and when the federal Constitution was drawn up, the failure of the delegates to include a similar clause, along with other basic freedoms, ignited a grassroots revolt that ended in the enactment of our Bill of Rights, in which Congress deliberately placed freedom of the press and religion as the First Amendment.

In practice, however, what the colonial people meant by ''freedom of the press'' was the freedom to express their own beliefs as against those who were loyal to the Crown. They saw nothing wrong, consequently, in suppressing opposite opinions. When John Mein's Boston *Chronicle* offended them with what they called Tory propaganda, a patriot mob attacked and beat the publisher so badly that he felt compelled to flee from the colony. When the flamboyant James Rivington's New York *Gazetteer* fought the rising tide of patriotism there, these same believers in the sacredness of a free press closed his shop and drove him out. (He returned, however, during the British occupation as the scourge of the Revolution and its leaders.)

There were many other such examples in pre-Revolutionary America, and, in fact, instances of violent censorship by the mob persisted through the Civil War and are not unknown in our own times. Those who promoted and sanctioned such actions believed they were making a distinction between liberty and license. In approving a boycott of Rivington, the Committee of Inspection in Newport, Rhode Island, set forth this distinction clearly. Asserting that it was the duty of "every friend of Civil Government" to protect and encourage a free press as long as it was employed in promoting "beneficial purposes," the committee then outlined a vital qualification:

> But when, instead thereof, a Press is incessantly employed and prostituted to the vilest uses; in publishing the most infamous falsehoods; in partial or false representation of facts; in fomenting jealousies, and exciting discord and disunion among the people; in supporting and applauding the worst of men, and worst of measures; and in vilifying and calumniating the best of characters, and the best of causes; it then behooves every citizen . . . to discountenance and discourage every such licentious, illiberal, prostituted Press.

This is more or less the philosophy of many Americans in our own time, and quite probably the inner belief of many presidents—that freedom of the press must be maintained unless it attacks us with what we think are lies, whether in fact they are or not. What is the "best of characters, and the best of causes" to one political party or set of activists may be the work of scoundrels to another. Often, too, it has taken the press, "exciting discord and disunion among the people," to depose those advertising their characters and causes as "best."

Put more succinctly, perhaps, by William Livingston in his essay, "Of the Use, Abuse and Liberty of the Press," which first appeared in the *New York Independent Reflector* in 1753, freedom of the press meant to the colonists, the men of the Revolution, and many of those who came after, "a Liberty of promoting the common Good of Society, and of publishing any Thing else not repugnant thereto." If the press was "prejudicial to the public Weal," said Livingston, "it is abused," and he added that "if . . . we suppose any broader Foundation for the Liberty of the Press, it will become more destructive of public Peace, than if it were wholly shut up."

If these early patriots were inconsistent in their beliefs, as seems so obvious now, they were not so within the ideological framework of their time. Few shared with Thomas Jefferson and James Madison the absolutist view of a free press that we call "strict constructionism" in the First Amendment debates of today. Jefferson's conviction that the First meant exactly what it said when it asserted that Congress must make *"no law"* restricting freedom of speech or the press, found little agreement among his contemporaries, no more than it does today. Colonial people, in fact, viewed the press as little more than a potent means of combating what they saw as excesses of power by those who governed them, and as a means of unifying people around the cause of freedom from these governors as the Revolution approached. In the years before the war the press had been chiefly valuable as a pamphleteering, propagandizing mechanism to unite the patriots behind a cause.

The concept of a free and *impartial* press lay far in the future. Those printers who issued newspapers were in the service of either Tory or patriot factions (mostly the latter), or they were political entrepreneurs in their own right. In any case, newspapers were not usually their chief business. Their presses turned out books and magazines as well from the same shop, and in the front of the building they sold these printed products along with a range of other items that made them the forerunners of the modern drugstore.

More important, however, the offices of these early printers were often intellectual centers, the breeding ground for growing rebellion against the Crown. In the case of the Boston Tea Party, the Boston *Gazette* provided at least one changing room for those activists who put on war-paint and feather disguise to dump tea in the harbor. Later, in reporting the war, the newspapers of the day made no pretense at coverage in the modern sense. Although they did print whatever news was available, they were primarily propaganda organs for one side or the other, and little of what they printed could be considered factually accurate.

When we talk about the "press" that awaited the first president, we are speaking of an institution that was only beginning to find a place for itself in American life. The end of the Revolution itself created a period of transition, during which many of the newspapers that had led the charge and helped sustain the war collapsed and died, their real purpose gone. In the decade before George Washington was elected as first president, others rushed to take their places. More than 60 new papers were started during the mid-1780s, and this growth continued for another decade; between 1783 and 1801, about 450 papers began publishing. Most failed to survive, but others flourished and a few attained a measure of brilliance. At the end of the century, however, only a dozen or so of the newspapers that had been important during the Revolution remained.

Growth did not mean a radical change in character. The press of Washington's two administrations was as partisan as it had ever been, and even went on to new excesses in the great struggle between the Federalists and Anti-Federalists, which divided citizens more thoroughly and bitterly than George III had done. Two major changes did occur, however. Where newspapers had been regarded earlier as only one of a printer's products in his efforts to make a living, now they were more often established to represent political parties and advance causes. That meant a change in their management. Now they were no longer the product of some printer but the work of an editor, a man who, for the first time, stood between the printer, whose work was merely mechanical, and the party men who supplied the money and the point of view, which the editor expressed well or badly, according to his capabilities. In that sense, the modern newspaper had been born.

II

When George Washington assumed the presidency, he brought with him a view of the press that could be expected from a Virginia Tidewater conservative and, in addition, a more personal antipathy derived from his experience as General of the Army. During his brief political career in the Virginia House of Burgesses he had regarded with satisfaction those newspapers that supported him, and with mild disapproval those that did not.

During the Revolution, however, Washington had been given far more reason to dislike the press. It was not entirely personal, by any means. In common with his field commanders, he deplored the carelessness of newspapers in printing information that would be useful to the British. In May of 1777, for instance, he complained to the president of Congress, "It is much to be wished that our printers were more discreet in many of their Publications. We see almost in every Paper, Proclamations or accounts transmitted by the Enemy, of an injurious nature. If some hint or caution could be given them on the Subject, it might be of Material Service."

The government did nothing, and there was little it *could* have done in its unstable condition, beset by far more serious problems and struggling against its own weakness. Washington consoled himself by having his aides carefully scrutinize the Tory press, which was equally as careless about valuable information and was frequently just as helpful to the patriots. The general also relied on patriot newspapers for news of what was occurring elsewhere, and he used the press adroitly to publicize court martial cases as object lessons to his frequently disgruntled troops.

Washington's feelings about the press in general when he came to the presidency were largely the result of the abuse he took from opposition newspapers, which had begun during the Revolution. He was particularly incensed during the war by James ("Jemmy") Rivington's New York *Gazetteer*, which was considered by the publisher's rival, Isaiah Thomas of Worcester, as an admirable publication even though it was on the other side. Thomas, the best of colonial printers and publishers, had little reason to love Rivington for any reason, yet wrote of him that "few men, perhaps, were better qualified . . . to publish a newspaper," and of his *Gazetteer* declared flatly, "No newspaper in the colonies was better printed, or was more copiously furnished with foreign intelligence." Yet this was the paper that did not hesitate to print the most scurrilous forgeries involving Washington, was ready to spread any kind of rumor that might damage the Continentals, and repeated every piece of gossip that came to hand.

General Washington was horrified by Rivington and his paper, and he was particularly sensitive to the editor's ridicule, an art at which Jemmy was a master. In the *Gazetteer* of August 6, 1780, Rivington wrote: "Our old acquaintance Mr. Washington we learn is approaching us Polyphemus-like, with hasty and ample strides, his dire intents (supported by myriads of heroes and in his train a thirteen-inch mortar drawn by eight charming lively oxen) are given out to be another coup upon Powles Hook." In one sense, however, Washington had the last word in the Revolutionary war of words. He gave his two-sentence dispatch reporting the surrender at Yorktown as an exclusive to the Philadelphia *Freeman's Journal*.

As president, Washington understood that newspapers represented a valuable means of communicating with his constituents, as they would always be for occupants of the highest office, but there were two obstacles. Not all of the voters could read, by any means, and the circulations of the papers were not large. Their combined subscribers numbered about forty thousand, but the readership was considerably higher since every copy was read by several people, a total impossible to determine exactly. One advantage was that those who did read the papers absorbed them carefully, down to the last advertisement. Americans had acquired the newspaper-reading habit during the Revolution to an extent unknown before, and their interest did not diminish in the turbulent days ahead.

One of the most devoted readers was Washington himself, and, as a result of his war experiences, he came into office well aware of what he could expect from a partisan press. It was as though he expected a hundred Rivingtons might be waiting for him, which was not far from the truth, but, on the other hand, he was human enough to believe that the adulation showered on him as war leader and as the first elected president, of a kind not seen before in public life, might silence most of his critics.

At the beginning of his first term Washington subscribed to at least five newspapers and three magazines, a number that steadily increased to about thirty as time went on. Stephen Decatur, Jr., described him as "an omnivorous newspaper reader, as he was anxious to keep in touch with public opinion, and for a time subscribed to all papers regardless of their political prejudices." Later, when Washington refused to subscribe to the journals that attacked him most virulently, he nevertheless contrived to get copies of them to read.

A man given to gloomy notions of himself and his future, Washington characteristically viewed his presidency as a duty fraught with peril. He had been elected unanimously (the only president ever to enjoy that distinction), but he was still able to write to Edward Rutledge shortly after he took office: "I fear, if the issue of public measures should not correspond with their [the people's] sanguine expectations, they will turn the extravagant (and I may say undue) praises which they are heaping upon me at this moment, into equally extravagant (that I will fondly hope unmerited) censures."

Washington's premonition was correct beyond his worst fears, for the press was now embarking upon what some historians of the media have called the "Dark Ages of Journalism." The great struggle between Federalists and Republicans needs no rehearsal here, but it is not an exaggeration to say that the rise of the two-party system which it signaled had the most profound influence on the relationship between the press and the presidency, although the nature of that influence changed radically with time.

From the beginning, and until about 1835, the press was a tool of these two contending philosophies in a struggle for power that not only shaped party politics as an institution in America but resulted in the rise of an entirely different kind of press. It was not until the arrival of James Gordon Bennett, Sr., and his New York *Herald* in 1835, that the press began to be controlled by powerful individuals rather than parties, in a manner that had not existed before except in a limited way.

Ironically Washington, the idol of the nation, and Jefferson, the prime architect and unyielding upholder of press freedom, suffered most from a press that was now free to publish anything short of libel (a law not often invoked by politicians in those days). They were fated to rehearse nearly all the problems that were to plague the relationship between press and president from that time onward to our own. For Washington, it was particularly difficult to be so enmeshed because it had been his policy from the beginning to hold aloof from

direct contact with the press as much as possible. But the press would have none
of it. There has never been a time in journalistic history when newspapers were
so noisily partisan, so utterly unrestrained in their language. There was not even
the pretense of objectivity; newspapers were either under the direct control of
party politicians or were totally committed to one side of the argument.

As has occurred in nearly every administration since then, there was a short
honeymoon between president and press during Washington's first term—longer
in the Great Man's case because of the extraordinary universal admiration in
which he was held. Washington contributed to this climate by taking unusual
pains to remove himself from possible criticism, as he did when he refused a
federal judgeship to his nephew Bushrod Washington, because he did not want to
be accused of nepotism. But the number of newspapers was steadily increasing,
rising with the tide of conflict between Washington's Federalists and Jefferson's
Republicans. It was inevitable that the president would not be spared for long.

As Allan Nevins pointed out long ago, a primary reason for the conflict that
now arose between press and president was the fact that no clear line existed
between the editor and the pamphleteer. Indeed editors were often pamphleteers,
including some of the greatest of them—Daniel Defoe, Benjamin Franklin, and
later William Cobbett. Consequently the important papers in the time of Washington and Jefferson, published in Boston, New York, and Philadelphia, were
more propaganda organs than newspapers.

Physically they were shabby products, small and badly printed on sheets
folded over once. While they contained a token quantity of news and advertising,
their main reason for being was their editorials, often long and constituting in
themselves a continuous political pamphlet, carrying on the same arguments
from day to day. A few were written by the editors, but in the beginning, before
the rise to some semblance of power by this new breed, the editorials were
written by politicians who disguised themselves under such grandiose classical
pseudonyms as "Cato," "Agricola," or "Publicola."

It was this kind of paper, coming to full flower in Washington's first administration, that so poisoned the climate of those critical first years of the presidency. For Washington, it was doubly frustrating to know that two members of
his own cabinet—Alexander Hamilton and Thomas Jefferson—bore the responsibility for establishing scurrilously contentious papers, which the others copied.

In the journalistic combat, it appeared at first that Hamilton might have the ·
better of it. The *Gazette of the United States,* which he established in 1789 as the
more or less official Federalist organ, had the benefit of the treasury secretary's
support. He and his influential friends had put up the money to start it, with more
to be provided if required, and they contributed their considerable writing talents. That was fortunate, because Hamilton had erred in his handpicked editor.
John Fenno, a Bostonian who had kept Gen. Artemas Ward's orderly book during the Revolution, had been an unsuccessful tradesman and a mediocre printer
before Hamilton hired him. It did not matter, in the circumstances, that he was
only an indifferent writer, and Hamilton saw to it that his paper got regular
transfusions of government printing contracts.

Jefferson, on the other hand, denied any connection with the *National Gazette,* the chief organ of the Republicans, but there is no reason to doubt Hamilton's charge in a letter to Washington at the height of his famous quarrel with the secretary of state: "I cannot doubt from the evidence I possess, that the *National Gazette* was instituted by him [Jefferson] for political purposes, and that one leading object of it has been to render me, and all the measures connected with my department, as odious as possible." Defending himself to Washington, Jefferson asserted: "As to the merits or demerits of [the] paper, they certainly concern me not. He [Philip Freneau, the editor] and Fenno are rivals for the public favor. The one courts them by flattery, the other by censure, & I believe it will be admitted that the one has been as servile, as the other severe." Jefferson went on to tell the president what he thought the role of newspapers should be in a democracy:

No government ought to be without censors, & where the press is free, no one ever will. If virtuous, it need not fear the fair operation of attack & defence. Nature has given to man no other means of sifting out the truth either in religion, law, or politics. I think it as honorable to the government neither to know, nor notice, it's [*sic*] sycophants or censors, as it would be undignified & criminal to pamper the former & persecute the latter.

While there is no doubt that Jefferson believed these words, it is also true that, inexplicably, he attempted to escape his responsibility for the paper. The evidence is clear that Jefferson and James Madison negotiated with Freneau to come down to Philadelphia from New York and start a national paper, after Jefferson had failed to persuade Benjamin Franklin Bache, proprietor of the Philadelphia *General Advertiser,* to make a national organ out of his paper. Part of the offer to Freneau was a job for him in the State Department, where he would have access to pertinent information in addition to the advertising that the secretary could throw his way. Pressed to explain why he had made Freneau a $250-a-year translator, Jefferson simply declared that the editor was "a man of genius," as in fact he was, and he had been glad to help this genius as he had helped other such men. Among his other notable attributes, Jefferson was the master of the equivocal statement, of which this is a splendid example. Later on, Freneau himself signed an affidavit denying that Jefferson had ever had anything to do with the *Gazette,* but near the end of his life he swore to the opposite, at the time citing Jefferson as the author of some of the paper's most violent pieces and producing a marked file to prove it.

It is difficult to understand why Jefferson was so anxious to disavow his connection with the *National Gazette,* particularly when Hamilton made no secret of his own sponsorship of the rival paper. Certainly there was nothing to be ashamed of in the paper itself. It stood well above nearly all the others of its time, not only because Jefferson and his friends wrote for it but because Freneau, a fine writer himself—he was America's first lyric poet of consequence—was also an excellent editor, far superior to John Fenno.

Washington was driven almost frantic by the brilliant, slashing attacks that came from Freneau's pen, which seemed to exist apart from the more sober, well-disguised Jeffersonian contributions. At the same time he held no particular brief for the means Fenno chose to defend him in the Federalist paper, especially on one occasion when the editor attacked the president's old and much admired friend Benjamin Franklin. As far as Washington was concerned, it was a case of calling down a plague on both houses, as he wrote to his friend Edmund Pendleton: "We have some infamous Papers calculated for disturbing if not absolutely intended to disturb, the peace of the community."

Disturbing the peace. That was the key to Washington's complaint about the press. Whether it attacked or defended him, the result was a further polarization of the nation he had believed he could unite by the sheer force of his reputation and sincerity. To find himself increasingly at the center of an unrestrained political battle violated his concept of both himself and the office he held.

Yet Washington was certainly not above using the press whenever it was possible. He was a firm believer in what came to be called "managed news" in John F. Kennedy's administration—that is, manipulating the media whenever and wherever it was feasible. On the other hand, Washington believed as a broad principle that the press had a duty to keep the public informed, and he shared Jefferson's deep conviction that only an informed electorate could make a democracy function successfully. Consequently he was against direct government censorship except in time of war, nor did he advocate indirect censorship through postal regulations or taxation. Nevertheless, in common with most, if not all, later presidents, he believed that there were some matters which were the business of government and others that should not be published if they hurt the image of the United States abroad.

What concerned Washington most about the role of the press in the developing quarrel between Hamilton and Jefferson, who used their newspapers as assault weapons, was his fear that the violent language and wild charges on both sides would divide the new nation irrevocably. Characteristically, Washington strove in his own mind for some kind of balance. "From the complexion of some of our Newspapers," he wrote to Gouverneur Morris in Paris, in 1792, "foreigners would be led to believe that inveterate political dissensions existed among us, and that we are on the very verge of disunion; but the fact is otherwise. . . . These kind of representations is an evil wch. must be placed in opposition to the infinite benefits resulting from a free Press."

To Stephen Decatur, after the *National Gazette* had focused its attack on the president himself, Washington was less sanguine. "These articles," he wrote, "tend to produce a separation of the Union, the most dreadful of calamities; and whatever tends to produce anarchy, tends, of course, to produce a resort to monarchical government." The articles, signed "Veritas," accused the president of various kinds of duplicity—notably in his handling of the neutrality proclamation—and repeated the Republicans' propaganda line that he behaved like a hereditary ruler, warning that he ought to beware of his "court satellites" who were deceiving him.

More than once such attacks sent Washington into a fit of temper that he found hard to control. Jefferson faithfully recorded two of those occasions in his diary. In the president's office one day, Jefferson and Washington were discussing

Freneau. Washington "adverted to a piece in Freneau's paper of yesterday." Jefferson reported:

> He [Washington] said he despised all their attacks on him personally, but there never had been an act of the government . . . which that paper had not abused. . . . He was evidently sore & warm, and I took his intention to be that I should interpose in some way with Freneau, perhaps withdraw his appointment of translating clerk to my office. But I will not do it. His paper has saved our constitution which was galloping fast into monarchy, & has been checked by no means so powerfully as by that paper.

Three months later, when Gen. Henry Knox, talking with the president and Jefferson, mentioned a lampoon in the *National Gazette* titled "The Funeral of George W———n and James W———n," the president's outburst was more spectacular. "The President was much inflamed," the secretary dutifully recorded in his diary,

> got into one of those passions when he cannot command himself, ran on much on the personal abuse which had been bestowed on him, defied any man on earth to produce one single act of his since he had been in the govmt which was not done on the purest motives, that he had never repented but once the having slipped the moment of resigning his office, & that was every moment since, that *by god* he had rather be in his grave than in his present situation. That he had rather be on his farm than to be made *emperor of the world* and yet they were charging him with wanting to be king. That that *rascal Freneau* sent him 3 of his papers every day, as if he thought he would become the distributor of his papers, that he could see in this nothing but an impudent design to insult him. He ended in this high tone.

Washington's outrage is understandable when one considers the venomous character of the attacks in the Republican press. Even more than Freneau's, the assaults made on him by Benjamin Franklin Bache, Franklin's grandson, stung Washington to the point of fury. Bache was only twenty-one when he began his paper, the Philadelphia *General Advertiser,* in 1790. His youth and ancestry made him known familiarly, if not always affectionately, as "Lightning Rod Junior," and his paper was popularly known as the *Aurora.* Where Freneau had brightened the pages of the *National Gazette* with his graceful poems, skits, dialogues, and epigrams, Bache contributed to the journalistic scene not only the first full account of proceedings in Congress, at painstaking length, but also a virulent campaign against Washington and the Federalists, couched in his slashing, brilliant, unrestrained prose style. Among other things Bache accused the president of overdrawing his salary and professed to regard most of his acts as unconstitutional. He also reprinted forged and long-since discredited letters of Washington, which the British had used in Rivington's paper in 1777.

Before Freneau and Bache had even appeared on the scene, however, Washington was smarting from the blows of Thomas Greenleaf's influential *New-York Journal.* Greenleaf, a Tammany sachem and friend of Aaron Burr, had been one of the earlier "patriot printers," going into business in 1774 at the age of nineteen. His *Journal* slurred Washington more indirectly, but it was outspoken about such new institutions as the State Department, decrying its size and expense. "Has America ever realized any substantial advantage from foreign ministers?" Greenleaf inquired rhetorically on September 17, 1790. Other cabinet members were regularly upbraided. Henry Knox, the stout, eminently respectable secretary of war, was not only treated bluntly and sarcastically for the treaty he signed with the Creek Indians, but in the issue for October 1 Greenleaf characterized the large regular army he advocated as one that would be composed of "disciplined ruffians."

The cries of Greenleaf and other Anti-Federalist New York editors followed Washington to Philadelphia when the government moved there from New York, and he was no more than settled down before Freneau and Bache were giving him his worst treatment yet. There were few committed Federalist editors in Philadelphia, so Washington could expect no support. His chief supporter in the press remained John Fenno, in New York, who brought Jefferson under attack at one of his weak points. Using letters from an otherwise anonymous contributor calling himself "T.L.," Fenno charged directly that "the editor of the *National Gazette* [Freneau] receives a salary from government." A little later, in the *Gazette of the United States* for August 4, 1792, another contributor, disguised as "An American," declared that Jefferson had attempted "an experiment somewhat new in the history of political maneuvers in the history of this country—a newspaper instituted by a public officer, and the editor of it regularly pensioned with the public money in the disposal of that officer." It was this charge which drew Freneau's affidavit, eventually repudiated, that Jefferson had nothing to do with the paper.

What was the real significance of this war of the editors? Was it simply a matter of party politics, when both the parties and the politics were new, and the press no more than a convenient instrument for the protagonists? Douglas Southall Freeman, in his monumental biography of Washington, raises other provocative questions that get below the surface of the controversy. Freeman inquired:

> Did Freneau's preoccupation with Washington in the months immediately preceding the second Federalist inauguration evince the bitterness of frustrated Republicans and mark the opening of a violent era in the war of parties and the battle of newspapers? Or was Freneau, the appointed journalist of Jeffersonianism, presenting a calculated plea to the best instincts of the President to renounce Federalism, as designed by Hamilton, in the years of office before him? Fenno attempted no analysis of the strategy of his opponents. . . . As Washington prepared to take the oath of the Presidency for the second time, one thing was certain: Just as a conflict of political philosophies was under way with no truce in sight, so, too, a contest in political journalism had begun in America with no prospect of peace.

Nor would peace ever come. The essence of that conflict has been the determining factor in relations between the president and the press from Washington's time to the present. A single incident from the second term serves to exemplify the basic nature of this struggle.

When John Jay returned from Britain in the early spring of 1795 with the carefully negotiated treaty that settled the outstanding issues left from the Revolution and would bear his name, Washington used the power of the executive to insist that it be considered first in secrecy by the Senate (with whom the president sat at that time) before its terms were made known to the public. The president knew the treaty would be attacked, and he hoped to discuss it with the Senate and gain as much support as possible before it was given to the public. But when Washington's intentions became known, the Anti-Federalists were quite naturally outraged. Bache's *Aurora* led the attack, calling the majority of Federalist senators who had agreed to this procedure a "Venetian Grand Council" and "the secret lodge at Philadelphia," while the New York *Augus,* among others, insisted that this continued secrecy during the debate was itself unconstitutional. Some members of Congress, most of them Anti-Federalists, agreed and decried any need for secrecy.

For the moment it was an impasse, but near the end of June there occurred the first major leak from government to press in the long and tangled history of that relationship. Bache printed what he described as an abstract of the treaty in the *Aurora* of June 29. It was signed "A Citizen." Two days later he advertised what purported to be the full text, available for twenty-five cents, together with an explanation by Sen. Stevens T. Mason, a Virginia Republican, that he had given Bache his own copy of the text so that the "false impressions" conveyed by the abstract could be corrected.

Nothing could have been more politically logical: an enemy of the Federalists had circumvented the attempt by the president and his party to keep the treaty's terms secret during Senate deliberations by the simple procedure of leaking his own copy to a leading opposition editor. Such practices have since become commonplace, but was this actually the case in 1795?

Scholars have disagreed, yet it seems clear now that Bache used Mason as his cover-up for the real source, probably the French minister, Pierre Adet, who in fact told the Committee of Public Safety in Paris that he had done so. Adet's copy was given to him by Edmund Randolph, no friend of Washington, and he was the man ultimately charged with the leak. If that was the case, it is astonishing that there was not more than one leak, since several copies of the treaty were circulating around Philadelphia by the time Bache came into possession of it. The *Aurora* claimed that Rufus King had shown a copy to the British minister, and Albert Gallatin had seen the full text before it was disclosed, although there was no suspicion that he had leaked it.

In any case, the disclosure precipitated a storm of protest and criticism from both the public and the Anti-Federalist press, which continued to fan the controversy. In one of his gloomy letters to Gouverneur Morris, Washington observed, "I have brought on myself a torrent of abuse in the factious papers in this country, and from the enmity of the discontented of all descripts therein . . . I have nothing to ask, and discharging my duty, I have nothing to fear from invective." But if he did not fear it, he continued to hate it, especially when he read in the *Aurora* that he had "violated the Constitution and made a treaty with a nation abhorred by our people; that he answered the respectful remonstrances of Boston and New York as if he were the omnipotent director of a seraglio, and had thundered contempt upon the people with as much confidence as if he had sat upon the throne of Industan.''

Washington refused to be drawn into controversy on any kind of personal basis. He made no efforts to justify his conduct of office and continued to rely on the public's good sense to counteract what the newspapers said. ''The Gazettes, which I presume you receive,'' he wrote to Thomas Pinckney,

> will show you in what manner the public functionaries are treated here. The abuse, however, which some of them contain has excited no reply from me. I have a consolation which no earthly power can deprive me of: that of acting from my best judgment; and I shall be very much mistaken, if I do not soon find that the public mind is recovering fast from the disquietude into which it has been thrown by the most willful, artful and malignant mis-representations that can be imagined.

Nevertheless, Washington's inner feelings could not have rested entirely on this lofty plane. He had always been a proud and sensitive man, with a thin skin where criticism of himself was concerned, and the personal bitterness generated in him by the controversy over the treaty was reflected in a letter to Hamilton, in which he said: ''Having from a variety of reasons (among which a disinclination to be longer buffited [sic] in the public prints by a set of infamous scribblers) taken my ultimate determination 'To seek the Post of honor in a private Station' I regret exceedingly that I did not publish my valedictory address the day after the Adjournment of Congress.''

It took courage and principle to remain silent as the storm deepened and Anti-Federalists from one end of the new nation to the other unlimbered their heaviest journalistic guns against the president. He was, it appeared, ''treacherous,'' ''mischievous,'' ''inefficient,'' guilty of ''stately journeying through the American continent in search of personal incense'' and of ''ostentatious professions of piety,'' accused of ''ingratitude'' and ''want of merit,'' characterized as a ''frail mortal'' like other men, ''a spoiled child, despotic,'' urged to ''put off your suit of buckram, and condescend to that state of humility, in which you might hear the real sentiments of your fellow citizens,'' and warned that ''posterity will in vain search for the monuments of wisdom in your administration.'' Other critics were even more extravagant in their condemnation, notably Tom Paine, who called Washington ''the patron of fraud . . . treacherous in private friendship . . . and a hypocrite in public life.'' The world, he said, would be ''puzzled to decide, whether you are an apostate or an imposter, whether you have abandoned good principles, or whether you ever had any?'' This from a man who had once been the president's good friend and ardent supporter. As the press historian James Pollard observed:

> The criticisms of Washington extended to all manner of things. In the eyes of his enemies every official action was open to suspicion if not to downright accusation. His personal affairs were bandied about and his private customs and habits were condemned alike for what he did or did not do. No item was too small to furnish the basis for new criticisms and accusations. Much of this kind of sniping was confined to whispering campaigns but some of it reached print also.

Washington's correspondence during his second term frequently reflects his more or less constant anger at the press, as well as his continued insistence on remaining personally aloof from it, even from those few editors who supported him. When at last it came time for him to leave office and return, thankfully, to Mount Vernon, it was understandable that he should decide not to give his Farewell Address (a written document, not a spoken one, as some mistakenly believe) to all the papers, to be published simultaneously, but to "manage the news" and give it as an exclusive to a Federalist paper that had, for the most part, supported him. This was the *Pennsylvania Packet and Daily Advertiser,* published by John Dunlap and David Claypoole, later to be the first morning daily in America and the nation's first truly successful daily newspaper.

The president prepared his address in consultation with Hamilton, to whom he sent a first draft in which he observed of the press that

> some of the Gazettes . . . have teemed with all the invective that disappointment, ignorance of facts, and malicious falsehood could invent, to misrepresent my politics and affections; to wound my reputation and feelings; and to weaken, if not entirely destroy the confidence you had been pleased to repose in me; it might be expected at the parting scene of my public life that I should take some notice of such virulent abuse. But, as heretofore, I shall pass them over in utter silence never having myself, nor by any other with my participation or knowledge, written or published a scrap in answer to any of them.

On his own initiative, Washington removed that paragraph from the final draft, characteristically reducing this and other references to himself to an absolute minimum. Then, after further consultation with Hamilton, he made his decision to give the document to the *Packet* for publication. Claypoole has left us an account of how this decision was carried out:

> I received a Message from the President by his Private Secretary signifying his desire to see me. I waited on him at the appointed time, and found him sitting alone in the Drawing room. He received me kindly, and after paying my respects to him, desired me to take a seat near him; then, addressing himself to me, said, that he had for some time past contemplated retiring from Public Life, and had at length concluded to do so at the end of the (then) present Term;—that he had some Thoughts and Reflections on the occasion, which he deemed proper to communicate to the People of the United States, in the form of an address, and which he wished to appear in the *Daily Advertiser,*—of which I was Editor.—He paused, and I took the opportunity of thanking him for having preferred that Paper as the channel of his Communication with the People. . . . He silently assented and asked when the Publication could be made.—I answered that the time should be made perfectly convenient to him,—and the following Monday was fixed on;—he then told me that his Secretary would bring me a copy on the next (Friday) morning, and I withdrew.

If Washington thought the Farewell Address, with its reference to newspaper abuse deleted, would constitute a dignified departure even in the eyes of the Anti-

Federalist press, he ws disappointed. When the address appeared, Bache greeted it scathingly in the *Aurora:*

> If ever a nation was debauched by a man, the American nation has been debauched by Washington. If ever a nation has suffered from the improper influence of a man, the American nation has suffered from the influence of Washington. If ever a nation was deceived by a man, the American nation has been deceived by Washington. Let his conduct then be an example to future ages. Let it serve to be a warning that no man may be an idol.

Even that was not enough. Washington's gloating enemies resurrected the seven forged letters attributed to him, first published in 1777 as British propaganda, and reissued them as a pamphlet. Washington once more denied the charges they contained in a letter, written on his last day in office, to Secretary of State Timothy Pickering. As Washington left Philadelphia for Mount Vernon, Bache delivered a parting editorial shot in the *Aurora,* March 6, 1797: "If ever there was a period for rejoicing, this is the moment—every heart in unison with the freedom and happiness of the people, ought to beat high with exultation that the name of Washington from this day ceases to give a currency to political iniquity, and to legalized corruption."

In the quiet of his plantation—which was immediately interrupted by a steady flow of visitors and a heavy correspondence—Washington at first canceled his subscriptions to most of the papers he read but discovered that he could not get along without them. Returning to their pages, he found them as irritating, partisan, and unreliable as ever. Bache, for example, had died in 1798, but his successor William Duane maintained the violent, partisan tone of the paper. Even as he lashed back in letters to his friends who were still in office, Washington nevertheless well understood the necessity of maintaining a free press, no matter how irresponsible. He might support the Alien and Sedition Acts on other grounds, but he told Pickering not long before he died that citizens must be well informed and that "concealment is a species of mis-information"—exactly what Jefferson and Madison had argued in pushing for the First Amendment.

However he might feel about the press's conduct, which continued to be reprehensible for the most part during the remainder of his lifetime, Washington nevertheless continued to read the newspapers until the day of his death. On the night before he died, as Tobias Lear, his faithful secretary, tells us, he still wanted to know what was in them. Of that last evening, Lear wrote:

> In the evening, the papers having come from the post office, he sat in the room with Mrs. Washington and myself, reading them, till at nine o'clock when Mrs. Washington went up into Mrs. Lewis's room . . . and left the General and myself reading the papers. He was very cheerful; and when he met with anything which he thought diverting or interesting, he would read it aloud as well as his hoarseness would permit. He desired me to read to him the debates of the Virginia Assembly, on the election of a Senator and Governor, which I did,—and, on hearing Mr. Madison's observations respecting Mr. Monroe, he appeared much affected, and spoke

with some degree of asperity on the subject, which I endeavored to moderate, as I always did on such occasions.

Before the next night had ended, Washington was dead, universally loved and admired by most Americans in spite of everything the press had written about him. Nothing the papers printed had the slightest effect on the virtual idolatry that has persisted from that day to this, unfortunately obscuring his essential humanity. An extraordinary man, but human—a fact that was more apparent in Jean Antoine Houdon's death mask than it was in Gilbert Stuart's thin-lipped portrait, which became his national image.

No president in office was so badly treated by the press except for Lincoln and Franklin Roosevelt, and although his resentment and anger sometimes came to the surface—occasionally in verbal responses, as with Jefferson, but much more often in letters—Washington never chose to debate the great principle of a free press that the Constitution had established and the papers of his time abused so grievously. Like Jefferson and Madison after him, he upheld that freedom in spite of the severest provocations. That was part of his character. It was not the character of many who followed him in the highest office.

John Adams: The First Test

With John Adams, a man presumably committed to Washington's policies, safely elected to the presidency, the Federalists had reason to believe that nothing the Anti-Federalists and their supporters in the press could say would be enough to shake their control. Yet it was Adams who, in spite of his undoubted intelligence and integrity, made a policy mistake of such proportions that it brought his own and the party's downfall after a single term.

The mistake was the Alien and Sedition Acts, which not only provoked the initial test of the First Amendment but challenged the Federalists' concept of government. Jefferson's subsequent victory brought the Republicans into power for the first time. Other factors were involved in this political transition, of course, but the acts were at the core of it.

That this particular piece of legislation should be the rock on which Adams's and the party's ship of state would founder was an irony in itself, for the second president was a writer, as his predecessor had not been, and before the Revolution had not only contributed to newspapers but had exhibited a shrewd knowledge of how to use them politically, in contrast to Washington's general attitude toward the press of aloofness and disdain. It was a talent John Adams shared with his cousin Samuel. In spite of their differences where revolutionary matters were concerned, they had worked together with the Sons of Liberty in Massachusetts and, as John put it, had "cooked up paragraphs" and "worked the political engine" in the offices of such patriot newspapers as the *Independent Advertiser* and the Boston *Gazette*. On the latter, they had joined forces with its young proprietors, Benjamin Edes and John Gill, to make it the principal organ of the Whigs and such an irritation to the Tories that they referred to it as the "Dung

Barge." The *Gazette*, in fact, became the chief organ through which the two Adamses and others attacked the Stamp Act, the Tea Tax, the closing of the port of Boston, and other measures of the Crown in a manner that did as much as anything else to stir the fires of revolt and unite patriots who had differing views of how to approach a break with England, or whether to break at all.

John Adams was involved in his kind of newspaper work right up to the morning of the battle at Lexington. The Boston *Post Boy,* a Tory paper, had published letters attacking the Continental Congress (they were written by Daniel Leonard, a local lawyer), and Adams answered them at length in a series he wrote for the *Gazette,* signed "Novanglus." But this debate ended with Lexington because, soon after, the *Post Boy*'s owners prudently went out of business before the patriots could accomplish its demise for themselves.

Few presidents have been such prolific writers as Adams; Jefferson, Lincoln, and Theodore Roosevelt are obvious comparisons. For more than forty years, Adams wrote letters, articles, and of course his famous diary. Yet he was never a regular newspaper or magazine writer. He viewed the press as most of his contemporaries did—a vehicle to be used for political purposes—and he had no close relationship with any paper after his *Gazette* days.

Adams's brief experience with the press, however, had convinced him that it was a primary source of political persuasion, and he found the idea of particular interest. Observing how it functioned in other countries, he was not reluctant to criticize the foreign press for its shortcomings. In Paris, during the Revolution, he wrote to Edmond Charles Genêt (that famed "Citizen" who became the new French Republic's first ambassador to America) about the exploits of an American naval captain, complaining, "There has not been a more memorable action this war; and the feats of our American frigates and privateers have not been sufficiently published in Europe," adding that they were seldom "properly described and published" in North America either. Yet, having observed the European press, Adams was well aware that the Americans had created something unique, as he wrote a month later to Elias Boudinot, the president of Congress: "There is not in any nation of the world so unlimited a freedom of the press as is now established in every State of America, both by law and practice. Every man in Europe who reads their newspapers must see it. There is nothing that the people dislike that they do not attack."

It was a vital sentence: *There is nothing that the people dislike that they do not attack.* Adams honestly believed this to be a virtue, since the American press in his lifetime had freed itself from licensing by government to attack, in the name of the people, the British Crown and all its works in America. It was to be a far different matter, however, when the voice of the people, reflected in the press, was directed against him as president.

From the nature of the man as well as the circumstances of his ascendancy to the office, it was predictable that Adams would find himself in conflict with the press, but nothing could have prepared him for the reality. For this proud New Englander who had a high (and no doubt well-deserved) opinion of himself, it had been galling to live in Washington's shadow. "I loved and revered the man,'' he wrote to Benjamin Rush after he left the presidency, ''but it was his humanity only that I admired. In his divinity I never believed.''

Idolatry of Washington was in full cry when Adams took office, and the cabinet he had inherited was well stocked with the general's strong supporters, including Secretary of War James McHenry, Secretary of State Timothy Pickering, and Secretary of the Treasury Oliver Wolcott—all of them under the influence of Alexander Hamilton, the leading Federalist ideologue, whom Adams despised. The new president had to establish his own identity among these men of his own party, and at the same time he was compelled to defend himself as best he could against the virulent Anti-Federalist press, which had simply resumed with him where it had left off with Washington.

There was something far worse brewing below the surface, however, as Adams began his presidency. It lay in the definition that the great English jurist, William Blackstone, had given to seditious libel, spelled out in English common law. In his landmark *Commentaries,* Blackstone was at pains to establish an assumption about the relationship between government and the people—an assumption that the colonists would reject in the course of fighting their Revolution. ''There is and must be in [governments],'' wrote Blackstone, ''a supreme, irresistible, absolute, uncontrolled authority, in which . . . the rights of sovereignty reside.'' British sovereignty, he went on, resided in Parliament, whose acts ''no power on earth can undo.'' It was exactly this presumed right that Parliament exercised in the Declaratory Act, asserting its right to make laws and statutes ''of sufficient force and validity to bind the colonies and people of America, subjects of the Crown of Great Britain, in all cases whatsoever.''

Americans rejected the idea of parliamentary sovereignty, substituting instead the principle that provincial assemblies were sovereign within the framework of a representative government and therefore independent of the British Parliament's control. The Declaration of Independence was the expression of American belief in the sovereignty of the people, but this idea was so new in the world, a theory which had yet to be proved in the crucible of reality, that the leaders of the new republic had not even worked out in their minds what the balance between legislative and popular sovereignty ought to be. As late as 1807, Adams admitted he did not know what republican government was and did not believe anyone else ''ever did or ever will.'' Americans, in fact, continued to debate the question from 1776 through the remainder of Adams's lifetime, and indeed they are still debating it today.

Where the press was concerned, Blackstone had laid down the principle of freedom but severely qualified it by limiting it to freedom from prior restraint, and that was how the Federalists conceived it. This interpretation had already brought the party into savage conflict with the Republicans during Washington's administration. After the so-called Whiskey Rebellion had been put down, under the general's personal direction (it was an uprising in Western Pennsylvania by settlers unwilling to pay an excise tax on whiskey), the House of Representatives began a debate about freedom of the press that went on for five days. Specifically, it concerned the right of public opinion, as expressed by the newspapers, to criticize the government.

Federalists were particularly irate about the Democratic Societies (called "Madisonian Societies" by the Federalist organ, the *Gazette of the United States),* which they asserted had precipitated the Whiskey Rebellion through their propaganda campaign in the Republican press. During the House debate, Congressman Theodore Sedgwick had denounced these societies as "a wicked, false and seditious misrepresentation of public men and public measures," which had been launched with "the seditious intention of slandering the measures of government and its administrations." Another congressman, William Vans Murray, was even more vehement: "The press is the rack on which they place the government, and it would have expired on the rack had it not been for the patriotism of the citizens" in putting down the rebellion, and he added, "This lesson calls the attention of the country to draw a line between the use and the abuse of the inestimable right of free opinion."

As a result of this debate, Congress proposed to censure the societies, their publications, and the papers supporting them, and quite naturally that drew the concentrated wrath of the Republicans. "Opinions are not the objects of legislation," Madison wrote sharply. "If we advert to the nature of Republican government, we shall find that the censorial power is in the people over the Government, and not in the Government over the people." He was vigorously supported by a Republican voice in Congress, William B. Giles of Virginia, who asserted that

> opinion whether founded in truth or error is a property, which every individual possesses, and which in this country he is at liberty to address to the public through the medium of the press. Any interference with the exercise of this right must terminate in the complete destruction of liberty of the press. . . . It should not be forgotten that in the United States the *rights* of every man and of every society are popular—*the rights of opinion, or of thinking and speaking and publishing, are sacred.*

But the Federalists did not think these rights were necessarily sacred. They put their faith in Blackstone and the English common law. In the Senate, which they controlled, they were able to pass a resolution condemning the Democratic Societies, but the House, under control of the Republicans, led by Madison, refused to go along. In any case, it was too late. The seeds of a major controversy had been well planted. The Federalists clearly believed that dissent was to be equated with disaffection and disloyalty, while the Republicans were in the process of creating a libertarian theory that defended the rights of a free press even when it might be in the hands of libelers whom the government considered seditious.

Madison set forth the substance of this argument clearly enough: If, he wrote to James Monroe, "the Government may stifle all censure whatever on its misdoings; for if it be itself the judge, it will never allow any censures to be just; and if it can supress censures flowing from one lawful source, it may suppress those flowing from any other—from the press and from individuals, as well as from Societies etc."

As the historian James Morton Smith points out, Madison and the other Republicans were arguing in 1794 as they were to do in 1798, and as they had done earlier during the period of Confederation—namely, that legislative sovereignty was not the sole reflection of the people. "By emphasizing the sovereignty of the people," Smith writes, "they fragmented the monolithic concept of the people into individuals; by stressing the power of the public in a republic, they put a premium on opinion expressed by the people at large, who could comment on the constituted authorities—individually or in self-contained societies, orally or in newspapers and pamphlets—without running the risk of prosecution for sedition."

It was this new theory of the relationship between governors and the governed, wrought in the Revolution's crucible, that was unexpectedly tested in 1798, when the threat of war between France and the United States had prompted the fear that subversive agents of the French were at large in the land, a possibility Congress dealt with by passing a series of acts. On June 18, the Naturalization Act extended residence requirements for citizenship from five to fourteen years. A week later "An Act Concerning Aliens" was passed, followed on July 6 by the Alien Enemies Act and on July 14 by a statute establishing punishment for sedition. Together, these laws, four of them all told, were known as the Alien and Sedition Acts.

They were fatally defective in more than one respect. While the Alien Enemies Act empowered the president in time of war, or the threat of war, to seize or deport all resident aliens who were citizens of the enemy, it was not to be effective unless war had been declared or there was danger of an imminent invasion. Agents of the enemy, meanwhile, could be carrying on works of subversion unapprehended; aliens who were not citizens of the enemy country could be just as subversive and yet were not subject to the law. The Federalists believed that refugee Irish and English aliens were a constant threat to their party, and therefore to the country.

But it was the treason and sedition bill, which Sen. James Lloyd of Maryland brought to the floor, that precipitated the historic uproar. Part of the bill seemed proper enough. Anyone, alien or citizen, who opposed or defeated the operation of any United States law, or "threatened any officer of the United States Government with any damage to his character, person, or property, or attempt to procure any insurrection, plot, or unlawful assembly or unlawful combination," would be subject to a fine of not more than $5,000 and imprisonment for not more than five years. While some might consider this language too sweeping, and possibly even subversive of the people's liberties in its own way, it was the second part of the bill that struck fire. The same penalties prescribed in the first part were to be applied to anyone found guilty of "printing, writing, or speaking in a scandalous or malicious way against the government of the United States, either house of Congress, or the President, with the purpose of bringing them into contempt, stirring up sedition, or aiding and abetting a foreign nation in hostile designs against the United States." Truth would be admitted as a defense (although this had not yet been established in libel law), and the act was to be void in two years. When this legislation reached the House, it was softened somewhat by requiring that malice and intent be proved and that the jury be the judge of law as well as fact. It passed by a narrow margin, and immediately drew heavy Republican fire as a plain infringement of freedom of the press as guaranteed by the Constitution, and so it would be seen today. Adams received a substantial share of the blame, even though he had had no hand in drafting the bill himself. Some historians have cited his subsequent support of it as strange and unworthy of the man, censuring him for precipitating the collapse of the Federalist party, which began with the subsequent furore over the acts. But Adams has also had some recent defenders. Page Smith, whose two-volume biography of Adams in 1962 was the first to make use of the opening to scholars of the voluminous Adams Papers, contends that the president might have had second thoughts about giving his support to the acts if he could have foreseen the consequences but believes he would have supported them anyway in the end. As Smith says, ''The United States was at war *de facto* if not *de jure*. The simplest right of a nation in peril had always been and would remain self-preservation. A self-preservation, certainly, that remained within the limits of the Constitution and the inalienable rights of Americans secured to them by its first ten amendments.''

The Federalists, however, had not even waited for the act to be passed before attacking the editors who opposed them and it. A justice of the United States District Court had issued an arrest warrant for Benjamin Franklin Bache, the Philadelphia *Aurora*'s publisher—that same ''Lightning Rod Junior'' who had so angered Washington—charging him with libeling the president and the government. Adams was delighted to hear that Bache had been arrested, which was understandable considering that the *Aurora* had accused the president of taking bribes from the British government to influence American affairs. It had also charged that the correspondence of Elbridge Gerry, which had been given to Congress by Adams in the wake of the XYZ Affair, was doctored and changed before the transmittal so that it would seem to support the Federalist position. As Page Smith points out:

> To Adams . . . the editor's accusation was of a piece with the innumerable lies and frauds which the man had published in his paper for years. Freedom of the press was one thing; deliberate distortion and falsehood that confused and misled the people was another. He saw no contradiction between his avowal that ''a free press maintains the majesty of the people'' and his endorsement of the Sedition Act. Nothing indeed would destroy a free press more quickly than its corruption.

Obviously the two Federalist presidents, Washington and Adams, did not understand the concept of press freedom, new and untried as it was, that had been established by the First Amendment. If Bache had libeled the president or his government, the libel law provided relief as it did to any citizen. If the Republican press was full of libel, as it unquestionably was, it was no different from the Federalist papers, which paid no greater attention to the truth. They had, for example, accused Bache of being in the pay of the French government. But the principle enunciated by the First Amendment was that the press was to be free to say *anything* it liked within the limits of the libel law, which the courts would determine, and that it was particularly free to criticize government, to be the people's watchdog over it, which Jefferson and Madison, as architects of the amendments, had intended it to be.

Adams had no philosophical sympathy whatever with the Republicans on this question. Look what had happened to the press in France after the Revolution, he told them, when editors dared to oppose Robespierre, Danton, or the Directory. If the Republicans, whom he equated with the Jacobins, wanted the French version of democracy in this country, he said, the press would soon find itself in serious trouble. Other Federalists pointed out that the Sedition Act was a good deal milder than common law libel statutes, which were still several years away from permitting truth as a defense.

The Federalist case, aside from its constitutional implications, rested on the belief that the new nation was threatened by the thirty thousand or so Frenchmen in America, many of whom were undoubtedly agents of their government, which seemed intent on deposing the president if possible, declaring war, or both. As noted, Adams and his government were also worried about the other thousands of Irish and English exiles, many of them veterans of revolutions in their own countries and avowed enemies of the Federalist government, no matter how sincere their beliefs might be. Adams considered it quite probable that many of them were desperately sincere in their hope of overthrowing him.

It was these enemies-at-home of the government that could be heard in the violent and vituperative Republican press, and although Republican papers were no worse than the Federalist press, the government considered what they said and wrote as seditious, and consequently had undertaken to protect itself through the Sedition Act. It was the same kind of fear, with far less reason, that inspired the laws enacted for the sake of ''internal security'' during the First World War, and later.

To Jefferson, the Alien and Sedition Acts were the prelude to tyranny, ''an experiment on the American mind to see how far it will bear an avowed violation of the constitution. If this goes down, we shall immediately see attempted another act of Congress, declaring that the President shall continue in office during life, and after that other laws giving both the President and the Congress life terms in office.'' As paranoid as the Federalists, Jefferson and the Republicans believed sincerely that this was Adams's aim and that he and his party would welcome the return of English rule. The only way to prevent such an outcome, the Republicans believed, was to advocate rebellion against paying the taxes that would support a military establishment, meanwhile fighting the Alien and Sedition Acts tooth and claw as ''against the constitution and merely void.'' Only state governments, they said, rehearsing their basic philosophy, were good and sound; they were the single source capable of resisting federal tyranny, which they said had become worse than George III's.

Adams's attempts to enforce the Alien and Sedition Acts produced twenty-five arrests, fifteen indictments, and eleven trials resulting in ten convictions. Common law actions brought the total of convictions ultimately to at least fifteen, of which eight were newspapers. The cases ranged from the absurd, as when an eccentric in Massachusetts erected a liberty pole with signs protesting the acts (he was fined $400 and given eighteen months in jail) to the serious, as when the government moved against the *Aurora*.

This move was the result of a direct complaint from Timothy Pickering, the secretary of state, to Adams about an edition of the paper for July 24, 1798, which the secretary thought was "imbued with rather more impudence than is common to that paper," and he added that he was passing on the issue to the government's attorney, William Rawle, asking him to prosecute the editor if he thought it was libelous. Adams replied:

> Is there anything evil in the regions of actuality or possibility that the *Aurora* has not suggested of me? You may depend upon it, I disdain to attempt a vindication of myself against any of the lies of the *Aurora,* as much as any man concerned with the administration of the affairs of the United States. If Mr. Rawle does not think this paper libelous, he is not fit for his office; and if he does not prosecute, he will not do his duty. The matchless effrontery of this Duane merits the execution of the alien law. I am very willing to try its strength upon him.

Apparently Adams blamed William Duane, Bache's associate editor, for what the *Aurora* was printing. Bache had been freed on parole, but a few months later, in September, he died during the yellow fever epidemic that swept Philadelphia. Duane succeeded him (and married his widow) and carried on the *Aurora* in a way that was, if possible, even more violent than the founder's.

If sedition alone had been the issue, it could be argued that Jefferson himself was just as seditious as Bache and Duane. After all, he had secretly written resolutions for the Kentucky legislature that implied a threat of secession and proposed for the first time the principle of nullification—that is, that a state had the right to reject acts of Congress which it considered unconstitutional. The real issue, however, was another principle in which Jefferson—paradoxically, as we can now see by hindsight—believed firmly, the press's First Amendment freedom.

In a resolution passed in May 1800, nearly two years after Pickering's original letter of complaint, Congress requested Adams

> to instruct the proper law officers to commence and carry on a prosecution against William Duane, editor of a newspaper, called the *Aurora,* for certain false, defamatory, scandalous, and malicious publications in the said newspaper of the 19th of February last past, tending to defame the Senate of the United States, and to bring them into contempt and disrepute, and to excite against them the hatred of the good people of the United States.

Duane was duly prosecuted. Bache had been dead nearly two years, and his successor had only deepened the heritage of Federalist hatred left behind. But as has often happened from that day to this, the case dragged on so long in the courts that it was ultimately dropped. The Alien and Sedition Acts themselves were a failure in every respect, not only unsuccessful in silencing the opposition press, as the Federalists hoped, but actually inspiring it to renewed attacks on the government and enabling it to use these obnoxious laws as one of the prime elements in bringing about the Federalist downfall and the election of Jefferson.

Sensing the futility of the acts, Adams in 1800 conceived the notion of establishing a government paper, an idea that Jackson carried to brilliant fruition a few years later. In doing so, Adams demonstrated once more that the principle of a free press still eluded him, for he pointed out that every European government had a gazette in its service and plainly saw no evil in such a controlled organ. "It is certain," he wrote, "that a President's printer must be restrained from publishing libels, and all paragraphs offensive to the individuals, public bodies, or foreign nations; but need not forbid advertisements." Adams seriously proposed the creation of such a gazette and printer in a letter to his cabinet members and asked their advice about the means of carrying out his idea, but nothing came of it.

Looking back from the standpoint of our twentieth-century values, we may view this as a somewhat shocking advocacy of the kind of government-controlled press characteristic of totalitarian countries in our time, whether right or left, but Adams was no totalitarian and his motives were basically honorable. What he proposed was no worse than having the press for the most part in the hands of partisan politicians. Like Jefferson, Adams believed in the vital importance of an informed public opinion in a democracy, but as to how that should be achieved, he and his successor were substantially in disagreement.

Adams could not understand the opposition to him and his beliefs. His often overweening ego would not permit him to think that he might be wrong, a failing he shared with lesser men, but, toward the end, vanity and frustration produced in him a bitterness that led him to blame his own misfortunes as well as those of his party on both the Federalist press and relentless Republican papers. On September 10, 1800, he wrote to Jonathan Trumbull:

> *Porcupine's Gazette* [William Cobbett's paper] and Fenno's gazette [*Gazette of the United States,* the chief Federalist paper], from the moment of the mission to France, aided, countenanced and encouraged by *soi-disant* Federalists in Boston, New York, and Philadelphia, have done more to shuffle the cards into the hands of the Jacobin leaders, than all the acts of administration, and all the policy of opposition, from the commencement of the government. . . . For myself, age, infirmities, family misfortunes, have conspired with the unreasonable conduct of Jacobins and insolent Federalists, to make me too indifferent to whatever can happen.

Four weeks after Adams and the party were swept out of office, he extended the area of blame to its widest limits in a letter to Benjamin Stoddert, his former secretary of the navy:

> No party that ever existed, knew itself so little, or so vainly overrated its own influence and popularity, as ours. None ever understood so ill the causes of its own power, or so wantonly destroyed them. If we had been blessed with common sense, we should not have been overthrown by Philip Freneau, Duane, Callender, Cooper, and Lyon [all eminent Republican editors], or their great patron and protector [meaning France]. A group of foreign liars, have discomfited the education, the talents, the virtues, and the property of the country.

Later, during the twenty-five years after he left the White House, Adams spent a good deal of time defending his administration, excoriating the French, berating his party, justifying himself, and damning the press. In an outburst to Benjamin Rush he wrote: "If I am to judge by the newspapers and pamphlets that have been printed in America for twenty years past, I should think that both parties believed me the meanest villain in the world. . . . Washington and Franklin could never do any thing but what was imputed to pure, disinterested patriotism; I never could do any thing but what was ascribed to sinister motives." To Thomas Jefferson, the foe with whom he resumed a friendly correspondence in his old age, he complained sententiously: "I have been disgraced and degraded, and I have a right to complain. But, as I have always expected it, I have always submitted to it, perhaps with too much tameness."

John Adams's tragedy was that a man whose voluminous writings had for more than forty years been devoted to the public good should have been tripped up in the highest public office by a vital lack of understanding of the nature of the government he was called upon to lead. He was the first president to suffer that misfortune, but he was not the last, by any means, nor was he the last to blame the press instead of himself for his troubles.

In retrospect it is clear that the Sedition Act which Adams supported was the most significant factor in his administration; it was termed by his grandson and first important biographer, Charles Francis Adams, as the Federalist party's worst and fatal error. In that biography Charles Francis wrote:

> It cannot be denied that the attempt to punish individuals for mere expressions of opinion of public measures and public men, to subject them perhaps to fine and imprisonment, and certainly to heavy and burdensome charges in their defense, for exercising a latitude of speech however extreme, in the heat and excitement attending the political conflicts of a free country, verged too closely upon an abridgment of the liberty of speech and of the press to be quite reconcilable to the theory of free institutions.

Yet it was fortunate that the question was raised so early in the history of the nation because it was one that badly needed to be clarified. Madison and Jefferson thought the First Amendment was unequivocally clear in its meaning, just as Justices William O. Douglas and Hugo Black interpreted it in our time, but a cloud of ambiguity surrounded it in the minds of public men, even in that earlier period. Adams was not alone.

In the struggle over the Alien and Sedition Acts that cost Adams his office, and his party its power, significant questions were raised, if not answered, which remain with us today. James Morton Smith, perhaps the most noted historian of the event, sums up neatly the importance of what happened in the Adams administration:

> The Alien and Sedition Acts played a prominent role in shaping the American tradition of civil liberties. Based on the concept that the government was master, these laws provoked a public response which clearly demonstrated that the people

occupied that position. The severity of the Sedition Law failed to prevent the "over-throw" of the Adams administration by the Jeffersonian "disorganizers." Indeed, the law furnished a ready text which the Democratic-Republicans used to incite the American people to legal "insurgency" at the polls; the election resulted in the repudiation of the party which tried to protect itself behind the Sedition Law. It elevated to power a party whose leaders stressed the concept that freedom of opinion is an essential part of an all-encompassing freedom of the mind; for Jefferson and Madison the First Freedom occupied a high, preferred position as the only effectual guardian of every other right. To them, as to the United States Supreme Court later, the defeat of the Federalists illustrated the common understanding that the First Amendment abolished the English law crime of seditious libel, of which the Sedition Law was merely declaratory.*

With the death of Federalism, a new political era began in which public opinion became "the basis of American democratic development," as Smith puts it. Most politicians could now agree with Madison's view of 1794 that "the censorial power is in the people over the Government, and not in the Government over the people." It would be a very long time before the Sedition Act of 1918 reversed that value, and even that was a wartime measure which was repealed three years later, not to be revived in essence until the Alien Registration Act of 1940, known as the Smith Act.

After Adams, however, the message was understood but not absorbed, and the new nation was still a long way from being out of the philosophical woods as far as the fundamental issues of press and presidency, the First Amendment, and the state versus federal power were concerned—as Jefferson and Madison were about to discover.

Jefferson and Republican Freedom

Thomas Jefferson was a man whose many-sided intellect cast reflections of itself in every direction, like a prism turning in the light, so it is hardly surprising that his views on the press can be, and often are, quoted to support a variety of opinions, some of them apparently contradictory. Revisionists have suggested that on occasion, like most politicians, he shifted ground according to his political circumstances. But in one respect, at least, he never wavered, and that was his belief in the absolute necessity of a free press in order to make democracy function as it should. There were times, admittedly, when he appeared to speak against the press, and against his principle, but those words rose out of the

---

*As Smith points out, the Supreme Court in 1812 (*U.S.* v. *Hudson and Goodwin*) dismissed the idea that the United States had common law jurisdiction over crimes of seditious libel, ruling that crimes against the nation had to be established by statutes. "Although this question is brought up now for the first time to be decided by this Court," the ruling said, "we consider it as having been long since settled in public opinion. In no other case for many years has this jurisdiction been asserted; and the general acquiescence of legal men shows the prevalence of opinion in favor of the negative of the proposition."

disappointment, anger, and frustration he felt when the newspapers of his time failed so abysmally to match his ideals.

This failure had its origin in the same reasons that had made Washington and Adams enemies of the press—that is, the newspapers remained primarily political organs. No matter how rapidly they were advancing in their news coverage, they were still, for the most part, in the hands of politicians who used printers as tools. The editors they employed were simply like-minded ideologues.

Since Jefferson knew no other kind of press, except in the ideal world his mind created, he was quite willing to be pragmatic about it and use the papers in his own interests whenever it was possible for him to do so. If they smote him, he turned the other cheek publicly, with words that have made him the primary champion of absolute press freedom. It was this Jefferson from whom Justices William O. Douglas and Hugo Black drew their inspiration for the Supreme Court opinions that echoed the third president's views, and those of Madison.

A prodigious letter writer, as were most of the public men of his time, Jefferson in his correspondence (of which about twenty-five thousand letters have survived) often asserted his ideas about press freedom. The most quoted, and most misused, is his letter to Edward Carrington of January 16, 1787, in which he declared that if it "were left to me to decide whether we should have a government without newspapers or newspapers without a government, I should not hesitate to prefer the latter." This is not the unqualified endorsement of press freedom it seems to be, although it is often quoted in that context. For Jefferson went on to say, "But I should mean that every man should receive those papers and be capable of reading them"—an ideal situation in his day as well as ours, and one not likely ever to be realized. But the principle is clear enough: a free press means nothing if there is no literate electorate capable of reading it—a cautionary observation with increasing relevance for our time.

In this quotation, taken whole, is the essence of Jefferson's view of the press. He believed that it must be free, but that its purpose in a democratic society was to inform, to circulate information among all classes of people, not simply the political aristocracy to which he himself belonged. The press informed the people, and they, in possession of the facts, would make democracy work. Nothing could be more sound in theory, or more difficult to attain in fact.

Again and again Jefferson pressed his beliefs, in different ways to various people. "Our citizens may be deceived for awhile, and have been deceived," he wrote to Archibald Stuart on May 14, 1799, "but as long as the presses can be protected, we may trust to them for light." Again, in 1804, the rural philosopher side of Jefferson was heard in a letter to John Taylor, asserting that it would be his principal aim as president "to subdue tyranny by intellect" and "to exhibit republicanism to the world, in an experiment, fair, full and final." He viewed the press as a prime instrument to be employed toward that end.

Not many Americans would have been prepared to argue that the press should *not* be free, except for those law-and-order advocates who still believed George III was not entirely wrong. But there were differing viewpoints about what curbs, if any, should be placed on it. Jefferson saw no paradox in his conviction that the press must be completely free, but at the same time must be free of libel.

What *was* libel, indeed? In Jefferson's time, as in ours, that was a matter of interpretation. The case of John Peter Zenger in 1735 is celebrated today as the cornerstone of press freedom, but no such illusion was widely held at the end of the eighteenth century. Jefferson and other knowledgeable leaders understood that the Zenger case, in fact, had established nothing more than the ability of a colonial jury to defy royal justices by bringing in a verdict contrary to the evidence. Truth was still no defense in a libel action, and it was only during Jefferson's second term as president that the New York legislature enacted the first state statute establishing that vital concept in press law. Even then, interpretations of "libel" and "truth" continued to vary from court to court.

Jefferson had incorporated his own free press ideas into law as early as June 1776, when he wrote a constitution for the new state of Virginia, in which one clause declared: "Printing presses shall be free, except so far as, by commission of private injury, cause shall be given for private action." It was this principle that he insisted on during the debates before and during the Constitutional Convention, even though he had to advance it by letter from Paris, where he was minister plenipotentiary to France. He laid down a barrage from this distance and found the most receptive target in his fellow Virginian James Madison, who had become a convinced supporter of a free press guarantee and eventually proved to be its chief architect. "I do not like the omission of a bill of rights," Jefferson wrote to Madison from Paris on December 20, 1787, referring to the absence of one in the document (they called it "The Plan") drawn up in Philadelphia. Such a bill, Jefferson told his friend, should provide "clearly and without the aid of sophisms for freedom of religion, freedom of the press, protection against standing armies, restriction of monopolies, the eternal and unremitting force of the habeas corpus laws, and trials by jury in all matters of fact triable by the laws of the land, and not by the law of nations."

Even with an ocean separating him from his country, Jefferson had put his finger on the essential omission committed by the gentlemen at Philadelphia, many of whom had shared Madison's original feeling that these liberties were implied in the Constitution, or agreement, that they had drawn up. But once more Jefferson had spoken for the people. The grassroots revolt that spread like a forest fire as the Constitution began to move through the state ratifying conventions guaranteed the basic liberties would be specifically protected in a Bill of Rights, generally regarded today as the heart of the Constitution. Twelve recommendations were sent up to Congress; ten suvived.

As the debate dragged on in the former colonies, marked by high language and some violence on the part of those who opposed the Constitution, Jefferson wrote again to Madison from Paris on July 31, 1788, once more setting forth his basic demand that the new Constitution contain "a declaration that the federal government will never restrain the presses from printing anything they please, will not take away the liability of the printers for false facts printed."

Eventually the Bill of Rights emerged out of the resolutions sent to Congress by the ratifying conventions. When Jefferson read a draft of these ten amendments to the new Constitution, sent to him by Madison, he replied candidly: "I like it as far as it goes; but I should have been for going further. For instance the following alteration and addition would have pleased me. Art. 4. 'The people shall not be deprived or abridged of their right to speak, to write or otherwise to publish anything but false facts affecting injuriously the life, liberty, property, or reputation of others, or affecting the peace of the confederacy with foreign nations.' ''

It was too late to change Article 4, but there were already sharply differing views in America of what freedom of the press actually meant, or could mean in the future. Alexander Hamilton, leader of the Federalist ideologues, was disdainful of Jefferson's free press notions, as he was of Jeffersonianism in general. In the Federalist Papers he had scoffed at the idea that the principle of press freedom could be made viable simply by embodying it in a constitution. Scornfully, and prophetically, he wrote in 1788:

> What signifies a declaration that "the liberty of the press shall be inviolably preserved" [Jefferson's phrase]? What is the liberty of the press? Who can give it any definition which would not leave the utmost latitude for evasion? I hold it to be impracticable; and from this I infer that its security, whatever fine declaration may be inserted in any constitution respecting it, must altogether depend on public opinion, and on the general spirit of the people and of the government.

In retrospect, this view does not appear to be the irreconcilable conflict the Hamiltonians and Jeffersonians of the day assumed it to be. By insisting that the people be able to read and understand their free press, Jefferson was reflecting Hamilton's belief that press freedom depended on public opinion and the spirit of the people and their government. The difference was that Jefferson and Madison thought it essential to get freedom of the press down in writing as a guarantee, which could then be protected by the Supreme Court, although at the time they only vaguely envisioned the role the Court would later play as interpreter. The machinery for it had been set up in the Constitution, but no one yet knew how it would work.

Thus Jefferson came to the presidency with a clear record of absolute support for press freedom, with the single limitation of the libel law. It would have been inconsistent with his philosophy for him to argue that a national law defining libel, and the grounds for suit when it was charged, would be a fitting companion to a national First Amendment that guaranteed press freedom. Hamilton would have considered that a legitimate Federalist idea, however. Instead Jefferson thought the states should have the right to impose their own restrictions on the press through libel laws and apparently saw nothing inconsistent in the fact that what would be considered libelous in one state might not be in another. "While we deny that Congress has a right to control the freedom of the press," he wrote to Abigail Adams, "we have asserted the right of the States, and their exclusive right to do so."

Unwittingly, Jefferson himself exposed the philosophical fallacy of that argument in 1803, when the Federalist press's scurrilous attacks on him were at their savage height. Writing to Gov. Thomas McKean of Pennsylvania on February 19 of that year, he observed that the press "ought to be restored to it's [*sic*] credibility if possible. The restraints provided by the laws of the states are sufficient for this if applied and I have therefore long thought that a few prosecutions of the most prominent offenders would have a wholesome effect in restoring the integrity of the presses. Not a general prosecution, for that would look like persecution, but a selected one.''

Here is a kind of speciousness not usually associated with Jefferson. He wants to restore the credibility of the press—that is, stop the opposition's lying attacks on him—by a few judicious, selected libel actions brought in the states where they are most likely to succeed, which if successful would put the fear of the law into the other papers so that they would restrain themselves. He prefers the selective process instead of a general prosecution so that he will leave his public image unblemished—an early triumph of public relations. So much for absolute freedom of the press.

Yet, in spite of attacks on him in the newspapers—the worst any president has had to endure, with the possible exceptions of Washington and Lincoln, and Franklin Roosevelt—Jefferson never brought any libel charges himself, even under the grossest provocation, nor did he, except rarely, reply to the press's attacks. It was not simply a matter of his political principles. Other aspects of his personality entered in, such as his dread of controversy that appeared to stem from his governorship of Virginia. Beyond that, he had an aristocrat's disdain (this man of the people) of general popularity, preferring the approval of informed persons; and he had a profound distaste for personal controversy, coupled with an innate politeness and amiability, as well as a strong dash of prudence.

After the passage of the Alien and Sedition Acts, on August 22, 1778, Jefferson reiterated his position forcefully in a letter to Samuel Harrison Smith, claiming that

> at a very early period of my life, I determined never to put a sentence into any newspaper. I have religiously adhered to the resolution through my life, and have great reason to be contented with it. Were I to undertake to answer the calumnies of the newspapers, it would be more than all my own time, & that of 20 aids could effect. For while I should be answering one, twenty new ones would be invented. I have thought it better to trust to the justice of my countrymen.

Jefferson's attitude toward the Federalist press was much like that of Washington's toward the Anti-Federalist papers. He was hurt and indignant to be the target of truly vicious political attacks when he considered that he had devoted his life to the service of his country, and he felt himself wholly undeserving of them. But where Washington was alternately furious and disdainful, Jefferson was usually resigned—"these moral evils must be submitted to, like the physical scourges of tempest, fire"—and unlike Washington, he came to the defense of the press whenever he saw the First Amendment challenged, even by implication.

Of all these defenses, perhaps the most significant was the episode related by Margaret Bayard Smith, wife of Samuel Harrison Smith, publisher and editor of the *National Intelligencer and Washington Advertiser,* which could have been called the Jefferson administration's paper. Mrs. Smith told about a visit paid to Jefferson one day by Baron Alexander von Humboldt, the Prussian minister, who had become friendly with the president. While he was waiting in an ante-room, the baron picked up a Federalist paper lying on the table and read with increasing ire a virulent attack on Jefferson. Still clutching the paper in his hand, von Humboldt strode into the presidential office when he was summoned and demanded to know why Jefferson permitted such libels to be published, why he did not suppress the paper and punish its editor. "Put that paper in your pocket, Baron," Jefferson told him, "and should you ever hear the reality of our liberty, the freedom of the press questioned, show them this paper—and tell them where you found it."

That was the essence of Jefferson's position; it has been noted earlier but bears repetition. He believed absolutely in freedom of the press. His detractors had a right to print what they liked, and he would defend them, only rarely defending himself. In short, he believed that it was more important to be informed than to be governed, an idea that has steadily lost ground since then.

If this was the ideal, however, the reality of newspaper practice in his era was something Jefferson deplored as much as other presidents, and with far more reason. As he told Lafayette, he truly believed that "the only security of all is in a free press. The force of public opinion cannot be resisted, when permitted freely to be expressed." Yet he could not condone everything the free press did, or even much of it, and no more when it was done in his own behalf, echoing Washington in that respect.

Jefferson was often made acutely uncomfortable by the partisan zeal of such Anti-Federalist editors as Benjamin Franklin Bache and William Duane. Conse-quently, when he moved from Philadelphia to Washington, he did not invite Duane and the *Aurora* to follow him, as the editor had fully expected. He even went so far as to deny Duane government printing contracts, which proved to be a fatal blow to the *Aurora*. It was a measure of Duane's Anti-Federalist fanati-cism that he continued to support Jefferson even after his former patron had turned on him.

By abandoning Duane, Jefferson meant to put his office above partisan squab-bling, but the practical effect, as he soon saw, was to give the Federalist papers a virtual monopoly on attack. He required a supportive organ of his own, one that would be moderate in political debate, as he was, and as he hoped all the press could be persuaded to become—a vain hope, at that moment. Samuel Harrison Smith's triweekly *National Intelligencer* was the only paper on either side that could be described as moderate. Its moderation, in fact, was an object of some scorn from the press of both parties. Smith, it was said, had carried nonpar-tisanship—or rather, unimpassioned support of Jefferson—to absurd lengths. They called the *Intelligencer* "Mr. Silky-Milky Smith's National Smoothing Plane."

Jefferson, by contrast, thought of it as more or less the way a newspaper should be, and indeed in these "Dark Ages" of journalism it shone like a beacon. It was never shrill or scurrilously partisan, like the others, and its foreign and domestic news coverage was the best of any in the young nation. While these qualities made the paper seem extremely bland by comparison with its contemporaries, they were also a guarantee that the *Intelligencer* would far outlast its raucous rivals. Changed to a daily in 1813, it remained one of the best papers in America until it disappeared in the flood of journals that followed the Civil War.

Although Jefferson flatly disavowed any connection with the *Intelligencer,* as he had earlier with the *National Gazette,* there is no reason to believe he was disinterested. Smith was his friend; they saw each other socially; and it was no accident that the *Intelligencer* was considered the administration's unofficial organ. Jefferson also enjoyed an asset in Smith's charming wife. She may have done more for his cause than her husband's paper. Margaret Bayard Smith and Dolley Madison were the forerunners of those Washington hostesses—Pearl Mesta, Evalyn Walsh McLean, and Gwen Cafritz, among others—who knew how to organize soirees where people might find themselves eating and drinking with their political enemies. At the salons Margaret Bayard presided over in their splendid country place Sidney, where Catholic University now stands, the Smiths encouraged a great deal of quiet politicking under the beneficent guidance of the host, a connoisseur of food and wine.

Whatever good was done by these occasions, however, could hardly balance the destruction caused by the paper that Jefferson's old enemy Hamilton set up in New York to carry on the ideology of the party now out of power. (Fenno, like Bache, had died in the yellow fever epidemic of 1798.) The editor Hamilton picked to operate this new Federalist organ, the New York *Evening Post,* was about as far from Smith in personality and talents as one could imagine. William Coleman was the prototpe of the big-city editor created later by Hollywood— a large, handsome man with a hearty voice, who loved women, alcohol, food, arguments, and politics. Earlier, as a lawyer in Massachusetts, he had been a rare combination of scholar and athlete, the kind of man who would read Greek in the morning and skate twenty miles from Greenfield to Northampton in the evening.

Hamilton, following Jefferson's example, dissociated himself from Coleman and the *Evening Post,* but there is little doubt that he and his friends were the paper's real founders; he carried on his philosophical and political debate with Jefferson anonymously in its columns. The *Evening Post* was pinched for funds at first, since the Federalists were now short of cash, being out of power, and so the first issues had to be printed on an old secondhand press. Even so, its quarter-size sheets found ready circulation in a city that by this time had grown to sixty thousand.

With the *Evening Post*'s arrival, a pattern of journalism was perpetuated that did nothing to alleviate the tensions between press and presidency. In his first issue of November 16, 1801, Coleman sounded a note of high principle, declaring that he abhorred "personal virulence, low sarcasm, and verbal contentions with printers and editors." He would not be swerved, he said, from "the line of temperate discussion." This kind of window dressing was increasingly common as the century wore on. Paper after paper appeared with high-minded declarations from the publisher on the front page of the first issue. They were promptly forgotten in the interests of politics.

Coleman was soon swinging the editorial ax with as much vigor as his predecessors in the Federalist press, and in his zeal he inadvertently opened the way to
another test of the relationship between the press and the presidency. It was a
testing, too, of Jefferson's Republican ideas about dealing with abuses.

A roundabout assault on Jefferson in the *Post,* a story written by Coleman
himself, provided an opportunity for the president to implement his theory that a
few libel cases brought under state laws might serve to discourage the worst
offenders. In his article Coleman had reported, without any attempt at qualification, that the "burden of the Federalist song" these days was the party's charge
that Jefferson had paid James Callender, the notorious editor of the Richmond
Examiner, to call Washington "a traitor, a robber, a perjurer; for calling Adams
a hoary-headed incendiary and for most grossly slandering the private characters
of men he knew well were virtuous." To this Coleman added, with self-righteous blandness: "These charges not a democratic Editor has yet dared or ever
will dare to meet in an open and manly discussion." The fact that Jefferson had
gotten Callender out of prison by pardoning him and other victims of the Alien
and Sedition Acts was not mentioned.

Coleman's story was picked up by an obscure paper, the Hudson (N.Y.)
Wasp, whose editor was Harry Croswell, a man who now became the first object
of Jefferson's method of curbing the libels of the opposition press. It was one of
the many paradoxes of this often paradoxical president that he saw no inconsis-
tency in his action, or, if he did, he never recorded it. He had rightfully condemned the Alien and Sedition Acts for what they were, a vengeful attempt to
intimidate if not supress the Anti-Federalist press. But there was scant philosophical or practical difference between the wrongful actions generated by the acts
and the libel action brought by the Jeffersonian Republicans at the plain suggestion of the president himself, who tacitly approved of it.

Croswell was convicted, which put the Federalists in the happy position of
being able to come forward as defenders of freedom of the press. Hamilton
himself joined the battery of Federalist lawyers who offered Croswell their talents in an appeal, and he went to Albany in January 1804 to argue in the Court of
Errors on a motion for a new trial. Before a packed courtroom Hamilton made his
famous defense of press freedom, "a pathetic, impassioned & most eloquent
address on the Danger to our Liberties," a contemporary called it.

As another Hamilton—Andrew—had done in defending John Peter Zenger,
this Federalist ideologue held up Croswell as an obscure "village printer" who
symbolized the struggle of English-speaking peoples for liberty. If the right to
criticize those in public office was "not permitted to exist in vigor and in exercise," he told the court,

> good men would become silent, corruption and tyranny would go on, step by step, in
> usurpation, until, at last, nothing that was worth speaking, or writing, or acting for,
> would be left in our country. . . . The real danger to our liberties was not from a few
> provisional troops. The road to tyranny will be opened by making dependent judges,
> by packing juries, by stifling the press, by silencing leaders and patriots. . . . The
> most dangerous, the most sure, the most fatal of tyrannies, was, by selecting and

sacrificing single individuals, under the mask and forms of law, by dependent and partial tribunals.

It was the same cause that Andrew Hamilton argued so eloquently—human freedom against government oppression—and ironically, it was this same cause that had inspired the attacks of both Jefferson and Madison on the Alien and Sedition Acts.

The core of the Croswell case was the same as it had been with Zenger. In the earlier trial the judge had ruled, properly, that Callender could not be called as a material witness to submit truth as a defense; that was still the law of the land, as it had been under British common law in Zenger's time. Jefferson and his friends must have been relieved by this ruling, however, because Callender was only too eager to get on the stand and repeat some of the charges against the president he had already made in pamphlets and in the Richmond paper, including dishonesty, cowardice, and worst of all, that Jefferson had had sexual relations with slave women on his plantation—perhaps the first public intimation of the Virginian's alleged love affair with Sally Hemings, which would become a matter of scholarly dispute nearly two centuries later.

Since truth could not be admitted as a defense, Croswell's conviction had been inevitable. In Albany, however, on the appeal, Hamilton contended that this was not a correct interpretation of the common law, that common law did in fact permit a defendant to prove the truth if libel was alleged. "I never did think truth was a crime," Hamilton asserted. "My soul has ever abhorred the thought, that a free man dared not speak the truth." Tyranny, he went on, could be found in a law which held "in the very teeth of justice and common sense that a man is equally guilty of having maliciously and wickedly published a *falsehood,* although every syllable is strictly *true.*"

Callender, as we know by hindsight, could not possibly have proved the truth of his statements, but the principle that he should be permitted to offer that defense was what Hamilton argued for. By this time, however, Callender himself had fallen off a ferryboat and drowned, possibly a suicide. One charge that Hamilton could well have proved, if he had been given the opportunity, was that Jefferson had contributed financially to Callender when the editor was an Anti-Federalist writer, before he turned against the president.

In delineating for the benefit of the appeals court his views on the rights of the press, Hamilton made his pilosophical difference with Jefferson in this matter absolutely clear. He saw no contradiction between positions he had taken in the past and what he believed now, although both he and the Federalists had changed their positions somewhat. He had never believed that the press should be entirely free of restraint and responsibility, he insisted. "The novel, the visionary, the pestilential Doctrine of an unchecked Press," he asserted, was a doctrine acceptable only to Jacobins and demagogues, and certainly he was quite ready to think that Jefferson and Madison, who believed the opposite, were both.

It was not conceivable, Hamilton went on, that anyone who treasured liberty and order could consider the press entirely free. And although he might be arguing for truth as a defense, he did not believe that it was always applicable.

Malicious intent could make a statement libelous even if it was true, Hamilton said, anticipating what future libel law would say. The "fundamental principle of jurisprudence," he asserted, was intent, where libel was concerned.

Here was the basic difference that separated not only Hamilton and Jefferson but others as well, and particularly influenced the attitude of presidents in their relationships with the press as time went on. Jefferson and Madison were believers in the absolute nature of the First Amendment. Hamilton and most of the presidents who followed Madison were First Amendment relativists, and several would have had no hesitation in abridging or denying the First's freedoms, if their interests were affected. They, like Hamilton, thought the press should have no more freedom than juries permitted it, since they were convinced that liberty was always secure with juries, where it might not be if power was given to courts or magistrates. Juries could determine both the truth and the law, and satisfy themselves about intent as well.

In Hamilton's curious line of reasoning, which seemed utterly sensible to him, it followed that the Alien and Sedition Acts were defensible because juries had been given these powers—and were not only defensible, in Hamilton's opinion, but were "an honorable, a worthy and glorious effort in favor of public liberty."

How would he define press freedom, then? "The liberty of the press," he said, "consists in the right to publish with impunity Truth with good motives for justifiable ends though reflecting on Government, magistracy or Individuals." Nothing could have been further from Jefferson's notion of it—or Madison's, for that matter. The First Amendment said nothing about responsibility.

Hamilton's eloquent appearance in Albany had two unexpected results. He was not surprised when the justices divided on partisan lines and deadlocked themselves, two to two, on his plea to give Croswell a new trial; the Republican judges were determined to punish Jefferson's defamer, and they certainly had no wish to let a jury look into the truth of his charges. The tie meant that a new trial was denied.

But Hamilton's arguments were widely reprinted and discussed, and a few years later the New York legislature passed a law that embodied most of the principles he had argued for. New York thus became the first state to admit truth as a defense in a libel action. Other states soon followed, and Hamilton's definition of libel was adopted as a model by several new states in their constitutions.

The other consequence of Hamilton's Albany appearance was far different. At a dinner party, he was said to have made a remark about Aaron Burr, his long-time rival, which, printed in a newspaper, led to the fatal duel on the heights of Weehawken, when Burr shot and killed Hamilton.

Jefferson's indirect method of dealing with his press enemies could be said to have succeeded in the case of Harry Croswell, but the president made no further moves in that direction, although the continuing attacks on him in the Federalist papers were so obnoxious that even their readers were sometimes shocked. The campaign charges of 1800 were dragged out periodically and rehearsed—that Jefferson was a dangerous demagogue, a man of no faith or morals, irreligious, dishonest, a coward during the Revolution, a slanderer of George Washington, and a man who aspired to be a dictator. A Boston paper, the *Columbian Centinel,* soon to be a thorn in Madison's presidential briar patch, ran a regular department called ''The Enquirer'' that retailed attacks on Jefferson's opinions, character, and career.

No wonder the president referred to such attacks, at the end of his first term, as ''the artillery of the press,'' in words still quoted: ''During this course of administration, and in order to disturb it, the artillery of the press has been levelled against us, charged with whatsoever its licentiousness could devise or dare . . . but public duties more urgent press on the time of public servants, and the offenders have therefore been left to find their punishment in the public indignation.'' It is a defense still employed by politicians at every level.

Nevertheless, it had been a rough first term, and Jefferson was not as unruffled by it as he wanted the public to believe. Nor was it only the assaults on him that he found disturbing. He wrote to Thomas McKean:

> The federalists having failed in destroying the freedom of the press by their gag-law [the Alien and Sedition Acts], seem to have attacked it in an opposite form, that is by pushing it's [*sic*] licentiousness & it's [*sic*] lying to such a degree of prostitution as to deprive it of all credit. And the fact is that so abandoned are the tory presses in this particular that even the least informed of the people have learnt that nothing in a newspaper is to be believed. This is a dangerous state of things, and the press ought to be restored to its credibility if possible.

Jefferson considered that his election to a second term was proof that a licentious press could not prevent the citizens of a democracy from returning a just verdict on its leaders. A successful candidate might well believe that, but the electorate had been far from ''cool and collected,'' as the president described it. In fact, the partisan press was still polarizing the country, and this virulent factionalism would soon, during Madison's administration, endanger the new nation's very existence.

Sometimes, in desperation, Jefferson was given to suggesting desperate remedies. When a seventeen-year-old boy, John Norvell, wrote to him and, saying he was considering a newspaper career, asked how a newspaper ought to be conducted, Jefferson replied (requesting that the letter not be published) at length. His inner anger was revealed in two sentences: ''I will add,'' he wrote, ''that the man who never looks into a newspaper is better informed than he who reads them, inasmuch as he who knows nothing is nearer to truth than he whose mind is filled with falsehoods and errors. He who reads nothing will still learn the great facts, and the details are all false.''

With some irony, and surely with tongue firmly in cheek, Jefferson went on to suggest that an editor could reform himself by dividing his paper into four ''chapters,'' headed ''truths,'' ''probabilities,'' ''possibilities,'' and ''lies.'' The first chapter, he continued,

> would be very short, as it would contain little more than authentic papers and information from such sources, as the editor would be willing to risk his own reputation for their truth. The second would contain what, from a mature consideration of all

circumstances, his judgment should conclude to be probably true. This, however, should rather contain too little than too much. The third and fourth should be professedly for those readers who would rather have lies for their money than the blank paper they would occupy.

These, however, were only the angry words of a president tormented for too long by a malicious, partisan press. The calmer Jefferson of an earlier time, who would rather have newspapers without government than government without newspapers, more closely represented the absolute upholder of the First Amendment. In fact, although he might lash out at it under pressure (and that seldom occurred), Jefferson was constantly fascinated by the press, primarily because he understood better than any of his contemporaries its crucial importance in making democracy work. He even collected newspapers, one of his several hobbies, establishing a file that covered the sixty years from 1741. He was correct in assuming that it was probably the only such collection in existence.

Moreover, Jefferson continued to correspond with a few journalists while he was in the White House, notably William Duane, to whom he gave more support as time went on than he had at the beginning. These letters concerned mostly matters of public policy, on which Duane was never reluctant to give his advice. Jefferson even replied to a letter from Noah Webster, who for a time edited a Federalist paper whose tone, in sharp contrast with its allies, was as moderate as the editor's personality. The president had no particular regard for Webster, however, viewing him as "a mere pedagogue, of very limited understanding and very strong prejudices and party passions," who might nevertheless be useful on occasion. In any case, it was much more agreeable to correspond with Thomas Ritchie, editor of the pro-Jefferson Richmond *Enquirer,* which began publishing in May 1804 and continued to be an influential organ for the next fifty years.

In the end, Jefferson's strong belief that public opinion would correct the press's abuse of its freedom was vindicated, in his own case at least, although he did not live to see the slow diminution of those abuses. The press remained noisily partisan during most of his lifetime, although its character began to change after 1810. Nor did the attacks on him end after he left office, since the world was no more ready to give him the peace and relative obscurity he professed to long for than it had been in Washington's case. Jefferson continued to insist that he read very little of the press, although the evidence suggests that there was more pose than truth in this statement. He subscribed to only one newspaper, he said, Ritchie's *Enquirer,* and did not even read all of that, although he continued to correspond with the editor, as he did with Duane, Smith, and one or two others.

"I have given up newspapers in exchange for Tacitus and Thucydides, for Newton and Euclid," he wrote to John Adams, "and I find myself much the happier." He made an exception for advertisements, which he regarded as the only truths in the press that could be relied upon.

Jefferson was constantly cautioning his correspondents in these later years not to divulge the contents of his letters to the press, a matter upon which he felt so strongly that, as he told John Adams, he believed unauthorized use of private letters ought to be made a crime. He had some reason to feel that way. An observation about Napoleon in a personal letter found its way into the papers in 1816, bringing down a storm of criticism on his head, even from his friends, and an official complaint from the French minister. This required more explanations from him, he complained, than any other event in his life.

Like so many other presidents, Jefferson continued to insist until the end that he was not hurt personally by newspaper attacks, but his correspondence shows that this was not the case. For example, he wrote bitterly to James Monroe in 1815: "A truth now and then projecting into the ocean of newspaper lies serves like headlands to correct our course. Indeed, my scepticism as to everything I see in a newspaper, makes me indifferent whether I ever see one." A year later, in another letter to Monroe, he added, "From forty years' experience of the wretched guess-work of the newspapers of what is not done in open daylight, and of their falsehood even as to that, I rarely think them worth reading, and almost never worth notice. A ray, therefore, now and then, from the fountains of light, is like sight restored to the blind."

Most of what Jefferson said about the press in his time was undoubtedly true, and correctly diagnosed the reason for it—it was not independent but in the hands of fierce partisans and politicians and simply reflected the intense political struggles of the times. That did not prevent him from deploring the state of journalism in the strongest terms until the end of his life, however. "As vehicles of information and a curb on our functionaries," he wrote of the newspapers to his friend Walter Jones, "they have rendered themselves useless, by forfeiting all title to belief."

Nevertheless, it was a grand paradox of Jefferson's life—so full of paradox—that in spite of the abuses of press freedom, which he had to endure personally to a degree that would not be seen for another half-century of the presidency, it was this same freedom, embodied in the First Amendment, that he advocated passionately until the day of his death. In the last letter he wrote, only ten days before he died, he expressed his faith once more in the free expression of opinion as the cornerstone of democracy.

That was the testing ground for the shifting relationship between the press and the presidency—how free the press was to be when its actions affected the president himself and, through him, the nation. Washington, Adams, and Jefferson had responded to this challenge in different ways. James Madison was now about to meet a test more severe than his predecessors had endured.

Madison and the First Amendment

All three of Madison's predecessors in the presidency had known what it was to deal with the press in peacetime, but it was his lot to face its political fury in a time of war, when the very existence of the nation was in question. No one except those who knew him best would have thought him equal to the experience.

A man who never doubted Madison's powers was his close friend Jefferson.

Their relationship has been called "no less than beautiful," and so it was. Together, they were a study in physical contrasts—Jefferson tall and graceful, Madison so short that he could scarcely be seen behind a podium, never in the best of health, an intellectual whose manner was considered by many to be indecisive and ineffective.

Jefferson knew better. He saw in his friend a man who was, like him, gentle in disposition, a believer in the same political principles, a holder of the same liberal views, a scholar who shared his unremitting passion for knowledge. Jefferson loved Madison as he would have a son; Washington admired and consulted him; the volatile Hamilton respected and for a time cultivated him. Years after both had left the public arena, Jefferson was still extolling Madison's "habits of self-possession which placed at ready command the rich resources of his luminous and discriminating mind," praising his language, which was "soothing always the feelings of his adversaries by civilities and softness of expression," and remarking on his "pure and spotless virtue which no calumny has ever attempted to sully."

Historians of our own time continue to disagree in their interpretations of both Jefferson and Madison—the origins of their political thought, their roles in the intellectual life of what is usually called Jeffersonian America, and their influence on the shaping of the Republic. Revisionism, however, has made little attempt to diminish their stature. As for the relationship of these presidents to the press, professional historians have paid little attention to this aspect of their administrations—surprising, since that relationship was so important to the men themselves. They were united in their devotion to a free press. What Madison said of Jefferson in a letter to Lafayette was equally true of himself: "Certain it is that no man more than Mr. Jefferson, regarded the freedom of the press, as an essential safeguard to free Govt., to which no man cd. be more devoted than he was, and that he never could therefore have expressed a syllable or entertained a thought unfriendly to it." In the hyperbole of the day, that sentiment may have been somewhat exaggerated, as we have seen, but it was true in its essence.

As a man brought up on a plantation, like Jefferson, and exposed from the beginning to the best cultural influences the new, raw country had to offer, Madison learned to appreciate what journalism could be when he read his favorite paper, the *Pennsylvania Packet,* a primarily commercial journal that was a cut above its rough contemporaries, or when he opened the imported pages of the London *Spectator* and found there the kind of material that would inspire "an appetite for knowledge and a taste for the improvement of the mind and manners" in young men like himself.

Madison shared Jefferson's fundamental belief that the press in general, with all its faults, was a necessary adjunct to a free society and must itself remain free of governmental interference. That was consistent with both men's ideal of political liberty as against subjugation to the aristocracy. It was in pursuit of this ideal that the twenty-five-year-old Madison, after taking his seat as an elected delegate from Orange County to the Virginia Convention in April 1776, quietly used his developing powers of persuasion to make certain that a free press was among the democratic political institutions he sought to establish.

As one of a forty-member committee entrusted with drafting a Declaration of Rights and then a Plan of Government, Madison saw to it that freedom of the press was incorporated in these documents. Article XIV of the declaration asserted: "That the freedom of the press is one of the great bulwarks of liberty, and can never be restrained but by despotic government."

This basic belief had its origins in Madison's study of the European political philosophers, although it is a subject of dispute which ones influenced him most. In this matter, however, he could not have failed to derive inspiration from those figures of the Enlightenment who were pointing the way toward an ideal system of government that they, unfortunately, were not yet in a position to enjoy. The American system that Madison, Jefferson, and the others created was the concrete expression of what the European philosophers had dreamed.

It was an eccentricity of character that led Madison to such political scholarship. Like Washington, he believed himself to be in precarious health and likely to die at an early age. As a young man, beset with these gloomy thoughts, he considered it useless to pursue a vocation and sought consolation in books beyond the law texts he was supposed to be studying. When he met Jefferson at the first sessions of the Virginia House of Delegates, his new friend offered him freedom to use the magnificent library at Monticello. The result was that Madison emerged from his reading as a self-made expert in political philosophy, not surpassed by any of the great men of his time in Europe or America. When he rose to speak at the Constitutional Convention, his voice may have been so nearly inaudible that everyone had to strain to hear it, but what he said stamped him as one who had no equal in America where knowledge of constitutional law and history was concerned.

Until shortly before the convention met, Madison had devoted little thought to the creation of a new constitution, but after his election as its secretary he organized the notes he had made during his years of study of the world's governments, from ancient Lycia to modern Germany. In them he sought to discover the strengths and weaknesses that would be likely to apply to the forming of a new government for America. His sole object was to develop a plan for a government that would overcome the defects of the Articles of Confederation, one the American people would accept.

Oddly enough, in his preliminary examination, and later in the actual work of the convention, Madison did not make a point of press freedom, and indeed joined the other delegates in ignoring it, along with other rights, in "The Plan." Presumably he thought, as they did, that these rights were implicit in the document they were composing. Nor did he discuss freedom of the press in the subsequent Federalist Papers, the historic arguments for a Constitution that he and Hamilton wrote. Not once is it mentioned in any of the papers clearly credited to him or assumed to be from his pen.

Nevertheless, when a ground swell of public demand led to the eventual enactment of a Bill of Rights, it was Madison's leadership in the initial session of the First Congress that brought about the passage of the ten amendments recommended. From his experience in the Virginia Convention, Madison was able to help materially in the adoption of a First Amendment that not only guaranteed press freedom but established the division of church and state, another principle in which he believed profoundly.

Madison also had some early education in how valuable a politically controlled newspaper could be when in 1791 he aided in bringing his Princeton classmate, Philip Freneau, to the temporary capital in Philadelphia to establish the *National Gazette*. Although the charge was denied, the *Gazette* was, in fact, created as an organ to attack the administration, greatly exacerbating the furious party warfare that was to plague both Washington and Jefferson.

As the first president's secretary of state, Jefferson had tried to explain why an opposition paper was necessary in a democracy, as we have seen. "No government ought to be without censors," he had written, "& where the press is free, no one ever will." Washington and most of the other Federalists could give only qualified approval to that sentiment. Madison agreed with his friend, however, as one might expect. In helping Freneau to establish the *Gazette,* he wrote, he "entertained hopes that a free paper meant for general circulation, and edited by a man of genius, of republican principles, and a friend of the Constitution, would be some antidote to the doctrines and discourses circulated in favor of Monarchy and Aristocracy and would be an acceptable vehicle of public information in many places not sufficiently supplied with it."

With these principles rooted so firmly in his mind, Madison's shock at the passage of the Alien and Sedition Acts was all the greater. "The Alien bill proposed in the Senate is a monster that must forever disgrace its parents," he wrote to Jefferson when the legislation was introduced. After discussing the matter with his friend, Madison wrote the Virginia Resolutions as a protest against the infringement of freedom of speech and the liberty of the press, which he saw as clearly inherent in the acts.

This episode was a turning point in Madison's political career. He had been a Federalist, a moderate supporter of strong central government, but now he joined Jefferson's Republican opposition to what he termed the Federalists' "absolute, or, at least, a mixed monarchy." Thus the Virginia Resolutions, with their strong support of state sovereignty, appeared to contradict the views he had expressed so eloquently in the Federalist papers. Yet, in combination with Jefferson's even more fiery Kentucky Resolutions, they were enough to be a major factor in the coming collapse of the Federalist party, with the ultimate result of bringing Madison himself first into the State Department and then into the presidency.

The Virginia Resolutions were important for another reason. They reflected Madison's evolving theory of free government and, in the area of press freedom, his challenge to the ancient doctrine of seditious libel, which had never been repudiated by libertarians. The resolutions represented a major step in the evolution of the meaning of the free-speech-and-press clause of the First Amendment.

At the same time, Madison was also learning how to use the press. Both he and Jefferson saw such manipulation as a primary means for reaching the public, and, in the manner of all presidents, they did not hesitate to manipulate it in whatever way they could. It was the bare beginning of what has become an art in our time, as government has become ever more powerful. When Washington was concerned about what would be the best way of conveying his intentions of serving a second term, there was not the slightest hesitation in Madison's counsel: "With regard to the mode, none better occurs than a simple publication in the newspapers." This advice was conveyed indirectly to Washington through a letter to Jefferson on May 5, 1798. Madison had learned that the press could also be approached indirectly, a method often employed by Jefferson, and so he sometimes sent him information that he thought should reach the public through newspapers, but left it to Jefferson as to how the information should be released.

Having observed the experience of three administrations, Madison as president was better able to deal with the press than any of his predecessors. He understood the dangers and the opportunities, and he had the cool intellectual ability to avoid the one and seize the other. Madison balanced his firm belief in freedom of the press with the practical realization that it was a good idea for a president to be circumspect in his relations with it, and he had no illusions whatever about the evils of the party press.

Both Madison and the press were changing during the years of his presidency. On the president's part, it was a change that led him away from liberal expedients and toward a delicate balancing act in which he continued to profess Jefferson's philosophy of state sovereignty and strict construction, while at the same time he practiced the principle of strong central government—fortunately, as it turned out, because the states were soon to be dangerously divided by the War of 1812. As for the press, it was beginning to emerge from the partisan morass it had been wallowing in since the pre-Revolutionary years, and it was also beginning to move toward a broader conception of itself, and to lay the foundations for a time not far off when the greatest editors would be nearly as well known and powerful as the leading figures in public office. Editors had been pamphleteers until now, and the newspapers themselves had been shabby sheets, folded over once, which had little real news, a few advertisements, and lengthy editorials in the partisan, frequently violent, pamphleteering tradition. They were not even editorials in a legitimate sense, because more often than not they were written by the politicians who used the newspapers as party platforms. Nor were the editorials of the single-subject kind we know today, but instead were a series of essays, carrying forward an argument and intended to have a cumulative effect. No politically independent newspaper had yet appeared.

Newspapers had an influence entirely out of proportion to their character because the electorate was so small, as Allan Nevins was first to point out long ago. Nearly everybody who voted read the newspapers, and if there was little but politics in them, that was hardly surprising, considering the cultural state of the new nation. "A raw young nation," Nevins wrote of it, "which had no independent literature, no drama, no art, no music, intent upon conquering a living from the wild forest and prairie—how much could this nation expect beyond politics; beyond underbred personalities, ill-tempered campaign harangues, and a none-too-intelligent discussion of fiscal topics? Certainly most journals gave it nothing better."

Historians of today may consider this an overly harsh judgment, but in the context of the times the verdict still seems largely true. The editorials of Madison's time were wooden in style, shrill and vituperative in tone, and lacking in perspective. Editors did not yet know how to handle news and usually made it part of their editorial commentary.

Nevertheless, when Madison viewed the press he hoped to influence as president, he could discern a few outstanding newspapers. One was Samuel Harrison Smith's *National Intelligencer* in Washington, Jefferson's old house organ. Another was William Coleman's *Evening Post* in New York, already the most distinguished of its contemporaries, having the benefit initially of both a great editor and a brilliant backer, Alexander Hamilton. These were established papers when a rival entered the field in 1811, Hezekiah Niles's *Register,* first issued in Baltimore and later moved to Washington. The *Register* is known to researchers of our time as a mine of historical information, but in its day it was also an effective editorial influence for Federalist, Whig, and protective tariff causes. There were also Thomas Ritchie's Richmond *Enquirer,* whose editorials soon achieved a countrywide audience, and Nathan Hale's (a nephew of the patriot spy) Boston *Daily Advertiser,* which bore the editor's fearless, responsible stamp.

Madison's chief support came from the *National Intelligencer* and the two co-editors who were now running it, both during his presidency and for a good many years afterward. They were Joseph W. Gales, Jr., who took over the editorship in 1819 and remained until 1860, and his brother-in-law William Winston Seaton, who joined Gales in 1812 and stayed with the paper until 1864. These men supported Madison during his term, later becoming the strong backers of John Quincy Adams, and still later supporters of Henry Clay.

The *Intelligencer* was a pioneer in the change that now began to take place in newspapers. Both Gales and Seaton were accomplished stenographers, and they covered the debates in Congress themselves, with an accuracy and fullness that put the other newspapers to shame. They were also students of government and history, which gave their editorials a perspective their rivals could not begin to match.

More significant for Madison, as it happened, than the support of the *Intelligencer* or any other Eastern paper was the growing influence on the electorate of papers in the West—meaning, in those days, the modern Middle West. John Scull's *Pittsburgh Gazette* had led the way in 1786, as the first newspaper west of the mountains, and Scull was closely followed a year later by John Bradford, who set up his *Kentucky Gazette* in Lexington. There were twenty-one newspapers west of the mountains by 1800. The subsequent rapid spread of the press was stimulated by a congressional act of 1814 mandating that all federal laws be printed in two (it was later changed to three) newspapers in each state and territory. That made it necessary to begin papers even in places not yet ready for them.

The Western press was vigorous, outspoken, and intensely regional, characteristics that played a large part in the outbreak of the War of 1812, that serio-comic drama which Samual Eliot Morison called "the most unpopular war that this country has ever waged, not even excepting the Vietnam conflict." Congress passed the bill declaring it by only seventy-nine to forty-nine in the House, and nineteen to thirteen in the Senate. This reluctance was more than justified by the events that followed, events that could have produced, as the historian Francis

Beirne has observed, these accurate headlines: "Detroit Falls," "Chicago Garrison Massacred," "New York Blockaded," "Enemy Fleet in Chesapeake Bay," "New England Invaded," "Maine Subjugated," "Boston Threatened," "U.S. Army Driven from Field and Demoralized," "Washington Captured," "Capitol and White House in Flames. President and Congress in Flight," "Baltimore Attacked by Land and Sea," and "British Army before New Orleans."

While every war has several causes, a sound case could be made that the initial impetus for this disastrous, needless conflict, one that nearly ended the American nation before it had scarcely begun, came from the Western press. It is part of American mythology, believed by generations of citizens, that the war was caused by national resentment over British abuses of free passage on the high seas and the forcible repatriation of former British naval ratings by "impressment." The myth asserts that these practices so outraged national pride and particularly New England maritime interests that the country was driven to war.

On the contrary, New England was deeply opposed to the war. Only eight out of ten senators from the region voted for declaring it, and only eleven of fourteen New York representatives in the House joined them. While these may seem like overwhelming majorities, the fact that there were any defections at all is significant, and the figures themselves do not reflect the serious reservations of many who voted in favor of the declaration from other states as well. Enthusiasm for the war was centered in the West and South, and, even at that, the War Department could get only ten thousand of the fifty thousand one-year volunteers it had been authorized to enlist; it was able to build the regular army to no more than half its authorized strength.

Western newspapers initiated their campaign for the war as early as 1810, when Tecumseh, the formidable Shawnee chief, began a last-ditch attempt to drive the white man back to the East by uniting the tribes of the Ohio Valley. The early results of this campaign were a bloody success, and the beleaguered settlers were consequently further outraged when they discovered that Tecumseh's forces were being supplied by the British through Canada. Anti-British sentiment flared, and some politicians began to press for war against Britain. Known in Congress as the "War Hawks," they did not care about any other aspects of the growing conflict—what was happening to seamen, or to New England merchants, or to other commercial interests suffering heavy losses from American shipping embargoes. They wanted action in their own interests and established themselves in a better position to get it by electing one of the most aggressive of their number, Henry Clay, as Speaker of the House.

All this became a primary issue in the election of 1812. Governor De Witt Clinton, of New York, Madison's opponent, was against going to war. But Clay had the votes, and if Madison wanted to win the election, he would be compelled to side with the War Hawks. Voters could choose between Clinton and peace, or Madison and war, since he was being offered to the public as the shipping interests' protector. Unwillingly, Madison found himself elected on that basis, and the opposition promptly labeled the conflict that followed as "Mr. Madison's War." He had not been given even one vote from the New England electors, while the West cast its electoral vote for him unanimously. The others divided about evenly.

The Western press played a strident, flamboyant role in these events, one that made Eastern editors realize they were not alone in the country any more. Embarking on his second term as president, Madison was uneasily conscious of the political debt he owed to these Western editors, who would soon help to put Andrew Jackson in the White House. But being the man of integrity that he was, Madison did not give his Western supporters particular favors, as Jackson was later to do. Madison was an Easterner, in any case, thrust unhappily into a war he did not really want, conscious of his great responsibility to hold together somehow a country that was deeply divided and in great danger.

Madison expected to be attacked by the opposition press, and he was, in the familiar virulent manner of the past, but he followed Jefferson's example and made no public reply, regardless of what was said about him. He seemed less prepared to deal with his partisans, who were unremittingly fierce. They were particularly aggressive on his behalf in Baltimore, a shipping port badly hurt by the conflict and strongly antiwar from the beginning. There the voice of the opposition was the *Federal Republican,* published by Jacob Wagner and Alexander Hanson, whose editorials and news stories as well were devoted to a continuing attack on Madison and the war, conducted in the most scurrilous manner.

For the first time since the Revolution, the troublesome question that is still with us today was raised: how far should press criticism be permitted to go when the country's security is threatened by an enemy? Everything in Madison's previous career was against that word "permitted." By his strict construction of the First Amendment, he believed it meant what it said, and he had no intention of censoring the *Federal Republican,* although conceivably he could have exerted the wartime powers of a president to do so.

That would have been ambiguous ground, however. It was not a question of disclosing the movements of troops and ships, where he could be expected to have the support of most people for suppressing or censoring a paper. It was partisan political attack, of the most familiar kind. Madison shied away from the mere idea of suppression—if, in fact, he ever seriously entertained it—in the belief that the rantings of one newspaper could not place the country in any more peril than it already was.

Madison's loyal supporters in Baltimore thought differently. When the *Federal Republican* protested the declaration of war with a series of violent attacks on Madison, cries of "treason" and "traitors" rose from the president's partisans. One day they poured out into the streets, attacked the paper's offices and printshop, and destroyed them, mangling the presses. The two editors saved their lives only because of a timely warning from their friend John Howard Payne, the composer, who was then far away from the "Home Sweet Home" in East Hampton, Long Island, which he later immortalized. Wagner and Hanson retreated to the comparative safety of Georgetown, while the mob rampaged through the Baltimore streets, burning and looting, beating up any Federalists they encountered, and completely intimidating the city's government.

Meanwhile in Georgetown, Wagner and Hanson, encouraged by their Federalist friends there, printed another edition of their paper and brought it up to Baltimore, where they intended to distribute it from Wagner's house. Anticipating the mob's reaction to this move, the editors' friends fortified the building against siege, which soon began, as rapidly as the antiwar mob had a chance to read this second edition.

What the *Federal Republican* (misnamed, in the circumstances) called the president was exceeded only by what his supporters called the paper, its editors, and its staff. The common word for Madison was "traitor," echoed on the other side in castigating the Anti-Federalists. The word seemed particularly ungrateful when applied to two men on the *Republican*'s staff—James Lingan and Henry ("Light-Horse Harry") Lee, who had been generals and heroes only a few years before in the Revolution.

These two men, other staff members, and the editors were in Wagner's fortified house when the mob came again. There was a short, furious battle that threatened to end in a bloodbath as the besiegers brought up a cannon. At this critical point, those who could still think prevailed and a truce was arranged, by which the staff was given safe conduct to a jail. But that was not enough to satisfy the mob. After the men were marched away to presumed safety, Wagner's house was destroyed, and then the infuriated zealots descended on the jail and assaulted it. This time there were no restraints. A few staff members escaped, but nine others were savagely beaten by the mob. Lingan was killed, and Lee was maimed for life.

Although he said little about it, Madison must have suffered during this episode. His own supporters had violated his firmly held principle of press freedom, yet he hardly dared denounce them. Worse, their actions were utterly alien to the president's character. But to have weakened the unity of his own party at this juncture might have been just enough to destroy the country's already precarious balance. A cherished principle had been flouted, at the very least, but the real issue was the nation's survival, and Madison well understood that he must do nothing.

Opposition persisted elsewhere as the war dragged on disastrously, and in the darkest hours it flared again in that stronghold of dissent, New England, with consequences that brought the whole issue to the fore a second time, in what seemed to some an even more dangerous aspect. The Federalist split over the war was at its worst in New England. Historians today are inclined to minimize the importance of this dissent, and it could be argued that Madison did not see the aspects of press freedom in it as significant because he did not take the party revolt there seriously. That might be, but, viewed in the context of the times, it is difficult to believe that Madison contemplated what was happening in New England with as much lack of concern as some contemporary scholars have thought.

It could have scarcely seemed less than threatening to him when such eminent men as Chief Justice John Marshall, Harrison Gray Otis, and Timothy Pickering joined the opposition. In Massachusetts there was a direct challenge from the state government itself. An address to the people was issued by the lower house of the General Court, advising them to "organize a *peace party* throughout your Country, and let all other party distinctions vanish."

Here was open defiance of the president by leading figures in his own party, coming at a time when the war he was committed to conduct seemed at the point of collapsing on the United States. The resistance in New England was not a matter of mobs in the streets but of old, rich, and respected families, particularly in Massachusetts, where only a few supported Madison. The academic community, especially at Harvard, opposed the war, and the state government went no further in support than it was compelled to by federal law. Every state government in the region joined in the opposition movement except New Hampshire's. Everywhere people spoke of Madison as "the little man in the Palace"—a forerunner of "that man in the White House," as President Franklin Roosevelt's opponents often referred to him.

When a war embargo was declared in 1814, effectively putting a stop to New England trade with the enemy, the region was outraged. Inflammatory memorials—that is, resolutions—began to issue at once from every quarter, and there were extremists who declared that if the Constitution permitted embargoes, even monarchy was preferable; it was suggested that New Englanders take their rights into their own hands. That kind of talk alarmed the moderates, and they moved quickly to dampen down fiery calls for a regional convention. Madison did respond, however, to the dangerous unpopularity of the embargo and repealed it.

In all these maneuvers the press played an accustomed role, not much changed since the Revolution. Coverage of the war itself was as haphazard as it had been in the earlier conflict, and otherwise newspapers divided on the usual partisan lines. Madison found little support from them in New England, particularly in Massachusetts, where the press continued to be the focus for dissent from the war, just as it had crystallized and propelled anti-British sentiment before and during the Revolution.

Thus, when Boston was threatened with invasion, Madison was not surprised but could well have been dismayed by the enthusiasm with which the Federalist press supported the disinclination of the party's leaders to do anything about defending the city. On the contrary, they talked of welcoming the invaders, who at least could be expected to respect private property—a fantasy in itself, as the British themselves proved after they took Washington. The ruthless treatment of that city jarred even the Federalist editors, who suddenly began urging the immediate fortifying of Boston. But then the British changed their minds, the fleet poised to attack sailed away, and press and politicians alike, relieved of danger, quickly revived their old resentments.

These culminated in that often disputed event known as the Hartford Convention. The idea originated largely with Harrison Gray Otis, who proposed a convention of the New England states, meeting at Hartford, to decide what they ought to do about the war they abhorred and opposed. The idea was to draft some constitutional amendments designed to protect the interests of New England and permit those states to conduct their own defense, if needed. The leader of this frankly secessionist group was no radical crackpot but a staunch Federalist who came from an old and respected Boston family—John ("Jack") Lowell, whom Jeffersonian editors, supporters of Madison, ridiculed as "Mad Jack."

The Federalist press became a prime mover in promoting Lowell's idea for a new constitution and new union that would encompass only the thirteen original states. With only one exception, the Boston papers considered it as a platform for the Hartford Convention, and the Boston *Gazette* predicted that if Madison was not out of office by July 4, 1815, "a new form of government will be in operation in the eastern section of the Union."

As the oldest and most respected of Boston's Federalist papers, the *Columbian Centinel* lent its prestige to promoting Lowell's scheme, advocating the new union in a series of articles whose tone recalled earlier excesses of the party press. Announcing Connecticut's and Rhode Island's acceptance to the Hartford Convention, the *Centinel* employed a graphics device it had used earlier to announce successive state ratifications of the Constitution. The two states, said the text, were the second and third pillars of a "New Federal Edifice Raised," and the accompanying drawing showed three columns in place for the edifice, with space for two more. A Republican paper, the *Yankee,* observed that the pillars looked more like snuff bottles in an apothecary's window, giving rise to that party's derisive description of the Hartford meeting as the Snuff Bottle Convention.

The *Centinel*'s continuing ardent advocacy of the convention brought support from Federalist papers. The *Federal Republican,* which had resumed publishing in Georgetown, after its destruction in Baltimore, printed an open letter to Madison, advising him to do "immediate justice to all the reasonable claims of New England," and to "withdraw . . . your disgraced and incompetent generals."

Madison's response to all this was silence—his customary policy. Again the question intrudes: was it because he refused to take Lowell's movement seriously, and regarded the Federalist press's ardent advocacy of it as just another series of partisan fulminations of a kind so familiar to him? Possibly, perhaps even probably, but it is unlikely that the architect of the First Amendment could have disregarded in his mind the implications posed by the press's exercise of it. The country, after all, was perilously involved in a war it could conceivably lose, and in the midst of it, here was a paper in Georgetown, in his own backyard, publishing what amounted to treason, not to mention what the New England gazettes were advocating. The question of how much freedom the press should have in wartime had at least been raised, although it was never seriously debated until Lincoln's time.

The problem was further exacerbated by the conduct of the press when the convention actually met in Hartford. For three weeks the remainder of the country read about its proceedings with fascination and, by many, with apprehension. The *Centinel* led off by presenting an address to the delegates that proclaimed: "At your hands, therefore, we demand deliverance. New England is unanimous. And we announce our irrevocable decree that the tyrannical oppression of those who at present usurp the power of the Constitution is beyond endurance. And we will resist.'' These sentiments were echoed by other Federalist papers, which added their own belligerent warnings to Madison.

As for the Republican press, it was busy denouncing what was happening in Hartford as treason. Editors asserted that the real business of the meeting was to set up a New England Confederacy, and the more fearful pleaded with the delegates not to precipitate a civil war. Madison's organ, the *National Intelligencer,* preached Republican doctrine to the dissidents, reminding them that the people retained sovereign power by their adoption of the Constitution, and the Richmond *Enquirer,* the South's leading Republican paper, proclaimed that "nullification or secession was treason and that the respectable gentlemen assembled at Hartford, if they attempted either course, should be treated as traitors.'' It was only forty-five years later that both Northern and Southern papers would be on exactly the opposite sides of this issue.

Press reports from Hartford, and the reaction elsewhere, raised public controversy to such a peak that the convention drove the war itself to a subsidiary position in the newspapers. As we know now, however, there was no substantial cause for panic. Of the five New England states, only three were fully represented at Hartford, and they were far from being unanimous in their views. Moreover, a moderate, George Cabot, was drafted (unwillingly) to be president of the convention, and he soon found that most of the delegates were not at all radical and had no intention of seceding from the Union, in spite of their disgust with Madison and his administration. Lowell complained that he did not know "a single bold and ardent man" among the Massachusetts and Connecticut delegations.

However, Madison took what the convention produced seriously enough to make an effort that he believed would appease the New Englanders on the single issue they considered immediate and vital—the raising of militia. He gave in completely to the convention's demands by signing a bill that authorized raising these forces but specified that they be employed only in the states where they were raised, or in adjoining states, and nowhere else except with the consent of the governor of the state where they were summoned to arms.

But the New Englanders wanted total surrender and demanded that Madison agree to let them deduct expenses for raising militia from federal revenues. To that end they sent three commissioners to Washington and instructed them to meet with Madison and demand this concession. While the commissioners were passing through Philadelphia, however, they were told of Andrew Jackson's victory at New Orleans, and by the time they arrived in Baltimore, news announcing the Treaty of Ghent (which would have made Jackson's battle unnecessary if it had gotten there sooner) arrived in Washington. The war was over. There was no issue, no ultimatum to be delivered; the Hartford Federalists and their "ambassadors,'' as they had been called, were left hanging in the air.

It was an outcome made to order for the Republican press, and its editors responded happily, with cartoons, poems, and editorials satirizing the Hartford Convention. It could all have turned out quite differently, of course, if the war itself had not come to an end, and while the secession of New England was not the mission of the "ambassadors,'' that could conceivably have been the result.

However, the myth that it *was* the mission of the three delegates was planted so firmly that, as late as 1967, President Lyndon Johnson, trapped in the Vietnam morass, employed it at a press conference in an effort to lower public dismay over the progress of the war.

No doubt Johnson learned this story, along with generations of other Americans, from his school textbooks and ornamented it with further erroneous details for his own purposes. In that respect he echoed the Republican newspapers of Madison's time, which were assiduous in spreading the story that a secession plot had been cut off only by Jackson's victory and the timely news of the signing at Ghent. Thus they successfully distracted the public from the real story, which was Madison's mismanagement of the war. Americans even believed that Jackson had won the conflict for them, although in fact the British expeditionary force in New Orleans had already been recalled before the ministers in London knew it was involved in what the Americans thought was a decisive battle.

So the affair of the Hartford Convention ended in anticlimax. Madison's failure to make any kind of point about the conduct of the press in what might possibly have been a treasonous movement, for all he knew at the time, was simply another confirmation of his belief that government had no right to censor newspapers regardless of what they said, even in such extreme circumstances.

In any case, Madison was not given to passion, whether in his public or private life. He bore little rancor toward Britain after the war, and even less against his enemies in the press. At the end of his life, still under attack in the papers, he wrote to Tench Coxe, November 3, 1823:

> Withdrawn as I am from the public Theatre, and holding life itself by a short thread, it would not be an unreasonable expectation that hostilities of every sort and from every quarter should cease. It has been my practice, through a long career, to let the various calumnies which I did not escape to die their natural death. . . . It is to be hoped that the friends of truth will have provided adequate corrections for errors of the former (curious and malicious) and libels of the latter, as time may bring them to light.

It was a salutary commentary on the period following his departure from office that came to be known as the Era of Good Feelings.

Monroe and His Doctrine

By the time James Monroe followed Madison into the White House, the nation was more than a little weary of partisan politics. There was a disposition to pause for breath in an atmosphere of calm while a regrouping took place beneath this placid surface. The Virginians were losing their lengthy grip on the government, and an expanding nation was beginning to boil with a new political ferment, but for the moment a relative quiet prevailed after the storms of the past.

No one could have been better qualified to preside over this lull than Monroe, a shy man who kept his feelings much to himself and was not disposed to engage his enemies, whether in the press or out of it. There was a reminder of the past about him in the old-style cocked hat he wore—the last president to wear one— but there was something quite new about his preoccupation with foreign policy rather than the domestic politics that had preoccupied his predecessors, with the exception of Madison.

This man, "whose soul might be turned wrong side outwards without discovering a blemish to the world," in his friend Jefferson's view, set the tone for his administration in an inaugural address that proclaimed national honor as "national property to the highest value"—a discreet bow to the Federalists—and at the same time reassured the Anti-Federalists that although the states were protected by a national government under a "mild parental system," they would still enjoy "their separate sphere" in a country where once again government was "in the hands of the people."

Soon after he took office, Monroe sought to spread his soothing philosophy among the electorate by a tour of the country, or at least the well-populated Eastern part of it—the first such tour any president had taken since Washington's excursions north and south in 1789 and 1791. Leaving the Federal City on May 31, 1818, Monroe was on the road until September 17, and, for the first time, there was full press coverage of a presidential journey. Local newspapers, of course, had recorded Washington's progress, but Monroe's tour was reported extensively in accounts given a wide circulation through reprinting elsewhere. Thus the editor of the New Haven *Herald* caught the spirit of Monroe's journey and saw his words carried widely around the nation:

> The dress of the President has been deservedly noticed in other papers for its neatness and republican simplicity. He wore a plain blue coat, a buff under dress, and a hat and cockade of the revolutionary fashion. It comported with his rank, was adapted to the occasion, well calculated to excite in the minds of the people, the remembrance of the day which "tried men's souls." It was not the sound of artillery, the ringing of bells, nor the splendid processions alone, from which we are to judge of the feelings and sentiments of the people on this occasion—it was the general spirit of hilarity which appeared to manifest itself in every countenance, that evinced the pride and satisfaction with which the Americans paid the voluntary tribute of respect to the rule of their own choice—to the magistrate of their own creation. The demon of party for a time departed, and gave place for a general burst of National Feeling.

This was exactly the impression the president wanted to create. To the nostalgic, his progress through the states must have revived memories of Washington, and the first president would surely have approved of his tour, if not entirely of him. With no pretensions to being of Washington's stature, Monroe nevertheless had many of his attributes. He was a military hero of the Revolution, a wounded one at that. His view of the nation was calm; he never found anything in it that was truly alarming. He viewed the presidency as the culmination of a lifetime of public service. He was deeply opposed to partisan politics and political wars. Like Washington, Monroe believed that everyone should work together for the greater glory of the nation.

Yet James Monroe could not have had pleasant memories of the Great Man, who had appointed him minister to France in 1794, giving him a post only a master diplomat could have filled successfully. His task was to convince the French that the treaty John Jay was negotiating with the British in London would not harm their interests and that Revolutionary France should give post-Revolutionary America the same cooperation that had helped to create it.

Monroe knew better. He was embarrassed by Jay's negotiations and unhappy with what was produced. Meanwhile, in a determined effort to win the support of France, where his sympathies lay, he made an unwise speech to the French National Convention, of such a glowingly partisan character that it brought him a stern rebuke from Secretary of State Edmund Randolph. The State Department sent Monroe arguments with which to defend Jay's treaty, but he virtually ignored them. Washington instructed Timothy Pickering, Randolph's successor, to recall Monroe in 1796, charging him with incompetence, being remiss in carrying out his duties, and pursuing incorrect courses.

All this had long since been forgotten by the public, if not by his few political enemies, when President Monroe's coach began rolling through New England. The press had already anointed him, and, surprisingly, the formerly virulent Federalist papers had been as loud as the others in his praise. Only two weeks before the inauguration William Tudor, Jr., editor of the *North American Review,* soon to be the nation's most distinguished periodical but at the moment a Federalist organ so partisan that the Anti-Federalists had called it the "North Unamerican," wrote a letter to the president-elect in which he declared, "I have heard in more than one instance solid respectable citizens express their belief in your magnanimity and generous feelings." He went on to suggest that the time was ripe for a reconciliation between Federalist Massachusetts and the national government.

With these comforting words in mind, Monroe entered Boston, the stronghold of federalism and home of the *Columbian Centinel,* which only the other day had been threatening Madison with New England's secession. If he had been apprehensive, he was no doubt greatly relieved to read in the *Centinel* of July 12, 1817: "During the late Presidential jubilee many persons have met at festive boards, in pleasant converse, whom party politics had long severed. We recur with pleasure to all the circumstances which attended the demonstration of good feelings."

That phrase, "good feelings," struck a popular chord, was picked up and repeated by other papers and came to characterize the two Monroe administrations as the Era of Good Feelings until well into this century, when modern revisionism disclosed that the good feelings were only a mask hiding turbulent political and social change building up beneath the surface. At the time, however, it seemed for the moment that Washington's dream of a one-party government might be realized after all. The administration's paper in Washington, the *National Intelligencer,* expressed this hope: "Never before, perhaps, since the institution of civil government, did the same harmony, the same absence of party spirit, the same national feeling, pervade a community. The result is too consoling to dispute too nicely about the cause."

Monroe was gratified by this astonishing harmony of press support, but it did not materially change his attitude toward newspapers. Where his friends Jefferson and Madison had been staunch defenders and supporters of a free press, believing in its absolute protection under the First Amendment, Monroe seemed to regard it more as a necessary evil. He was mildly appreciative of the press when it supported him, but when the inevitable turning point came, he viewed it with the same disdain he directed toward others who might assault the pedestal of the presidency.

Monroe returned from his presidential tour, however, with its general approbation still soothingly in his mind. Ostensibly traveling to view the work on coastal fortifications and frontier outposts for which Congress had voted large sums of money, his real purpose was to heal the raw wounds of party conflict, a task in which he was greatly aided by the newspapers as they covered his progress meticulously. He could not escape criticism entirely, however. Even members of his own party complained that he was spending time and money that could have been better employed in solving the pressing problems of the new administration.

Back in Washington, he turned to those problems, but he did so without seeming to feel it necessary to convert the unprecedented support he was getting from the newspapers into a weapon he might use to advance his policies. Monroe appeared to believe his position was so secure that he did not need to make any effort to influence public opinion, which in any case was on his side.

Consequently he made no particular attempt to use the *National Intelligencer,* which had spoken for his party since Jefferson's time, as a mouthpiece. His relationship with it was perfunctory, although it continued to be the administration's unofficial organ. Not that Monroe disdained the papers. He read them regularly and, as his correspondence shows, used them as a valuable source of information. As had been the case with previous presidents, he was sent dozens of papers by editors who gave him free subscriptions, for various reasons of their own. And as Washington particularly had done, Monroe resented the practice. On March 21, 1821, he wrote rather testily to Madison:

> Since I have been in this office, many newspapers have been sent to me, from every part of the Union, unsought, which having neither time nor curiosity to read, are in effect thrown away. I should have stopped this practice, but from delicacy to the Editors, & expecting also that they would subject me to no charge. Lately I have been informed that the same practice took place in your time, & had been tolerated till you retired, when the Editors sent you bills for the amount of the subscription to their papers, for the eight years, making an enormous sum. Be so kind as to inform me whether this was the fact, as in case it was I may write to the Editors (a few excepted & a very few) not to send them.

If Monroe had taken more notice of the newspaper on his doorstep, the *Intelligencer,* he might have better appreciated what an ally he had. In some ways, as journalism's eminent historian, Frank Luther Mott, has told us, it was the best of a long line of Washington dailies. Founded by Joseph Gales, Sr., it had come into its own under the ownership of Samuel Harrison Smith, an era described earlier. Smith had learned shorthand from Gales, and had won a brilliant reputation in Philadelphia before Jefferson persuaded him to come down to the new Federal City (no more than a rough village then) and issue a paper that would be the administration's official organ. Thus the *Intelligencer* was established as a triweekly on October 31, 1800.

Soon after, Smith became the semiofficial reporter of the debates in the House, and for a long time his was the only record made, which as a by-product gave the *Intelligencer* a distinct advantage over every other paper. Until 1825, or a little later, the remainder of the press had to base its news about what was happening in Congress on the *Intelligencer's* reports. As a newspaper, it was modest enough—running a mere four pages for years, with only advertising on the first and fourth pages, and Congress's proceedings, interspersed with other news, on pages two and three. Unlike nearly all its contemporaries, but very like Monroe himself, it was not politically belligerent or noisy in any way.

When Smith retired in 1810, the paper had fallen into the hands of the founder's son, Joseph Gales, Jr., who two years later took a partner, W. W. Seaton, who had worked for his father and married his sister. These brothers-in-law proved to be an ideal team. Both were expert shorthand reporters, and both devoted this talent to recording what happened in Congress, one sitting on the Speaker's left hand in the House, the other taking a similar position with the president of the Senate. They even shared these dignitaries' snuff boxes, or so it was said.

The *Intelligencer* became a daily in 1813, and by the time Monroe came to the White House it was solidly established not only as the party's newspaper but, in a nonpartisan sense, as the printer to Congress. It lost that favored position later, as we shall see, but for more than fifty years it continued to be the leading American newspaper, in the judgment of Mott and others, although that may be disputed today. It was a sound, reliable, informative paper of a kind not seen before its advent, and not to be equaled for solid, dispassionate reporting until the New York *Times* was founded in 1851.

Such was Monroe's powerful ally, whose support he treated so casually. Perhaps it was the president's natural modesty and shyness, as well as his overriding preoccupation with matters of state, that made him less forceful about the press, either pro or con. Nevertheless he knew that the papers had to be dealt with, and that task he left to his secretary of state, John Quincy Adams, whose voluminous diary tells us most of what we know about Monroe's press relations. Here, for example, is the president's typical method of working with the *Intelligencer,* as Adams tells it in his diary entry for July 24, 1818:

> The Florida business and General Jackson absorb so much of his cares and anxieties that every other subject is irksome to him, so that he can give little attention to it. He had given Gales the paragraph prepared for that purpose by Mr. Wirt. Gales told him it had got abroad that there was a division of opinion among the members of the Administration on the point of approving or disavowing Jackson's proceedings [his campaigns in Florida]. He had answered there had been diversity of opinion, as

naturally happened upon all important measures, but that all were agreed upon the result, and he said Gales wanted to add that the opinion of the members of the Administration had been unanimous.

Here was a situation quite unlike our own times—a president acknowledging to an editor that there was a split in the administration on a matter of policy but nevertheless presenting the face of unanimity, and then hearing the editor advise him to *emphasize* the unanimity. Gales was intensely loyal to Monroe, but apparently he changed his mind, because the article he had discussed with the president appeared in the *Intelligencer* four days later without any mention of cabinet unanimity. The omission did not escape Adams, who had no confidence in the press. He wrote in his diary four days later:

> There is in the country a great mass of desire to be in opposition to the Administration. It is a sort of instinctive impression that Mr. Monroe's Administration will terminate by bringing in an *adverse* party to it. This of itself engages all the newspapers not employed by public patronage, but desiring it, and many of those possessing it, against the Administration. This propensity to blame it is still increased by an affectation of showing their independence, and escaping the charge of subserviency to the Executive.

Monroe was well aware that a large part of the press was highly critical of Andrew Jackson's forays against the Spanish and the Indians in Florida and was not likely to applaud his administration's approval of them, unanimous or not, even though to some people Jackson was already a hero. To many newspapers, particularly the Philadelphia *Aurora,* the general was a "tyrant," a "ruffian," and a "murderer." Monroe's interest in the affair was the acquisition of Florida, and he was not overly finicky about the means used to acquire it, whether it was Jackson's ruthlessness or his own stretching of the implied powers of the Constitution to their limit. He seemed to perceive no contradiction in his restriction of these same powers when it came to internal improvements, apparently willing to leave this matter to the states.

In shrewdly estimating that the public's delight in getting Florida would far outweigh both Jackson's behavior and his own, Monroe proved to be correct. He did not damage his extraordinary relations with the press over this issue. In the matter of the Missouri Compromise, however, it was a different matter, and here Monroe became the first president to find himself embroiled in the deep passions generated by the slavery issue, which so divided press and public that no occupant of the White House could hope to avoid attack (as well as defense) from the media—that is, newspapers, magazines, and books, all of them involved in the great issue of the century.

The divisions over the compromise were the first real cracks in the cocoon of "good feelings" that had enveloped Monroe and the press. The president was beginning to feel that even the *Intelligencer* could not be trusted. Adams found Monroe one day in an irritable mood over publication in that paper of an item reporting that he had not offered the post of secretary of the navy to Commodore

John Rodgers. Monroe told Adams that Rodgers would be "mortified" if he did not contradict this assertion, but if he did, on the other hand, another man who was actually going to get the job would be equally upset. Monroe summoned Gales to his office, demanded an explanation, and presumably reprimanded him, although Adams gives us no further details.

Monroe scrupulously refrained from setting down any of his opinions about journalists, but he often talked about them to Adams, who carefully recorded them in the omnivorous diary. Thus we learn that Monroe thought Thomas Ritchie, editor of the Richmond *Enquirer,* "a vain and presumptuous man, affecting to have great influence, and inconsiderately committing himself upon important political subjects without waiting to understand them thoroughly." Again Adams records at length Monroe's no doubt partisan belief that William Duane, editor of the Philadelphia *Aurora* and still a fervently unshaken Anti-Federalist, was "as unprincipled a fellow as lived" and his newspaper "the most slanderous in the United States"—opinions he shared with Washington and all the Federalists who had followed him.

Before his second term began, Monroe could see that the *Intelligencer* was no longer an unquestioning ally, although it continued to be in general a presidential organ and printer to Congress, as it would remain for a time in the succeeding administration of John Quincy Adams. The president himself had little contact with Gales and Seaton any more; the editors dealt with him chiefly through Adams. When the treaty whereby Spain ceded Florida to the United States was awaiting ratification in 1820, they called on the secretary and asked if they could contradict a story that had just appeared in another paper, the Washington *City Gazette,* reporting that Monroe had refused to receive the ratified treaty Gen. Francisco Vives had brought with him and then refused to accept Vives as minister of Spain, emphasizing this diplomatic insult by avoiding any interchange of civilities with the general at a private party.

The chief preoccupation of Monroe in his second term was the threatening aspect of France, Spain's seeming determination to recolonize South America, and Russia's territorial designs on the northwest corner of the North American continent. Monroe believed he could negotiate with Russia, but he thought stronger measures were needed against the European powers. All this led to the enunciation of his famous doctrine of December 2, 1823, which in effect made the Caribbean an American lake and asserted the right, with American backing, of the South American and Central American states to establish and maintain their own governments, free of foreign interference.

Gales greeted the Monroe Doctrine with alarm, telling Adams he saw it as a war message and warning that dispatches from Europe were reporting that an army of twelve thousand Spaniards was about to embark for South America with the intention of subduing it. Adams viewed the rumor with chilly skepticism and told Gales the president was "singularly disturbed" by it. He himself had advised Monroe to use even stronger language, disregarding the opposition from press and public that might be expected. In his diary he wrote: "I have much more confidence in the calm and deliberate judgments of the people than he has. I have no doubt that the newspaper scavengers and scape-gibbets, whose republicanism runs in filthy streams from the press, would have attempted to exhibit this reference to the Holy Alliance in a false and odious point of view, but I would have trusted to the good sense of the people to see through their sophistry and their motives.''

The seeds of America's ambiguous policy toward her southern continental neighbors were planted by Monroe's determination to foster anticolonialism and independence in South America, just as he had been sympathetic to French republicanism early in his career. He sent a mission to the provinces of La Plata (contemptuously refusing to accept a suggestion that Duane be made a member of it) as early as 1817 and continued to press for their independence, even if it was necessary to send the military there to protect American commerce ''and to countenance the patriots.'' Yet he held no theoretical agreement with republicanism, nor did he have much confidence in the ability of the new South American states to govern themselves. He expressed doubt about any similarity between the revolutions in North and South America.

Almost without exception, the press stood behind the president in the pronouncement of his doctrine, even those papers that had for years been pouring invective against the foreign policies of earlier presidents. There were a few reservations, however. Ritchie's Richmond *Enquirer* politely expressed its doubts about the imminence of a Spanish invasion: ''The President takes bold ground. We are solicitous to know what attacks are meditated; and we presume that Congress will call for such information as may be in the power of the Executive to give, and which it might be expedient to submit, calculated to shed any light upon this interesting subject.''

As might be expected, most of the opposition to the president's stand came from Federalist papers in the North, especially New England, the stronghold. In New York the *Advertiser* thought the president had used language ''too broad and comprehensive for the occasion. We much doubt whether our country will be satisfied to go to war with France and Spain on this account'' (meaning to prevent reconquest of the South American colonies). Both the Salem (Mass.) *Gazette* and the Boston *Advertiser* questioned the danger to the United States of despotic governments in exotic places. The Boston paper's editor spoke in words that could as easily have been said in our own time. ''Is there anything in the Constitution,'' he demanded, ''which makes our Government the Guarantors of the Liberties of the World? Of the Wahabees? of the Peruvians? the Chilese? the Mexicans or Colombians? . . . In short, to reduce it to the actual case, though we acknowledged the disturbed and unsettled governments of South America as being de facto independent, did we mean to make that act equivalent to treaties offensive and defensive? I hope not.''

There were reservations in Congress, too, but the public generally supported Monroe, and so did the press. By virtue of the doctrine, its supporters saw, the country might well draw a sigh of relief. Florida, so long a festering sore, was healed through incorporation into the nation. The irritating series of quarrels with Spain had ended, at least for the time being. Monroe could truthfully say, with his press supporters, that cautious but firm diplomacy had paid off.

It was not all sweetness and light, however. As the campaign of 1824 began to arouse partisan feelings again, even a year and a half before the election, neither Adams nor the president had any confidence that the *Intelligencer*'s support could be relied upon. Gone were the days when, for example, Gales could ask for a copy of the Florida treaty to publish in his paper and be told that it was impossible because the details would take two or three more days, and, in any case, the public would find nothing new in the treaty—and in response, Gales could answer that these reasons had escaped his attention "and declared himself satisfied," as Adams noted with satisfaction in his diary.

Now the *Intelligencer* could not appear to make up its mind between Secretary of the Treasury William H. Crawford, the dispenser of patronage, and Adams. Never one to let weakness in a possible opponent go unnoticed, Adams quietly made an issue of an *Intelligencer* account of a convention just made with Great Britain for suppressing the slave trade. He considered it both incomplete and erroneous. Specifically, he asserted that Gales and Seaton had "suppressed" two extracts from House committee reports of 1821 and 1822, which had been attached to the president's message to the Senate about the agreement, "on the pretence of a want of room for them." Yet, Adams went on accusingly, "nearly a whole column of counter-argument against the Convention was introduced. . . . And at the same time, while the *Intelligencer* of the morning published the documents thus mutilated, the Washington *Gazette* of the evening charged the suppression of the omitted papers to me, as if they had been withheld from the Senate to screen me from the public indignation."

For the *Intelligencer,* the handwriting was beginning to appear on the wall. Adams went to the president with his complaint and then instructed the State Department's chief clerk to tell Seaton that the "suppressed" documents were going to be given to his rival, Peter Force's *National Journal,* for publication, with the notation that the *Intelligencer*'s story had been incomplete. The clerk was then to arrange with Force "to have the documents accurately published." These moves brought an apology from Seaton, who insisted nevertheless that he had only published what was in the Senate's proceedings.

It was hardly surprising, then, that in the midsummer of election year, a showdown occurred. Charles Francis Adams, who edited his father's diary, described it many years later:

The newspapers grew more and more violent. The *National Intelligencer,* in some sense used as the official organ of the Administration, though anxious to avoid a breach with any of its Departments, was yet cautiously paving the way to the support of Mr. Crawford against all others. The first manifestation was made in the paper of the 1st of July, which was thought by the rest of the Cabinet so hostile to the Administration that it drew forth not merely a formal reply, but a recourse to a different press, ominous of the rise of a rival official newspaper. This press had taken the name of the *National Journal.* The *Republican,* heretofore referred to in this work as the organ of the friends of Mr. Calhoun, after two years of not ineffective labor in impairing the prospects of Mr. Crawford, had not proved equally successful in advancing those of their own candidate, and therefore was brought to a sudden close, having lasted about two years. The *National Journal* now took its place, conducted by still other editors, and opened to a different influence.

A few days later Peter Force, the *Journal*'s editor, bought the *Republican* and began to publish three times a week, hoping to establish the paper soon as a daily. Meanwhile Monroe had called in Gales, and, as Adams was told later, the president, "with great severity, reproached him for the treacherous manner in which the newspaper has for a long time been managed." The *Journal* was now, at least for the moment, the administration's (and Adams's) more or less official newspaper.

While Monroe's general policy was to ignore the press as much as possible until he thought it interfered with his interests, as in the *Intelligencer*'s case, Adams remained a cynical analyst of its shifting allegiances and the reasons for them. As the election neared, and it was clear that an influential portion of the press was pushing for Crawford's election, Adams wrote:

> Among the most powerful of his agents have been the editors of the leading newspapers. The *National Intelligencer* is secured to him by the belief of the editors that he will be the successful candidate, and by their dependence upon the printing of Congress; the Richmond *Enquirer,* because he is a Virginian and a slave-holder; the *National Advocate* of New York, through Van Buren; the Boston *Statesman* and Portland *Argus,* through William King; the *Democratic Press,* of Philadelphia, because I transferred the printing of the laws from that paper to the *Franklin Gazette;* and several other presses in various parts of the Union upon principles alike selfish and sordid.

John C. Calhoun, the South's candidate, also had his ardent supporters, Adams noted. "The newspaper war between the presses of Mr. Crawford and Mr. Calhoun waxes warm," he wrote.

> This day the *City Gazette* has three columns of brevier type of the foulest abuse upon McKenney, and upon Mr. Calhoun personally. . . . The *Republican* replies this evening with firmness and moderation to the *National Advocate* and *Boston Statesman,* and reviews its own progress hitherto. If this press is not soon put down, Mr. Crawford has an ordeal to pass through before he reaches the Presidency which will test his merit and pretensions as well as the character of the nation.

Did all this journalistic marching and countermarching have any real influence on the voters? Not much, to judge by the results. The voters had been satisfied enough with Monroe's policies to give his anointed successor, Adams, 109,000 votes. Andrew Jackson, the national hero whose star was rising but whose powerful newspaper support was not yet mobilized, polled even more, 150,000, but because he failed to win a majority in the electoral college, the election was thrown into the House for the second time under the Constitution, and there John Quincy Adams, with the timely help of Henry Clay's supporters, won the presidency on the first ballot.

John Quincy Adams: The Policy Tested

So much for the Era of Good Feelings. It ended with the supposed revelation that Adams had been elected through a "corrupt bargain." A letter from George Kremer appeared in the *Columbian Observer,* of Philadelphia, charging that, in spite of the fact that Jackson had polled the most popular votes, Clay had agreed to throw the election to Adams in the House, in return for the position of secretary of state.

There was no provable truth in the charge, but once made, it could not be withdrawn, and Adams was compelled to begin his administration in a defensive posture that appeared to cripple it. The new president, like his predecessor, had a vision of establishing national policies, but sectional rivalries stood firmly in the way as two ambitious men, Jackson and Clay, carried on their struggle to attain the White House. Adams's election had merely postponed Jackson's success.

As he began his presidency, Adams had no illusions about himself, viewing his character much more objectively than most people, particularly politicians, could be expected to do. "I am a man of reserved, cold, austere, and forbidding manners," he wrote in his diary; "my political adversaries say, a gloomy misanthropist, and my personal enemies, an unsocial savage" who did not, as he confessed, possess the pliability to reform his "defect." Yet there was always a paradox in his self-view. Thus he deplored the fact that his intellectual powers were not greater, because if they were, the monumental diary that was his closest companion might have become, he asserted with a straight face, "next to the Holy Scriptures, the most precious and valuable book ever written."

Adams thought he knew what press and public expected of him—high character, rather than high intellectual abilities. Americans wanted from their president firmness, perseverance, patience, coolness, and forbearance, and he meant to practice those qualities. Unfortunately, he observed, the practice might be overshadowed because he was by nature irritable, tactless, aggressive, and humorless. The paradox within himself was reflected in his presidency. Here was a man who had considerable talent for abstract theory and its practical application to American nationalism, with its push toward leadership among nations begun by Monroe, yet he found himself unable to lead the country out of a growing sectionalism.

Given his character, Adams's relationship with the press during his brief tenure was predictable. He was even less able than Monroe to deal with journalists, and his encounters with them were not only infrequent but increasingly antagonistic as he felt his political enemies and an unsympathetic public closing in on him. Through it all, he professed his faith in the calm and deliberate judgment of the people—but only, apparently, when that judgment was in accord with his own.

While Adams had no talent whatever for publicizing himself through the media, he understood that it would be an advantage to him and seized upon any small opportunity to do so. He had exhibited no reluctance in permitting his friend, Joseph E. Hall, editor of the *Port Folio* in Philadelphia, to publish in 1819 an anonymous sketch of his life and public service up to the year 1808. He wrote this document himself, but his father, a better man with the pen, undertook to rewrite it in the final version. This sketch became a campaign biography in 1824, reprinted discreetly as a series of letters to the Baltimore *American,*signed "Tell," but containing information that left no doubt Adams had to be its author.

Adams, in fact, had first come to public attention between 1791 and 1793 through a series of articles on current issues that appeared in that fortress of Federalist opinion, the *Columbian Centinel* of Boston. It was his criticism of Citizen Genêt and the French Revolutionary government in these articles that attracted Washington's attention and led him to appoint Adams as minister to The Hague, where he began to play a small role in setting the stage for American foreign policy that would endure for the next century. The *Centinel* "letters" (the form in which they appeared) also inspired Washington's famous warning about entangling foreign alliances in his Farewell Address, echoing Adams's praise of "impartial and unequivocal neutrality" for reasons of morality, interest, and policy. Further echoes could be found in the Monroe Doctrine. It was, in fact, Adams's reputation as a diplomat and a spokesman on foreign policy that brought him the presidency, since he had no political following to speak of, no party machinery to back him (of the kind Jackson and his supporters were quietly organizing), and only lukewarm support from his own party.

The papers supporting Jackson had been Adams's chief attackers during the campaign, and they continued to be during his single term in office. Unfortunately for him, the new breed of aggressive editors that was beginning to rise in the national press contained more able Jacksonians than Adams supporters. Peter Force's *National Journal* was loyal enough, supplanting the *Intelligencer* as the more or less official administration organ, but Force was no match for Duff Green and his *United States Telegraph.* In New York, the pro-Adams Charles King and his *American* never got the advantage of Mordecai Noah's *Enquirer,* and there were no editors in all the Adams camp who could equal Isaac Hill, of the *New Hampshire Patriot,* Thomas Ritchie of the Richmond *Enquirer,* or, most of all, the brilliant Amos Kendall whose *Argus of the Western World,* in Frankfort, Kentucky, would become one of the most powerful forces propelling Jackson into the White House.

Adams's irritability with the press, and the press's with him, was not entirely political. As president, he was able to control the dispensing of government printing contracts, which had become another form of patronage, and it was hardly surprising that publishers who possessed and lost them, or failed to get them at all, were unsympathetic to the administration. When, for example, Adams replaced the *Democratic Press* in Philadelphia with the rival *Franklin Gazette* as the holder of these contracts, he provoked what he called "a battery of scurrilous abuse."

Other presidents, even Jefferson, had subsidized favorable newspapers in one way or another, but Adams had strong views on that subject. As a politician he understood well enough that, as he put it later, "in our Presidential canvassing an editor has become as essential an appendage to a candidate as in the days of chivalry a 'squire' was to a knight,'' but he flatly refused, from the beginning, to subsidize any newspaper. ''I would take not one step to advance or promote pretensions to the Presidency,'' he wrote in the diary during his candidacy. ''If that office was to be the prize of cabal and intrigue, of purchasing newspapers, bribing by appointments, or bargaining for foreign missions, I had no ticket in that lottery. . . . I had neither talent nor inclination for intrigue. . . . I will have no stipendiary editor of a newspaper to extol my talents and services and to criticize or calumniate my rivals.''

Even before his election, Adams expected nothing from the press, and seemed more or less resigned to it. Writing to his friend Robert Walsh during the campaign, he noted that the Richmond *Enquirer* ''does not approve of me for next president of the United States,'' and he went on: ''This declaration is fair and candid, nor have I a word to say in objection to it; but when in setting forth my sins it charges me with a proposal to let the British into the heart of our country, it is neither fair nor candid, nor true. And as it considered me *hors de combat* for the Presidency even before the last kick which is to prove my *coup de grace,* to join in the slander upon me was as needless as it was ungenerous.'' Two months later he wrote to his wife Louisa:

I well know how hopeless a task it would be to attempt the refutation of the falsehoods which are constantly circulating against me in the newspapers. For every amputated head of the hydra there will always be two new ones to shoot up. Slander is the first and most efficacious of the electioneering engines among us, but newspaper slander is not that which has operated or will operate most unfavorably to me. An undercurrent of calumny has been flowing and will continue to flow in every direction throughout the Union, nothing of which appears in the newspapers, but it goes in whispers and in private correspondence. It is a branch of the caucusing system.

Adams was not paranoid about the ''undercurrent of calumny'' he sensed was flowing through the Union. It had been flowing since Washington's day, and it would continue to seep through every level of society down to the present. The difference was how much overflowed into the media. Already there were a few efforts at restraint here and there, which probably led Adams to write ''nothing of which appears in the newspapers,'' but the newspapers were still light-years away from the kind of restraint that has kept facts as well as gossip about sitting presidents from seeing print in our time.

Indeed, those who thought during the Monroe interlude that the ''Dark Ages'' of violent, partisan journalism were slipping into the past were profoundly mistaken. As the intense passions that led to the Civil War intensified between Adams's and Lincoln's time, a new, and even worse, violence characterized the press, not only in what it printed, reaching a new peak with Lincoln, but in its relations with the public and its own intramural quarrels.

Mark Twain made hilarious fun of this era in his celebrated ''Journalism in Tennessee,'' published after the war, but while his official biographer, Albert

Bigelow Paine, viewed it as one of his "wilder burlesques," the burlesque was based on solid truth. Lambert A. Wilmer's *Our Press Gang,* published in 1849, documented (although with some fanciful ornamentation) how editors not only attacked politicians but in turn were set upon by irate readers and other outraged editors. "Five editors of the *Vicksburg Sentinel* were killed, in street fights, within ten years," he wrote. "For a time, shooting editors seemed to be the favorite amusement of the Mississippians. Recently, however, these people have become less wasteful of their ammunition, and find it more economical and convenient to *flog* their journalists, when some kind of discipline is necessary."

Wilmer noted that readers might wonder why there was less flogging of editors in Boston, New York, and Philadelphia than in some other parts of the country. One might think it was because the tone of the press had improved on the Atlantic coast and that the editors there were more courteous and dignified, Wilmer answered, but, on the other hand, "The flogging of editors may happen to be less in fashion, or more inconvenient, in one place than in another. . . . There are *various* mollifying influences which dispose the people of the Atlantic cities to be patient under great provocations, and even to tolerate some of the worse offenses of journalism."

What was happening to journalism, although Adams and his contemporaries were not aware of it, was the rise of strongly individualistic editors of newspapers, who might be committed to one party or the other but were no longer owned by them and considered themselves as freewheeling entrepreneurs. There were "giants" among them, in New York, Chicago, and elsewhere, proprietors of what would soon become highly profitable and influential business enterprises. But there were thousands of others who simply loved printer's ink, the news, politics, the whole vast panoply of human affairs—the mix that makes journalists practitioners of their craft.

Attacks on presidents and other politicians in the period before the Civil War were worse, if anything, than they had been in the "Dark Ages" of journalism during the Revolution and in the two or three decades after it. Since one factional newspaper reprinted from another, every insult was capable of getting the widest possible circulation. Thus in 1821 Adams read an article in the Washington *City Gazette* that, as he said, republished "the vilest and falsest ribaldry" against him from papers in Tennessee and Georgia. He returned no answer. "I never that I recollect but once," he said, "undertook to answer anything that was published against me in a newspaper, and that was at a time when I was in private life. To answer newspaper accusations would be an endless task. The tongue of falsehood can never be silenced, and I have not time to spare from public business to the vindication of myself." Washington—and John Adams, Jefferson, and Madison—wrote much the same thing, and they were right. To engage in a dialogue with editors during these early days of the Republic would have been useless, and dangerous as well.

Among John Quincy's opponents in and out of the press, there was some real fear that he meant to be an autocratic ruler, reviving the fears that had haunted the Anti-Federalists for so long. In his inaugural address he had for no discernible reason recalled that it had been said "all Adamses are monarchists," and then this man whose father had signed the Alien and Sedition Acts, still an unpleasant memory for many, went on to say that he had even more dangerous ideas of consolidation and central government, which he called "Liberty with Power." No wonder many of those who read this address joined in the outcry that went up from the opposition papers. William Branch Giles declared ominously that these words reflected "an admitted despotism of the worst tendencies."

Adams was far from being a convinced despot, however, or even a mildly practicing one. He went about his administration in what he believed was a conciliatory manner, but because of the circumstances of his election and the fearful reaction among many that greeted his inaugural address, some historians have been led to conclude that the story of his administration ended in the first year.

Certainly these early events were not calculated to make it easy for him to continue what Monroe had begun—spreading a vision of American nationality and establishing the nation as a continental power in the world. To do that it would be necessary to harmonize, conciliate, and unite all the country's partisan factions—a task quite beyond Adams or anyone else. When he proposed a national bankruptcy law, a national university, a national astronomical observatory, a national academy, national research and exploration, and a new Department of the Interior to help administer increasing national business, a substantial part of press and public saw only threatening autocracy in these proposals. Congress would not act on them, and the opposition press began to abuse the president, in the traditional way.

Moreover Adams presented himself to the public as he really was—a man of moral righteousness and unsocial nature, always a natural target for the less righteous and the more social. He could bear with stoicism the charge that he had been elected because of a "corrupt bargain," which only added to the humiliation of being elected by the House rather than being given the mandate of the electorate. He could even endure the added charge that he had bargained for Daniel Webster's support by promising offices to Federalists that he then failed to deliver as president. Nor could he expect the party's old and faithful loyalists to forgive him for his reluctant support of Jefferson's embargo in 1808, perhaps his most controversial act.

What he found hard to endure was the extraordinary and ridiculous slander spread by the opposition press that pictured him as a kind of pimp for the Tsar Alexander of Russia during the time he was minister at St. Petersburg, between 1809 and 1813. The story first appeared in an electioneering life of Jackson published by Isaac Hill in New Hampshire during the campaign of 1824, and was widely circulated later. In it Adams was depicted as attempting to make use of a beautiful American girl "to seduce the passions of the Tsar Alexander and sway him to political purposes"—an early example of a covert operation, if it had been true. The girl, as it turned out, was one Adams had hired to take care of young Charles. She had written letters home in which she retailed current stories of the Tsar's amours. Since mail from foreigners was carefully examined by the government, her gossipy missives were read at the post office in St. Petersburg and sent on to the Tsar, who found them amusing and even showed them to his wife. They were curious to see the girl and invited her to the palace, where she arrived with her small charge, was treated courteously, and suffered only fright and embarrassment.

This was but one of the stories spread by Jacksonian editors in their papers. Even Louisa Adams did not escape, to her husband's disgust. She was accused of being English, not American, in retaliation for charges made by papers supporting Adams that Jackson's mother was a mulatto. This kind of nastiness was not above even a man like Peter Force, later a noted historian and mayor of Washington, who, in the administration's paper, the *National Journal,* first renounced any intention to indulge in personalities, particularly any reflections on "female character," then printed a pamphlet by Thomas D. Arnold, a congressional candidate from Tennessee, asserting that Jackson's "irregular" marriage "would have subjected any other to an indictment in the County Court for open and notorious lewdness."

Legends were created from facts. It was true, for example, that Adams, as part of his walking and swimming health program, often swam for two or three hours at a time in the Potomac, with a black cap on his head and a pair of green goggles on his eyes—and nothing else. He always left his clothes on a favorite rock. But it was the stuff of legend that Anne Royall, whose small newspaper, *Paul Pry,* later known as the *Huntress,* was the forerunner of the gossipy tabloid, pursued the president in search of a story and found him swimming in the river, whereupon she perched herself on his clothes until he gave her the story she was after. This tale was part of American mythology for decades, in spite of the plain fact that Mrs. Royall was scarcely in Washington during Adams's administration and did not found her paper until 1831. Moreover it was unlikely that Adams would ever have left such an incident out of his omnivorous diary; he withheld few secrets from it. He did meet the eccentric Anne twice, once in 1824, when she called on him in pursuit of a Revolutionary War pension claim, and again three years later, when he was attempting to take a short vacation in Quincy, Massachusetts. Both times the president was fully clothed.

Some of the invented stories in the opposition press bordered on the absurd. A newspaper in Philadelphia, which Adams failed to identify in his diary, charged him with negligence in his dress, asserting that not only did he often go about with neither tie nor waistcoat but even went barefoot to church on occasion. Of this story, Adams wrote bitterly: "It is true only as regards the cravat, instead of which, in the extremity of the summer heat, I wear around my neck a black silk riband. But, even in the falsehoods of this charge, what I may profitably remember is the perpetual and malignant watchfulness with which I am observed in my open day and my secret night, with the deliberate purpose of exposing me to public obloquy or public ridicule."

Nevertheless, in the ordinary course of White House events even representatives of the opposition press might appear at such affairs as the "drawing room," by which was meant more or less regular receptions (Washington called them "levees," much to the disgust of some Jeffersonians), where the president received official Washington. One of these occasions, in the spring of 1828, led to Adams's only real crisis with the press.

The players in this small but intense drama were the president's son John and Russell Jarvis, a writer for the *United States Telegraph,* edited by Duff Green and described by Adams, with some accuracy, as "a scurrilous and abusive print set up by and for the opposition." Nonetheless, Green had been elected as printer of the Senate by that body. John, who had been expelled from Harvard the year before for participating in a student riot, was presently serving as his father's private secretary, which sometimes involved carrying presidential messages from the White House to Congress.

At the "drawing room" of April 2, 1828, John saw Jarvis come into the reception and, indignant at seeing a man from the *Telegraph* making such a brazen appearance, remarked in a loud voice that, as his father wrote later, "if Jarvis had the feelings of a gentleman he would not show himself here." Apparently Jarvis did not hear this remark because it was nearly a week later before he wrote a note to John, sending it by messenger, saying that he had been told the president's son had "spoken of him disrespectfully" at the affair and inviting him to send any explanation he might have by the messenger. According to protocol, this was really an invitation to a duel. John repeated what he had said to the messenger and refused to give any written answer, adding that Jarvis could not expect one from him later.

Next day the president sent his son to deliver messages to both the House and the Senate. After delivering the first, he was on his way through the House rotunda with the second when Jarvis, according to the president, approached John from behind, "accosted him by name, asking if he had given him his final answer, and, upon John's answering him that he had, struck him on the face, and retreated back, so that John could only strike at him in return before they were parted" by a passing congressman.

It was evening before Adams heard about this scuffle, and he immediately saw in it something more than a question of personal honor. John, after all, had been on an official errand when he was attacked. Such an assault, if ignored, might set a dangerous example. What if Jarvis had been an assassin? What if he had been a man intent on seizing a confidential message for political reasons? Adams hesitated, then consulted his cabinet, which urged him to send a special message to Congress on the subject. Adams was still inclined to do nothing precipitate, but Clay thought a message should be sent, and at once. Each man drafted one, and Clay's was adopted after a little editing.

Adams had scant faith that Congress would do anything about the matter. "Under this Congress," he told his diary, "it is doubtful whether any remedies for such brutalities will be found, short of being provided with arms for self-defence." The message was sent two days after the event, and seeming to contradict Adams's cynicism, both houses named special investigative committees. Some thought the opposition party would have to make some kind of gesture disapproving, at least, of Jarvis's conduct, but Adams remained skeptical. By this time he suspected the opposing party and the press representing it of more sinister motives. "They brought him here for the purpose of assassination," he wrote, "and they cannot punish him for laboring in the very location to which they called him."

Nevertheless the House committee, at least, made some pretense of looking into the matter. John was called to testify before it, and there he was closely cross-examined by Duff Green, whom the committee admitted as Jarvis's counsel. In the end, however, the president proved to be right, and neither committee pursued the matter or came to any conclusions, much less taking the step the president had suggested in his message of passing a law or making a regulation that would ensure the security of messengers on official business between the White House and Congress, or prevent disorders within the Capitol itself.

The incident only served to deepen Adams's deeply felt but carefully suppressed (except from his diary) anger and contempt for his political opponents and the editors who spoke for them. In one diary entry, for example, written even before he became president, it was possible to look into the murky depths of these feelings and see there not only a corrosive hatred of the press in general but just a touch of anti-Semitism as well. The entry concerned Mordecai Noah, editor of the clever New York *Enquirer,* "a Jew," Adams wrote in his diary on September 7, 1820,

> who was once Consul at Tunis, recalled for indiscretions, and who has published a Book of Travels against Mr. Madison and Mr. Monroe. . . . He is an incorrect, and very ignorant, but sprightly writer, and as a partisan editor of a newspaper has considerable power. . . . He is, like all the editors of newspapers in this country who have any talent, an author to be let. There is not one of them whose friendship is worth buying, nor one whose enmity is not formidable. They are a sort of assassins who sit with loaded blunderbusses at the corner of streets and fire them off for hire or for sport at any passengers whom they select. They are principally foreigners; but Noah is a native.

Again he interpreted a complaint that his administration had failed to support its friends as no more than an insinuation that he should give more patronage to printers. He wrote: "There is much money expended by the adversaries to the Administration, and it runs chiefly in the channels of the press. They work by slander to vitiate the public opinion, and pay for defamation, to receive their reward in votes."

Yet Adams was an assiduous reader of newspapers, as his diary often attests, and he was not above using the *National Journal*'s semiofficial status to further his own political ends, even contributing an occasional anonymous editorial. Peter Force had devised a slogan for his paper that adroitly identified the administration with the whole nation: "For our Country and our Country's Friends." Even its opponents had to read the *Journal* because it conveyed what Adams was thinking at the moment, and besides it carried excellent news summaries, both foreign and domestic. Its tone was partisan but not shrill or vituperative. Editorially, the *Journal* preached Adams's causes—the American System; centralized domestic government, particularly in land policy; and continuation of

Monroe's foreign policy. It was constantly reminding its readers of the general prosperity that flourished during the president's term, urging national unity (another Adamsian theme) to maintain it.

Sadly, while the *Journal* spoke of large issues, an increasingly frustrated and embittered president was immersing himself more and more in administrative details that should have been left to others. His friends were distressed to see him spending so much time and energy on such questions as whether cadets at West Point must strip naked for physical examinations. The diary was his only confidant. His private letters were few, and Adams blamed that on the press as well: "I can never be sure of writing a line that will not some day be published by friend or foe. Nor can I write a sentence susceptible of an odious misconstruction but it will be seized upon and bandied about like a watch-word for hatred and derision. This condition of things gives style the cramp. I wrote also the weekly letter to my son. These at least will escape the torture of the press."

In the end, too, Adams could blame the newspapers for the rupture between him and his successor, Andrew Jackson, which made the transition a historically chilly affair. The general did not remember, or chose to forget, that it was Adams, during Monroe's administration, who had defended his wild, lawless, but effective campaign in the Spanish possessions. Monroe and most of the cabinet had opposed his methods, even though the public was pleased by them. Adams was the exception. He was in favor of offering Jackson the post of minister to Mexico and even thought of him as a vice-presidential candidate until the general became his rival for the presidency.

How did the break occur then? Adams thought he knew. In the diary, he wrote: "I had seen in the *Telegraph* an anonymous statement that it was because he knew that I had caused or countenanced abusive charges against Mrs. Jackson in the newspapers. The fact was not so. I never had cause or countenanced, directly or indirectly, any such publication. But General Jackson had never asked of me the question, and I did not deem it necessary to notice anonymous charges in the *Telegraph*." The two men were never reconciled.

In the election of 1828, the result was a foregone conclusion. Few presidents running for reelection have ever faced a more hopeless prospect. In fact, Jackson had been running against Adams ever since the election of 1824, which he and his followers were convinced he had lost by fraud. While a growing popular tide for Jackson swelled through the country during the next four years, an antiadministration Congress was busy destroying Adams's domestic program and hampering his other policies. Moreover the country was dividing into a new political alignment, soon to result in the creation of the Democratic party. The Adams and Clay people were becoming known as the National Republicans, while the Jacksonians were the nucleus of what had once been Jeffersonian Democracy, with William Crawford, John Calhoun, and Martin Van Buren among its chief movers.

In the 1828 campaign Jackson's able managers—practical men who were devising a new and enduring pattern of political organization—marshaled every charge made against Adams in a propaganda barrage that flooded the press. First, of course, there was the alleged "corrupt bargain" with Clay by which he had been elected. Then came the accusation that his patronage was as excessive as his spending of the public money in a wastefully extravagant way—charges that must have been particularly galling to Adams, the Puritan enemy of both patronage and spending. The tale of the "beautiful American girl" whom Adams was supposed to have used for the seduction of the Tsar Alexander was rehearsed again, and there were endless snide bits about the president's purchase of such items as a set of ivory chessmen and a billiard table for the White House. These emerged in the papers as a "gaming table and gambling furniture."

Not that the administration's journals showed any particular restraint. In their columns Jackson was pictured as a man who enjoyed gambling and cockfighting, who drank too much and traded in slaves, a liar, even a murderer. Jackson, the administration papers asserted bluntly, was ignorant, cruel, bloodthirsty, and probably insane. And, of course, the worst charge, from Jackson's viewpoint, was the old story that he had married Rachel before she was divorced. "Ought a convicted adulteress and her paramour husband to be placed in the highest offices of this free and Christian land?" one editor wanted to know. It was the general's conviction that Adams countenanced this kind of writing which drove the irrevocable wedge between them. There was, in short, at least some substance in the comment by Isaac Hill, Jacksonian editor of the *New Hampshire Patriot,* that "Clay is managing Adams's campaign not like a statesman of the Cabinet, but like a shyster, pettifogging in a bastard suit before a country squire."

The triumph, if it could be called that, of the Adams forces was what came to be known as the Coffin Handbill, a broadside conceived by John Binns, editor of the Philadelphia *Democratic Press,* which retold the now familiar story from the Southern campaign of how Jackson had approved the execution of six militia deserters after their conviction by a military court. But the day of broadside effectiveness, which had played so large a part in pre-Revolutionary days, was over. Most people who saw the Coffin Handbill seemed inclined to agree with Hill's retort: "Pshaw! Why don't you tell the whole truth? On the 8th of January, 1815, he murdered in the coldest kind of cold blood 1,500 British soldiers for merely trying to get into New Orleans in search of booty and beauty."

In the election Jackson swept the electoral college, 178 to 83, but his popular vote was not as overwhelming as one might have expected—a margin of little more than a hundred thousand. The general marched into Washington on the heels of his triumph and immediately broke precedent by failing to make the usual courtesy call at the White House, a slight duly noted in the papers. On Inauguration Day, Adams departed from precedent himself by not accompanying Jackson to the ceremony and issuing a statement to be published in both the *Intelligencer* and the *Journal* requesting citizens and his friends to refrain from calling on him, again according to usage, thus dispensing with that formality.

So Adams slipped out of the presidency quietly, with as much dignity as possible in the circumstances. One might have thought he had tasted enough of politics and its humiliations, but that would have been contrary to the Adams heritage. Politics was as firmly ingrained in this family as New England principles. Adams not only stayed on in Washington but ran for Congress from his

Massachusetts district of Braintree and won, serving from 1831 until he died in 1848.

In Congress, Adams engaged himself in a final crusade, depicting himself, old and infirm though he might be, as an upholder of the public good against the forces of evil. There was some truth in this perception, since he fought in defense of the Constitutional right of petition and against the House gag rule.

Once more the villains of the opposition press opposed him. "I occupied the whole of this day in continuing my defence before the House," he wrote in the diary. "I charged the newspapers of this city and District with injustice to me, the *Globe* being daily filled with abuse and invective upon me while I am here on my trial, and the reporters of the *Intelligencer* suppressing the most essential parts of my defence." On the following day he added: "No report of my yesterday's speech in the *National Intelligencer,* but a blustering notification that, as I have chosen to complain of their reporters, they will report no more without my own authority. This is a mere subterfuge to suppress the publication of my defence and the exposure which I made of the conspiracy in and out of the House against me."

Like the presidents before him, with the possible exception of Washington, Adams understood the value of influencing public opinion through the press, but he was the first to make no concessions whatever in his relationship with the papers, even those that supported him. Such inflexibility assured his unpopularity and was an important factor in limiting his tenure. Neither Peter Force nor any of the other editors who supported him could make such a president seem other than what he was. Unfortunately, too, the most talented editors of his time were on the other side. Adams was not a victim of the press, as he thought himself to be; he was simply his own worst enemy, and the opposition merely took advantage of it.

PART TWO

The Rise of Manipulation

Jackson and the Corruption of the Press

Jackson and his times have been a scholarly battleground fought over at times with as much academic gore as the general himself managed to distribute in real blood across southeastern America. In the lull that took place in the 1970s, primarily due to the switch from political to social history, the guns were subdued but never quiet, and in the early 1980s new fusillades were heard. Not much was said about the role of the press in Jackson's career during any of these exchanges, and, even discounting the minimal interest of professional historians in that relationship, it still seems strange in view of the fact that no president's life was so powerfully influenced by newspapers and newspapermen as Jackson's.

Jacksonian revisionism got under way in the late 1940s, soon after the publication of Arthur Schlesinger, Jr.'s, landmark volume, *The Age of Jackson,* and it culminated in the early 1980s with Robert Remini's multivolume biography. Richard Hofstadter, Lee Benson, and others demolished the myth that Jackson was the Man of the People who championed the workers and small farmers against the rich and the elite politicians representing wealth and privilege. In the new scenario, Jacksonians were depicted as ruthless political entrepreneurs, many of them either already rich themselves or planning to be so, whose goal was to get and keep power. The general himself was seen as an opportunist, a land speculator who engaged in dubious maneuvers, a political fraud, even a strikebreaker.

For a time historians chewed over these concepts in the new view of history they represented. But inevitably, questions were raised, and in the late 1970s the revisionists were beginning themselves to be revised. As Sean Wilentz, an analyst of these events, has observed, "the revisionists had construed politics far too narrowly," in the view of their critics, "and thereby distorted social relations, social consciousness, and the exercise of political power."

In the succeeding revisionist period, social historians argued among themselves about the role of power, politics, and party in social history, disputes in which Jackson himself all but disappeared. By the mid-1980s a new social his-

74

tory of politics was being created, and a new interpretation of the Jacksonian period appeared to be in the offing. One result has been to see the Age of Jackson not in the traditional way, as a phenomenon by itself, but as a phase in an Age of Revolution that began in 1776 and ended in the political disintegration that took place between 1848 and 1854. In this view a coherence between social and political history begins to take shape.

Jackson's arrival on the political scene coincided with the new era in journalism that began in Monroe's and John Quincy Adams's time and came to an initial flowering in his second administration. The press in this period was more of a force to be reckoned with in the influencing of public opinion than it had been before, simply by virtue of its increase in numbers .Between 1810 and 1828 the number of newspapers rose from 359 to 852, with the annual number of copies printed increasing from twenty-two million to sixty-eight million, in round figures. By 1830, there were a thousand newspapers or more in the nation, a growth only partly accounted for by the westward movement of population, since, with the exception of Ohio, the states showing the greatest growth in this period were in the East, with Pennsylvania leading. During the same period, the figure for issues per person virtually doubled. As the editor of the Boston *Daily Advertiser* pointed out, nearly half the total amount of reading done by at least half the people in the country, and a great part of what the other half read, was the daily or weekly newspaper. Many people relied on a single newspaper for their information.

One aspect of the press had not experienced any substantive change, however. Newspapers in Jackson's time still served the purposes of political candidates and parties and were often subsidized by them. Nearly every candidate had his own newspaper, with its loyal editor, whether he had any organization behind him or not. Until Jackson, political party organization had been so weak that newspapers were a prime element in the ability of a candidate to function. When he solicited funds, the money was needed largely to buy the support of newspaper editors—the practice John Quincy Adams had viewed with so much disgust.

It was the last gasp of the old system, however. Beginning in 1835, with the arrival of James Gordon Bennett, Sr., and his New York *Herald,* a new era in journalism began in which editors might be just as partisan, and might even be involved in politics themselves, but at the same time were independent entrepreneurs who could afford to be independent because they were the proprietors of money-making newspapers that did not need the support of politicians or parties to survive. It was a major turning point in the relationship between the press and the presidency—and, for that matter, politicians in general.

The Jacksonian era, then, was a watershed from which all else in this relationship flowed. However one may view the period, it was both revolutionary and unique. Certainly no president before or since was quite like Andrew Jackson. National military heroes were not strange to American presidential politics—Washington had been the first, of course—but no one like the implausible figure of the general had yet appeared, or would appear again. This tall, craggy, rough, deeply opinioned man was about as far from the Virginia dynasty as one could get.

There were those who wondered whether Jackson was physically able to take on the rigors of the presidency. He was in constant physical pain from two bullets lodged in his body, the result of a duel and a gunfight, and he also suffered from recurring dysentery, severe congestion of the chest, a persistent cough, occasional pulmonary hemorrhaging, a rheumatism that increased with age, and poisonous effects from a prescribed medical treatment of sugar of lead and calomel, which also led to tooth decay.

Small wonder that Jackson's usually short temper made him increasingly irascible as he fought the steadily growing pain in his body. Where his predecessors had been content with condemning the press in relatively polite terms, the general flared out at the papers with the enthusiasm of a cavalry sergeant. Once a note that had fallen accidentally to the floor of the House came into the hands of Francis Blair, editor of the administration's paper the *Globe*. It expressed the opinion that the story of how Jackson had shed his blood in the Revolution was only an electioneering tale. Blair described the note to Jackson, who flew into a rage and bellowed, "The damned, infernal scoundrel! Put your finger here, Mr. Blair." The editor gently placed a digit on the long dent in the president's head, a reminder of the British officer's sword that had been applied there when Jackson refused to clean the Redcoat's boots, fifty years before.

Whatever else might be said about him, including his sometimes uncontrollable temper, no one doubted that Jackson was a sincere and ardent patriot. The military had taught him loyalty and the conscientious performance of duty. Life had convinced him there were grievances and personal slights that could neither be forgiven nor forgotten. Above all, there was his relentless pursuit of fame and his unshakable conviction that he represented the people against aristocracy and privilege.

Jackson's ideas of government were wholly consistent with his character. He agreed that there should be three equal parts of government, as the Constitution had decreed, but he insisted that he was the first among equals, as the popular voice responsible for policy. Jackson was the first modern president in the sense that he used his office for purposes of national leadership, to bring the people and their government closer together. It was an interpretation of the role of presidential authority later strengthened and carried out by Lincoln, both Roosevelts, and Woodrow Wilson. Still later, global war and the threat of nuclear war brought an explosion of presidential power in which presidents waged undeclared wars, bombed neutral nations, impounded funds appropriated by Congress, and insisted on sweeping claims of executive privilege—in short, what Arthur Schlesinger, Jr., has called the "imperial Presidency." In the broad sweep of this developing power, the press has played an important and relatively neglected role, which began in the Age of Jackson.

As the campaign of 1828 began to take shape, the general heard a clarion call to governmental reform, and he perceived that the press was a valuable tool to bring it about. Along with his party, he viewed Adams's election in 1824 and the subsequent appointment of Henry Clay as secretary of state as a fraud, and he suggested to his Tennessee campaign manager "that the papers of Nashville and the whole State should speak out with moderate but firm disapprobation of this corruption, to give a proper tone to the people, and to draw their attention to the subject."

In this climate Jackson's progress to the White House began. For the first time a presidential campaign was organized from the grassroots upward, not only to elect Jackson but, so it was said, to reaffirm the principles of republicanism of the Jeffersonian variety—that is, debt reduction, minimal government, and states' rights. In the election of 1828 these broad issues were addressed only in the broadest way, and the more specific questions before the voters—tariffs, land policy, internal improvements—were never dealt with directly by either the candidates or the newspapers. Instead, the press lost whatever ground it had gained since the "Dark Ages" and engaged in the old style of invective and reckless charges. Although neither side held a preponderance of support in the press, each imagined that the other had superior resources. Thus Ritchie's Richmond *Enquirer* asserted that the Adams people had enlisted four hundred presses in their service, while the administration in turn charged that the opposition had raised a fund of $50,000 to establish newspapers guaranteed to support Jackson. It would have been impossible to validate either of these figures, but it is safe to say both were exaggerated.

Meanwhile Jackson and his backers were busy organizing a powerful coalition, drawing into it astute politicians and businessmen, as well as some of the new editors—not yet independent entrepreneurs, by any means, but on the way. In doing so they were creating what would become the Democratic party. At the center of it were the general's cronies in Nashville, "good old boys" who were trusted and reliable. To these were soon added sympathizers in Nashville and elsewhere in Tennessee, most important among them, perhaps, followers of Calhoun and Crawford. Together they formed the Nashville Central Committee, which began to operate as all political parties have since learned to do, with regular handouts to the press, letters written to politicians everywhere in the nation, and visitations to local and state central committees, not forgetting the central committee in Washington. From Nashville came a steady outpouring of propaganda and campaign material.

In the year before the election Jackson acquired the newspaperman who was to become one of his most important allies. Amos Kendall, editor of the *Argus of the Western World,* in Frankfort, had been a friend of Clay and once tutored his children. Long after his career with Jackson, he would be Samuel F. B. Morse's partner in the first extension of the nation's telegraphic system. Like Jackson, Kendall was a rough diamond and looked the part. Thin and stooped, almost "spectacularly homely," as the historian Robert Remini has called him, he, too, suffered from chronic illness and went about his nearsighted way as though he were a walking medical case, his yellow complexion accented by prematurely white hair. There was nothing infirm about his prose, however. When he wrote, the words came out with as much force and velocity as though Old Hickory himself were speaking. Kendall was known as a "quiet man," but that was only his public persona. With pen in hand, he became a tiger.

According to John C. Rives's candid description, Kendall was "bent, near-sighted, badly dressed, with premature white hair, sallow complexion, and a hacking asthmatic cough." Even on the hottest days he wore a white broadcloth greatcoat, buttoned to the throat, and, because he was subject to migraine head-aches, he sometimes had a white handkerchief tied around his head. No wonder that a bemused congressman remarked on the floor of the House: "Poor wretch, as he rode his Rosinante down Pennsylvania Avenue, he looked like death on the pale horse."

It was Kendall who first approached Jackson, offering in a letter proof of Clay's "perfidy, meanness, and wickedness" and pledging his support unto the day of victory and beyond. Jackson accepted him gladly, and with him, Kendall's associate on the *Argus,* Francis P. Blair. No one has recorded what the general thought when he viewed this strange pair for the first time, for if Kendall presented an odd appearance, to say the least, what could be said for Blair? John C. Rives, the third member of this remarkable trio (who were soon to be famous as Jackson's Kitchen Cabinet), described Blair in the most unflattering terms. He was, said Rives,

about five feet ten inches high, and would be a full six feet if his brain were on the top of his head, instead of being in a *poll* behind it. He looks like a skeleton, lacks but little of being one, and weighed last spring, when dressed in thick winter cloth-ing, one hundred and seven pounds, all told . . . flesh he has none. His face is narrow, and of the hatchet kind, according to his meat-ax disposition when writing about his enemies. His complexion is fair, his hair sandy, and his eyes blue—his countenance remarkably mild.

Rives himself was another giant, shaggy Kentuckian, who had worked for Duff Green's *Telegraph* and came to Jackson recommended by that editor. He was later to be the *Globe*'s business manager. Of the three, Rives was the least noticeable, and even Blair was overshadowed by Kendall.

Other, less colorful but also influential editors joined the Jackson camp. Ritchie and his *Enquirer* were enlisted by Martin Van Buren, who also brought in Edwin Croswell (Harry Croswell's nephew) and his Albany *Argus.* Isaac Hill and the *New Hampshire Patriot* were a certain addition, and briefly there was the New York *Enquirer.* Among the others were Nathaniel Greene's Boston *States-man,* Gideon Welles's New Haven *Journal,* Dabney S. Carr's Baltimore *Repub-lican,* and other ardent Jacksonian editors in various parts of the country. The National Republican camp was justifiably alarmed, and charged that the Demo-crats had put together "a chain of newspaper posts, from the New England States to Louisiana, and branching off through Lexington to the Western States." To these editors, furthermore, could be added such aggressive, imaginative politi-cians as Thomas Hart Benton and Henry Lee, among others.

Of all the newspapers enlisted in the Jackson cause, perhaps the most signifi-cant was Mordecai Noah's New York *Enquirer,* not only because it was so well written and edited but because it produced in the person of James Gordon Ben-nett, Sr., the first Washington correspondent, who went on to become, with his

New York *Herald,* the first real publisher-editor in the modern sense. This tall, slim, aggressive young man was a Scottish immigrant who had arrived in Halifax, penniless, only a few years before, and had gone through a period of struggle in Boston and New York before he got a job on Noah's paper, where his satiric, vitriolic, amusing pen soon brought him to public notice. When W. G. Graham, Noah's chief assistant, who wrote frequently on the evils of cardplaying, gambling, and dueling, was killed—ironically, in a duel over a game of cards—Bennett took his place.

Late in 1827 Bennett arrived in Washington as the paper's political reporter (he also covered New York, Albany, and Saratoga Springs), and for the next four years he was Jackson's ally and the scourge of the opposition. His first story, unsigned, was sent to the *Enquirer* for its edition of January 2, 1828, describing the annual New Year's Day party at the White House. In subsequent dispatches he set a new style of reporting from the capital—chatty and often windy but also knowledgeable and informative. A sample: "The Adams party are afraid of losing the advantage of riding the Tariff hobby. The animal is sliding from beneath them. They try to catch his tail, as the witch did that of Tam O'Shanter's mare, but their vociferations, etc., will not avail them. It will be found that the Jackson party are the truest friends of the country, and that they will encourage every interest, but favor none." Another sample, written a few days later: "The House of Representatives has been engaged for some time on a subject, trivial in itself, but involving warm feelings—the paying for a slave killed in the service of the United States at New Orleans. This brings up the question whether slaves are property under our constitution; and everything touching on slavery fires all the gunpowder feelings of all sides, which are always so ready to catch and explode." Reporting of this kind brought hundreds of new subscribers to the *Enquirer* every week. Bennett was on his way.

Bennett was in Washington when Jackson swept to triumph in 1828. Only New England voted solidly for Adams, while nearly all the Middle Atlantic states, the Western states, and Pennsylvania, Ohio, and Kentucky combined to give the general 647,276 popular votes to 508,064 for Adams; the electoral college was a landslide, 178 to 83. Clearly something extraordinary, even revolutionary, had taken place in presidential politics, whether it was the "howl of raving democracy," as one disgusted National Republican asserted, or a triumphant majority representing the "ardor of thousands," as Hezekiah Niles, proprietor of the Jacksonian *Register,* proclaimed it.

As the historian Robert Remini and others have pointed out, the figures were somewhat misleading. There were nearly 13,000,000 people in the nation, but only 1,155,340 white males voted. Still, it was 800,000 more than had voted in the previous election, and nothing could diminish the fact that Jackson had won an astounding victory. It was deeply shadowed by the loss of his beloved wife, Rachel, who had told him, "I had rather be a doorkeeper in the house of God than to live in that place at Washington." She was buried on Christmas Eve. A tablet placed over the grave carried Jackson's conviction that her death had been caused, at least in part, by the slanders against her that had been trumpeted in the National Republican press. She was, said the tablet, "a being so gentle and so virtuous, slander might wound her but could not dishonor.'' Jackson came to Washington with that conviction, and it colored all his associations with the press.

Although his heart was "nearly broke," as the weeping old soldier said, he had recovered enough by Inauguration Day, March 4, 1829, to make that event one of the most memorable in the annals of American political life. Even before it took place, Jackson had appointed what has been called one of the worst cabinets in that century and thus laid the groundwork for a relationship with the press that could only be stormy.

The general was well aware, however, that his staunchest friends were the newspaper editors who had worked so hard for his election and had played such a vital role in it. Consequently he welcomed them when they came around to call in February, particularly Kendall, whom he and others considered the most impressive of the lot. The two men genuinely liked each other, and since Kendall made it clear that he had come to Washington solely to help Jackson reform the government, it was plain (and the February interview confirmed it) that the editor was going to be close to the president.

Kendall conveyed the president-elect's views and intentions to a select group of his fellow editors who met more or less regularly at the home of the Reverend Obadiah Brown, who was a Post Office Department clerk during the week and a Baptist minister on Sundays. In his parlor Kendall met with Hill, Nathaniel Greene, Duff Green, Gideon Welles, and Noah. The subject was patronage, and all the editors expected to get something from the new administration as a reward for their efforts. Whatever high-minded feelings about reform they may have brought to these meetings evaporated in the practical discussion of patronage, and its easy translation into spoils for the victors.

The inauguration itself has often been written about, either as a celebration of the spontaneous explosion that accompanied the installation of the first "people's president" or as a sad commentary on the sometimes disgraceful scenes that destroyed the dignity traditionally surrounding this national occasion. It was a wild affair, at times nearly a riot, as the White House itself was turned into a shambles of half-drunken celebration. Yet in the end it was no more than a completely unrestrained expression of love for Jackson and happiness that he had come to power. Unfortunately the revelers nearly suffocated him to death, and he had to be physically protected and removed to the safety of Gadsby's Tavern in Alexandria.

Something of all this was conveyed in Bennett's description of the inauguration, done in his exuberant, high-flown style:

> The Chief Justice of the United States then administered the oath of office; and thus, in the sight of Heaven and the surrounding multitude, was Andrew Jackson declared the chief of the only free and pure republic upon earth. The welkin rang with music and the feeling plaudits of the populace; beauty smiled and waved her kerchief—the first spring birds carolled their notes of joy, and nature poured her various offerings to the Giver of all good. The very marble of the pediment seemed to glow with life— justice, with a firmer grasp, secured her scales—"Hope, enchanted, smiled," and

the Genius of our country breathed a living defiance to the world. What a lesson for the monarchies of Europe! The mummery of a coronation, with all its pomp and pageantry, sinks into merited insignificance, before the simple and sublime spectacle of twelve millions of freemen, imparting this Executive Trust to the man of their choice.

Twenty-one of the eminent Jacksonian editors were on hand for the celebration, and they decided to call on the president in a body to offer their congratulations and best wishes officially. Hill suggested that Noah lead the delegation, but the New Yorker demurred. "No," he said, "I'm too fat and in too good condition. If Old Hickory sees me, he will think that editors require no office. Our deputation must be headed by our worst looking—the lean, the halt, the blind." And with that in mind, he nominated Blair, Hill, and Kendall to lead them.

Once in office, Jackson did not forget his editor friends when the patronage began, over the bitter protests and opposition of both the National Republicans and members of Congress. While the extent of his dispensations was not quite as scandalous as it has been depicted—as the revisionists have assured us—it was generous enough in the case of the journalists. John Quincy Adams tells us how these awards appeared to him and his remaining followers: "The appointments, almost without exception, are conferred upon the vilest purveyors of slander during the late electioneering campaign, and an excessive disproportion of places is given to editors of the foulest presses. . . . The appointments are exclusively of violent partisans; and every editor of a scurrilous and slanderous newspaper is provided for."

In the Senate, Daniel Webster labored hard to save the country from, as he called it, "the typographical corps," and in some cases he was successful. The Senate rejected Jackson's nomination of Hill for a job in the Treasury Department, but the editor later ran for the Senate and was elected. It also refused to confirm Noah for a government job. When the vote came on Kendall's confirmation as fourth auditor for the Treasury Department, the result was a tie, and Vice-President Calhoun cast the deciding vote that got him the job. Later Kendall became postmaster general, but his real job was to be Jackson's confidential adviser—in much the same role as Harry Hopkins to Franklin Roosevelt, Sherman Adams to Eisenhower—and to direct the operation of the administration's own newspaper, the *Globe,* with Blair as its editor and Rives as business manager.

This was the trio that came to be known as Jackson's "Kitchen Cabinet," a cozy relationship of intimate, "good-old-boy" companions. Kendall noted down the president's ideas, often as the president lay back on a couch and smoked his pipe, and later he and Blair would write, or rewrite, what was said into stories for the *Globe.* It was a highly profitable partnership for everyone concerned, through both the Jackson administrations and Martin Van Buren's as well. Thus the general emerged as the first presidential manipulator of the press, in a practical, systematic way that far surpassed any earlier attempts.

The *Globe* was started from scratch, without plant, facilities, or subscription list. Creating the latter was no problem for the Kitchen Cabinet. Half-secret (and wholly improper) pressure was put on federal officers earning $1,000 a year or more to subscribe or, it was clearly implied, to be out of a job. Kendall also passed the word around to department heads that the president wanted to see departmental printing shifted to the new paper. To ensure that this was done, Jackson issued an executive order requiring all cabinet members to give him monthly reports on how much money had been spent for printing and who had been given the contracts. It was made clear, however, that favors were to be given, not returned. When a Jackson supporter offered Blair a $100 contribution with the implicit understanding that the *Globe* would support his private interests, Blair sent back the money.

Since everyone knew that the *Globe* was the president's personal organ, its circulation naturally increased because in its pages could be seen what the president was thinking and assiduous readers might even anticipate what he might do. Governments abroad read it more carefully than any other American paper. In an episode rich with intimations of the future, the Russians complained about some items in the *Globe* they considered unfavorable to them, and when James Buchanan, the American minister, assured them the paper was not under the control of the government, they greeted this denial with as much frank disbelief as it would have received in Washington.

Placed in such an enviable and unprecedented position, the *Globe* prospered, and within a year had four thousand subscribers and congressional and departmental printing contracts worth about $50,000 annually. Many of these had been taken away from the *Telegraph*, the opposition's leading paper, which could not survive the loss and eventually had to suspend, leaving the *Globe* virtually alone. With this powerful instrument in hand, Jackson meant to use it and the other papers as a weapon to achieve the second term he had decided to seek even before the first one was half finished The press would be needed to pull off the political coup he intended—that is, to run without Calhoun, and without the members of his cabinet he believed were disloyal, whom he meant to purge.

As the man at the editorial controls of this engine, Blair looked anything but a powerful political journalist—mousy, weighing less than a hundred pounds, resembling a walking cadaver, as some thought. But he enjoyed the president's warm confidence, and when he spoke in the Kitchen Cabinet, or to Jackson alone, it was with enthusiasm for beliefs and opinions shared by the president and held dear by him. Jackson considered Blair the ideal editor, and those who doubted it at first became believers, too, when they read his clear, penetrating, lucid, often wicked prose, with which he scalded the administration's enemies and advanced its viewpoints.

The two households became socially entangled. Blair's wife knitted woolen socks for Jackson, and his daughter copied letters for the president, while one of his sons got into West Point with Jackson's help. Another son got a navy appointment by the same route. Jackson and the Blairs entertained each other often, and the general treated his favorite editor like a son. Remini, Jackson's most recent biographer, has summed up the balance in this relationship succinctly:

> In the coming years few men surrounding Jackson matched Blair's influence in the formulation of policy and the definition of issues.

But one reason for Blair's longevity as a presidential adviser was his recognition that only Old Hickory decided policy, ran the Democratic party, and headed the government. Blair might make important contributions to the President's thinking, as did other men, but he knew who ultimately held the reins of power and made the final decisions. Blair never stepped out of line. He served loyally and effectively. As a consequence he gave the President a "blaring" trumpet to sound his call around the nation and summon the American people to follow him as he continued to reform and reshape the structure of American politics.

Aside from politics, it had been a warm, human relationship between the two men from the day Blair arrived in Washington, summoned from Kentucky, to edit the new paper—an assignment he welcomed eagerly since he was $40,000 in debt. His stagecoach had overturned as it neared Washington, and a black patch covered a head wound he suffered in the accident. Jackson was assuredly startled to see him, but within minutes they were friends. The president talked to him about his political problems, and then, inviting Blair to sit beside him on the sofa, he put an arm around the editor's shoulder and began to speak about the loss of his wife.

Blair treated the president with the same openness, and as it was nearly dinner time, Jackson invited him to stay. When the hour came, however, Blair was horrified to find that the other guests, gathered in the East Room, were ambassadors and similar dignitaries, all splendidly dressed, in vivid contrast to his scarecrow appearance. He shrank into a corner, "abashed and miserable," but when Jackson entered, he sought out Blair at once and insisted on placing him at the head of the table, in the place of honor at his right.

Jackson believed that the *Globe,* under Blair's direction, should not only give the public authentic information about the government, since he considered himself merely the people's representative in Washington, but that it should also keep the electorate informed about his adversaries—"the spies," as he called them. His "faithful sentinel," the editor Blair, would uncover and expose these dangerous enemies. Whenever any such information came to his attention, the president would say at once, "Give it to Blair."

The editor was a tireless worker. Sitting on a stool behind the door of his office, and using a lead pencil, Blair wrote so quickly that two boys were hired to carry copy to the typesetters. "We have known him," said Rives, "to send one of the boys after the other to overtake him, and get the last word on the last sheet sent off."

Jackson himself was the *Globe*'s most faithful reader. A voracious peruser of newspapers before and after his presidency, he confined himself during his term to the Bible, his correspondence, and the *Globe.* In its columns he saw not only the information he had conveyed privately to Kendall but official messages, such as his announcement that he was available for a second term. "We are permitted to say," the *Globe* reported on January 22, 1831, "that if it should be the will of the Nation to call on the President to serve a second term in the Chief Magistracy, he will not decline the summons." There were occasional complaints in Congress about the president's conveying of information through the administration's paper that properly should have gone to the legislators first, but Jackson paid no attention.

As the campaign for the second term began, the overwhelming political character of the *Globe* was evident as even the most important news had to take second place to the political maneuvers the Democrats were making. A cholera epidemic in Washington was noticed only in the official reports of the Board of Health, but there was room for columns of quotations from Democratic papers on the veto of the bank bill.

Blair calmly refused to publish speeches by the opposition. There was no space for these long, tiresome orations, he said. If he published them, there would be no place for the good news he wanted to print or for the speeches made in Congress by the president's friends. Those who wanted to read about what the opposition was doing could find everything they desired in the opposition press. Besides, as Blair pointed out equably, those newspapers did not publish the speeches of Democrats.

Thoroughly political though he might be, Blair did not fill his staff with hacks but hired the best reporters available, regardless of their politics. The paper also faithfully reported the daily proceedings of Congress, with a minimum of bias and a maximum of coverage. This was the kind of service, as well as its role as spokesman for Jackson, that kept the *Globe's* circulation climbing. When the hard-pressed opposition papers charged that the paper was being distributed gratuitously, financed by taxpayers' money, Rives replied with an affidavit swearing to the legitimacy of the circulation.

During July, August, and September of 1831, new subscriptions were coming in at an average of nearly a hundred every week. Blair got numerous letters from farmers, laborers, and other devoted Jackson followers instructing him to strike their names from the subscription lists if he ever deserted Old Hickory. There was not the slightest chance. The *Globe* continued to prosper, and its rivals struggled to stay alive. But it was an unequal battle, and the National Republicans' chief organ for so long, Duff Green's *Telegraph,* died in 1837.

As the *Globe* rose to the peak of its power during Jackson's second administration, Blair gradually came to take Kendall's place as the president's confidant, at least where the paper was concerned. Jackson's scrawled messages tell the story—"Your note was received & answer returned that you could get a message tonight if you would come up," and "Send up your confidential man if you cannot come up in the morning" to get Jackson's message on the land bill. Rives confirms that the president consulted chiefly with Blair after 1830.

There was no separation, however, among the three Kentuckians who constituted the Kitchen Cabinet, so called because they entered the White House through that room. Kendall was considered to be more powerful in shaping Jackson's policies than any cabinet member except Secretary of State Van Buren. A contemporary observer described him as "secretive, yet audacious in his political methods, a powerful and ready writer, and the author of many of Jackson's ablest State papers." He helped Blair with the longer argumentative articles and with other editorial problems. The two men remained the closest of friends until 1843, when they fell out over who would become the public printer, but they were reconciled before Jackson's death.

Outside this White House circle the most militant of the Jacksonian editors was Isaac Hill. He lacked Kendall's depth and constructive powers, nor did he have Blair's literary polish, but he was a highly talented phrasemaker who was most valuable in the heat of a campaign. A biting paragraph from him, it was said, could be as valuable as one of Kendall's editorials. As a kind of *ex officio* member of the Kitchen Cabinet, it was Hill who constantly urged Jackson to exploit the spoils system to the limit.

Jackson, of course, preferred not to call it "spoils." When he expelled people from office and filled the vacancies with his own men, he termed it reform, not patronage. Those removed from office were considered tainted with corruption, guilty of contributing to the concentration of power, and Jackson's mission as he saw it was to root out corruption and diminish that power in order to protect American freedom. This pious rationalization was later improved to become the principle of rotation. "Rotation in office will perpetuate our liberty," he declared. The newspapers were not fooled, and many of them could not choke down Jackson's rhetoric. They called it a housecleaning demanded by the people. But in fact, as Remini has pointed out, no real purge took place, and the number of dismissals was not exorbitant, although this Jacksonian cleansing of the Washington stables has passed into American mythology.

Nevertheless, there was enough in the cleansing to make even Jackson's editorial supporters, or at least some of them, apprehensive about his methods and intentions. Thomas Ritchie of the Richmond *Enquirer,* leader of the Jacksonians in Virginia, "scarcely ever went to bed . . . without apprehension that he would wake up to hear of some coup d'état by the General," according to Van Buren. Ritchie complained to the secretary: "We are sorry to see the personal friends of the President appointed; we lament to see so many of the Editorial Corps favored with the patronage of the Administration." It was true, he went on, that many were well qualified and had "fought manfully to put out a corrupt coalition," but what about the effect these appointments had made, he wanted to know. "Under the profession of Reform changes will be made to the public injury. . . . The contest will be for office and not for principle."

Oddly enough, the truly limited extent of Jackson's "spoils" was documented by the leading opposition paper, the *Telegraph,* before it went into its fatal decline. As of September 27, 1830, the paper said, giving figures that have not been substantially altered by later research, the president removed only 919 out of about 11,000 officeholders, or roughly one-eleventh of the total. Few removals were made after that time. Jefferson had fired a larger number, and Van Buren, William Henry Harrison, and Zachary Taylor were to oust far more in their administrations. Lincoln made a clean sweep when he came to office. Thus the revisionists of today insist that Jackson did not create the spoils system, as generations of Americans were led to believe, but merely gave it new conditions.

As for the appointment of newspapermen, the *National Journal* offered some illuminating statistics. In the spring of 1830 it printed a list of fifty-six editors, proprietors, printers, and others connected with the press who had been rewarded by Jackson up to that time. Undoubtedly there were some others who were offered positions that they declined, but the number is impossible to determine. In any case, no one disputes the fact that Jackson did build up his newspaper patronage with journalists who had worked for him faithfully against long odds.

Still, it was the appointment of newspapermen that elicited the loudest protest from the opposition. As everyone knew, partisan editors of Jackson's time were more often than not hack writers for whom even their own employers had little respect, and it was customary to reward them with government printing contracts, not government jobs. Even historians examing the period long after it had ended were distressed to find so many "press writers" on the lists of patronage jobs. Many of the loudest complainers at the time were lawyers, who until then had held the majority of public positions, and they were understandably annoyed to see Jackson become the first president to support the power of the press by offering its editors the privilege of governmental influence. Jackson defended what he was doing vehemently. "Why should this class of citizens be excluded from offices to which others, not more patriotic, nor presenting stronger claims as to qualification, may aspire?" he wrote, in a long letter.

Inevitably there were Jacksonian editors who broke away from the Great Kentucky Crusade. In New York, for example, Col. James Watson Webb, whose *Courier* had merged with Noah's *Enquirer* to make the *Courier and Enquirer,* was initially kept better advised of what was going on in the White House than any other editor outside Washington, through his friends Van Buren and Calhoun. He was also greatly helped by having James Gordon Bennett, who had come along with the merger, as his Washington correspondent. The new paper grew rapidly in circulation, thanks in large part to Bennett, but the two men were prickly associates. The correspondent was an individual of notoriously short temper, and Webb was an irascible blusterer of even more substantial ego; the time would come when they would brawl on the streets of New York. Bennett had reason to be angry with his employer. As Noah had done before him, Webb never gave his young correspondent credit by name for any of his brilliant work, and later both these publishers refused to acknowledge what everyone knew— that Bennett was the man whose provocative letters from Washington had brought prestige and a steady cash flow to their papers. It is difficult to understand why they thought it could be kept a secret, not only because of Bennett's unmistakable style but because they must have known, sooner or later, that many of the correspondent's Washington sources saw his dispatches before they were sent.

For a time Webb's ardent Jacksonianism was a substantial help to the administration, but it quickly became something of an embarrassment when his wordy battle with Duff Green in the pages of their newspapers went beyond verbiage, and Webb came down to Washington determined, as he said, to punish this "St. Louis upstart." He ambushed Green in the Capitol rotunda, denouncing him as a "poor, contemptible, cowardly puppy." Green drew a pistol—"about eight inches long," according to Webb—but prudence restrained him from using it.

It was Bennett whose friendship with Van Buren, carefully manipulated by that astute politician, resulted in persuading Webb to back Van Buren for the vice-presidency in the 1832 elections. Bennett had also convinced the publisher to support Jackson, but when the president's struggle to reform the federal banking system reached its most intense stage, in 1832, Webb split with Jackson on this issue, swung around to the other side, and so lost Bennett, who had been the prime factor in making the *Courier and Enquirer* the best paper on the continent. It was said that the big bankers—always a target of Bennett's enmity and his investigative reporting—had "gotten to" Webb, but whatever the reason, his switch to Nicholas Biddle, head of the Bank of the United States, cost his paper its supremacy and its influence in the White House. When a congressional committee disclosed that the Bank of the United States had loaned Webb nearly $53,000 in the year before his defection, the publisher took out his wrath on Bennett, attacking him viciously.

There was a brief period, subsequently, in which Bennett made two preliminary attempts to be a publisher himself, first with the New York *Globe* (a sincere tribute to its Washington counterpart), and then with the *Pennsylvanian,* in Philadelphia. The failure of both led him at last in 1835 to found the New York *Herald,* the first real newspaper in the modern sense, a paper so successful that it made Bennett's political influence in Washington far greater than he had ever dreamed.

But these were largely post-Jacksonian events. During his second term Old Hickory emerged more and more as a chief executive who had raised manipulation of the press to a fine art. In this he was always the practical man, accepting newspapers as they were, and using them to the best effect possible. His early radical attempts at reform, however, and the ruthless way that he and his kept press dealt with people made a good many enemies, and in his second term he did not have the support of a majority of the press—if, indeed, he ever truly had it.

One reason was that the opposition press at first, and some of the Jacksonian papers later, perceived correctly that Jackson was far from being an absolutist about freedom of the press, as Jefferson and Madison had been. He aroused the Northern press, for example, by recommending a kind of censorship, in the form of a penalty for circulating in the South any newspaper that "intended" to instigate insurrection—meaning, to advocate abolition. In his first years as postmaster general Kendall had actually permitted the Charleston, South Carolina, postmaster to refuse delivery of the *Liberator* and other abolitionist newspapers, and in his 1835 annual report, he also suggested (presumably with Jackson's approval) that the president empower his department to refuse "giving circulation to the obnoxious papers in the southern states." When Calhoun saw this proposal after it was sent to his committee, he declared it unconstitutional and drafted another to replace it, but it was defeated by a narrow margin.

In the growing conflict over slavery, there were evidences of things to come in the press. Some Southern states passed laws against "incendiary publications," although widespread condemnation of antislavery people and publications was in itself a heavy censorship. There were also fairly frequent mob attacks on antislavery newspapers, notably the one that resulted in the murder of the Reverend Elijah P. Lovejoy, in Alton, Illinois, in 1837, after he had established the *Observer,* a religious antislavery newspaper.

Kendall's moves against infiltration of the South by the antislavery press had the effect of strengthening Jackson and his party in that region. In the North the opposition press was daily accusing the president of such tight party control that any criticism of it meant a personal attack from his controlled press, and if the critic happened to be a party member, he would be compelled to withdraw. "THE KING UPON THE THRONE: THE PEOPLE IN THE DUST!!!" read one Republican newspaper headline in the election of 1832. Savage as its attacks frequently were, however, the Republican press was never as vigorous, or as vicious, as the Democratic newspapers.

One example was the Republican pamphlet titled, *A Retrospect of Andrew Jackson's Administration,* which was documented with more thoroughness than one would expect from this kind of electioneering. The president struck back in the usual way, by directing his editors to attack it, which they did with willing vigor and scant regard for the facts. Isaac Hill's *New Hampshire Patriot* carried a story headlined, "Twenty-one Reasons Why Henry Clay Should Not Be Elected President." Reason No. 20 was a fair sample of the others: "Because . . . he spends his days at a gaming table and his nights in a brothel."

No president ever had a supporting press more vociferously loyal, or more intolerant. Even such a respected figure as William Cullen Bryant, who had been editing the New York *Evening Post* with a decorum not seen since its founding in 1801, went so far as to cane a Clay supporter as he walked along Broadway. Jackson's influence was so pervasive that, when it reached its peak in the election of 1832, one Republican editor wrote that he had "no heart to publish election returns." Yet when those returns came in, they showed that the percentage of Jackson's popular majority had declined by more than 1.5 percent, the first time it had done so in a president's reelection.

There were multiple reasons for that drop and the president's subsequent decline, which have been analyzed endlessly by historians and are not the subject of this volume. It might have been a lesson for the press, too, but in that respect the editors were totally blind. Although Jackson's party continued in power with the election of Martin Van Buren in 1836, it was clear that a highly popular president, even a national hero, with an unprecedented political organization and a loyal cluster of powerful newspapers and their editors who willingly permitted themselves to be manipulated—all this was no proof against the strong and shifting undercurrents of public opinion.

The president's superbly effective grassroots organization was in itself a spur to greater public participation in the voting when it stirred opposition on such issues as the federal bank and tariffs. A powerful press could also elicit a powerful response if it offended enough people. And Jacksonian supremacy had revived the American fear of too great a power in the presidency, which had begun with Washington.

Jackson had shown what could be done with a manipulated press to hit people on the head with the hammer blows of an aggressive presidency. It would take the Little Magician, Van Buren, to demonstrate how the press could be used to persuade without the hammer blow. Unfortunately he was a little late. Violent passions were rising in the country over the slavery issue, and a new breed of editors was about to come into its own—editors who could declare themselves independent of any political party or candidate and not only survive but become rich and more successful than any of their predecessors.

Van Buren: The Triumph of Persuasion

On a Hudson River steamer making its way up to Albany in 1830, Martin Van Buren became an object of speculation by two newspapermen who had observed him leaning against the railing, deep in contemplation of the valley's celebrated scenery. They gazed with admiration on the "Red Fox of Kinderhook," as the press sometimes called him, because journalists already were well aware of Van Buren's talents as a master manipulator, the ability that had earned him his other familiar epithet, the "Little Magician." The delicate finesse he displayed with political problems was equally masterful when he applied it to relationships with the press—first on behalf of Jackson, later in his own presidency. John Randolph described this technique perhaps better than any other observer. Van Buren, he said, "habitually rowed to his object with muffled oars."

As they watched Van Buren, the two journalists on the Hudson steamer began to talk about the impossibility of getting this genius from Albany to make a definite statement. Could they make him express an opinion? Could they persuade him to say something—manipulate the manipulator? A bet was put down between them on that possibility, and they approached their quarry.

"Fine day, isn't it, Mr. Van Buren?" one of them remarked affably.

Van Buren turned from the rail and regarded them equably. "Now that depends on what you mean by a fine day," he replied. "There are all sorts of fine days. This particular one . . ." and he continued with a description in itself equivocal, while the reporters looked at each other with resignation. All bets were off.

The secretary of state, soon to be president, had other distinctions, of course—the first president to be born a citizen of the United States, the first New Yorker to be elected—but he was known to all, and especially to his frustrated opponents, as the nearest approach to Talleyrand the American political system had yet produced. His rise from obscurity to eminence was a lesson in statecraft, and his lasting contribution was a patronage system that became at once the strength and the curse of both parties.

More than any president who preceded him, Van Buren possessed a native ability to grasp the interrelationship of the press and the public mind. Yet what he wrote about both was hardly full of brilliant insight. "In this matter of personal popularity," he wrote in his autobiography, "the working of the public mind is often inscrutable. In one respect only does it appear to be subject to rule, namely in the application of a closer scrutiny by the People to the motives of public men to their actions." In the same volume, speaking of the opposition papers, he gives us the opinion common to all politicians: "Their press had been for a long time and was at that very moment teeming with the most outrageous calumnies against me on the same general subject."

The press's view of Van Buren was summed up in the coined word it gave to current language, "vanburenish," meaning noncommittal, straddling the issues, or seeming to be uninvolved with behind-the-scenes maneuvering to gain public office. But Van Buren saw himself quite differently, as he disclosed in his auto-biography, where he noted that the Albany *Argus* "gave rise to the charge of my pursuing a non-commital [*sic*] policy in regard to the administration of Mr. [John Quincy] Adams." The "extraordinary success of this partisan accusation and of its striking illustration of the power of the Press," he went on, was quite contrary to his "universally known intention to oppose the reelection of Mr. Adams."

In fact, Van Buren pursued a deliberate policy in this matter, with a specific goal in mind. It was true that he had an aversion to Adams, which he shared with many New Yorkers, but he believed that a noncommittal position would separate national from state politics, thus avoiding conflict and helping to make peace between the Jackson and Crawford factions of the party.

The Little Magician may have complained on occasion about the Albany *Argus,* but this paper was an important factor in his rise to power in New York State. He contributed to it often and in time came to own it. In its day the *Argus* was a paper of some distinction. It was founded after ninety-one Democrats had signed a prospectus seeking its establishment to replace the *Register.* The first editor was Jesse Buel, whose management was as safe and discreet as Van Buren could have desired. He and other party leaders wrote strong and powerful articles for it, and it was soon the leading organ in the state, outside of New York City, and the official voice of the new Democratic party.

Buel made his money out of it, particularly from state printing contracts, and sold the paper in 1821 to Van Buren's brother-in-law Moses J. Cantine and a man named Isaac Q. Leake. Cantine died two years later, just before the last $1,500 payment was due, and Van Buren became responsible for his debt. He was intent on getting a good, solid party man to run it, one who would hew discreetly to the party line. "Without a paper thus edited at Albany," he wrote to his lawyer Jesse Hoyt, "we may hang our harps on the willows. With it, the party can survive a thousand such convulsions as those which agitate and proba-bly alarm most of those around you." Eventually a third partner, Edwin Cros-well, became sole editor when Leake retired in 1824, and his first act was to make the paper a daily. Van Buren, now a senator, continued to write for it, along with those other leaders who formed the party machine known as the Al-bany Regency, which controlled state politics.

By the time Van Buren got into presidential politics, there was a powerful journalistic impulse behind his rise and that of the Democrats. As Frederic Hud-son has written, "When the *Globe, Argus,* and *Enquirer* spoke, there was an echo from every corner of the nation. They made cabinet officers and custom-house weighers, presidents and tide-waiters, editors and envoys. They regulated state legislatures and dictated state policies. They were the father confessors to the democracy of the country."

Of these three papers, the *Globe* had long been a power in Washington, the *Argus* was the voice of the Albany Regency, and the Richmond *Enquirer* (there were several other papers by that name) was the spokesman for Thomas Ritchie, its proprietor, the leading radical in the Old Dominion. He exchanged articles with the *Argus* and maneuvered a union between the Regency and its Southern equivalent, the Richmond Junto. The result, as Ritchie put it in the *Enquirer* of April 27, 1827, was a union of the "planters of the South and the plain Republicans of the North."

Ritchie had come to Jackson's support with some reluctance, and it was Van Buren's persuasion that brought him to it. The two men became firm allies. "From the first moment of my acquaintance with you, I have been your personal and political friend," he wrote to Van Buren on July 2, 1838. Thus Van Buren became the catalyst who brought Ritchie, Amos Kendall, Francis P. Blair, Duff Green, and Isaac Hill together in a solid journalistic phalanx of formidable influence, a major factor in electing Jackson and revamping the Jeffersonian Republicans into the new Democratic party.

The *National Intelligencer,* always alert to such trends, was the first to sense what was going on, in this "congeniality of feeling" between Croswell's *Argus* and Ritchie's *Enquirer*. No doubt there was some hidden "identity of purpose," the paper hinted in its opening shot. Croswell agreed, but he denied there was anything secret about it. He argued, "Professing a common political faith—members of the same great national party—and mutually seeking to promote its welfare, such an 'identity of purpose' was not only natural, but we are free to say for ourselves, desirable."

Quite naturally, the *Intelligencer* never forgave Van Buren for his role in depriving it of public printing in 1827. Before then, as a senator from New York, he had been useful to the paper because of his support for Crawford in 1824. The temporary alliance ended, however, when Van Buren rose in the Senate to observe that "the condition of the press might be improved and respect for the Senate and accuracy in publication of its proceedings better secured by a judicious revision of the laws relative to the public printing at large."

Gales and Seaton, the *Intelligencer*'s editors, regarded this observation as an insult to their journalistic reputation, and they also saw in it a plan to control the press through controlling the Senate's printing contracts—which, of course, had been going on since Jefferson's time. In their response they charged Van Buren with what he was, in fact, doing—that is, organizing a new and potent party. Van Buren, said the editors, was a "Master Spirit" by whose agency "machinery had been established to substitute the regular operation of the Government, and to control the popular election by means of organized clubs in the States, and organized presses everywhere." The editors also exaggerated, in the familiar partisan manner, when they asserted that Van Buren was an arch-villain who was plotting to subvert the democratic institutions of the country. "There are intrigues on foot," they wrote, "to place the election of President and Vice President of the United States within the control of a Central Junta in Washington, of which Mr. Van Buren's happy genius is the ascendant influence."

All the opposition editors failed to notice the great paradox in the character of this man they both feared and admired. Van Buren had committed himself to Jackson, the Hero of the People, and he had been one of the chief instruments installing the people's choice in the White House, yet he himself had no love for the people. He dreaded and distrusted the commonality of the electorate, and in his own person he remained the aristocrat, in spite of his humble origins. In becoming the close ally of Jackson he was only accepting what he knew was the politically inevitable and seeing in the general a helping hand on his own road to power. Yet there was nothing superficial or self-seeking in his personal relationship with Jackson. He was speaking from the heart when he wrote in his autobiography: "From that [first] night to the day of his [Jackson's] death . . . sometimes official, always political and personal, [relations] were inviolably maintained between that noble old man and myself, the cordial and confidential character of which can never have been surpassed among public men."

While Jackson remained in office, Van Buren never lost sight of his own goal—to be president himself. He had learned his political lessons well, understanding among other things that it would be necessary to spend money on editors and pamphleteers in order to keep his name in the public eye. The expenses were heavy, and to replenish his accounts he was not above employing inside information from the Treasury Department for his own speculative purposes. But in the end the press subsidies, in spite of their effectiveness, did not save him from direct and indirect attacks by the newspapers.

One of the rising young editors he had to deal with was James Gordon Bennett, who had been so useful in the early Jackson days, as we have seen. At a low point in Bennett's life, however, Van Buren took the risk of antagonizing him on a matter of principle, or so it seemed. In essence it was more of an artful dodge.

Bennett had fallen out with James Watson Webb and his *Courier and Enquirer* when the colonel made a last-minute switch to the anti-Jackson forces, as noted earlier, and for a time he had floundered. The pro-Jackson New York *Globe,* which he established, immediately sank under the pressure of its owner's lack of capital and credit and his inability to get any money from the Jackson camp. Bennett made another try with a small Philadelphia daily, the *Pennsylvanian,* buying a small interest in it and acting as its editor. Since he continued to assault the bank barons and Wall Street, a crusade he had begun on the *Enquirer,* there was no reason to expect the banks to come to his financial aid when the *Pennsylvanian* found itself in trouble.

At one point during these travails, Bennett went to Washington and attempted to use his Jacksonian loyalty to extract a job from Francis Blair on the administration's *Globe.* Blair turned him down, and in fact it was he who suggested the Philadelphia paper as a possibility. But that required money, so Bennett asked his friend Van Buren for help, through Jesse Hoyt. Refusing, Van Buren took a typically ambiguous stand that at the same time made him look like a man of principle. "I cannot directly or indirectly afford pecuniary aid to his press," he wrote to Hoyt. "I can only regret it, but I desire no other support. Whatever course he pursues, as long as it is an honest one, I shall wish him well. He does not understand the relation between the editors he quarreled with and myself, or he would not complain of me for their acts. They are as independent of me in the management of their papers, as I wish him to be and remain."

Bennett was not fooled by this disclaimer, and he did not forget it when the New York *Herald* became influential enough to make politicians think twice before antagonizing its eccentric owner. No doubt that was a development the astute Van Buren did not foresee. He was more concerned with avowed opponents readily at hand.

One of these was Thurlow Weed, who had begun his newspaper career on the *Argus* in Albany before he fell out with the Jacksonians and started his own opposition paper in Rochester to fight the Albany Regency. Later, as a political boss himself, he supplanted the Regency with his own machine and his own Albany newspaper, the *Evening Journal.* The machine elected William H. Seward as governor of New York, and the *Journal* became a tough competitor for the *Argus.*

When Van Buren began his campaign for the presidency, he found himself in the unaccustomed position of being on the receiving end of abuse from the press. The worst he had known before was Duff Green's charge in the *Telegraph* that he had furthered his own career at the expense of Calhoun's. His denials did not stop the accusations. As a candidate, he came under the blows delivered by Webb's corrosive pen. "Every paper almost that we open speaks contemptuously of Van Buren's prospects for the presidency," the *Courier and Enquirer* asserted, "but they speak without knowledge of . . . the vast machine of intrigue and corruption that he has set in operation in every part of the Union—they do not see the fox prowling near the barn; the mole burrowing near the ground; the pilot fish who plunges deep in the ocean in one spot and comes up in another to breathe the air." Like an echo, the New York *American* declared: "Mr. Van Buren consorts most naturally with the degraded and vile—for among them he is a superior. . . . The good we desire we may not be able to attain; but the evil we dread, the great and menacing evil, the blighting disgrace of placing Martin Van Buren, illiterate, sycophant, and politically corrupt, at the head of this great republic . . . we can avert it and such a consummation is surely worth some trouble."

In our day the campaign biography illuminating the virtues of a candidate is commonplace, but in the nineteenth century it was equally common for the opposition to publish a hastily put together book that would have been slanderous, libelous, or both in other circumstances. As it was, a politician might be enraged, but he was not foolish enough to sue. Thus it was not surprising that an already legendary figure like Davy Crockett, once a soldier and frontiersman of outsize proportions and now a congressman from Tennessee, should write a campaign biography of Van Buren on behalf of (and supposedly paid by) another candidate, Sen. Hugh L. White, also of Tennessee. What Crockett wrote was typical:

> What have I to say vs. Martin Van Buren? He is an artful, cunning, intriguing, selfish, speculating lawyer, who, by holding lucrative offices for more than half his life, has contrived to amass a princely fortune. . . . His fame is unknown to the history of our country, except as a most adroit political manager and successful officeholder. . . . Office and money have been the gods of his idolatry; and at their shrines has the ardent worship of his heart been devoted. . . . He can lay no claim to pre-eminent services as a statesman; nor has he ever given any evidences of superior talent, except as a political electioneerer and intriguer.

In spite of Jackson's open support of Van Buren, such attacks were effective.

The legislature of his own state refused to endorse him, even though he saw to it that every member got three copies of the Washington *Globe,* sent under presidential frank and addressed in his own handwriting, attacking Senator White, the legislature's choice, in vituperative language. The Whig press in Tennessee and elsewhere, as hopelessly split as the party and finding no unanimous candidate of its own to support, continued to characterize Van Buren as "that dandy" who strutted and swaggered "like a crow in the gutter . . . laced up in corsets such as women in town wear, and if possible, tighter than the best of them."

With the Whigs in disarray and the issues ill-defined, the election itself was something of an anticlimax. Van Buren won rather easily over William Henry Harrison, 170 to 73 in the electoral college. With a failing party organization of his own and a generally hostile press, Van Buren had triumphed because he had the support, politically and journalistically, where it counted, and because, it must be said, none of the alternatives was exciting enough to whip up any enthusiasm among the electorate.

The national mood was reflected in the inauguration itself. Old and feeble though he was, Jackson rode in triumph with his friend Van Buren to the ceremony, and, as Sen. Thomas Hart Benton observed, the cheers of the thousands along Pennsylvania Avenue were directed more toward the outgoing than the incoming president. Again, as Jackson walked toward his carriage after the swearing-in, a spontaneous sound burst from the waiting crowd, the kind of tribute, as Benton noted, "as power never commanded, nor man in power received. It was affection, gratitude, and admiration . . . the acclaim of posterity breaking from the bosoms of contemporaries."

It was the kind of tribute that Van Buren could not hope to inspire—nor any of his contemporaries, for that matter. No one could imagine this precise and proper man, well and expensively dressed, doing what Jackson did a few days later—dropping into Frank Blair's house, lighting his pipe, reviewing his political career, and remarking that he had made only two mistakes—not shooting Clay and not hanging Calhoun.

A meditative man, Van Buren must have found more than a little irony in the fact that he was no sooner in office than he had to deal with some other mistakes Jackson hadn't mentioned, which were about to bring on a national economic panic. One was the Distribution Act, designed to dispose of the federal surplus of $36 million, and the other an act requiring cash payment for the purchase of all public lands. To some, it was an affirmation of what the Whig papers had been saying, that Van Buren's oblivious solution was to order the White House refurbished at a cost of $25,000. However exaggerated the partisan attacks might have been, it was undeniably true that the new president loved patrician elegance and, at the same time, had a certain disdain for the public that was paying the bills.

In the storm that swirled around Van Buren in the panic of 1837, he could still count on Blair and the *Globe* to support him, even though some Democrats were already turning against the party leaders as a result of the economic crisis. His press support elsewhere was always uncertain and shifting. James Gordon Bennett, for instance, was now rapidly becoming one of the country's most successful editors with his New York *Herald,* and, although he remained a Democratic supporter, his enthusiasm for Van Buren was lukewarm. No doubt he found it hard to forget that Jackson and Blair had turned him down in his hour of great need.

When Bennett made a tour of the South in 1839, the first by any New York editor of consequence, he stopped to call on the president—the first independent presidential interview—and wrote his usual meticulous if overblown account of the visit:

> When my turn came I went up to His Excellency. He held out his hand. It was soft and oily. I took hold of it, gently, by the very hand, too, which has quizzed him most unmercifully during the last four years. . . .
>
> "How do you do, Mr. Bennett?" said Mr. Van Buren, with a half smile.
>
> "Pretty well, I thank you," I responded, with another half smile.
>
> I looked into his face—his eyes wandered over the carpet, probably thinking at that moment of the meeting of Agamemnon and Achilles. I was almost on the verge of bursting into a horse-laugh, at the vagaries of human nature, but being in the presence of the Chief of the Democratic Party, I restrained myself.
>
> I sat down on the sofa, crossed my legs, and looked very knowingly into the fine hickory fire blazing on high.

What did these two talk about? "A little on local politics," Bennett reported, "a little on land speculation—a little on the weather." Nevertheless, as a good reporter, Bennett could not conclude his account of the meeting without paying Van Buren at least a halfway tribute: "Ten years ago I knew Mr. Van Buren as a senator, when he had no more idea of being president than I had. What a remarkable illustration of the free institutions of this land! Forty or fifty years ago, Mr. Van Buren was a poor boy in Kinderhook, unnoticed, unknown, unheralded—now he is President of twenty millions of people, and a territory second in size to all Europe."

Whatever else the poor boy from Kinderhook might be, he was a shrewd politician and knew he could not count on the likes of Bennett. Far better to rely on Blair, who was nearly as adept in political infighting. Jackson's editor knew how to use the *Globe* and other sympathetic Democratic papers to whip up the masses by accusing the Whigs of trying to break the local banks. An "able and inflexible editor," said the president of Blair, and with the daily support of the *Globe,* Van Buren pursued his policy of extending the Specie Circular to include postal receipts and even recommended that Congress adopt a policy which would require all government receipts to be in gold and silver. That led the president into a historic struggle with Congress over his proposal to establish an independent treasury. Here the *Globe* became a useful weapon, as it carried a series of articles by the secretary of the treasury, reassuring the South particularly that the president meant strict construction of the Constitution and favored the interests of all classes by adopting a sound currency.

Blair must have been well aware that Van Buren was not really interested in all classes, and certainly not all classes of the party, as his predecessor had been.

Consequently he devoted much of his editorial space to a continuing defense of Jackson, to which he had pledged his journalistic life. The friendship between Blair and Van Buren was a firm one, characterized by respect on both sides, but it had none of the warmth of Blair's relationship with Old Hickory. Van Buren was too cool, distant, and wily for Blair, who could not forget how warm-hearted and trusting Jackson had been with him. As a result, the *Globe*'s support of Van Buren's presidency continued with slowly diminishing degrees of enthusiasm. There were occasional aggravations in this relationship, too. For instance, Van Buren was determined to follow Jackson's policy on the federal bank, but at the same time he urged Blair to tone down his caustic editorials on the subject, even though he knew that their substance came directly from the Hermitage, from which Jackson was still trying to exert his influence on national affairs.

After his interview with the president, Bennett had delivered one of his *ex cathedra* editorial judgments that "there is a strong presentiment here that he will be re-elected, in spite of all that the Whigs can do. And even that he will name his successor." But those who read other papers, or even the *Herald,* were less optimistic as the administration struggled along. Van Buren simply could not muster public support as Jackson had, and he was vulnerable on several issues. In general, the newspapers took a negative stand against him; they spoke of his silence "upon the great and interesting topics of the day." He appeared to enjoy associating with the rich and the powerful, so antipathetic to homespun Jacksonianism, and when this was taken in conjunction with the continuing hard times generated by the panic, Bennett was only echoing the thoughts of many others in and out of the press when he editorialized, "Martin Van Buren and his atrocious associates form one of the original causes of the terrible moral, political, and commercial desolation which spreads over the country."

Even his supporters in the press were disturbed by his frankly antislavery views, particularly the influential New York *Evening Post,* and they could not even begin to defend his continued extravagances at a time when the country was wallowing in a state of economic fear. He had bought an English coach to travel about Washington, and those who dined at the White House were quick to note the golden spoons in the table service. (They were not so quick to note that the spoons had been bought by a previous administration.) Van Buren's son John was conspicuous for his lordly ways, and the Whig press referred to him as "Prince John." All this was a vivid contrast to the simple ways of the Jacksonians.

The president seemed curiously removed from the abuse in the newspapers and appeared not to hold grudges against even the worst of his detractors. When William Leggett, who had attacked the president regularly in the pages of the New York *Evening Post,* found himself stricken with tuberculosis and was advised by his doctor to settle in a warmer climate, Van Buren was told of it and immediately appointed him to a diplomatic post in Guatemala. Unfortunately, Leggett died a few days before he was to have sailed.

Van Buren had used his masterful knowledge of government and his superb political craftiness to gain the presidency. Though lacking both popular affection and party loyalty, he was available, subservient, and a party regular, and therefore became the Democratic candidate for president in 1840 without serious opposition, since the party had no viable alternative. In this contest he had to face again a national hero, Gen. William Henry Harrison, the victor in the Battle of Tippecanoe, a man cast somewhat in Jackson's image as the Champion of the People as against Van Buren, whose basic philosophy was that the federal government had no right to interfere with business and that the president had no duty to restore prosperity, leaving that to the private sector. The Whigs, as divided as ever, could not unite on Henry Clay, their logical choice, because it was plain he could not even get the nomination, so they had turned to electable military heroes, choosing Harrison over Gen. Winfield Scott only because Thurlow Weed threw his support to the hero of Tippecanoe, although Harrison's other qualifications were minimal and he had already failed to win in 1836.

The campaign itself, as Stefan Lorant has put it, was "the most exuberant, exciting and nonsensical campaign in American presidential history," an unbelievable circus in which the Whig press presented Harrison to the public as a simple backwoodsman, although he was, in fact, the son of a governor and the rich owner of two thousand acres. Against this sitting target the Democratic papers leveled a barrage of ridicule. A correspondent for the Baltimore *Republican* gave a devastating account of how a friend of Clay's had told him after Harrison's nomination, "Give him a barrel of Hard Cider, and settle a pension of $2,000 a year on him, and my word for it, he will sit the remainder of his days in his Log Cabin, by the side of a 'sea coal' fire and study moral philosophy."

This quotation served the Harrison strategists well. Their papers were soon presenting the general as "the log-cabin and hard-cider candidate," until they had the public believing that he lived in a log cabin, never drank anything stronger than hard cider (not considered a serious drink), and tilled the fields like any frontiersman. Log cabins and hard cider became the symbols of his campaign, along with various Tippecanoe handkerchiefs, badges, breastpins, and coonskin caps. What a pale comparison was Van Buren's chaste image—this "Old Kinderhook," as he was called (the origin of "O.K.," some believe), dragging the dead weight of the depression behind him. Once more it was mass emotion opposed to a serious discussion of issues. The voters didn't believe or even care about the Democratic papers' accurate depiction of Harrison as an unreconstructed old Federalist. They much preferred to read in the Whig papers about Van Buren's "Blue Elliptical Saloon" in the White House, with its gilt mirrors and chairs at $600 a set; a presidential bedroom with an ornate French bedstead; Royal Wilton carpets on the floors; and tables set with gold and silver. And this man calls himself a Democrat? the Whig papers inquired contemptuously.

In all the clamor the public scarcely noticed that John Tyler, an aristocrat from Virginia fully as patrician as Van Buren, had been chosen as Harrison's running mate. They thought about it a month after the inauguration, however. Harrison had won in a surprisingly close election as far as the popular vote was concerned (he polled only about 150,000 votes more), although his electoral vote was 234 to 60, and he had ridden triumphantly down Pennsylvania Avenue on a white charger (shades of Jackson!) to his inauguration.

The Whig papers were triumphantly proclaiming, "Our republican institutions are redeemed from the grasp of tyrants. Let the people . . . rejoice." But there were more sober voices. For the first time several important newspapers had remained neutral in a presidential campaign, and some had shared Bennett's view. He had declared himself an "armed neutral" at first, and the *Herald* became the first newspaper in journalistic history to give equal prominence to both candidates, but at the last minute he gave his support to Harrison, observing, "I don't like Harrison—but I like Martin Van Buren even less."

One of the steadfast neutralists had been the Philadelphia *Public Ledger,* and in the midst of Harrisonian victory fervor, it gave its own sober conclusions about the election:

> For two years past, the most ordinary operations of business have been neglected and President-making has become every citizen's chief concern. The result being uncertain, some have been afraid to engage in new enterprises, others have retired from business, others have not dared to prosecute their business with the old vigor. Millions of dollars will now change hands on election bets; millions of days have been taken from useful labor to listen to stump orators, and millions more to build log cabins, erect hickory poles, and march in ridiculous, degrading, mob-creating processions; millions of dollars have been wasted in soul- and body-destroying intemperance, in paying demagogues for preaching treason and bribing knaves to commit perjury and cast fraudulent votes. However high the hopes inspired by the election of General Harrison, they will prove to be delusive.

Whatever these presentiments for the future conduct of American politics may have been, the importance of the *Public Ledger*'s editorial lay in its assertion of the independence now taking hold in the press. It was not that the partisan press was dying or dead. Newspapers continued to be as partisan as ever, and real efforts to attain objectivity were still a long way off, particularly in the case of political news, but the ownership of journals was falling rapidly into the hands of individual enterpreneurs, independent of party both financially and ideologically, and the papers were becoming business enterprises. Advertising revenue was beginning to be a factor, but increasingly circulation was the decisive element in the failure or success of a newspaper, which meant that every publisher had to find, and expand if possible, the public for his particular product.

There were those at the time who were skeptical about the nature of this transition, believing that control of the press had simply passed from the politicians to the bankers and rich merchants who supplied the publishing entrepreneurs with capital and support. That viewpoint was shown to be wrong, however, as the new publishers attacked social institutions and beliefs which the bankers and other members of the elite supported, to the extent that the "better people" of New York attempted to carry on a Great Moral War against Bennett, who regularly abused Wall Street, the churches, corrupt businessmen, and others who displeased him.

Recent journalism scholarship has tended to look for the roots of objectivity in the rise of the penny press, and to denigrate further the "great man" concept of the new journalism's rise. But these sociological speculations hardly detract from the reality of men like Bennett, Charles Anderson Dana, Horace Greeley, and Henry J. Raymond (to name only those in New York), who unquestionably shaped the character and function of the press for the remainder of the century, or at least until the advent of Joseph Pulitzer and William Randolph Hearst. Nor do these studies offer any real proof that "objectivity," however defined, was a characteristic of the new journals.

In fact, the chief difference between old and new presentations of the news, especially political news, was the beginning of an *attempt* to be objective in the news columns, which Bennett and the others succeeded finally in separating from editorial comment appearing on an editorial page. The editorials themselves continued to advocate the views of the newspapers' owners, whatever they might be; the essential fact was that these views were individual, neither paid for by politicians, nor necessarily dictated by party loyalty or affiliation. As for the news, it was far more comprehensive than it had been, and an attempt was made to get the facts and present them in a relatively unbiased fashion for the times. There was, of course, still a long way to go.

The effect of these developments on the relationship between the press and the presidency was profound. In the two decades before the Civil War, candidates and presidents alike had for the first time to deal with a press that, by and large, they could not buy with direct or indirect patronage. Further, they were compelled to recognize that the larger, more important papers, with growing circulations extending beyond their cities, were exerting a national influence with which they had to reckon. Horace Greeley's New York *Tribune,* to cite the most conspicuous example, became virtually a spokesman for the nation's farmers, who liked the kind of populism Greeley was preaching in his editorials.

In the other media, too, the traditionally independent magazines now commanded substantial national audiences, thanks to the growth of education and literacy, and they were becoming national forums for the discussion of public issues, particularly *the* public issue of slavery. Books were playing the role they had played from the beginning, as the disseminators of ideas, but now as a result of that marvelous invention, the cylinder press, which had so greatly changed the nature and influence of all the media, books, too, could work upon public opinion to an extent politicians could not ignore. Harriet Beecher Stowe, with her best-selling *Uncle Tom's Cabin,* may not have been "the little lady who started the great war," as Lincoln is supposed to have called her, but her novel certainly played as great a role in rallying Northern opinion and further alienating the South as the speeches of any politician.

In brief, a new era was dawning as the Little Magician succumbed to the hoopla of the Harrison campaign that the *Public Ledger* had deplored in its plague-on-both-your-houses editorial. From now on, the adversary relationship between the press and the presidents would become, as White House occupants of our time would have put it, a whole new ball game. It was not an instantaneous transition, but a surprisingly rapid one, measured by historical time. The consequences for both press and presidency were serious and far reaching.

William Henry Harrison: A Jacksonian Postscript

We can only speculate what role William Henry Harrison might have played in this new configuration, because his sudden death from pneumonia after only a month in office deprived him of the opportunity. His brief political career, however, provides us with a capsule summary of the old order's style.

When he became a politician, Harrison found that he had first to defend his record in the War of 1812 against charges made by subordinates reflecting on both his courage and his command abilities, which in retrospect appear exemplary considering that he was, admittedly, not a great general and was called upon to face nearly impossible challenges. At least it could be said of him that he was victorious where so many others were defeated. Nevertheless, when Capt. Robert McAfee's *History of the Late War* was published, an account favorable to him, it was at once challenged by Gen. James Winchester, who replied to the book in a series of articles that ran in the *Intelligencer*. Harrison responded with his own version of events, first in the *Kentucky Reporter* in November 1817, and two years later in the *Intelligencer*.

Winchester's charges were rehearsed again when Harrison ran unsuccessfully for Congress in 1822, to his professed "shock," but in the meantime he had made some helpful friends among the editors of various journals who began assiduously to build up the military reputation that would be so useful to him in the presidential campaign of 1840. Among them was Moses Dawson, of the Cincinnati *Advertiser,* who published an excessively flattering biography of the general in 1824. It was a newspaper, the *Pennsylvania Intelligencer,* that first suggested Harrison for the presidency in 1834, but he was opposed by party leaders and their Washington organ, the *National Intelligencer,* because of the shadow that lingered over his military career in spite of everything partisan editors could do.

When they were not recalling the supposed errors of the 1812 conflict, Harrison's opponents in the press liked to emphasize his age, which was only sixty-three when he first ran for the presidency in 1836. They asserted he was already "in his dotage." This kind of slur was still prevalent in 1840, but that campaign was a far different one, made easier for the Harrison forces by the character of Van Buren and his disposition to run for office from the White House rather than on the hustings, where the general's three-ring circus was producing a state of hysteria far removed from the real issues the president hoped to talk about.

If Harrison had a point of real vulnerability, it was his pretense of being the poor man's candidate, scarcely rising above a state of poverty himself. Van Buren's editorial supporters were quick to point out that the general drew about $6,000 a year from his clerkship and that his substantial farm, run for him by a host of in-laws, was highly profitable. If there was a log cabin on his estate, they noted, it was one the general had never lived in and was merely a wing maintained as an antique. As for hard cider, the liquor of the proletariat, upon which the general was pictured as having been nurtured, it was never served at the

Harrison manor, where good wine and whiskey were no strangers. As we have seen, however, the Whigs succeeded in making Harrison the log-cabin, hard-cider candidate just the same.

A more serious problem in electing Harrison was the religious one of the reaction to him. In the papers the general had emerged as a Messiah come to deliver the Chosen People into the Promised Land, just as Jackson had done—a land where they would subsist on $2 a day and roast beef, instead of "Matty's" fifty cents a day and French soup. The log cabin became a symbolic temple in this scenario. As a gospel, the Harrison notion of political immortality spread with enthusiastic fervor. There were songs and poems; the naming of babies, animals, and boats for Harrison, Ty, and Tip. Even a newspaper, Horace Greeley's old *Jeffersonian,* was renamed the *Log Cabin,* while in Ohio there sprang up several variations on this theme—the Chillico *Log Cabin Herald,* the Cleveland *Hard Cider for Log Cabins,* and the Steubenville *Log Cabin Farmer.* These journals were published for campaign purposes only, but they were, none-theless, successful. The circulation of Greeley's paper, for example, climbed from forty-eight thousand to eighty thousand, increasing at a rate of nearly five thousand per week.

There were pious citizens and religious leaders who considered that this secular Harrisonian religion was being carried too far, and there were protests in the pulpits and the religious journals, but in the end these objections were not strong enough to matter. The general's managers believed they had more practical problems, among them the necessity to keep their candidate from saying too much in public, since they had no illusions about his intellect. His silence led to his being dubbed "General Mum" by the Democratic press, and when a Whig editor from New York, James Brooks, asked him if he would care to respond to this implicit accusation, he answered, "There is scarcely anything I am not asked and if I were to answer all the correspondence I should have no time for anything else."

But the attempt to muzzle him was alien to an old soldier accustomed to command, and, during a swing through Ohio, Harrison ignored his advisers on one occasion. In a speech at Greenville he declared: "You have undoubtedly seen it oftentimes stated in a certain class of newspapers that I am a very decrepit old man, obliged to hobble about on crutches, that I was caged up, and that I could not speak loud enough to be heard more than four or five feet distant; in consequence of which last misfortune, I am stigmatized with the cognomen of 'General Mum.' You now perceive, however, that those stories are false. . . . Ask the subsidized Press," he went on, "what governs its operations, and it will open its iron jaws and answer you in a voice loud enough to shake the pyramids—MONEY! MONEY! I speak not at random—facts bear me testimony."

After this honest outburst, the Harrison managers might have believed they had made a mistake to keep the general's voice muffled, but in Dayton he was asked a question on national finances and replied, "Methinks, I hear a soft voice asking, Are you in favor of paper money? I am." That was *too* honest for political managers. However, the issues were seldom discussed except in the briefest terms, and Harrison's mere appearance at a rally was enough to win over the audiences who contemplated his authoritative military figure, as opposed to Van Buren's almost receding presence.

One of the casualties of this unprecedented campaign, in which the press was used to an extent it had never been before, was Francis Blair, who was old-fashioned enough to believe that it was issues which really counted. Futilely he swam against the tirades against Van Buren issuing from the talented pens of Bennett, Greeley, William Lloyd Garrison, and Mordecai Noah, among others. Blair attempted to convince the slaveholders that there was no substantial difference between the principles of Northerners and Southerners, and he invoked the horror of disunion to his readers. This was something of an editorial high-wire act, since it meant somehow justifying the *Globe*'s attacks on abolition and maintaining a discreet silence about Van Buren's opposition to the annexation of Texas, which ultimately contributed to his downfall.

In the *Globe,* Blair dutifully campaigned for Van Buren, but without much conviction. He was sharply accurate in his argument that the question was not whether Harrison lived in a log cabin, but whether he was a friend of the people who lived in such humble dwellings. In column after column he tried to turn the public's attention to principles or issues, but it was no use. He was joined in his efforts by his old friend and co-worker, Kendall, who overreached his physical and financial reserves in the cause, eventually having to resign as postmaster general so that he could restore his health, wealth, and family relations. Blair came to his aid by hiring him to write editorials and supervise the circulation of the *Extra Globe,* the paper's dollar edition, published "to neutralize the poison which the Federal party" was "laboring to instill into public sentiment. The *Extra Globe* was part of the Democrats' effort to match the Whigs' log-cabin campaign organs. Other newspapers of this genre bore such feebly imitative names as the *Coon Skinner,* the *Dry Cider Barrel,* and the *Rough Hewer.*

For a time Blair was carried away by the extraordinary character of the campaign. He wrote in the *Globe:* "This is the most violent political struggle there has been since 1800. The excitement is great and universal, pervading the whole population, of all ages, classes, and conditions; in the city and in the country, in all the public thoroughfares, in steamboats and in railroads, at the public hotels and in the field and workshops, and in every family circle, you hear nothing but politics, politics." He seemed hypnotized by his own prose and predicted confidently to Jackson that Van Buren and Jacksonian principles would win. By November, however, he had lost hope, and he sailed for Cuba with his daughter in an effort to restore her health.

At last it was over, and the general came to Washington. He delivered a long inaugural address, partly ghostwritten by Daniel Webster, not one of the great orator's better efforts. In it was a paragraph devoted to the press, in which the prose may have been Webster's but the voice was authentically Harrison's. He would not, said the new president, use the power of his office to interfere with press freedom, particularly by manipulating public printing contracts, and he continued:

There is no part of the means placed in the hands of the Executive which might be used with greater effect for unhallowed purposes than the control of the public press. The maxim which our ancestors derived from the mother country that "the freedom of the press is the great bulwark of civil and religious liberty" is one of the most precious legacies which they have left us. We have learned, too, from our own as well as the experience of other countries, that golden shackles, by whomsoever or by whatever pretense imposed, are as fatal to it as the iron bonds of despotism. The presses in the necessary employment of the Government should never be used "to clear the guilty or to varnish crime." A decent and manly examination of the acts of the Government should be not only tolerated, but encouraged.

Having spoken, Harrison made one of his first acts in office the dismissal of the *Globe* as printer to Congress, costing it both money and status. That was understandable, however, since Blair had greeted the victory with accusations of fraud and of profiting from the English capitalists, besides charging his party with maneuvering a puppet who would be led around by Webster and Clay.

In his brief month of life remaining, Harrison also rewarded the journalistic faithful, appointing Duff Green as governor of Florida Territory, although the editor would have preferred to head the mission to Texas. Green's son Todd was made minister to Russia, and Col. John S. Todd, editor of the Cincinnati *Republican,* one of the most vociferous of the Harrison organs, was made the president's private secretary. Harrison's rejection of Greeley for any post at all, and his cold indifference to the remainder of the press during the few weeks he was in office, was no doubt an accurate forecast of how it would have been if he had finished his term.

But even his death did not end the general's editorial war. Virtually over the grave the *Globe* ran a story purporting to be an account of the deathbed scene, in which Harrison was reported as giving "utterance to the secret thoughts that oppressed him. Sometimes he would say, 'My dear madam, I did not direct that your husband should be turned out. I did not know it. I tried to prevent it.' On other occasions he would say, in broken sentences, 'It is wrong—I won't consent—'tis unjust.' Again,—'These applications, will they never cease?'" The inferences of party manipulation were obvious, and the *National Intelligencer* called the story an example of "shocking depravity. We should have thought, until we saw the *Globe* of Thursday evening that party ferocity would have relented on approaching a scene hallowed by the regrets of a whole nation, and would not have dared so revolting an outrage on truth and decency." The paper added a letter from a personal friend of the president's, denying that this scene ever took place.

The *Globe* was not the only dissenter, however, from the national mourning that now took place. In New York the *Evening Post* refused to employ the traditional black borders that every other paper was using, and in an editorial seemed to express regret only because Harrison had not lived long enough to demonstrate his unfitness for office. Given his attitudes and the kind of opposition existing even after his death, there is no reason to believe that Harrison would have improved the relationship between press and presidency had he lived. The circumstances of his political life only emphasized the death agonies of the party press and forecast the kind of adversary relationship that could be expected from the new commercial entrepreneurs.

Tyler and the Twilight of the Party Press

In the wake of the campaign clamor and the president's sudden death, there remained a quiet Virginian, John Tyler, whom no one much esteemed and who now became the first vice-president to succeed as president. He made the usual gestures of peace and good will toward the other party and the press in general, but these were quickly forgotten in the tide of events that soon engulfed his office, leaving him, as James Pollard has put it, "one of the most abused and least understood of the Presidents. A century later he was still the victim of misunderstanding and doubt." The press played a large role in creating this unfortunate situation, but it was only reflecting the intense political pressures of the time, and in retrospect it seems doubtful whether anyone who occupied the White House during this period would have fared much better.

The effect of this pressure on Tyler after only two years in office was plainly visible, as it has been with so many other presidents. Charles Dickens, on his memorable visit to the United States in 1842, saw Tyler in the White House and, with his novelist's (and reporter's) eye, noted: "He looked somewhat worn and anxious, and well he might, being at war with everybody—but the expression of his face was mild and pleasant, and his manner was remarkably unaffected, gentlemanly, and agreeable. I thought that, in his whole carriage and demeanour, he became his station singularly well."

The cause of the president's growing trouble was clear enough. He had inherited a bagful of serious problems from the two previous administrations, notably the vexing question of a national bank, the tariff, and how to distribute public land sale proceeds. To the solving of these problems, Tyler brought his own personal dilemma. His entire political career, including his election to the Senate in 1827 and his nomination to the vice-presidency in 1840, rested on the support of those powerful politicians who were against the doctrine of states' rights and for a broad construction of the Constitution. Moreover, his Senate victory had been at the expense of the most distinguished supporter of states' rights in his generation, John Randolph. Whatever he might think about the questions of public policy now confronting him, Tyler could count on enmity from some quarters and, worse, the necessity to conform with the wishes of his backers.

Nevertheless, as the drama of Tyler's administration developed, the war against everybody that Dickens had noted was without any substantial cause. In the circumstances Tyler did well with the short rope given him. But his shortcomings were exaggerated into damning faults, and his weaknesses into imbecilities, while his virtues were depicted as vices. Unlike other presidents he did not rail against the injustices and sink into malice or bitterness. He was able to forgive his enemies most of the time, and that was his salvation.

Another complication, however, was the fact that the campaign slogan, "Tippecanoe and Tyler too," implied that Tyler shared the views of his running mate, as a good vice-presidential candidate was expected to do, but in fact this was not the case. The differences between them had been glossed over, and Tyler knew they were likely to emerge almost at once. However, he feared what the press would do with this ideological dichotomy when it was discovered. Consequently, only two months after he took office, he declined an invitation from his friend, former governor of North Carolina James Iredell, Jr., to make a speech in that state on behalf of the Whig cause, because, as he said, he could not do it "without being subjected to assaults from the newspaper press which at this time I feel desirous of avoiding."

Tyler may have felt vulnerable for another reason. He was only fifty-one, the youngest man to sit in the White House until that time, and it is possible he felt the weight of seniority around him, notwithstanding that he had had more experience in government than any president before or since. He had spent his life in politics, first in the Virginia House and Senate, then in the governor's mansion in Richmond, and finally in the House and Senate of the United States.

Along the way, Tyler had acquired the rhetoric of politicians who understood that the press represented itself as the champion of the people, to whom every officeholder had to express devotion, but, at the same time, it was necessary to appear to rise slightly above the journals. Thus he declared: "The barking of newspapers and the brawling of demagogues can never drive me from my course. If I am to go into [political] retirement, I will at least take care to do so with a pure and unsullied conscience."

There was something of Van Buren in this man. He could be warm in private, but was not often so in public. His success derived from his powers of oratory and his campaign methods rather than an ability to endear himself to the voters. He much preferred the society of his social and intellectual peers to that of those beneath his station. In short, he was a patrician of the old school that had run the business of the Republic for so long, but he was living in a time of populist ferment.

Tyler believed that the press should be free and should never act as merely the mouthpiece of a political party, yet he was no different from those who came before and after him in deploring the press's freedom when it was directed against him. Nor, apparently, did he see anything contradictory in establishing his own party press or in attacking the Northern abolitionist journals with the implication that they should be suppressed. As early as 1835, in a speech at Gloucester, Virginia, Tyler was condemning the abolition press: "It has established numerous presses, four of which circulated from the city of New York, with copies of three of which they had been *so extremely kind* as to favor me through the mail. These papers were circulated gratuitously among us, and at mere nominal prices to actual subscribers. . . . I propose to show you the cheap rate at which these papers are delivered out to actual subscribers."

When he assumed office as president, Tyler had more immediate problems to confront than the abolition press. First, as always, was the question of patronage, and here he tried to deal with an equable hand. Although the Richmond *Enquirer* accused him of "wholesale removals" of Democrats from office with the view of succeeding himself, no evidence exists that anything of the kind occurred. In fact, at the time the accusation was made, most of the federal offices were held by men opposed to the president. Tyler named nine members of his family to various positions, but, except in two cases, he did not give federal jobs to editors who had supported him. Indeed, he denied the ambassadorship to the Court of St. James's to Mordecai Noah simply because he *was* an editor.

Once past the patronage tangle, Tyler had to confront what he would do about his principles. If he maintained them, he would have to break with Clay, Webster, and most of those who had gotten him nominated. But if he followed Clay and the others, he would certainly appear unprincipled, and that was what the opposition press confidently expected him to be. "Tyler is to become the tool of this poor braggart and disgraced politician, Clay," Frank Blair wrote to Jackson only a month after Tyler had taken office. "He veils his intention about the Bank but thinly. . . . I have no doubt he was fully pledged at Harrisburg. . . . I shall trace him down. . . . The monstrous corruption disclosed in the old Bank's business will make a proper mire to drag him through."

The test came almost at once, with the passage of a new bank bill. When it reached his desk, Tyler vetoed it as unconstitutional. To the astonishment of nearly everyone, he had come down hard on the side of principle, and he could not have been unaware of the outburst of rage that would follow his action. "In Wall Street there is considerable blasphemy," wrote the New York correspondent of the Washington *Madisonian*. "Some Whigs are very obstreperously taking large oaths never to vote for a Virginian again or a man who has a cousin in Virginia. All this gas is well to flow off at once as to keep souring on the stomach. I think the most obstreperous will feel calmer and cooler tomorrow."

One of the less cool recipients of the news was James Gordon Bennett, who saw an opportunity to make circulation capital. He had the complete text of the veto brought up to him by a specially chartered train and, as soon as it arrived, printed an extra morning edition of the *Herald* containing it. By noon the extra was a sensational success. "Up to this time," a *Herald* correspondent wrote, "I think that no less than 100,000 copies of it have been issued from our several printing offices and greedily snatched by the eager multitude. The broker in his den, the merchant at his desk, the hod-man at his dinner, the carman between jobs—all are reading Veto, Veto!"

The opposition press was dumbfounded, but quick to respond. Blair wrote in the *Globe* of August 17, 1841: "The Veto brings with it a moral. It punishes the most atrocious fraud ever attempted upon a nation. . . . We make our acknowledgments to Mr. Tyler for his deliverance. If he maintains his position firmly, he will be acknowledged as a public benefactor." In the familiar manner of the time, but rather startlingly familiar in this case, the *Madisonian*'s man in New York commented, "For my own part, I think John might have been a little favorable towards us forlorn Bank Whigs who are not yet convinced that a national bank, or at least a national currency of some kind, is desirable and necessary."

Tyler found it easy to forgive the disrespectful "John," but he was not ready to excuse the *National Intelligencer*, the administration organ he had inherited, for its backing of Clay in the bank dispute. In September 1841 he made the

Madisonian the official newspaper, observing, "I can no longer tolerate the *Intelligencer* as the official paper. Besides assaulting me perpetually, directly, it represses all defensive articles, as appear by the *Madisonian* of Saturday. There is a point beyond which one's patience cannot endure."

That point had also been reached by Tyler's cabinet, which resigned in protest after the veto, all except for Daniel Webster, his secretary of state. In the columns of the *Madisonian,* Webster continued to defend Tyler and denounce his enemies in unsigned editorials, the kind he often contributed to friendly newspapers. On the other side, Secretary of the Treasury Thomas Ewing, who did resign, complained that Robert Sutton, the Washington correspondent of the New York *Herald,* not only treated the cabinet badly but also betrayed a few of its secrets. There may have been some truth in the accusation. Already in Washington there was enough leakage to the press in high places to make secrecy more a hope than a fact.

Journalistically, the veto cleared the air for Tyler. He now had a few papers he thought he could rely on. Besides the *Madisonian* in Washington and Bennett's *Herald* in New York, the president had blandly ignored his earlier statement of principle and, employing the customary apparatus of patronage, had established administration papers in nearly every state, notably in Philadelphia and Boston. The march toward independence had only begun, obviously; there were still a good many newspapers and editors for sale to politicians.

One of the president's shrewdest moves in this direction was to make Mordecai Noah editor of the new official party paper in New York City, the *Union.* Through the veteran editor and his paper, Tyler hoped to gain control of the divided Democratic party in New York State, believing that a Tammany-trained professional like Noah, who knew his way about the incredible complexities of city and state politics, could be of great help to him.

Nevertheless, the *Union* was not a success. The New York Democrats were not about to permit Tyler to gain control of their party machinery, especially after the bank veto. Noah resigned, and the paper quietly merged with the New York *Aurora,* which had begun in February 1843 with presidential support. The resulting product failed to rouse the president's continued interest. When he was asked later if he wanted to try to keep the paper going at any cost, he replied candidly that he did not "care a God damn about it," and so the *Aurora* slid into another merger with Levi Slamm's New York *Plebeian,* which was temporarily, at least, pro-Tyler.

The most effective support for the president came from Bennett's *Herald.* A tireless worker himself, the editor was pleased by Tyler's application to his job. "Nothing can exceed the industry of the President," Bennett editorialized. "He arises early and retires late. Every hour of the day is devoted to his duties. He is compelled to look over papers and decide on a great mass of matters that would be handed over to the action of his secretaries if they were really his friends."

By this time, Bennett had six correspondents in his Washington bureau, the first of its kind in the business, and they reported regularly in much the same way bureau men do today, except that their dispatches had a more intimate, personal tone than modern news writing—not unlike British dailies of our time. Bennett's criterion was to get the news, and get it first. The reporters in Washington were so good at this that the *Herald* was able to report, shortly before the event: "We learn, by an intimate friend of ours, and a personal friend of Mr. Tyler's, who arrived last night from Washington, that beyond doubt the Bank Bill will be vetoed. There will be a terrible fuss—no row—much blowing off of steam, and unquestionably a reconstruction of the Cabinet. One, and perhaps two, members of it will remain in office. There is no mistake in this."

How far journalism had come since the days of the partisan press, at least in the best papers, could be seen by comparing this dispatch with the style of a provincial paper like the Richmond *Whig,* which was still wallowing in the invective of the past. The *Whig*'s rival, the *Enquirer,* reprinted a few choice samples as models of Whig frustration: Tyler was "the accident of an Accident," "a famished Charles City pettifogger, whom nature never intended to elevate above the trial of ten dollar warrants upon plain cases, a man destitute of intellect and integrity, whose name is the synonym of nihil," "if so miserable a thing can be called a man," "base, selfish and perfidious," "a vast nightmare over the Republic," and exclaiming with Shakespeare, "O! for a whip in every honest hand—To lash the rascal naked through the world!" Such language was still common enough in the provincial papers, but more polished editors of large city dailies like the *Herald* denounced their enemies in elegant language, for the most part, and were making an effort to bring sanity into the writing of political stories.

There was now an element of professional jealousy, too, even among political allies, where coverage of the news was concerned. The *Herald* frequently hinted that it had direct lines into the White House, but the *Madisonian,* believing its official position threatened, on September 16, 1841, denied even the possibility:

> The *Herald* employed in this city during the late session of Congress, in addition to a "corps of professional reporters," a special *correspondent,* whose sole business it was to gather all the information within his reach and to write down the results and his own speculations. The correspondent, we judge from his works, devoted himself assiduously to his special duty, and succeeded better than most letter writers in producing correct statements and making pretty accurate predictions. But he made no discoveries, as we have seen, but such as were in the reach of practical observers, familiar with public men and parties. The topics treated of in those letters were such as were generally discussed here, and the information communicated, whenever true, and of any consequence, was such as was known to us and numerous others of the President's friends, and in fact current in this city. We have seen nothing in them worthy to be regarded as a special revelation of the President's mind. The speculations in advance of the Veto were such as any shrewd person could have detected from an examination of the bill and a study of the President's character and past opinions.

The *Herald*'s correspondents had also come to the attention of Congress, where the anti-Tyler men were beginning to fear that the ability of Bennett's reporters to get news, sometimes before Congress itself knew what was happening, was getting out of hand. Consequently, Sen. Samuel L. Southard, of New

Jersey, president pro tem of the Senate, invoked an old rule by which the privilege of the floor was limited to two men from each *Washington* paper, thus barring the *Herald* entirely. In his characteristically breezy way, Bennett dismissed this action. The rule, he said, was only designed to protect the lazy Washington papers from competition, and to help them rob "the public treasury, under the color of public printing." As for the *Herald,* he declared, it would continue to give the congressional debates a daily coverage and circulation "better and more comprehensive" than any of the other papers, and without taking a cent from the public treasury.

Nevertheless, Bennett appealed the banning of his reporters from the Senate floor to Clay. It was costing him $200 a week to maintain a Washington bureau, he said, and barring his men was "hostile to the public interest." Moreover, he went on, the rule was "illiberal and injurious both to private enterprise and public advantage." Clay promised to work out some kind of accommodation, but the Senate was having none of it for the moment. His proposals were buried in committee. Bennett's reporters continued to rely on their ingenuity rather than access for the time being, and their publisher continued his protests, particularly when he learned that the foreign press was exempted from the rule.

Tyler himself antagonized the press needlessly by issuing an executive order to the postmaster general, instructing him not to appoint editors of partisan political newspapers as postmasters—a practice common since pre-Revolutionary days. The word "partisan" stuck in every editor's throat. What did "partisan" mean? Nearly every newspaper of general circulation in America could be termed partisan in one degree or another. It was a difficult decision to defend, but the *Madisonian* made a gallant try at it. The president's order, it said on October 7, 1841, "as we understand it, [is intended] to secure *equal rights to all editors.*" There were few believers.

Having twice vetoed a bank bill, to the outrage of the Whigs, Tyler compounded his difficulties by vetoing the tariff bills of 1842, for which he was attacked harshly by a House committee. Responding to the committee's report, the president did so through an address published by his son, John Tyler, Jr., in which he duly noted the role of the press in this affair.

> What means of protection had I against the assaults which were to be made upon my character, and of the intention to make which I was apprised in advance, private and public? The *Madisonian* was, I believe, the only political paper that sustained me; its circulation was limited and confined. The New York *Herald* did me justice, and the neutral press assisted; while an affiliated press, organized, and which it has required years to affiliate, opened their batteries upon me. The shout was raised from one end of the country to the other; indignation meetings were everywhere held; effigy burnings took place, and a universal roar of Whig vengeance was heard in every blast.

It was even worse than he thought. A movement to impeach the president was initiated by Tyler's fellow Virginian, Congressman John Minor Botts, the aggressive and often violent voice of the Whigs in the House, but he was unsuccessful. Tyler defended himself indirectly through his son, who wrote an editorial for the *Madisonian,* countering the congressman's assertions.

As his term neared its end, the president had succeeded in alienating nearly everyone, not only the Whigs *en masse* but even some influential Democrats. Both the *Globe* and the *Intelligencer* were now joined against him. Even the faithful but always fickle Bennett had turned to the attack. As Clay observed, Tyler had become a president without a party. In fact, although he had been elected as a Whig, in the end he seemed closer to the Democrats.

The final straw was the annexation of Texas. Oddly, the president's other excursions into foreign policy, while not spectacular, had been successful but largely unreported by a press that was preoccupied with domestic controversy. When it came to Texas, Tyler saw in its annexation a highly important step in the territorial expansion of the country, but neither his party nor the electorate was solidly behind him, and in fact his actions laid the groundwork for the bitter divisions in the nation with which his successor, James K. Polk, would have to contend.

There was a strong feeling—as it turned out, an accurate one—both in Congress and among the people that annexation would mean a war with Mexico. Horace Greeley was warning of it in his new paper, the New York *Tribune,* in March 1845, when he wrote, "We have adopted a war ready made, and taken upon ourselves prosecution to the end." And new accusations were made against Tyler—that he wanted annexation because of sordid motives involved with land speculation in Texas, that he was guilty of the high crime of sectionalism, and that he was the captive of stock and land speculators. Tyler employed two of his sons, Alexander and Robert, to circulate replies to the charges in the New York and other Northern newspapers, so that people would understand why he thought annexing Texas was a matter of national importance. Even Tyler's second wife Julia was engaged to do what she could with coquetry where reason might fail. The first Mrs. Tyler, Letitia, had been a retiring woman, seen infrequently at White House affairs because of her invalidism, but Julia did her best to charm senators and congressmen. The *Herald* regarded all these efforts as the dying gasps of an administration already consigned to the dust heap. Bennett advised his readers to forget about Tyler as a force in American politics, "for that once distinguished man, whom the steamboat left on the wharf—lady, trunk and all— has long since ceased to possess any influence for either good or evil."

As the election of 1844 drew nearer, Tyler still had friends and adherents who were loyal to him, but as he himself said, "the question with me is between Texas and the Presidency." The treaty to annex Texas was still pending, and he had a choice of either defying or giving in to the majority Whig opinion in Congress opposing it. Whatever he decided, it would be at the cost, as he said, of "false ascriptions of motive and base assaults upon my character, which would be reverberated throughout the Union by the affiliated presses, while I should find but a most circumscribed defense in the columns of a single newspaper, and that, at the time, of a limited circulation."

It was plain that the Democratic party would not nominate him; they nominated Polk on the same day Tyler's supporters held their own convention, encouraged by resolutions of endorsements adopted by New York City Democrats, and came out for "John Tyler and Texas." In the end, however, the president decided to withdraw, and might have withdrawn earlier, he told his friends (speaking of himself in the third person), but "it would not aid the Democratic cause, for that his friends were so exasperated by the assaults of the *Globe* and other presses, that if he withdrew, they should either remain neutral, or many of them join Mr. Clay."

This action drew a letter from Jackson to Frank Blair, instructing him to soften his onslaughts against Tyler in the *Globe,* since it was more important to defeat Clay and Whiggery. There was some consideration that Tyler should run as a third-party candidate. But Mordecai Noah had long since advised him that this was a vain idea. "The only hope you have," he had written from New York, "must rest on the chance of erecting a party of your own. This you cannot do. You possess patronage, to be sure; and you can use it, without violating any principle; but if it were ten times as extensive as it is, it would not enable you to create a party of sufficient consequence to justify you in accepting a nomination even if you could obtain one. The whole Executive patronage is but a drop in the ocean." And so it had proved. Friendly newspapers and magazines remained open to Tyler, especially in the South, where he was much more popular, but there was no hope. The way was open for James K. Polk.

In his retirement Tyler continued to defend himself and carry on controversies in the press, and even found good things to say about old enemies. Of the *Intelligencer,* he observed that it was "a paper which deservedly ranks amongst the most respectable journals of the day, and which, along with others of the same high class, will hereafter be regarded as one of the lights of history." As for Ritchie, whose *Enquirer* had once scourged him, Tyler called him "that able and talented editor" and asserted that his course had been "sensibly felt on all questions of public policy for more than a quarter of a century." The remainder of the press could be dismissed. For "the thousand and one newspaper paragraphs which would fain persuade the country that I was in leading-strings during my term of service," Tyler wrote, "I care but little."

As the crisis that led to the Civil War developed, Tyler became an assiduous writer of letters to the editor, arguing his views on this and other public questions. Following Virginia into secession, he was elected to the Confederate Congress, but he died before he could assume his new office—a final irony in the life of this quiet man who moved unswervingly toward goals that always eluded him. If he did not truly understand the press, it could also be said that the press did not understand him. There was some loss on both sides.

PART THREE

The Power of the Presidency

Polk and the Mexican War

"Who is James K. Polk?" the Whig press inquired sarcastically, when the Democrats nominated him at Baltimore in 1844. Who, indeed? We are still trying to answer that question more than a century later, and whatever answer is returned, an inevitable ideological halo surrounds it, even among scholars. For Polk became the symbol of American expansionism, if one did not care to use the ruder word "imperialism," and the questions raised by his role in the Mexican War were not answered then, or later in the Spanish-American War, or still later in the Vietnam War. Polk himself might well be a fit study for the psychohistorians of our time. A victim of his own rigid character, he fought a successful war in the field but lost a battle against the pressures of office, to which he presented a stone wall of inflexibility, steadily losing ground until he died only a few months after leaving the White House.

In several other ways, Polk was unique. He was the first dark horse candidate for the presidency, the first ever to announce unequivocally when he assumed office that he would not seek renomination for a second term, and one of only three presidents (John Quincy Adams and Rutherford B. Hayes were the others) who kept full diaries while they were occupants of the White House.

Was he "Polk the Mendacious," as the late-nineteenth-century historian Hermann Von Holst called him? Or was he "Polk the Mediocre," as Allan Nevins, a historian of our own time, would have it? There were a scattered few of his contemporaries who saw a far greater good in him. George Bancroft, his secretary of the navy, who later as a historian examined the Polk papers, saw a different aspect. "His character shines out in them [the Polk Papers] just exactly as he was," Bancroft wrote, "prudent, far-sighted, bold, excelling any Democrat of his day in undeviatingly correct exposition of his democratic principles; and in short, as I think, judging of him as I knew him, and judging of him by the results of his administration, one of the very foremost of our public men, and one of the very best and most honest and most successful Presidents the country ever had." Nevins gives us a succinct picture of Polk:

He was a man to command respect, but neither liking nor awe. In person he was spare, of middle height, angular in his movements, with a small head, long grizzled hair brushed stiffly back behind his ears, penetrating and rather chilly grey eyes, and a stern mouth. His countenance was usually sad, but sometimes lightened by a genial smile. . . . He was intense, laborious, humorless, pedestrian, immensely aware at all times of the responsibilities which he bore, and inclined to make everyone with whom he came in contact aware of them.

Nowhere were all these qualities more obvious than in Polk's relationships with the press. He repeated the mistakes of the past, even the recent past, because that was the way things had always been done; and when he was confronted with press hostility in a country sharply divided by his war policies, he ignored it for the most part and hewed straight to the line, undeviating, certain he was right.

Polk had seen during the presidential campaign, for instance, how futile it had been for Tyler's supporters to buy up several Democratic papers, put their own men in the editor's chair, and then launch a propaganda effort through them to prove that Tyler was really a regular Democrat. In the more influential days of the party press that strategy would have had some effect, but in these days of its declining power only the already convinced believed what they read, and the result was a waste of money and effort.

But Polk had always understood that this was how politics worked, and it never occurred to him to break away from the past. In Tennessee, early in his career, he had in a sense acquired his own paper through the support of Jeremiah George Harris, editor of the Nashville *Union*. It hardly mattered that the *Union* was distinguished by extravagant statements and personal abuse or that the Whigs contemptuously called it "Harris's buzzard," referring to the paper's logo, a fierce eagle with outspread wings that dominated the front page. Harris's support was important in helping Polk to achieve seven terms in Congress (he was Speaker of the House) and a term as governor of Tennessee—notwithstanding that it failed twice to get him reelected.

This alliance came apart in the maneuvering before the 1844 convention, when Polk, who was trying to throw the support of Tennessee Democrats to Van Buren, failed to convince a later editor, John P. Heiss, that he should support the former president. At that point Polk saw himself as a vice-presidential candidate, with Van Buren.

Now the Washington *Globe* became a factor in the affair. It was a strong supporter of Van Buren but had no particular love for Polk and, in fact, charged him with cowardice and taunted him about his two defeats for the governorship, concluding that he would not "add one particle of strength to the ticket in any State of this Union," and Democrats should not "jeopardize their success by vain attempts to force upon the people of Tennessee a man whom they have twice refused to honor." Meanwhile Polk had brought in a former editor of the *Union*, Samuel H. Laughlin, to take the editorship of the paper, guaranteeing money from the party coffers to help support it and making sure it would back Van Buren.

That was how matters stood as the Democrats met in Baltimore, where a surprising shift of forces took place. Until then it had been supposed that they would nominate Van Buren to oppose Henry Clay as the Whigs' candidate. But then the rapidly growing argument over the annexation of Texas caught up with them. Secretary of State Calhoun had concluded a treaty for its acquisition, and Tyler had submitted it to the Senate to be ratified.

Annexation had now become the overwhelming political issue, and both Clay and Van Buren were compelled to declare themselves on it. They outlined their positions in letters that were published by the newspapers of both parties. Both were against annexation, Clay because he thought it meant inevitable war with Mexico and Van Buren for the same reason, adding that in such a conflict the United States would be perceived by the world as a morally wrong aggressor. This was not, of course, the Democratic position, and because of his unflinching honesty, Van Buren in effect denied himself the nomination.

Since the Whigs met only four days after Clay's letter appeared in the *National Intelligencer,* it was too late to head him off, and he won the nomination by acclamation from a united party. A month later the Democrats met, and Van Buren found himself unacceptable to most of the delegates, even though the *Globe* tried hard to convince both delegates and public that he had not lost as much as one supporter, asserting that the whole movement against its man was the work of that devious villain Calhoun. There was turmoil on the convention floor, of a kind soon to become a commonplace in political life, as North and South fought over Van Buren and Lewis Cass of Michigan. It was clear the regions were irreconcilable, and on the ninth ballot Van Buren withdrew to restore peace. Polk, who had appeared for the first time on the eighth ballot, became compromise candidate. New York began the parade to him, and the resulting stampede led to his unanimous nomination.

The result was flashed from Baltimore to New York by way of Samuel F. B. Morse's new telegraph—the first such transmission of political news, heralding a new era in communications, particularly for newspapers. In their case, it was an invention fully as significant as that of the cylinder press. The latter had created a mass audience that was nevertheless discrete; the telegraph bound these parts together.

As the campaign developed, it followed the familiar, violently partisan lines in the press. Polk was pictured, incongruously, as both a duelist and a coward. His paternal grandfather, it was said, had been a Tory in the Revolution. These and other charges were hotly denied, not only by the *Union* but by the *Globe,* which for the time being was on Polk's side. Only one of the Whig attacks proved clever (or absurd) enough to get into the history books, where it has long been known as the Roorback (or Roerback) Hoax. A traveler named Roorback, so the story went, was making a trip through the South in 1836 when he observed forty-three slaves being taken to auction. Each of them was branded with the initials J.K.P. Obviously, it was a tale designed to undermine Polk's support in the North.

After considerable uproar on both sides, the Albany *Argus* disclosed the real story. It had been based on an incident related by a British traveler named Featherstonhaugh, who indeed had made a tour of the South in 1834, but his account had been altered to include Polk's initials and then planted in a Whig paper, the Ithaca *Chronicle,* after which it was picked up on exchange by the Albany *Patriot,* and then by Thurlow Weed's prestigious *Evening Journal,* where it was advertised as being an extract from "Roorback's Tour through the Western and Southern States in 1836."

Thrown on the defensive by the *Argus*'s exposé, the *Evening Journal* attempted to defend itself by asserting it had taken the story from an exchange paper and printed it in good faith. James Gordon Bennett was among those who were not convinced by the alibi. In the *Herald,* with his customary talent for understatement, he called the hoax "one of the most infamous fabrications to be found in the records of falsehood."

Quickly the whole affair became a national scandal, and an occasion for satire and ridicule by Democratic papers everywhere. To the partisan *Madisonian* the story was "The Way a Man's Character Is Destroyed," as an editorial headline declared, but to a more literary, sophisticated paper like the New York *Evening Post,* the matter became the subject of irony: "Distinguished Arrival.—We are told that the celebrated traveller Roorback has just arrived in town and has taken lodgings at the Astor House. It is surmised that the object of his visit to this city is to get the Harpers to publish a second edition of his popular 'Tour in the Western and Southern States &c.' revised and corrected by—an exchange paper."

Otherwise, the campaign of 1844 was one in which the Democrats demonstrated how well they had learned the lesson given them by the Whigs in propelling Harrison into the White House. If "Log Cabin" and "Hard Cider" slogans could make a president, they reasoned, it was easy enough to invent catchy phrases for their own candidate. Thus Polk and his supporters made the slogan "Fifty-four forty or fight" (meaning that the northern boundary of the Oregon country should extend to 54° 40′ north latitude) a lasting part of the American language, and the less famous "All Oregon or none," an effective echo. By contrast, "Hooray for Clay" seemed dismal.

Nevertheless Clay was a more popular candidate. To many people it seemed improbable that a candidate so personally colorless as Polk could defeat "Harry of the West," as the brilliant, dashing Clay was often called, with his proven record of leadership. Some historians believe he would have been elected if the third party in the race, James G. Birney's Liberty party, had not taken ten thousand or so votes away from Clay in New York, giving Polk a plurality in that decisive state. In the end, however, it was the annexation of Texas and the passions it aroused that carried the day for Polk. He had supported this popular move without equivocation, while Clay, a born compromiser, had waffled. In the close popular vote, Polk won by a mere thirty thousand, in round numbers; he did better in the electoral college, 170 to 105.

Among the disappointed losers was a young Illinois politician named Abraham Lincoln, who had fought for Clay and believed he would have won if the Whig abolitionists in New York had stood firmly for him. Lincoln did not mention it, but there was more fraud in this election, or at least more blatant evidence of it, than had been seen before, with thousands of aliens quickly (and quite often illegally) naturalized so they could be guided to the polls by Democratic party workers. Other Democrats were conveyed up the Mississippi by steamboat on election day, stopping off here and there to vote. Newspapers took due note of such fraudulent voting, in a partisan way, but there was not yet any compulsion toward public-minded investigative reporting as there would be in time. Fraud was too common in both parties, although more so among the Democrats, and the independent papers were only beginning to be concerned about it. The others were too partisan to care.

How partisan the press remained could be seen from the fact that before the election President Tyler ordered the three hundred newspapers holding federal contracts for publishing the laws to follow the *Madisonian*'s line opposing Van Buren's nomination. Not one thought of disobeying, or at least made any effort to do so. Yet the *Globe,* presumed to be an administration organ, was said to hold Tyler "in as much contempt as the Whigs do."

As a president about to "inherit" the *Globe,* Polk had a low opinion of it because of the "coarse brutality" the paper had displayed in attacking Tyler and, on the other hand, its "coldness or indifference" to his own candidacy. Knowing that Frank Blair spoke for Jackson, Polk persuaded the ailing old general to use his influence with the editor, and the party's patriarch agreed to do it. "My dear friend," he wrote to Blair, "permit not Col. Benton to have controle [*sic*] over your editorial column, as he will ruin your paper." Within a few weeks, Polk was satisfied that the *Globe* was fairly supporting him.

After his election, however, Polk still believed it would be necessary to do something about Blair and his paper. Its support had been lukewarm; it had never made any secret of its loyalty to Van Buren; and its general approval of his own ideas seemed unstable at best. If Blair remained as editor of what had so long been considered the party's administration organ, Polk said later, "I had every reason to believe that he would have labored more to advance the ambitious aspirations of others than to promote the glory and success of my administration. . . . If he had remained, I could not have regarded him as my friend and could have had no confidential communication with him."

To make a change was not as easy as it might appear. There were the sensibilities of the dying Jackson to be considered, as well as a number of other political considerations. But Polk needed a reliable organ to represent his administration, and he meant to have it, in spite of Jackson's strong support of Blair and the *Globe.* Was a quiet deal made in the maneuverings that followed? No proof is available, but the possibility certainly suggests itself.

It was first proposed that the *Madisonian,* the *Spectator,* and the *Globe* be merged, but there was not enough enthusiasm for this idea to overcome the difficulties involved. Then Polk had what he considered a splendid idea—to bring the party's editorial stalwart, Thomas Ritchie, up from his Richmond *Enquirer* and give him Blair's job. When he heard about this proposal, Jackson came loyally to his old friend Blair's defense. He warned Polk, with his usual bluntness, about the dual dangers of replacing the *Globe* with the *Madisonian,* and Blair with Ritchie. The first move, he wrote in a letter of December 13, 1844,

> would blow you sky high & destroy the Republican party—The second would be an insult to the Editor of the *Globe* & seperate [*sic*] him from you, whose administration he is determined to support—Keep Blairs [*sic*] *Globe* the administration paper, and William B. Lewis, to ferret out & make known to you all the plotts [*sic*] & intrigues Hatching against your administration and you are safe. . . . Ritchie is a good Editor, but a very unsafe one—He goes off at half bent, & does great injury before he can be set right.

Jackson believed that the merger plan was a "plott," but he did not attribute it to Polk, and meanwhile he advised Blair to hold fast and not listen to any notion of a co-editorship with Ritchie. As for Ritchie, he was not about to be enticed into any of these schemes. He wrote Polk that he was in no position to buy the *Globe,* and, in any case, he could not bring himself to leave Richmond after forty-one years of newspaper work there.

After Ritchie's refusal, Polk renewed his effort to get Jackson's support for a change at the *Globe.* "There is at present no paper here which sustains my administration for its own sake," he wrote.

> The *Globe* it is manifest does not look to the success or the glory of my administration so much as it does to the interests and views of certain prominent men of the party who are looking to succeed me in 1848. The arrangement which above all others I prefer would be that, the owners of the *Globe* would agree to place it in the hands of a new Editor,—still retaining the proprietorship of the paper if they choose. You may rely upon it, that without such an arrangement, the Democratic party who elected me cannot be kept united three months. If Majr Donelson would take charge of the Editorial Department—all the sections of the party would be at once reunited and satisfied.

(By "Majr Donelson," Polk meant Andrew J. Donelson, Jackson's nephew, namesake, and adopted son, presumably an editor of whom Jackson would certainly approve. Polk had already offered the job to his old friend J. G. Harris, of the Nashville *Union,* who had refused.)

On the eve of his inauguration Polk remained firm in his intention. "As to the *press* which may be regarded as the Government organ," he wrote to Cave Johnson, "one thing is settled in my mind. It must have no connection with, nor be under the influence or control of any clique or portion of the party which is making war upon any other portion of the party—with a view to the succession and not with a view to the success of my administration. I think the view you take of it proper and of the proposed arrangement the best that can be made. I hope it may be effected." At that point Polk still had Ritchie in mind as the "arrangement," but party leaders, understanding that a change was going to be made, with all kinds of implications and opportunities involved, were casting about in other directions.

When Polk came to Washington in February, the matter had not been decided, and he was faced with reluctance from every quarter. Ritchie had declined. Blair and Rives had rejected "with scorn" the proposal by speculators that Rives should buy Blair's interest, and they also opposed Polk's plan for a new editor and controlled editorial policies. And to everyone's surprise, Donelson declined the appointment.

With the problem still unsettled in March, Polk gave his inaugural address to the editors of all the Democratic papers in the city, directing them to publish it simultaneously so that no one would have a particular advantage. There is some confusion about this, however, and another version seems more likely. In this scenario, Polk gave the address as an exclusive to the *Globe,* which encouraged both Blair and Jackson to think the president had given in to them. A few days later Blair read in the *Madisonian* that no decision had been made yet about an administration paper, and he went directly to Polk for some kind of clarification. It was a long interview, in which the president again suggested that Blair abdicate in favor of Donelson, the editor gave him a noncommittal answer, and Polk agreed to write once more to Jackson. In a lengthy letter of March 26, 1845, Polk again showed his mastery of practical politics:

> Blair called on me on the evening of the 24th and desired to know whether the *Globe* was to be considered the administration organ or not. I answered that no organ had as yet been selected. He entered into a full and as far as I felt or know a friendly conversation upon the subject. I explained to him the reasons which induced me to desire that he would if consistent with his views of propriety retire from the Editorial Department of the paper; retaining if he chose the ownership of the establishment, and of course dividing the profits. I suggested to him that such a man as Majr Donelson (if he would accept) at the head of the paper would be acceptable to the whole party, North and South, and to my branch of it. . . . [He] would not yield to any of my suggestions, and seperated [sic] from me with the distinct understanding, that if the *Globe* was my organ, I must take it just as it was, and if I did not choose to do that, I must take my own course.
>
> . . . The inference I drew from the tone of Blair's conversation was, that he was acting on the belief, that I was helpless and defenceless without the *Globe.* I feel this, and am unwilling to remain in so defenceless a position. I must be the head of my own administration, and will not be controlled by any newspaper or particular individual whom it serves.

If Polk had ever thought of continuing with Blair, the idea did not linger after the editor began calling on him to complain about his cabinet appointments. The president treated him coolly, but Blair appeared insensitive. "I shall get on well with the new powers," he wrote to Jackson confidently. "They knew me & I knew them—and we shall therefore be able to make allowance for one anothers [sic] infirmities. The *Globe* will roll on its course and will carry the administration with it." Blair persisted in dropping in on Polk, as he had done with Jackson and Van Buren, seeking suggestions for his editorials, but he continued to follow his own ideas when he wrote them, or else reflected the opinions of those who opposed the president's Texas policy, thus further alienating many Democrats.

The president was also not getting much support from other prominent newspapers, particularly Horace Greeley's New York *Tribune,* in which Polk found himself under the lash of this new independent editor whose influence was growing. Of the inaugural address, Greeley had written that it was a "mixture of verbal piety and practical knavery," and of Polk's warning of European intervention in the Texas affair, he scoffed, "All the gas is the paltriest fishing for thoughtless huzzas, worthy rather of a candidate for constable than President of the United States." Speaking of Polk's views on the tariff expressed in the inaugural address, the Charleston *Mercury* called them "oracular nonsense" and added, "Putting green spectacles on a horse and feeding him with shavings may do for once, but in the long run even an ass would rebel against it."

If these were minority views, they were no less uncomfortable. But Polk could take some solace in the editorials of the New York *Herald,* at that moment the nation's most influential independent newspaper. There, in his grandiloquent way, Bennett was asserting that "Mr. Polk, in one bound, has leaped from the obscurity and common place [*sic*] of a country town in Tennessee, to magnificence and sublimity in the foreign and domestic policy of the United States, and in the history of the world."

The existence of deep divisions in an administration only just begun was an added incentive to solve the *Globe* matter quickly, so that Polk and the Democrats could have a strong, reliable administration organ. At this point Blair reversed himself and intimated through Secretary of State James Buchanan that he might be willing to sell the paper and retire. About the same time Ritchie appeared in Washington, owing his creditors $20,000 and on the point of leaving his unprofitable paper to start a school. Meanwhile, too, Buchanan had suggested to Blair that Polk might appoint him on the forthcoming mission to Spain in an attempt to negotiate land claims—an unlikely proposition, to say the least—if he gave up the *Globe.* John P. Heiss, former publisher of the Nashville *Union,* was also in town, apparently interested in buying the *Globe,* and Polk was extremely hopeful that this would open the way for a joint editorship by Ritchie and Donelson, whose initial reluctance now seemed diminished.

In the end the pressure proved too much for Blair, especially after Polk told him plainly that, if he did not give up, the administration would start a competitive newspaper. In this threat Blair and Rives foresaw the ruin of the party as well as their own. They agreed to sell out to Heiss and Ritchie, who promptly renamed the paper the *Union,* with the Richmond veteran as editor and the Nashville entrepreneur as business manager. The new paper appeared first as a daily on May 1, 1845, but four days later it went to semiweekly publication. Thus the *Globe,* which had done the party so much service, disappeared, but Blair, who had made this organ the powerful paper it was, lived to fight again, as one of the Republican party's founders and a Lincoln adviser.

The circumstances surrounding the *Union*'s birth were suspicious at the time, and continue to be. The price was $35,000, a third due at once, the remainder in two annual payments. Since Ritchie was nearly bankrupt and Heiss was not a rich man, it may well be that Polk was able to channel some federal funds into the purchase, although that has never been proved. Everyone involved professed complete innocence. Ritchie said he had no knowledge of where the money came from, that Heiss had made all the arrangements. Polk declared he was ignorant of the finances. Heiss said nothing at all. Some investigators have speculated that federal funds were used, but that they were repaid out of the profits from government printing contracts.

In retrospect all these alarms and excursions over the demise of the *Globe* may seem like a political tempest in a journalistic teapot, hardly worth so detailed a retelling. But the story aptly summarizes the state of the relationship between press and presidency in these declining days of the party press before the Civil War, when a transition was beginning to take place. Whether correctly or not, Polk sincerely believed it was absolutely essential to both his own and the party's success to have an administration-controlled newspaper in Washington. That what was why he spent what seems like such an inordinate amount of time and energy on the matter, even risking his own political capital at times. There were several reasons for this conviction, but prominent among them was the long shadow of Jackson, whose help and influence were sought nearly up to his deathbed. He and his party organization had shown conclusively what could be done with a bought-and-paid-for party press at the local and state levels, surmounted by a paper in Washington that was clearly recognizable as the voice of the president and his party.

Earlier presidents, of course, had had their fiercely partisan press supporters, and on occasion they had subsidized individual editors, but the Jacksonians had raised this branch of politics to a fine art and Old Hickory's successors had learned the lesson well. Partisanship was not about to end with their departure, and the vituperative character of most papers would be slow to improve, but the time would soon come when great individual editors like Bennett, Greeley, Charles A. Dana, Henry J. Raymond, William Cullen Bryant, and others would dominate the newspaper business. These giants of the trade could not be bought by politicians or parties, at least in the old literal sense and not significantly in any other way. Their support or opposition could be important to a president or a party, but not necessarily crucial, as Polk supposed the administration's paper in Washington to be.

Was he right in attaching so much importance to it, even as late as 1845? Would he and the Democrats alike have been destroyed if Blair had elected to stick it out, perhaps with the help of Polk's enemies, and the president had been compelled to carry out his threat of launching a rival paper on his own behalf? With the advantage of hindsight, it does not seem likely, but at the same time, it is easy to understand why Polk was convinced of it. As it turned out, however, the coming crisis of the Mexican War would prove to be a much better illustration of what a president had to fear or discount from a hostile press.

Following custom, Polk passed out a few plums to deserving journalists at the start of his term. He made Donelson his minister to Berlin, and Harris was given a navy purser's appointment, while Laughlin was appointed a recorder in the general land office. Another purser's job in the navy was given to John O. Bradford, a member of the Nashville *Union*'s staff. One of the Washington *Union*'s first tasks was to defend these and other appointments on the ground that Polk's only criterion had been whether a man was honest and capable.

It was important politically to counter the generally held idea that the administration's new paper was really the administration's puppet, although any practical observer considering the conditions of its creation would have found it difficult to believe otherwise. Nevertheless, the loyalist press worked hard to create the opposite impression. The New York *Herald* sent a man to investigate the situation, and he produced this ingenuous account:

> I made inquiries the other day in a very unsuspicious manner, and was informed that the editor is seldom in communication with the President, and very rarely consults him about the course the *Union* is to pursue. He teases the President, I am told, sometimes, to read his editorials—wishes him to advise him about this and about that—but Mr. Polk always has one reply: "Do as you like, Mr. Ritchie; you know my principles; they are the same the democratic party hold, and have held; we have no shifting or shuffling in our measures, or our plan of action. You know what are our views in regard to all the great movements of the time. Before you came to Washington, I had long been satisfied you was a true friend of democratic principles. You are free, and you know I have never bound you, and never will; our views harmonize in the main and other matters are unimportant, and you must take just such a course as you think best." I happen also to know that Mr. Polk seldom knows what is coming out in the *Union,* til he reads it.

One may reasonably doubt that Polk ever made such an improbable speech to Ritchie or anyone else, but the *Herald*'s account was duly picked up and solemnly reprinted by both the *Union*s, with sententious editorial approval. Ritchie denied ever "teasing" the president, but he confirmed everything else and asserted an independence the paper could not possibly have had.

How the real situation between president and editor must have been can be seen in Polk's own account of an occasion in the spring of 1846 when the Washington *Union* carried an article on certain resolutions by Congress, the tone and substance of which were conceivably offensive to the president. The postmaster general brought the story to Polk's attention, and his omnipresent diary continues the episode: "I told him I had known nothing of the article until it had appeared in the paper, and upon a casual reading of it this morning there were portions of it which I did not approve. Mr. Ritchie called afterwards and I told him the article I thought was exceptionable. He was much concerned about it and said it had been prepared in hurry and confusion at a late hour of the night." Later, responding to a suggestion from Buchanan that the *Union* might be a stronger paper if Blair were brought back to co-edit it, Polk recoiled from the idea and remarked, "I told him Mr. Ritchie meant well, but might occasionally make mistakes, but he was always ready to correct them when informed of them." So much for editorial independence on the administration's paper.

But now came a critical test of press opposition to the presidency, as the questions of Oregon and Texas came to the point of decision. In approaching them, Polk increasingly disclosed himself as devoted to a nationalistic and expansionist ideology. He demonstrated little feeling for the moral aspects of slavery and expansionist aggression, and his literal mind led him easily to favor military solutions for hard problems. Polk had the true imperialist's scorn for other nations. At home, he was determined to keep the country on an expanding continentalist course, regardless of what the rest of the world, much less his domestic political enemies, might think.

These views were set forth baldly in the Washington *Union* and many other Democratic papers. "For who can arrest the torrent that will pour onward to the West?" Ritchie inquired rhetorically on June 2, 1845, speaking with the voice of Polk. "The road to California will open to us. Who will stay the march of our western people?"

When it appeared that there were Americans ready to arrest the torrent, Ritchie declared that the Rio Grande boundary would never be surrendered and that those editors who were protesting that an invasion of Mexico would be "utterly infamous" were traitors. "Is it the part of an American to take the Mexican side against the rights of the United States?" Ritchie demanded on September 19. "There [on the Rio Grande] our boundary is planted, and [neither] the bullets of the Mexicans, nor the paper shot of their friends in this country will be able to shake the determination of our Executive upon this question."

War with Mexico split the nation apart, as had the War of 1812, and as the Vietnam conflict would again in our time. Modern historians have found threads linking all three, although the circumstances were different in each. What they have in common, as John H. Schroeder tells us, is that they are cases "in which the president was unable to convince an overwhelming majority of Americans that war was either advisable or imperative." In all three conflicts, too, there was a considerable antiwar movement that failed in varying degrees to overcome determined presidents, although in the case of the Vietnam War the degree of failure is much more arguable. The press led these movements, although the media were by no means the only element involved. In the War of 1812, as we have seen, Madison did not resist the primarily New England papers that preached what could have been called treason in those days, with loose talk of secession, and even though the conflict was branded as "Mr. Madison's War," the president emerged triumphant. In our time the opposition of the media, acting to expose what was going on secretly as well as to report what was occurring openly, was certainly a decisive factor in the defeat of President Lyndon Johnson and a focus of the pressure brought on President Richard Nixon and Secretary of State Henry Kissinger to end the war.

In 1846 the opposition press also pinned the label of "Mr. Polk's War" on the conflict, but in the end it was unable to turn the president from his course. The best that can be said of its efforts is that by helping to generate so widespread an opposition to the war, and by acting as the spokesman for many diverse interests, it may have mitigated the harsh terms Polk might otherwise have imposed on Mexico.

The details of the war itself, fascinating though they are and still far from accurately understood by the general public, are not germane to this volume. It is necessary to confine ourselves to a brief examination of the press's opposition to the conflict and its relationship to the presidency. In essence, the beliefs of the opposition and its press have been admirably set forth by Schroeder:

> In the opinion of its numerous critics, the Mexican War was unnecessary, impolitic, illegal, and immoral. Furthermore, the outbreak of hostilities was shrouded by highly suspicious circumstances. War critics charged that a secretive, evasive, and high-handed president himself had provoked Mexico into firing the first shots. And once under way, the war soon manifested the Polk administration's intention to obtain territory by invasion, conquest, and plunder. Horrified by such an immoral spectacle, opponents argued that the most basic democratic precepts of the United States were violated in her thirst for land.

Opposition was broad. Not surprisingly, Whigs led the list of dissenters, but there were substantial numbers of Polk's own party who opposed the war. Reformers and clergymen were also predictably against it, including such noted individualists as Henry Thoreau, William Lloyd Garrison, John C. Calhoun, Theodore Parker, and Daniel Webster. Here, obviously, was a wide spectrum, broad enough to include ardent abolitionists like Garrison and proslavery conservatives like Calhoun, idealists such as Parker and practical politicians of Webster's stripe.

Angry though they were, these opponents were thoroughly frustrated by the nature of war itself—that is, once it started, they could not vote in Congress against anything that might endanger Gen. Zachary Taylor's forces. Outside Washington, most of the dissenters were in New England, as they had been in 1812, but unlike those earlier days, they had no such platform as the invasion of their rights to stand upon. The war was being fought by volunteers, not draftees; and government loans, not increased taxes, were financing it. Consequently no significant attack on the president and his policies could be organized, particularly when it was clear that he had the bulk of the electorate behind him.

Behind the dissent were larger issues, of course, most notably, perhaps, the argument over the ends and means of American imperialism, or whether it was imperialism at all—an argument far from concluded today. But also there was the rising importance of the slavery issue, now tied to the question of expansionism. It would soon dominate everything else in American politics, replacing such traditional concerns as tariffs and fiscal policies. Polk was presiding over the first stages of a period of transition, in which sectional antagonisms were sharply increased, parties were splintering, and a new kind of national politics was being shaped.

These divisions were also reflected in journalistic opposition to the war. Commercial papers—the New York *Journal of Commerce,* for instance—were gloomy about the conflict, anticipating serious disruption of business. Among the general newspapers opposition centered in New England, where the journals served as the outlet for a loose coalition of Whig politicians, editors, clergymen, and social reformers. Antislavery sentiment was strong in this region, and the annexation of Texas had therefore also been bitterly opposed. New Englanders feared that the acquisition of new territory, especially in the South and West, meant only the addition of more slave states.

The Boston *Courier* was one of the leaders in the attack, and it achieved fame as the first paper to print the opening poems in James Russell Lowell's satiric antiwar verse cycle that later emerged as *The Biglow Papers*. In other regions of the country press opposition sprang up largely where the most abolitionist sentiment existed, principally in Ohio and western New York State. In New York City, Horace Greeley's *Tribune* took the high moral ground, as was the editor's custom, and condemned the war, while Bennett's *Herald* supported Polk in this as it had in his earlier policies. But there were Democratic papers, most prominent among them the New York *Evening Post* and the Charleston *Mercury,* which sought to bring editorial pressure on the president to end the war quickly and were generally opposed to the whole idea of territorial conquest. A few Whig papers did not follow the party's lead in condemning the war, including the Baltimore *American,* the Nashville *Republican Banner,* and the Chicago *Daily Journal*. The others generally followed antislavery, antiwar themes, although most of them carefully adhered to the *National Intelligencer*'s party line of attacking the war as unjust and immoral but nevertheless pledging support for the military.

Polk's conduct of the war was under constant criticism in the papers, and especially his treatment of the two leading military commanders, Winfield Scott and Zachary Taylor, both of whom emerged as possible presidential candidates before the conflict was over. It was a sordid quarrel between the generals and the president, the press lining up on both sides and providing a platform for the charges and countercharges. Using this controversy, the astute Thurlow Weed began to employ his Albany *Evening Journal* as a launching pad to obtain the 1848 Whig nomination for Zachary Taylor, much to the surprise of the general, who was nevertheless highly flattered. It was a move that convinced Polk he had a Whig enemy in Taylor and further soured relations between them.

The president stuck to his guns stubbornly in spite of all opposition, knowing that he had the general support of the country, whose patriotic and nationalist citizenry responded to such stirring military episodes as the repulse of Antonio López de Santa Anna at Buena Vista, the storming of the fortress at Chapultepec, and Gen. Stephen Watts Kearny's long march with the Army of the West from Fort Leavenworth to Santa Fe and Los Angeles, not to mention the conquering of California. The opposition was widespread and strong, to be sure, and war weariness began to settle in rather early even among Polk's strongest supporters, but on the whole he pushed forward with justified confidence that he would win.

In Washington itself, Polk had to deal with the opposition forces in Congress, and there in 1847 he took his first and only stand on freedom of the press. It was a pale reprise of Madison's steadfastness on that issue in the War of 1812—true, under far more serious provocation—but the incident attests again to the president's rigid adherence to principle, whether right or wrong.

The Washington *Union,* Polk's now faithful organ, precipitated the affair by printing an anonymous letter signed "Vindicator" (a practice still common in those days), in which the writer castigated the Senate for not supporting the administration in some specific military matters relevant to the conduct of the war. Several Whig senators were irked by this criticism, and they were further irritated by the *Union*'s reporting of a subsequent Senate debate, which seemed to them less than respectful as well as inaccurate. Resolutions were forthwith introduced, one of them citing Ritchie as having libeled the Senate and calling for his expulsion, and the other demanding the exclusion of *Union* reporters from the press gallery. What followed is summarized graphically by Polk in his diary:

> Saturday, 13th February, 1847.—About six o'clock p.m. I learned that the Senate had expelled Mr. Ritchie from the privileged seats of that body, in consequence of the publication in the *Union* a few days ago over the signature of ''Vindicator.'' It is a second Duane case, and strikes a blow at the liberty of the press. The foul deed was perpetrated by the votes of the undivided Federal [Whig] Senators, and Senators Calhoun and Butler of South Carolina and Yulee and Westcott of Florida. These four gentlemen constitute what Senator Turney denominated in debate a few days ago the Balance of Power party. They have more frequently voted with the Federalists than the Democrats during this session.
>
> After night an unusual number of members of Congress called. They were Democrats and were most excited at the expulsion of Mr. Ritchie from the Senate today. I learn that the public opinion and sympathies are all enlisted in his behalf, and that this act of the Senate is condemned by public opinion, as far as it has been expressed in the city.

The uproar resulted in two days of Senate debate, during which the issue of press freedom was all but lost in political posturing with the next presidential election in mind. Votes were taken, and the resolution expelling the reporters was withdrawn, while the one designed to throw out Ritchie was approved twenty-seven to twenty-one—not enough to pass. Skeptics might question whether Polk would have been as vociferous in defense of press freedom if a Whig paper had been the one involved, and the criticism directed at his enemies, but few of those who have read his diary would believe that on matters of principle he would do other than rise above politics. Polk's belief in a free press may not have been ardent, but it was sincere.

While the war staggered on, the president became the first occupant of the White House who relied on the press to supply him with information he might be slow in getting or unable to obtain otherwise, foreshadowing the practice much more extensive in Lincoln's administration. In this war, for the first time, there were correspondents in the field covering the action in the manner familiar today, and at least some of their dispatches could be speeded by telegraph, which was also useful in carrying the news swiftly from one major city to another.

Polk learned, too, how to use these correspondents for other purposes, as he disclosed in his diary:

> After night Mr. Buchanan called and read me a letter which he had received this evening from Moses Beach of the ''New York Sun,'' written in the city of Mexico and dated on the 17th of March last. In his letter Mr. Beach describes the revolutionary condition of Mexico, but expresses the opinion that a treaty may be made which

would be satisfactory to the United States, and leaves the inference that he made such a treaty. Mr. Beach was in Washington on November last and had several interviews with Mr. Buchanan and one with me. . . . [He] from his intimacy with General Almonte expressed the opinion that he could exert a favorable influence on him and other leading men in Mexico, with a view to the restoration of peace. He induced Mr. Buchanan and myself to believe that he could do so. Mr. Buchanan informed him confidentially of the terms on which we would treat, and it was deemed advisable to constitute him a secret agent to Mexico.

There was somewhat more to this story than the diary entry suggests. Moses Y. Beach, one of the enterprising Beach family who acquired the *Sun* from its founder, Benjamin Day, in 1837, had gone to Mexico as the secret agent of Secretary of State James Buchanan in 1847, and in March of that year he was instrumental in fomenting a church-supported uprising in Mexico City. As editor of the *Sun,* he was presumably there on a business trip, but his real mission was to find out whether a settlement with Mexico was possible; his contacts with American Catholic leaders were considered valuable. Beach supposed that, with those who opposed the Mexican general, Santa Anna, in power, a settlement was more likely to be worked out. But when Santa Anna heard about the revolt, he hurried back to Mexico City, overthrew his rival Valentín Gómez Farías, and assumed the office of chief of state that he had momentarily vacated. The plot had failed. Beach turned out to be a far better newspaper manager than a spy or diplomat. Yet Polk had trusted Beach to the extent that even if the editor had exceeded his powers in making a treaty, if it proved to be a good one the president was ready to waive Beach's authority to make it. He would then have submitted it to the Senate for ratification.

Even while he was using this representative of the press, however, Polk had to fight off disclosure by other newspapers of what was happening in the secret negotiations, of which Beach's mission had been only one aspect. More important was the negotiation the president was entrusting to the chief clerk of the State Department, Nicholas P. Trist, which was to be conducted in the utmost secrecy. (As a small political irony, it may be noted that Trist carried with him a proposed treaty, and if the Mexicans insisted on discussing it further, Buchanan was to take over this process, since it was essential for Democratic glory to have a Democratic cabinet member achieve the diplomatic victory.) Polk was extremely apprehensive that the papers would find out what Trist was up to and thus destroy the entire mission, as his diary tells us:

Had his mission and the object of it been proclaimed in advance at Washington I have no doubt there are persons in Washington, and among them the editors of the *National Intelligencer,* who would have been ready and willing to have dispatched a courier to Mexico to discourage the government of that weak and distracted country from entering upon negotiations for peace. This they would do rather than suffer my administration to have the credit of concluding a just and honourable peace. The articles in the *National Intelligencer* and Federal [Whig] papers against their own government and in favour of the enemy, have done more to prevent a peace than all the armies of the enemy. . . . If the war is protracted it is to be attributed to the reasonable course of the Federal editors and leading men.

In spite of every precaution, however, the leak Polk feared occurred, and no doubt he was unsurprised to find that Bennett's enterprising *Herald* had dug out the story, or more likely, had it handed to one of the paper's Washington reporters. When he read the account, Polk declared himself as never more "vexed or excited" since he had entered the White House, as he told his diary, and he went on to describe the episode in much the same terms Washington had used in the leak of the Jay treaty, and as presidents would do for generations afterward. Everyone, it appeared, would have to learn the simple truth that in a free society government suppresses and the press discloses, which was the kind of balance Jefferson had in mind. Polk wrote:

> The statement is so accurate and minute that the writer must have obtained information on the subject from someone who was entrusted with the secret. It was a profound Cabinet secret, and was so expressly declared by me to be, and was communicated to no one but to Mr. Trist himself and to Mr. Derrick a clerk in the Department of State. . . . I cannot believe that any of my Cabinet have betrayed my confidence, and conclude, in the absence of further information on the subject, that the disclosure must have been made by Mr. Derrick, the clerk in the State Department recommended by Mr. Buchanan as worthy of all confidence, and who was employed in preparing the writing. . . . The success of Mr. Trist's mission I knew in the beginning must depend mainly on keeping it a secret from that portion of the Federal press and leading men in the country who, since the commencement of the war with Mexico, have been giving "aid and comfort" to the enemy by their course. . . . That this has been the effect of the unpatriotic and anti-American course of the *National Intelligencer* and other Federal papers all know.

How familiar the words sound in our ears today, nearly a century and a half later!

By this time, Polk had become more than a little paranoid about the press. He was beginning even to distrust Ritchie and the *Union*. When he was preparing his annual message to Congress, he had showed Ritchie the parts of it relating to the war in final form, but he was careful to explain that the editor had not previously seen any part of it, or known what Polk was going to say. "The truth is," Polk wrote, "that the old gentleman's passion to put everything he learns into his newspaper is so great that I did not think it prudent to entrust its contents to him at any earlier period."

In the end Trist did succeed in his mission and negotiated a treaty with the Mexicans. Ironically, the news was brought to the president by a newspaper reporter, James L. Freaner, of the New Orleans *Delta,* who had been with the army as a correspondent. He also brought with him dispatches from Scott. It was a circumstance that underlined the importance of New Orleans papers in reporting the war and in establishing the modern tradition of war correspondence. No other war, anywhere, had ever been covered so thoroughly, and because the New Orleans journals were so near the scene of action, they became the chief source of news for nearly all the other American papers. Only a few of the affluent New York gazettes had their own men on the scene. There were nine highly competitive newspapers in New Orleans at the time, of which the *Picayune, Delta,* and *Crescent* were the most prominent.

To get the news first, the *Picayune* employed the same technique James Watson Webb had inaugurated with his *Courier and Enquirer* and Bennett had perfected in the *Herald*—that is, sending out fast packets to meet incoming ships from Europe carrying dispatches from European correspondents, to be rushed to composing rooms and so beat the other papers by a few hours. The *Picayune* went the *Herald* one better. Its fast boats were equipped with composing rooms so that when they met the incoming ships from Vera Cruz, the dispatches could be set at once and printed as soon as the packets reached land.

The Mexican War also produced the first of the dazzling war correspondents who were to enliven nineteenth-century journalism, reaching an apotheosis in the Spanish-American War with the ineffable Richard Harding Davis. He was George W. Kendall, one of the *Picayune*'s founders, whose colorful, informative dispatches were sent back from the front by a pony express system he set up. It came to be called "Kendall's Express," and a few of its daredevil riders lost their lives to guerrilla fire as they carried back the correspondent's stories and official dispatches as well. Once, in a gesture of a kind Ben Hecht would later elevate to an art form with the Chicago *Daily News,* Kendall went far beyond horses and spent $5,000 of the *Picayune*'s money to carry dispatches from Vera Cruz to New Orleans on a chartered steamer.

In spite of such heroic efforts, the president and other Americans experienced agonizing waits for news of a war that was happening more than two thousand miles away. It usually took anywhere from two to four weeks to get the report of an event across the rugged, hostile Mexican terrain to the Gulf of Mexico, where slow steamers carried it to the American mainland, and then by horse and stage over miserable roads. The Baltimore *Sun* achieved a beat on the conquering of Vera Cruz, but it did not reach print until twelve days later, and it was five weeks before the Boston *Evening Journal* broke the news of General Taylor's victory at Buena Vista.

The telegraph, which would make so great a difference in Civil War reporting, did not extend south of Richmond in 1846, and the Southern railway system was so sketchy that virtually nothing existed through the vast reaches of Mississippi and Alabama. Horse expresses had to be employed to cover this gap, so news from the front could be put on the wire at Richmond. It was a process so expensive that newspapers were compelled to share the costs. It could reasonably be said, then, that what the Polk administration lost in its attempted secret conduct of the war was compensated for by what both president and public gained in the press's extraordinary coverage of this controversial struggle that had so divided them.

To the end, however, Polk fought gamely to conceal what the papers were intent on revealing. When the *Herald* attacked him through one of its correspondents, John Nugent, who signed himself "Galvienses," the president suspected that Buchanan must be the source of the stories since he was friendly with the reporter and vowed to fire the secretary if he could prove it. Buchanan admitted the friendship but denied the leak. Then, when Polk submitted a confidential message to the Senate along with the Mexican treaty, he was angered to find it printed in full in the *Herald*. Polk blamed that on an opposition senator. There were a Senate inquiry and a cabinet discussion of the matter, and once more Buchanan was compelled to profess his innocence, because again it had been the ubiquitous Nugent who obtained the documents. Nugent himself refused to provide any details whatever about how he got the story.

A little later the New York *Evening Post* published an exchange of letters between Frank Blair and Benjamin Tappan, a former Ohio senator, describing the methods by which the resolutions annexing Texas were passed by Congress and quoting Polk's conversations with several of those involved. The president angrily denied the accuracy of these gossipy accounts but felt that he could not "descend" into newspaper controversy while he was still president. Perhaps later . . .

Even Polk's last annual message to Congress did not escape the press's revealing eye, and it was the unfortunate Ritchie who discussed it prematurely in the *Union,* prompting the president to lament once more the editor's "infirmity"— his inability to keep a secret. What Polk always considered an "infirmity," however, was simply continuing evidence of Ritchie's journalistic enterprise, the natural instinct of a man who had been in the news business nearly a half century. But the ritual dance had to be performed. Polk reprimanded his editor, and Ritchie was, as always, "much mortified" and repentant, so that the president could write one more time in his diary: "He meant no harm, I am satisfied. It is a constitutional infirmity with him, I believe, that he cannot keep a secret: all he knows, though given him in confidence, he puts into his newspaper. My sympathies were excited at seeing his mortification, and I relieved him by telling him to let it all pass."

No one could fault Ritchie on the devotion he gave his work, however. His capacity for it amazed everyone; John Heiss, his partner, believed that he slept no more than two hours out of every twenty-four. Heiss worried that Ritchie attended too many dinner parties, but making these rounds was not part of a frivolous nature. Ritchie had already learned what later generations of Washington reporters came to accept as commonplace—that the city's social events were actually political affairs, a prime source of news. He may have been regarded as "the kindest and most genteel old fogy who ever wore nankeen pantaloons, high shirt-collars, and broad-brimmed straw hats," as a contemporary described him, but over a long and often tempestuous career Ritchie proved that he was first and foremost an astute and highly competent newspaperman.

After four years of tension and turmoil, the Polk administration came to a close in anticlimactic quiet. The war was over, Zachary Taylor was elected, and, on the eve of retirement, Polk gave a dinner for the newly elected president. It was one of those typical affairs so often seen in politics where opponents who have done their best to destroy each other sit down together and bask in the unspoken awareness that it is all only an elaborate game—deadly, but still the greatest game they know.

At the retiring president's dinner General Taylor sat down with Lewis Cass, who, as the Democrats' candidate, had just finished excoriating him in the campaign. Millard Fillmore was there, too, another quiet man on his way to the White House. W. W. Seaton, senior editor of the *National Intelligencer,* was present, appearing also in his dual capacity as mayor of Washington, and breaking bread with Ritchie, the editor who had been at his throat for years. "It passed off well. Not the slightest allusion was made to any political subject," Polk recorded in his diary.

But the struggle had been too much for him. Fifteen weeks later, he was dead, at fifty-three.

Taylor and the Compromise of 1850

In electing Zachary Taylor in 1848, the voters turned to a military man, as they had done before and would do so often again. The turning in this case was carefully engineered in advance by Thurlow Weed, the New York political boss who had his own mouthpiece, the Albany *Evening Journal,* to launch the candidate.

As other Americans had done, Weed first became aware of Taylor early in the conflict with Mexico when the newspapers, particularly that New York journal called with endearing simplicity the *War,* reported on his "gallant defense" of Fort Harrison. At the same time the *National Intelligencer* gave an entire page to the official report of the battle. Subsequently the *Intelligencer* and other papers reported that President Polk had been "pleased to confer the brevet rank of major on Captain Z. Taylor." It was the first brevet of any kind ever awarded by the United States. Still later, victories at Palo Alto and Resaca de la Palma added to Taylor's reputation, as the press described these conquests in exotic and perilous locales.

Nevertheless Weed confronted a formidable challenge in promoting Taylor as the Whig candidate for president. Despite his military exploits, the general was an obscure man. With the possible exceptions of Franklin Pierce, Grover Cleveland, and Jimmy Carter, no other president was less known to the American people when he was nominated. Although the word "image" was not yet a cliché in American life, the creation of one for Zachary Taylor was what Weed achieved. When his name was first proposed, the general made the customary modest disclaimer that he had no interest in political office; he was simply a professional soldier, dedicated to his country's service. This was elementary good politics, as Weed, who had suggested it, well knew. In time of war a general should avoid politics and concentrate on military matters. Such concentration could only add to his political luster, and Weed already had a name for the sum of Taylor's vote-getting personality. "Old Hickory" and "Tippecanoe" had passed into American legend. Now there would be another charismatic nickname: "Old Rough and Ready."

Rough, indeed, but not truly ready until after the victory at Buena Vista, where Taylor beat Santa Anna's army, the best the Mexicans could put in the field. All the better that, in the continuing quarrel between commander and president, Old Rough and Ready had undertaken this campaign without administration support. News of the victory provided Taylor with spontaneous and widespread recognition, easily translated into support for his candidacy. "Rough and Ready" clubs emerged in both parties, and in every section of the country. There were even "Rough and Ready" newspapers.

By this time, however, Weed was having a few second thoughts. It had occurred to him and other Whig party leaders that William Henry Seward might be a better candidate because he was against the extension of slavery, a primary Whig blank, and it was also assumed that he would attract the immigrant vote. Henry Clay could hardly be overlooked either. A veteran of the political wars, he was still the outstanding Whig, but he had made a fatal though principled error by coming out firmly against any kind of annexation involving the extension of slavery, thus antagonizing those Southerners known as the "Cotton Whigs." On the other hand, the Great Compromiser had made some proslavery pronouncements in the past, and so had lost those New England abolitionists known as the "Conscience Whigs."

Among the major newspaper editors, Greeley with his *Tribune* was Taylor's foremost opponent. "Uncle Horace," as he was coming to be known among his devoted readers, referred to the general as "an old-fashioned Kentucky Whig," and he professed publicly to support Clay. Privately, however, he confessed that he was less pro-Clay than anti-Taylor. But Greeley had little company. Most Northern and Southern editors came out for Taylor, including not only Weed's *Evening Journal* but the Philadelphia *North American,* Bennett's *Herald,* Webb's *Courier and Enquirer,* and Alexander C. Bullitt's New Orleans *Picayune,* now one of the best Southern papers.

Weed had advised Taylor to keep a low profile and not talk about politics, but the old general was too straightforward and unsophisticated politically to understand the wisdom of this counsel, and he wrote a letter to the Cincinnati *Morning Signal* that could not help antagonizing Southerners. When the editor, a Free-Soil Democrat and an old Van Buren man, baited him with a letter soliciting his views on several delicate subjects, Taylor compounded his indiscretion, honestly enough, by indirectly endorsing the editor's opinions. Taylor's friends cried "forgery," but it was too late.

Thus the general, in spite of all Weed's maneuverings, moved toward the nomination with extreme reluctance. Since he was not a strong party man, he said, it was impossible for him to be a convention candidate. In a letter to a Philadelphia friend, which was soon widely printed in the newspapers, he repeated that "if I were nominated for the presidency by any body of my fellow-citizens, designated by any name that they might choose to adopt, I should esteem it an honor, and would accept such nomination provided it had been made entirely independent of party considerations."

Conceivably Weed and his friends might have made do with this ambiguous statement if it had not been for the almost simultaneous appearance in the newspapers of another Taylor letter, dated two days before the first, in which he declared that he would reject a Whig nomination unless he were "left free of all pledges, and permitted to maintain the position of independence of all parties in which the people and my own duty have placed me.'' At the same time he branded as untrue statements in the papers that he would withdraw from the campaign if the Whigs nominated Clay. That was never his intention, Taylor asserted in a letter to the Richmond *Republican.*

These epistolary barrages in the newspapers underlined Taylor's old-fashioned character. Using letters to the editor to advance political positions was older than the Republic itself, but it would soon die out as the nation grew too large for candidates to be certain that reprinting would carry their messages widely enough and as the press conference, in rudimentary form, came to be a more effective way of reaching the public.

As matters stood, however, the letters cost Taylor a large part of his early newspaper support. The Syracuse *Journal,* which had been a strong supporter, lowered his flag from its masthead. The Boston *Courier,* a Whig stalwart, refused to endorse him, and the leading Whig newspaper in Indiana deserted him for another candidate. Only the party professionals clung to him; they could see the victory beyond the hero of Buena Vista. The Louisiana state convention was first to announce him as a nominee, and by the time the Whigs met in Philadelphia for the national convention, there was enough strength to make Taylor the party's candidate, with Millard Fillmore of New York chosen as a safe running mate. The party was so badly splintered that it could not pass any resolutions or even set forth a platform. There were simply too many factions to achieve agreement on any set of principles. The coming winds of the slavery storm were blowing harder now.

Those winds were blowing the Democrats about, too, and they were hardly more united than the Whigs. Their divisions produced a picturesque split in the New York delegation, where the conservatives were known as "Hunkers," because they "hunkered" for office, and the radical antislavery wing was called "Barnburners," in memory of the legendary Dutch farmer who burned his barn down to get rid of the rats. In the end the Democrats nominated an ardent expansionist, Gen. Lewis Cass of Michigan. Now it was a case of one military man against another.

In this carnival of reluctance, Greeley was a chief barker. The *Tribune*'s editor proclaimed that he had been sure of Taylor's success from the beginning, but, on the other hand, he deemed the nomination "unwise and unjust," and while he recalled that he had always "spoken with respect" of Taylor, at the same time he wished there were a "more deserving, more capable, more popular" candidate. Greeley, and others in the North, could not forget that Taylor had won his nomination only because of the slave states' support. If it had not been so serious a business as electing a president of the United States the whole affair would have assumed all the aspects of comedy, particularly when Taylor, whose mail had grown so voluminous that his expenses for nonpayment of postage were becoming burdensome, refused receipt of the letter of nomination sent to him, and it was some time before this essential piece of protocol could be straightened out.

Reluctance extended beyond the nominating conventions into the campaign itself, to which Taylor contributed little more than further letters to the newspapers. They did not do much to clarify his views, if indeed he had any clear ones. Both parties had tried to evade the slavery issue, since both were too divided to come to terms with it, but it appeared anyway.

When the election was held, the split in the Democratic party between Cass and Martin Van Buren, hero of the New England antislavery Whigs, who ran on the Free-Soil party ticket, proved to be worse than the other party's indecisions, and the Whigs won by little more than a hundred thousand popular votes, 163 to 127 in the electoral college. (It was, incidentally, the first time that election day came on the first Tuesday after the first Monday in November, according to an act passed in 1845.)

As Stefan Lorant has pointed out, the election had results both political and literary. The size of Van Buren's vote as the Free-Soil candidate was so large that it was clear the slavery issue could no longer be pushed under the rug. Literarily, the customary clean sweep of federal appointments by the president after his election cost Nathaniel Hawthorne his job in the Salem Custom House, freeing him to write *The Scarlet Letter,* while, in a similar upheaval, a failing Democratic newspaper employing Walt Whitman failed even further as a result of Taylor's victory and fired the poet, who then had time to work on *Leaves of Grass.* Lorant might have added that Taylor's victory also proved the efficacy of the campaign slogan once more—"Old Rough and Ready" had been a far better vote getter than "Father of the West," as Cass was known.

Eased into the White House after this confused and unemotional working of the democratic process, Taylor emulated his predecessors and at once established an administration paper. Its creation was in keeping with the tenor of his political life. The *Republic,* as he called it, had enjoyed an earlier life beginning in April 1847, with Charles W. Fenton as editor, and had been first to suggest Taylor's name for the presidency immediately after the Battle of Buena Vista. The *Republic* had failed during the campaign, and now Secretary of State John M. Clayton urged the president to revive it, with A. T. Burnley and G. S. Gideon as owners.

The revival began auspiciously with the appointment of two outstanding editors, Bullitt of the New Orleans *Picayune* and John G. Sargent of the New York *Courier and Enquirer.* "These selections were considered excellent," says Frederic Hudson, the pioneer of journalism history,

> but whatever these writers may have been in the editorial rooms [of their own papers] . . . they were neither vigorous nor strong enough for the leading paper of their party in the national capital. Besides the cohesive power of public plunder, it required boldness and brains to keep the lesser lights of a party in order, and under a good state of discipline. These editors did not possess the requisite facilities for this work. They needed audacity. They lacked the journalistic confidence of the nation. The result of this was failure.

In common with other new papers of that day, the first issue of the *Republic* on June 13, 1849, contained a high-minded statement of purpose, declaring that it would "acknowledge no allegiance inconsistent with the dignity and independence of the press, nor come under obligations incompatible with the utmost

freedom of thought, and the largest liberty of action.'' Similar pronouncements
by other editors in their initial issues had been repudiated so rapidly that few took
them seriously, but it seemed singularly naive for the *Republic*'s editors to think,
if they really did, that a paper founded by and dedicated to the administration,
existing on its bounty, could be accepted as a free and independent journal. More
likely Bullitt and Sargent considered it merely the usual bombast.

Certainly the *Republic* exhibited no evidence of independence from its second
issue onward. It employed its columns largely in a defense of everything Taylor
did, as it was expected to do. The attacks, locally at least, came principally from
Ritchie's *Union,* which saw no more virtue in Taylor than its editor had in Jackson—as the *Republic* liked to remind its readers, clucking an editorial tongue
over such unpatriotic disparagement of national heroes.

This clash between the two leading Washington papers quickly degenerated
into the familiar kind of vituperative name calling that had always characterized
the party press. The *Union,* said the *Republic* on July 11, 1849, was ''a journal
which has marked out for itself a career of infamy; which has assailed, with
venomous malice the purest and best citizens of the Republic; which stoops at no
defamation, however indecent, of a soldier who has won the admiration of the
civilized world by his brilliant achievements, and the affections of his countrymen by a blameless life.'' Bullitt and Sargent were particularly sensitive to the
Union's characterization of their paper, frequently repeated, as the kept organ of
the administration, living on the subsidy provided by the public printing contracts given to it. On February 16, 1850, they undertook to define their position
in an editorial that was more an elaborate rationalization of a dying institution,
the presidential newspaper:

> The *Union* styles the *Republic* a ''pensioned'' organ of the Cabinet. The *Union*
> knows that the charge implied in this epithet is unfounded. The reference is to the
> fact that we have been selected by President Taylor as the *third* paper contemplated
> by the law for the publication of the Government advertisements. The law gives
> these advertisements for this District to the two papers having the largest circulation
> and to one paper selected by the President. It is true that in the first instance we
> received these advertisements by the favor of President Taylor. . . . It was consistent
> with the purposes we had avowed in the establishment of our journal. . . . If the time
> should come when we should so far differ with the President in our views of public
> measures as to render it irksome to us to remain under any formal obligation to him,
> we shall then resign the appointment which we enjoy by his selection. If the time
> should come when we should cease to repose confidence in President Taylor's Ad-
> ministration we shall cease to occupy a position which may subject us to the appear-
> ance of incurring an obligation to it. We owe no favors and no allegiance as a public
> journal in any quarter but to the Whig *people of the United States.*

There were some elements of truth in this statement. The editors' definition of
the law was correct, but it was also true that the ''third paper'' had unquestionably been created by the party for the sole benefit of the president. Bullitt and
Sargent were not without integrity, however; they were only taking advantage of
long-established practice, and the time would soon come when they would be

compelled to take the kind of stand they prophetically envisioned, with the result they promised.

In New York, Taylor had the friendly support of Bennett, at least for the time being. In him could be heard the authentic, if flamboyant, voice of the independent editor, especially in the letter Bennett wrote to Taylor after the election, recalling their only meeting at the Cataract Hotel in Niagara Falls during the summer of 1840 and his subsequent support of the general:

> You are now elevated to the high honor of President of the United States by the spontaneous outburst of the popular will. I joined in the movement simply from a conviction of your patriotism and capacity, but I want nothing, personally, of any administration but wisdom in its management, and the public good for its leading purpose. As an independent journalist and an early friend of your election, I can offer you a warm support when you may be right and erring before Heaven, yet I have every hope that your administration of this great Republic will be as wise, patriotic, and successful as that of the Father of his country.

Before he was well into his presidency, however, Taylor provoked a journalistic storm over the familiar issue of patronage. No president could hope to avoid controversy when it came to replacing the old with the new, and in Taylor's case he had made a not unfamiliar error in advertising lofty intentions that there was no possibility of fulfilling. Like so many others, he had campaigned on the proposition that he would not be a party president but president of the whole country, and consequently his appointments would not be on a partisan basis.

At first, after the election, he appeared to mean what he said when he gave offices to only a few loyal Whigs. But then came the more visible removals, and the storm broke over his head. It seemed a small matter to fire a man from his Customs job in distant Salem, Massachusetts, but if the man was Hawthorne, it was easily predictable that there would be outraged public objections from such notable citizens as George Ticknor, Rufus Choate, and Horace Mann. Salem Whigs had accused Hawthorne of writing partisan articles for the *Democratic Review,* and, on the advice of his cabinet, the president removed him—this "inoffensive man of letters" who had never acted as a politician, banished from his "pitiful little office," as his admirers put it. No matter that the charge was true. Taylor was perceived as a heartless politician, an enemy of arts and letters—about which, in fact, he cared little.

Hawthorne's departure was followed by hundreds of others. Democratic editors, keeping gleeful score, counted 54 of them in one day from the Post Office Department alone—132 in one week. Taylor was reviled by the New York *Globe* and in Washington particularly by Ritchie's *Union,* spitting out its disgust: "What a commentary on no-party pledges." The blame was directed more at the cabinet than the president, however. Ritchie called these gentlemen "low-minded, unprincipled, and shameless politicians, who are intent only on avenging themselves upon their enemies, and seizing the 'spoils of victory'"—as though that were something new in political life.

Sen. Truman Smith assembled statistics showing that the Democrats held so many offices at the end of the Polk administration that Taylor's removals had only equalized the position of the two parties, but it did no good. Matters were unexpectedly complicated when a scandal involving three members of the cabinet suddenly came to public notice. Details of the "Galphin claim" affair are still murky, but in essence it concerned interest on government debts that Attorney General Reverdy Johnson ruled was not only authorized but required by an act of 1848. On those grounds, Secretary of the Treasury William Meredith paid the claim without further investigation. The amount was nearly $200,000, half of which went to Secretary of War George Crawford, who it turned out had an interest in the claim. Was it cozy collusion or simple bungling? The Democratic press scarcely bothered to find out in celebrating the event.

Taylor took a great deal of the newspaper abuse personally, even when it seemed directed at the cabinet. He believed, sincerely, that he had never sought the presidency and that his only motive for holding the office at all was to promote the welfare of the whole nation. Consequently he saw no reason for the flood of criticism pouring out on him and his administration, and he was shaken and hurt by it.

Bullitt and Sargent had stood by him, but now they, too, felt pushed beyond conscience by what was happening in the administration. They blamed the cabinet rather than Taylor, but their support for both was becoming noticeably half-hearted, so that Bullitt was called in by the president for what the editor described as "long and affectionate" conversations, which resulted only in making their differences appear irreconcilable. There was, indeed, affection in these talks, however, as was demonstrated by the way in which Bullitt and Sargent gracefully withdrew, announcing that their retirement was because of "personal differences" between themselves and members of the cabinet "that are inconsistent with the relations in which we stand towards President Taylor and the Whig Party" because "our confidence in President Taylor is unimpaired." The editors wanted to place no obstacle in the way of party harmony, they concluded.

The paper's financial backers now took over, principally A. T. Burnley, who tried first to get some financial assistance from members of the cabinet. Failing, he settled down to negotiating with Bullitt and Sargent to buy their interests in the paper, and, after a week of tough bargaining, a deal was concluded. Explaining the terms to a friend, Burnley wrote: "The understanding is that they have sold out to me, but I tell you in confidence, as I am incapable of speculating on two friends whose confidence in me is so great, I shall make their fate & my fate in this enterprise *the same*. I shall furnish them with what money they want now & periodically, & tell them to call on the 4th of March 1853, & I will inform them what the *terms* are on which I bought them out."

Meanwhile Burnley and his other original partner, G. S. Gideon, hired Allan A. Hall of Nashville as editor. Hall not only had a satisfactory record of Whig loyalty in Tennessee but twenty years of newspaper experience as well. He came at once to Taylor's support, unequivocally, and there were no further difficulties at the *Republic* during the general's brief tenure.

Taylor had another reason for replacing the two editors. He did not like Bullitt's sympathy for the compromise Henry Clay was proposing for the new territories coming into the Union as a result of the Mexican War, and it was this controversy over whether they should be slave, free, or permitted to decide later that occupied the remainder of his time in office, as in fact it was dominating the entire political scene. The long, relentless drive toward Civil War was beginning.

All the issues that had been present when Taylor assumed office were now coming together in a complex tangle: organizing California as a state or a territory, with or without slavery; organizing the remainder of the Mexican cession; the boundary dispute between Texas and the inhabitants of New Mexico territory; the South's demand for a more effective fugitive slave law; and the North's demand for abolition of the slave trade, if not slavery itself, in the District of Columbia. Talk of "disunion" had been heard in the first session of Congress after the general's election.

As a possible solution of these problems, which were threatening the "peace, concord and harmony of the Union," as he put it, Henry Clay came out of retirement to propose his famous compromise in January 1850. It would admit California as a free state and establish territorial governments without restricting slavery in the remainder of the territory acquired from Mexico; settle the Texas–New Mexico boundary dispute; assume the preannexation public debt of Texas if she gave up all her New Mexican territorial claims; abolish slavery in the District of Columbia only if Maryland and the people of the District agreed, and with just compensation to slave owners; prohibit slave trade in the District; enact a stricter fugitive slave law; and deny Congress the right to interfere with slave trade between the states.

The proposal prompted a historic debate in Congress, one of those dramatic moments in American life by which everything else is measured. To the country, if not to the press, it was a gathering of nearly legendary giants—Henry Clay, John C. Calhoun, and Daniel Webster, masters of an oratorical style that made the pronouncements of editors seem like the yapping of small dogs. If what they said was often more rhetoric than substance, that was not important. These great figures of the past were doing a last reprise on the national stage, and all of them would be dead within the next two years. Clay, at seventy-three, was already so racked with consumption that it was considered miraculous he could hold the Senate floor for nearly two days. Calhoun was so ill (he was dead in less than a month) that Sen. James Murray Mason of Virginia had to read his speech for him. Only Daniel Webster, strongly supporting the compromise, could produce his old persuasive vigor and thunderous oratory.

Taylor was opposed to Clay's proposals with all his heart, and he fought them at every opportunity as the debate passed from Congress to the country, where it would go on until September. He fought even though he was threatened with impeachment if he used federal troops in Texas, as he had said he might. Always the press was at his heels, reflecting the bitterness that was beginning to tear the nation apart.

It must have been a pleasant respite for Taylor on July 4, 1850, when he went out to attend ceremonies at the unfinished Washington Monument. But it was a hot day, and the general suffered from the heat in the vast open space around the monument site. Thankfully he returned to the cool retreat of the White House, where he drank large amounts of ice water and cold milk as he washed down some wild cherries and other fruit. That night he came down with what the *Republic* called "serious cholera morbus," in the mistaken medical language of the day, but in reality it was acute gastroenteritis. On July 9, he died.

The times were violent, as the newspapers testified every day, and Taylor had tried to rise above the struggle, but one of his most conspicuous failures had been his inability to raise public attitudes toward his administration above the tepid level on which they began. A man who hated display and was utterly unable to reach out to the electorate through the papers, even those that supported him, Taylor had no talent whatever for manipulating the growing power of the press. Yet even those who opposed him most could not dislike him as a human being. One thinks of Horace Mann, who was against virtually everything the general stood for, writing of the president after dining with him at the White House: "He really is a most simple-minded old man. He has the least show or pretension about him of any man I ever saw; talks as artlessly as a child about affairs of State, and does not seem to pretend to a knowledge of anything of which he is ignorant. He is a remarkable man in some respects; and it is remarkable that such a man should be President of the United States." Horace Greeley may have reflected the attitude of the more thoughtful editors when he wrote after the president's death:

> I think I never saw General Taylor save for a moment at the Inauguration Ball, on the night after his accession to the Presidency. I was never introduced, and never wrote to him; and, while I ultimately supported and voted for him, I did not hurry myself to secure his election. . . . Zealous Whigs apprehended that he might, if elected, shrink from discharging the office-holders appointed by Tyler and Polk; but, after giving him a trial, they were constrained to admit that he "turned out better than had been expected." He was a man of little education or literary culture, but of signal good sense, coolness and freedom from prejudice. Few trained and polished statesmen have proved fitter depositaries of civil power than this rough old soldier, whose life had been largely passed in camp and bivouac, on the rude outskirts of civilization, or in savage wastes far beyond it. General Taylor died too soon for his country's good, but not till he had proved himself a wise and good ruler, if not even a great one.

It was a fair judgment from one of the few editors capable of making such an estimate.

Fillmore and the Politics of Slavery

Millard Fillmore occupies a unique place in presidential history. Alone among the chief executives of the past, he has had to endure the ridicule and even contempt usually visited on current occupants of the White House. Worse, it is not a partisan matter. Fillmore has become a synonym in both parties for the obscure man who occupies a position of power although he is without merit or distinction. His name has become a part of American mythology and humor, the butt of jokes by comedians who can barely spell it.

Professional historians, including recent revisionists, have done what they could to rehabilitate Fillmore, but it is a lost cause as far as the general public is concerned. The injustice is plain to anyone with even a casual knowledge of his career. Fillmore may not have been a great president, or even a particularly good one, but he was no worse than the succession of mediocrities who occupied the office between Jackson and Lincoln.

While it may be hard to understand why Fillmore has been singled out for scorn, there is nothing particularly mysterious about his obscurity. At the beginning he suffered that sudden propulsion from virtual anonymity to fame that vice-presidents who succeed presidents must endure, and he was not equal to it. In office, he was caught up in the struggle over slavery and annexation. It would have required a far greater man to place an easily definable imprint on the chaos of his time; consequently evidences of presidential power are almost nonexistent in his administration. Most significant, perhaps, he was a president who shunned the press and any kind of publicity, even though paradoxically he had used newspapers shrewdly throughout his career to advance his political fortunes and was thoroughly familiar with their uses.

Fillmore was the ultimate political animal, a man who devoted his life to politics, as essential to him as meat and drink. While this total absorption brought him at last to the White House, albeit by accident, it also meant that the machinations involved with seeking office often appeared to take more of his time and energies than dealing with larger affairs. In the process he neglected to exploit several opportunities that might have enabled him to find a national platform for his views with such influential editors as Greeley.

We see this careful lawyer and politician beginning to ply his trade in the press as early as 1832, when he published a series of lectures in the Buffalo *Patriot,* entitled ''An Examination of the Question, 'Is It Right to Require any Religious Test as a Qualification to Be a Witness in a Court of Justice?' '' He signed these letters ''Juridicus,'' in the style that still persisted from colonial days, and saw to it that they were reprinted in pamphlet form because, as the preface put it modestly, they were important and their author wanted to make them available ''to the world in a more extensive and substantial manner than the limited circulation and evanescent nature of a country newspaper would permit.''

Fillmore had chosen the *Patriot* to advance his early career, but even though the paper changed its name to the *Commercial Advertiser* in 1834 and became a daily instead of a weekly, he thought it lacked aggressiveness and concluded that Buffalo Whiggery needed a stronger voice. To that end he began negotiations with the publisher, Hezekiah A. Salisbury, to hire a new editor. The choice fell on Dr. Thomas M. Foote, a young doctor from Fillmore's native East Aurora, who was ready to switch careers for his patron and friend. Foote bought a third interest in the *Commercial Advertiser,* and for the next two decades gave his unqualified support to Fillmore as his benefactor (so Foote considered him) maneuvered his way through the jungles of New York State politics to the White House.

As state comptroller at one point during his rise, Fillmore did not hesitate to use the columns of the state's chief Democratic paper, Edwin Croswell's Albany *Argus,* to advance the interests of his office, and incidentally his own. But no one could achieve political success in New York State, at least in the Whig camp, without the blessing of the redoubtable Thurlow Weed and the Albany *Evening Journal* he had established, whose remarkable influence we have seen in operation before.

Relations between Fillmore and Weed ran a long course, during which they were both friends and enemies. On the way up, their relations were cordial, but as president, Fillmore did not hesitate to repudiate whatever political debts he may have owed the Albany boss and to oppose Weed when he thought it was necessary. Something of this ambivalence was evident as soon as Fillmore arrived in Washington in 1833 as a newly elected congressman. He wrote to Weed: "Immediately on my arrival here I told the clerk to order me your semiweekly paper on Gov't ac. [account]. He tells me he has done it, but yet I have not rec'd it. Will you look to it?" Only four years later Fillmore was writing testily to his friend about an omission in a story involving him: "Two paragraphs containing the whole discription [*sic*] of the outrage. Was this by design? If so, there is undoubtedly a good reason with which on suggestion I shall be fully satisfied. But it certainly gives me a very *awkward* appearance."

At the same time the correspondence between the two reflected Fillmore's dependence on Weed's political good will. Despondent over Whig party prospects, the young congressman consented to be a candidate for a vacancy in the state vice-chancellorship under Gov. William H. Seward, one of Weed's protégés and allies, but came to feel that the state's Whig machine, Weed's creation, was less than enthusiastic about him. He "felt a little mortified in the cavalier manner in which I have been treated," he wrote to the boss, and added, "The intimacy of our relations, and the frankness due it will justify me in soliciting from you—if you know it—the reason of so determined a hostility to my nomination."

In Washington, as part of the Whig struggle for power, Fillmore saw the capital's newspapers as pawns in the conflict, mere instruments of propaganda without any value as conveyers of news. To him the *Extra Globe* was "a perfect *Behon Upas* [poisonous tree] in the field of truth and virtue. Its noxious leaves are falling in every town and hamlet and rumor says the deputy marshalls [*sic*] for taking the census are to be converted into special agents for the distribution of this poison to every family throughout the United States." He worked behind the scenes in the effort, recounted earlier, to replace the *Intelligencer* with an invigorated *Madisonian* as the national Whig newspaper. Assessing the former, he told Weed that it was "no partisan paper. It is good in its sphere but worth nothing to meet the vile slander and base fabrication of the *Globe.*"

Weed used Fillmore at times as though he were no more than a piece in the elaborate game the party boss was playing. In 1844 he concluded that Fillmore would be most useful as governor of New York State and succeeded in getting him nominated, even though his candidate wanted neither the nomination nor the job. It was a move that failed.

When the Poughkeepsie *Eagle* had first proposed his name as a vice-presidential candidate in 1842, Fillmore had begun to feel that stirring in his bones which led Bernard Baruch in another century to observe that it was enough to make a man rise from his deathbed and walk to Washington. He sent two copies of the clipping to Weed, with the suitably modest notation, ''You may publish them or return them as you think best—for I regard them only as a passing compliment from an unknown hand.'' The result was a meeting of the two men with Seward and other party leaders, at which it was decided that Seward would not run for any office for the time being, that both he and Weed would support Fillmore for vice-president, and if the candidate failed to get the nomination at the Baltimore convention, he would not become a candidate to oppose any other Whig choice. Horace Greeley was another party to this agreement. As Weed's principal editorial backer in New York at the moment, Greeley began a campaign in the *Tribune* for Fillmore's nomination.

Nothing better illustrates Fillmore's attitude toward the press and the meticulous attention he paid to his career than his action at this strategic moment to establish a German-language Whig paper in his home base of Buffalo. He realized that a few votes might change the election outcome in Ohio, New York, or Pennsylvania, and he was acutely aware, as were other politicians, that the tremendous influx of German immigrants taking place could be decisive if they were informed and voted, as was likely to be the case. Buffalo had a substantial population of these immigrants. With the help of two other Whig leaders in the city, Fillmore succeeded in finding a capable German editor and establishing a newspaper called the *Freimüthige und West New Yorker Anzeiger*. He sent a copy of the first issue to Weed, calling attention to its lead editorial, which he had requested be published in both German and English.

Until he was successfully nominated and elected as vice-president, Fillmore maintained his cordial relations with Weed, and the two men used each other in the ancient manner of politics. In late February 1849, on the eve of the new vice-president's departure for Washington, they dined together in Albany, along with Seward, now a senator, and the occasion could only be called a love feast. Of that evening, Weed wrote in his autobiography, ''The Vice President and Senator were to consult from time to time (it was agreed), as should become necessary, and agree upon the important appointments to be made in our state.''

Understandably reluctant to disclose his own duplicity, Weed did not record in his memoirs that he held a knife at Fillmore's back. By this time he was closer to Seward and apparently had serious doubts, as others would later, about the vice-president-elect's real views on several matters, questioning his authentic Whiggishness. Moreover, he did not trust Fillmore's ability to divert the proper stream of patronage jobs to the New York machine, and so he had instructed Seward to sabotage whatever influence the vice-president might have in the dispensing of plums.

This backstage maneuvering soon moved into the fore, and it was not long before there was open warfare between the Fillmore and Weed factions in the party. It was a naked struggle for power. Weed learned that a political hack named Levi Allen had been appointed collector of the port of Buffalo over Fillmore's candidate for the job, and the boss's papers picked up this small triumph and made much of it. "We could put up a cow against a Fillmore nominee and defeat him," one of them taunted. The effect of the press campaign was to draw unpledged members of the party into the Weed camp.

In this critical battle, the worst of Fillmore's career, the vice-president's best qualities emerged. His partisan biographers were not exaggerating by much when they asserted, "That quiet and undramatic perseverance that kept him constantly on the edge of greatness began to show." It was frustrating for Weed, no doubt, that a man whom he probably considered his creature, raised to high office by the party, should stand in his way, defying the power and cunning of the Albany machine and its master.

Fillmore showed an uncharacteristic aggressiveness in this struggle. He made plans to start a rival paper in Albany, even though newspapers friendly to him existed elsewhere in the state. Such a paper, he predicted, "would restrict and tame Weed and his dependencies—harmonize and strengthen the party—protect our friends from proscription and slander, and weaken, if it does not destroy, this arbitrary and over-shadowing central influence."

When, predictably, Weed attacked both him and the idea in the pages of the *Evening Journal,* Fillmore ordered John T. Bush, who had been given the task of raising enough money to start the paper and find an editor, to delay his work temporarily and see if it was possible to buy the *Evening Journal* itself, even if it cost as much as $10,000. At the time, a capital fund of $2,000 would have been enough to start a paper. To G. R. Babcock, Fillmore wrote:

I have urged a purchase of the *Journal* even at a sacrifice of $10,000 rather than establish a new paper. These are still my sentiments, as all I ask is an independent Whig paper, devoted to the Whig party and the Whig cause, and to nothing else. . . . But this paper is about to be started. I trust it will be discreetly conducted—sustaining no *clique,* and opposing no men or set of men, who act with the Whig party. Such a paper may do good, and will receive my cordial approbation and support.

Since Weed was not about to sell the *Evening Journal* for any price, especially to Fillmore, the vice-president went ahead with his original plan, and in March 1850 the new paper, called the *New York State Register,* emerged. Its capital of $10,000 had been raised by Bush from ranking state Whigs and New York City merchants. Fillmore himself had contributed $250. Bush had also found two competent editors: Jerome Fuller, a former state senator whom Fillmore knew, and Alexander Seward, former owner-editor of the Utica *Gazette* and an opponent of Weed.

The vice-president believed that even the unusual sum of $10,000 would not be enough to arm the *Register* against Weed, and he sent Fuller to New York City to solicit more funds. There the editor encountered convincing evidence of a change taking place in the business community on the question of slavery. "The tendency," he reported, "is to be less ultra." That meant there was now a considerable sentiment among businessmen to support quick settlement of the territorial issues, since they feared that further struggles over them could only hurt business, particularly those firms with substantial Southern trade. Upon his return to Buffalo, Fuller gathered a group consisting of "the strongest and some of the wealthiest men in the city" and told them that if they gave money to the newspaper, it would pursue zealously the goal of settling the territorial question. They, too, contributed generously. Only in the context of the times can it be understood that these successful businessmen were so unperceptive as to believe that the *Register* or anything else could hold back the powerful forces now gathering.

Even before the new paper appeared, the knowledge that Fillmore meant to carry out his threat had alienated Weed still further from his former protégé. When the two men met by chance in New York, both on their way to Washington, they did not make even a pretense of politeness, but exchanged cold accusations of treachery. It was a meeting that prepared Fillmore for his new ordeal as president, after his abrupt elevation occurred. During the previous sixteen months he had been the target of an unremitting attack from President Taylor's cabinet, carried on largely through the papers controlled by the Weed faction. The papers supporting Fillmore fought back in kind, at times joining the chorus of Democratic journals when scandal struck the cabinet, as noted earlier.

Once in office, Fillmore knew that he must change the cabinet immediately, which he did with a ruthless hand. The chief figure to emerge in a position of power regained was Daniel Webster, named as secretary of state. At the same time the *National Intelligencer* was also rehabilitated as the official party organ, replacing Taylor's *Republic,* which had sided against Fillmore. Webster had frequently written for the *Intelligencer.*

To the nation, however, concern did not lie with these internal affairs. The politics of slavery dictated only one question that must be answered: Would the new president support the annexation policy of his predecessor, or would he support Clay's compromise, which Taylor had fought against? During Fillmore's first week in office there was endless speculation in the press. Washington correspondents of leading papers theorized that the differences Fillmore had with Seward, Weed's ally, would ensure his coming out on the side of the compromise, but others suspected that he was really a strong abolitionist who would support Taylor's plan.

One can only sympathize with Fillmore. Presidents usually had four months between Election Day and inauguration to work out their policies. But the man from East Aurora had only one night, which he spent sleeplessly behind locked doors after his hasty taking of the oath, to formulate some kind of stand. The territorial issues would not wait for quiet deliberation. Texas, the Southwest, and beyond them the great question, slave or free, had to be faced.

There had been a warning signal from Congress. Only three days before, 91 congressmen, using the Treasury scandal as a reason for their action, had passed a motion of censure against President Taylor. Their real motive, however, was to rebuke him for purportedly instructing Col. James Monroe to resist Texas to the last man if it came to conflict. And there were other signals of trouble ahead. Two weeks earlier, 180 Southern leaders had met in Nashville to demand as a minimum condition for peace with their region the right to carry their slaves into the Southwest when migration into the new territories began.

In the face of these formidable, even terrifying, problems lying just ahead, Fillmore underwent a remarkable transformation. All his life he had been the apotheosis of the party man, wheeling and dealing, always advancing his own cause. Now he seemed to leave that way of living and thinking behind him. His friends as well as his enemies were astonished to see a new Fillmore emerging, one who appeared to be putting the national welfare ahead of personal ambition and party politics. It was an unusual and to some an exhilarating spectacle. Practical men like Seward and Weed found it hard to believe. The new course Fillmore set for himself was based on compromise, not vengeance. Anticipating Lincoln, he believed that the prime necessity was to save the Union. In that spirit he signed the Fugitive Slave Act over the protests of the antislavery people in his party as a gesture of peace toward the South.

As an old hand at manipulating the press, Fillmore realized that if he continued to employ it as a propaganda medium, in the traditional way, he could not gain the confidence of both sides; consequently he began a policy that had its own dangers, virtually closing off the administration to the press, although the *Intelligencer* was still the "official" paper. A veteran correspondent, who signed his dispatches "Gath," recounted later how he and other reporters got at least some of the news in the White House. "In Fillmore's administration," he recalled, "some of the correspondents used to get into the reception room next door to the Cabinet room, and overhear the discussion. Daniel Webster discovered it, and had a door interposed."

Not all the correspondents were compelled to eavesdrop, however. Benjamin Perley Poore, a Washington reporter for thirty years who signed himself "Perley," recorded in his memoirs that the best correspondent in the Fillmore administration was Erastus Brooks, one of the editors and owners of the New York *Express*. Poore recalled: "What he did not know about what was going on in political circles, before and behind the scenes, was not worth knowing. His industry was proverbial, and he was one of the first metropolitan correspondents . . . to write with a vigorous, graphic, and forcible pen. Washington correspondents in those days were neither eavesdroppers nor interviewers, but gentlemen, who had a recognized position in society, which they never abused." Poore was something of a gentleman correspondent himself during his more than three decades in Washington, from Jackson to Grover Cleveland. He was a correspondent for the Boston *Evening Journal,* became the first editor of the *Congressional Record* in 1869, and was one of the founders of the Gridiron Club.

If he virtually shut himself away from the press, Fillmore nevertheless did not stop reading it carefully—the habit of a lifetime. In a letter to Webster, for example, he enclosed a clipping from the New York *Herald,* one of Bennett's editorials declaring that "it is high time to have an interpretation of the Nicaragua treaty. It either means something or nothing. That the British agents in Nicaragua regard it as a dead letter, we have the satisfactory proof in the late outrage and in the authority upon which it was committed." In his letter the

President asked Webster: "It seems to me to be in direct violation of the treaty. Is there any information on the subject in the State Department?"

Nor did the president's new seclusion preclude him from rewarding friendly editors—another lifetime habit. In a letter to Webster he noted: "I perceive also that Mr. Sanderson, the editor of the Philadelphia *News,* is very strongly recommended by the whole Pennsylvania delegation for the Chief Justiceship [of the state supreme court]. That paper has done good service to the Administration and been specially devoted to you. If he is willing to take the Assistant Judgeship, and is all that he is recommended to be by the delegation, I would submit whether he had better not be nominated."

Following his policy of impartiality, Fillmore withdrew only one appointment urged by Weed in the first three months of his administration, but he could not resist that one. It was the hapless Levi Allen, whose appointment to the Buffalo port collectorship Weed had used in the *Evening Journal* and elsewhere to ridicule the president. In its turn the *Evening Journal* appeared with an editorial praising Fillmore for his annual mssage to Congress, a switch so extraordinary that it drew from the president's former Buffalo law partner a sarcastic query: "What's the matter with Weed? Is he sick?"

It was a brief truce. The *Evening Journal* resumed its customary attacks on Fillmore for several months, but Weed was discouraged to see that these campaigns were not only without effect but were beginning to reflect on him. Discouraged, he went off to Europe, leaving a much quieter *Evening Journal* behind him. At the core of the renewed rivalry had been Weed's conviction that Fillmore had gone to the White House as an ardent abolitionist, like any conservative Whig, and had almost immediately turned around and become a friend of slavery. The *Evening Journal* had been fond of reminding the president that his conduct was no different from what he had criticized Tyler for doing eight years before.

No matter what Fillmore did, even his attempt at impartial patronage, it was not enough to placate the Weed faithful, if not Weed himself. Thurlow Weed Barnes, his grandson, sums up their feelings in his memoirs: "All federal officeholders suspected of fidelity to 'the Dictator' were requested to resign. Mr. Weed's friend, Mr. Benedict, Postmaster at Albany, was summarily removed. The post-office department interfered with the subscription lists of Mr. Weed's paper. . . . Hoping to keep up the division, Democratic papers took a hand in the quarrel, doing what they could to strengthen the administration."

"Dictator" was a word frequently applied to Weed himself, even by his friends and allies. Seward, shortly after they met, remarked that he had not "known that dictators could be such amiable men." Certainly this tall, somewhat awkward, good-natured party boss was a dictator in the way he ran the New York State Whig machine, but he was no more evil than his similarly situated contemporaries.

In New York State, Fillmore could counter whatever mischief the *Evening Journal* might be up to through the Buffalo *Commercial Advertiser,* where Dr. Thomas Foote had now replaced John Bush as co-editor. Foote, the original editor, had left to serve President Taylor as chargé d'affaires in Bogotá, and Fillmore had sent him briefly to Vienna. He was now more fully in the president's confidence than he had ever been before. (It is worth noting that Weed became editor of the *Advertiser* after his political career virtually ended with Seward's failure to gain the Republican nomination in 1860.)

During his short two years in the White House, Fillmore continued to pursue his general policy of expanding commerce, particularly abroad, and maintaining domestic peace at whatever reasonable cost. It was not without results. Seeking to develop trade with China, he opened up trade to Japan, kept Hawaii out of foreign hands, and sought vainly to bridge the Central American isthmus with a railroad or a canal, anticipating Theodore Roosevelt. He was not particularly a believer in what would be called Manifest Destiny; he simply thought that these aggressive actions he took were the proper methods by which a president could use his authority in order to promote commerce that would benefit the whole nation. As for domestic politics, his prime objective was to save the Union, and if that seemed impossible, at least he would leave the Whig party dismantled and useless to the Weed-Seward wing. It was clear to him, as it was to a number of angry editors and discouraged Whig politicians, that nothing could now save the party.

Fillmore's attempt at an impartial administration cost him the nomination in 1852. Since he was not unequivocally on their side, the Northern Whigs considered him a friend of the South and a closet advocate of slavery. Their inclination was to turn to another military hero of the Mexican War, Gen. Winfield Scott, as a guaranteed kind of vote getter. Daniel Webster's candidacy, however, complicated their plans, and the delegates balloted fifty times without getting a clear vote for Scott, who led Fillmore by a small margin. Webster's managers offered the Fillmore people a deal: if Webster could get forty-one more votes from the North, the Fillmore votes would be released to him. But the Northerners were adamant, Webster withdrew, and Scott was nominated on the fifty-third ballot. Then the platform was voted on and accepted, and it appeared that these same Northerners had agreed to Clay's compromise laws "as a settlement in principle and substance" and pledged to insist on their strict enforcement until further legislation was needed.

In the uproar that followed, a new journalistic voice was heard, that of young Henry J. Raymond, who had founded the New York *Times* in 1851. In the usual declaration of principles appearing in its first edition, Raymond had written: "We do not mean to write as if we were in a passion—unless that shall really be the case; and we shall make it a point to get into a passion as rarely as possible." Old hands in politics and journalism had greeted these words with utter disbelief. A newspaper not in a passion, at a time when passion seemed to be the partisan keynote of every other paper's editorial policy, and when the whole country was being seized by increasingly strong feelings? Impossible, they agreed—just another example of lofty promises so often published and so soon broken. But Raymond meant them, and the *Times* would soon become what it has always been, the nearest thing to journalistic objectivity that the business has known.

The fact that it was even being attempted made the *Times*'s arrival a landmark in the history of the press.

But if that was so, the skeptics inquired at the time, what was Raymond doing at the convention, charging that the Whigs who had secured the nomination for Scott had done so by making a deal with the Southern delegates by which they would be allowed to dictate the platform if the Northerners could have their candidate? "It's a lie," the Southerners shouted, but there was more truth in it than the party faithful excluded from the smoke-filled rooms wanted to believe. If there was a seeming ambivalence here in Raymond's behavior, it was because he was something new in journalism—an editor who was also a politician, as Greeley would also become, and a few others after them. Weed too could be counted among that number, although he was predominately the politician.

As for Fillmore, he left Washington unemployed, broke, seemingly dead politically, and without visible prospects. But while old politicians may die, they seldom fade away if they can still run for office or mix in party affairs. Consequently, we see the former president having one more try at the White House in the next election, as the Whig and Know-Nothing candidate. (There were cynics who thought one designation described the other.) It was another bitter campaign, in which Fillmore's candidacy nearly threw the election into the House. A change of about eight thousand votes from Buchanan to Fillmore in Kentucky, Tennessee, and Louisiana would have given him those states, and the House would have had to decide. Nevertheless, the struggle had made him such a whipping boy for his enemies in the party that warring factions among the Democrats sought him out for political endorsements.

In fact, Fillmore began to seem indestructible. He was among those who greeted Lincoln when the president-elect traveled through Buffalo on his way to the inauguration, and although his later opposition to the administration's conduct of the war, and the war itself, led to his being accused as a Copperhead, he was never entirely out of favor. But hatred pursued him relentlessly. When Lincoln died, Fillmore happened to be absent from Buffalo and so was late in draping his front door with black. An irate passerby smeared his house with black ink, and the news stories reporting this vandalism made it appear that a great throng of Fillmore's respectable fellow townsmen had gathered in front of the house to insult the former president. No one seemed to remember that Fillmore had headed a citizens' committee appointed to meet the Lincoln funeral train at Batavia, and escort it to Buffalo.

Having fortuitously married a rich widow in 1858, Fillmore refused to disappear from national politics. In September 1873 the New York *Herald* ran a long interview with him in which he pontificated genially on the questions of the day, observing generously that "General Grant is undoubtedly a greater general than statesman; and perhaps, there should be some allowance made for his want of experience."

By that time Fillmore had even made his peace with Weed, as disclosed in a New York *Times* account of the reconciliation in the summer of 1869, which reported:

It will afford the friends of both distinguished gentlemen infinite pleasure to learn that the long personal estrangement between ex-President Fillmore and Mr. Thurlow Weed was brought to a happy close a few days ago at Saratoga, by a meeting or reconciliation so *magnanimous,* creditable and characteristic of both sides, that we trust we violate no private confidence in stating the facts. Mr. Fillmore made the first advance by intimating to Miss Weed [Thurlow's daughter] on the occasion of an accidental meeting at the dinner-table of the hotel, that if he were sure it would be agreeable to her father he would call upon them at his rooms. On hearing this, Mr. Weed immediately sought the rooms of Mr. Fillmore, where, with scarcely a momentary reference to bygones, personal or political, hearty good neighborhood and kindly understanding were restored, and these great co-workers in the old Whig vineyard, both grown gray in the service, are again friends, after an estrangement of nearly twenty years.

Thus, with nothing more to be gained or lost on either side, the two old enemies became friends once more.

Does Fillmore deserve obscurity and latter-day scorn? The facts argue strongly against it. Robert J. Rayback, a historian of our time, has summed up the case for him succinctly, as a president who "possessed extraordinary strength of character and an enviable tenacity of purpose—as well as an admirable personality."

Pierce and the Failure of Power

In the tumultuous decade before the Civil War, the worst fears of the early Federalists about the evils of party politics appeared to be realized. As the need for power in the presidency became greater, the lack of strong leadership in the White House was more evident. Fiercely partisan politics, fueled by a still highly partisan press, was the law of the political day. Among the rising leaders of the independent press, particularly in New York, a sense of disgust and frustration about the machinations of both parties could be seen in the editorials, if not in the news columns.

Among the papers most influential in forming public opinion, and therefore with the greatest effect on the presidency, was Greeley's New York *Tribune,* because of the editor's extraordinary national popularity, followed closely by Raymond's *Times* and William Cullen Bryant's *Evening Post.* Bryant, whom most Americans remember (if at all) as a minor poet they read in American literature courses, was in reality an intellectual leader of his time, editor of what in many ways was the most distinguished paper in America. Outside New York, the only papers to rise above competent mediocrity, and whose editorial voices were heard in Washington, were Samuel Bowles's Springfield *Republican* in Massachusetts and the Chicago *Tribune,* whose editor, Joseph Medill, would soon play an important role in Abraham Lincoln's presidential nomination.

The editorial page itself, as a distinct part of the newspaper, had come into being with Greeley—a page admirably defined by Allan Nevins as "treating a wide variety of topics in a variety of manners, though pursuing a consistent policy; achieving a level of genuine literary merit; produced by a body of editors, not by a single man, and representing their united judgment and information; and earnestly directed to the elevation and rectification of public opinion.''

Not every page fulfilled these requirements by any means. Greeley's and Bryant's probably were closer than the others, and the *Times* was already becoming the model it would be later. Bennett's *Herald* concentrated on the news, however, and the editorial page suffered from the publisher's excesses in both style and cerebration, but its importance during this decade cannot be discounted, as it argued the cause of the Southern slaveholders and so was read eagerly not only in the South but by Northern businessmen fearful of losing their trade in the disputed region.

Nevins believed that the *Tribune* was ''one of the great leaders of the nation, and its role in the particular drama which ended with the Emancipation Proclamation was as great as any statesman's save Lincoln.'' That judgment may be challenged, even ridiculed, by some historians today, but it would be difficult to deny the major role the *Tribune* played in rallying the North against the spread of slavery. If the paper became greater than its editor, as Nevins thought, that was because of Greeley's personal inability to control and direct the magnificent political engine he created—an inability rooted in a personality tinged with madness, like both the Bennetts, father and son.

One can easily understand the skepticism, and in some cases derision, with which these leading newspapers viewed Franklin Pierce's entry on the presidential scene. And it mattered what they thought. The days of the bought press and the official administration organ were rapidly coming to an end. Greeley's power can be understood by the fact that the *Tribune*'s weekly edition was circulated even in the smallest Western settlements, and since magazines were still too expensive to be read by a mass audience (although they were proliferating at an astounding rate), it was passed along and read by entire communities. Greeley could say with confidence that he spoke to all the Free-Soil states and territories with a force previously unknown in the history of American journalism. In 1854 the weekly's circulation was 112,000, and Bayard Taylor, on a lecture tour, was not exaggerating when he declared that ''the *Tribune* comes next to the Bible all through the West.''

Pierce was another product of convention maneuvering, in which James Buchanan's managers, frustrated after thirty-three ballots, sought to prove that none of the other candidates could get the nomination. They encouraged Pierce, as the dark horse from New Hampshire, believing he would prove their point, but instead a stampede toward him began on the forty-ninth ballot, and in the end he got all but six of the votes.

No one knew much about Pierce, and so he had acquired no enemies of consequence. Smiling, bland, well-mannered, he had supporters in both the North and South, and there was an added attraction in his youth—he was only forty-eight—which appealed to a party weary of old war heroes. But even Nathaniel Hawthorne's campaign biography admitted that ''he did not, at the outset, give promise of distinguished success,'' and although Hawthorne applied his considerable talents conscientiously, he could not get much beyond the ''moderate

talents'' of this unknown politician. Much of what he wrote had to be drawn
from a sketch of Pierce that had appeared in the Boston *Post.*

There was not much to encourage a campaign biographer in Pierce's career to
that point. He had been at the bottom of his class in Bowdoin and, in his mortification, even dropped out for several days, hoping to be expelled. Returning
after the persuasion of friends, he applied himself with such devotion that he rose
at four in the morning to study and went to bed at midnight. No one could have
done more, but in the end he graduated only as the third scholar in his class.
''The key to the secret of Pierce's development,'' his most recent biographer,
Roy F. Nichols, has written, is that ''too little of his life was taken by struggle
with outward circumstance; too much, by fighting or more often regretting personal weakness. . . . [Starting] at Bowdoin . . . he was determined to conquer
himself.''

Whatever his success in doing so, Pierce in the White House was merely a
reflecting mirror for his party, a man seemingly devoid of inspiration and initiative, both in politics and in his relations with a hostile press. It was not a case of
ignorance. Pierce had been brought up with a proper understanding of the part
newspapers played in the politics of his time, as he demonstrated in his maiden
speech as a legislator in New Hampshire, when he upheld the ''fundamentally
important political agent—the press.'' At issue was official publication of the
laws, which had previously been done in all papers, most of which were not
Jacksonian. Now the Jackson majority in the state legislature proposed to confine
publication to their party's press, passing it off as an economy measure. Pierce
helped the Jackson partisans to victory.

In New Hampshire, Pierce had become friendly with Isaac Hill, editor of the
Patriot, whose abilities as a supporter of Jackson we have already seen displayed. Hill was considered as the man who first brought Pierce to national
attention and by some as the major influence behind his election. The two men
shared a conviction that a republic without parties was a complete anomaly. As
the protégé of an editor known to be Jackson's intimate friend, advertised by Hill
in the *Patriot* as ''the most popular man of his age that I know of in New Hampshire,'' Pierce made the natural progression to Congress with ease, and there
quite naturally became a part of Jackson's inner circle. He was already a devoted
party man. When the New Hampshire Democrats seemed dangerously split,
using similarly named papers, the *Patriot* and the *New Hampshire Patriot* as
dueling weapons, Pierce stepped in as mediator. In the process he formed a
political friendship with still another editor and fellow congressman, Edmund
Burke, of the *Argus and Spectator,* who employed the paper as his mouthpiece in
Sullivan County politics. Burke was later one of the Washington *Union*'s editors.

In Washington, Pierce proved to be singularly ineffectual. He lacked the self-
assertiveness to put through any bill, even one proposed by his brother-in-law
involving reforms in the pension system. None of the bills he sponsored ever
became law, and he retired from public life momentarily without a record to
stand on. Moreover he had alienated his original sponsor, Isaac Hill, who now
attacked him in *Hill's Patriot,* the paper this irascible editor had established after
he sold his original paper and found himself unable to get it back. *Hill's Patriot*

charged Pierce with numerous political crimes: opposing the program of "radical" farmers who were resisting the building of railroads on their lands until he was hired as counsel by the landowners; conniving at the passage of the bankruptcy law while voting against it; franking mail after he had resigned from the Senate; and a few lesser misdemeanors. Pierce denied everything.

Eventually Pierce made peace with Hill, and was instrumental in combining the two *Patriots* and finding a new editor. Burke was the most obvious candidate, but he wanted to continue his political career in Washington. Pierce chose instead, displaying his usual lack of tact, a man his friend Burke hated, William Butterfield.

By this time Pierce was ready for the political wars again, and he was encouraged to believe he might become president. But on the eve of setting out for Concord to present himself as a candidate, he made a serious tactical error. A Richmond, Virginia, editor named Robert G. Scott sent him a letter soliciting his opinions about the issues involved in the Compromise of 1850, in the belief that they might be made the basis of the Democratic platform. Three questions were posed to him: "Would you do everything in your power to sustain the compromise and the Fugitive Slave Law? Would you do all you could to prevent change in the Fugitive Slave Law to make it less effective? Would you veto a law impairing the Fugitive Slave Law?"

Everything in Pierce's character revolted against giving an unequivocal answer to these questions. Any public statement he might make could conceivably endanger his candidacy. Instead of consulting someone knowledgeable, like Hill, he went to an old friend from Mexican War days, Maj. F. T. Lally of Maine, who would be a delegate at the national convention in Baltimore. Taking the major's advice, Pierce framed a careful reply, which was forwarded to Lally at the convention. In it Pierce made the proper demurrer that his name would not come before the delegates, but as for the compromise issues, he wrote, "I intended . . . liberty." It was an answer that might have been received with more joy by the Whigs, however it was interpreted, but fortunately this masterful equivocation was read the other way, as liberty for the upholders of the Fugitive Slave Law.

Pierce was nominated in the manner already described and immediately launched into a campaign distinguished by the inevitable newspaper abuse. Almost at once he was accused by the Boston *Evening Journal* of cowardice during his Mexican War service. It was alleged that he was carried from the field of action after suffering a "fainting spell." Pierce denied the charge furiously (he was particularly sensitive about his war record), and military friends came to his rescue with testimonial letters, couched in general terms.

By way of further defense, and anticipating what was yet to come, Pierce arranged for the writing of two campaign biographies, one by a Boston *Post* reporter named Charles G. Greene and the other that reluctant eulogy by Hawthorne quoted earlier. When he was asked to write it, Hawthorne had given Pierce a true writer's answer: "Whatever service I can do you, I need not say, would be at your command, but I do not believe that I should succeed in this matter so well as many other men. It needs long thought with me, in order to produce anything good.''

Hawthorne did his best with the material at hand, but the result was half-hearted, extremely mild, and hardly enough to counterbalance the kind of barrage that was being laid down by the Whig press, in which Pierce was called not only a coward but anti-Catholic and a drunkard. On the last charge he was particularly vulnerable. It was an ill-kept secret that he had suffered with an alcohol problem for years, unable equally to refuse liquor or handle it. Again he had to resort to testimonial letters certifying his character, this time from medical and clerical friends.

The anti-Catholicism charge was more difficult. Every politician knew that the massive influx of Irish immigrants (providing a large new class of readers for the New York papers) had to be taken into account, and, in Pierce's case, there was also the troublesome problem of certain anti-Catholic provisions in the state constitution of New Hampshire, as well as in other states. It was not an easy charge to counter, but, if he failed to do so, untold numbers of Irish Catholics, most of whom were Democrats, might switch to Scott. Pierce turned once more to letter writing as a solution, sending off pleas for help to Charles O'Conner in New York, George M. Dallas in Philadelphia, and George F. Emory in Boston, who had considerable influence with such Catholic newspapers as the *American Celt* and the Boston *Pilot*. On his own behalf he wrote a typically vague letter declining to attend a Fourth of July celebration in Philadelphia, in which he contrived to insert a laudatory mention of the services rendered by foreigners in the American Revolution.

In all the campaign minefield, however, the hardest potential disaster to avoid was the issue that underlay everything else—slavery. Both parties had accepted the compromise, with reservations and qualifications of various kinds, and a great many doubts, but the issue continued to seethe below the surface. Pierce's previous stand on it was in keeping with his general style. In a speech at New Boston the previous winter, he was said to have described the Fugitive Slave Law as inhuman and against moral right, but at the same time declared it ought to be accepted and enforced as part of the compromise. When New Hampshire congressmen were asked to explain this small puzzle of contradictions, they were hard put to do so, and Pierce offered them no help by asserting that he didn't remember precisely *what* he had said because he was ''unwell'' during the speech and had employed a rapid-fire manner of extemporaneous speaking. In any case, he said, he had difficulty with recall.

This astonishing explanation led to a brief Battle of the Affidavits. Several were produced from those who had heard the speech, testifying that the words had never been spoken, and the opposition offered counteraffidavits providing that they had. These were followed by a flurry of pamphlets from both sides, while Pierce refused to offer a definite denial but kept repeating that the truth had been distorted.

This phase of the campaign was enough to carry it through the summer, until in September a new charge surfaced. A Baltimore newspaper, the *Old Defender*, asserted that Pierce, while he was serving in Mexico, had been slapped on the face by a brother officer, John B. Magruder. Outraged, Pierce shot off a telegram of denial to the paper and soon after produced a letter from Magruder himself, now living in California, who said there was no truth in the charge. The *Old Defender* had to withdraw the accusation. Pierce also directed that paper and others to a sentence in Hawthorne's biography: "There was not a man of his brigade but loved him, and would have followed him to death, or have sacrificed his own life in his general's defence."

Meanwhile Scott was having no easy time of it himself. Northern Whigs were split between him and the platform, and some of the party's newspapers joined the Democrats in attacking the general, particularly those sympathetic to the Southern Whigs, who suspected that Scott was the puppet of Senator Seward, whose antislavery views they feared. Scott was an easy mark in other respects. A vain and pompous man, he was a particularly choice target for ridicule by the political cartoonists in the popular press. Worse, his sympathy for the Native American party, with its xenophobic views about foreigners, was well known which virtually guaranteed that he would get little support from Irish and German voters. Like Pierce, he also avoided coming out flatly for or against the compromise.

Northern antislavery Whigs finally refused to support Scott, held their own rump convention, and nominated candidates for what they called the Free Democracy party, whose candidates ran on a generally liberal platform of "Free soil, free speech, free labor and free men." Other splinter groups sprang up, all with their own candidates and supporting newspapers: the Liberty party, the Democratic Southern Rights Convention, and a loose coalition of New England Whigs and Union Democrats in favor of Webster. But all these small movements accomplished was to split votes away from the main parties, and somehow to diminish the usual campaign excitement. Since none of those in the field had offered credible policies of their own, it came down to a contest of personalities.

In the newspaper war truth was the victim, as always. The Democratic newspapers tried to counter the charge of Pierce's "fainting spell" on the battlefield with the facts—that a knee injury the day before had given him so much pain he could no longer function—but this mundane explanation was lost in the verbal melee. Democratic newspapers, for their part, also had wicked fun with General Scott's nickname, "Old Fuss and Feathers," which was considerably less heroic and reliable than "Old Hickory" and its successors. The charge by these papers that Scott was against foreigners had to be taken more seriously, however, and the general had to take to the stump, seeking out German and Irish audiences so that he might declare his impartial devotion to everyone.

As for Pierce, he stayed home and said little during the campaign, a strategy that proved its wisdom when he won the election easily, carrying every state but four. The results were a requiem for the Whig party. It was hopelessly splintered, and during the campaign its two great leaders, Clay and Webster, had died. The new Republican party would soon rise from its ashes.

Pierce was in office only four months before he began to have trouble with his press relations. He and those around him had stepped out on the wrong foot by shutting themselves off as far as possible from communication with the papers.

That included what could still be considered the official administration organ, the Washington *Union,* which had been under the direction of Robert Armstrong since 1851, when Ritchie had resigned his post; it appeared to be only lukewarm in its support.

Armstrong was the publisher, but he was not in direct editorial control. Two editors, Charles Eames of Massachusetts and Roger A. Pryor of Virginia, actually ran the paper, and the editorials were written, for the most part, by Caleb Cushing and John W. Forney, clerk of the House, whose most notable years on newspapers were still ahead of him.

A complicated power struggle over the paper now ensued. The *Union* expected to have its contract as official printer continued, since tradition dictated it be given to the publisher of the party organ. Congressional Democrats who were disenchanted with the paper revolted in both houses, but Armstrong won easily. No doubt that gave him the courage to refuse when Pierce wanted his friend Alfred O. P. Nicholson to take over the paper. There were skirmishes and counterattacks. Armstrong fired Pryor, and Pierce arranged for Nicholson to replace Eames. He also brought onto the staff an old friend from congressional days, Harvey Watterson, whose son "Marse Henry" Watterson would achieve journalistic fame as the noted editor of the Louisville *Courier-Journal.* Briefly there was a plan to start a new administration paper in New York and put Forney in charge of it, but nothing came of it. In the middle of the power struggle, Armstrong died.

The men now in charge of the *Union* were not inconsiderable journalists. Nicholson had political experience, Cushing was a highly talented editorial writer, and Forney would prove to be the best of the lot, but still the paper could not give Pierce and his administration a political edge in the continuing battle. There were too many disgruntled Democratic editors opposed to what was happening in Washington, and there was a rising tide of exceptional Republican newspapers and editors, particularly in New York. The *Union* found itself overshadowed by this kind of competition.

Inevitable disappointments over patronage appointments not granted by the president also hurt the administration. C. Edwards Lester, New York correspondent of the London *Times,* was one of the disappointed and in retaliation he wrote a series of negative letters about Pierce. Another frustrated office seeker, Francis J. Grund, capital correspondent of the Philadelphia *Public Ledger* and the Baltimore *Sun,* attacked the administration for its apparent favoritism toward states' rights advocates.

Far more damaging than these, however, was the opposition of the two leading newspapers in New York (and in the nation), the *Herald* and the *Tribune.* Bennett had been angered initially because Pierce had thanked him for his campaign support through a third party. "I have not been insensible to the vast influence of the *Herald* throughout the late canvass," the president wrote to a mutual friend. "Will you assure Mr. B. when you write him that I appreciate both the motive and the ability, and at the same time present to him my sincere acknowledgments."

Bennett might have overlooked this snub, but as soon as Pierce reached the

White House, the *Herald*'s proprietor, in his customarily immodest fashion, let him know without much subtlety that he expected to be named minister to France in return for his support. When the president appointed someone else, he not only lost Bennett's support but came under the *Herald*'s heaviest editorial guns. In Greeley's case, this editor demonstrated why the *Tribune* had come to be known as the "Great Moral Organ" by thundering against the administration as "tools of the slave power."

Nor was this the end of Pierce's misfortunes by any means. He also found himself opposed in the distinguished columns of the New York *Evening Post*, whose Washington correspondent sent back a dispatch not unrepresentative of the way that paper and others viewed their president:

> We walked in unheralded, and soon found ourselves in the reception room, where Mr. Pierce was talking with a bevy of ladies. Immediately on seeing us he approached, received us very politely, and introduced us to Mrs. Pierce. The President impressed me better than most of his pictures. He had whitened to the true complexion of a parlor knight—pale and soft looking. Though not what I could call elegant, his manners are easy and agreeable. He is more meek in appearance than he is usually presented as might be expected of a man who has submitted to be drawn into the position of tail to Senator Douglas's kite. . . . The President evidently feels the Presidency thrilling every nerve and coursing every vein. He is so delighted with it that he is palpably falling into the delusion of supposing himself a possible successor of himself! Could fond self-conceit go further?

Pierce did have his admirers, but they were not among the new lords of the press. Anne Royall, for example, who had been a fixture on the Washington scene since Madison's day and was now eighty-five years old, had revived her former journal, the *Huntress*, her third venture as a publisher, and in June 1854 she wrote of her own visit to the president:

> For the first time since he has been President, we have had the pleasure of seeing the patriot and statesman, Franklin Pierce, a few days ago. He looked stout and healthy but rather pale. . . . His fine blue eye is still bright while his deep, placid forehead clearly bespeaks the mind of the man who has won the admiration of his countrymen by his independence and strict political integrity. His soft and pleasing voice is attuned to melody itself, and his engaging manners readily captivate the beholder, though he rarely smiles.

No doubt Pierce was pleased to have such a flattering portrait, but it would take more than the approval of an eccentric editor of a small-circulation paper to enhance his reputation, and one can be sure he knew it. In fact, that not always reliable correspondent "Gath" is credited with saying that "Frank Pierce was so sensitive about newspaper correspondents, that he had printers set his message in the White House." In short, if they did not admire him, no more did he trust them.

There was never any improvement in this relationship as long as Pierce remained president. While it was true that he tried to conduct his administration with far too much secrecy, at the same time it must be remembered that, no matter what he did, he could expect to be abused not only by the opposition press, which he anticipated, but by the most influential Democratic papers as well. When historians study his state papers today, they see the record of a president whose efforts were, in the main, designed to be strictly constitutional, impartial, and patriotic. One would never know it from reading the newspapers of his time.

Central to Pierce's difficulties, however, was something far larger than the man himself—the tremendous social and political changes occurring in his era, which scarcely anyone could comprehend. Western expansion, Eastern industrialization and urbanization, and above all the overweening questions of slavery and states' rights were transforming the nation, but the politicians of the day were too immersed in party and sectional warfare to understand that, while even the best of the newspaper editors could offer few insights into what was happening to America. A great deal seemed to be going wrong at once, and while Pierce was in Washington, much blame fell on his otherwise blameless shoulders. Events occurred that he could not control, although he had pledged to do his utmost to prevent them. He was manipulated by those in the party to support legislation that could only encourage more unrest.

Matters might have been somewhat smoother in the White House if Pierce had taken the trouble to read the papers himself, but he was among the first of the presidents, perhaps the first, to do what is commonplace now. He arranged to have the contents of the press and what else was known about public opinion filtered through to him by someone else—in this case the presidential secretary Sidney Webster, who read to him "such items as he thought he ought to hear."

Oddly, Pierce seemed not to listen to the divisive voices in his own party, much less those outside it, and continued to believe for some time that he might be reelected. As his term ran out there was scarcely a newspaper of consequence he could count on for support, and even the *Union* was doubtful because Forney, the editor now running it, was close to his fellow Pennsylvanian, James Buchanan, who was about to make his second run for the office. The *Union,* in fact, was so erratic in what it supported or opposed that it could no longer be viewed as an administration organ. Even though Pierce had declared that "all hell" could not persuade him to break with Forney, the editor stopped visiting the White House and finally left the paper to Nicholson's direction.

As the conventions neared, the divisions among the Democrats appeared to be irreparable, as they would be for a long time to come, but the antislavery Whigs had formed the new Republican party in 1854 while the struggle over the new territories, slave or free, raged in and out of Congress. The national mood was slowly coming to a boil.

At this moment of crisis, the Democrats met in Cincinnati, only a week after abolitionist John Brown and his sons had deliberately murdered five proslavery men in Kansas. The convention opened amid scenes of incredible confusion, and the delegates began to choose from among Pierce, Buchanan, Stephen A. Douglas, and Lewis Cass. The issues had divided these candidates. Douglas had introduced the Kansas-Nebraska Act, which rendered the Missouri Compromise void by permitting slavery in the Kansas Territory; Nebraska Territory was to be free. Pierce had signed this act, so both were opposed by the delegates from the anti-slavery North. Buchanan, who had not been involved with the debate on either side because he had been serving in London as minister, won the nomination on the seventeenth ballot when Douglas released his supporters to him.

With this act, Pierce slipped unobtrusively back into the obscurity from which he had emerged. He came to public attention only once more, during the Civil War, when his public opposition to Lincoln's policies led to a quarrel with Seward. It created a brief flurry in the newspapers and served only to increase the public's already unfavorable opinion of him. Later some papers suggested unkindly that no one in his native Concord would speak to him. It was not that bad, but when Pierce died in October 1869, he slipped away from the scene leaving scarcely a ripple on the surface of American life—not simply unsung, but ignored in a way no other president, even Fillmore, had to endure. It was a fate not entirely deserved.

Buchanan: A Second Failure

James Buchanan's career as president is a study in frustration. In broad terms that is understandable because he was another weak man in the White House at one of the great crisis points in American history, when far more was required of him than he had the ability or character to produce. But in his relationship with the press, which is our concern here, his professed devotion to its freedom was more than balanced by what seemed at times an excessive preoccupation with how it regarded him—his "image." At a time long before the invention of public relations techniques, Buchanan had no idea how to defend himself, and his attempts only bred further misunderstanding, even contempt, among press and public, and utter frustration on his own part.

There was a particular flaw in Buchanan's personality. He always appeared to stand outside himself; even his memoirs were written in the third person. The self-portrait he constantly looked upon was not the one others saw, and often, with some desperation, he besought them to confirm his own observations. In the same manner, he watched his friends from afar, with a cool detachment, and advised them with little regard for their inner feelings. This was the man who presided over the collapse of the Democratic party—it would not elect another president until 1884—and over the end of the official administration newspaper, a decline that had begun with Polk when government printing contracts began to be spread among party newspapers rather than concentrated on the Washington organ.

The *Union* was still the party's Washington paper, but it continued to be unreliable under the editorship of Buchanan's friend, John Appleton, whose salary was paid by Cornelius Wendell in consideration for the printing and binding the *Union* did for the executive departments. Albert J. Beveridge, who had seen an impressive amount of corruption in his time, wrote in his Lincoln biography that Wendell was "one of the most corrupt men in political history," but this judgment may be excessive. As Ben Poore pointed out, it was Wendell who got a copy of the Supreme Court's Dred Scott decision at a time when it was being suppressed by court order and the clerk of the court was peddling copies of it in manuscript for $750 each. Wendell had it printed and distributed free—a small but significant blow for freedom.

One of the causes of Buchanan's troubles was that too much had been expected of him. No one had appeared to be better prepared for the presidency since John Quincy Adams. He was given particularly valuable experience in foreign affairs by acting as minister in both Great Britain and Russia, although in each of these assignments he exhibited those unfortunate traits that would later cause him so much trouble.

In London, following Secretary of State William Marcy's instructions to ambassadors that they appear at court "in the simple dress of an American citizen," Buchanan had worn what we would call today a plain business suit when he met Queen Victoria, thereby scandalizing Maj.-Gen. Sir Edward Cust, master of ceremonies at the court. Telling Marcy of Sir Edward's curt reproof when they met at the Travellers' Club, Buchanan tried to make the secretary understand that if he were compelled to wear "simple dress" he would not be invited to the queen's balls and dinners, valuable sources of information. Marcy did not answer, Buchanan was not invited to the opening of Parliament, and the whole affair created a sensation in the British and American press.

Later, during his time in London, Buchanan did manage to engage the English cardinal, Nicholas Wiseman, in a long conversation at a dinner, during which he was careful to inform His Grace of his great admiration for Archbishop John Hughes of New York, a political power in the city. "That dinner," Thurlow Weed asserted later, "made Mr. Buchanan President of the United States," no doubt an exaggeration, but certainly the good impression Buchanan made that night filtered down to Hughes and had some influence on the Catholic vote in New York.

While he served as Jackson's ambassador to Russia, Buchanan continued his early campaigning for the presidency. Knowing the importance of newspaper support at home, he found an occasion to praise the American press and at the same time made what must have been one of the first attempts to explain to the Russians why it was not like that of any other country, particularly Russia. The occasion came when a certain Baron Sacken, temporarily the Russian chargé d'affaires in Washington, complained to Secretary of State Edward Livingston about articles in the *Globe,* the administration's organ, dealing with the conduct of Russia toward Poland. Livingston tried to explain that the Constitution rendered the government powerless to control the press in America—although he did not mention that the *Globe* was without any doubt under Jackson's control. In St. Petersburg, Buchanan was apprised of the whole affair by Livingston and instructed to lay the matter before Count Karl Robert Nesselrode, then in charge of foreign affairs. At their meeting Buchanan explained the nature of the American press all over again.

There was more than a touch of hypocrisy in this diplomatic double-talk. While it was certainly true that the government did not control the press in America, as both the president and Buchanan had good reason to know, it was also true that Frank Blair would suppress or disclose in the *Globe* whatever Jackson told him to, so the American minister could be sure (barring an outburst of Jacksonian temperament) that no more would be heard from the *Globe* on this subject if the president willed it. He wrote to the home office at once, suggesting specifically what the paper should do, that is, "abstain at least from severe editorial paragraphs respecting the emperor of Russia" and "the publication of a strong editorial paragraph in the *Globe,* expressing a proper sense of the good feelings of the emperor of Russia, evinced towards the United States in making us an exception to his general policy by concluding the commercial treaty." Successful conclusion of the treaty was, of course, the point of this exercise.

These passages written in St. Petersburg and London made good preliminary precampaign reading back home. There was no doubt that Buchanan already had his eye on the White House, but he wanted to be invited to it rather than struggle in the open arena. As early as 1841 he was writing to his strong supporter, John W. Forney, then publisher of the Philadelphia *Press,* asking him not to mention his name as a candidate for the presidency because any premature movement in that direction might injure his chances. He wanted, as he said, to "let events take their course." Meanwhile he was not above submitting those like Forney, who were dependent on him for political or financial favors, to a little emotional blackmail, threatening to withdraw from politics if they were remiss in fighting his cause. Forney, a man who was brighter and cleverer in many ways than Buchanan, understood that this transparent weapon could easily be turned the other way, and when he needed something—a loan of several hundred dollars, for example—he would tell his patron that he had decided to leave his newspaper for the law, or for some other reason, and Buchanan was sure to respond with a kind letter and the money.

As editorial mouthpiece for Buchanan, Forney in these earlier years, first as editor of the Lancaster *Intelligencer* and then in Philadelphia with the *Press,* provided the launching pad for his patron's candidacy. In some respects he was a dangerous ally because he had a quick temper and a tendency to exact revenge, qualities that sometimes got Buchanan into trouble. In addition Forney viewed himself as his friend's confidential political manager and challenged anyone he thought might be a successful rival for that position, which often caused resentment. Nevertheless, it was largely owing to Forney's editorial efforts that Buchanan became known to the public. Through the medium of the exchange system, by which Forney's words in Lancaster or Philadelphia were spread by newspapers all over the country, voters were made aware of his clarion call to the polls: "The Union is in danger and the people everywhere begin to know it."

The party press, which was still strong in a way it would not be after the Civil War, was also a potent factor in launching such political careers. For example, about 50 million copies of newspapers circulated in the South annually, and since these papers were overwhelmingly Democratic, the party's message was widely and continuously broadcast. The new Republican party would fare better in the North in 1856 because the annual newspaper circulation there was 175 million copies, and both parties (as well as several splinter groups) got through to the voters. The rise of the great independent dailies in New York and elsewhere was beginning to change this traditional pattern, but because the nation was now sharply divided on party as well as along regional lines, their full effect would not be felt until after the Civil War.

Since Buchanan had withdrawn himself as far as possible from these divisions and had permitted others to fight for him, he became the available man at the convention, the only one on whom a majority could finally agree. When the Republicans met as a party for the first time, in Philadelphia, they, too, chose an available man, another dashing soldier, John C. Frémont, explorer of the West, believing that the other candidates, Seward and Salmon P. Chase of Ohio, were too radical on the slavery issue. They overlooked an obscure young Illinois lawyer, Abraham Lincon, as Frémont's running mate, giving him only 110 votes on an informal ballot and selecting instead a deservedly obscure man who would remain so, William L. Dayton. Millard Fillmore, rising briefly from the political ashes, was the candidate of a third party, the Know-Nothings, on an anti-Catholic, anti-immigrant platform of bigotry and hatred. (They were not called "Know-Nothings" out of public contempt but because they habitually answered, "I know nothing," when they were asked about their political beliefs.) The remaining dissident Whigs also supported Fillmore, believing that both the major parties were leading the country into war.

In the campaign the slavery issue was the major one for the first time. It was a drama played out against a virtual civil war in Bleeding Kansas, and it was the freshly minted Republicans who carried the abolitionist banners, bearing their slogan, "Free soil, free speech, and Frémont." The best of the Northern newspapers supported them, and so did the country's leading intellectuals—Bryant, Ralph Waldo Emerson, and Henry Wadsworth Longfellow, among others. In this crusade for morality, Greeley's Great Moral Organ led the journalistic parade, which was being joined daily by Whig and Republican converts.

Yet, as we know, Buchanan won. The Democratic papers hammered away on a simple theme: if the voters elected Frémont, the South would surely secede and there would be no more Union. In the South itself, where that outcome might have had many sympathizers, Buchanan was nevertheless sure of victory because Southerners were addicted Democrats and Republicans had no party organization—their candidates did not even appear on the ballot in eleven of the region's states. Pennsylvania was considered a key state, and the Democrats tried hard to secure it. There were charges that the party's Wall Street backers, highly apprehensive that a Republican victory would mean the civil war they feared as disastrous to business, supplied a half-million dollars to secure Pennsylvania, by fair or devious means.

Such heavy campaign contributions—August Belmont alone was said to have given $50,000—put the new and struggling Republican party at a serious disadvantage and contributed to its defeat. Not only was Pennsylvania lost to it, but four other critical states as well. Buchanan won the election easily, by nearly five hundred thousand popular votes, 174 to 114 in the electoral college.

Once in office, Buchanan was faced with the crowding events that would lead to war, but more immediately with personal problems that no doubt seemed important to him at the moment. One of those problems was Forney, who he had hoped would become editor of the *Union* in the new administration. But Forney, with Buchanan's consent, had supported Pierce up to the time of the convention and was therefore wholly unacceptable to many Southerners, especially the Virginia Democrats. That meant he was also unacceptable politically to the president. But what to do with this man who had done so much for him, and who had already written that he was "sick at heart" over his situation? If the editorship of the *Union* was an impossibility, placing Forney in the cabinet was equally so. An imminent election in Pennsylvania to choose a new senator offered an escape route; Buchanan believed Forney would be safe there. The attempt was made, but an ardent abolitionist won the election so Forney was left more distraught than before. In desperation Buchanan offered him the job of consul in Liverpool, the only position available at the moment, but Forney refused with some indignation. Deeply in debt, supporting five children, and without the lucrative political post he had believed was his due, he began to drink heavily. He would have mortgaged his remaining property if the president had not intervened on behalf of Forney's wife and children.

In the end this embittered man accepted—he had no choice—Buchanan's offer of a temporary job as paid correspondent for several Democratic papers. It was not enough. Forney wrote to Buchanan, "I have suffered deep and bitter humiliation since you have been elected, the gibes of false friends and the open exultation of open foes." Buchanan must have replied, but there is no record of it. Something of what he felt, however, was expressed to his friend Joseph B. Baker, collector of the port of Philadelphia, in January 1858: "I mourn over Forney. I fear he can never return to us, & yet he must feel awkward in his new associations. . . . I would, however, do nothing harsh towards Forney. . . . I repeat, I mourn over Forney."

The editor had left the party, as well as the inner circle of Buchanan's supporters, but the president felt the loss more keenly in terms of friendship than politically. Forney had been extremely useful, but it was the help of such powerful editors as Greeley and Bennett that Buchanan really needed. As he was about to enter the White House, the president-elect made a deliberate move to end the state of war that had existed between him and the unpredictable Bennett, editor of what should have continued to be a leading Democratic paper. No doubt Buchanan hoped in the bargain to smooth away some of the bitterness generated by the campaign, in which Greeley had referred to Bennett and his paper as "nigger drivers," to which Bennett had responded in kind, calling Greeley a "nigger-worshipper" and "Massa Greeley." In defending the Kansas-Nebraska Act, Bennett had proclaimed that "through good and evil report, the New York *Herald* has been the only Northern journal that has unfailingly vindicated the constitutional rights of the South." Such a policy had made the *Herald* unpopular among Northern abolitionists, quite naturally, but it was read eagerly by Southern businessmen from Richmond to New Orleans.

Since Buchanan's policy toward the South, whatever his real feelings, was one of appeasement, he recognized that Bennett's influence was important to him and wrote on February 20, 1857:

I rejoice that our former friendly relations are about to be restored. I can assure you I am truly sorry they were ever interrupted; & this not only for my own sake but that of the Country. The New York *Herald,* exercising the influence which signal ability & past triumphs always command, can contribute much to prostrate the Sectional party which now so seriously endangers the Union & to restore the ancient friendly relations between the North & the South. . . . I confess I had calculated with the most perfect confidence you would be as you had been my friend. It has been throughout us a Comedy of errors, in which I have been the sufferer. But let by-gones be by-gones; & when we again get together, I feel that we shall never separate.

To which Bennett responded on April 14: "I have received with great pleasure your kind letter—your very kind letter. I reciprocate most warmly the desire you so kindly express that we may soon meet not to separate by any comedy of errors—however, my dear sir, I am not altogether to blame for recent separations."

On the day Bennett was writing this letter the president was writing to Bennett's wife, who apparently had been the intermediary between them:

I am glad to learn that Mr. Bennett has promised you "to stick by my administration through thick and thin." Thus far he has given it a powerful support with occasional aberrations, for which I am always prepared and do not complain. He is an independent man and will do just what he pleases—though I know there is an undercurrent of good will towards me in his nature and he is disposed to treat me fairly. The *Herald* in his hands is a powerful instrument and it would be vain for me to deny that I desire its music should be encouraging and not hostile. Mr. B. makes his mark when he strikes and his blows fall so fast and heavy it is difficult to sustain them. . . . It is my desire as well as my interest to be on the best of terms with him. Justice is a kind providence. I hope that my administration may equal your friendly wishes. I shall do my best with all honest purpose and leave results to Heaven.

It was, nevertheless, an uneasy alliance. Neither man trusted the other. Bennett did not trust any politician, and the president was well aware that the day had gone when any party and its incumbent president could employ their combined weight to keep even the newspapers of its own persuasion in line. No one, he knew, was going to control men like Bennett and Greeley; a new dispensation had begun in journalism.

If Bennett stuck by Buchanan "through thick and thin" during his administration, it was only because the president did nothing to displease him. Buchanan's policy, in general terms, was one of drift on the stormy national sea, coupled with appeasement of the proslavery people, North and South, and that was the *Herald's* policy, too. If the administration was denounced in the House itself as "the most profligate and corrupt Administration ever known to this government since its organization," Bennett dismissed such talk as the mad rantings of abolitionist agitators. As a practical politician, Buchanan felt that such support deserved its rewards, and he was careful to see that the *Herald* got them. Its reporters were often the happy recipients of advance information about important administration actions, especially changes in policy or personnel.

Fortunately Buchanan never tested Bennett's loyalty by doing something that departed from their silently agreed-upon policies. If he had, he would have found, as others did, that Bennett was the prime herald of the new journalistic day in his determination to print what politicians did rather than simply support their causes. He had a single purpose—to tell all that was worth telling about everybody and everything. His newspaper had been built on its devotion to news values, and he did not intend to depart from that purpose for partisan reasons. Besides, it was a policy that had made him a great deal of money.

Viewing his character in this light, one can only speculate whether Bennett did not feel a touch of contempt along with natural journalistic exhilaration when he opened the mail one morning and found an advance copy of Buchanan's first annual message to Congress, accompanied by a note dated December 7, 1857, from the president that read: "I inclose you one of my messages and know I can implicitly trust to your honor that this copy will not be used for printing before 12 o'clock tomorrow. You will have an opportunity of perusing it and forming your own opinion of it in advance. Another copy for the *Herald* is in the bundle of papers to be delivered. . . . With many thanks for your very kind and very efficient support."

It would have taken more than the support of Bennett, however, to shield Buchanan from the attacks of the abolitionists and their friends. These attacks came from both press and pulpit. In the summer of 1857 a memorial was sent to him, signed by forty-three distinguished citizens of Connecticut, including several eminent clergymen, informing him that he had violated his official oath and that they prayed the Almighty to preserve him from the error of his ways.

Slavery was not the only issue. The opposition press fought Buchanan savagely on the question of Cuba, whose acquisition was the keystone of his Latin American policy. He had carefully not mentioned the subject in his first annual message, but he had already authorized the American minister in Madrid to make inquiries about the possibility of negotiating for the island. During the following year he made a forthright proposal to buy it, asking Congress to appropriate funds for an advance payment. When the Senate, on January 1, 1859, called for an appropriation of $30 million "to facilitate the acquisition of the Island of Cuba by negotiation," Buchanan immediately became the target of a newspaper war that broke out in Europe as well as America.

Hostility in the press and elsewhere was now beginning to reach a dangerous point. Not only was Buchanan perceived as a friend of slavery, but his foreign policy was denounced as aggressive and adventuresome. The *National Intelligencer* called the roll of administration proposals:

The great Napoleon himself, with all the resources of an empire at his sole command, never ventured the simultaneous accomplishment of so many daring projects. The acquisition of Cuba . . . ; the construction of a Pacific Railroad . . . ; a Mexican protectorate; international preponderance in Central America, in spite of all the powers of Europe; the submission of distant South American states; . . . the enlargement of the navy; a largely increased standing army . . . what government on earth could possibly meet all the exigencies of such a flood of innovations?"

Small wonder that Greeley, aghast at ideas that went so much against his grain, called the president "insane," while the Northern papers referred to him regularly as a "secessionist." The latter was a case of guilt by association. The pro-Southern editorials of William Browne that appeared in the Washington *Constitution,* regarded as a semiofficial administration paper, were presumed to reflect the views of the president. Buchanan, however, was not responsible for what Browne wrote and, in fact, was not in accord with most of what he said. The president compelled Browne to insert notices that the newspaper's editorials did not represent his views and one Christmas Day actually rebuked him for an editorial frankly advocating secession, informing him at the same time that he had withdrawn any support of the paper through government patronage.

In spite of the virulent press abuse directed at Buchanan—a precursor of the far greater storm that broke over Lincoln—historians of our time have come to view him in a different light. Those who argue that the Civil War was neither necessary nor worth the terrible price point to the president's moderation under extraordinary stress and praise his efforts for compromise. Those who believe the opposite—that the war was necessary and justifiable to destroy slavery and preserve the Union—can cite his insensitivity toward Northern abolitionists, which contributed to the movement toward war. When the struggle over Kansas resulted in the so-called Lecompton Constitution, which made the territory "as much a slave state as Georgia or South Carolina," in the president's view, only one out of twenty newspapers in Kansas supported the new constitution, but the Southern press and Buchanan's official Washington *Union* lauded it, to the scorn of most Northern newspapers. In reassessing Buchanan's presidency, then, it appears that only those who believe the war could and should have been avoided owe him nothing.

All this is hindsight, however. At the time, mounting criticism of Buchanan resulted in something unprecedented, a five-member congressional committee, appointed by the Speaker of the House, "for the purpose, first, of investigating whether the President . . . has, by money, patronage, or other improper means, sought to influence the action of Congress, or any committee thereof, for or against the passage of any law appertaining to the rights of any State or Territory; and second, also to inquire into and investigate whether any officer . . . prevented or defeated . . . the execution of any law or laws." Such an investigation, it was believed, might well lead to censure of the president.

In this extremity Buchanan turned to his uncertain ally, Bennett, and in an extraordinary letter to him, dated June 18, 1860, and marked "Private & Confidential," sought his help:

> I thought I should never have occasion to appeal to you on any public subject, and I knew if I did, I could not swerve you from your independent course. I therefore now only ask you as a personal friend to take the trouble of examining yourself the proceedings of the Covode Committee and the reports of the majority and minority, and then to do me what you may deem to be justice. . . .
>
> In performing my duty, I have endeavored to be not only pure but unsuspected. I have never had any concern in awarding contracts, but have left them to be given by

heads of the appropriate departments. I have ever detested all jobs, and no man, at any period of my life, has ever approached me on such a subject. . . .

I shall send a message to the House in a few days on the violation of the Constitution involved in the vote of censure and in the appointment and proceedings of the Covode Committee. I am glad to perceive from the *Herald* that you agree with me on the Constitutional question. I shall endeavor to send you a copy in advance.

For the moment the president did not misplace his confidence. Bennett roared to the rescue, quoting part of Buchanan's letter, particularly the part about endeavoring to be "not only pure but unsuspected," and castigating those who would censure with the grandiloquent invective of which he was an acknowledged master. It is doubtful whether this had the slightest effect, but in the end this congressional aberration came to nothing, as is so often the case. No report from an investigating committee was ever issued during the few remaining months of Buchanan's presidency.

The charges refused to die, however, even after the president had left the White House. On December 15, 1862, a resolution was introduced in the Senate by Garrett Davis of Kentucky, charging Buchanan with "sympathy with insurrection" in the Southern states for which "he should receive the censure and condemnation of the Senate and the American people." The resolution did not pass, but Buchanan was wounded anew, and one can hear the anguish in his cry, "If two years after a Presidential term has expired the Senate can go back & try, condemn, & execute the former incumbent, who would accept the office?"

By this time even Bennett had forsaken Buchanan. The *Herald* was accusing him of appropriating for his personal use pictures of Queen Victoria and other members of the royal family that had been presented to him for the White House by the Prince of Wales. Greeley's *Tribune,* never his friend, had already accused him a few months earlier of forwarding an engraving of Harriet Lane, his niece, ward, and White House hostess, to the publishers of the *Almanach de Gotha,* the social register of European royalty, with the suggestion that it be included because "our Republican rulers had a right to appear in the company of the reigning families."

Buchanan left office with his press relations in a shambles. He could not make anyone understand that he was not proslavery but interpreted the Constitution to mean that it was protected by this document he was sworn to defend. On Christmas Day, 1860, he had broken with the Washington *Constitution* because, although nominally the administration's organ, it had opposed his views on the right of secession, outlined in his fourth annual message to Congress.

The loss of Bennett's support, even though he was now out of office, further embittered him. He wrote to his former secretary, J. Buchanan Henry: "The *Herald* . . . from a spirit of malignity, & supposing that the world may have forgotten the circumstances, takes every occasion to blame me for my supineness. It will soon arrive at the point of denouncing me for not crushing out the rebellion at once, & thus try to make me the author of the war. Whenever it reaches that point, it is my purpose to indict Bennett for libel." Matters never did reach that extremity, however.

There remained only one paper Buchanan could count on in the last year of his presidency and afterward. Gerard Hallock of the New York *Journal of Commerce* remained his friend and strong supporter. But oddly enough, his old enemy, the *National Intelligencer,* provided him with a forum to defend himself in a lengthy debate with Gen. Winfield Scott that erupted in its pages six weeks before the end of his term. Scott had published his "Views" of the dangers threatening the Union in this paper on January 18, 1861, without informing the president he was doing so, an action equivalent to insubordination, since he was ranking general in the army of which the president was commander in chief. Buchanan replied, and the debate dragged on for months. Scott refueled it as soon as Lincoln was in the White House by giving the new president a report censuring Buchanan's policy towards forts in the South and having it published subsequently in the *Intelligencer.* These charges and countercharges were widely circulated as other newspapers across the country picked them up and reprinted them. Nothing could diminish the hostility of the New England papers, however. The Boston *Post* refused to print Buchanan's letters to Scott, and the former president wrote regretfully to Nahum Capen, "New England, except Connecticut, is a sealed book."

Buchanan became a man obsessed with defending his record in office, using the press with an ingenuity and initiative he had not shown while in the White House. And the papers continued to attack him. The New York *Evening Post,* digging into the past, recalled an alleged incident at the 1856 convention in Cincinnati in which Buchanan was supposed to have given several politically unwise pledges to Judge J. S. Black, who later became his attorney general. Buchanan did not take the *Evening Post,* but he saw the story when the *Tribune* picked it up and at once wrote a reply to the *Evening Post,* pointing out that Black was not only not a delegate to the convention but was more than five hundred miles from Cincinnati while it was in session.

There was no way of stopping such a delectable political morsel, however, and Republican papers reprinted it as soon as they saw it. In protesting and denying the story through letters to editors, Buchanan demonstrated that he had learned something about public relations. Writing to Greeley on May 23, 1865, for example, he pointed out that, even though he realized the two had always been opponents, he confessed that he had been a constant *Tribune* reader for years, so that he could "obtain a knowledge of the principles and policy of the Republican party, from their ablest and most influential expounder."

But Buchanan could not really forgive Greeley. The wounds were too deep. Writing to another New York supporter, Manton Marble, editor of the New York *World,* on January 30, 1867, to thank him for "the vindication of my views against Mr. Greeley's assault," he declared: "No man who was not on the spot at the time can justly appreciate the influence which the *Tribune* exerted in inducing the Southern people to believe they might secede with impunity. Against Mr. Greeley I have no feeling of hostility. He is often guided by honest & generous impulses; but from his nature and 'his head over heels' manner of writing he is incapable of becoming a discriminating and unbiased historian. Accuracy is certainly not his forte."

Nor was it Buchanan's. He collected all the letters to the editor he had written, added still more material, and published them as a book entitled *Mr. Buchanan's Administration on the Eve of the Rebellion.* It was a long and often tedious exercise in self-justification, blaming Congress for failing to stand behind him, accusing cabinet members of betraying their office as well as himself, and, most of all, condemning the press for deluding "the cotton States into the belief that they might leave the Union without serious opposition," as he had first put it in his letter to Marble. In a final salute to the *Tribune,* he charged that it had "contributed much to this delusion." Harking back to the Covode Committee, he recalled that the first knowledge he had of testimony before it had come from the New York journals opposing him.

No amount of letter writing or book-length self-justification, however, could hide the fact that it was Buchanan's weakness as a leader that had encouraged Southern extremists to press their advantage. It also made possible the formation of a strong Northern faction in open revolt against administration measures and encouraged the Republicans to be more resolute in their opposition to slavery. His lack of force quickened the conflict by steeping one party in pretensions and goading the other to desperate resistance.

Lincoln: The Triumph of Power

Standing at the foot of this Everest of presidents, we can only gaze up at the lofty summit with awe, not simply for who he was but for the vast range of peaks looming up behind him—the mountains of explication of what he did. Lincoln and the Civil War he presided over have become an industry, manned by an army of specialists, subspecialists, and ardent amateurs, churning out books and monographs without end. Snowfalls of revisionism and counterrevisionism have fallen on these mountains, and all we can be certain of is that there will never be a consensus school of historians about Lincoln and the war. The best and most respected of synthesizers could not now produce a work that would be immune to attack.

Even in the relatively narrow area with which the present volume deals, there are at least two books devoted entirely to Lincoln's relationships with the press and many other books and monographs concerned with various aspects of it. Curiously the great landmarks of general history—Allan Nevins's eight volumes, J. G. Randall's several studies, among others, as well as the work of Kenneth Stampp and other revisionists of our time—pay scant attention to the role of the press in Lincoln's life, although it was substantial, both before and during his presidency. The implication is that its significance is relatively minor compared with the multitude of other influences surrounding Lincoln and the great conflict. This belief, in fact, seems to be dominant in the work of professional historians of other periods as well. Since the press is seen by them as an unreliable source for their scholarly investigations, the tendency is to denigrate, or simply ignore, its influence on men and events.

This belief could be challenged on a broad front, but in the case of Lincoln it

seems particularly inappropriate because he, of all the presidents, was most involved with the press, owed the most to it, and suffered the most from it. There
were also far larger matters involved. In Lincoln's administration the issue of
press freedom arose for the first time since the War of 1812, in terms dwarfing
the partisan wrangling of the earlier conflict. The Constitution had not foreseen
civil war, and so severe a test of the First Amendment had never been envisioned. There were no precedents to guide Lincoln in resolving the conflict between press freedom and what would now be called national security; he had to
make his own decisions, and in retrospect it can be seen they were not always the
right ones. There developed an unprecedented struggle between the federal government and an opposition press far surpassing anything that had been seen before, strong enough to threaten the Union that Lincoln had dedicated himself to
saving. His first concerns, of course, were the battlefronts where the struggle was
being fought out amid dreadful carnage, but at home he had to fight another war,
with a so-called Copperhead press that opposed him savagely, creating a major
problem with a variety of ramifications.

The conflict extended even to the papers that supported him. Here the issue
was how much freedom the press should have in reporting the war from the front
and how free from criticism the commanders in the field should be. The generals
were inclined to brook no such freedom and took matters into their own hands
until they were restrained. With one that proved nearly impossible. Gen. William
Tecumseh Sherman carried on a private war with the correspondents, and, in the
case of a *Herald* reporter whom he insisted on treating as a spy, precipitated an
issue so explosive that the president was compelled to act, as we shall see.

The Republicans, and Lincoln, came to power in 1860 not only because they
were far better organized than they had been four years earlier; they now also had
an array of newspapers supporting them of a strength and character not seen
before. The era of what has come to be called "personal journalism" was in full
sway by this time. Journalism had always been personal, if nothing else, but now
the leading newspapers were in the hands of formidable editors, reaching larger
audiences than ever before, largely independent of political subsidy as a whole.
They offered to politicians not a fanatical, screaming party press as in the past
(although fanaticism and screaming had far from gone out of style) but a national
debating platform. As Allan Nevins has observed, "What gave power over opinion to the great Republican journals . . . was the homogeneity of their audiences,
the vogue of their weekly editions in village and country, and the power with
which they combined editorial argument and news-gathering vigor."

Who were these new editors? In New York there was preeminently Horace
Greeley, whose rising importance we have already observed. Greeley was a master showman, an amiable medicine man, an eccentric with high principles, a
mass of unresolved contradictions. A biographer, William Harlan Hale, describes his "moon-faced stare, his flopping trousers, his squeaky slang, his sput-
tering profanities, his unpredictable oddities, and his general air of an owlish,
rustic sage." Wearing his frock coat and white hat, Greeley was highly visible to
New Yorkers, with his "round moon-face, eyes blinking through spectacles, and

a fringe of whiskers that invited the pencil of the cartoonist,'' as Vernon Parrington has described him.

The leading editor of his time was also a legendary eccentric. People repeated stories about him with more affection than scorn. They told how Greeley, an ardent vegetarian, once absentmindedly ate a large steak under the impression that it was graham bread. On another occasion a visitor poured out a tirade in his office, and when the editor seemed to be paying no attention, exclaimed, "I've treated you like a gentleman, which obviously you're not." To which Uncle Horace responded mildly, "Who in hell ever said I was?" He was a strong-minded man who kept a goat in the backyard behind his house on East Nineteenth Street and refused to give it up when his neighbors complained.

In the *Tribune,* Greeley created a newspaper as legendary as he was, a training ground for other editors, a forum for every liberal idea directed to the betterment of humanity, without regard for its real merits, since the editor's agile mind leaped from idea to idea, like Eliza among the ice floes, and he was likely to go whooping off after another before his readers had fully absorbed one. He had worked his way up from poverty to affluence on his journey to becoming the foremost editor in the nation.

Greeley deployed a news staff that was unexcelled. Washington correspondence was sometimes written by Charles Anderson Dana, later the noted editor of the *Sun* and soon to be a "spy" for Lincoln; he was also city editor, and rose to be managing editor. J. S. Pike covered the capital, too, and sometimes the Washington news bore the byline of "H.G." himself. Whoever wrote it, the result could be guaranteed as both colorful and expert. Other correspondents covered the Western regions and even the South, their reports tending toward emphasis on the agricultural; farmers were prime readers of the *Weekly Tribune,* the auxiliary in which much of Greeley's influence reposed. A brilliant editorial page was written by Dana, Greeley, George Ripley, and others—"a magnificent combination of argument, invective, and news," as Nevins puts it. Margaret Fuller was literary editor for a time, and Bayard Taylor contributed travel sketches and occasional editorials. Karl Marx was briefly the paper's London correspondent, but he quit when Greeley cut his $10-a-week salary to $5.

New York papers either Republican or leaning in that direction also included William Cullen Bryant's *Evening Post* and the most recent addition, Henry J. Raymond's New York *Times.* Raymond had gotten his training on the *Tribune* before founding his own paper, which meant to be nonpartisan in a highly partisan period. Its owner was a born middle-of-the-roader, but paradoxically he was also in love with politics. While he preached rational fairness in the columns of his paper, he practiced Whig and then Republican politics in the state legislature and elsewhere.

There was always Bennett to be considered, and the Republicans never failed to consider him, but he could never be depended upon. Bennett was much more of an opportunist than the others, an eccentric whose eccentricity sometimes could not be distinguished from simple flamboyance. His son, now in training as a careless man-about-town, would demonstrate what real eccentricity was when he took over the paper after the war.

Outside New York there were Republican stalwarts like Samuel Bowles and his Springfield *Republican,* Joseph Medill and the Chicago *Tribune,* the Philadelphia *Press,* and the Cleveland *Leader.* Party organizers were also busy, in the traditional way, trying to bolster the circulations of other Republican papers, and they encouraged people to read such magazines as the *National Era* and the *Independent,* both of them powerful and influential in the shaping of political opinion toward Republican goals.

It was significant that "the press" now had to include these and other magazines. The ideological issues of the day were debated in them, often at greater length than in the newspapers, and their readers were likely to be what we call opinion makers today. *Harper's Weekly,* for example, carried well-written articles from Washington and by people in public life; during the war it rivaled the best newspapers in battlefield coverage, far surpassing them in one sense because of its superb pictures, primarily woodcuts.

As Herbert Mitgang reminds us, the press of Lincoln's time "was a direct, unpolled reflection of the shades and fervor of clashing public ideologies." For this and other reasons, the Civil War years were a major transition point in the history of American journalism, and one feels the temptation to discuss its role in the Civil War more broadly. But it will be more than enough here to focus on Lincoln's relations with it, which are extensive, well documented, and unique in the history of the presidency itself.

No president, until Warren G. Harding, came into office with a better understanding of the press and how it worked. Although he lived in a village as small as New Salem, Illinois, during his early years Lincoln was not sequestered in some rural backwater. The level of education and sophistication in New Salem was well above that of most small towns, much of it the result of a small flood of newspapers from everywhere in the nation flowing into the post office where Lincoln presided for a time as postmaster, and many of which he read. Until then, growing up in the back country of Indiana, he had first been introduced to newspapers, according to Harlan Hoyt Horner, one of his numerous biographers, by neighbors who passed on to him copies of the Louisville *Journal* and other Midwestern papers. By the time he was ready to leave Indiana for Illinois in 1831, he had acquired the newspaper habit.

Arriving in New Salem, Sangamon County, Illinois, in that year, Lincoln became at once a devoted reader of the local weekly, the *Sangamon Journal* (later the *Illinois Journal*), whose slogan was "Not the glory of Caesar, but the Welfare of Rome." It had just been founded by Simeon Francis, and for the remainder of Lincoln's life it was to be his home-town supporter and never failing ally. Moreover, his life became involved with the Francis family. It was the editor's wife, Rebecca, who brought Lincoln and Mary Todd together again after their failed engagement. Francis himself remained a devoted admirer of Lincoln, so much so that he virtually turned over the columns of his paper to the young politician. William Herndon, Lincoln's law partner, tells us, "Whatever he wrote, or had written, went into the editorial page without question." Editor and aspiring politico spent long hours together in the new brick building fronting on the Public Square, "north-west of the Court House, Up Stairs."

Lincoln used a newspaper for political purposes when he wrote a letter to the editor of the *Journal* that appeared on June 13, 1836, endorsing Hugh L. White for president. Lincoln was then twenty-seven years old and a candidate for re-election to the Illinois state legislature. It was not the first time he had appeared in the *Journal,* however; on March 15, 1832, he had announced his candidacy for the General Assembly in a "Communication to the People of Sangamon County," signed "Your friend and fellow-citizen, A. Lincoln."

Later, as a practicing lawyer in Springfield as well as a politician, Lincoln was embroiled with the partisan press when he carried on a running feud with the *Illinois State Register* of Springfield, which charged him with trying to swing public printing to the *Journal* and, as part of the Springfield Junto, with hand-picking candidates for United States representative. He endured much worse in the violent campaign of 1840, when he supported Harrison and was himself reelected for a fourth term in the state legislature.

Elected to Congress in 1846, Lincoln came upon the national scene and was soon drawn into the controversy over the Mexican War. He strongly favored the Whig position that the war was "unnecessarily and unconstitutionally commenced by the President." When he introduced resolutions in the House demanding that Polk disclose the exact "spot"—a word he used eight times—where Americans had first been killed by Mexicans, he drew the fire at home of his old enemy, the *Register,* which led the Democratic papers in calling him "Spotty" Lincoln and otherwise vilifying him.

Lincoln had already been noticed by the editor who would be perhaps the most important factor in his presidential press relations, Horace Greeley. Before going to Washington the congressman-elect had attended a river-and-harbor convention in Chicago, covered by newspapermen from the great Eastern cities, among them Greeley. When Lincoln was bold enough to reply to a statement by the well-known New York lawyer, David Dudley Field, Greeley carefully recorded for his *Tribune:* "Hon. Abraham Lincoln, a tall specimen of an Illinoisan, just elected to Congress from the only Whig District in the state, was called out, and spoke briefly and happily in reply to Mr. Field." Greeley himself served briefly in Congress, filling a vacancy, in 1848, and although Lincoln addressed him as "Friend Greeley," they were already at odds.

After a second term in the House, Lincoln returned to his law practice in Springfield, where he was beginning to be involved with the growing question of slavery, avidly following the course of the controversy in the pages of the seven newspapers to which he subscribed: on the Northern or antislavery side, the Chicago *Tribune,* Greeley's *Tribune,* the *Anti-Slavery Standard,* the *Emancipator,* and the *National Era;* and on the other side, the Charleston *Mercury* and the Richmond *Enquirer.* He also read the party's organ, the *National Intelligencer,* and the Washington *Congressional Globe.*

When Sen. Stephen A. Douglas introduced the Kansas-Nebraska Act in 1854, which repealed the Missouri Compromise, Lincoln entered the lists against a man whom he had already debated here and there and would debate historically again. He began with an editorial in the *Journal,* and when the extension of slavery began to be a serious national issue, the argument was transferred to the speaking platform. Then, as events moved more rapidly, Lincoln was propelled into the heat of the national spotlight. The Kansas-Nebraska Act had become the focus of controversy, precipitating such unseemly acts as the caning of Sen. Charles Sumner of Massachusetts in the Senate chamber by Congressman Preston Brooks of South Carolina. A week later, the Republican party had its formal birth in Illinois, as some historians contend, at a convention in Bloomington, where Lincoln, as delegate from Sangamon County, made his now famous Lost Speech.

This "grand effort" of Lincoln's life, as Herndon called it, was heard by some of the leading newspapermen in the Middle West. One was John L. Scripps, editor of the Chicago *Press.* Among the others were Joseph Medill, part owner and manager (at that point) of the Chicago *Tribune* (briefly the *Press and Tribune*), and his partner and editor Dr. Charles H. Ray. Yet the speech was never published, although it was lauded editorially in extravagant terms. Scripps, for example, wrote of it in his paper:

> Abram Lincoln [a frequent misspelling that followed him into the White House] of Springfield was next called out, and made the speech of the occasion. Never has it been our fortune to listen to a more eloquent and masterly presentation of a subject. . . . For an hour and a half he held the assemblage spell-bound by the power of his argument, the intense irony of his invective, and the deep earnestness and fervid brilliancy of his eloquence. When he concluded, the audience sprang to their feet, and cheer after cheer told how deeply their hearts had been touched, and their souls warmed up to a generous enthusiasm.

Yet not one of those eminent reporters and editors present gave their readers the speech in its entirety. For years it was generally accepted that they had all been in the same state as Medill in his well-publicized admission that he had not taken any notes because he was in a "sort of hypnotic trance, forgot what he was there for, and joined in the wild applause and cheering along with the others in the crowd." When he recovered he found he had taken only a few notes, and the other newspapermen were in the same condition.

This is a most unlikely story. Robert Harper, a historian of Lincoln's press relations, speculates that the speech was "lost" deliberately. There was no opposition press present, because editors tended to ignore the opposition at the local level and often did not report what the other party was doing. In this case, it was well known to the Republican papers who *were* represented that this was going to be a radical antislavery convention; the managers of it had imported some antislavery agitators from Kansas for the occasion, even though up to that time, for purely political reasons, the new Republicans had shied away from being branded as abolitionists. But Lincoln had nonetheless given what was unquestionably an abolitionist speech, and a brilliant one. Being good party men as well as editors, it may be, as Harper says, that they imposed a self-censorship to avoid being labeled a little while longer.

Whatever the reason, the Bloomington speech had another result. Presumably it convinced Joseph Medill and Charles Ray that Lincoln was a man to watch and to push toward greater things. While many historians have given them short shrift in chronicling Lincoln's rise to the presidency, the evidence is impressive that it was their politicking and their *Tribune*'s influence, more than anything else, that were responsible for Lincoln's nomination in 1860.

The relationship soon became a close one. Medill and Ray, along with four other financial partners, had rescued the Chicago *Tribune* from its financial problems in 1855, eight years after its founding by John Scripps and two businessmen, and by 1859 the paper was surpassed in power and influence only by its namesake in New York. Already it had established an editorial pattern that would be perpetuated into the twentieth century—aggressive, opinionated, extensive in its news coverage, and always highly political. Even at that early date it believed that God was on its side, a conviction it shared with its hated Eastern rival, the New York *Herald*. As an early and firm supporter of Lincoln, it referred to Douglas and the Democrats as the "anti-American party."

In a study of Medill that is still regarded as the best extant, Tracy Elmer Strevey sums up the editor's character as follows: "Medill was clearly a devout Republican from the beginning and throughout this entire period never deviated from the platform of his party nor from the principles for which it stood. He was intensely partisan and apt to take extreme views. . . . He looked upon the Republican party as the product, in part at least, of his own efforts." Medill boasted, and with some accuracy, that Chicago was "the pet Republican city of the Union, the point from which radiate opinions which more or less influence six states." To which the neighboring Cleveland *Plain Dealer* replied acidly, "The principal productions of Chicago are corner lots, statistics and wind."

Medill did not support Lincoln without preliminary hesitation. He admired some of the other Republican hopefuls, particularly his friend Salmon P. Chase, but in the end he settled on Lincoln because, as he said candidly, "The one committed to the cause and who can concentrate the greatest number of votes is the man." That led to the *Tribune*'s historic editorial of February 16, 1860, urging Lincoln's nomination, followed by a Medill report from Washington, where he had gone to write a series of letters intended to launch Lincoln as a candidate and to lobby for him in Congress.

By this time Lincoln was clearly the leading candidate, as far as the Middle West was concerned, and his oratorical powers, although homely as opposed to the orotundity of Douglas's speeches, had made him much in demand as a speaker. But he needed greater exposure, and so welcomed the invitation from the Young Men's Central Republican Union of New York in February 1860 to speak on February 27 in New York. The letter was addressed to "Abram Lincoln." Obviously the East needed to know him better.

On the way to New York, Lincoln stopped off in Chicago to consult Medill and Ray about his speech, showing them the manuscript and asking if they would look it over. The editors were only too glad to oblige. Understanding the importance of this appearance, they were eager that their candidate make the best possible showing. As Medill described their work later:

Ray and I buckled down to the delicate task. One read slowly while the other listened attentively, and the reading was frequently interrupted to consider suggested improvements of diction, the insertion of synonyms, or points to render the text smoother or strong, as it seemed to us. Thus we toiled for some hours, till the revision was completed to our satisfaction, and we returned to the office early next morning to re-examine our work before Lincoln would call for the revised and improved manuscript. When he came in we handed him our numerous notes with the reference places carefully marked on the margins of the pages where each emendation was to be inserted. We turned over the address to him with a self-satisfied feeling that we had considerably bettered the document and enabled it to pass the critical ordeal more triumphantly than otherwise it would. Lincoln thanked us cordially for our trouble, glanced at our notes, told us a funny story or two of which the circumstances reminded him, and took his leave.

When Medill and Ray finally got the text of that famous Cooper Union speech from New York, as it was printed in Greeley's *Tribune,* they looked eagerly for the evidences of their handiwork. There were none; Lincoln had not used even one of their suggestions. "Abe must have lost the notes out the car window," Ray said.

It was Lincoln's first direct contact with the New York press, and he scored a triumph, at least with the papers friendly to him. He was introduced to an audience of 1,500 people who had braved a snowstorm—the greatest gathering of "intellect and moral culture" since the days of Clay and Webster, said the New York *Tribune*—by William Cullen Bryant, editor of the *Evening Post.* Greeley was among those on the stage, prepared to speak briefly after Lincoln finished. In the front row sat men with pads and pencils—reporters from all the leading papers.

Afterward Greeley invited Lincoln to the *Tribune*'s offices to read proofs of his speech. If he had read the account of it that Noah Brooks, the *Tribune*'s reporter, was writing, he would certainly have been flattered: "The tones, the gestures, the kindling eye, and the mirth-provoking look defy the reporter's skill. The vast assemblage frequently rang with cheers and shouts of applause. No man ever before made such an impression on his first appeal to a New York audience." Next morning, reading the papers in the lobby of the Astor House, where he was staying, Lincoln was happy to see that four of them had reprinted the speech in full, and he was told there would also be a pamphlet reprint. The *Tribune*'s coverage was highly laudatory, as one would expect. The *Times* was brief (one paragraph) but friendly. In the *Evening Post,* Bryant echoed the *Tribune*'s enthusiasm. The opposition papers ignored him, again as expected.

Events moved rapidly toward the nominating convention in Chicago, where a huge barn of a place called the Wigwam had been erected on the site of the old Sauganash Hotel, at the corner of Lake and Market streets. Five hundred delegates and more than forty thousand onlookers of one kind or another gathered there in May. Seward, regarded as Lincoln's foremost contender, arrived without the support of either Greeley or Medill. Ray, Medill, and the leading Midwestern Republicans had been working since December on their plan to nominate Lincoln, a plan based on horse trading, in the style of fundamental democratic politics.

While the Chicago *Tribune*'s editors and others worked the convention floor, a half-dozen or more party stalwarts were busy in the Tremont House, Lincoln's headquarters (he himself remained at home), securing the votes of such important states as Pennsylvania and Indiana. Promises of offices in exchange for votes were traded freely, entirely without the candidate's knowledge. Ray told Medill, "We are going to have Indiana for Old Abe, sure." "How did you get it?" Medill wanted to know. "By the Lord, we promised them everything they asked," Ray told him.

That was typical of what was occurring. Nevertheless, after the first day's balloting, Seward appeared to be so certain of winning that his people prematurely opened up three hundred bottles of champagne at his headquarters. Greeley was among those already convinced. He filed two successive dispatches expressing his conviction that Seward was a sure thing. But when Lincoln's name was presented to the convention, Murat Halstead, then of the Cincinnati *Daily Commercial,* wrote of the demonstration that followed: "Imagine all the hogs ever slaughtered in Cincinnati giving their death squeals together. . . . I thought the Seward yell could not be surpassed; but the Lincoln boys . . . made every plank and pillar in the building quiver. The New York, Michigan, and Wisconsin delegations sat . . . very quiet. Many . . . faces whitened."

The trading had nearly done its work, even though Lincoln had telegraphed from Springfield, "I authorize no bargains and will be bound by none." But when his managers were confronted with this blunt statement, one of them solved the impasse by exclaiming, "Lincoln ain't here, and don't know what we have to meet, so we will go ahead as if we hadn't heard from him, and he must ratify it." Trading continued unabated.

After the second ballot Lincoln was on the edge of victory, and Medill whispered in the ear of David Carter, a lawyer from Massillon, Ohio, that Chase (for whom the Ohio delegation was still holding) could have anything he wanted if the state swung to Lincoln. A switch of four votes in the delegation was required, and Carter got them. Halstead argued afterward that other delegations were clamoring for recognition at that moment, more than enough to ensure Lincoln's nomination, but the chairman's eye had fallen on Carter first; when the convention was over, there was some newspaper speculation about the identity of the Ohio men who had changed their votes. In any event, and in spite of what Lincoln had said, Carter was rewarded by being appointed minister to Bolivia, and later the president named him chief justice of the District of Columbia Supreme Court.

Abraham Lincoln was duly nominated, and there was a great outburst of emotional tension from the delegates, which spread across the city and into the nation. Thurlow Weed found it hard to hold back tears; all he had worked for was lost. Greeley wrote to a friend that it was a fearful week, and he hoped never to see it repeated. In the *Times,* Henry Raymond charged that Greeley had gone to Chicago solely to preside over the defeat of Seward and that Lincoln's nomination was "purely an accident." The editorial battle between them was widely circulated in other newspapers and did not augur well for the unity that the Republican party now badly needed—and was not to attain, as disgruntled Republican editors, unhappy over the convention's choice, joined the Democratic press in fighting Lincoln during the campaign. As for Greeley, Seward and Weed got their revenge the following year when the editor sought the nomination for senator and was beaten as a result of Weed's behind-the-scenes maneuvering.

If the story of Lincoln's rise to the presidency seems overly familiar, it is rehearsed here only to underscore the vital role in it that was played by influential editors and their newspapers and by Lincoln's own knowledge of the press and how to use it, which was far greater than any of those who had preceded him. In fact, the intimate relationship with the press that Lincoln had already displayed was unprecedented, and there was much more to come.

After his nomination the candidate was in frequent correspondence with various important editors, particularly Medill, who volunteered that he intended to go to New York and call on "His Satanic Majesty," meaning Bennett, to attempt to win his support, or at least his neutrality. The latter was a vain hope indeed, but Medill explained that it would be better than his support, which might mean a political kiss of death in some quarters. Medill had a carrot ready to offer, he told Lincoln. Bennett did not need money, but his ambition was to bring his wife and son to the White House as guests of the president.

For a short time Springfield became a center of editorial activity. Ray came down to offer his advice. George D. Prentice, poet-editor of the Louisville *Journal,* arrived in an attempt to convince himself that Lincoln could lead the country. Greeley stopped off during a lecture tour to discuss matters, and incidentally to suggest the names of *Tribune* men he thought ideally qualified for diplomatic posts. John Forney, editor of the Philadelphia *Press,* came to talk about a cabinet appointment and the possibility of government printing contracts. A faithful recorder of these events was Henry Villard, now covering the candidate for the *Herald,* the Cincinnati *Daily Commercial,* and the *Missouri Democrat.* This young reporter, only twenty-five, an immigrant who still took notes in his native German script, was soon to play a role in the Lincoln press drama and in time become one of the nation's most noted editors.

As the campaign developed that autumn, it was soon apparent that the country was witnessing one of the most ferocious newspaper wars it had yet seen, which was saying a great deal. For that matter, it has hardly been exceeded since. Nor was it taking place only in the North. The conflict was even worse in the South, where three parties had emerged, each convinced that it was the only one to defeat Lincoln, the "Black Republican," as he was known to them. One scholar, Robert S. Cotterill, has written, "Every Southern political editorial contained the ingredients of a duel; many of them were potential invitations to homicide." In fact, several editors were involved in acts of violence, recalling the bloodier days of the early partisan press. Reading the Southern papers, which were fighting it out for their individual candidates, it was possible to believe that any one of them was a greater enemy than Lincoln. In the last month of the campaign they were united on only one thing—the question of whether the South would submit to Lincoln's election. The answer was no.

Lincoln was depicted as the personification of evil, a man who would, if elected, destroy the South and all her institutions. A particularly vivid picture of what might happen was drawn by the Corsicana (Texas) *Navarro Express:* "As soon as Lincoln is installed into office . . . he will wave his black plume Southward. With the army and navy . . . he will invade us. He will issue his ukase, enfranchising the negroes, and arming them; he will confiscate property, and commend us to the mercy of torch and steel. Of this we are not left to doubt."

The Southern press hinted that there was black blood in the Republican ticket itself, and some of its editors retailed the allegation that Lincoln's running mate, Hannibal Hamlin, was a mulatto. One Alabama paper inquired wrathfully: "A free nigger to preside in the United States Senate: How would Southern Senators like that? The humiliation and disgrace of the thing would certainly be something, but the smell would be awful." A Memphis paper simply took it for granted that Hamlin had black blood, for, as it said, "in all the acquirements of mind, manners, morals, form, features, complexion, woolly hair and all, he comes nearer being a negro than any one we have ever seen who claimed to be a white man." This must have been something of a surprise to Hamlin, who came from Maine and looked as New England as a Downeaster could.

Submission was out of the question, the Southern rights editors insisted vehemently, and since they believed to a man that emancipation was the ultimate goal of Lincoln and his party, secession would be the only alternative to racial equality and equal political rights for blacks, both of which were universally abhorred in the South. There were a great many doubters in the North, too, where the abolitionists did not reign supreme, as many Americans think to this day. The Republican press was sharply divided over Lincoln and the direction the party was taking. That, combined with the fact that Lincoln was still such an unknown quantity to most voters—some journals still could not decide whether he was "Abram" or "Abraham"—accounted in large measure for the closeness of the election, although many other factors were involved. Lincoln won only 39.8 percent of the popular vote, and his electoral vote was just 180, twenty-eight more than he needed for election. He had carried the large Northern states by a substantial margin, and that proved to be decisive.

The result stunned the Southern papers, as though the reality of the outcome they had so frequently predicted and dreaded was too hard to believe. The future looked so grim to them that it perversely inspired caution, and a few papers in the upper South began looking over Lincoln's speeches and trying to find some reassuring conservatism about slavery in them. There appeared to be a general feeling in the Southern journals that Lincoln might well follow a policy of conciliation for the benefit of all, and, in any case, there was no precedent by which to measure what a new party like the Republicans would do.

Greeley had tried to soothe the common agitation in the North by predicting editorially that Lincoln would restore harmony and that peace was still possible. He was not widely believed. The phrase "irrepressible conflict," derived from one of Seward's speeches, was the catchword of the day, even seeping into advertising when Knox, a New York hatter, proclaimed that he, too, was irrepressible and would keep on selling "the best, the neatest and most stylish hats and caps in the city at the very lowest prices."

In Washington itself the news of Lincoln's election was received in a Southern spirit, as the *Herald* reported:

> "The effect . . . upon the people of this District can be more easily imagined than described. There is no place in the United States where the officeholders, for nearly everybody has an office—feel it more disastrously. The defeat of Lincoln was a matter of life and death with them, and when it was announced that he was elected, curses loud and deep went up from these infuriated individuals. They were for forming a Southern Confederacy at once, and some of the more resolute and determined donned the cockade, and indicated their willingness to shoulder their muskets and resist the inauguration of Lincoln."

Events were rapidly moving beyond control. In December the retiring Buchanan delivered his contradictory message to Congress, asserting that states had no right to secede, but at the same time arguing that neither Congress nor president had a right to coerce individual states. Sen. John J. Crittenden of Kentucky proposed a Peace Congress in an effort to avoid disunion, but South Carolina responded on December 20 by voting at a state convention to secede. Mississippi, Florida, Alabama, Georgia, Louisiana, and Texas followed within a few weeks. In Charleston, Maj. Robert Anderson moved his garrison from Fort Moultrie to Fort Sumter and prepared to defend it. Early in January a mob destroyed the printshop of a Galveston newspaper that had published an editorial against secession. In February the seceding states formed the Confederate States of America in Montgomery, Alabama, with Jefferson Davis as provisional president. The stage for a national tragedy of epic proportions was set.

Meanwhile, in Springfield, the president-elect was preparing to make the long trip to Washington and preside over a disintegrating nation. Bennett sent his best man, Henry Villard, to cover the event. It proved to be a wise choice because this young reporter, who had been an immigrant unable to speak or write English only a few years before, was now one of the best newspapermen in the nation, and his subsequent dispatches provided a clear and objective view of the new president. He had already won distinction through his coverage of the Lincoln-Douglas debates, so that when he reached Springfield he was given a cordial welcome as one who had shared the rigors of the campaign trail. Lincoln introduced him at once to John G. Nicolay, his new secretary, and the equally new assistant secretary, John Hay, only twenty-two, who had been a reporter for the *Missouri Democrat*.

Villard reported carefully and vividly on the president-elect's daily routine, particularly on the overwhelming flood of visitors, all of them wanting something, and the noxious tide of hate mail threatening Lincoln's life. Wild rumors were set afloat, and requests for denial came from worried supporters like Raymond of the *Times*. Bryant officiously attempted to tell Lincoln who should be in his cabinet. Thurlow Weed arrived and expressed satisfaction that his man, Seward, was to be secretary of state. Most of all, however, there was the steady flow of office seekers in and out of Springfield, numbering as always a good many editors and correspondents who had supported Lincoln. Among them was Greeley, who firmly denied that he was seeking any office but nevertheless spent hours with Lincoln. Writing of this interview in the third person, he reported that Mr. Greeley had not asked "anything either for himself or friends."

At last it was time. On February 11, a chill, drizzly day, Lincoln climbed onto his special train, spoke a few heartfelt, somber words to a weeping crowd of friends and well-wishers, and set off for Washington. Aboard with him was Villard, the only correspondent from a metropolitan paper, who was already reproaching himself for not taking down Lincoln's parting remarks—indeed, a curious omission in so good a reporter. He asked the president-elect if he would repeat what he had said extemporaneously, and Lincoln obligingly wrote it down for him, in a somewhat more polished style. Villard incorporated that text into the story he filed at the next stop, and wrote of the occasion: "Toward the conclusion of his remarks himself and audience were moved to tears. His exhortation to pray elicited choked exclamations of 'We will do it; we will do it.' As he turned to enter the cars three cheers were given and a few seconds afterward the train moved slowly out of the sight of the silent gathering."

II

Abraham Lincoln came to Washington with the closest associations to the most responsible elements of the press that any president had ever enjoyed, and with the avowed purpose of preserving the Constitution that he would swear to defend on Inauguration Day. During the next four years, as Arthur Schlesinger, Jr., tells us, this is what he did:

> He asserted the right to proclaim martial law behind the lines, to arrest people without warrant, to seize property, to suppress newspapers, to prevent the use of the post office for treasonable correspondence, to emancipate slaves, to lay out a plan of reconstruction. His proclamations, executive orders and military regulations invaded fields previously the domain of legislative action. All this took place without a declaration of war by Congress.

Lincoln suspended *habeas corpus,* a keystone of democratic free government, and he suppressed newspapers. But as Schlesinger notes, there was never an effective censorship imposed by his administration, and Lincoln repudiated most of the attempts at it, nor was any Sedition Act in the John Adams vein ever proposed, or an espionage act either, although there was some justification for both, since the press displayed a reckless disregard of what today would be secret information about the movement of troops.

Why did Lincoln behave in what might appear superficially to be a contradictory way? First and foremost, it was because he had dedicated himself wholly to the preservation of the Union, a principle he placed above the abolition of slavery. If that meant he had to invoke the last refuge of tyrants—the end justifying the means—he was prepared to do it for the sake of a whole nation. But because he understood so well how important the press was to the conduct of the war, far beyond what it would do for him personally, he stretched toleration of its excesses to the breaking point.

If reporters in the field on occasion seemed to think themselves as important as the commanders, he would overlook it. If editors appeared to take on the task of running the war themselves, he would ignore them as diplomatically as possible. That it was a forbearance routinely abused is made plain by the historian J. G. Randall, who reminds us: "The location of Grant's guns secretly placed against Vicksburg in 1863 was published; his proposed concentration upon City Point in July, 1864, was revealed; Sherman's objectives in his Georgia march and the disposition of his various corps were proclaimed; full details concerning the land and sea expedition against Wilmington, North Carolina, in December, 1864, were supplied." The South could get more information from Northern reporters than from its own spies, Schlesinger adds, and Robert E. Lee became a devoted reader of the Northern papers. In his second inaugural address the president observed dryly: "The progress of our arms, upon which all else chiefly depends, is as well known to the public as to myself."

Yet, for all that, the press proved to be as indispensable to Lincoln as it was to the public. The latter depended on it for news of what was taking place on the battlefields, for the long listings of those killed and wounded. This was vital information that only daily newspapers could supply, and although war raged on the editorial pages as well, it was the news pages that mattered most. So great was the demand that the press flourished as it never had before in terms of circulation. People in general were against Sunday newspapers, and many deplored the generals' insistence on Sunday fighting, but, rather than let a day go by without news, they would accept a Sunday edition, especially if the papers placed a Sunday dateline on the first page and a Monday one inside. Morning and afternoon editions of the same paper appeared for the first time, and there were sometimes afternoon "extras" of other papers. The Chicago *Tribune* began to publish three editions—morning, afternoon, and evening—in December 1861.

It could reasonably be said that the press came of age in these war years, for the first time understanding that the chief business of a newspaper in a free society is to provide news. Celebrating its fiftieth anniversary in 1901, the New York *Times,* looking back on its early years, noted that

it was during the civil war that the New York newspapers [and others as well, it could have said] gained their first realizing sense of two fundamental principles that have made them what they are today—first, the surpassing value of individual, competitive, triumphant enterprise in getting early and exclusive news, and second, the possibility of building up large circulations by striving unceasingly to meet a popular demand for prompt and adequate reports of the day-to-day doings of mankind the world over.

To Lincoln the press was indispensable for somewhat the same reason. It was his direct link to the battlefields, not simply from what the papers reported but the firsthand accounts given to him by correspondents (they were called "specials," and by themselves, "bohemians") who often came from the front directly to his office to make personal reports. He was close to the Washington correspondents as well, treating a few of them as familiars. Whether their editors were for him or against him, Lincoln did not often make invidious distinctions, although it was only natural for him to favor the representatives of friendly editors, what few of them there were.

Lincoln set the tone of his press relations as soon as he arrived in Washington. At the Union Ball celebrating his inauguration, Stephen Fiske of the *Herald* asked him if there was any message he could take back to his boss. "Yes," Lincoln said in that half-jocular way that endeared him to many and outraged others. "You may tell him that Thurlow Weed has found out that Seward was not nominated at Chicago." When the president did not immediately perform miracles during his first month in office, and the *Tribune* was demanding irritably, "Come to the Point!" Raymond went down to Washington for a talk with him and was told, "I am like a man so busy in letting rooms in one end of his house, that he can't stop to put out the fire that is burning in the other."

Journalists from abroad who came to examine the new Yankee phenomenon found it hard to understand what was going on. When William Howard Russell arrived to represent the London *Times,* he was greeted like a visiting dignitary and presented to the president by Secretary Seward. "I'm very glad to make your acquaintance," Lincoln told him, shaking hands, "and to see you in this country. The London *Times* is one of the greatest powers in the world—in fact, I don't know anything which has much more power—except perhaps the Mississippi. I am glad to know you as its minister." The two men talked for a moment, and, as Russell reported later, their conversation was "enlivened by 2 or 3 peculiar little sallies, and I left agreeably impressed with his shrewdness, humour, and natural sagacity."

Lincoln already knew that he had to be on his guard against reporters less well certified than Russell. There had been the strange case upon his arrival in Washington when a journalist named Joseph Howard, purporting to represent the New York *Times,* had wired to that paper an account of the president-elect's coming in which he wrote: "He wore a Scotch plaid cap and a very long military cloak, so that he was entirely unrecognizable." The *Times* printed this story, and it quickly spread around the world, presenting Lincoln in an incongruous and ridiculous light.

Howard's imagination, which made him notorious after this and later incidents, was regrettable, but there was a somber story behind the story. So hostile had been the reception at some points along the way between Springfield and the capital, reflected in many of the newspapers, that Lincoln's advisers had persuaded him, against his wishes, to slip through Baltimore, with its Southern sympathies, on a midnight special and in disguise. In New York, Lincoln had been given a new beaver hat and a soft wool hat by a friend, consequently his disguise, he decided, would be the wool hat and an old overcoat he had brought with him. Later he asserted that he never believed he would be assassinated in Baltimore, but had decided not to take any unnecessary risk.

A more accomplished journalistic fraud in Washington was Malcolm Ives, ostensibly a correspondent for the *Herald,* whose past was so checkered it was impossible to be sure of anything in it. His present was clear enough. He was a smooth, plausible, unconscionable liar. A well-dressed, good-looking, black-haired con man, Ives was supposed to have been educated in Rome and Vienna and therefore fluent in several languages. The aura of Europe hung about him. It was said he had been a Catholic convert and a priest who was later unfrocked for writing in unflattering terms about the Spanish Inquisition, and for getting married. In New York, Ives had first worked in the Custom House, a job obtained through the influence of the notorious Copperhead, Mayor Fernando Wood.

Arriving in Washington, Ives established himself in the Willard Hotel, and during the next few weeks he managed to involve himself in a scandalous affair. First, however, he endeared himself to Bennett by sending him a series of confidential dispatches purporting to be inside information from cabinet members and generals, with whom he claimed to be intimate. One February day he went over to the War Department and told Assistant Secretary Peter Watson that unless he was given an exclusive story he would turn the *Herald*'s guns on Stanton's management of the war. Informed of this ultimatum, the secretary, irritated beyond measure by what he considered Bennett's long-range insolence, had Ives arrested and confined to Fort McHenry, in Baltimore, as a spy. (Other versions of this story—and there are many—describe Ives's conduct as even more outrageous.) Bennett gave Ives no support, even denying that he was a regular member of his staff and praising Stanton's prompt action. It could have been, as the historian Bernard A. Weisberger speculates, that the astute editor of the *Herald* simply did not want to endanger his contacts with the War Department and was quite willing to sacrifice Ives.

Another of Bennett's colorful mistakes was Henry Wykoff, an even more plausible liar than Ives, whose road to the boss's heart lay through his flattering, intimate dispatches about Mrs. Lincoln, founded apparently on an actual friendship with the lady, who was otherwise not well liked. But when *Herald* printed the excerpts of Lincoln's December 1863 message to Congress before its delivery, and Wykoff was identified as the source, he was summoned before the House Judiciary Committee. Refusing to disclose his informant, he was confined in the basement of the Old Capitol prison. A surprise (and incredible) witness then appeared before the committee—the White House gardener, a Mr. Watt, who testified under oath that he had seen the message on the president's study table, memorized large parts of it, and passed them on to Wykoff. Before anything else could happen, however, the committee suddenly dropped the entire matter, and Wykoff was released.

The reason was not disclosed for years. Benjamin Perley Poore, the Boston *Evening Journal*'s Washington correspondent, reported that Mrs. Lincoln had been so enchanted by Wykoff's stories about her that she had rewarded him with confidential information, including the president's speech. When he learned about it, Lincoln (or so Perley said) appealed to leading House Republicans to scuttle the inquiry before an unsavory scandal developed. Once more Bennett had been embarrassed by his own reporter, to the enjoyment of his rivals, and only the Cincinnati *Daily Commercial* reminded its readers: "The upshot of the whole disgraceful business will, of course, be to advertise the New York *Herald*—already sufficiently notorious—and no advantage will accrue to the cause of truth and fair dealing."

Clearly Lincoln had to exercise considerable caution in dealing with the correspondents from all over the country who now swarmed about the capital, so unlike previous administrations. He spoke freely, or reasonably so, with many of them, but only one remained on close personal terms with him throughout his presidency. That was Noah Brooks, a young man from Castine, Maine, who began as a house painter but drifted into journalism at age twenty, worked for papers in Boston, and then went west to Dixon, Illinois, where in 1856 he first met and covered Lincoln for the *Telegraph* there. Later he was a Kansas homesteader, journeyed by ox team to California, and in November 1862 went to Washington as a correspondent for the Sacramento *Daily Union*. For that newspaper Brooks wrote a series of 258 dispatches, signed "Castine," which later became a book, *Washington in Lincoln's Time*. As Herbert Mitgang, who edited a recent modern edition, wrote of it, "It is outstanding for its intimacy and insight. The book is filled with insight and anecdote; many of these have been source material in the studies of Lincoln's life and actions in Washington."

Brooks was more than a friendly reporter. He was the president's old friend, was often seen in the White House, and even went with Lincoln on his trips to the front. The president sometimes asked his advice, but Brooks was able to resist what would have inflated the egos of many reporters in such a situation beyond manageable proportions. He never presumed on the relationship, never used it unfairly.

To his journalistic friend Lincoln was candid about his own opinion of the press. It was, he said, likely to be "ahead of the hounds, outrunning events, and exciting expectations to be later dashed into disappointment." On a subsequent occasion he was more explicit. To a *Herald* correspondent he said: "You gentlemen of the press seem to be pretty much like soldiers, who have to go wherever sent, whatever may be the dangers or difficulties in the way. God forbid I should by any rudeness of speech or manner, make your duties any harder than they are. . . . If I am not afraid of you, it is because I feel you are trustworthy. . . . The press has no better friend than I am—no one who is more ready to acknowledge . . . its tremendous power for both good and evil."

While the press conference had not yet become a White House institution, Lincoln was usually so approachable that sometimes he seemed to be conducting a continuous one. Reporters were astonishingly free with him, measured by today's standards, not hesitating to send in inquiries written on their cards even when he was in conference. If he could, Lincoln would come out and answer them in person; otherwise he wrote out his answer on the card and sent it back.

Few of the president's official family approved of such accessibility. Secretary of the Navy Gideon Welles deplored the president's weakness in permitting "the little newsmongers to come around him and be intimate," but he added: "He has great inquisitiveness. Likes to hear all the political gossip as much as Seward.

But the President is honest, sincere, and confiding—traits which are not so prominent in some by whom he is surrounded.''

Of those cabinet members who had better opinions of the press, Seward, Secretary of War Simon Cameron, and Secretary of the Treasury Chase were the most accessible. Seward was highly susceptible to flattery; Cameron was talkative and adept at leaking information helpful to him that would nevertheless not be attributed; Chase was simply a worldly man who knew how to handle reporters. As for the others, a low-grade state of war existed between the press and both Welles and Edwin M. Stanton (later secretary of war), both of whom were disliked with varying degrees of fervor by the reporters, who called Welles ''Marie Antoinette'' and dealt with his assistant, Gustavus Fox, whenever it was possible. Their particular hatred was reserved for Stanton, however. One of the *Herald*'s Washington men wrote to Frederick Hudson, the paper's managing editor: ''Stanton absolutely stinks in the nostrils of the people and the army. His manner has made him offensive to everyone who approaches him.'' Bennett always maintained a battery of guns trained on Stanton; he could never forgive the secretary's jailing of Malcolm Ives, justified though he pretended it was.

Even those in the administration who were most friendly to the press, however, including Lincoln, could not help being appalled at times by the reckless disregard for the truth shown by a few sensational papers and by some of the correspondents in the field. There was sharp criticism from the press itself, in fact, especially in the early days of the war, when several of the Midwestern papers were harshly critical of the New York papers' Washington correspondents and the kind of news they put on the wires. The Cincinnati *Daily Commercial* spoke bluntly:

> The fact is, with these gentlemen it is . . . sensation or nothing. They hang about the Department offices; they button-hole the unhappy ushers; they besiege goers and comers; they read physiognomies; they absorb the contents of all leaky vessels like a sponge; they study hotel registers as faithfully as a monk his breviary; they ''spot'' ''distinguished arrivals'' as quickly as a detective, and pursue them like Death in the Apocalypse. And if these resources fail, there is a bank that never fails, a supply that never gives out, in their fertile imaginations. Rumors are recorded as facts with an amazing indifference, and, like the Fate that unravels in the night what she knits in the day, they contradict as flatly as they publish confidently.

But as one careful historian, J. Cutler Andrews, assures us: ''Much of the inaccuracy in Civil War reporting . . . was accidental, or at least unintentional; comparatively few war reporters were chronic liars. In many cases the misstatements which cropped up in news stories were not so much a matter of willful misrepresentation as they were the result of haste and confusion involved in newsgathering, especially after a battle.''

In the first year of the war, however, it was clear in Washington that a great deal of information was leaking to the enemy, and Lincoln, acting through Secretary Seward, Gen. George B. McClellan, and others, was determined to curb it. Meetings with editors and correspondents were held, at which the press placed the blame on an efficient rebel spy and courier system. That might be so, Mc-Clellan, commanding the Department of the Ohio, told them, but the newspapers must not help them with their work. Ground rules were agreed upon at a conference with him; these were set down in writing and distributed to newspapers in all the "loyal states" and the District. McClellan signed this gentleman's agreement first, followed by representatives of a dozen major papers and the Associated Press. There were only three holdouts. The New York *Times* and the Philadelphia *Press* decided not to send a representative to the conference, and the Chicago *Tribune*'s Washington man said he was too busy to attend.

This document lasted five days, an extremely short life for what could be called a treaty. The War Department abruptly took over the matter, apparently not trusting what McClellan had done, and invoked the Fifty-seventh Article of War of 1806, aimed at spies and traitors. It could also apply to offending newspapermen, the department concluded. Secretary Cameron issued an order, which was approved by the president, and it became General Order No. 67, declaring that "all correspondence and communication verbally, or by writing, printing or telegraphing" concerning army operations, or military and naval establishment affairs, were forbidden, unless consented to by the commanding officer and authorized by him.

No doubt it was because Lincoln knew the press so well, and was so close to it, that he could not bring himself to trust it and consequently approved General Order No. 67. His skepticism was justified again and again. Noah Brooks records a particularly flagrant example in 1863, when a decision was made to reinforce Gen. William S. Rosecrans with the Eleventh and Twelfth Corps of the Army of the Potomac. The War Department sent an officer to every correspondent in Washington and requested each one, in the name of the president and the secretary of war, to make no mention of this movement. They agreed, and notified their papers not to print anything about the matter if it came to their attention in some other way, explaining the circumstances.

Nevertheless, only a short time afterward, the New York *Evening Post*, considered a strong supporter of Lincoln and edited by the responsible Bryant, published all the details on a Saturday afternoon, and the Washington Sunday papers had little choice but too follow. Brooks writes:

> It is a curious illustration of the muddled condition of things at that time, that the Monday morning papers in Washington discreetly held their peace, and printed not a word of news or comment concerning the whole affair. The *Evening Post* explained its position by saying that its Washington correspondent was not responsible for the "rumors" which had appeared in the Saturday edition, and that the paper had been imposed upon by others. When this comical imbroglio began, the Washington correspondents were in despair, Stanton raged like a lion, and Lincoln, I am bound to say, was exceedingly angry.

Brooks wrote that Lincoln had a small cabinet in his White House office, its interior divided into pigeonholes, in which he kept copies of letters (his own and other people's) that were of particular moment. These pigeonholes were lettered in alphabetical order, and Greeley had one all to himself. Another was labeled "W & W," and one night Lincoln asked Brooks if he had any idea what the letters stood for. Brooks did not, and Lincoln explained. "Well," he said, "that's Weed and Wood—Thurlow and Fernandy," adding with a chuckle, "That's a pair of 'em!" Wood, of course, was the Copperhead mayor of New York mentioned earlier.

The unpredictable Greeley needed a separate compartment because it was this editor and his *Tribune* that caused the president so much mingled pain and satisfaction. Lincoln and Greeley had been of one mind on the issue of slavery at the beginning, but there was a vital difference. Lincoln would not countenance disunion for any reason. Greeley, on the other hand, believed that slavery was the greater evil, and for a time he was willing for the "Cotton States," as he called them, to secede. Yet the president was anxious to keep Greeley's friendship and support, knowing how popular his paper was among Republicans and how widely it was circulated across the nation.

By the summer of 1862 Greeley found himself in the throes of disillusionment with the president over the presumed imminent issue of the second and final Emancipation Proclamation, which Greeley was against and many doubted would ever appear. He wrote one of his characteristic letters to Sen. Charles Sumner:

Do you remember the old theological book containing this:
CHAPTER I. HELL.
CHAPTER II. HELL CONTINUED.
Well, that gives a hint of the way Old Abe ought to be talked to in this crisis of the Nation's destiny.
Still, I comprehend the wisdom of not breaking with the Chief of the Republic in this hour of her fiery trial, and shall respect it. Only you must do all his puffing; for I can't help you. He's a bad stick.

By 1863 Greeley had a long shopping list of complaints about the president and was casting about in the political waters for someone to oppose him in 1864. He told James Gilmore, a rich New Yorker who often acted as his liaison with the president, that Lincoln could not be trusted. He had not kept his agreement to give the *Tribune* "early information," meaning judicious leaks, but instead, so Greeley complained, had used him in various ways to test the public pulse, making him look like an officious meddler. Greeley concluded: "No . . . I can't trust your 'honest old Abe.' He is too smart for me. He thinks me a damned fool; but I am never fooled twice by the same individual." Lincoln, the editor went on irritably, thought God was managing the war and that he (the president) was vice-regent. Someone else would have to be found, someone more "suitable."

Greeley had declared as early as November 1861 what his ideas were about the role the press should play in its relation with government. In a two-column editorial, "The Government and the Press," he argued that the government must recognize the press's ability to serve the country through honest and fearless criticism, not indiscriminate praise. He added: "But let the Government and the

Press do justice to each other's motives; let the Press realize that the Government, though it may err in judgment, cannot possibly be wrong in purpose; and let the Government feel that the Press, where it ventures to criticize the acts of the Nation's chosen leaders in this struggle, does so only because the triumph of the Republic is in its view above all personal considerations, and all will yet be well.''

Everything was *not* well, of course, and Greeley fell out not only with Lincoln but with the antiwar portion of the New York public. When the bloody Draft Riots of 1863 occurred, and mobs raged through the streets of the city for days, burning and killing, until troops summoned from the battlefields were called in to subdue them, one of the chief targets was the *Tribune,* regarded as a prime mover in the war. Windows were broken, doors battered in, and the ground floor wrecked, but before the editorial rooms and presses could be attacked by the mob, a countercharge by massed policemen broke up the riot, or at least that part of it.

Stories circulated later, no doubt spread by jealous rivals, that Greeley himself fled to the shelter of a nearby restaurant and hid under a table, but the facts display Greeley in a far more characteristic way. William Harlan Hale, one of his biographers, writes that Gilmore, who was present, and Charles Congdon, a top editorial writer, tried to persuade the editor to slip out the back way and leave town, but Greeley told them he would go out, all right, but only for dinner. "If I can't eat my dinner when I'm hungry, my life isn't worth anything to me," he said. Then, as Hale tells it, "He clapped on his hat, took Theodore Tilton of the *Independent,* who had been calling on him, by the arm, and stepped out into seething Printing House Square. The editors watched him stalk through the crowd arm in arm with Tilton, hat pushed back on head, specs hanging on his nose, and his face wearing its expression of unshakable benignity. No one in the mob touched him. He steered Tilton into Windust's Restaurant nearby." This was an act of considerable courage, considering the fact that the rioters had been chanting, "We'll hang old Greeley to a sour apple tree, And send him straight to Hell."

Bennett's reaction to the riots was not so admirable. The affair occupied the front pages of every paper in the city but his. The *Herald*'s reports were brief and somewhat disconnected, running on an inside page. Obviously, whether his reasons were personal or political, he had given orders to play down one of the greatest news stories, perhaps the most remarkable, he would ever see in his city—and this from the man who boasted that the news came first.

The *Herald* and Bennett had already gone through its own confrontation with mob violence. Soon after the attack on Fort Sumter, mobs surged through the New York streets, looking to destroy "friends of the South," which they believed included the *Herald.* They surrounded the paper's building, demanding that Bennett appear and the American flag be flown over the building. The *Herald* later denied that its sudden display of the national emblem had anything to do with the riot, which it claimed was not a riot at all but merely excited citizens trying to read the latest bulletins posted outside or to buy papers. In fact, Bennett did not even have a flag and had to send an office boy to get one from a bunting store. When it was finally unfurled, he appeared and stood as close to it as he could get and, thus sheltered, bowed to the mob. Later he prudently stocked the office with rifles and ammunition in case of later trouble, but it never came. Even more prudently, he gave his yacht to the Union navy, with attendant publicity, and announced that his son, almost certainly with a stern parental push, would go into the navy—a sacrifice that was to have far-reaching consequences for Bennett, Jr., and the postwar *Herald*.

Bennett's conversion to the Union cause was political and self-serving, but Greeley's move in the opposite direction was the result, as always, of his convictions, shifting though they might be. He broke with Lincoln on the Emancipation Proclamation, and the break was never repaired. But they agreed that slavery should be abolished, and Lincoln firmly believed Greeley's support on that issue was worth a hundred thousand men in the field. In the end the editor came to see the president in a truer light, as he observed in a postwar lecture, declaring that "the one providential leader, the indispensable hero of the great drama, was Abraham Lincoln." But stubbornly—and characteristically—Greeley remained convinced until nearly the end that the man from Illinois was not big enough for his job.

In retrospect, however, Greeley can be seen as a poor judge of character. On February 23, 1864, he wrote of the president: "He is not infallible—not a genius—not one of those rare great men who mold their age into the similitude of their own high character, massive abilities and lofty aims." Less than five months later, on July 1, he was declaring: "Mr. [Salmon P.] Chase is one of the very few great men left in public life." Behind it all was Greeley's deep conviction that he could run the country better than any of the men elected to do it, a notion he was to test, disastrously, in 1872.

In the case of Bennett, relations with the president were governed by opportunism rather than principle. Yet Lincoln could not ignore him. At the time the war began, the *Herald* was proclaiming itself as "the most largely circulated journal in the world," and although that might have been disputed by some, its daily printing of eighty-four thousand copies was certainly the largest in the United States, and it would increase sharply during the war. Its editorial page appeared to reflect no consistently held principles, but its news and feature pages were brilliantly alive. On the eve of Fort Sumter the *Herald* had proclaimed that the only hope of avoiding civil war was to overthrow Lincoln and his "demoralizing, disorganizing, and destructive sectional party."

After Sumter was fired upon, and Bennett had suffered his confrontation with the angry mob outside his office, the editor abruptly switched to the opposite side. He summoned his Washington correspondent, Henry Villard, to consult with him, driving with him in his carriage to his resplendent residence on Washington Heights, plying him with questions about Lincoln all the way. After dinner he outlined a message to be given to the president, promising support for putting down the rebels by whatever means were necessary. The offer of his yacht and his son was included in this tidy package.

For his part, Lincoln was worried about the *Herald*'s arrogant, even insolent, tone, particularly its anti-British sentiments, because it was the only American paper to have any significant influence or circulation in Europe, where the president feared it might be giving the wrong impression of America and of his policies. He was anxious not to lose European good will in the struggle ahead. Consequently, as Thurlow Weed wrote later in his memoirs, Lincoln brought up the subject of Bennett at an early cabinet meeting, and it was decided to approach the editor and see if the *Herald*'s editorial course could be trimmed a little.

Oddly enough, Weed was chosen to do the job—a curious choice, since he and Bennett were old political enemies. Seward told Lincoln that sending Weed would ensure the mission's failure, but the president persisted, so the veteran Republican boss was invited to Washington to discuss the proposition. At their meeting Lincoln remarked that he understood Weed had "considerable experience in belling cats" and described the cat belling he had in mind. Weed insisted he should be the last person to be considered for the task, but Lincoln prevailed.

Weed secured an appointment, took the "cars" up to Washington Heights one afternoon, was greeted at the station by Bennett, who had taken the same train, and driven to the mansion, where they had a pleasant dinner. Over the fruit course at the end, Weed introduced the subject of his visit, concluding his effort at persuasion with the observation that the president would rather have the *Herald*'s support than a victory in the field.

Bennett rewarded him with one of his customary flamboyant, self-righteous sermons. The Whigs had provoked a war he had been warning them against for years, he said, and now they had no right to ask him to help them get out of their troubles. He interspersed these remarks with denunciations of Greeley, Garrison, Seward, Sumner, and Weed himself, among others. In his own account of the meeting, Weed asserts that he replied calmly, not taking issue, but simply stating the other side of the matter, disclosing some inside information in his possession to support his argument. It was no use. Bennett remained unconvinced. Weed prepared a gloomy report of the meeting and was astonished to learn that Lincoln and the cabinet were "greatly gratified" by it.

Subsequently, however, the *Herald* supported the war, in a somewhat lukewarm way, although it was against emancipation. Its battlefield coverage was exceptional, including some first-rate reporting by the editor himself. Often during the war Bennett denounced the president in his editorials, demanding that so-called Radicals be removed from the cabinet and opposing abolitionists of every stripe. But in 1864 he came to Lincoln's support for reelection. Historians have speculated since that Bennett was told privately he would be offered the post of minister to France in return for his support, but it has never been proved. This temptation does not seem unlikely, however, since the president actually did make the offer after he was reelected, but Bennett declined. In any case, his support did not prevent Gen. George McClellan, the Democratic candidate, from carrying New York City.

Lincoln could never count on much from the New York press in any case. Only five of its seventeen papers supported him in any degree—the *Times, Evening Post, Sun, Tribune,* and *Commercial Advertiser.* Nine of the others were frankly proslavery, and, of these, five were firmly in the Copperhead camp. The president was never popular in New York and twice failed to carry it.

Bryant and the *Evening Post* remained firm supporters, for the most part, although the paper was often critical of Lincoln's conduct of the war—in good part, perhaps, because Bryant fancied himself as a military strategist, as did some of his fellow editors, and kept up a running correspondence with generals in the field. Bryant found fault with all of them except Ulysses S. Grant, whom he supported to the end.

The New York *Times* could usually be found on the side of Raymond's friend and political ally Seward, but the editor continued to steer his paper on as much of a middle course as it was possible to take, and most of the time that meant it supported Lincoln. The president had few more constant supporters, and it was particularly valuable to him in 1864 that Raymond was chairman of the Republican National Committee and personally took charge of the campaign that re-elected him. As a by-product of that effort, Raymond himself was elected to Congress.

Lincoln did have the support of several excellent party journals outside of New York. Samuel Bowles of the Springfield *Republican* followed Raymond for the most part, although he also shared Greeley's feeling that Lincoln did not have the ability to "rise to the height of this great Argument," as Bowles put it. Bowles did his best to rally the Massachusetts press around the administration's flag, but there was no more unanimity there, in the heart of abolitionist country, than there was anywhere else.

Elsewhere John Forney, the reliable Republican editor of the Philadelphia *Press,* led the party's journalistic forces in Pennsylvania and issued a weekly edition called the *War Press,* which was distributed to the troops, keeping them informed and, so Forney hoped, inspired. Forney also established a paper in Washington in 1861, the *Chronicle,* which came as near to being an administration organ as that nearly dead institution could muster. Forney was an editor Lincoln could always count on.

Less reliable was Joseph Medill, who had done so much to get Lincoln elected. From the beginning the Chicago *Tribune* took a hard line toward the South, and Medill's differences with the president arose mostly from his recurring conviction that Lincoln's line was not hard enough. Medill was rewarded in a nonpolitical way. The affluence that came to most newspapers as a result of greatly increased circulation during the war years was enough to save the *Tribune* from the bankruptcy it had faced in 1860 and established it as one of the nation's leading newspapers.

Whatever their intermittent differences might be, Medill came only once into direct confrontation with the president, and, as he himself recorded it, this sublimely arrogant editor found himself in disorderly retreat. In 1864 a mass meeting of Chicago citizens was held to protest the new draft quotas, which these Midwesterners considered too high for their city. Medill was appointed to head a committee that would go to Washington and take up the matter with Secretary Stanton, who adamantly refused to make any concessions. Medill then appealed directly to Lincoln, who promised only to go with him to Stanton's office and listen to both sides of the argument. The president listened carefully, and then, as Medill recalled later, he turned to the committee sternly and said:

Gentlemen, after Boston, Chicago has been the chief instrument in bringing this war on the country. The Northwest has opposed the South as the Northeast has opposed the South. You called for war until we had it. You called for emancipation, and I have given it to you. Whatever you have asked for you have had. Now you come here begging to be let off from the call for men which I have made to carry out the war which you have demanded. You ought to be ashamed of yourselves. I have a right to expect better things of you. Get home and raise your 6,000 extra men. And you, Medill, are acting like a coward. You and your *Tribune* have had more influence than any paper in the Northwest in making this war. You can influence great masses, and yet you cry to be spared at a moment when your cause is suffering. Go home and send us those men.

Medill went on: "I couldn't say anything. It was the first time I ever was whipped, and I didn't have an answer. We all got up and went out, and when the door closed, one of my colleagues said, 'Well, gentlemen, the old man is right. We ought to be ashamed of ourselves. Let us never say anything about this, but go home and raise the men.' And we did, 6,000 men, making 28,000 in the war from a city of 156,000.''

Lincoln could tolerate and deal with the dissenting editors in his own party, but the opposition Democratic press and the Copperhead papers were a different matter. In them one could see the past reflected, as the excesses of the early partisan press were resurrected for one more reprise. The president was the subject of the worst invective ever to be visited on a chief executive, with the exceptions noted earlier. The wildest charges were made against him. It was asserted that he drew his salary in gold bars, that he was frequently drunk, that he gave out pardons in exchange for votes, authorized needless slaughters of soldiers for the sake of victory, and even the ultimate lie—treason. The rhetoric employed by these character assassins was at least colorful. Lincoln was referred to as "a slang-whanging stump speaker," a "half-witted usurper," "mole-eyed," "the present turtle at the head of government," "the head ghoul at Washington." There were others even less complimentary.

Most of this abuse came from the Copperhead press. Southern sympathizers in the North had earlier been called "Doughfaces," but the Detroit *Free Press* is credited with first using the word "Copperhead" for them as early as 1831. Not all those who opposed the war were Copperheads, of course, but sometimes it was difficult to tell the difference. That the true Copperhead papers were permitted to exist at all in wartime, when censorship was being exercised in other respects, is a tribute to Lincoln's firm belief in the system he was struggling so hard to preserve. It was as though, to cite a modern instance, pro-Nazi papers in major cities were permitted to publish and circulate in the years of the Second World War.

In New York the *Daily News* (not related to the present paper of the same name) and the *Day-Book* were among the chief offenders. Edited by Benjamin Wood, brother of the openly Copperhead Mayor Fernando Wood, the *Daily News* never supported either Lincoln or the war effort for a moment, denouncing both with equal fervor. Until Lee surrendered, it continued to insist that news of

Northern victories was either fabricated or exaggerated and that the South would never be conquered.

Lincoln moved against the *Daily News* in a way that was plainly unconstitutional, no matter how justified. Throwing the First Amendment out the window, as John Adams had attempted to do, he ordered the paper's postal privileges denied in August 1861, compelling it to find other means of distribution. Then a United States marshal seized three thousand copies that had been sent to Philadelphia, and a month later the *Daily News* was suspended, not to reappear for eighteen months, as uncompromising as ever. No further action was taken against it, however. The *Evening Journal* of Philadelphia, another Copperhead organ, was also suspended in 1863, this time by Maj. Gen. Robert Schenck, who sent its editor as a prisoner to Fort McHenry, from which he was released a few days later after a written apology and a promise to reform.

In the Middle West a fiery Copperhead journal was the Columbus *Crisis,* the work of Samuel Medary, who was also editor of the *Ohio Statesman.* It was Medary who sheltered and supported C. L. Vallandigham, the notorious Copperhead activist, and actually put up his name for the governorship of Ohio at a time when this violent antiwar crusader was banned from the Union. Such advocacy was not tolerated by Medary's prowar neighbors, who completely wrecked the *Crisis* plant in 1863 and would have sacked the *Statesman*'s office as well if they had not been restrained. Indicted the following year for treason by a federal grand jury, Medary died before his trial date.

Medary, at least, had the sincere courage of his convictions, however wrong we may believe them now. Not as much could be said for the nearly legendary editor of the Chicago *Times,* Wilbur F. Storey. Like the other great nineteenth-century editors, he had an acute sense of the news, and like both the Bennetts, father and son (to which could be added Greeley, Medill, and later Joseph Pulitzer), he was an eccentric. This dissipated tyrant, with his flowing wild white hair and beard, was a familiar figure in Chicago, particularly in the courts, where he once had twenty-four libel suits pending against him simultaneously.

The war, and Lincoln, brought out the worst in Storey, although he scarcely needed any stimulation. His *Times* was not only the worst excoriator of the president but it spared no one else, high or low, and consequently the editor was frequently called upon to defend himself against physical assaults. The most memorable of these was the attempt by Miss Lydia Thompson, star of a pioneer burlesque troupe called British Blondes, to horsewhip Storey for uncomplimentary remarks made about her art in his paper.

In one sense the *Times* was not untypical of Democratic journals that began by supporting the war and ended by turning on Lincoln after emancipation was proclaimed. But even in such a violently partisan era, what the *Times* called the president and his generals was insupportable. Medill, rushing to the defense against his chief Chicago rival, tried to act as Lincoln's one-man journalistic army against their common enemy, but that only precipitated a war between the two papers so virulent that the day came when both camps waited in their offices, fully armed and barricaded, for the other to come and launch an assault.

The president made no pretense about trying to suppress the *Times,* which was plainly a danger to public order as well as unquestionably treasonous. There were boycotts and military orders directed against it, but Storey sat in his armed camp behind the barricades and defied the world. Even so, Lincoln remained ambiguous about using the military force available. He had the opportunity in June 1864 when Maj. Gen. Ambrose E. Burnside, on his own initiative, sent his troops into the *Times* office at four o'clock in the morning, stopped the presses, ordered the employees out, and took possession.

It was not the first time Burnside had assumed such authority. He was the officer who had sent troops to arrest Vallandigham in Dayton, Ohio—another middle-of-the-night affair. In the subsequent rioting Vallandigham's followers attacked and burned the plant of the Dayton *Daily Journal,* the town's Republican paper, disabling the fire engines and slashing their hoses so that not only the *Journal*'s offices went in the flames but a half-dozen other buildings as well. The paper's pro-Vallandigham rival, the *Daily Empire,* published a violent protest against the activist's arrest, and General Burnside suppressed it immediately, sending its editor to prison in Cincinnati.

In the case of the Chicago *Times,* Secretary Stanton had already been told by the governor of Illinois, Richard Yates, that loyal citizens were demanding its suppression, and Burnside obliged them. The results, however, were not what they expected. Storey went into federal court and got a temporary injunction (although it was already too late), but Judge Thomas Drummond refused to grant a permanent one on technical grounds, giving it as his personal opinion that the Constitution had probably been violated. The Illinois legislature, after hearing the news, passed resolutions censuring the seizure, by a decisive vote, again citing it as unconstitutional. Businessmen and prominent Republicans, appalled by what had happened, joined in signing a petition to the president requesting him to revoke the suppression order. Sen. Lyman Trumbull of Illinois, who had worked to elect Lincoln, and Congressman Isaac N. Arnold, one of the president's close friends, joined in the appeal. A bipartisan, bi-party mass meeting of twenty thousand people was held in protest, and some of those who had no love for Storey were talking about burning down the *Times.* The Chicago militia had to be called out.

Next day General Burnside sent Storey a telegram revoking the suppression, "by direction of the President of the United States." Robert Harper, one of the historians of these events, tells us what happened: "Lincoln was 'embarrassed' by Burnside's suppression of the newspaper; while he desired to do right by the military and give it every support, he was faced by the question of liberty of the press. He was reflecting over the course he should follow when he received the telegram from Trumbull and Arnold. His order to revoke the suppression resulted."

Everyone except Medill appeared to be satisfied. In the Chicago *Tribune* he wrote that the revocation was "a most unfortunate blunder. As the matter stands it is a triumph of treason." Nor was Storey in the least appeased. When it was announced in 1864 that Burnside was about to visit Chicago, the *Times* greeted him: "The butcher of Fredericksburg and attempted assassin of the liberty of speech and of the Northwest is coming to Chicago. . . . He was not the head butcher and assassin, he was only the creature, the mean instrument, the puppet, the jumping-jack of the principal butchers and assassins.'' And the *Times* hailed Lincoln's second inaugural address, since so much admired, with these words: ''We did not conceive it possible that even Mr. Lincoln could produce a paper so slip-shod, so loose-jointed, so puerile, not alone in literary construction, but in ideas, its sentiments, its grasp.''

The affair of the *Times*'s suppression did not end with Lincoln's revocation. A basic question had been raised, for the first time in a national sense. The question was the right of free expression, guaranteed by the First Amendment, in a time of war. Madison wrestled briefly with this proposition during the War of 1812, but he was not compelled to act on it, as Lincoln had been. In this civil war, paradoxically, when no foreign enemy was threatening (or so it seemed), the question had become a national issue.

In an attempt to come to practical grips with it, representatives of fifteen daily and weekly newspapers in New York met under Greeley's chairmanship to debate the matter. This ad hoc committee produced a set of highly ambiguous resolutions, perhaps a reflection of the chairman's character, asserting that the press had no right to uphold treason or rebellion, but, on the other hand, it had a constitutional right to criticize civil and military government, which was what the *Times* and other antiwar, anti-Lincoln papers had been doing all along.

Whatever the government and the editors might decree, however, meant nothing to the mob, just as in the days of the Revolution and the War of 1812, and to a small extent in the Mexican War. Lawless, vengeful partisans were constantly attacking and often destroying Copperhead newspaper plants. At one point anonymous bill posters flooded New York with this sinister warning: ''The freedom of the press is subordinate to the interests of a nation. Let the three southern organs issued in this city beware!'' Toward the end of the war, as the anti-administration papers clamored more loudly than ever for peace at any price and against the draft, mob violence rose to a new climax. ''Loyal citizens'' destroyed literally dozens of newspapers—at least a half-dozen in Oregon and the same number (or more) in Ohio. In the nation's agony following Lincoln's assassination, mobs in their grief and frustration once more fell upon Copperhead papers across the country, destroying five in San Francisco alone.

It must not be supposed, however, that the president's problem with the press was entirely one of lofty constitutional principle, or what ranting editors like Storey might say about him or his generals. Rather it was what to do on a day-to-day basis with reporting from the field, in that perpetually uneasy relationship between the military and the press that has no universally satisfactory solutions. Generals, like governments, always want to conceal except what may be to their advantage, while the press's mission is to disclose. Since some secrecy is essential for the protection of troops, the question becomes what may be disclosed and what may be withheld.

In the Civil War no one expected the kind of relative objectivity from the field that reporters would not achieve to any great extent until the Second World War. Reporting on both sides was often as highly partisan as political comment in the papers, and no one was surprised to read in the New York *Tribune* about a dead

Confederate soldier "sacrificed to the devilish ambition of his implacable masters, Davis and Lee."

The trouble was that newspapers so often went beyond these expected boundaries and printed information about troop movements and other military matters that could reasonably be argued as direct threats to national security. There is no question that lives were lost as a result, and even battles fought unnecessarily. J. Cutler Andrews has pointed out that the primary fault, however, was not with the reporters but their editors, who often failed to exercise the prudent self-censorship so obviously required. When Lincoln or a government official called them to account, they simply pointed to the official censorship already existing and argued that they were therefore relieved of responsibility.

The press had, in fact, been officially censored since April 1861. Censorship was applied mostly to telegraphic dispatches, but on occasion to mail and express. The censors themselves were frequently inept, particularly in the early stages of the war, before they had learned from experience. A whole dispatch might be suppressed if it had a single fact in it that might be censorable, but then later the censors began to send along those portions of the dispatches they had cleared without showing the reporters what they had done, resulting in a mutilation of correspondents' stories that drove them to desperation. This desperation took the form of evading censorship whenever it could be done, and the inevitable result was direct action by military commanders in a great many cases— arrests, military trials, expulsion from the lines.

Nowhere was the conflict between field commander and reporters so intense as it was in the progress of Gen. William T. Sherman through the war. Sherman had his own view of the First Amendment. "Freedom of speech and freedom of the Press," he wrote in October 1863, "precious relics of former history, must not be construed too largely." Acting on that belief, as John F. Marszalek tells us, Sherman "threatened to hang several reporters. He banished a number from his army. He even court-martialed one correspondent. On numerous occasions, newspapermen wrote that Sherman was insane. Throughout the Civil War, this famous general battled the press in a conflict which rivaled the intensity of the fighting between Union and Confederate soldiers. The controversy focused on one issue: the meaning of the term, freedom of the press."

Sherman, Lincoln and his administration, and the press itself were navigating uncharted waters here, it must be remembered. The Bill of Rights, as has been noted, had never been a major issue in wartime before, and, in fact, the question would not be argued in the Supreme Court until after the First World War, and even then the case concerned the home front, not the battlefield. It was not until 1971, in the case of the Pentagon Papers during the undeclared Vietnam War, that the Court concluded the government could not exercise prior restraint against newspapers even in wartime.

People who opposed Lincoln and his administration believed that the Constitution must be strictly interpreted; consequently they believed most of the president's actions were unconstitutional. On the other hand, the Radical Republicans (whose "radicalism" and identity are now under scrutiny by the revisionists), believed that the Constitution was invalid in wartime. Lincoln's view was that the Constitution was not only in effect, but that it gave government extraordinary powers to conduct the war effectively. He prevailed, and, in Marszalek's words, "The war was fought with the Constitution stretched but unimpaired." Presidents have taken the same position in our century, and they have been backed by the Supreme Court.

For the press the question was whether it should retain its First Amendment rights during the war, without restriction, or should that protection be suspended for the duration. Another alternative was for government to regulate the press within the limits of the First Amendment—a thorny question of definition. Regulation became the chosen path, and there was no real censorship of newspapers during the entire conflict.

As we have seen, there was brutal censorship by the mobs and arbitrary censorship by a few generals, but the government's efforts were confined largely to controls over telegraphic transmission, which was aimed also at the Confederate spy network. As they always have, furthermore, reporters found ways to avoid censorship, sometimes by such simple methods as delivering the dispatches in person or by using the United States mails. The postmaster general closed the latter loophole at least partially, and in another way, by forbidding the mails to certain newspapers in 1861, and a year later the press was notified that a paper would be excluded from using the mails if it published anything that had already been censored on the telegraph. This became the government's chief weapon during the war in its effort to control reporters in the field, but it was never fully effective.

Voluntary censorship was also attempted, as we have already seen with McClellan's gentleman's agreement, but these agreements often broke down after a time. Far more of a threat to the press was the invocation by Lincoln's administration of the Fifty-seventh Article of War, a law passed in 1806, which subjected reporters to the death penalty if a court-martial found them guilty of publishing anything that might help the enemy. It would have completely throttled the press if it had been strictly enforced, but in the event it was virtually ignored—by everyone except General Sherman.

There was nothing impulsive or arbitrary about Sherman's actions. He had given a great deal of consideration to the question of First Amendment rights in wartime, and when he reached his deeply felt conclusion that the press had no rights, he had the strength of his convictions. Many generals, before and since, have held strong antipress views, but Sherman went a step further. He believed in a direct relationship between censorship and military victory; one was a prerequisite for the other. Where other commanders in later years learned to manipulate the press (as Gen. Douglas MacArthur, for example, did so deftly) Sherman elected to fight a war within a war against the newspapers, following his conviction that the Bill of Rights should be suspended in wartime. But, as Marszalek has pointed out, this inner war became one of personal conflict, not a struggle over constitutional issues.

Sherman's press war culminated in the case of Thomas W. Knox, one of the New York *Herald*'s correspondents, who filed what the general considered damaging information without first submitting it for censorship. He had Knox arrested as a spy and court-martialed. And Knox was not the only offender, in Sherman's opinion. His deep contempt for the press could be seen at its worst in his observation that his camp sheltered "some half-dozen little whipper-snappers who represent the press, but are in fact spies, too lazy, idle, and cowardly to be soldiers."

The court-martial verdict did not order Knox shot as a spy, which Sherman no doubt wished, but only demanded that he stay outside army lines. Sherman had told his wife that he intended to inform Lincoln that he would never again command an army if the president interfered with this or any other court sentence, but Lincoln was compelled to do exactly that because Sherman himself was dissatisfied with the verdict. He complained that the main issues had not been dealt with and demanded that the matter be referred to the judge advocate general and to Lincoln himself.

Meanwhile Knox's fellow correspondents had decided to make an issue of this case, since all of them heartily disliked Sherman. They drew up a petition, signed by a dozen of the most prominent among them, and sent a delegation to call on Lincoln. The president received them amiably, told them a funny story— and equivocated. He wrote in their presence a "To-whom-it-may-concern" letter, revoking the sentence only to the extent of permitting Knox to return to Grant's headquarters, where that commander would decide whether to let Knox return to the lines. The reporter went to St. Louis to argue his own case, and, after hearing him, Grant requested him to write a letter to Sherman and ask if he was willing for the reporter to return. But Knox could not bring himself to do that, and the stiff note he wrote to Sherman had no word of apology or plea for leniency. As for Sherman, he wrote an angry letter that not only completely rejected Knox but regretted any conclusion by the court that the correspondent had been guilty only of "technical offenses." There was no possibility of reconciliation. Knox went off to report in other theaters of the war and was present at the climactic Battle of Gettysburg. After the war he wrote more than forty books about his experiences as reporter and traveler.

Out of this affair came the tacit recognition, never spelled out, that journalists could accompany military units only if field commanders accepted them—in short, what we now call accreditation. Thus ended the only recorded military trial of a newspaperman in our history. For Sherman, his unremitting hatred of the press continued to the end, as well as his contempt for anyone, including Lincoln, who disagreed with his stand.

By 1864, that bitter year, the press had come a long way from the earlier confusion and was proving itself to be much more responsible. When reporters went with Grant into the Battle of the Wilderness, they did so with a prudence and reserve that brought some satisfaction, at least, to both sides.

Lincoln observed all these conflicts with the press from a distance, involving himself only when it was essential. He did little reading of the newspapers himself, largely ignoring the marked copies editors sent him advising him how to run the war. When he looked at the papers, he read the telegraphic news and ignored the editorials. If there was anything the editors were doing that seemed important for him to know, his able young secretaries, Nicolay and Hay, kept him informed. They *did* read a broad selection of all the important papers.

Correspondents who knew the president personally found him always courteous and willing to give interviews, seemingly anxious to tell them everything he could. Sometimes he had serious arguments with editors, but he tried not to permit these quarrels to develop into lasting hostility. When generals were rough with correspondents (some of them shared General Sherman's feelings, at least in part), he often interceded on behalf of the reporters, but never in the sense of giving orders to his commanders. He did not complain about how the press treated him personally, although certainly he had abundant cause, but he was not averse to expelling William Russell of the London *Times* after he had written what many believed was a highly exaggerated account of the Union army's panic at the Battle of Manassas. Carl Sandburg has summarized Lincoln's general attitude (and that of the administration as a whole): "The press was seen as an institution of mixed benefits and evil results, a few editors having printed their opinion placing 'newspapers and politicians' first in blame for the war. Lincoln undoubtedly agreed with whatever Artemus Ward had in mind in pointing to the aboriginal Red Men of America having 'no Congress, faro banks, delirirum tremens, or Associated Press.' "

Lincoln certainly knew of the corruption that existed in the Washington press corps, but he overlooked it, perhaps because it was a small patch on the corruption that prevailed in other quarters. Reporters sometimes used their inside knowledge of events to speculate in Wall Street, according to Noah Brooks, an honest observer of the scene, and there were a few who even acted as spies for brokers. If the president closed his eyes to these activities, he opened them when he read a dispatch attributing an off-color joke to him. On that occasion he sent for the reporter and issued one of his rare reprimands.

One man he always welcomed at the White House was Mathew Brady, the master photographer to whose skill we owe the best photographic record of Lincoln, and of the war as well. The president would not support Brady's ambitious plan to be the official chronicler for the War Department, but he did give him a card on which he had scrawled, "Pass Brady," and that enabled the enterprising photographer to go wherever he wanted to travel, and so produce the record he wanted anyway, official or not.

In assessing Lincoln's long relationship with the press, somehow one always comes back to the human side of it, as is so often the case with this president. The contentious editors, the imperious generals, the large questions of policy seem less meaningful than the kind of intimacy Lincoln was able to establish because of the humanity for which he is revered today, alone among all the others who have occupied the White House. The instances are so abundant that it would be hard to choose one exemplifying the rest, but perhaps two incidents from the life of Henry E. Wing, the *Tribune* correspondent, will do.

Lincoln had a few favorites among the regular Washington reporters, foremost among them Noah Brooks, but he relied most on those correspondents who came into Washington, exhausted and battle-worn, with firsthand reports from the battlefield. On them he depended for news that was often well ahead of official dispatches.

Such an occasion occurred when Grant vanished with his army into the Wilderness, and for three days nothing was heard from him, leaving an anxious president and public. Stopping at the War Department's telegraph office early on a Friday evening to read the latest news, as he often did, Lincoln was told that a *Tribune* correspondent was at Union Mills, twenty miles from the capital, and had telegraphed for permission to talk with Assistant Secretary of War Charles A. Dana. That was natural. Dana, once Greeley's managing editor, had been employed by Lincoln early in the war to follow Grant, on a pretense of gathering information for a pension system, and report on the general's conduct and character. As a result of Dana's careful account, Lincoln elevated Grant to the top command post and later rewarded his "spy" with the assistant secretaryship of war.

Of course the reporter would rather talk to Dana if he had a problem rather than to Stanton; one newspaperman would better understand another. But Dana had happened to be away from his desk, and Stanton had already been given the request, after which the secretary had demanded that the correspondent give him the message. Wing, the *Tribune*'s man, refused to do so, and an infuriated Stanton had ordered him shot as a spy the next morning.

Lincoln was incredulous and asked the operator to find out if Wing would talk to him instead. Wing replied that he would if the president would permit him first to send a hundred words to his paper. Lincoln agreed, then sent a special military train with Dana aboard to talk with Wing, after which the assistant secretary would go on to the front and Wing would return to Washington on the special train.

It was nearly two o'clock on Saturday morning before Wing reached the White House, where he found Lincoln and the entire cabinet waiting for him, desperately anxious for news from Grant. Wing told them only a little more than the information contained in the hundred words he had already communicated, and when the cabinet members learned that he knew nothing of what had happened in the past twenty-four hours, since Grant had ordered an attack, they went unhappily away. Wing was the last to leave, seeming to hesitate, and Lincoln asked him if he wanted to say something more. Yes, Wing replied, he had a message for the president from Grant, which was to be given only when they were alone. The message was: "There will be no turning back."

It was the kind of message Lincoln had waited for three years to hear, and, overcome, he put an arm around the reporter's shoulder and kissed him on the cheek. Then he sat Wing down in a chair, and, to the intently listening president, Wing poured out all the things he could not have said before, of the confusion and the intramural warfare among the officers at headquarters, and of how Gen. George Meade had even argued for pulling back until an implacable Grant had ordered, "We shall attack in the morning."

They talked until nearly four o'clock, when Lincoln broke off the interview, asking Wing to come see him that afternoon. But the exhausted Wing had scarcely fallen asleep, fully clothed, on a bed in the National Hotel when he heard newsboys outside, shouting the news he had telegraphed earlier from Union Mills. Hurrying out of the hotel, he rushed to the *Tribune*'s bureau office and found his chief, Sam Wilkeson, trying to deny the story, not knowing his reporter was in Washington. When the editor and the crowd found that the correspondent was indeed there, and the story of Grant's intentions was true, Wing was an instant hero.

Later that day Wing told the president that he had to go back at once to rescue his horse, Jess, which he had left tied up when Confederate soldiers were closing in on him. Lincoln gave him a train and an escort of soldiers, who had to fight off guerrillas until they reached the thicket where Jess stood waiting for his master's return. The entire party, including Jess, returned safely to Washington that night.

After the struggle in the Wilderness came the bloody Battle of Cold Harbor, through which Wing dragged himself on the crippled leg he had suffered at Fredericksburg. In pain, and horror-stricken by what he had witnessed, he returned to Washington, filed his stories, and went to his hotel room, determined to resign next day. Rising that afternoon after a restless, nightmare-haunted sleep, he was told at the *Tribune* bureau that Lincoln had learned of his arrival and wanted to see him. J. Cutler Andrews, the best historian of these events, has given us a moving picture of the scene between them, which tells us much about both Lincoln and the press:

> It was evening before he was admitted to the President's study; Lincoln was alone, his face drawn and gray, his eyes filled with anguish. The President greeted his visitor kindly, however, and seemed anxious to learn what he had seen and done since his last visit to Washington three weeks before. Under the spell of the President's gaze, Wing talked freely. He spoke of many things which the censorship had not permitted him to write: of men driven to slaughter which was sheer murder; of quarrels between those in high command so jealous of their own prerogatives that they would stop in the midst of a frightful struggle to accuse each other, to threaten, to weaken their own ability by hate and self seeking. Wing went on to picture camps of men sleeping on their arms, attacks on entrenchments which defied the strongest efforts, incessant marching through swamps and across swollen streams in sunlight and during heavy rains. He told of how he had tramped over the battlefield on the night after Cold Harbor, looking for the bodies of the Connecticut boys he knew and taking down messages from the dying for delivery to their loved ones back home.
>
> Lincoln listened intently to this recital and after Wing had concluded exclaimed with considerable feeling:
>
> "And after that you go back to the army—are going back again! Why, boy, you shame me. You've done your part; anybody would say that. You could quit in honor, but you stick. I wonder," he mused thoughtfully, "if I could do that. I don't believe I would. There's many a night, Henry, that I plan to resign. I wouldn't run again now if I didn't know these other fellows couldn't save the Union on their platforms, whatever they say. I can't quit, Henry; I have to stay. But you could, and you don't." The two men had risen; they stood facing each other. Perhaps the President sensed the latent rebellion in the younger man, for he added in a pleading manner, "I reckon we won't quit, will we, Henry?"

"No, Mr. Lincoln," replied Henry, "we won't quit," and so after taking his leave he returned to the army.

The vast drama wound down to its final scene. On the night Lincoln went to Ford's Theater for the last time, he invited Noah Brooks to go with him, but his favorite newspaperman was too ill with a bad cold and stayed home. Thus we were deprived of a firsthand account of the climactic moment by the reporter who knew Lincoln best. And after four years of bitter conflict, and the most intense competition to report it ever seen in the newspaper business, it was the Associated Press, even then a symbol of relative neutrality, which got the beat on the Greeleys, the Bennetts, and all the other fierce competitors. On that fateful April night in 1865, Lawrence Gobright, the AP's man in Washington, flashed the first bulletin: "The President was shot in a theater tonight, and perhaps mortally wounded."

With that, the presidency and the press alike passed into a new era.

PART FOUR

The Aftermath of Power

Andrew Johnson: The Limits of Power

Rewriting the history of Reconstruction has become almost a cottage industry among historians during the past two decades. Eric Foner has observed, ''In the past twenty years, few periods of American history have been the subject of so thoroughgoing a reevaluation.'' Yet, as Foner goes on to point out, the study of Reconstruction is still in serious crisis because, in spite of all the substantial new revisionist literature, historians have failed to define and describe this event within a specific time frame or as a societal response to the results and consequences of the Civil War and Lincoln's historic Emancipation Proclamation.

The role of the press during this period has scarcely been examined at all, one supposes largely because historians consider it relatively unimportant. Yet it was an influence in the convergence of events that resulted in the impeachment of President Andrew Johnson. Further, the press demonstrated during this period the power it now exercised as the result of wartime affluence and its dominance by strong-minded editors in New York, Chicago, and elsewhere. All this had to be reckoned with by the president and his administration.

Johnson came to the White House at a time when the old guard was beginning to change in the nation's great dailies. Henry J. Raymond, having established the New York *Times* as the voice of reason in a partisan world, would soon die prematurely in 1869, at forty-nine—strangely, for a man presumed to be unemotional, soon after leaving the arms of his mistress, Rose Eytinge, the star of Wallach's. Greeley remained a substantial force at the *Tribune,* but more and more he was turning to the pursuit of his political fortunes, which were to end so disastrously in 1872. Bryant, by now an elderly man, was slipping gradually away from direct control of the *Evening Post,* leaving it in the hands of his managing editors. In Springfield, Samuel Bowles was in the final fifteen years of his career on the *Republican.* As for Bennett, Sr., he welcomed his son home from service with the Union navy by putting him through an apprenticeship on the *Herald,* then retiring in 1867 to leave him in charge of the paper. The father, who was at the least eccentric, had been a master at getting the news; the son proved himself a genius at making it happen and pushed eccentricity to the verge of madness. What he lacked was his father's deep involvement with politics.

There were new voices in the land. Charles A. Dana, having served with distinction in the War Department, spent two unhappy years in Chicago journalism before returning to New York, where he bought the failing *Sun* for $175,000, with the help of such backers as Cyrus Field and Alonzo Cornell. Equipped with a brilliant staff, Dana made the *Sun* as preeminent in the news department as the *Herald* had been ("the newspaperman's newspaper," it has been called), and on the editorial page, with the addition of several first-rate writers, he produced essays that were models of style. Unfortunately his own were also models of cynicism and the sardonic; they gave a tone to the page that considerably weakened any political influence the *Sun* might otherwise have had.

Nevertheless, the *Sun*'s editorial page was to produce phrases that became popular catchwords across the country, political weapons in themselves to influence public opinion. "Turn the rascals out," directed at the Grant administration, would become a part of the language. Others were much less memorable, effective for a specific time. Contemporaries would not forget that it was Dana's mocking characterization of Gen. Winfield S. Hancock, the Democratic candidate in 1880, as "a good man, weighing 240 pounds," that contributed to his defeat by James A. Garfield.

More of a mover than any of these, however, was the unlikely person of Edwin Lawrence Godkin, that austere, aloof Anglo-Irish immigrant who made his fame in America as E. L. Godkin, editor of the New York magazine called the *Nation* from 1865 until the end of the century. This magazine merged with the *Evening Post* in 1881, becoming its weekly edition, and Godkin wrote more than a thousand editorials for Bryant's old journal, reprinting them in the *Nation*. He was also editor-in-chief of the *Evening Post*.

Godkin's audience never exceeded thirty-five thousand, but his influence on the political opinions of his generation of intellectuals was profound, as Greeley's had been before the Civil War. What Godkin wrote went far beyond his immediate audience, trickling down through a network of other journals, pulpits, college classrooms, and by word of mouth into the national consciousness. Of him, William James truly wrote, "To my generation, his was certainly the towering influence in all thought concerning public affairs, and indirectly his influence has assuredly been more pervasive than that of any other writer of the generation, for he influenced other writers who never quoted him, and determined the whole current of discussion."

Godkin came to the editorship of the *Nation,* a new political weekly, on July 6, 1865, in the chaos that followed the war, possessed by the determination, as the historian William M. Armstrong puts it, to purify the political life of the United States—surely a hopeless task for even the greatest of editorial writers, as Oswald Garrison Villard called him. "For the next thirty-five years," writes Armstrong, in his study of this idealist,

> Godkin strove valiantly and, as he thought, vainly toward that goal. When, at the end of 1899, he abandoned the struggle, an era had passed. The progress of the Industrial

Revolution and the passing of the frontier had wrought great changes in American life since the Civil War. The disunited country with a semi-handicraft economy to which Godkin had come hopefully as a young man was gone; the United States in 1900 was a modern industrial nation—and a world power.

Andrew Johnson stood unhappily on the threshold of that new age, in the wake of a national tragedy, suddenly entrusted with uniting a torn and bleeding nation, and with the great question of the day settled only by force of arms, not by conversion or conviction. He desperately needed support from the press, or at least the most influential part of it. There were the lords, old and new, of the New York press, and out in the countryside rising new editors, such as Henry W. Watterson ("Marse Henry") of the Louisville *Courier-Journal,* who in his person and his policies seemed to Southerners the journalistic leader of the Lost Cause. Medill, in Chicago, was looking into politics himself and would soon be mayor of that city. There were other local editors to be considered, and now there were also the magazines, particularly *Harper's Weekly,* whose war coverage had been as good as any newspaper's. It had a circulation of 120,000 and a political editor, George William Curtis, whose views politicians would have to take into account. And he had strong views about the questions of Reconstruction.

To make an impression on these editors was important, but Johnson had a public relations problem at the very beginning that would have staggered even the most eminent counselors of our time. The truth was that no man had ever entered national public life under more disgraceful circumstances, and even though there were reasons for his conduct, the general public was not immediately aware of them.

Johnson had become Lincoln's running mate in 1864 because of his record in Tennessee, where he had been military governor after Grant first drove out the Confederates. He had held tenaciously to his office while the war tides ebbed and flowed across that embattled state, taking a dictatorial, unbending line with everyone who opposed him. When the war was over, he hammered Tennessee into line as a Union state by disenfranchising those who still supported the Confederacy, rigging a constitutional convention, and pushing through an amendment abolishing slavery.

As a reward, the Republicans (temporarily renamed the National Union party as a vote-getting device) nominated Johnson in 1864 as vice-president. Late the following February he set off for Washington to be inaugurated. It was a doomed journey from the first. Johnson was just recovering from a bout of typhoid fever, and when he reached Washington he was still weak. On the night before the inauguration, instead of getting the rest he needed, he was duty bound to attend a party in his honor, where he had far too much to drink. Next morning he suffered from the inevitable hangover, and in that condition made his way to the Capitol for the ceremonies. Feeling faint and ill, he asked Hannibal Hamlin, the departing vice-president, if he had any good whiskey. Hamlin readily produced a bottle (said later to be Tennessee bourbon), and Johnson took two stiff drinks, telling his benefactor, "I need all the strength for the occasion I can have."

The result, however, was not strength but a half-drunken state, enhanced by the poor ventilation and suffocating heat of the packed Senate chamber. When Johnson began to speak from the rostrum, what emerged was more like what his amazed listeners might have expected to hear in a tavern after a long evening. His voice slurring over the words, he declared: "I'm a-going for to tell you— here today; yes, I'm a-going for to tell you all, that I'm a plebeian! I glory in it; I am a plebeian! The people—yes, the people of the United States have made me what I am; and I am a-going to tell you here today—yes, today, in this place— that the people are everything." It went on that way, until Johnson stopped for breath long enough so that Hamlin could intervene and swear him in.

For the press, it was an extraordinary story. The *Herald*'s correspondent spoke for many of the others when he wrote:

> During all this time [before the oath of office was administered] Andrew Johnson— for such he simply was then, not having taken the oath of office (would to heaven that it could still be said in behalf of the country that he was still Andrew John- son!)—continued his speech. Such a speech! It might have been appropriate at some hustings in Tennessee, but it certainly was far from being appropriate on this occa- sion. It was not only a ninety-ninth rate stump speech, but disgraceful in the extreme. He had not proceeded far when Senators on the Republican side began to hang their heads, sink down in their seats, and look at each other as much as to say, "Is he crazy, or what is the matter?"

Did Johnson say anything at all? The papers reported several different versions, each one colored by the correspondent's (and his paper's) political complexion. The *Globe,* with a straight face, printed a "cleaned-up" version, which con- veyed what sense there was in the speech, ignoring the manner of its delivery. In it were reflected the simplicities Johnson had always believed in: the people's sovereignty, the marvel of his rise from lowly origins, the benevolence of a government that made such a rise possible, faith in the Constitution, and the loyalty of Tennessee.

Some of the Democratic papers tried to reproduce the rustic vernacular, drunken garbling and all, in which the speech had been delivered. The *Herald*'s man, like most of the others, was content to note that what Johnson said was "so disconnected, the sentences so incoherent," and the excited babbling of the spec- tators so distracting that he, the reporter, could hear only snatches of it, so he could do no more than offer the gist. There was a single oblique reference to the probable cause. The new vice-president "evidently did not shun Bourbon county, Kentucky, on his way here," the *Herald* murmured.

After he had taken the oath, Johnson began to make a second speech, but those around him prevented it, and Lincoln, who had sat with his head bowed in humiliation, whispered to Sen. John B. Henderson of Missouri, who was at his side, "Don't let Johnson speak outside." The second inauguration of Lincoln, with his own memorable speech, took place without further incident.

Administration supporters in the press tried to make the best of it. Greeley's *Tribune* gave a single sentence to Johnson's inaugural and merely noted that he was present at a White House reception that evening. The New York *Times,* another supporter, quoted Johnson's speech in a version greatly revised by the reporter. But a new radical magazine, the *Independent,* reprimanded those newspapers trying to suppress the disgraceful affair and printed what everyone was saying privately—that Johnson had "presented himself to take his solemn oath of office in a state of intoxication." As one would expect, the Copperhead papers drew out the stops. Johnson had made "the most incoherent public effort on record," the *World* asserted, and next day it called the vice-president's performance an "exhibition of drunken impertinence," concluding prophetically, "to think that one frail life stands between this insolent, clownish creature and the presidency."

There were a few sympathizers. Frank Blair and his son, Montgomery, who had seen a good deal of both politics and newspapers, invited Johnson to come and shelter with them until the affair blew over, in their country place at Silver Spring, Maryland. On the Senate floor, however, indignation continued, and a resolution demanding Johnson's resignation was introduced but never came up for debate, much less for a vote. As the true nature of his plight on Inauguration Day became better known, even the *Independent* was compelled to retreat and to admit that the vice-president had been "in a shattered condition, resulting from a severe illness and severe labor," and probably would "never have committed the terrible blunder" if he had been well.

It was not the first time Johnson had fallen under political attack. In his often stormy rise to prominence, he had been charged in the press with being a Catholic (a capital crime in some quarters), with being an atheist, and even with being an illegitimate child. There was one thing he was not, however, according to the testimony of the president himself. When an anxious member of his cabinet came to discuss the demands of some Republicans that the new vice-president resign, Lincoln told him: "I have known Andrew Johnson for many years. He made a bad slip the other day, but you need not be scared; Andy ain't a drunk." Lincoln had some reason to know. Responding to rumors, he had ordered an investigation of Johnson on this score before the Republican convention and concluded that, although Johnson drank—an activity virtually universal among politicians—he did not do it habitually to excess. There were a good many public officials of both parties about whom not as much could be said.

Johnson did the wise thing and kept a low profile in Frank Blair's Maryland place until late March, when he came back to Washington intending to stop only briefly before returning to Tennessee to take care of family matters. But the news that Grant had taken Richmond, foreshadowing the end of the war, caused him to postpone his departure. He conferred briefly with Lincoln, for the first time since Inauguration Day, on Friday, April 14, and that night history overtook him, when a pounding on his hotel door as he lay asleep brought him the news of the assassination. Twelve hours later, in the parlor of the Kirkwood House, he was sworn in as the seventeenth president of the United States.

Considering what had gone before, Johnson began his administration on surprisingly good terms with the press. He was courted by Col. John Forney, Buchanan's former editor, now secretary of the Senate and publisher of both the Philadelphia *Press* and the Washington *Chronicle.* In the *Press,* Forney called

Johnson, with considerable exaggeration, "the most popular man in America." Even the radicals in Congress who wanted the South treated as harshly as possible supported Johnson in the beginning because they remembered his uncompromising stand toward the Tennessee rebels. Another helpful supporting voice in Congress was that of Henry J. Raymond, editor of the New York *Times,* who now sat in the House.

It could be expected that leading Democratic papers like the New York *Evening Post* and Greeley's *Tribune* would oppose Johnson. After the inauguration episode the *Evening Post* had even demanded that he either resign or apologize formally to the nation, but the assassination of Lincoln apparently produced a change of attitude in the mind of its editor, Bryant, no doubt in part the result of his natural generosity. When his correspondents in the South reported a widespread desire for reconciliation there, he swung around to support Johnson's mild policies toward the defeated rebels and attacked the vindictive acts proposed in Congress.

Important support also came from Horace Greeley, who had opposed Lincoln's renomination but supported the choice of Johnson as the president's running mate. During his first few weeks in office Johnson was the object of commendatory editorials in the *Tribune,* asserting that he was gaining "steadily in public confidence and esteem." The paper's Washington correspondent termed him "not only one of the nation's foremost patriots and statesmen" but also "a fitting type of a modest, yet self-reliant and accomplished gentleman."

When the president delivered his first annual message, it was greeted by the influential press in the North with a more or less united chorus expressing both amazement and approval. E. L. Godkin called it "frank, dignified, and manly," but he wrote a cautionary note to Johnson, saying, among other things, "I trust you will adhere to it in the face of any hostility." Raymond's *Times* hailed the speech as "full of wisdom," and the *Herald* called it a message "any Democrat as well as any American may well read with pride," although Bennett couldn't help adding that it was surprising so much sagacity and insight could emanate from a tailor who was supposed to be rude, unlettered, and unenlightened. The *Tribune,* usually on the Radical Republican side, doubted "whether any former message has contained so much that will be generally and justly approved, and so little that will or should provoke dissent."

There was enough dissent in the Radical press, however, to balance the praise. Forney's courtship of Johnson had been brief, and now that he held an official position and possessed lucrative government printing contracts given him by Congress, he switched to the side of his benefactors. In his Washington *Chronicle* he declared the president's demand that the Southern states, "now almost as rebellious as they were a year ago . . . should be at once rehabilitated, will send a thrill of dismay to every loyal heart."

The Radicals soon had company. Other newspapers began to turn against Johnson's Reconstruction policies, urging sterner measures with the South. A harsh note came from Joseph Medill, in Chicago, warning the president not to confuse the political opinions of twenty million Americans with what he might read in the columns of the New York *World* or the *Herald.* Before Johnson condemned the Radicals, Medill said, he should remember "their votes made you President, their bayonets and principles put down the Southern rebels, and held their allies, the Northern Copperheads, by the throats. . . . They control 20 states in both branches of Congress. Four-fifths of the soldiers sympathize with them. Can you afford to quarrel with their two millions of votes? . . . For God's sake move cautiously and carefully. Don't show so much eagerness to rush into the embrace of the 20,000 Rebels."

The day of the more or less official administration newspaper was over, but there were Johnson supporters, particularly within his cabinet, who hoped that the idea could somehow be revived. Frank Blair, who had now become one of Johnson's intimates, was urged by conservatives around the country to find some means of doing what he had done for Andrew Jackson. Writing to Blair, the publisher of the Philadelphia *Ledger,* George W. Childs, asked him to tell the president that his paper's columns were at the administration's service. The independent press of the country would support him, Childs asserted, "and we hope he will carry out the wise policies of Mr. Lincoln." Blair's answer to the pressures from these conservatives was to recommend using the loyal and sympathetic *National Intelligencer* as much as possible in the absence of an administration paper in the old sense. But cabinet members were divided on the question of whether to give government advertising to the *Intelligencer,* some favoring the *Chronicle* because Lincoln had done so in this matter.

One reason it was difficult to envisage any newspaper as an "official" organ was the fact that the press as a whole was stridently partisan, yet at the same time undependable in its loyalties. The *Intelligencer,* for example, was nominally pro-Johnson, yet it carried an article on the cabinet that Ulysses S. Grant complained about, charging that it teemed with "many and gross misrepresentations." But "official" or not, the paper continued to be as much of a mouthpiece for the administration as it was possible to be.

Under attack from within and without Washington, Johnson seemed determined to stand fast and to seek support from the most powerful newspapers, however unreliable they might be. Thus he wrote Bennett a note of thanks

> for the able and disinterested manner in which you have defended the policy of the Administration . . . the more highly appreciated because it has not been solicited. . . . Now is the time for the principles upon which the government is founded to be developed, discussed and understood. There is no man in America who can exercise more power in fixing the government upon a firm and enduring foundation than you can. I do not intend to be drawn from my purpose by taunts and jeers, coming whence they may, nor do I intend to be overawed by pretended or real friends, or bullied by swaggering or pursuing enemies.

Bennett thought it a "noble letter" and continued to support Johnson until after the 1866 elections, when he swung his support to Grant for the presidency. The reason for the switch was disclosed by the *National Intelligencer:*

> Bennett had sent for Phillips [W. B. Phillips, the *Herald*'s chief editorial writer] on the night of February 22 and had outlined a "new program" to him. Bennett estimated that the Radical strength in Congress was so formidable that the contest would

be long and fierce, the grounds of opposition being really political, with the next presidential election in mind. Thus the "true way" to aid Johnson in bringing peace to the country was to advocate General Grant! Bennett had a high opinion of Grant and a not less exalted opinion of Johnson himself. He would be as ready, and perhaps more ready to go for [Johnson], if political conditions should then be favorable. Bennett deemed it good policy to keep Grant attached to Johnson.

While Bennett had been unpredictable and independent from the beginning, his behavior in this instance was not untypical of the new era of press "giants." The men who now ran the nation's major dailies could no longer be counted on individually or *en bloc* to support a president. And with the virtual disappearance of the "official" administration newspaper as an institution, presidents could not expect unwavering loyalty even from the press of their own parties. They had not yet learned how to orchestrate public opinion from the White House; that would not come until the days of Theodore Roosevelt. Meanwhile the influence of these papers on the electorate could not even be measured; that, too, would come later. Modern historians who minimize the influence of the press in elections may or may not be correct, but most presidents have believed it to be important, although in varying degrees.

If Andrew Johnson had possessed the machinery of our time—the whole panoply of image-making devices—he might have saved himself from the disaster that awaited him. As it was, he had to depend for support on the passing fancies of publishers, many of whom considered themselves as important as he was. Thus it was frustrating but hardly surprising to find Bennett in Grant's camp after 1866, and then to see him urging Johnson's impeachment when the crisis came—and for no better reason, or so W. B. Phillips thought, than the publisher's wish to cast the *Herald*'s support always on the side of the strongest party.

As Bennett's chief editorial writer, Phillips was inclined to give his employer the benefit of the doubt, explaining that he was "not without patriotism or generous sentiments, nor are these apparently fitful moods without a motive," a judgment whose truth may well be doubted. Phillips's assessment of Bennett, Jr., who would soon succeed his father and with whom other presidents would have to deal, was shrewd and correct, however: "Young Mr. B. . . . is more changeable than his father, while his judgment is more defective and his information limited."

Editorial turnabouts in support of a president could work both ways, as the case of the New York *World* clearly demonstrated. This paper had attacked Johnson in the old style of vituperation from the moment he had been nominated with Lincoln and later referred to him in such tender terms as "an insolent drunken brute in comparison with whom Caligula's horse was respectable" and "an insolent, vulgar, low-bred brute." Yet, when the president faced impeachment, the *World* hastened to his defense because it believed this procedure should be used only in an extreme case.

Johnson's Radical enemies in Congress, however, were not above any kind of maneuver that would undermine him. One of the incidents that gave impetus to the impeachment movement was a wholly erroneous story cleverly planted with the Washington correspondent of the Philadelphia *Bulletin,* who took it in good faith and failed to follow sound journalistic practice by verifying it. The story said that Johnson had asked his attorney general for advice on five separate questions involving the constitutionality of actions taken by the Congress and of measures he might take to counter them. George Childs, now the *Bulletin*'s editor, found this deception deeply humiliating.

There was no protection whatever from the assault on Johnson leveled by three master propagandists who operated in different spheres of influence. One was David R. Locke, who as "Petroleum V. Nasby" contributed dialect humor to the Toledo *Blade* that was reprinted and widely read across the country, earning him an enduring place among the nation's humorists. This kind of homely ridicule, which newspaper readers could easily read and understand—as they would Will Rogers in this century—was subtly devastating to Johnson's public image. No less so were the cartoons of Thomas Nast, appearing in *Harper's Weekly* and other publications, depicting "King Andy" in various unsavory guises, among them as a Roman emperor complacently permitting Seward to crown him while mercenary soldiers slaughtered captives in the arena below. Nast's brutal and bitter cartoons were shocking even to *Harper's Weekly*'s editor, George William Curtis. The third of these propagandists, although he was less deserving of the label, was James Russell Lowell, better remembered today as a poet but then editor of the *North American Review,* well on its way to becoming one of the most prestigious magazines in America. Lowell's contempt for Johnson was profound, and it permeated the pages of his magazine, which was widely read by opinion makers.

In Johnson's power struggle with Congress over his Reconstruction policies, most modern historians believe that his rejection by veto of the civil rights bill was the blunder that led to his eventual downfall. As a result of the veto, allies turned into enemies, and the Moderates and Radicals were given something they could unite on against him. The veto made clear that the quarrel was not over black *political* rights, an argument the president would have no doubt won, but *civil* rights, an issue he could not possibly win. Not only did the veto effectively end any realistic hope he might have had of being elected president in his own right but it stirred up the kind of opposition that would ensure his continued impotency in office.

The veto and reaction to it led to the National Union movement, by which Johnson hoped to marshal enough supporters to give him a third-party victory over the Republicans in 1866 and thus secure majority support in Congress until 1868. To rally the troops the president resorted to a strategy that had worked for him since his beginnings in Tennessee, that is, to make a swing around the country and exhort the voters—in short, old-fashioned stumping. Johnson frequently reiterated the oldest of political clichés, one still healthy in our own time: "I have great faith in the people, I believe they will do what is right." He sincerely believed that, if he could only talk directly to the voters, everything would turn out well for him. Johnson's friends and advisers tried hard to talk him out of making the tour, but he seemed to have sublime confidence in his oratorical powers and simply refused to listen. He had left the press out of his calculations, however, and the reporters who covered his trip drove what would prove to be the decisive nails in his political coffin.

The president left Washington in late August 1866, while his future was being debated in pro- and anti-Johnson conventions, accompanied by two cabinet members, Seward and Welles, and General Grant. Even before his departure Petroleum V. Nasby was entertaining readers with crude cartoons showing Johnson packing for the journey, stowing away jugs and bottles of whiskey and a pistol. Accompanying this was an account of the president's life that began: "The subject uv this sketch wuz at an early age apprenticed to the tailoring bizness, which wuz a most fortunate and appropriate selektion, becuz fust, the aspirant is only required to be the ninth part uv a man."

As an official excuse for the tour, Johnson had accepted an invitation to speak at the dedication in Chicago of a monument to Stephen A. Douglas, a statesman for whom he had exhibited little but contempt when the great orator was alive. To reach Chicago, Johnson had planned a circuitous route, with many speaking stops scheduled. The first of these was in Baltimore, where Greeley's *Tribune,* which was currently referring to the president as "Judas Johnson" and had given the swing no advance coverage, was compelled to admit reluctantly that he addressed a "simply enormous" throng.

From that point on, however, the president encountered a storm of denunciation in the press, epitomized (or summarized) by the *Tribune*'s declaration that Johnson had "turned a solemn journey to the tomb of a celebrated American into the stumping tour of an irritated demagogue." Godkin's *Nation* characterized his speeches as "vulgar, egotistical and occasionally profane," while Lowell in the *North American Review* called the tour "an indecent orgy." What Lowell meant by an orgy was the repeated charge that Johnson was drunk during many of his speeches, particularly one he gave in Cleveland, although it was shown at his impeachment trial that there was no truth in this particular allegation. The drunk in Cleveland was, in fact, General Grant, who had to be spirited aboard a steamer bound for Detroit to conceal his condition; it was intended that he should sober up under the cooling breezes of Lake Erie and rejoin the tour in Detroit.

In Ypsilanti, Michigan, carried away by his own oratory, Johnson attacked the *Tribune*'s accusation that he was a Judas by shouting rhetorically, "If I have played the Judas, who has been my Christ that I have played the Judas with? Was it Thad Stevens? Was it Wendell Phillips? Was it Charles Sumner?" A cry came from the crowd: "Why not hang Thad Stevens and Wendell Phillips?" "Yes," Johnson shouted back enthusiastically, "why not hang them?" No wonder that the New York *Evening Post,* one of the least partisan of papers, observed disgustedly that the president's speeches had "driven people's blood to their heads and aroused a storm of indignation throughout the country."

The "Drunken Tailor," an epithet repeated in newspapers again and again, clung to Johnson like a burr; he was never to shake it. Nearly as damaging was his constant repetition of stock words and phrases—ready ammunition for the satirist's pen. His constant description of his trip as "going around the circle" was picked up with delight by Nasby and became "swingin' round the cirkle," "around the Southern side of the cirkle," "swung around the entire cirkle of offices,'' and similar variations. In every speech the president denied that he was even making a speech, protested that he had no personal ambition because he had filled so many public offices ("the entire cirkle of offices," said Nasby), compared his pardon of Southern rebels to the forgiveness of sinners by Jesus, and declared that if it took crucifixion to save the country, he was prepared.

Since all of this was reported assiduously, and often in extremely biased but detailed form, by the swarm of reporters who followed Johnson, audiences found themselves listening to speeches they had read in some newspaper or magazine and were soon bored. Crowds became unruly, and often there were cries for Grant or Adm. David Farragut. There were times when the commotion created a real danger for the president, and the conductor would order the train to leave before he was finished speaking.

As the trip wound down, disorder became chaos. A riotous crowd prevented Johnson from speaking in Indianapolis; in Ohio he was shouted down by angry mobs, an incident repeated in Pittsburgh. Grant left the tour in Cincinnati, declaring that he was no longer willing to "accompany a man who was deliberately digging his own grave." Seward was stricken with a severe illness in Louisville and had to leave the train in Harrisburg. In the border cities of Louisville and Cincinnati, the crowds were much more friendly because of Johnsonian remarks that would be considered racist today.

Johnson had believed that if only the voters could hear him directly they would support him, but in fact they heard and rejected him. Soon after the tour virtually all the major newspapers that had once supported him, including the New York *Times* and the *Herald,* now turned against him. In the case of the *Times,* Raymond had his own career in Congress to think about, but for both papers it was obvious that their circulations would be seriously hurt if they continued to support the President. The *Times,* the last to desert, had lost a third of its circulation and suffered a financial loss of $100,000 within a few weeks. In the November election, the people finally repudiated Johnson, giving Republicans control of every Northern state and increasing their already large majority in Congress. The president had dug his own grave, as Grant said, but the press could take some credit for the digging.

Later Secretary Welles asserted that the president's speeches were "poorly reported, and often misreported and misrepresented." There was more than a little truth in this complaint. A St. Louis publisher even had to fire a reporter whose account of a Johnson speech proved to be largely imaginary. As Johnson's biographer George F. Milton characterized coverage of the tour: "The type of thing that the Radical press had to say about this President of the United States shows to what low estate journalism had fallen. Editorially and in their news columns, such papers as Joseph Medill's Chicago *Tribune* and Horace Greeley's New York *Tribune* gave vent to vituperation which a decent man would be asked to apply to a convict." While the president refused to defend himself publicly, he did tell Welles that "slander upon slander . . . vituperation upon vituperation of the most virulent character, has made its way through the press."

At a low point in his fortunes during the spring of 1867, bereft of whatever political power he had possessed, Johnson demonstrated considerable courage by turning around and fighting back. Surprisingly, he did it by using that same press that had slandered and deserted him. As his most recent biographer, Albert Castel, has observed, "More than any of his predecessors Johnson endeavored to reach the people through reporters." Employing in an embryonic form the "bully pulpit" technique developed with such devastating effectiveness later by Theodore Roosevelt, Johnson laid down a barrage of messages, speeches, and press interviews in a desperate effort to convince the voters they were mistaken about him.

His first approach, in March 1867, was one that would become standard operating procedure. He called in Charles G. Halpine, regarded as one of the most influential journalists in the business under his byline of "Miles O'Reilly," and gave him an exclusive interview. In it Johnson tried to distract attention from his current problems with Congress by raising an entirely different issue—whether the national debt should be paid or repudiated. Predicting that a war of finance would be the next national conflict, he declared that this struggle would soon overshadow everything else and adroitly (so he thought) defined his own battle to uphold the Constitution against "Congressional usurpation" (as he put it) in terms of prevented repudiation.

But the public, much less the political parties, refused to be distracted by economic issues: Reconstruction was much easier to understand. There was some movement in Congress to cope with the debt problem, but Johnson made little progress as a result of the Halpine interview, largely because he tried to work both sides of the inflationist-contractionist street, satisfying no one and laying himself open to new charges of demagoguery. The president also asked Halpine to do what he could with the New York editors, and this loyal journalist agreed to act as go-between. He was able to persuade Greeley to take a strong stand against the whole idea of impeachment, which was now being talked about openly, but he had no luck at all with Bennett.

Inexorably, the tide swung against the president. A report by the House Judiciary Committee called for impeachment, but a minority report by the chairman denied that there was any legal basis for such an action, and when it came to a vote, the House rejected its own committee's recommendation. The press greeted this decision with a measure of relief. It would be expected that the *Intelligencer,* the only newspaper of consequence supporting the president, would proclaim "The Death of Impeachment," but here was the New York *Times* headlining "End of the Impeachment Folly," and the Chicago *Tribune* praising Congress for what it had done.

Nevertheless the move toward impeachment continued as the president resumed the grave digging he had begun on his trip around the circle. It was a political and personal tragedy too well known to be rehearsed here. What is important for purposes of this study is that in the end Johnson stood alone without support from the press except for the sometimes doubtful loyalty of the *Intelligencer.*

The big guns of the newspaper establishment were trained on him as his trial began. The tone of much that was printed could only be called spiteful. Colonel Forney's Washington *Chronicle* reported, erroneously, that even the president's counsel saw no hope of acquittal. Greeley and Medill led the pack of big-city editors urging their readers to persuade uncommitted senators to vote for conviction. Someone, perhaps Greeley himself, saw to it that one of the *Tribune*'s acid editorials on the subject was placed in the hands of every member of the Supreme Court.

Only the New York *Times* found reason to modify its stand. It called the *Tribune*'s treatment of the impeachment proceedings "so far-fetched, so untenable, and withal so ludicrous, as to render the *Tribune*'s excitement exceedingly absurd." At the same time it saw "no reason to change the opinion we have already expressed that the President will be found guilty and removed from his office." But when Johnson's St. Louis speeches during his tour were cited as evidence that he was illegally assailing Congress, Raymond was outraged and on April 27, 1868, the paper declared that this constituted "an admission that the facts in which the House founded its resolution of impeachment are insufficient to sustain a verdict of guilty." When the legalities of the situation were satisfied, however, the *Times* reverted to its former low opinion of the president. "We care but little for the immediate result of the impeachment trial," it said. "Whether Johnson stays in office ten months longer or not, is of very little consequence to the country. . . . He is the merest shadow of an Executive that ever sat in the Presidential chair."

Most of the country appeared to agree, and the press reflected a general feeling that it was impeachment itself that seemed intolerable rather than anything the president might have done—a feeling echoed more than a century later in the case of Richard Nixon. Godkin, in the *Nation*, thanked by name those who had voted for acquittal, not because of their vote "but for vindicating . . . the sacred rights of individual conscience. . . . We shall hear no more of impeachment and we are glad of it." This sentiment was affirmed by a broad spectrum of such Republican journals as the Chicago *Tribune*, *Harper's Weekly*, the Boston *Advertiser*, the Providence *Journal*, the Cincinnati *Daily Commercial*, and the Hartford *Courant*.

For all his problems with the press, Johnson left the White House with a better record than most of his predecessors (except Lincoln) in his direct relationships with it. Not only had he given the first exclusive, formal White House interview, but he had granted the most frequent interviews of any president until that time. Most of these were informal, often impromptu, as Johnson tried to get his message to the people and gain their support in his fight with Congress.

Unlike many presidents Johnson was a regular reader of newspapers. That was a part of his daily routine, between his rising at 6 A.M. and his breakfast two hours later. He was familiar with the individual work of reporters, and he had his favorites, a few of whom could go into his office without being announced, something that even Lincoln had permitted only sparingly. One of these was Simon P. Hanscom, editor of the Washington *Republican*, who was considered an "office broker" for job applicants. It was Hanscom who arranged an interview with Johnson for Charles Dickens in 1868, which resulted in one of the best descriptions we have of the president as an individual. "He is a man with a remarkable face," Dickens wrote, "indicating courage, watchfulness, and certainly strength of purpose. It is a face of the Webster type, but without the 'bounce' of Webster's face. I would have picked him out anywhere as a character of mark. Figure, rather stoutish for an American; a trifle under the middle size; hands clasped in front of him; manner, suppressed, guarded, anxious. Each of us looked at the other very hard."

When he left the White House, a private citizen for the first time in thirty years, Johnson went first to the house of John Coyle, proprietor of the *National Intelligencer*. On the way home to Greeneville, Tennessee, a few days later, he told a newspaper correspondent accompanying him, "Yes, there's a good deal of life in me yet." To some, it sounded like whistling in the wind, but he proved them wrong.

Johnson had no inclination whatever toward peaceful retirement. Instead he was determined to vindicate himself and his policies, and to revenge himself upon his enemies. That could only be done in Washington, and so, less than a month after he returned to Greeneville, he was laying plans to run for the Senate from Tennessee. He failed by one vote on his first attempt; there were enough Confederate Democrats and opposition Republicans around who were not as forgiving as he was, and they prevailed. Three years later he tried again, running in a special election for congressman-at-large, and wound up a disappointing third. At that point he appeared to be finished politically and began to drink again—or still, as some would have it. Once, in Nashville, when he was called upon to speak, he was too drunk to utter a sound. Then he was stricken with yellow fever in an epidemic that struck East Tennessee in 1873, but he survived that too, and in 1874 ran a third time for a Senate seat. He won, and in March 1875 returned triumphantly to Washington.

It was a display of courage and indomitable persistence that brought him tributes from the newspapers which had once scourged him. In the *Herald* his election was termed "a national victory," and the *Times* declared: "He went out of the White House as poor as he entered it, and that is something to say in these times. We shall not be sorry to see him again in public life."

Johnson did not live long to enjoy his victory. Four months after his return to Washington, he was dead following a brief illness. But indomitable he was to the end. The press duly reported his last speeches. They were attacks against his old enemy, Ulysses S. Grant, who now sat in the White House.

Grant: The Rise of Investigative Reporting

Ulysses Grant's military reputation is as secure today as it was in his lifetime, and, conversely, there is nearly as much agreement that he ranks among the worst presidents. The litany of his faults in office remains unchanged: poor selection of cabinet members and other associates; an inexplicable failure of leadership from a man accustomed to command; inability to learn from his mistakes; a blindness (if indeed it was) to flagrant corruption within his administration, even his own family; a failure to formulate definite policies about most matters of public concern—the list could go on.

We have come a long way in our estimate of Grant, however, from William E. Woodward's scathing *Meet General Grant,* a product of the debunking era, to recent revisionist attempts to portray him as a decent if misguided man with human faults, surrounded by unfortunate associates and controlled in some degree as president by a strong-minded woman, his devoted wife Julia. But even making every possible allowance for what he may or may not have been as a person, it can hardly be disputed that his eight years in the White House were among the most politically corrupt in the nation's history.

Grant had no consistent policy toward the press, any more than he had toward most other matters, and he was abused by it where once he had been its hero—a common enough fate. Although the journals did not play a decisive role in Grant's presidency, they did rise to new heights in exposing corruption. Newspapers (and some magazines as well) had always carried out this function as part of their perceived mission to inform the public and monitor the excesses of government, but, during Grant's two terms, they employed the techniques of what we now call investigative reporting, foreshadowing the era of the muckrakers soon to come.

This unsavory period began with a campaign and an election in marked contrast to the usual quadrennial hoopla. The nation was temporarily weary of bloodshed and partisan wrangling. As a man who had never been an office holder, an office seeker, or a partisan politician, Grant seemed the ideal candidate. When the Republicans met in Chicago four days after Andrew Johnson's acquittal, the business of nominating a presidential candidate was such a foregone conclusion that the entire procedure took just forty-eight hours. Grant's name was the only one before the convention. What more could the delegates have asked for than a war hero, admired by everyone except those Southerners who still hated him, a man who spoke very little and who had never done anything that could reasonably be attacked, except possibly drink too much? He liked people, horses, and tobacco (besides liquor), not necessarily in that order. Most of all, he was not a professional politician, a breed unpopular with the voters for the time being.

There was one small difficulty. In 1856, the only time he had ever voted, Grant had cast his ballot for the Democrats, and in fact he could easily have been the Democratic candidate for president if it had not been for his break with Johnson, which cast him in the role of Radical Republican. The general did not seek to be president and insisted modestly on being wooed, but on the other hand he would have been disappointed if a grateful nation had not given him what he clearly believed he deserved.

When the Democrats met at Tammany Hall, in New York, they were as contentious and divided as usual. On the opening day an address from Susan B. Anthony was read, asking the party's support for at least the principle of woman suffrage. It was received with howls of laughter and dismissed. After days of wrangling over a variety of candidates,essentially a struggle between Eastern and Western interests, the choice fell on the convention's permanent chairman, Horatio Seymour, the Great Decliner, who had refused the honor emphatically when it was first offered and declined even more emphatically when the tide began to flow toward him. He would have refused a third time, but friends virtually kidnaped him, hurried him out a back door, and carried him off to the sanctuary of the Manhattan Club, where he was said to have encountered a friend and, with tears on his cheeks, uttered the melancholy cry, "Pity me, Harvey! Pity me!" Thus a man who did not know until twenty minutes before the event that he would be the Democrats' candidate was chosen in a scene of wild excitement and, still weeping, accepted the honor. No potential president was ever more reluctant to be one. Almost overlooked was Frank Blair's nomination as vice-president—the only time a newspaper editor had been so honored.

The campaign was conducted in an atmosphere of mutual recrimination, as turmoil in the South over the likelihood of Grant's success touched off riots and the Civil War was fought all over again verbally. The Democrats called Grant a "Man on Horseback" and warned of a military dictator in the White House. Meanwhile their man Seymour had to be prodded into campaigning. The prospect of an overwhelming Democratic defeat was so likely that the New York *World* suggested both Seymour and Blair should retire in favor (unbelievably) of Johnson and Chief Justice Chase. John Quincy Adams II, grandson of the president for whom he was named, observed sourly that it was too late to change candidates, and the Democrats might as well accept Grant's inevitable victory.

That victory, when it came, was surprisingly tarnished. While Seymour got only 80 electoral votes from eight states, in contrast to Grant's twenty-six states and 214 votes, the general's popular vote margin was not much more than 300,000, with 5,750,000 people voting. There was another surprise. Six of the eight former Confederate states voted for Grant, the balance tipped by black voting. More than any other factor, however, it was the Republican campaign slogan, "Let us have peace," that appeared to have touched hearts and minds everywhere in the country.

As the inauguration approached, the new era of investigative reporting was ushered in by an enterprising reporter for the New York *World,* who wrote a story presenting what purported to be Grant's views of various men in public life, including some prominent editors. These opinions were offered as direct quotations, but in fact they represented a composite of statements from Grant's friends and others close to him, since the president-elect himself would not be interviewed. The story consequently had to be suspect, but, since Grant never denied the authenticity of what was attributed to him, and since much of it was well known to represent his views, one can accept that this was, in substance, what the general really thought. The result may have given the subjects a few moments of discomfort, but coming from a man who was anything but a good judge of human nature, these estimates were not far from the mark.

Of Horace Greeley, Grant said (or so the reporter paraphrased him):

Mr. Greeley has published some unpalatable things about me, but I have no doubt he thought at the time they were true. Greeley is a good man, a great man, and a faithful, honest and efficient advocate of the cause of human liberty. He always seemed to me to exaggerate the bright side of human nature, and underrate the dark side. . . . Such men are always the dupes of men of inferior abilities, who are cunning and dishonest. . . . The world is better for Greeley having lived in it and erred in it. I like Greeley better than I have any reason to suppose he likes me.

Of Charles A. Dana, who had just begun his new career as owner and editor of the New York *Sun:*

Dana is a man for whom I ought to have a great contempt, but to whom I owe nothing but good will. He came to me a spy upon my conduct. He reported favorably. If it had not been for his favorable report, I should probably have been removed from my command. . . . So far as I know he is not an applicant for office under me. He is eminently fitted for journalism, and I should consult his interest in declining to remove him to any other sphere.

Of James Gordon Bennett, Sr., who had now turned over control of the *Herald* to his son, Bennett, Jr.:

Bennett is a Scotchman; no man born in Scotland ever became acclimated in this country. . . . I am of this descent myself, and therefore speak candidly. . . . Bennett, like a true Scotchman, is ever ready to trade upon the misfortunes of his adopted country. He cares not how terrible a time it is for the country, if it is only a good time for newspapers. He made his paper famous by making it infamous. It mattered nothing to him who was harmed, so that he made money.

On the whole, Grant did not feel unkindly toward newspaper editors in general as he took office, particularly those who had favored him. He appointed the irascible James Watson Webb, Bennett's old enemy on the New York *Courier and Enquirer,* as minister to Brazil, and a Wisconsin editor named Horace Rublee as minister to Switzerland. He even considered Greeley briefly for a position in the cabinet, but wisely decided against it.

Yet it was clear from the beginning what Grant's policy (if it could be called one) toward the press was going to be. He intended to tell it as little as possible about what he was going to do, an aim made easier by his naturally secretive nature. Even Julia Grant did not know who his cabinet choices were going to be. When the nominations were sent to the Senate, however, the outcry began. Dana, who had written a campaign biography for the general, and Henry Raymond of the *Times,* who had supported him, were appalled by those selected. Partly it was because so many of the nominees were obscure. "Who in the world is Borie?" the New York *Herald* wanted to know. (The remark has also, erroneously, been attributed to Medill and the Chicago *Tribune.* Adolph E. Borie, the designated secretary of the navy, was in fact a blameless Philadelphia millionaire, a merchant whose country house a dozen miles or so from the city contained Grant's oil painting of an Indian family and a trader, which the general contemplated with justifiable pride on visits otherwise occupied with endless card games.)

But the chief burden of the outcry against Grant's appointments was that so many of them went to relatives of either the president or his wife—a number estimated at anywhere from twelve to forty-eight. There was nothing particularly unusual about this kind of nepotism—many previous presidents had been especially kind to deserving kinfolk—but some Democratic newspapers were very disturbed by the large number of Dents (Julia Grant's maiden name was Dent) who appeared on the appointments list. "A plague of Dents," one called it, even worse than the similar plethora of Todds in Lincoln's administration.

Grant did not appear to be especially upset by these attacks. He even gave frequent interviews to the New York *Herald*'s Washington correspondent, G. De. B. Keim, although Bennett, Jr., at this juncture was generally sympathetic to the Democrats, as his father had been. Like so many other presidents, the general continued to be an assiduous reader of newspapers, perusing the Washington journals as soon as he arose at 7 A.M., before he had breakfast at eight-thirty.

In spite of his initial calm, Grant had not been in office more than two months before an uneasiness about him, which was not particularly partisan, began to be apparent in the press. The Chicago *Tribune,* which had supported his candidacy, gave voice to it in an editorial complaining that the administration's moral power "has been frittered away by small absurdities" and that "there never was an administration with more good intentions at heart and less aptitude for carrying them into effect."

Other disturbing signs of trouble began to appear. In spite of the fact that Grant had sound democratic instincts, as those who knew him best could testify, at the same time he had developed a taste for luxury, perhaps a reaction to the hardships and bleak realities of military life. He enjoyed visiting Borie's splendid country place so much that he found himself unable to resist the gift of houses from admiring citizens—one of them a modest enough place in Galena, Illinois, but another a $60,000 mansion in Philadelphia. His stables held no fewer than eighteen horses, all but two presumed to be gifts. Moreover, most of his friends were rich men, like Borie. The gratitude of the country, indeed, appeared to have no limit, even after his scandal-filled presidency; the New York *Times* began a campaign in 1880 to establish a $250,000 fund that would give him an income of $15,000 a year for life. At the same time other friends raised $100,000 to buy him a third house in New York City.

One and all, these friends plainly saw Grant as a good and honest man, and so he may have been. Still it is difficult to believe now, as many of the best editors doubted then, that the president knew nothing of the wholesale corruption around him, particularly when his own family was involved in it. Unfortunately for him, his sister Jennie had married a notorious Wall Street speculator named Abel Rathbone Corbin, who was a plundering associate of Jay Gould and Jim Fisk, scourgers of innocent investors. These devious highflyers saw in Corbin's family connection a heaven-sent opportunity to rig the gold market with the help of the White House. Corbin introduced them to his father-in-law, who appeared happy to associate with such celebrated financiers, and the financiers in turn used the connection to advertise themselves favorably to the victims they intended to deprive. Gould also entertained the Grants handsomely in various expensive ways.

The conspirators neglected, however, to consider the newspapers in their plans. No one of such prominence as Gould and Fisk could have carried on so open a mating dance with the White House without attracting skeptical attention.

Bennett, Sr., if he had still been in charge of the *Herald,* would have smelled out the gold plot at once, but Horace Greeley, an astute and knowledgeable observer, would not be far behind him, and it was Greeley who blew the whistle. In an editorial he exposed the budding conspiracy and called on the Treasury, which had a great deal of gold to sell, to act without delay. The conspirators responded by getting Corbin to send a letter directly to Grant, urging him not to let the Treasury throw any gold on the market.

A more sophisticated president would have seen through this transparent maneuver at once and acted decisively, but Grant, vaguely disturbed and sensing trouble, did no more than ask his wife to drop a note to his sister, telling her that he was worried about what his brother-in-law was doing in "The Street" and urging her to use her influence in stopping it. Julia's letter was signed, discreetly, "Sis," a term she had never used before with Jennie.

Inevitably, Gould learned about the letter from Corbin and, anticipating possible disaster, moved quickly to save himself. Meanwhile Greeley shot off another editorial gun, again demanding that the Treasury act. That alarmed Grant enough to make him confer with Secretary of the Treasury George Boutwell on the question of whether, or when, to sell the government's gold. But even as he did so Gould was taking an extraordinary step to preserve the plot. He knew that if Corbin withdrew, or if Julia Grant's letter got out, his conspiracy would be ruined; consequently he offered Corbin what amounted to a $100,000 bribe to stay in with the speculators. This scene took place early in the morning in the Corbins' home, where a fearful Jennie persuaded her husband to reject the offer on the spot.

During a later Senate investigation of this affair, Corbin told of Gould's reaction to the refusal: "Mr. Gould stood there for a little while looking very thoughtful—exceedingly thoughtful. He then left—about 10 o'clock—and went into Wall Street." What Gould did when he got there, of course, was to begin selling his gold anonymously, as fast as he prudently dared, while he let it get about that Corbin was still in the market with him, with the implication that the White House approved.

The result was that historic Black Friday on Wall Street, which occurred after Grant and Boutwell decided to sell $4 million worth of government gold, and the price of the precious metal fell from $160 to $140 in the first ten minutes after the sale was announced. Before the day was over, ruined speculators were strewn about the landscape. Others, who had taken the opposite gamble, got rich. Corbin was not one of them. Although he got rid of his gold, he did not do it in time to realize enough money to cover the loan he had obtained to buy it. He and Jennie soon had to move to Jersey City, in less opulent surroundings.

But Grant was saved. A general recession did not occur, like the one in 1857, as he had feared; that would not come until 1873. There was enough odor of fraud in the air, however, to produce a Senate investigation by a committee whose chairman was an up-and-coming politician from Ohio, James A. Garfield. Since the Republicans were in control of Congress, it was axiomatic that the trail of Gould and Fisk would not be followed to the White House by the investigators if it could be covered up, and Garfield did his best. Committee Democrats tried to insist on calling Julia Grant and Jennie Corbin for their testimony in the matter, since it was widely believed by everyone except Republican loyalists that Julia had put some money of her own in the Corbins' gold account, and so was a party to the conspiracy, whether knowingly or not.

Was she? And could she have done it without the president's knowledge? There is no proof in either case, and the revisionists, who take a kindly view of Grant, tend to doubt it. But even though the Republicans managed to block a summons for the president's wife and his sister, they could not suppress evidence that a packet of money had been delivered to Mrs. Grant that fall. Whether it contained $2,500 or $25 was a matter of dispute, and whether it had come from gold speculation or not was never proved. In the end all the satisfaction the Democrats got was to see the assistant secretary of the treasury, Daniel Butterfield, whose appointment Corbin had secured through his White House connections, fired as a result of the investigation when it turned out that he had an account in the same gold market he was supposed to be regulating.

While the Democratic papers rejoiced in these events, they did not play much of a part in them. They came into the controversy after the fact, when the conspirators began to quarrel among themselves. Corbin tried to deny, through a letter to the New York *Sun,* that he had anything to do with Fisk, but Fisk angrily denied that, using the *Herald* to confess his own part in the scheme and going much further by asserting that "the President himself was interested with us in the corner." Fisk then took a *Herald* reporter with him as witness and went to call on Corbin, who simply went on denying that he had any connection with "such men" as Fisk and Gould.

The press was ready to convict Corbin on this evidence, and Fisk himself was self-confessed, but what about Grant? The *World* was convinced of his innocence, but not so completely that it failed to chide him. "The President compromised his independence by his indiscreet acceptance of courtesies," it said, apparently referring to Gould's lavish hospitality, which Grant had accepted gladly. A professional moralist like E. L. Godkin could not be expected to let the president off so lightly, and he did not disappoint his readers. "One thing is certain," the *Nation* concluded, "bankers here see traces in the operation of the hand of somebody in authority. Let us know who that person is."

At this point Robert Bonner, who had been Washington correspondent for the *Times,* offered the president a platform to clear himself, if he wished. The paper had already given Grant such a platform, as the Senate investigators had disclosed, through interviews with John Bigelow, the editor, in which the president took advantage of an invitation to make clear his views about the country's financial condition and prospects. Gould and the others had cleverly used a resulting *Times* editorial, headlined as "Grant's Financial Policy," to spread the idea among investors that this was a semiofficial statement of government policies whose consequences could only be higher gold prices.

Bonner's offer was in the form of a letter to the president, in which he said:

In the present disturbed state of the public mind concerning the recent gold combination, is it not the quickest and surest way to set at rest the great excitement and

uneasiness which prevail for you to make a brief denial over your signature of all
foreknowledge of that combination, in order to relieve yourself entirely of all responsibility for the acts of others? Of course, those who know you personally, do not
require such a disclaimer; but the great public . . . will be, it seems to me, at once
satisfied and quieted by such a statement. . . . I do this with less hesitation because
you did me the honor, after your election, to confide in me pretty fully your views.

Grant replied:

I have never thought of contradicting statements and insinuations made against me
by irresponsible parties, as these are alluded to in your letter; but as you have written
to me on the subject in so kind a spirit, I will say that I had no more to do with the
late gold excitement in New York City than yourself, or any other innocent party,
except that I ordered the sale of gold to break the ring engaged, as I thought, in a
most disreputable transaction. If the speculators had been successful, you would
never have heard of any one connected with the administration as being connected
with the transaction. P.S. I have written this in great haste, and without exercising
judgment as to the propriety of writing it, but I submit it to your judgment.

In short, not guilty. Still, Bonner must have read one sentence thoughtfully:
"If the speculators had been successful, you would never have heard of any one
connected with the administration as being connected with the transaction." This
was presidential naîveté that taxed credulity. If Gould and Fisk had succeeded in
their fraudulent scheme and gotten away with it, of course, the Corbins and Julia
(if indeed she had been speculating, too) would have been shielded from any
public notice, as would the conspirators themselves. Who could doubt it? For
that matter, General Butterfield would still have his job in Treasury.

One of the disbelievers when these letters were released was Charles Anderson
Dana, whose renascent *Sun* was already the envy of other editors. There was
little Dana did not know about politics. He had trained under Greeley on the
Tribune; he knew Grant intimately as a result of his secret "spying" mission for
Lincoln; and he knew the inside workings of government as a result of his service
in Lincoln's War Department. What he saw now was enough to convince him
that he had been wrong in supporting Grant.

The *Sun* had been critical of the president, however, as early as six weeks after
his inaugural, citing his "frightful blunderings and flounderings" and declaring
prophetically that he was in the hands of "charlatans and adventurers." But it
had continued to regard him with mild hopefulness until the Black Friday episode. Then, slowly and reluctantly, Dana began to turn against him, until he
could no longer avoid a full confrontation when Grant was nominated for a second term.

There were other skeptics, too, besides Dana, but their motives were different.
Greeley, who had stoutly defended the president from the beginning and assailed
his critics in the press, found himself less enthusiastic when Grant allied himself
with the Roscoe Conkling faction, Greeley's perennial enemies in New York
State politics. That was the opening wedge. The split widened further in 1871, as
the *Tribune*'s formidable editor scented the possibility of holding the high public

office he had craved desperately for so long. The tantalizing prospect of the White House itself had now been raised.

The Republican press as a whole remained cautiously hopeful about Grant until near the end of his first term, balancing the slashing attacks of the Democratic papers, which had now abandoned any semblance of respect for the war hero president. The New York *World* habitually called him "Kaiser Ulysses." By 1872, however, even the most loyal Republican editors could not escape the realities of life in Washington, where patronage, graft, and fraud were now the order of the day. The fact that so many of those involved were friends or relatives of the president could hardly escape notice. There were those who argued then, as they do today, that Grant was such a simple and honest man that he did not see what was going on around him or, if he did, refused to believe or accept what he saw. There were many others, however, who found it equally difficult to believe that any president could be so blind or so simplistic.

The result was a deep split in the Republican party. Those who demanded sweeping reform, calling themselves the Liberal Republicans, broke off and put up their own ticket at a national convention in Cincinnati. As in most reform movements, the delegates who assembled proved to be a mixed bag, with widely varying motives. They were united on only one thing—to block Grant's renomination and purge the Republican party of corruption.

Behind this movement were four of the most noted newspaper editors in the country: Horace White of the Chicago *Tribune*, Sanuel Bowles of the Springfield *Republican*, Murat Halstead of the Cincinnati *Daily Commercial*, and Henry Watterson of the Louisville *Courier-Journal*. These men came to be known collectively as the Quadrilateral, a reference to the four fortified towns in northern Italy that supported the Austrian occupation. They held regular meetings, formulated policies, and used their papers in an effort to organize public opinion in support of their goals. They were encouraged by other influential journalists and editors, such as Carl Schurz, who helped write the Liberal platform—a devastating indictment of Grant.

When it came to choosing a candidate, the prevailing sentiment appeared to be in favor of Charles Francis Adams, whose only drawback appeared to be his chilling personality, which the Quadrilateral was prepared to overlook. On the eve of the nomination, however, the plans of the Liberal leaders were upset by the sudden appearance of two gentlemen from Missouri, Gov. B. Gratz Brown and Sen. Francis P. Blair, Jr. They did not want Adams, and they were ready to be spoilers. Blair, ironically, was the youngest son of Frank Blair, Jackson's great editor, who had been a pillar of the Democratic party. The son, who had risen to be a Civil War general, was now nominally on the other side, although his main objective was only to unseat Grant.

In the balloting Adams led on the first time around, but Horace Greeley ran a suprising second, to his great joy, because he had not until then been taken seriously as a candidate. Governor Brown himself ran fourth, and after the balloting he rose to say that he was withdrawing, and then eloquently urged the convention to vote for Greeley, who had been his candidate all along and whose nomination he had come to Cincinnati to secure. Brown's speech threw the hall into an uproar, with one of those outbursts of spontaneous emotion that often characterize political conventions. The Greeley bandwagon was rolling, and on the sixth ballot, when several states swung over to him, he was nominated, with Governor Brown as his running mate.

Greeley, always emotional, was overcome. He could see the ambition of his life, the White House, shining in the distance, almost within his grasp. There were a good many other delegates, however, who considered the convention's decision a disaster, and they were just as emotional as the candidate. Meeting after the vote, some were in tears, others in transports of frustration and rage. Carl Schurz expressed his anger by pounding on the top of a piano with his fist. Governor Brown and his friend Blair were denounced as intruders.

One might have thought that Greeley's fellow editors would have rallied to his support, since he was the first of their number ever to be nominated for the presidency, but they deserted him *en masse*. The voice of E. L. Godkin could be heard in the New York *Evening Post*'s outraged pronouncement: "With such a head as is on Greeley's shoulders, the affairs of the nation would not, under his direction, be wisely administered; with such manners as his, they could not be administered with common decorum; with such associates as he has taken to his bosom, they could not be administered with common integrity." And the usually soft-spoken New York *Times* came as near to thundering as it ever did, wondering whether "so eminently shrewd a people as this would ever place such a man as Greeley at the head of their government. If any one man could send a great nation to the dogs, that man is Mr. Greeley." (This figure of speech, it must be noted, had been used in essence by every opposition editor since Jefferson's day to predict the downfall of the Republic if a candidate it did not support was elected.)

When the Republicans met in Philadelphia, not a word about corruption in Washington (or Wall Street) was heard, and Grant was nominated unanimously. Vice-President Schuyler Colfax was pushed aside, however, in favor of Sen. Henry Wilson of Massachusetts. Colfax had made the mistake of intimating he could be persuaded to take the nomination himself, and Grant would have none of him.

The Democrats, meeting in Baltimore, were expected to endorse the Liberal Republican candidates, in the practical expectation that the combined strength of the two factions would be enough to beat Grant. Many of the delegates had a difficult time swallowing Horace Greeley, however, since he had been a lifelong Republican and the *Tribune* was a mouthpiece for the party during much of the time. Only their frank conviction that they would vote for anybody who could defeat Grant carried the day for Greeley. The governor of North Carolina spoke for most of them: "If the Baltimore Convention puts Greeley in our hymn book, we will sing him through if it kills us."

But again there were dissenters, enough of them to hold a separate convention, where they denounced the action in Baltimore as a sellout of the party. These "Straight-out Democrats," as they called themselves, nominated Charles O'Conor, an undistinguished party wheelhorse. The Labor Reform party and the Prohibition party also put up candidates.

It proved to be one of the strangest campaigns in American political history, and in the confusion poor Greeley stood out as a man obviously marked for martyrdom. Because he and the *Tribune* had been so well regarded across the nation for so long a time, he had a profound faith that the people would follow him now as they had always done through the editorial columns of his newspaper. He took his case to these people and pleaded it well. James G. Blaine recorded later that he

> presented his case with an ability which could not be exceeded, and [his speeches] added to the general estimate of his intellectual faculties and resources. He called out a larger proportion of those who intended to vote against him than any candidate had ever before succeeded in doing. His name has been honored for so many years in every Republican household, that the desire to see and hear him was universal, and secured to him the majesty of numbers at every meeting.

But one would not know he had ever been honored at all, in light of the vicious assault on his life and character that his fellow editors launched against him. His moonlike face and general picturesque appearance had always made him the delight of cartoonists, but these artists now turned savage pens against him, particularly Thomas Nast, the most noted of them all, who hacked away at Greeley week after week in *Harper's Weekly*. Greeley clung to his faith in the people, but nevertheless he was hurt and bewildered by the assault.

Thus, predictably, the effort of the first editor to run for the presidency ended in tragedy. Grant, who had said almost nothing during the campaign because he had so little to say, took a great deal of abuse from his fellow Republicans among the editors, as he had been doing all along, but the blatant corruption in his administration was never really an issue with the voters, who plainly wanted honest old Ulysses, the man who whipped the South. He carried thirty out of thirty-seven states, and a stunned Greeley realized that his "people" had deserted him and that he had taken the worst beating of any man who had ever run for the presidency.

It was a devastating blow, compounded by the death of his much-loved wife Mary, just a few days before the election. Greeley was also losing control of his paper to Whitelaw Reid in the aftermath of the election, as he lay in a state of physical and mental exhaustion at the house of a friend on Fifty-seventh Street. "I am not dead, but I wish I were," he wrote to a friend. "My house is desolate, my future dark, my heart a stone." His mind gave way under such stress, and after being removed to a private mental hospital in Pleasantville, New York, he sank into a coma and died less than a month after the election.

Greeley had asked for a simple funeral. "Plant me in my favorite pumpkin arbor," he had written, "with a gooseberry bush for a footstone." Instead he was given a church funeral on Fifth Avenue, and among the prominent pallbearers and mourners were Grant, who had killed his dream, and the *Tribune* men who had been struggling to take control of his paper. The people, however, belatedly returned to him. The funeral cortege wound down Fifth Avenue between solid walls of them, most in tears.

In his second inaugural address Grant acknowledged the abuse that had been directed against him by the press, in words employed by nearly every previous president. He had never asked for anything but to do his duty, he declared piously, but "notwithstanding this, throughout the war, and from my candidacy for my present office in 1868 to the close of the last presidential campaign, I have been the subject of abuse and slander scarcely ever equaled in political history." In equally immortal words he added that he could disregard this opposition "in view of your verdict, which I gratefully accept as my vindication."

A sea of troubles awaited Grant in his second administration. Offshore, in the Caribbean, the first calls for expansionism in that American lake were being heard—or if not the first, since the urge to acquire Cuba by one means or another predated the Civil War, at least they were becoming more urgent as the Cubans began an insurrection against Spanish rule. Most Americans of both parties sympathized with this revolution, and the revolutionaries were being aided with arms, supplies, and even volunteer soldiers from the United States. Cuban agents fanned the fire on the mainland.

One result was a giant public demonstration for Cuban independence from Spain, held in New York, about three weeks after Inauguration Day. The mayor of the city was permanent chairman of this event, and Dana acted as temporary chairman. Henry Ward Beecher was a speaker. All the major newspapers in the city supported the Cuban cause; two of them, the *Herald* and the *Sun,* wanted immediate American intervention. Only the Democratic *World* remained coolly on the other side. Elsewhere, newspapers divided along party lines on the question.

Grant's handling of the Cuban crisis was regarded as singularly inept by all these editors, and so was his approach to the controversy over whether Santo Domingo should be acquired. The newspapers were more closely divided on this question, but they were virtually united in their criticism of Grant's role in it. A bill of annexation was defeated in Congress.

At home another shadow of scandal hung over the general even as he was being reelected—the Crédit Mobilier affair, in which (to simplify a complex scam) promoters of the Union Pacific Railway tried to divert fraudulently into their own pockets, through creating a dummy company, some of the profits derived from building the line. Dana's *Sun* had exposed this brazen grab, which involved Vice-President Colfax and several highly placed Republican politicians. As the story of the scheme unfolded in the *Sun* and other papers, so many of the administration's people appeared to be involved in it that much of the public was beginning to believe there were few honest men in and around the White House.

The Crédit Mobilier scandal might have demolished another president, but Grant, as we have seen, rode serenely to a second victory even as the plot continued to be exposed. It was more difficult to avoid blame for the panic of 1873, but again Grant ducked his head until the worst of it was over, when he gave a guarded exclusive interview (he called it a "conversation") with the Washington correspondent of the New York Associated Press, in which he offered some vague conclusions and possible courses of action, none of which were taken. Dana remained unconvinced. His *Sun* continued to blame Grant for the panic and also revived the charges of presidential drunkenness. (Strangely, Dana had not believed that Grant's admitted drinking problem would prevent him from commanding the Union army, in his report to Lincoln on the general's abilities.)

The clouds of scandal continued to thicken as the second term progressed, and other papers, employing methods not too distant from today's investigative reporting techniques, began to dig into the formidable mass of corruption. In 1876 the *Herald* unearthed a fragrant mess in the War Department and demanded an investigation. The House took up this challenge and found that Secretary of War William W. Belknap had taken bribes for selling trading posts in Indian Territory. He was impeached, resigned to avoid trial, and then was surprisingly acquitted anyway by the Senate. All but two of those who had found him not guilty said later that they had voted for acquittal because they thought they had no jurisdiction over an official who had resigned. Neither did they have jurisdiction over the president's brother, Orvil Grant, who was also involved in this shady business, along with a relative of Julia Grant's, and one of the secretary's relatives.

At about the same time the St. Louis *Democrat*'s able editor, G. W. Fishback, exposed another fraud which came to be known as the "Whiskey Ring." This was a conspiracy of revenue officials, led by a Grant appointee, and a group of distillers who joined to defraud the government of tax money in St. Louis and other cities. It was a scheme so complex and widespread that 238 people were indicted for the crime, including Gen. O. E. Babcock, Grant's private secretary, who was saved from conviction only by the president's personal intervention.

Did Grant know nothing of all this corruption under his nose, in his very office? To the end he maintained earnestly that he did not, and much of the public believed him. Many newspapers were skeptical, and some of them (including Republican journals) were frankly disbelieving. Yet in his final defensive message to Congress the president referred to these sordid events as "errors of judgment," so far as his part in them was concerned. He asserted it was inevitable that

> differences of opinion between the Executive, bound by an oath to the strict performance of his duties, and writers and debaters, must have arisen. It is not necessarily evidence of blunder on the part of the Executive because there are these differences of views. Mistakes have been made, as all can see and I admit, but it seems to me oftener in the sections made of the assistants appointed to aid in carrying out the various duties of administering the Government.

Grant, in short, simply wrapped himself in the majestic mantle of the presidency and blamed others, even unto the assistants of those he had appointed, as responsible for the nearly total corruption of his administration.

It was too much for Dana. His own experience in Washington had made him doubly cynical about all politicians, and, with Grant's defection from virtue (as he saw it), no president thereafter could please him. When Grant had the temerity to dream of a third term, it was Dana's memorable demand in the *Sun*, "Turn the rascals out!" that not only helped derail Grant but added a phrase to the American political lexicon. In the disputed election of 1876, which followed, Dana supported Samuel Tilden and simply refused to recognize Rutherford B. Hayes as president as long as he remained in office, referring to him as the "Fraudulent President." He considered James A. Garfield in 1880 as not much better than a common thief. He found no good reason to oppose Grover Cleveland but did so anyway because Cleveland had refused him a political favor; Cleveland's only consolation was that Dana had an even worse opinion of the other candidate, James G. Blaine.

During the last unhappy years of his second term, Grant remained as he had been from the beginning, turning his back on the press for the most part, rarely granting interviews, making no attempt to generate good will, seemingly oblivious to what was being said and written about him, on the defensive. Through it all his extraordinary hold on the public remained relatively intact. The electorate would simply not believe anything derogatory about its hero, and later, when he returned from a trip around the world, during the Hayes administration, he was greeted on his journey across the country as though he were a returning conqueror. It was a triumphal progress. Buoyed by this demonstration of public affection, Grant was the more bitterly disappointed in 1880 to be refused another nomination.

The Democrats had already made sure there would be no third term by introducing a resolution in Congress in December 1875 that it would be "unwise, unpatriotic and fraught with peril" to depart from the two-term tradition for presidents. The resolution was approved by an overwhelming number of both Republicans and Democrats, and, while it did not have the force of law, politicians of both parties saw the handwriting.

For Grant, it was the end of ambition. He had traveled a long way, from initial eclipse in the early days of the Civil War to being the hero of the North, from triumphal entry into the White House to a departure from it that was darkly shadowed by events over which he asserted he had had no control. He was not in disgrace, as far as the public was concerned, but it was clear that his political career was over. Moreover his fortunes continued to decline. The $100,000 he had invested in his son's Wall Street brokerage house, Grant & Ward, was lost when the firm collapsed in another scandal, and meanwhile, the throat cancer that would kill him was drawing more and more of his strength as he struggled to finish the memoirs that he hoped would save Julia from a widowhood of poverty.

Unable to speak at last, he communicated by scribbling notes, one of which, near the end, was directed to something he had read in the New York *Times*. "I had that newspaper article, with a reply to write, to worry me," he scrawled on his notepad. "Mrs. Grant was very much excited on reading the article." A little later, in another note, he added, "I see the *Times* man keeps up the character of his dispatches to the paper. They are quite as untrue as they would be if he described me as getting better from day to day. I think he might spare my family at least from reading such stuff."

Some admiring biographers have charged that Grant endured more abuse from the press than nearly any other president, but that judgment appears to be more than a little excessive. He was certainly abused, but not nearly as much as Washington, Lincoln, and Johnson before him, or Cleveland, Wilson, and Franklin Roosevelt in later years. Moreover, while he may have been as honest and innocent as his defenders assert, Grant deserved many of the assaults upon his administration if for no better reason than his stubborn refusal to see, for eight long years, a cesspool of corruption that lapped at the doors of the White House.

From the standpoint of the press, the Grant administration marked another turning point in its relationship with the presidency. Approval of a president, or attacks on one, could no longer be conveniently labeled as the work of Republican or Democratic editors. There would always be party partisanship, of course, but Grant's two terms demonstrated that where corruption existed, it would be exposed by a competitive, investigative press no matter which party was in power. Newspapers would continue to divide according to the party leanings of their managements, but now the news came first, regardless of party. It was, in a way, a declaration of independence from pure politics.

Hayes: The "Fraudulent President"

As a man who early in life concluded that reading newspapers was a waste of time, Rutherford B. Hayes came to understand, if not appreciate, that he owed the most significant event of his life—his election as president—to one editor and one newspaper. Curiously, this singular fact (if one concedes that it *is* a fact, which some historians would not) has been overlooked or ignored by all the standard chroniclers of journalistic history. The newspaper in question was the New York *Times,* but in its semiofficial history, *The Story of the New York Times,* by that estimable reporter, Meyer Berger, the name of Rutherford B. Hayes does not even occur.

This omission is in keeping with the generally erroneous impression of Hayes that has come down to us, a perception created by the press of his own time and never revised in the public consciousness. To those Americans who now think of Hayes at all, he is forever categorized as the winner of the famous Hayes-Tilden disputed election in 1876. How he won, and what happened afterward, is more or less forgotten.

Hayes was far from being the monster the opposition press made him out to be. Born in Delaware, Ohio, educated at Kenyon College, he grew up to be a serious young man, well read, something of a moralist, his view of life and the world shaped by his Midwestern background. He entered Cincinnati politics as a Whig in 1851, supported Lincoln, served as a judge-advocate and as an infantry brigade commander in the Civil War, rose to be a commissioned brigadier general and a brevetted major general of volunteers, and was elected to the House from Ohio before he was out of uniform. He resigned from Congress to be governor of Ohio and served two terms, proving himself to be an astute and able administrator.

Able but not brilliant. That was the verdict of many politicians in his own time, and of historians afterward. He came upon the national scene at a time when the country was weary of corruption in Washington, tired of its war hero president who appeared to be always defending the corrupt, and, most of all, sick of the war's aftermath, with its Radical Reconstruction policies and spirit of vengefulness. Peace was what the electorate wanted, and a peaceful man to administer it.

When the Republicans met in Cincinnati to nominate their candidate, it appeared that James G. Blaine of Maine, former Speaker of the House, possessed of considerable charisma, might well be their man. The great Illinois orator, Robert G. Ingersoll, presented him to the delegates in rotund phrases, one of which clung to him. "Like an armed warrior, like a plumed knight, James G. Blaine marched down the halls of the American Congress," Ingersoll shouted, "and threw his shining lance full and fair against the brazen forehead of every traitor to his country." Thus Blaine became the "Plumed Knight."

The enthusiasm aroused by this speech almost swept the Speaker into nomination on the first ballot, and his opponents sought an adjournment before the vote in order to organize themselves, but fearing that they would still lose in the voting, they thoughtfully cut the main line providing gas illumination in the hall, and adjournment was compelled. Next morning Blaine led on the first four ballots, but there was enough competition to convince party leaders that a dangerous split was developing, and, as always in such cases, they sought a compromise candidate. Hayes was offered to the delegates, but the Blaine vote seemed only to increase until Kentucky broke away from its own candidate and swung to Hayes, beginning the usual stampede.

When the Democrats met in St. Louis, they nominated a rich bachelor, Gov. Samuel J. Tilden of New York, who owed his fame to his prosecution of the notorious Tweed Ring, thereby earning the enmity of Tammany Democrats. His path to the nomination represented something new in American politics, since it was largely the result of a coalition of editors, writers, advertising copywriters, and one of the early advertising agencies, the felicitiously named Goodsell Brothers, who had combined their talents to promote him. The Goodsell firm had made a public opinion survey (not, of course, employing the presumably scientific techniques of today) to ascertain where support might exist or be created. It had also loosed a flood of publicity releases and cartoons to local newspaper editors, who were always happy to get free material. Some of this propaganda was targeted directly to people whose influence might make a difference. No wonder that when Tilden got to Cincinnati, he was well known to most of the delegates. Manton Marble, editor of the New York *World,* wrote the Democrats' platform, a document which cleverly outlined a reform campaign that obviously could be carried out by no one but Tilden. The result was that the governor overcame the uncompromising opposition of the Tammany chieftains and won the nomination easily.

In the campaign Hayes had the active support of such stump speakers as Carl Schurz, Blaine, General Sherman, Ingersoll, Garfield, and even Mark Twain, who had been impressed by Hayes's letter of acceptance, in which he not only went beyond the Republican platform but announced that it was his "inflexible purpose" not to run for a second term. Tilden, on the other hand, had the powerful support of Henry George, Manton Marble, Henry Watterson, Charles Dana, and other eminent editors and publicists. Oddly enough, the New York *Times* did not support Tilden even though he had prosecuted the Tweed gang, whose larcenous City Hall activities the *Times* had exposed in another notable instance of early investigative reporting. William Marcy Tweed had tried to save himself by offering a $5 million bribe to George Jones, then the paper's editor, which was scornfully refused.

On election night, November 7, it seemed clear that Tilden had won, and far away in Ohio a disappointed Hayes retired to bed, convinced he had lost his opportunity. For what followed, we have the testimony of a contemporary who was in a position to know. While historians customarily have no more faith in the memoirs of editors than in the newspapers they edited, there is no reason to doubt the recollections of Edward P. Mitchell, editor in chief of the *Sun,* one of the most accomplished newspapermen of his day in the opinion of his boss, Dana, and many others. Due allowance, of course, must be made for the fact that Mitchell knew and liked Tilden, who visited the *Sun*'s office occasionally during the campaign. Mitchell gives us this intimate view of the man Dana believed to his death had been defrauded of the presidency:

> The characteristic attitude in conference of that great political philosopher and past-master of political detail was not such as to indicate either the dimensions of his intellect or its really human and even humorous perceptions. He would sit on the edge of his chair, leaning forward slightly, and mysteriously whisper communications that might refer to literature or art or the wine cellar or the dogs at Greystone [his country place] but sometimes seemed to an unhearing onlooker as if they must be sinister suggestions for the overthrow of the Republic. The drooping eyelids that half-veiled the gray-blue pupils gave his countenance an expression of exceeding sagacity. . . . Dürer's little etching, "The Peasant at Market," is a capital likeness of him. The Democratic candidate of 1876 suffered in his sixties a partial paralysis of the left side, which made him look older than he was. He was slow of movement, unimpressive of utterance, deliberate in his judgments, unexcitable of temperament, capable of absolute personal detachment even from a situation that greatly concerned himself, capable likewise of momentous decision, though his characteristic phrase when such matters were put up to him was the half-audible "I'll see you later." Those who knew him best . . . appeared not only to trust him, but also to love him. . . . In the uncertainties following that memorable election day, however, hundreds of thousands of Democrats came to think of Tilden, first of all, as a whisperer and a procrastinator.

In the early morning of November 8, Mitchell recalls, the Republican leaders had conceded Hayes's defeat and gone to bed, not all of them sober. The New York morning papers were on the street announcing Tilden's victory—with one exception. At the *Times,* John C. Reid, the paper's news editor, and three of his city room colleagues were still going over the latest returns and bulletins, stubbornly refusing to admit that Hayes was beaten. Mitchell describes Reid as "an indomitable manipulator of election returns," but that can be put down to professional jealousy, since there is no evidence that Reid ever "manipulated" anything, then or at any other time. What the editor did do was to perceive that, if the still incomplete returns from South Carolina, Florida, and Louisiana placed these states in the Hayes column, Tilden's victory would be doubtful and might be reversed. Mitchell calls this "perhaps the most sensational illustration in all history of the influence an obscure newspaper desk can exert upon the course of national events."

Reid wasted no time. He hurried uptown to Republican headquarters in the Fifth Avenue Hotel, where the only official about was William E. Chandler, the National Committee's secretary, who had just returned from voting in his native New Hampshire. Reid conveyed his discovery and also told Chandler that before he left the office the New York State Democratic chairman had wired him, "Please give your estimate of electoral votes secured for Tilden. Answer at once." That meant the Democrats were not themselves certain of Tilden's election because they were not sure of the results in the South.

Together Reid and Chandler rushed upstairs to awaken (an unfortunate similarity of names) Zachariah Chandler of Michigan, the National Committee chairman. It was no easy task. The chairman had consoled himself with a friendly bottle before drifting off, but, once awake, he was sober enough to join in an excited discussion of the situation. It was decided to send telegrams to the party chairmen in the three contested Southern states saying, "Hayes is elected, if we have carried South Carolina, Florida, and Louisiana. Can you hold your state? Answer at once."

Reid was well aware that any attempt to reverse the outcome in such a close election could lead to violence, especially in the South, and, with the assent of the others, a call was put through to President Grant, then in Philadelphia, securing his promise to send federal troops if they were needed in order to get a "fair count." Mitchell tells us that Grant was reached "by way of Jay Gould's private wire," indicating that Black Friday was already forgotten by the president and his friend.

A delayed second edition of the *Times* reached the streets at 6:30 A.M., and in it the electoral count was put at 184 for Tilden and 181 votes for Hayes, with the assumption (unjustified at the moment) that Louisiana and South Carolina would be for Hayes. This meant that Tilden needed one more vote to secure the majority of 185 required for election. Florida, with four votes, was still doubtful, and the *Times* asserted, with little foundation, "If the Republicans have carried that state, as they claim, they will have 185 votes—a majority of one."

Later in the morning Zachariah Chandler, assuming an air of utter confidence, issued an announcement: "Hayes has 185 electoral votes, and is elected." When Hayes got the word in Cincinnati, he told a local reporter bluntly, "I think we are defeated in spite of recent good news. I am of the opinion that the Democrats have carried the country and elected Tilden." Nevertheless, as the *Ohio State Journal* reported, he "received those who called in his usual cordial manner, and was very unconcerned, while the greatest office on the American continent was trembling in the balance."

Hayes's lack of concern was no doubt the result of his disbelief in what was occurring. Oregon, as well as the three Southern states, was not certain, and he was particularly doubtful about Louisiana. Party leaders and his friends rushed to reassure him, however, and by early December he was able to tell Carl Schurz in a telegram: "I have no doubt that we are justly and legally entitled to the Presidency."

If Hayes now had no doubts, there were millions of others who did. And at this point the foundations for the later charges of "fraud" were laid. Republican emissaries fanned out to the disputed states and held meetings with members of the Returning Boards, who had to certify the electoral votes when the electoral college met in December. Whether or not the "visiting statesmen," as they were called, bribed these members has never been proved, but since all three boards ultimately certified for Hayes, something more than a suspicion was raised, particularly in the case of Louisiana, where the Democrats had apparently won by a six-thousand-vote margin.

The Democrats did not give up easily. Democrat electors from the three states appeared with their Republican opposites at the electoral college meeting, where the situation was further complicated by Oregon, whose Democratic governor had disqualified a Republican elector and given his place to a deserving Democrat. Obviously the final decision was going to be made in Congress, where it would be no easier because the Senate was Republican and the House Democratic. One would certainly nullify the votes of the other, no matter what procedure was adopted in a situation not foreseen by either the Constitution or the Twenty-second Joint Rule, governing the counting process.

In this deadlock Congress turned for an answer to the creation of a special Electoral Commission, consisting of five senators, five representatives, and five Supreme Court justices, equally divided politically but including one presumed independent, Justice David Davis, who was nevertheless believed to favor Tilden. Unfortunately for the Democrats, before the commission met he retired from the Court to become an Illinois senator, and his place was taken by a colleague, Justice Joseph P. Bradley, an avowed Republican. Predictably, commission voting on the disputed returns divided along party lines, and since there was now one more Republican, the Hayes electors from the Southern states were accepted.

A great outcry rose from the Democratic press, soon echoed across the nation in cities and small towns. There was talk of a filibuster in Congress, which would mean an Inauguration Day without a president to be inaugurated. The newspapers generated a rising tide of popular excitement that took on an ugly tone. A slogan, "Tilden or blood," began to circulate, and it appeared that the election promise, "Let us have peace," might be instead converted to a call for more civil strife. And so, possibly, it might have been if Tilden had been a different kind of man. He was not a fighter, however, and the stroke mentioned by Mitchell had left him in health so uncertain that it often took precedence over everything else. He shuddered away from even the possibility of another civil war in the nation, and, rather than take such a risk, he refused to contest the matter any longer.

Even so, the retreat was not accomplished without a further political deal, in which Republican emissaries again met with Southern Democratic leaders, this time in Washington. As president, the Republicans suggested, Hayes would pur-

sue a conciliatory policy toward the South, and, in particular, he would withdraw
troops from South Carolina and Louisiana. That would pave the way to restoring
white rule in those states and Florida, where carpetbag governments had been in
power—a restoration that had been the real goal of the Southern Democrats.

As a result Hayes was duly certified on March 2—185 to 184—and was inaugurated two days later. But after these tumultuous events, his administration was
something of an anticlimax, although he made a conscientious effort to carry out
what he had promised to do—conciliating the South, trying to realize the party's
reforms outlined in the platform, and pursuing a conservative financial course.

In doing so, Hayes was compelled to break away from the old guard in the
party, the very men who had followed John Reid's election night lead and eventually secured his election. Conciliating the South was not what they wanted;
promising the Southerners was one thing, fulfilling the promises was another.
The two Chandlers involved in the election night drama deserted Hayes in anger
and contempt. William Chandler published a temporarily famous pamphlet titled
vaguely, *Can Such Things Be and Overcome Us like a Summer Cloud without
Our Special Wonder?* In his memoirs Mitchell says of this Chandler, ''I am
sure I am not misrepresenting his sentiments two years after the electoral count
when I say that the memory of his share in it had for him the bitterness of gall.''
Other prominent Republicans, Mitchell recalls, spoke privately to him about
Hayes ''in terms that would scarcely bear reporting,'' and as for the other
Chandler, Zachariah, he was heard to say (Mitchell records), in an excess of
disappointment and disgust: ''If I owed the devil a thousand liars and he
wouldn't take Hayes and give me a receipt in full, by heaven, I'd go into
bankruptcy!''

There were similar expressions in high places. Justice Nathan Clifford, one of
the five representatives of the Supreme Court who sat on the commission, had
voted with the Democratic minority, and after the final decision, considered
Hayes as a usurper and never entered the White House while he was in office. A
prominent Republican, Parke Goodwin, son-in-law of the *Evening Post*'s publisher William Cullen Bryant, wrote: ''R. B. Hayes, commonly supposed to be
Rutherford B. Hayes, clearly means Returning Board Hayes. Let the *Sun* fasten
the name on him.''

All this was mild indeed compared with the obloquy heaped upon the president
by Dana and the *Sun*, leading the pack in a running press attack on Hayes that
sometimes recalled the bad old days. As noted earlier, the *Sun* never referred to
''President Hayes,'' but always called him the ''Fraudulent President.'' It
printed his picture with ''FRAUD'' in capitals lettered on his forehead. The shock
can well be imagined, then, when the paper one day got a letter on White House
stationery, signed by the president's private secretary, a former Western clergyman, asking to be put on the free list for this valued journal, ''for use in the
Executive Mansion.'' Isaac England, the publisher, brought the letter upstairs to
Dana, and asked him what to do. ''Write him politely the truth,'' Dana said,
''that our rule is to issue no unpaid copies. Then have his letter framed and hung
up in the business office to certify our standing with the present administration.''

Once in office, Hayes made a determined effort to unite the country by making trips through New England, Ohio, Kentucky, and as far south as Atlanta. In this effort he had the advice and help of three newspapermen. One was his close personal friend, William Henry Smith, a fellow Ohioan who was the Associated Press "agent," as bureau chiefs were called then, in Chicago, and later on in New York. Among his other friends in the press were Maj. W. D. Bickham, editor of the Dayton *Journal,* and William Dean Howells, an old newspaperman himself, who had graduated to higher literary levels. These men wrote to the president frequently, talked with him on many occasions, and offered advice he often took. They—and particularly Smith—were a valuable liaison between the president and the press. It was Smith, for example, who monitored the gossip among Washington correspondents about which of them, or their editors, were angry with Hayes, and why. Smith then helped Hayes's efforts to patch up the differences where the president considered the withdrawals of support to be important.

By this time the Washington correspondents had become a formidable body whose influence was growing. There were now more than 150 of them, supplemented by women correspondents who were, of course, expected to confine their reporting to social affairs. The dean of these intrusive females was Mary Clemmer of the New York *Independent,* and there were also Mrs. R. B. Mohun of the Cincinnati *Daily Commercial,* who employed the *nom de plume* of "Raymonde," the ubiquitous "Miss Grundy" of the New York *Daily Graphic* (not related to the sensational tabloid of the 1920s), and Fayette Snead of the Louisville *Courier-Journal.*

These correspondents, male and female, faithfully recorded, with varying degrees of accuracy, Hayes's attempt to deal with the problems of an expanding America, which he did not always understand; his mind was firmly anchored in the past. Those in his government and in the press who sought to deal with the future were confronted with the necessity to understand and explain a nation undergoing profound change. Big business was in the ascendant as the great postwar fortunes were accumulated by the men building industrial America. Labor was becoming a counteractive force, and the era of bloody strife in mines, factories, and elsewhere had begun. Women were in the workplace on a larger scale than ever, and they were beginning to press harder for their rights. Technology was accelerating at a bewildering pace with the invention of the telephone, the electric light, and, soon, the automobile. Photography was beginning to transform the appearance of the media, which were being read by increasing numbers of people as education spread at every level. Periodicals were entering a second golden age.

Hayes was much more successful in assimilating these cultural changes than he was in grasping the great political and economic questions of his day. A cultivated man himself, he bought from a prominent Cincinnati bookseller six thousand volumes of Americana, a valuable collection; no president since Jefferson had exhibited such a love of literature. In the White House, with the help of his adored wife Lucy Webb, he presided over a general revival of presidential hospitality not seen since the reign of Dolley Madison. Lucy, the first wife of a president to be a college graduate, was a teetotaler, refusing to serve liquor of any kind in the White House, thus causing her to be known in the press on occasion as "Lemonade Lucy." But she and the president more than made up for the lack of alcohol by the sheer quality of their entertainments.

The president also tried to attract into government service men of distinction from the intellectual community. George William Curtis, editor of *Harper's Weekly,* and Whitelaw Reid, who had succeeded Greeley as editor of the New York *Tribune,* were offered diplomatic posts but refused. Several other men of letters, however, including James Russell Lowell, Bayard Taylor, and Bret Harte, accepted nominations to head legations in Madrid, Berlin, and a German consulate, respectively.

The reaching out did not extend to the working press. Hayes looked upon the accuracy of newspaper reporting with deep suspicion and was always checking what he read in the papers with other sources, either to confirm or refute press dispatches. The president also continued the system that would later be commonplace—clerks who read newspapers to sample opinion about the administration. Henry C. Morton led this staff, whose further job it was to paste up pertinent clippings in scrapbooks so the president could look them over later.

Hayes was also the third president to keep a diary, following in the footsteps of John Quincy Adams and Polk. It was a journal with a purpose, as his campaign biographer William Dean Howells (the president's cousin by marriage) pointed out. Hayes, wrote Howells, "had the habit of compiling history from the newspaper as it was made, and from these collections he has been able at any time to confront an opponent with the record of that opponent's political life from the outset." What distinguished this diary (he was speaking of the early journals) from others kept by young men, Howells said, was "the evidence they afford of his life-long habit of rigid self-accountability and of close, shrewd study of character in others."

From the diary, as was the case with both Adams and Polk, it is possible to get a more intimate view of this president's relations with the press. For instance, after an interview in May 1876 with a *Herald* reporter, Hayes wrote: "I said enough to induce him, as I hoped, not to publish as an interview what I was saying. But in this morning's [*Ohio State*] *Journal* I see extracts from his letter showing that with reasonable fidelity he has given my talk. . . . But I do not think it consistent with the rule I have laid down for my conduct to write a letter for publication." Like many other White House occupants, Hayes professed to be above abuse from the press. "The sort of falsehoods which the partisan press gathers up, or fabricates . . . are not believed and do not annoy me a great deal," he wrote. But not long afterward he confided to his diary that "the only slander that has given me annoyance is the one referred to"—meaning the charge that he had appropriated the money of a Civil War deserter. Sometimes Hayes used his diary to prepare for an interview with a reporter. One of these rehearsals, intended to be given to the Cincinnati *Daily Commercial*'s correspondent, occupied three pages, but apparently the interview did not take place because nothing of what he wrote was ever published.

Cultivating the press was not part of Hayes's presidential style. When he was criticized, he responded dispassionately, if at all, preferring to let the public record speak for him. The idea of making a personal attack on an editor or a politician who struck at him was foreign to his nature. At the most he would draft a short memorandum of the facts in a dispute and ask a friend to circulate his rejoinder quietly. As others had done before him, he took his case directly to the voters when he believed it was necessary, and because he was such a skillful speaker—Carl Schurz called him "the greatest master of rhetoric in the United States"—he was effective, giving his cordial, earnest speeches in an easy and enthusiastic manner. Even Dana admitted at last that the *Sun*'s unremitting onslaught had been materially blunted by the president's exemplary conduct.

Yet Hayes felt that he had few supporters in either the press or Congress. When the newspapers, as was their custom, attempted to draw up a balance sheet after his first year in office, he considered the result an unfavorable verdict. In the diary he summarized his feelings about the relationship:

> The end of the first year of my Administration furnishes a topic for the press. There is enough of favorable comment from independent papers like the New York *Post,* the *Gazette,* the *Commercial,* the Boston *Advertiser,* the Philadelphia papers, and notably the religious newspapers; but the body of the party papers of both parties are the other way. The main point is that the President has so few supporters in Congress and among the newspapers. It is to be remarked that a nonpartisan President or Administration will of course be feebly supported, if at all, in Congress or by the press.

To counteract criticism William Henry Smith urged him to use papers particularly friendly to him, like the San Francisco *Bulletin,* as a sounding board for his views and policies, and he made some ineffectual attempts to do so. But in general, these attempts were failures. "The truth is 'the Administration is not well edited,'" he wrote sadly, quoting the verdict of a friend. "None of my excellent associates possess the editorial talent or experience." Smith might have winced if he had read those words.

Hayes was resigned to his situation, however. After his second annual message, which drew considerable praise along with the usual rain of acid, Hayes wrote in his diary: "Such Stalwarts and irreconcilables as the New York *Times* are severe in their strictures upon it. No doubt the Bourbon press, which represents the extreme sectionalism of the South, will be equally bitter. This was to be expected. It will doubtless continue to the end of my Administration."

And so it did, whether the problems were trivial or substantial. There was, for example, the admitted mistake made when the press corps was accidentally left off the guest list for a diplomatic reception. Hayes wrote of it in his diary: "We did not include among 'officials' the reporters—the gentlemen of the press. Strictly they are not officials. But their connection with Congress is so intimate and important that they might properly be included with the officers of the Congress. Nothing sinister was intended. It was not considered. But it has caused great irritation, and accounts of the affair, corresponding with the feelings of the writers, have been sent out."

On larger matters the president fared best with the press when he was truly presidential, as he demonstrated in a long session of Congress (seventy-five

days) during which he vetoed five bills, sent down several special messages, and
in general behaved like the shrewd and purposeful politician he was. As a result
Hayes recorded in his diary: "The great newspapers, and the little, have been
equally profuse of flattery. Of course, it will not last. But I think I have the
confidence of the country. When the *Tribune* can say, 'The President has the
courtesy of a Chesterfield and the firmness of a Jackson,' (!) I must be prepared
for the reactionary counterblast."

Godkin attacked Hayes frequently in the *Nation* on the question of civil service
reform, a subject about which the editor was particularly zealous, but Hayes
refused to make a public reply on this or any other question. He simply observed
in his diary that he was in general agreement with Godkin, but he could not push
for reform until he was sure he had public opinion and Congress behind him. If
he admitted his shortcomings in this matter, he added later, they would not be
what Godkin said they were.

A charge made frequently against the president, not only while he was in
office but repeated long afterward, was that he had enriched himself through the
presidency. Although he made no personal reply to these attacks, Smith persuaded Hayes to approve a statement about his financial affairs, which the AP
man then released. It appeared to appease all but the most intransigent of his
critics. As Hayes wrote to Smith shortly after the election of 1880, he was in fact
leaving office owing anywhere from $22,000 to $25,000 but with his credit
unimpaired, his real estate holdings intact, and in no need of either help or
sympathy.

As he departed from the White House, Hayes could take comfort from an
editorial in the New York *Graphic* that represented the view of most papers:
"Take him for all in all, Hayes will step out of office on the 4th of March next
with more peace and blessing than any President in fifty-six years. Who since
Monroe has gone out so *willingly* and regretted?"

The president's last public appearance before the inauguration of his successor
was at a dinner of the Baltimore Press Association, where, as he noted somewhat
wryly in his diary, he was "well received and with much enthusiasm, viz., three
cheers as I closed." In that speech Hayes paid tribute to the press as a powerful
force in American life, remarking platitudinously that the author of a book could
hope to speak to only relatively few people, while newspapers reached millions.
He took a conciliatory view of what the press printed, merely observing that it
took everything that was good and gave it to the world, along with "some rub-
bish," which would be overcome by the "pure stream of truth." In his peroration, according to the New York *Times* of February 13, 1881, Hayes declared
grandly: "The truth of the newspaper was like gold and would be eternal. He
would, therefore, honor the man who would give to his country a good newspaper."

Much of the abuse directed toward Hayes could be put down to unadorned
political partisanship, and certainly there was nothing in his conduct to merit
Dana's unremitting contempt for him, which even extended to disassociating
himself from a move to erect a memorial to the president at Harvard, where both
had been students. Dana was a superb newspaperman who created a great news-

paper, but in his views of public life he represented the classic bitterness of one who had begun life as an ardent idealist and then swung slowly across the spectrum to an extreme cynicism—in his case, induced by his constant rediscovery, often at first hand, that idealism is the stuff of political theory, not political practice.

But one cannot be too judgmental about Dana either. The politics of his time were exceptionally corrupt, and it would have been difficult for an editor as intelligent and knowledgeable as he was *not* to be cynical. The election of 1876 enraged him, and justifiably so. There was not only the highly dubious and almost certainly corrupt matter of vote counting in the Southern states, and the part played in it by the Republicans, but there was the usual outpouring of fraudulent Democratic voters in New York, many of whom were temporarily jailed until the polls closed. Both parties did not hesitate to use intimidation or bribery of voters, and even brutal violence, in their drive to gain a victory. Following on the outrages of the two Grant administrations, and considering the general climate of the times, Dana's cynicism seems less excessive.

Hayes was not unhappy to leave political life and the White House behind him. "Gladly" was the word he would have used, he said, rather than the *Graphic*'s "willingly." He lived for another dozen years, during which he maintained his association with the newspaper friends mentioned earlier, sometimes writing corrective letters to editors but always specifying that they were not for publication, and still refusing to grant interviews. He could not even be induced to write for publication, although he had many invitations to do so. An exception was made for Garfield's assassination, an event that shocked him, when he made some written comments. Hayes was in Cleveland at the time of General Sherman's death, and this event compelled him to break, for once, his rule about interviews, giving them to two local papers, the *Leader* and the *Plain Dealer*.

The president retained his definite views about interviewing, however, as he made plain just before his death in a letter to a correspondent not identified. "There are two ways of dealing with offhand talk," he wrote. "One is for the reporter in his own words to briefly sketch the topics—the persons named, the general character of the talk, etc., etc. The other is a perfectly full *verbatim* report by a skilful hand. But you have caught the editorial frailty. No bargain is binding that interferes with the paramount duty to furnish the news. The victim has no recourse but submission. To correct one error would be an endorsement of all the others."

Hayes may not have been a brilliant man, but he knew who he was and what he believed, and he filled his office with an integrity not always seen in the White House. If he understood the value and uses of public opinion and public relations, yet failed to comprehend how the press could be used to further both, much less how it functioned in a democracy, he was no worse a failure in that respect than many of those who came before and after him. It was unfortunate that he made no attempt to establish any kind of formal relationship with the press. Both might have been the better for it, not to mention the nation itself. In the end he could have had the satisfaction of knowing that he was right, generally speaking, and the press was wrong. But then he never doubted it.

Garfield: Uneasy Ally of the Press

To call Garfield the press's "uneasy ally" is to sum up one of the most ambiguous aspects of an ambiguous man's character. Even recent efforts of historians to throw a little more light on Garfield and place him in better perspective have not entirely resolved the nagging questions raised about him in his lifetime, and for decades afterward. Was he the true American leader who rose *From Canal Boy to President,* as Horatio Alger, Jr., pictured him, the apotheosis of Algerian mythology? Or was he a shrewd Ohio politician who shared in the general corruption of the day on his journey to the White House? What kind of president he would really have been, we can never know because an assassin's bullet removed him only 120 days after his inauguration; his death in Elberon, New Jersey, 79 days later ended a presidency that had only begun.

In his relations with the press Garfield was quite as ambivalent as he was in other respects. On the one hand, he had many influential friends among the editors on his upward path to Washington, as an ambitious politician should have, but somehow these personal relationships remained no more than that—personal, but not official. In his brief tenure as president, Garfield maintained the same kind of silence toward the press that Hayes had before him, declining to explain any of the few executive actions he was able to take and establishing a distance between him and the correspondents that, presumably, would have continued had he lived.

Garfield was no better able to understand the function of the press in a democracy, and its relationship to the presidency, than most of those who had gone before him. This appears clearly in the only speech he ever made on the subject, an address before the Ohio Editorial Association in 1878. He began promisingly with the modest admission that, as a layman, he was "wholly ignorant of the art and mystery of your profession." Nevertheless, he went on, it seemed plain to him that the public's first and greatest demand upon editors was that they should "obtain and publish the news—that they shall print a veritable and intelligible record of important current events." No one in the audience was prepared to quarrel with that definition. But then Garfield disclosed how deeply his mind, like that of Hayes, was rooted in traditional politics. As he spoke, the press was struggling toward an independence, even an objectivity, that it had never known or attempted previously, but Garfield told the Ohio editors flatly that he believed in a party press. "The journal should have opinions of its own, and should advocate them," he declared.

> I have no sympathy with the Utopian idea of "independent journalism." . . . It is fair to presume that every intelligent man has convictions upon leading public questions. . . . Let the journalist defend the doctrines of the party which he approves; let him criticize and condemn the party which he does not approve, reserving always his right to applaud his opponents or censure his friends, as the truth will require, and he will be independent enough for a free country.

. . . Believing as I do in parties and in a party press . . . I hold it equally necessary to liberty and good government that the press shall comment with the utmost freedom upon the public acts and opinions of all men who hold positions of public trust. . . . The only just limitation is that it shall adhere to the truth.

The chief danger which threatens the influence and honor of the press is the tendency of its liberty to degenerate into license. . . . [Yet] the character of the press has greatly improved during the last half century.

On that last point Garfield was indubitably right, but on the others he was lost in a forest of ambiguities, which almost certainly escaped his listeners, most of them small-town editors who thought he was reading them a declaration of independence, with a cautionary note on liberty and license whose origins lay in the early Republic. He was applauded generously, a tribute to what Garfield did best—make speeches. And this in a man who had proclaimed, "The age of oratory has passed. The newspaper, the pamphlet, and the book abolished it. Only plain speaking—argument and fact that may be printed—are of any great value now." Lincoln, the plain speaker, was his model.

It was Garfield's admiration for Lincoln, in fact, that had inspired his most dramatic flight of oratory—or did he actually make that speech? Again the evidence is conflicting, indecisive. In his campaign and memorial biographies, according to his most recent biographer, Justus D. Doenecke, there was always a chapter titled, "Garfield Stills the Mob," which described how he went to Wall Street on business the morning after Lincoln's assassination, heard the dreadful news, and watched an agitated mob of fifty thousand people milling about the area, ready to lynch Southern sympathizers and wreck the office of that Copperhead paper, the *World*.

At this ugly moment, according to that "distinguished public man who was an eyewitness to the exciting scene," always quoted without being named, Garfield appeared on the balcony of the Custom House, holding a small Union flag. The sudden appearance of the general, who had been a Civil War hero, momentarily quieted the mob, and Garfield cried out to them: "Fellow citizens! Clouds and darkness are round about Him! His pavilion is dark waters and thick clouds of the skies! Justice and judgment are the establishment of His throne! Mercy and truth shall go before His face! Fellow citizens! God reigns, and the Government of Washington still lives."

The effect on the crowd was "tremendous," the anonymous eyewitness reported; it was completely hushed by this "greatest triumph of eloquence" the "public man" had ever seen. He turned to ask a bystander who the orator was, and the answer came back in a low whisper (why a whisper was necessary, or could even be heard in that situation, is not explained), "It is General Garfield of Ohio."

Other observers on the scene included reporters from the New York *Herald* and the *Tribune*, both of whom wrote what purported to be verbatim accounts of Garfield's speech, but neither of their reports even approached the eloquence or the brevity of the speech as it was recalled by the "eyewitness," nor did the newspapermen mention that it pacified the angry mob, whose subsequent actions were anything but pacific. Chauncey A. Depew and a reporter from the Brooklyn *Eagle* also said they had heard the speech, but they were vague and contradictory about its contents. In his autobiography, Charles Townsend Harris also came forward as a witness to the event, but his testimony is shadowed by the fact that he remembered hearing Garfield speak while the general was working on Wall Street during the gold panic of 1869, not an easy feat since Garfield was out of New York at the time. Strangely, considering that it came to be considered one of the best-known incidents of his career, Garfield himself never mentioned it, nor was there any family oral history of it. Garfield's son Harry went to a good deal of trouble to authenticate the tale, but without success, and it remains a part of Garfield's puzzling legacy.

Garfield was also a diary keeper, not counted among the other presidential writers only because he had no opportunity to practice his art in office. From early entries, however, we can see the shaping of his attitude toward the press. As an eighteen-year-old student at Geauga Seminary in Chester, Ohio, he was appointed one of the editors of the *Human Elevator,* a small periodical published at the school, but he was obviously not destined for the press because, as he told his diary, he "felt incapable of doing it justice." No budding journalist would have made such an admission.

Four years later Garfield was in New York, taking a guided tour of the *Tribune*'s printing plant before going on to Barnum's Museum, which impressed him more. He was, however, a reader of the *Tribune,* says the diary, and also of the *Atlantic Monthly.* He loved and admired Goethe and wished he had more time to pursue literature, but politics was already beginning to erode his leisure. As the diary shows, he did not hold journalism in high esteem from the beginning; there are numerous disparaging references to individual newspapers and editors.

After hearing Henry Watterson give an address on journalism to the Indiana Press Association in Indianapolis, Garfield came away unconvinced in spite of Marse Henry's celebrated oratorical prowess. As a profession, Garfield wrote, journalism was now "in the Goth-Vandal period." Again, much more frankly (one supposes because it was written in the heat of political battles), he reports: "The Cincinnati newspapers are making a savage assault, charging me with the loss of the election and demanding that I shall not be appointed on the Committee on Appropriations. It remains to be seen how far the reckless assaults of public journals can go in ruining public men. I am not sure but a friend of mine is right who says that the greatest danger this country has to confront is the corrupt and reckless press."

It was a familiar refrain by this time, a tune sung frequently by politicians, but especially by presidents or those aspiring to be. Always, it appeared, they were misquoted, or they were deliberately misconstrued. Often there was truth in their complaints, since the press still possessed many of its unsavory pre–Civil War characteristics. But whatever progress had been made, it did not satisfy, and would never satisfy, public men (especially presidents) who saw everything that was said or done in terms of more or fewer votes for themselves or their party. This common anxiety is demonstrated in one of Garfield's diary entries: "The

Tribune of this morning has a letter from a correspondent detailed [detailing] a view of my opinions in which something is said that will doubtless be construed unpleasantly and contrary to my meaning. I dread the newspaper talk that will doubtless be opened up on public men this Winter. It is one of the features of public life that has of late had a rank overgrowth.''

In his daily routine Garfield did not much expose himself to what the news-papers were saying. Not only did he spend little time with the journals, but he believed that the public at large was doing itself damage by neglecting books for newspapers, the contents of which were in large part "of only passing interest," useless alike for "mental training and culture." The general read one New York paper a day to get the news and a northern Ohio journal for the news, mostly political, from his source of strength. He also read one of the New York weeklies specializing in critical writing, and he managed to scan most of the major magazines.

In the manner of Hayes, Garfield did not permit his distrust of the press to interfere with the friendly relations he maintained with some of its representa-tives. He recognized that the small corps of Washington correspondents had become "a powerful body in this country," and he prudently did not go out of his way to antagonize its members. Besides, he could not help enjoying the company of newspapermen, particularly those who had shared his Civil War experiences, and he often went riding with both reporters and editors, or dined with them.

Among these favorites were his good friend Whitelaw Reid of the *Tribune,* who had made that paper a far more dependable ally than it had been under the erratic Greeley. Other friends among the editors included George A. Benedict of the Cleveland *Herald and Gazette* and Manton Marble of the *World.* The favored reporters included Donn Piatt, Washington correspondent of the Cincinnati *Tri-bune,* who founded, with George Alfred Townsend of the Chicago *Tribune,* a weekly called the Washington *Capital,* which gave Garfield generous support.

There were still other close friends and advisers among newspaper people. For example, W. C. Howells, William Dean's father and editor of the Ashtabula *Sentinel;* and Lyman Hall and his son, Hawley R. W. Hall, co-editors of the Ravenna *Democrat.* It was these editors, and their papers, who were among Garfield's earliest supporters and who, joined by a large part of the Ohio press, began to generate the public enthusiasm that led to his nomination for the presidency.

Nor was it entirely an Ohio native-son movement. Such papers as the New York *Times,* the Duluth *Tribune,* and the Springfield *Republican* were early ar-rivals on the bandwagon, whose beneficiary was not even yet a candidate and who proclaimed, according to custom, that he was not seeking the office. The press was not fooled by this disclaimer. The editors knew that Garfield was presidential material, even though he did not have the experience of Blaine or Sherman—or, for that matter, Grant, who was still hopeful of a third term now that Hayes had broken the succession.

Dissent was splitting the Republicans once more, however. On one side were the conservative, antireform "Stalwarts," led by the New York State political boss Roscoe Conkling; and on the other were the "Half-Breeds," led by Blaine and professing, at least, to be more liberal. There were those in and out of the party who could see no significant difference between these factions and regarded them as no more than loyalists of two deeply antagonistic political leaders. The Stalwarts wanted Grant again, while the Half-Breeds leaned toward Blaine. There were a few other possibilities, but it was clear that Grant would outvote all of them collectively at the convention unless the forces opposing him could unite.

That would mean, eventually, a compromise candidate, but when the Republicans met in Chicago, the anti-Grant people realized that the former president would get the nomination on the first ballot if the unit rule were enforced, and so their first task was to defeat its acceptance. The man who successfully organized and carried out this maneuver was James A. Garfield, the senator from Ohio. After the adoption of a platform even more meaningless than usual, the convention got down to the nominations. Conkling, as planned, placed Grant's name before the delegates to wild applause, but, before the echoes were quiet, Garfield, the plain talker, rose and nominated Secretary of the Treasury John Sherman in one of his more eloquent speeches. Then the balloting began.

It was interminable and indecisive, going through thirty-three rounds before Sherman threw his support unexpectedly to Garfield, who had not even been nominated but seemed a likely choice, perhaps the only one, who could break the deadlock. Garfield got seventeen votes on the thirty-fourth ballot and rose on a point of order to protest that he had not given his consent to be a candidate, but the chairman overrode him, and the balloting went on, gradually gathering steam for the senator, who was finally nominated on the thirty-seventh round. The Republicans knew they had to throw a sop to the Stalwarts, without whom they would not be able to win an election, and so they nominated, fatefully, as Garfield's running mate, Chester A. Arthur, a machine boss from New York who was opposed to any reform that would interfere with the comfortable tenor of Republican ways in the state or city of New York.

When the Democrats met in Cincinnati, they were even more badly divided. The Northerners were split along Civil War lines between traditionalists and Copperheads, while the Southerners divided between Jacksonian Democrats and the conservatives, known as "Bourbons." The only solution was to nominate a man so devoid of strong opinions that he would offend no one, and that man, as it proved, was another Civil War general, Winfield S. Hancock, called for political but no other reason, "The Superb." He had commanded troops at Gettysburg, and he had been liked (a rarity in itself) as military commander in Louisiana during Reconstruction.

The press took more note of the Democrats' platform than it had of the Republicans' platform. In the *Nation,* Godkin observed sardonically that it was "a singular document, and suggests the conclusion that all the conventions have now begun to treat the platform as a joke. It appears to have been the composition of Mr. Watterson, of the Louisville *Courier-Journal,* and reads like a highly inflammatory 'editorial' from that paper." If the platforms of the two parties made less sense than usual, it was because there were no real issues at the moment to be fought over, unless it was the question of tariffs. Consequently the campaign concentrated on the public and private lives of the candidates. There was little to be found in Hancock's blameless life, but Garfield was more vulnerable, as the Democratic press soon made clear. Was he really the poor but honest canal boy who rose to the United States Senate? The Democrats begged leave to doubt it. Meanwhile Garfield, instructed to make no promises to anyone, wisely stayed on his farm in Mentor, Ohio, conducting a front-porch campaign and letting people come to him, supporting the political adage that what a party wants is not a good president but a good candidate.

The Democratic papers were soon recalling that Garfield was alleged to have been given a $329 dividend from the Crédit Mobilier and then had been less than frank about it when he was testifying before the Senate committee investigating the affair. Garfield had also been vague about a paving contract negotiated while he was chairman of the Appropriations Committee, which also had come under investigative scrutiny by his fellow senators.

Dana spent considerable space in the *Sun* attacking Garfield's army record, charging that he had been responsible for removing Maj. Gen. W. S. Rosecrans from his command of the Army of the Cumberland after Chickamauga. This was *chutzpah* of a superior kind, since it had been Dana himself who was chiefly responsible for that action, acting in his capacity as assistant secretary of war. The charge set off a controversy in and out of the press that persisted long after the election was over.

In the Washington *Post,* Garfield was attacked for leaving the army in 1863, preferring, as the *Post* said sententiously, "a comfortable seat in Congress to a life in the tented field." In fact Garfield had consulted Lincoln on that matter, and the president had advised him to stay in Congress, where Republican votes were needed.

There were also charges that Garfield had been a heavy drinker while he was chief of staff for Rosecrans, that he favored the election of senators for life, and that he advocated disregarding property rights. There were biting editorials in such papers as the New York *Tribune,* the Chicago *Daily News,* and the Springfield *Republican* on all these and other accusations. Thomas Nast, king of the political cartoonists, was so opposed to Garfield that, even though his editor strongly supported the Republican candidate, he refused to include the general in the cartoons he drew for *Harper's Weekly.*

The most damaging blow, late in the campaign, came from a forged letter in which Garfield was purported to have advocated importing Chinese labor to California, an explosive issue in the West. Thousands of copies were distributed there, after its first appearance in an obscure penny paper, the New York *Truth,* and Garfield himself believed it cost him the electoral votes of California and Nevada. The forgery itself was a crude one, containing two grossly misspelled words; whatever else he may have been, Garfield was an excellent speller.

Throughout the campaign Dana harped on the Crédit Mobilier scandal day after day in the *Sun,* on the editorial page and in the news columns. Garfield might believe that Dana had "sold his claims to the respect of all his friends for the money he could make by editing a vile paper," but there was just enough smoke in this fire to make it uncomfortable. It was true that Garfield had given an interview to the Cincinnati *Daily Commercial,* in which he said he had "never subscribed for a single share of the stock, and that he never received or saw a share." But then came the revelation of the $329 dividend, and when Garfield testified before a Senate committee, he failed to tell the whole truth.

Dana's unremitting, often vicious assaults on Garfield's character and conduct were picked up and repeated over and over by the Democratic papers, without any attempt to give him the opportunity of denial or explanation. That concept of fairness was still in the future. But on the other hand, even Dana could not stomach the circulation of the blatantly forged "Morey Letter," as it was called, which had so offended the West. Garfield made a major political blunder by not declaring it a forgery at once, and Dana wrote in the *Sun* of October 30, 1880, "If a party requires such infamous aids, that party by whatsoever name it may be called, deserves to perish."

Nothing that Dana or the Democratic editors wrote kept Garfield from the White House, thus supporting the idea that voters were not decisively influenced by the press, but the campaign charges affected enough of them to convert what was expected to be an easy Republican victory into a close contest. Garfield's popular majority was less than ten thousand in a total count of more than nine million; the electoral margin was 214 to 155.

As soon as he entered the White House, Garfield was under fire again, but this time on more customary political grounds. To stay in power, he knew, the Half-Breeds and the Stalwarts had to unite, and that meant the president, in filling cabinet posts, must consult Conkling, who advised him, among other things, to refuse posts to New York men who had disobeyed the instructions of the New York State convention by voting against Grant at Chicago. Conkling was supported by Joseph Medill, the Chicago *Tribune*'s editor, who advised Garfield to reward at least some of those who *had* supported Grant. Since it was no secret that a deal had been made with Conkling in Chicago, the president was now naturally accused of making still another deal with the New York boss. It was true, but the object had been party unity, without which there would be no effective government.

Garfield compounded the problem by refusing to explain his actions to the press, just as Hayes had done before him. This policy of presidential silence had failed before, and it failed now. It would surely have led to another embittered presidency if Garfield had not become the second American chief executive to be assassinated. As he entered the Washington railway station on July 2, 1881, on his way to a twenty-fifth reunion of his class at Williams College, he was shot and fatally wounded by Charles J. Guiteau, a known Stalwart and one of those office seekers Garfield had refused to appoint. Those who liked to blame the press for everything that was wrong with American life pointed to the fact that the assassin carried a marked copy of the *Herald* in his pocket, in which Garfield was harshly criticized for his alleged "sellout" to Conkling. There is no proof that the *Herald* story inspired Guiteau, but, conversely, no proof that it did not.

So the Stalwarts had won after all, and the compromise vice-president, Chester A. Arthur, was to become president. Garfield was removed at considerable risk from the intense Washington heat and taken by special train to the cottage in New Jersey he had enjoyed so much, where he died a few weeks later, on September 19. Arthur was sworn in the next day.

In death, the press briefly elevated Garfield to a position beyond any of his accomplishments during his short term. It took Godkin, in the *Nation,* to make the best estimate. When Garfield took office, Godkin said, he might have been "fully competent to take charge of any executive department of the government, but he never took charge of his press relations." Nothing in his character or previous career indicates that he ever would have. And with the funeral behind them, the Democratic papers resumed their invective against him, which diminished but did not end with time. As late as forty years after his death, in 1921, a completely false story was circulated that he and his wife had been alienated by his alleged domestic infidelities. It is reasonable to assume that Garfield would have made no attempt to explain this situation if he had been still alive. He would have let ambiguity hang in the air, and refused to deal directly and forthrightly with his pursuers in the press.

Arthur the Pacifier

For the Stalwarts, Arthur proved to be a cruel disappointment. A man who had shown himself to be a master at the corrupt art of political patronage and who would presumably be against any effort to reform a system that had so greatly benefited his career, this plump, amiable, accidental president, with his ferocious mustaches, astonished everyone by doing exactly the opposite of what was expected. He was no sooner in office than he advised Congress of his belief that "original appointments should be based upon a certain fitness"—exactly what the reformers had been saying all along. As for the other controversial question—tariffs—Arthur again took the high road, urging reform.

How much was the press responsible for this sudden conversion? We can only speculate, of course, but we do know that in the two months he waited, a virtual prisoner in his own house, while Garfield moved agonizingly toward his death, Arthur had more than enough time to contemplate what awaited him in possessing the prize he had never hoped to achieve on his own. He remembered the harsh criticism Garfield had endured during his short term in office, and the prospect of nearly four more years of such attacks, directed at him, could not have helped but be unnerving.

Arthur was acutely conscious that he was not bringing a positive national reputation to the White House, as his three predecessors in the accidental presidency (Tyler, Fillmore, and Johnson) had done. He had been a compromise candidate, named only to placate his powerful boss, Conkling, who represented the worst elements in the party. Meanwhile, as he waited to see whether the stricken president would die, Arthur was reminded daily by the press that his public image was already clouded.

Dana, who liked accidental presidents no better than those duly elected, rehearsed again a speech Arthur had made at Delmonico's, in which conviviality had led him to make loose statements that appalled even his admirers. The *Sun* also investigated charges that the potential president was not even an American but a British subject, a canard which so worried Arthur that he issued a full and detailed denial after he took the oath. There was also the ugly rumor, given a spurious dignity by some Democratic newspapers, that Conkling and Arthur had conspired to assassinate Garfield, using Guiteau as a useful tool. It was recalled that the assassin shouted after he pulled the trigger, "Arthur is president now!" It was a charge that shocked and outraged Arthur, who issued a pained and indignant denial, declaring that no one deplored the national calamity more than he and Conkling.

But Conkling was unquestionably a heavy weight around Arthur's neck. They had certainly been thick as thieves, which many people thought both of them were. Only three years earlier, when President Hayes had forced Arthur's dismissal as collector of the port of New York, the odor of Conklingian corruption had arisen from the incident like cheap perfume. There was no doubt that Arthur, as chairman of the New York State Republican Committee, took his orders from the handsome, haughty party boss whom a grateful populace had sent to the Senate.

Conkling's hold on the voters, aside from those he had bought, was sometimes beyond belief. The press had been overjoyed to publish all the details it could get about his notorious romance with Kate Chase Sprague, daughter of Salmon P. Chase, who had been a secretary of the treasury and chief justice of the Supreme Court. Kate was married to William Sprague, the alcoholic governor of Rhode Island during the Civil War and later a senator from that state. It had been a political marriage, which she had endured by virtue of her father's insistence and her husband's money. But when her father died and the fortune diminished, she turned to Conkling, who was also married but long since estranged from his wife.

Shortly before the election of 1880, the papers thought that Conkling would be ruined by a startling episode in the Sprague home, when the husband found his wife in the arms of her lover, chased Conkling from the house with a gun, and later in a nearby restaurant engaged him in a heated quarrel within sight and sound of several shocked but delighted bystanders. The Conkling machine had enough clout to get this story suppressed by several of the New York papers, circulating a dubious cover-up account to replace it. Such an event could not be contained, however, and soon newspapers all over the country were running stories about this triangle in high places. Hayes wrote optimistically in his diary: "The Conkling scandal is the newspaper sensation of the times. This exposure of C's rottenness will do good in one direction. It will weaken his political power, which is bad and only bad." Contemplating this sordid landscape while Garfield lay dying, Godkin wrote in the *Nation,* with his lofty contempt: "It is out of this mess of filth Mr. Arthur will go to the Presidential chair in case of the President's death."

Through that long, hot summer, when the nation's nerves were frazzled and no one was quite sure what to do if Garfield lingered on and no full-bodied president sat in the White House, Chester Arthur stayed home and made all the right moves, astutely counseled by Conkling's experienced advisers. He made himself available to those who would talk with him, but he refused to be drawn into the national debate about what the Constitution meant, if anything, by the gaping hole it had left in the matter of a president unable to perform his duties. It was recalled that during his four months as vice-president, while Garfield was showing his independence by rejecting most of the demands for patronage coming from the Conkling forces, Arthur had continued to maintain business as usual in New York politics, and since he was regarded as Conkling's right-hand man, he not only antagonized the reformers who thought the new Republican team had not gone far enough but also the Conkling men who believed the president had gone too far, taking the vice-president with him.

In the press Arthur was charged with having too little respect for his office. Nast pictured him in *Harper's Weekly* as a bootblack, shining Conkling's shoes. John Hay wrote a sharp editorial for the *Times*, headed "A Public Scandal," and the *Tribune* of July 7, 1881, declared bluntly: "The manly figure of the Vice President of the United States still stands at Albany under a sign which reads: 'Political dickering and other dirty work done here.'" No paper was more scathing than the New York *Times*, which declared:

Active politicians, uncompromising partisans, have held before now the office of Vice-President of the United States, but no holder of that office has ever made it so plainly subordinate to his self-interest as a politician and his narrowness as a partisan. . . . While his succession to the Presidency of the United States depends simply on the issue of a strong man's struggle with death, Arthur is about the last man who would be considered eligible to that position, did the choice depend on the voice either of a majority of his own party or of a majority of the people of the United States.''

Thus Arthur came to the presidency under a cloud thicker than most other incumbents had faced, enough to have smothered a lesser man. But the press and his other critics overlooked his better qualities. First of all, he looked presidential, exuding a dignity befitting the office. Then it had to be admitted that he was an intelligent man who knew politics down all its steamy corridors. It had to be conceded, too, that during those trying summer months he had behaved with such cool restraint, always correct and respectful, that critics found it hard to fault him. While the press was projecting a stereotypical image of him, Arthur was creating his own persona through his conduct, so that by the time Garfield actually died, a large and influential portion of the press saw him differently. As one of his biographers, George Frederick Howe, observes, he was "pictured as a gentleman of good intentions but small ability, instead of as a low politician of evil objectives and great force. The danger . . . would be his dependence on Conkling for advice. He himself could look forward to support from his worst critics of the past for every future act in the public interest, but he would be held to strict account."

Arthur assumed office knowing exactly what he had to do. He must push for civil service and tariff reform, since that was plainly what the people as well as the Half-Breeds wanted. That would alienate some of Conkling's most ardent supporters, but he could appease them by not going too far with it. He could not afford to ignore Conkling and would have to seek his advice, but at the same time he would make gestures of independence to offset these excursions. It was a course calculated to offend everyone in some degree, but Arthur believed it was the politically wisest path to take.

Above all Arthur knew that if he were to carry out this plan successfully, he would have to distance himself from the press as much as possible and hold firmly to the conviction that, whatever the editors might say about him, the people wanted calm, not adventure. He intended to project an image of quiet, confident independence, meanwhile carrying out a conservative program on currency and tariff reform, banking, and taxation, minimizing the role of government. He was certain that would impress the business community, and it did; many of its leaders thought Arthur was the most effective president since Lincoln.

It was a mistake, however, to believe that Arthur did not need the press, that he could shut it out so thoroughly. It seemed not to occur to him that he could never communicate his ideas and plans to the public whose good will he sought without the newspapers. Washington correspondents, who thought they had made at least a little headway with Hayes, were dismayed to find that Arthur did not intend to have any regular dealings with the press and that he was nearly as adamant as Hayes about refusing interviews. When he did grant one, the meeting was useless because the president simply refused to discuss political or personal affairs. Taking a cue from him, his cabinet followed suit. Reporters had to depend on Arthur's friends and visitors, or even his enemies, who could at least be depended upon for rumors. This policy has led Howe to conclude that Arthur's administration was "one of the really arid spots in the long history of the Presidential relations with the press."

Not surprisingly, it was a policy that only stimulated press criticism, about which the president proved to be extremely sensitive. One of Conkling's Stalwarts thought Arthur had a "mental fear of newspapers." That had been evident long before he came to Washington, when he had made very effort to keep the details of his job private, believing correctly that spoilsmen operate best behind closed doors. Beyond that, he was extremely jealous of his reputation, and he could never forgive the press for its treatment of him (no worse, it must be said, than of any other public figure) before he reached the White House. Once there, it was easier simply to withdraw from reporters rather than to overcome his prejudices and try to influence them on his behalf. In common with most other presidents, he could never understand or accept the fact that a president lives in a goldfish bowl where every action, every utterance, is scrutinized, not excepting his private life—the rock on which so many president-press relationships have shattered.

Arthur's desire for privacy within the White House for himself and his family was understandable although impossible, for him or any other president, at least to the extent he (or they) would have desired it. In Arthur's case, however, there was another element. When he snapped at a prying White House visitor,

"Madam, I may be the President of the United States, but my private life is nobody's damned business," he was not only expressing the normal irritation of a private man trapped in public life but also displaying a certain aristocratic disdain for the public. He sincerely believed that it was undignified to share any of his thoughts with the public, except for formal messages and occasional dedicatory speeches.

Arthur, in fact, did not like living in the White House. "You have no idea how depressing and fatiguing it is to live in the same house where you work," he told a reporter. "The down-town business man in New York would feel quite differently if after the close of his day he were to sit down in the atmosphere of his office to find rest and recreation instead of going uptown to cut loose absolutely from everything connected with his work of the day." Consequently, during the summer and whenever it was possible at other times, Arthur fled to a cottage he had set aside for him on the grounds of the Soldiers' Home on the outskirts of Washington—the forerunner of Camp David. He even went so far as to suggest to Congress that a separate presidential residence be constructed on Lafayette Square. The response varied from apathy to horror, and nothing came of the idea.

In his attitude toward the White House, Arthur was inviting criticism from Congress, the public, and the press. The Democratic newspapers made much of the fact that he would not consent to live in it until a great deal of refurnishing and repairing was done. A man of taste accustomed to elegance, Arthur intended to bring style into the old place, and he did so, to an extent not seen again until the Kennedy administration. His refurbishing got nearly as much attention from the press as he gave to it himself, supervising the entire process.

To begin with, twenty-four wagonloads of existing White House furniture and clothing were auctioned off, including the birdcage that had belonged to Grant's granddaughter Nellie and a pair of Lincoln's trousers. A tea table was replaced by a punch bowl. One of the changes designed to enhance presidential privacy was a Tiffany glass screen between the public entrance hall and the corridor connecting the East Room to the dining rooms and conservatory. Japanese leather paneling was installed on some of the walls, and Limoges china appeared on the president's table. For the first time a French chef practiced his art in the White House kitchen. Conkling's steward was stolen away to preside over the household. Arthur had his own resident barber, and from a friend he borrowed an imposing-looking black man named Alec Powell to be his valet. Powell took his title and his job seriously. When the *Sun* referred to him as "the servant," he wrote a letter to the editor expressing the hope that "in the next edition of your paper you will correct the same to 'the messenger.'"

Arthur's person matched the elegance of the mansion he lived in so reluctantly. He was always impeccably turned out, the very figure of a proper gentleman. Some people found all this stylishness impressive and in keeping with the status of chief executive, but others, including many newspapers, looked upon it in much the same way the Anti-Federalists had regarded George Washington's splended furnishings, clothing, and equipages—as too aristocratic by half in a democratic nation.

While he thought such criticism trivial and unwarranted, Arthur was politician enough to understand that his life-style would be a problem if he ran for a second term. When he did not win renomination in 1884, Congressman Joseph ("Uncle Joe") Cannon, of Illinois, who would one day be the celebrated Speaker of the House, declared that "Arthur was defeated by his trousers." (Cannon himself was in no danger of suffering that fate; he had been known as "the Hayseed Member from Illinois" before he was "Uncle Joe.")

It appeared that Washington society members and newspaper editors who admired the president's taste and manners were far outnumbered by those who did not. The *World* printed a long list of the cooks, the valet, the barber, the stablemen, and all the other domestics who were ministering to Arthur's personal comfort. It was not so much that this paper and others begrudged Arthur his creature comforts. It was the belief that they were being paid for from public funds rather than private money, which Cannon called "a cruel misrepresentation."

Arthur's self-justification for both his life-style and his conduct was that he never sought the presidency, he did not like it, and he did not intend to seek it again, actively at least. Given those assumptions, he believed himself fully justified not only in living as he did but in erecting a wall between himself and the press. Moreover, as his term in office lengthened, he had two things to hide from the reporters. One was knowledge of the fatal illness that would kill him shortly after he left Washington, and the other was the decision already made that he would not seek reelection because of it. Arthur had no illusions that he would be drafted. While his reform record seemed exemplary, he knew it was not enough for the party's reformers and too much for the other Republican faction.

There was a personal reason, too, why Arthur kept his distance from the press and from the public as well. Not long before he was nominated as vice-president, his wife Ellen had died, and he was still grieving over her. When the news of his nomination was brought to him at his New York house on Lexington Avenue, he had broken down and wept because he could not share the honor with her. Not even his love for his little daughter Nell could prevent him from saying, "There is nothing worth having now." Not even the presidency would be enough.

There were two quite different sides to this president, which the press did not understand, compounding the barrier between them. The correspondents saw Arthur acting the gentleman, but they also saw him drinking with the most disreputable ward heelers. Some, like a Boston *Herald* reporter who first tried to analyze it, thought the dichotomy arose from political necessity. Others thought it simple hypocrisy. These doubters could not forget the way Arthur had actively electioneered for Garfield and himself in Albany, the acknowledged seat of Republican iniquity; they considered such campaigning undignified.

Nor could they forget that famous speech at Delmonico's, at a testimonial for Sen. Stephen W. Dorsey, just before Garfield's inauguration. It had been a rambling, jocular speech, sometimes veering on the silly, the kind that could be expected in a gathering of political cronies who had absorbed a quantity of spirits. In it Arthur had talked about "the secrets of the campaign," which he said he did not want the reporters to discover for "what they might make of it before the inauguration takes place.'' One of the "secrets" was his description of what could have been construed as the corrupt use of funds in Indiana, and the reporters did with it what Arthur had half-seriously feared. Later he denied categorically that any such campaign practice had taken place and went beyond the denial to charge that the reporters had invented it, which did not recommend him to the press.

The paradox of Arthur's character was clearly evident as his administration progressed. The New York *Times* spoke editorially of the "beauty and brilliancy of the entertainments given in the Executive Mansion," asserting that nothing in previous administrations could equal it. Other papers talked of Arthur's impeccable manners and charming conversation, how he bowed with elaborate courtesy to everyone he met. Even the lap robes in his carriage, monogrammed C.A.A., testified to his style. This early version of Camelot at the White House had made Arthur the most "universally popular" president since the Civil War, one Washington paper observed. So many people came to his public receptions that at one of them Gen. Phil Sheridan had to make his entrance through a window and the president had to run a gantlet of three thousand admiring women before he could reach the Blue Room.

Yet this was a president whom some thought of in retrospect as a lonely man. At the unveiling of his statue in Madison Square, New York, in 1899, McKinley's secretary of war, Elihu Root, asserted: "Surely no more lonely and pathetic figure was ever seen assuming the powers of government. He had no people behind him. . . . He had no party behind him. . . . He had not even his own faction behind him. . . . He was bowed down by the weight of fearful responsibility." As his more recent biographers tell us, Arthur was increasingly isolated from both the press and his associates. His schedule listed no time or occasion for the papers, and, in practice, it seemed that he could be found more often at play than at work.

This was a distorted impression, however. Arthur was not indolent; it was simply that his work habits were not like other people's, or like what a president's were supposed to be. He rose late because he rarely retired before two in the morning. During the day he worked hard enough at official business and, by all accounts, handled it well, but in the evening he was eager to retreat from responsibilities and to give small suppers for any congressional leaders willing to listen to him. As General Sherman recalled later, "When he threw off the cares of office he seemed at his best. I have sat up with him till midnight, and then, when I excused myself, he would say, 'Oh, General, don't go; stay and let us have a good time.'"

The press was puzzled by the president's conduct. It was eager—and vied competitively—to give the public a behind-the-scenes view of Arthur's life of a kind that has always greatly intrigued readers, and it found no difficulty in showing Arthur as an epicure, a "high liver . . . who ate and drank too much and died young from the effects of overindulgence," as was said of him later. On the other hand, the newspapers, politically oriented as most of them still were, could not bring themselves to view Arthur's conduct of the presidency with the same half-envious equanimity they gave to his private life. Revisionists have changed the perception of Arthur as a weak, ineffective president, but at the same time his general policy of conciliation was calculated to offend large numbers of people, including many in his own party. For example, Arthur pointedly contributed funds to a black church and personally awarded diplomas at a black high school in Washington. When the Supreme Court nullified the Civil Rights Act of 1875, the president assured Congress that he would unhesitatingly support any "right, privilege and immunity of citizenship" it might pass. That brought him the endorsement of a growing black press, and the enmity of those in both the South and the North who were not ready to accept civil rights for black people. (Interestingly, out of 120 black journals then extant, only two—the New York *Age* and the Washington *Bee*—thought blacks should form their own party. These two editors backed Blaine in 1884.)

In the arena of foreign policy Arthur appeared to have a chance for real successes, but the promise was never wholly realized because of Blaine's influence. The "Plumed Knight" had been Garfield's choice as secretary of state, but after the assassination Arthur replaced him with Frederick Theodore Frelinghuysen. Blaine revenged himself for this rebuff by attacking his successor's policies (which were, of course, also Arthur's) through exclusive interviews that he gave to the Washington *Post* and in unsigned editorials written for the New York *Tribune*. When these were combined with the serious divisions in the party itself, and Arthur's worsening illness, the administration's foreign policy foundered.

What little support Arthur got came chiefly from his intimate friend, Charles R. Miller, editor of the New York *Times,* his only close relationship with a newspaperman. Nor was he pursued by the Washington press corps in an attempt to understand him better. The modern tradition of presidential news gathering had not yet been established, although current practices were about to be changed, along with the business itself, by the advent of Joseph Pulitzer, the Hungarian immigrant who had just bought the New York *World.* For the time being, however, Arthur did not seek newspaper support, nor was he sought out by the press. He relied on the convenient instrument used by his predecessors, the campaign biography. While he had disavowed any intention or interest in serving a second term, he prudently solicited the veteran Washington correspondent, Ben Perley Poore, to write such a biography in case the unimagined occurred and he was renominated. It was a book carefully tailored to his wishes. He told Poore, for example, not to mention the trip he had made to Albany in 1881, while he was still vice-president, to campaign for the reelection of Senators Conkling and Thomas Platt, a journey that had earned him accusations of boss rule.

If Arthur's policy toward the press was to remove himself from its notice, and in general to make himself as inconspicuous as possible, he succeeded. As a customs collector, even as vice-president, he had not been much in the public spotlight. As president he was nearly invisible, generating less news than any chief executive before him. His tour of duty in the White House marked perhaps the lowest point in the long history of the president-press relationship, in the sense that it barely existed for three and a half years. Arthur shielded not only himself but his son and daughter from the newspapers, so that they could not even print the usual trivia about family life in the White House.

Ironically Arthur prevented the public from understanding fully how much better a president he was than anyone, including himself, had expected when he was thrust on stage. At best, he earned a kind of cautious respect from press and public alike. Worst of all, by isolating himself in this way, he also alienated politicians of every kind, friends as well as enemies. Blaine, of course, would have none of him, and with Blaine went the Half-Breeds. The Stalwarts could not find anything congenial about Arthur either, and only the more conservative reformers found something to approve in what he was doing. Moreover, by coming out for Charles J. Folger as governor of New York, in a mistaken effort to ensure that the state would be Republican in 1884, Arthur succeeded only in helping to secure Albany for Grover Cleveland, who would soon use it as the launching pad for his own ascent to the White House. In addition, the victory became part of a Democratic sweep that gave the party a troublesome (for the president) majority in Congress during the final two years of his administration. Once again there was proof that presidents who dabbled too openly in machine politics might well find themselves in trouble with the voters.

In his last two years Arthur suffered under a running campaign of character assassination in the press, engineered by his political enemies for a variety of reasons. Attacks were made on both his public and private life, and Arthur smarted under what he could rightfully consider injustices. Poore, struggling with the just-in-case campaign biography, recalled in his own memoirs: "I well remember with what sadness and indignation he referred to the manner in which he had been treated."

Arthur's failing health led him to travel frequently in the last months of his presidency. On a trip to Florida he was accompanied by his close friend Miller of the *Times* and four reporters; on an expedition to Yellowstone Park, one reporter was part of the entourage of a dozen people. It was during this latter trip that the Chicago *Daily News* conducted a national poll of what would now be called "opinion-makers" to assess the Arthur administration, and the results filled fifteen columns. The president was gratified, and somewhat surprised, to see that he was highly regarded.

But as the 1884 convention drew nearer, the opposition papers began to renew and concentrate their attacks on him, especially his personal style of living, and particularly the elegance of the White House and its elaborate staff, which the *Herald* charged was paid out of public funds. The Arthur coat of arms reflected his Irish ancestry, but the *World* produced a book written by the president's father that traced the family to British sources. The heavy implication, for the benefit of Irish voters, was that the family had been ashamed of its Irish origins. The old charges involving machine politics were also revived, along with assorted innuendoes about his penchant for high living.

After the election, of course, most of the papers treated the departed president in friendly, "let-bygones-be-bygones" terms, with the exception of the New York *Tribune,* which conceded nothing. It mattered little to Arthur now. His health failed rapidly, and he died only twenty months after leaving office. The major papers marked his passing with the kind of editorial respect they had failed to give him, for the most part, while he sat in the White House.

Cleveland the Reformer

Stephen Grover Cleveland (he dropped the Stephen when he entered public life) was a remarkable president in several ways, and not simply because he was the first Democrat to be elected in twenty-eight years. Of him Allan Nevins wrote in 1933: "His honesty was of the undeviating type which never compromised an inch; his courage was immense, rugged, unconquerable; his independence was elemental and self-assertive. Beneath all this was a virility or energy which enabled him to impose his qualities upon others in any crisis—reform in 1885 and financial error and class and sectional antagonism in 1893."

The revisionists have somewhat reduced Cleveland's stature. When rating the presidents first began as a national pastime in 1948, the Harvard historian, Arthur M. Schlesinger, Sr., polled fifty-five experts, most of them professional historians, and Cleveland emerged as eighth in the list, just below Theodore Roosevelt, and ranked with John Adams and Polk among the "near great." These results were attacked by other historians, but in 1962 Schlesinger repeated his polling, this time querying seventy-five experts, fifty-eight of them historians. The results of the first poll were more or less confirmed, but this time Cleveland had slid to eleventh, at the bottom of the "near great" category, just above Madison, who at that time had not been able to work himself above the "average" classification.

In 1981 the historian David M. Porter asked forty-one of his colleagues to rate the presidents, and this time poor Cleveland had sunk to the fifteenth rung, mired in the middle of the "average" presidents. He did a little better in a Chicago Tribune poll of 1982, ranking thirteenth, and in a more scientific procedure that same year, conducted by two historians, Robert K. Murray and Tim H. Blessing, employing modern opinion-research techniques for the first time, Cleveland finished seventeenth, at the bottom of the "above average" category. (It may be worth noting that in these polls, taken over a period of thirty-five years, Warren Harding finished dead last every time.)

In looking back on Cleveland's far from undistinguished career, it is difficult to understand why he ranks so low in the opinions of those presumably best qualified to judge. His presidency was unique in many of its aspects, his accomplishments not inconsiderable, and his relationship with the press, while it did not depart from the strictures of the past in any great degree, nevertheless raised important questions and foreshadowed the radical change that lay just ahead.

Perhaps, after so many decades of political corruption, the American public could not readily absorb a man as honest as Cleveland. As for the press, since it had been given little reason to believe in political honesty, in Washington or anywhere else, its skepticism and disbelief about Cleveland were not surprising. However, that hardly excuses its treatment of the president, which was frequently shabby and sometimes cruel. The conduct of the press appeared even worse than it was by comparison with Cleveland's courage and integrity.

By conventional standards, Cleveland was the ideal candidate for the presidency, as juicy a piece of apple pie as Mom could bake. Horatio Alger never wrote a better script. A small-town Presbyterian minister's son, born in Caldwell, New Jersey, the fifth of nine children, Cleveland moved with the family to the town of Holland Patent, in central New York, when he was still very young. There he learned the dominant cultural values of small-town America, dutifully memorizing both *Pilgrim's Progress* and the Westminster Confession, faithfully (if compulsorily) attending prayer service every evening in the family bosom.

Cleveland's father died when he was sixteen, and young Steve—already called "Big Steve" by his friends; Grover was a very large boy—had to go to work. Like the Alger heroes, he went to New York City, where he worked for a year as bookkeeper and assistant superintendent at the New York Institute for the Blind. But life in the city was too difficult for him, and he returned home long enough to borrow $25 from one of his father's church elders before leaving again, this time going westward with a young friend. In Buffalo his uncle, Lewis F. Allen, helped him get a job in a law firm, even though he had no more than a public school education, and not all of that.

For the next twenty-eight years, Cleveland struggled upward in Buffalo, living out the reality of the Alger dream. His first object was to become a lawyer, for which he studied half the night for years, getting little sleep, until he was admitted to the bar in 1859. A portrait of him in those days shows us a young man with fierce handlebar mustaches, a clenched fist, and a look of solid determination on his handsome face. Determined he was, and also independent to a fault, stubborn, impatient when he was crossed, but already with such a reputation for honesty that he was in demand as a lawyer, a profession regarded by the general public as deficient in that quality since colonial times. Cleveland hewed to the line of ambition and purpose, forgoing marriage, turning down jobs that might distract him, steering straight toward a political career that he meant to achieve by following an astonishing route—the avoidance of machine politics. To rise any other way than with the help of the bosses was virtually unheard of in those days, when the corrupt machines dominated political life.

But this public facade did not represent the entire Cleveland persona. He had other all-American qualities as well. Big Steve was a beer-drinking cigar smoker, an ardent hunter and fisherman, a compulsive worker, a man who enjoyed spending his none too frequent nights out with the boys, whooping it up with them in the more respectable Buffalo watering places. When it was time, he prudently eased himself out of this pattern, began to wear good clothes and a top hat, and helped to organize the City Club.

This careful man committed only one known indiscretion, but it was enough to threaten his political future later on. He fell in love (or it may have been no more than the mutual attraction of two lonely people) with an unattached widow named Maria Crofts Halpin. She has been described as amusing, attractive, and cultured, which must have been a refreshing change from the often seedy companions who accompanied Cleveland on his visits to German beer gardens. What may or may not have been the result of this liaison was a boy named Oscar Folsom Halpin; his mother asserted that Cleveland was the father, but others said the paternity might have resembled a corporation more than an individual.

In any case, although Cleveland did not marry the lady, he looked after the boy's welfare. In the belief that Mrs. Halpin had become an alcoholic, he persuaded a friendly judge to sign an order removing Oscar from her custody. After a temporary stay in an orphanage, Oscar was adopted by one of Cleveland's friends and later became a prominent physician. Mrs. Halpin moved away from Buffalo and remarried, later filing a suit for the return of her child, which her brother-in-law persuaded her not to press. Instead she surrendered all claims, signed a release, was given $500 (presumably by Cleveland), and dropped out of sight, permanently lost from view if her former dear friend had not run for the presidency.

Meanwhile, in spite of his resolve to avoid the machine, Cleveland moved actively into politics in 1858 by working for the local Democratic organization and then moved smoothly up the ladder from delegate to the city convention in 1862, election as ward supervisor at twenty-five, appointment as assistant district attorney, and, after losing a race for his boss's job in 1865, five years later becoming sheriff of Erie County, winning by a thin margin of 303 votes. On the way up he took one step that would have been fatal to a politician in later years: he avoided Civil War service by sending a substitute. Since this practice was so common, however, it was never held against him.

To be sheriff to Erie County was a job no other lawyer of promise would have wanted. Buffalo was a tough waterfront town whose 673 saloons were populated by a rowdy collection of canal hands, sailors, roustabouts, vagabonds, and a miscellaneous assortment of riffraff. Crime was a way of life in the city, and the sheriff was an object of disdain. Nevertheless, during his three years in office Cleveland attracted public attention by his integrity in a position where graft had been considered a business expense, and by sending two notorious murderers to their deaths.

Buffalo rewarded him by making him mayor. The citizens had learned to respect this large man who had become a partner in one of the city's best law firms and was known to be extremely hardworking, taking only brief vacations and saving his money. They did not consider it a fault that he was known to put away prodigious amounts of beer and sausage in Schenkelberger's Restaurant, raising his weight to 250 pounds; being fat was a bourgeois virtue in an increasingly prosperous America. The further knowledge that he was an accomplished poker player and the proud owner of a celebrated bird dog and had fought a public fist fight in a political argument only added to his fame in this macho society. But above all, it was Cleveland's growing reputation for honesty in a sea of public corruption that was pointing him toward future political success.

Reform was in the air. The newspapers and magazines were full of rural discontent, strikes and the rise of unions, the growth of trusts, robbery in high places, and, most of all, the abject state of political office, which had led *Harper's Weekly* to call the United States Senate "a club of rich men . . . not sensitive to the charge of voting upon questions in which they have a pecuniary interest.'' It was a Senate, said this influential magazine, that was not only corrupt but cared nothing whatever about public opinion.

In this atmosphere, and given Cleveland's reputation, it was natural that a reform group in Buffalo should have approached him to be mayor, another post with few takers. He did not disappoint his backers, winning the office without making any political deals or spending money unwisely. Moreover, when he was in office, he saved the city a million dollars at once by throwing out fraudulent contracts for municipal services and pointing an accusing finger at the numerous grafters around City Hall. To disillusioned voters, he was an astonishment. He seemed actually to hate dishonesty. And when he publicly admitted one of his own mistakes, a virtually unknown act by a politician, it was clear that the only proper reward for such a man was the state governorship.

The reform movement that propelled Cleveland into Albany was so strong that it even attracted a respectable number of Republican voters who swallowed and voted Democratic. And, once more, he disappointed no one. No one, that is, except the press. By this time, Cleveland was on a stage large enough to attract national attention, and in New York State he represented a power base that was always under partisan fire in fierce political wars.

At this juncture Cleveland was a formidable man in more ways than one. He weighed more than 300 pounds (he would never reach Taft's 350, a presidential record), and it made him uncomfortable, particularly in the torrid Albany summer when, as usual, he worked hard at his desk while others sought mountain and shore. Consequently he was more than ordinarily irritated when rumors spread, unaccountably, that he was enjoying the fleshpots of Newport, Rhode Island, while Albany sweltered. It was his first major conflict with the press.

At a press conference of sorts, a Brooklyn *Eagle* reporter inquired, with transparent guile, ''I hope, Govenor, that you enjoyed your visit in Newport?'' Cleveland put down his pen and swung around in his chair. ''Newport?'' he repeated. ''I have not been to Newport.'' The reporter's surprise was equally transparent. ''Why,'' he said, ''the papers of New York City announced you as spending some days there.'' ''Yes, I know they did,'' the governor answered curtly. ''I received an invitation to go to Newport, but I declined it, for the reason that I had so much business here to do. But that fact did not prevent certain of the newspapers of New York from stating it as if it were really so.

''How is it,'' Cleveland went on, warming to a subject that had only begun to irritate him,

that they get these things in the newspapers out of nothing? Alongside of the very columns announcing my presence in Newport were statements of doings here in this chamber showing that I was here at work. Yet, notwithstanding that, the New York *Times* read me a lecture on its editorial page nearly a column long about my ''junketing'' and roaming about for pleasure. ''Junketing'' would have been far pleasanter than working at this desk hard all day. When an officer junkets and is blamed by the press for it I suppose he has the consolation and compensation of having had a very good time. When he doesn't junket and yet is criticized he has the consolation of duties performed. The *Sun* about the same time said I was away pleasuring, and that the lieutenant-governor was the governor. Those papers keep well informed.

The sarcasm was deserved, but unfortunately for Cleveland this was only a trivial foretaste of what was to come. Meanwhile he pursued his uncompromising way. He made moves that his fellow Democrats considered suicidal. When the legislature passed a bill to reduce the fare on New York City's elevated railway, controlled by the popular villain, Jay Gould, from ten cents during off hours to five cents at all times, Cleveland vetoed it on the grounds that such a reduction without any regard for the company's finances violated the railway's First Amendment rights. No matter how dubious this may have been legally, his veto message was so convincing that his constituency was hardly damaged. Worse, however, his refusal to appoint the incompetents and party hacks proposed by the Tammany Hall leader, John Kelly, was considered to be a death blow to his political future in the state. Instead, it had just the opposite effect. The electorate was charmed by this governor who defied the bosses of his own party, challenged the integrity of his supporters, and proved himself over and over to be a sworn enemy of corruption.

Virtue had never been so popular as the parties gathered for their convention in 1884. When the Republicans met in Chicago, in June, their chaplain's opening prayer petitioned God to see to it that "the coming political campaign may be conducted with that decency, intelligence, patriotism and dignity of temper which become a free and intelligent people." Heaven's ear was deaf. It was quickly apparent that the convention would be a duel between the machine Republicans who dominated it and a small group of reformers whose leader was the noted journalist Carl Schurz, but which also included Theodore Roosevelt, President Charles W. Eliot of Harvard, the eminent Brooklyn clergyman Henry Ward Beecher, Charles Francis Adams, Jr., Leverett Saltonstall, and Henry Cabot Lodge. These gentlemen were treated with contempt by the party leaders, and when, as expected, the name of James G. Blaine was once more brought before a convention that had refused him the nomination on two previous occasions, it was clear what would happen. "Nominate him," said Judge West, rising to do so, "and the campfires and beacon lights will illuminate the continent from the Golden Gate to Cleopatra's Needle. Nominate him and the millions who are now waiting will rally to swell the column of victory that is sweeping us."

Those words touched off one of the wildest demonstrations ever seen at an American political convention, an institution never noted for restraint. The dignified president of Cornell, Andrew D. White, who was present as a delegate at large, looked on with affronted dignity and wrote later that the scene was "absolutely unworthy of a convention of any party, a disgrace to decency, and a blot upon the reputation of our country." Nevertheless, it carried the Plumed Knight into the nomination at last, and a symbolic helmet surmounted by a white plume was carried up in triumph to the platform. It took five more hours and sixteen more speeches nominating Blaine before enthusiasm was exhausted. There was only token opposition next day, and Blaine was nominated on the fifth ballot.

Blaine's supporters were dismayed by the reaction that followed. In the aftermath of the convention there was a wave of public indignation, and many Republican newspapers failed to support the candidate, while reform factions and independents within the party united to oppose him. It was one of those rare occasions when the best elements in both parties meet on common ground; Democratic leaders were told by their Republican counterparts that, if they could produce a satisfactory candidate, support and vote-switching would be forthcoming.

The Democrats acquired an important ally in E. L. Godkin, by this time the most influential editorial writer in the country. The troika that had been running the *Evening Post* was now reduced to a duo with Carl Schurz's resignation. Godkin had almost complete editorial control of the paper and was busy remaking it in the image of the *Nation,* his true love, so that it was becoming something like a daily edition of the respected weekly. Many of his editorials first appeared in the *Evening Post,* then were reprinted in the *Nation.* Godkin opposed Blaine because, in common with a growing number of others, he saw the Plumed Knight's plume as badly tattered by his shadowy affiliation with corruption. As Godkin put it, this was a man who had "wallowed in spoils like a rhinoceros in an African pool."

Thus, by the time the Democrats gathered in Chicago, there was obviously only one man among them whose entire political reputation was built on honesty, who could be guaranteed to drive sin from Washington and, more important, attract the votes and support of the Republican independents. That man was Grover Cleveland. He had only to overcome the opposition of John Kelly, the Tammany boss, who had his own candidate, Gen. Benjamin Butler. But Kelly could not control his New York delegation, and, when the Brooklyn delegates deserted him for Cleveland, he was utterly frustrated. How utterly was expressed by the *Sun*'s reporter: "Fire and smoke burst from the nostrils of Tammany. Their henchmen paced the lobbies raging like lions." In spite of this incendiary display, Cleveland was nominated on the second ballot.

The press stood back for a moment to examine the man who had achieved so remarkable a triumph, viewing him with the candor that the papers still exhibited in their political stories. "Cleveland," said the Boston *Advertiser,*

is stout, has a well-fed look, is indeed a good liver, has the air of a man who has made up his mind just how he ought to behave in any position where he may find himself. He is getting bald; he is getting gray—though his white hair does not show conspicuously, as his complexion is sandy. He dresses well, carries himself well, talks well on any subject with which he is familiar, and on any subject with which he is not familiar he does not venture to talk at all.

So began a campaign that, in spite of high-minded purpose in the Democratic camp, degenerated into one of the ugliest ever seen in American party politics. The Independent Republicans, as promised, organized and campaigned for Cleveland, calling themselves "Mugwumps," said to mean "chief" in the Algonquin language. Their former Republican friends, however, asserted it meant they had their "mugs" on one side of the fence and their "wumps" on the other.

Nevertheless they and the Democrats had soon mustered the support of some of the country's most influential newspapers and magazines, including the New York *Times,* the *Herald, Harper's Weekly,* and of course the New York *Evening Post* and its satellite *Nation.*

It was the latter combination that meant most to Cleveland's managers. Whatever else might be thought of him, Godkin was regarded as an editor of the highest morality, whose words were quoted across the country in other publications and heard from pulpits and in the mouths of prominent educators and public men. At first his advocacy of Cleveland was greeted with horror by some of his readers, who could barely imagine voting for a Democrat, but Godkin saw the election as a moral issue, the kind he gloried in, a clear-cut case of a man, Blaine, who had used his official position for private gain. Godkin wrote to Lord Bryce in England, "The Blaine movement is really a conspiracy of jobbers to seize on the Treasury under the lead of a most unprincipled adventurer."

In the streets the campaign was fought on a much lower level. Since there were no great issues at stake, the arguments were reduced to what the candidates had done, or had not done, in their private and public lives. Blaine was the most vulnerable. As Godkin and other editorial writers reiterated again and again, his activities while he was in Congress had been extremely murky. There was the matter of how he had obtained bonds and large loans from the Northern Pacific, Union Pacific, and Little Rock & Fort Smith railroads, in return for votes favoring their interests. There was also his predilection for waving the "bloody shirt" as a good Republican who had never forgiven the South, and, most of all, his hardly concealed conviction that the spoils system was a good thing.

Cleveland, on the other hand, was the virtuous honest man. Or was he? The ghost of Maria Halpin appeared on the political ramparts to haunt him when, on July 21, 1884, the Buffalo *Evening Telegraph* appeared on the streets with flaming headlines: "A Terrible Tale. A Dark Chapter in a Public Man's History." And on into the subheads: "The Pitiful Story of Maria Halpin and Governor Cleveland's Son," "A Prominent Citizen States the Result of His Investigation of Charges against the Governor—Interviews Touching the Case."

It was all very well for the Albany *Argus* to hail Cleveland in equally large headlines as the "Man of Destiny" and the "Agent of Providence." But there were the Republicans marching in the streets and chanting,

> Ma! Ma!
> Where's my pa?
> Gone to the White House,
> Ha! Ha! Ha!

The marching Democrats had their own chant:

> Blaine! Blaine!
> James G. Blaine!
> The con-ti-nen-tal liar
> From the state of Maine.

And, in a reference to a postscript Blaine had written to Warren Fisher, a businessman implicated in his schemes, "Kind regards to Mrs. Fisher. Burn this letter," the campaigners roared,

> Burn this letter!
> Burn this letter!
> Kind regards to Mrs. Fisher.

It became a popular slogan.

Mrs. Halpin's ghost was finally exorcised by a group of noted clergymen, led by Henry Ward Beecher, who investigated the charges against Cleveland and (since they were all good Cleveland men) exonerated him. The public accepted their report, so that particular issue lost its impact.

Cleveland had an opportunity to shame the resurrectors of his lost love and enhance his own reputation when he was presented with a packet of letters supposedly disclosing scandalous details about Blaine's marriage. At the time he had first been confronted with the assault on his own private life, and his managers had asked him what to do, he had replied simply, "Whatever you do, tell the truth," an admonition widely quoted. Now, faced with an opportunity to smear Blaine in kind, he climbed to even higher moral ground, took the presumably incriminating letters, tore them up, and asked a porter to burn them. "The other side can have a monopoly of all the dirt in this campaign," he said, another remark well circulated by friendly newspapers, which now included nearly all the powerful Eastern journals, from Boston, Albany, and Springfield to New York.

Just the same, the smears were having their effect on impressionable voters, and it became clear late in the campaign that it would probably be an extremely close election. A few of the Mugwumps, fearing embarrassment, drew their mugs and wumps together. Among them was Theodore Roosevelt, now a Republican assemblyman in Albany, who had denounced Blaine at the convention but now supported him.

There was one important defection in the press—the New York *Sun*—but then Dana had given Cleveland and the party only lip service from the beginning. The reason was personal and petty. As governor, Cleveland had refused to appoint one of Dana's friends to his military staff. The editor would have supported Blaine outright, but the stench of corruption, which he had spent his editorial life assailing, was too much for him. "Cleveland may not be satisfactory as a Democrat," he wrote in an editorial, "but Blaine is not honest as a man."

It was Dana's mistake. By virtually forsaking the party's candidate, the *Sun* was no longer regarded as the leader of Democratic opinion, and the eternal crusade for the Great Cause fell into the waiting lap of the *World,* rising rapidly under its new owner and editor, Joseph Pulitzer. While *Sun* circulation fell from 137,000 to 85,000, the *World*'s increased dramatically, heading toward that milestone which would make it the first American newspaper to top one million. Moreover, Dana had removed his paper from the company of leading journals all over the country, even the most conservative Republican organs, which were now beating their editorial drums for Cleveland.

Pulitzer, for the moment, was a valuable ally. Dana had used the Halpin affair to break completely with the party, calling on the "moral elements" of the nation to cast out Cleveland and urging that the Democrats withdraw him as a candidate. If this man were elected, Dana wrote in his usual style, so reminiscent of the past, he "would carry his harlots with him to Washington and lodge them in the White House."

Attacking his fellow publisher in return, Pulitzer declared that only a paper with such a "filthy record" and possessed of a "cankered imagination" could paint Cleveland as "a sensuous beast and an animal." Pulitzer would go no further than admit that Cleveland, as he quaintly put it, once "had a sporadic association with a middle-aged female," but "if Grover Cleveland had a whole family of illegitimate children . . . he would be more worthy of the Presidential office than Blaine, the beggar at the feet of railroad jobbers, the prostitute in the Speaker's chair, the law-making broker in land grabs, the representative and agent of the corruptionists, monopolists, and enemies of the Republic."

While Pulitzer would have nothing to do with the supposedly incriminating letters about Blaine that Cleveland tore up, the Indianapolis *Sentinel* exhibited less restraint and published a story based on them, which suggested that the Plumed Knight's oldest son had been born without benefit of clergy. Pulitzer applauded Blaine's decision to sue the *Sentinel* for libel, disclosing that the *World* had been getting scores of letters with allegations about Blaine's private life and had emulated Cleveland by destroying all of them.

In this campaign it was easy to be carried away by moral indignation. Even Godkin, that most careful of men, was sued for alleging, falsely as it proved, that a Brooklyn clergyman who was a Blaine supporter had once been charged with what was called in those days "moral turpitude." Cleveland demonstrated his gratitude for Godkin's support by offering to pay half his legal fees, and the editor—inexplicably, by later standards of newspaper morality, and amazing even then in Godkin's case—took the money.

Given the alternate images projected by the candidates, it may seem curious that elements of the press and public continued to hesitate between Blaine and Cleveland. It seemed clear that Blaine was a venal man, knee deep in corruption, while Cleveland, the honest politician, was only the possible father of an illegitimate child, whose existence he had never tried to cover up, and indeed he had behaved honorably in the entire affair. By the standards of the times, however, bribery was so common that voters could be stirred by it only to a point, while adultery, although not unpopular in the private lives of these same voters, was considered a capital crime and a direct route to hell. After all, while the committee of prominent clergy that had investigated the Halpin affair had returned a verdict of "no seduction, no adultery, no breach of promise, no obligation of marriage," there was nevertheless a "culpable irregularity of life . . . for which it was proper and is proper that he should suffer."

Consequently, in the closing days of this historic campaign, it appeared that Blaine might win after all, but then occurred one of those political accidents that so often determine the course of elections—usually an unguarded remark or gesture. In Blaine's case it was the result of a seemingly innocuous rally of Protestant clergymen, held in the Fifth Avenue Hotel, at which the Reverend Samuel Burchard, giving the address of welcome, uttered an oratorical flourish that earned him an unwanted place in history. "We are Republicans," he proclaimed, "and we do not propose to leave our party and identify ourselves with the party whose antecedents have been . . . Rum, Romanism, and Rebellion!"

A politician as experienced and astute as Blaine should have risen instantly to repudiate those words, recognizing their great danger clearly, but the Republican candidate, one must remember, was at the end of a long and exhausting campaign trail and understandably was only half listening, his mind no doubt on more important matters. He simply did not hear the fatal words. Too late, he heard them next morning when he opened the *World* and read Pulitzer's gleeful comment on the story his reporter had brought back from the hotel. "Romanism indeed. What are Blaine's Irish supporters supposed to think of that?" he inquired, and went on: "Mr. Blaine and his friends, in their eagerness to clutch at every chance of making political capital, have not hesitated to inflame religious prejudices and to drag creeds into politics. . . . Let the party of 'Rum, Romanism, and Rebellion' resent the insult at the polls." No one but the historians would remember Blaine's rueful answer, "The good Lord sent me an ass in the shape of a preacher."

Nor was that the end of this day of disasters for Blaine. In the evening, after leaving the clergymen, he was due to attend a banquet in his honor at Delmonico's. Worried friends urged him to find some excuse for not attending. They pointed out that his hosts were to be Jay Gould, Russell Sage, and other rich men generally regarded as despoilers of the public virtue—people it would be well to avoid in the closing hours of a tight campaign. Blaine, however, believed it would be an even worse mistake if he failed to appear. After all, one does not gratuitously snub large contributors to the party treasury. A single defense was set up: reporters were not to be admitted, but, again, a fatal concession was made. The Associated Press was permitted to report the speeches, and among them was Blaine's. Fueled by excellent food and quantities of vintage wine, it was oratory of a kind that any of the money changers present could have given.

In the morning the *World* was not only aflame with "Rum, Romanism, and Rebellion" but it had a front-page story headlined "BELSHAZZAR'S FEAST." Spread across the page was a cartoon by Walt McDougall, captioned "The Royal Feast of Belshazzar Blaine and the Money Kings." It showed Blaine and his millionaire friends eating Monopoly Soup, Lobby Pudding, and Gould Pie, among other delicacies, while at the lower left corner of the table a ragged man and his wife, in obvious poverty, stretched hungry hands to catch any crumb that might fall from the table. Some political historians regard it as perhaps the most effective political cartoon ever published in this country.

Blaine regarded it as a disaster, and he felt worse when he read the editorial page, with Pulitzer's scorching attack on the event:

From "Rum, Romanism, and Rebellion" at the Fifth Avenue Hotel, Mr. Blaine proceeded to the merry Banquet of the Millionaires at Delmonico's, where champagne frothed and brandy sparkled in glasses that glittered like jewels. . . . The mask is off, and Blaineism stands revealed in its true colors. . . . Read the list of Blaine's banqueters who are to fill his pockets with money to corrupt the ballot box. Are they

the friends of the workingman? What humbug! Are they in sympathy with labor?
Fraud! Are they not mostly railroad kings, Wall Street millionaires, greedy monopolists, lobbyists, and speculators, who have grown wealthy on public grants, legislation, and special privileges? . . . Do the people believe that the Jay Goulds, Sages,
Fields, and others who banqueted at Delmonico's last night poured a corruption fund
into Blaine's pocket without a consideration? . . . Shall Jay Gould rule this country?
Shall he own the President?

There had been other notable cartoons in the campaign, some of them, like
Thomas Nast's in *Harper's,* ultimately famous, but "Belshazzar's Feast" burst
on the country like an incendiary bomb. The happy Democrats had it made up
into posters that were attached to every vacant space available across the country.
A populace still suffering from a national depression could not help being persuaded by it, as they were by Pulitzer's editorial, reprinted by virtually every
paper supporting Cleveland.

Still, adultery, even the suggestion thereof, proved to be just as potent a factor. The election was as close as everyone had predicted. Cleveland won by a
slim twenty-three thousand popular votes, carrying Connecticut, New Jersey,
New York, and Indiana in the North, and the Solid South entirely. After twenty-
four years, the nation had a Democratic president again, but it was a perilously
close call for Cleveland.

Political veterans recalled the Tilden-Hayes count that election night as the
World proclaimed its candidate's victory in its last extra, while Whitelaw Reid's
New York *Tribune* was on the streets with the assurance that Blaine was elected.
A sense of *déjà vu* gripped the city rooms as it became evident that New York
State's vote was so close the election could go either way, with normally Repub-
lican upstate returns remaining in doubt.

By the morning after election, everybody has the fever; it's Tilden and Hayes
all over again, people are saying. Thousands crowd Park Row in New York,
where the major papers still have their offices, reading the latest returns being
posted on the bulletin boards outside. Suddenly they stop for a time, and an
ominous murmuring rises from the crowd as rumors pass from lip to lip. It's
being said that Jay Gould, who controls the Western Union Telegraph Company,
is deliberately holding up the returns, and that the Associated Press is helping
him do it. "Let's hang Jay Gould," comes a lynch mob cry from the street, and
it is taken up by hundreds of honest citizens and voters, who surge toward Dey
Street and Broadway, where Gould has his offices. "We'll hang Jay Gould from
a sour apple tree," they sing, marching along democratically. The police arrive
and restrain them.

In the end Cleveland won by 219 to 182 electoral votes, with the popular
plurality little better than a dead heat. The *World* was jubilant. "The beauty of
this close contest," Pulitzer exulted, "is that it enables every political factor that
strove for the election of Cleveland to say, 'We did it!' . . . While claims for the
defeat of Mr. Blaine and the preservation of the Republic are coming from every
quarter, permit us also to say that the New York *World* did it!" This was more
than the usual editorial bombast, as Cleveland himself acknowledged years later,

on the occasion of the *World*'s twenty-fifth anniversary. In his letter of congratulations he wrote of the paper in that critical 1884 election: "It was here, there, and everywhere, showering deadly blows upon the enemy. The contest was so close that if it had lacked the forceful and potent advocacy of democratic principles at that time by The New York *World* the result might have been reversed."

There were several fallouts from the occasion of importance to both press and presidency. One was the result of Godkin's action in taking an independent course, leading the parade of other Republican papers in support of the Democratic candidate. This was a further weakening of that monolithic partisanship that had characterized the press from the beginning. Among the nation's largest and best newspapers, it was now clear that a well-defined party press no longer existed, as it had in the past. The new generation of editors might be zealous for one side or the other, but they were no longer reliable extensions of the party. The new spirit was evident in Pulitzer's editorial after the election, in which he declared: "The *World* is chained to no conqueror's chariot. It will gladly and zealously support all that is good in President Cleveland's administration, but it will oppose anything clearly wrong or mistaken. *The* World *is as great a public trust as the Presidency.*"

Another result of the 1884 election was the emergence of the *World* as a national newspaper, as the *Tribune* had been and the *Times* would be. It would soon be not only the nation's largest paper but one whose voice had to be respected by presidents. Its extraordinary publisher, Joseph Pulitzer, was revolutionizing the newspaper business as James Gordon Bennett, Sr., had done when his *Herald* appeared on the scene in 1835.

Pulitzer would prove to be the most formidable press figure with whom the office of the presidency had yet contended, and he would soon be joined by an entirely different kind of publisher, William Randolph Hearst, who would bring further change. Together they ushered in a period in which the conduct of newspapers became a matter of vital concern for both presidents and public.

To his historic career with the *World,* Pulitzer brought journalistic genius, a certain eccentricity in the vein of the Bennetts and Greeley, and a crusading zeal that aptly coincided with the social movements of his time. A crusader had a great deal to occupy his time and conscience in late nineteenth-century America.

Born in 1847 in Mako, Hungary, of a good Hungarian-Jewish family, young Pulitzer left an unhappy family situation at seventeen to join the army—any army, he did not care which one. But even in a Europe torn by wars and revolutions he could not find one that would have him. His appearance must certainly have been against him. His biographers describe him then as "tall, scraggy, with long, thick black hair, large head, and oversized nose. . . . About six feet two and a half inches tall, ungainly in appearance, awkward in movement, lacking entirely in the art of human relations." Turned down by the Austrians, the French, the British, and even by old sea captains in Hamburg, when he tried to ship as a common seaman, Pulitzer fell into the hands of Union army bounty hunters, busy hiring young men who would get passage to America, where they would be substitutes for men who, like Cleveland, did not want to be drafted. Such recruits were worth $500 each.

Details about Pulitzer's early life are vague, and he may or may not have jumped ship in Boston harbor and collected the bounty himself (it would have been like him), but in any case he enlisted at once in the First New York (Lincoln) Cavalry, organized by Carl Schurz. He found army life intolerable. As a young man who asked questions incessantly and despised anyone who withheld information, he was bound to be in constant conflict with the military; he fought more skirmishes in the barracks than on the battlefield and was nearly courtmartialed for striking a noncommissioned officer.

Out of the army in 1865, alone and broke in New York, Pulitzer made his way to St. Louis and got his first newspaper job on the *Westliche Post,* the city's leading German-language daily. He was soon recognized as the best reporter in town, especially on the political scene, where he spent much of his time. Persuaded to run for the state House of Representatives, he became briefly a politician himself, although hardly distinguishable from the explosive reporter he had been. He once shot and wounded a well-known lobbyist and had to be saved from jail by his friends. Later he was one of the city's three police commissioners and helped nominate Greeley in 1872 as a Liberal Republican. Greeley's failure made a Democrat of him.

Returning to the newspaper business, he acquired a part interest in the *Post,* sold it at a profit, bought the bankrupt *Staats-Zeitung* for next to nothing, sold its AP franchise to the *Daily Globe* for a substantial profit, took some of those profits to study law, was admitted to the bar, married a distant cousin of Jefferson Davis, and then stood at a crossroads in his life. There was no doubt he could be a successful politician if he liked, or he could be a publisher. Pulitzer chose the press. He bought a failing St. Louis paper called the *Dispatch* for $2,500, merged it with the *Post,* and so established the St. Louis *Post-Dispatch,* still one of the nation's best newspapers.

With his paper Pulitzer became a crusader against corruption, an activity that made working on the paper dangerous but quickly gained it public acceptance and respect as a fearless organ of unblemished integrity. Pultizer was soon a rich man, ready to conquer New York at the first opportunity. On his way to Europe in May 1883, he stopped in that city, where Jay Gould's representatives sold him the *World* for $346,000; it had been struggling for years.

On the first day of publication under its new owner the *World* printed the customary statement of purpose, which proved to be something more than the grandiloquent rhetoric of the past. It was an expression of journalistic idealism that seemed to set a new tone for the press. The purpose of a newspaper, said Pulitzer, was to be

an institution that should always fight for progress and reform, never tolerate injustice or corruption, always fight demagagues of all parties, never belong to any party, always oppose privileged classes and public plunderers, never lack sympathy with the poor, always remain devoted to the public welfare, never be satisfied with merely printing news, always be drastically independent, never be afraid to attack wrong, whether by predatory plutocracy or predatory poverty.

Since Pulitzer ardently believed in every item on this list, as his enemies discovered, he meant to stand on that platform and he had a shopping list of goals to go with it—the taxing of luxuries, inheritances, large incomes, and monopolies; abolishing all special privileges possessed by corporations; tariffs for revenue only; civil service reform; the severe punishment of corrupt officials; and punishment for employers who tried to coerce employees in elections, a common practice at the time.

But Pulitzer was also a shrewd businessman who knew advocacy alone did not sell newspapers, and so he offered a refined version of the formula that Bennett, Sr., had invented and Dana had improved upon—that is, sex, scandal, and corruption emphasized in the news columns and on a front page intended for the workingman, while the editorial page would preach crusading idealism for intellectuals. This formula did not entirely please either class. Workers did not know what Pulitzer was talking about on the editorial page, and the intellectuals deplored the *World*'s sensationalism. Nevertheless, it was a formula calculated to elevate circulation, and it did so remarkably.

Pulitzer added another element to his formula, a professional one, which was also new to the business. He laid down a famous dictum: "Accuracy, accuracy, accuracy." It was the first movement toward some kind of objectivity in writing the news, and, while the *World* often violated its own rule, a long step toward the modern newspaper had been taken. Until then newspapers had made little attempt to report the news fairly and accurately. As we have seen, the press was intensely partisan in political reporting, and careless in everything else.

The idea of objectivity has recently come under critical attack as an evasion of responsibility, but this rather bizarre notion is contradicted by the change in reporting that began with Pulitzer and the *World* and, by the early years of the next century, had transformed the general character of newspapers. For a time, the flamboyant personal style of news writing remained substantially the same, but the impersonal attempt to realize the ideal of fairness and accuracy (rather than an admittedly unrealizable objectivity) had begun. The hundred years since then have witnessed further substantial change.

If there was one politician in the United States who could have been expected to endorse Pulitzer's broad principles, it was Cleveland, and the publisher was first to realize it. James Barrett, the *World*'s last city editor and one of Pulitzer's biographers, believed that the publisher had set down Cleveland as a marked man on the first day he edited the paper, May 10, 1883, when he presumably instructed his Albany correspondent to play up the governor in an otherwise routine story. "Governor Cleveland," said the story, "apparently likes work and exhibits no desire to shirk it. He is thoroughly Democratic in his manner and modes. He is always accessible."

It was Pulitzer who, a month later, first raised the possibility of Cleveland's presidency in an editorial titled, "Another Cleveland," in which he said that the only way to drive the Republican rascals out of Washington was to find a man like Cleveland, and, if the governor was not available, since he was doing so well in Albany, it would have to be someone like him. "The Democrats will find a national Cleveland,'' Pulitzer predicted. By early June of 1884 the *World* was proclaiming that the party need look no further than Albany and came out flatly for his nomination, the first major paper to do so.

It appeared to be the beginning of an unprecedented romance, but as soon as the triumphant election was over, Pulitzer began to understand that he had misread his man, at least according to his own lights. As president-elect, Cleveland came to New York in February 1885 and met the press for the first time. He brought some emotional baggage with him. Cleveland had editor-friends upstate—Daniel Manning, owner of the Albany *Argus,* who would become his first secretary of the treasury; Harold Frederic, editor of the Albany *Evening Journal;* and E. Prentiss Bailey, editor of the Utica *Observer*—but he could not forget the false accusations of how he spent his time in the governor's chair, made by the New York dailies. Much less could he either forgive or forget the campaign attempts to blacken his reputation by resurrecting Mrs. Halpin and implying that he had consorted with ladies of no reputation in Albany. Consequently Cleveland let the assembled reporters know, in his almost daily contacts with them, that they did not have his high regard. "I came for information—the idea of this trip is to widen my information on public needs," Cleveland advised them blandly. He quickly discouraged prying, too. "Young man," he told one correspondent who had asked him a particularly penetrating question, "that is an issue too big to be brought up in a brief interview that is rapidly drawing to a close."

Those New York meetings were an accurate forecast of things to come. As Cleveland assumed office, it became clear that he meant to follow the example of most of his predecessors and hold the correspondents in Washington, now an increasing tribe, at a distance. If he thought it necessary, he would issue a statement about a particular matter, for the benefit of all papers, but he had no intention of confiding anything. Correspondents were asked to submit their inquiries through his secretaries, and he would answer whichever ones he cared to. Occasionally he would agree to see an individual reporter, but the interviews were infrequent, and anything approaching an off-the-record conversation was rare. Naturally the press found all this frustrating and irritating.

In the person of George F. Parker, an old newspaper friend, Cleveland had what amounted to a press secretary, although Parker had no official title, merely serving as a personal buffer state between the president and the press and advising him on his relations with the media. In his later *Recollections of Grover Cleveland,* Parker set down the best and fairest summary extant of the president's press relations, and since it remains the most authentic contemporary analysis we have, it may be worth quoting at what would otherwise be undue length:

> While he [Cleveland] held close relations with the editors and owners of papers in the smaller cities, he never relaxed his attitude of watchfulness in dealing with those in New York. He was still more shy of correspondents and reporters. He wanted them to have real news, but he objected to giving it as a favor. . . . As no paper could have any claim to represent him, he was equally free from any such connection with any writer. He never gave his full confidence to any man so related to a metropolitan paper, whether editor or reporter. . . .

It is almost impossible . . . to comprehend the rigidity of Mr. Cleveland's attitude toward the press. . . . He made opinion so long as he was active, not by courting at every turn the various forms in which it found expression, but by maintaining a personal dignity that became him and his place in the world; not by antagonizing it, in the last resort, but by giving it something real and substantial upon which to carry his message laden with ideas and principles. . . .

He was particularly wary of newspapermen, whether in their collective or individual capacity. He had grown to have a strong aversion to them as a class, although not, as was generally thought, to individuals among them. From the beginning of his public career he was unsympathetic with most of the owners of metropolitan papers—the controlling spirits. As he had had some disagreeable experience with them, he reached the conclusion that, in the main, they sought to maintain friendly relations in the hope of getting inside information, or interviews, or news. In like manner, he felt no attraction for the editors of these newspapers. Two or three of them pushed themselves upon him with considerable persistence, and, from this, tried to make their public believe that they were close to him. . . . I never heard or knew of him asking advice from the proprietor or editor of a New York paper. In one or two cases when he had been drawn into giving an interview with the representative of one paper upon any given question, he would advise with me as to the best means of keeping the news from becoming exclusive, or for arranging that it should be distributed through the press associations or other mediums.

Obviously, this was not the kind of relationship Pulitzer had in mind, nor was it an attitude that would endear the president to the press in general. It was, in fact, an open invitation to attack, and that was not long in coming. Moreover, it was a guarantee that Cleveland would come to believe, as had his predecessors, that the press deliberately misrepresented him. "I don't think that there ever was a time when newspaper lying was so general and mean as at present," he wrote to Joseph Keppler, editor of *Puck,*

and there never was a country under the sun where it flourished as it does in this. The falsehoods daily spread before the people in our newspapers, while they are proofs of the mental ingenuity of those engaged in newspaper work, are insults to the American love for decency and fair play of which we boast. . . . If you ever become a subject of newspaper lying, and attempt to run down and expose all such lies, you will be a busy man, if you attempt nothing else.

Amplifying these opinions a few days later, he added: "The only qualification I would make, if any is needed, is that I do not include all the newspapers . . . nor cast any reflections on careful and conscientious correspondents who are known to be such to everybody."

Cleveland needed Parker's advice in what would be a state of constant confrontation with the press, and he got it from a man who was not only an experienced working journalist but a natural public relations man, a talent he made into a later career when he founded the nation's first public relations firm, Parker & Lee, in 1905, with the legendary Ivy Lee. Parker hoped to make the president's life easier by presenting him to press and public as more human—the image, as we would learn to call it, as distinct from reality.

This was not an easy concept to project, since Cleveland not only kept the press at a distance but nearly everyone else as well. He was a workaholic who spent more hours in his office than any president since Polk and had little time for the frivolity he had once enjoyed in the German beer parlors. His sister Rose had come to Washington with him, and Parker was careful to see that the press conveyed her highly respectable image to the public. She was a model of propriety, appealing particularly to the president's religious and temperance constituency, which was a large one.

But then Cleveland fell in love, or, perhaps more accurately, reached the critical point of a long relationship. Frances Folsom was the daughter of one of his Buffalo law partners, who had died in 1875, leaving him as her virtual guardian, even though her mother survived. A lushly pretty young woman, with dark eyes and flowing black hair, Frances and her mother had been entertained at the White House for ten days soon after the president had moved in, and after her graduation from Wells College, Cleveland proposed to her and was accepted.

It was a story made to order for the newspapers—a dour bachelor president, forty-nine years old, being married to a twenty-one-year-old girl he had known since her childhood. Cleveland, however, could not conceive of the public interest such a marriage would arouse, or the lengths to which newspapers would go to satisfy that curiosity. The issue of a president's privacy had not really been tested before; the "right to privacy" concept itself had never met a court test. Pulitizer had instructed his reporters to ask questions freely and aggressively, but most Americans still considered their private lives as private, and in the upper classes it was believed by many that a lady's name appeared in the papers only three times—birth, marriage, and death. The notion that a celebrity, and particularly a president, had forfeited his right to privacy would have seemed farfetched to most people. Consequently Cleveland was wholly unprepared for what followed his proposal to Frances Folsom. He wanted a nice quiet wedding and a secluded honeymoon; it never occurred to him that a president could expect neither.

Cleveland's first mistake was not to announce his plans at once, and so he gave free rein to rumor and speculation. The *Herald* printed the first rumor, as would be expected from a paper prepared to make news where none existed. Since Miss Folsom and her mother were traveling in Europe when the unconfirmed news first broke, she was tracked down by both European and American correspondents, prompting a cry of pain from her fiancé in a letter to Congressman John B. Weber, an old Buffalo friend, over the manner in which a "scandalous press and thoughtless people of the country" had begun "to hunt down an absent and defenceless girl, as if she were a criminal." To his sister Mary he complained even more angrily that Frances and her mother "will be subjected from the time of their arrival [in New York] to the impudent inquisition of newspaper correspondents, and if this latter dirty gang were not entirely satified, our friends would probably be dished up in a very mean way." He did not excuse the public either, assuring Mary that people had "acted in such a mean way" about the matter and expressed no interest in helping.

For a time Cleveland fenced with the press about his marriage plans, while the papers friendly to him either said nothing or denied everything. But then there was, as always, a leak. After a visit with the president, Dr. Winslow Pierce, of New York, spoke to a reporter from the *World,* the most avid of the seekers for truth, and the paper promptly printed what he said about the approaching wedding on page one in its Sunday edition next morning. Later it dutifully reported that the president was angry and irritated by the newspaper talk of his coming marriage.

So the president and friendly papers like the Cincinnati *Commercial Gazette* (the result of a merger in 1883) continued to deny, and the press in general continued to speculate, until Miss Folsom arrived in New York, and on that day the official announcement was made—a story worth six and a half columns of type in the New York *Times* and an "I-told-you-so" editorial in the *World* by Pulitzer, who further observed that a newspaper's business was "to publish news and not to play the part of flunkeys and suppress the facts."

The wedding itself on June 2 might have been an anticlimax if the papers had not treated it as an event of the first magnitude, employing the kind of type and space usually reserved for declarations of war. Since Cleveland was a Democrat, only the Republican *Tribune* placed it in a more limited, if partisan, perspective. But the *Times* story ran five columns on page one, and the *World* was not far behind.

All the accounts were secondhand. Not surprisingly, Cleveland had ordered both reporters and photographers excluded. Standing outside, however, they could not help hearing the Marine Band, led by John Philip Sousa, play the Wedding March. As a small concession, photographers were to be permitted in the White House next day so that the elaborate decorations would be preserved for posterity in pictures.

By that time the honeymooners had slipped away by special train, unseen, to their honeymoon cottage in Deer Park, Maryland, where the president hoped to do some trout fishing while he was shattering the bonds of bachelorhood. As day broke over the happy couple on their first morning of marital life, an express train pulled into the Deer Park station, bearing a half-dozen eager reporters and photographers, who pitched camp immediately in a pavilion a few hundred yards from the cottage. It was only the vanguard.

Such a scene would be commonplace in our time, but to Cleveland this massive invasion of his privacy was unprecedented and contemptible, even though he had anticipated it to some extent and brought along eight or nine detectives from the Baltimore and Ohio Railroad to guard the place. He emitted a bellow of indignation against the entire press:

They have used the enormous power of the modern newspaper to perpetuate and disseminate a colossal impertinence, and have done it, not as professional gossips and tattlers, but as the guides and instructors of the public conduct and morals. And they have done it, not to a private citizen, but the President of the United States, thereby lifting their offence into the gaze of the whole world, and doing their utmost to make American journalism contemptible in the estimation of people of good breeding everywhere.

"Good breeding" was the key phrase, setting apart the rich and respectable bourgeoisie from the clamorous and insolent masses represented by the press, which impertinently insisted on breaking the rules agreed upon by the best people. This attitude was expressed later by Joseph Bucklin Bishop, who analyzed these events in an article entitled "Newspaper Espionage," which appeared in a new magazine, the *Forum.* The conduct of the press, Bishop wrote, had served "to call public attention to the intolerable lengths to which the modern system of press espionage had been carried. . . . Why should not a newspaper be governed by the same principles which a gentleman follows in his personal conduct?"

Cleveland's "good-breeding" condemnation appeared, quite naturally, in the one paper that had stood apart from the Deer Park skirmish, Godkin's *Evening Post,* and the *Nation,* its satellite. It was the voice of that great moralist editor which asserted the day after the wedding, "Nobody has a right to know everything about anybody on any occasion in life, except the police about a man convicted of a crime." Later, on June 10, when the honeymooners had returned to Washington, Godkin observed: "Nothing has been too silly, or too trivial, or too vulgar to be printed, and the result is a mess of balderdash such as probably has never before been laid before a civilized community as a product of the human mind." If journalism, Godkin went on, his editorial voice rising to a piercing moral howl, demanded that its practitioners do or say anything to increase sales, "it was the lowest occupation, not absolutely criminal, known to modern society—in some respects, worse than keeping a brothel or gambling house."

Here Godkin was enunciating what would become an integral part of American folklore—that reporters (or editors, or publishers, as the offender might be) would print anything, no matter how false or vile, to sell papers. It remains a part of popular belief long after television and other social changes have virtually ended the competition of most newspapers with each other for circulation. At the time, however, with Pulitzer and soon Hearst ushering in what would be known as the era of yellow journalism, there was more than enough truth in the charge to justify it, although it could not be applied to all newspapers, just as it applies to only a handful of them today.

Godkin, in this discussion, contributed the descriptive phrase "keyhole journalism" to the language, one still in use. It was an issue hotly argued for a few weeks, a debate in which even the *World* admitted that the correspondents may have carried their news-gathering efforts too far, but, as it also observed, on June 15, with some accuracy, "Is it not true that the president first drove journalism to the keyhole by shutting the door of information rudely in its face?"

In spite of the clamor, the honeymoon apparently went so well that the chief complainer mellowed in his attitude. The *Tribune* quoted Cleveland as telling the detectives that the reporters "appear to be a gentlemanly lot of fellows, and with the legitimate object only of gathering news and I shall not interpose any obstruction to their getting all the points they need as long as they do not intrude upon my privacy." There were different versions of these words in various papers, but the upshot was that the president held a brief, impromptu press conference for a few (perhaps only two) of the reporters and showed them some of the letters and telegrams the couple had received, answering their questions affably enough.

In the end it remained for the New York *Times* to put the Deer Park affair into some kind of perspective. In a long story summarizing the event, it first set down the facts—that six reporters were on the scene on the morning of the first day, and a half-dozen more by afternoon. By nightfall they had filed thirty-two thousand words, and forty thousand more by the end of the next day. Only its man and the *Herald*'s correspondent, the *Times* insisted, were actually received by the Clevelands, and at no time did the entire assemblage have any more than a distant view of the cottage. The reporters, it said on June 10, could see the president

> when he came outdoors or when he drove on the road 300 yards away, but never got nearer to him in the hope of seeing him, excepting in one or two petty instances. All in all, they were a self-respecting set of men, who had gone to Deer Park in the line of their business in response to a good-natured, unobtrusive popular demand, and they found means through callers and in ways perfectly legitimate and inoffensive to get enough information for truthful and entertaining reading. That was all they wanted to do.

It took them four hundred thousand words in five and a half days to do it.

Thus the Deer Park incident ended on a sober and conciliatory note, but important questions had been raised that would persist as the new journalism and what would soon be the new presidency advanced together. The mountain of honeymoon trivia reported by the papers, some true and some manufactured, was not important in itself. It was the question of the *right* to report that had been raised.

Cleveland appeared to be softening rapidly under the influence of his young wife as they took up life again in Washington, but those who thought the president had forgiven and forgotten did not know their man. That fall, in a speech commemorating the 250th anniversary of Harvard College, Cleveland stirred his Cambridge audience with a sudden, violent attack on at least certain members of the press. It is worth quoting, even at some length, because in it he set forth an idea held by many presidents, that the chief executive should be treated in the papers like any other citizen in respect to his private life. Deer Park had not been forgotten. He said:

> The close view afforded our citizens of the acts and conduct of those to whom they have entrusted their interests, serves as a regulator and check upon temptation and pressure in office, and is a constant reminder that diligence and faithfulness are the measure of public duty. And such a relation between President and people ought to leave but little room in popular judgment and conscience for unjust and false accusations, and for malicious slanders invented for the purpose of undermining the people's trust and confidence in the administration of their government. No public officer should desire to check the utmost freedom of criticism as to all official acts; but every right-thinking man must concede that the President of the United States should not be put beyond the protection which American love of fair play and decency accords to every American citizen. This trait of our national character would not encourage, if their extent were fully appreciated, the silly, mean and cowardly lies that every day are found in the columns of certain newspapers, which violate

every instinct of American manliness, and in ghoulish glee desecrate every sacred
relation of private life.

Everyone knew who the "certain newspapers" were: the *Sun* and the *World* in
New York, Dana and Pulitzer respectively, and the *Commercial Gazette* in
Cincinnati.

But now it was time to get on with the presidency, and life in the White House
was strikingly different. Mrs. Cleveland lit up the place with an active social life,
and her husband was plainly a more relaxed man, more willing to leave his desk
and take an occasional vacation, better able to improve his personal relations
with Congress, and in general less irritable about everything. As for the press, an
armed truce existed, and civilities were maintained. The White House staff, and
especially the secretaries, constituted the buffer state and the transmitting medium for ordinary intercourse. But Cleveland, following the practice of the past,
made himself available to individual reporters, or to a group of them, only if he
thought there was a good reason for it. Beyond these question-and-answer sessions, Cleveland did grant an infrequent full-scale interview, and he used the
press, as had all presidents, to reach the public with official statements.

This first term was preoccupied with two problems—patronage and the tariff.
On the former, much was expected of Cleveland, the reform candidate on whom
Democrats and Republicans had united to drive out the rascals and reform the
system. Editors like Pulitzer and Henry Watterson, editor of the Louisville
Courier-Journal, were not likely to let him forget his implied promises. Yet
Cleveland was faced with an impossible task, on the one hand to satisfy the
regular Democrats who swarmed upon Washington, jubilant that the long pa-
tronage drought was over, and on the other to preserve the support of those
Independent Republicans who had made his election possible. He was compelled
to give at least some jobs to deserving Democrats, but it was not enough for the
Regulars and far too much for the former Mugwumps.

Nevertheless, even Cleveland's worst enemies in the press, notably Pulitzer
and Dana, had to admit that here was a president who was trying to run an honest
administration. The cabinet he appointed was the most competent in decades; he
was the avowed scourge of waste and corruption; and he had the exceptional
courage to veto swollen pension bills introduced for the benefit of GAR veterans.
Moreover he kept a careful eye on government expenditures and, to the surprise
of some cynics, actually appeared to believe that public office was a public trust.

Cleveland could ride out the patronage problem, even though he satisfied no
one, but the tariff question was another matter. He perceived clearly that the push
toward ever higher tariffs was a policy that could only lead to serious trouble. He
felt so strongly about it that he took the unprecedented step of devoting his entire
annual message to Congress (what we would call the State of the Union speech
today) to the problem. He wanted tariffs reduced and those on raw materials
removed completely, and he offered substantial reasons for taking these steps.
His much quoted words, "It is a condition which confronts us, not a theory,"
were part of this address.

There was no hope that a Senate controlled by Republicans, the party of high tariffs, would do what he wanted. His hope lay with persuading his fellow Democrats, who dominated the House, and they responded with the Mills bill, a modest effort in the right direction, but the Senate killed it. These actions drew the lines along which both parties expected the next election would be fought.

The press divided along much the same party lines, and Cleveland had no more than the customary complaints to make about its conduct toward him. But he continued to resent, and with some bitterness, the zeal with which his wife was pursued as she went about her activities, even the most casual shopping trip, and much more so the idle gossip that Republican newspapers printed about both of them, implying that poor Frances was the victim of an unhappy, sometimes a brutal marriage. It was sheer partisan fantasy, of course, but the president's wife finally was forced to deny it all explicitly while her husband raged in private.

So Cleveland's first term wound down to what, in spite of his honesty and dogged purpose, was seen as a probable defeat for reelection. There were simply too many powerful people who wanted high tariffs, and too many in the electorate who did not understand such a complicated issue. Nevertheless, there was not much question about his renomination. He had not only rank-and-file support, but the workers generally favored him, and there were influential money men who could forgive him his stand on tariffs as long as he stayed with his hard-money and antisilver policies. When the Democrats met in St. Louis, Cleveland was nominated by acclamation, and the platform drawn up endorsed his policies.

To some it may have seemed incredible that the Republicans would think once again of James G. Blaine, that tarnished Plumed Knight whom they had already rejected twice, but nevertheless more than four hundred delegates to the Chicago convention declared themselves for him a month before the event. Blaine himself, who was in Europe, had written in January that he did not want to be a candidate, but no one who knew politicians or Blaine believed such a disclaimer.

Blaine's hold on the party was extraordinary. Notwithstanding his previous rejections and the fact that a great many Americans regarded him as a thoroughgoing crook, he was still said to be "the greatest living Republican," and the party obviously wanted him. In June he wrote another letter from Europe, this time to Whitelaw Reid, again expressing his disinterest in the nomination, but this time the denial was a little ambivalent. His supporters proclaimed that he was available, and when the convention opened the presence of the absent Knight dominated it, although he was the last of fourteen nominees on the first ballot.

After four more inconclusive tries, the delegates adjourned for the weekend, during which it was feared that Blaine's supporters would organize an overwhelming boom for him. There was frantic behind-the-scenes maneuvering by the anti-Blaine people, attempting to find a candidate upon whom they could unite. Blaine, now in London, was still insisting by cable that he was not a candidate, and Andrew Carnegie, his host there, was implored to persuade him. Carnegie discovered that Blaine meant it, and both men advised the party to unite behind the splendid figure of Benjamin Harrison, grandson of the ninth president, William Henry Harrison, a strong Blaine man. They did, and the portly Civil War general was nominated on the eighth ballot.

There was nothing much to be said against Harrison. Since he had virtually no political record, he had not accumulated a collection of enemies, and that he had been a commander in the Great War, was a grandson of a president and a great-grandson of a signer of the Declaration of Independence, were positive appeals to the voters. What could be said *for* him, from the party leaders' standpoint, was that he would do what he was told—or so they believed.

By contrast with the madness of 1884, the campaign was a mild one. There was only one real issue, the tariff. It was hardly exciting to hear the Harrison supporters chant, "Trade, trade, no free trade!" or to hear the Cleveland partisans reply, "Don't, don't, don't be afraid; only low tariff so don't be afraid!" These were not inspirational slogans. But what did inspire and excite the Republicans was the amount of money being poured into their efforts by rich high-tariff supporters among the nation's industrialists, who contributed the unprecedented sum of $3 million. Many of these benefactors put slips in their employees' pay envelopes, advising them that they would be unemployed if Cleveland were re-elected. Blaine campaigned vigorously for the General, but Cleveland thought it was too undignified to go on the stump and forbade his cabinet members to do it either.

But once more, in spite of everything, it was a close election, and Harrison won it by virtue of that combination of fraud, intrigue, and bribery which had elevated so many candidates into political office. As usual the Democrats carried the South, but they got the electoral votes of only two others, Connecticut and New Jersey. Harrison took the two states he had to take, New York and Indiana, which gave him 233 electoral votes to Cleveland's 168, although the president had a popular majority of one hundred thousand. The general took New York as the result of a political deal between Tammany Democrats, Cleveland's old enemies, and the Republicans. In Indiana the vote had to be bought, and the Republican bosses did it by organizing the "floaters," that is, voters who sold their ballots for the highest price they could get, which in this case the Republicans were well able to pay. The floaters were voted in groups of five.

"Providence has given us the victory," Harrison exulted when he heard the news. That was too much for Matt Quay, the Republican National Committee chairman who had so efficiently organized the corruption. "Think of the man!" he exploded. "He ought to know that Providence hadn't a damn thing to do with it."

Benjamin Harrison: The Party Man

When Benjamin Harrison took office, the party bosses got what they had so ardently desired, a man who would sign whatever bills the Republican Congress could produce without demurring, who would look after the interests of the rich industrialists who had financed his rise to power, and who could be guaranteed to dispense the patronage of which the party faithful had been deprived for four long, thirsty years. It was only the people who voted for him, whatever the illusions that inspired them, who were cheated and betrayed.

Harrison already had one known and deadly enemy in the press—Godkin—who knew exactly what to expect and had fought hard to avert it from the moment Harrison was nominated, an event he greeted with instant condemnation: "The advocate of centralization, the defender of reckless pension schemes, the friend of Hennepin Canal jobs, is not a safe man to be President." The Hennepin Canal to which Godkin referred was a Chicago sewer system project, more redolent of fraud than the sewage it carried; he called it "the most gigantic and unequalled piece of jobbery" ever attempted of its kind. After the election Godkin observed sourly in the *Nation:* "Well, the first battle has been lost, by a narrow vote. What follows?" Certainly it was not what the more trusting Republicans expected. Their hopes were embodied in Bernard Gillam's cartoon captioned, "His Own Boss," which appeared in the humor magazine, *Judge,* on January 12, 1889. It depicted Harrison firmly astride and driving a GOP elephant, with six leading Republicans, among them Blaine, riding in the howdah behind him, a position permitting the caption to be read either way.

What kind of man was this general whom no one knew much about? Physically, he was an inconspicuous five-foot-six, slightly rotund army veteran with a full white beard, but one of his biographers tells us that he had a graceful, energetic, and commanding presence. On the other hand, as this same biographer, Harry J. Sievers, points out, Harrison was also so austere and withdrawn that Speaker Thomas Reed was moved to characterize the White House as an icebox whose chief occupant was an iceberg. There were those who said he had outstanding intellectual abilities, but if so, he did not choose to exhibit them.

In 1927, when Henry L. Stoddard ranked Cleveland, Theodore Roosevelt, and Wilson as the three outstanding presidents between Lincoln and Calvin Coolidge, he wrote: "I feel as though I were doing an injustice to Benjamin Harrison not to crowd him into the three, for, intellectually, he outdistanced them. He was the ablest of them all." More recent rankings by historians, however, place Harrison at or near the bottom of the "average" category, and that is surely where he belongs. Perhaps his basic problem, as the historian Arthur Wallace Dunn puts it, was that he had a fatal gift for "doing the right thing in the wrong way." Austere and with absolute confidence in himself, Harrison succumbed only to great pressure, but the point was that he did, in fact, succumb—and often.

As expected, the first months of Harrison's presidency saw an unprecedented rush for patronage, in which a number of deserving Republican editors who had supported the party faithfully were among the front runners. Indeed, the first beneficiary the president selected was Col. W. Halford, who resigned as editor of the Indianapolis *Journal* to become Harrison's private secretary. He was followed by a deluge of others. Benjamin H. Bristow, who had been Grant's secretary of the treasury and now served Harrison, wrote that "every dead-beat whom we used to know in the army and about Washington after the [Civil] War has turned up as an office-seeker." Bristow believed that everyone who had been turned out of office by Cleveland had returned to ask for his job back and that thousands of others sought appointment on the ground that they had never been so employed.

There was one appointment Harrison could hardly deny. To keep Blaine out of the secretary of state's office would have been an unimaginable betrayal of party trust, and the Plumed Knight got his expected reward. Just as certainly, the Democratic papers took this as the fulfillment of their direst prediction, that Harrison was merely a "caretaker" president on behalf of Blaine and the spoilsmen. They were not surprised that Harrison filled his cabinet with good Republican businessmen and that the Republican National Committee gave every appearance of running the government.

Certainly the spoilsmen were hard at work. The Post Office was a perennial home for deserving party workers, and in Harrison's first year thirty-one thousand out of fifty-five thousand postmasters were changed. When the veterans came with their congressional hands out, Harrison did not veto their demands as Cleveland had done; during his time the number of GAR pensions doubled. And when the industrialists and manufacturers came to him for the high tariff bill that Cleveland had struggled so hard to deny them, he approved the McKinley Tariff, which some historians regard as the most damaging piece of economic legislation ever passed in Washington; it resulted in staggering profits for big business.

Joseph Pulitzer viewed all this with dismay from the beginning. He predicted that "Gen. Harrison's administration is predestined to failure. It will go down in history as a parallel of that of Rutherford B. Hayes." Godkin joined in the chorus with nearly every issue of his papers, carrying on an unremitting barrage of barbs. He was particularly unsparing of his fellow editors who were seeking patronage plums from Harrison, including Charles E. Fitch of the Rochester *Democrat and Chronicle,* Joseph W. J. Morgan of the Buffalo *Commercial Advertiser,* John M. Francis of the Troy *Times,* and Elliot Shepard of the New York *Mail and Express.*

Heading the list of editors who now found themselves suddenly in the foreign service was Whitelaw Reid, who was made minister to France. Later *Tribune* historians were blunt about it. Harry Baer wrote that

> The *Tribune,* independently of its connection with Blaine, was the chief Republican newspaper in the country, and it was clear that some recognition of services rendered was due. . . . Reid's desire was the mission to London. But Blaine, whom Harrison had somewhat reluctantly given the headship of the State Department, pointed out to John Hay that the *Tribune* had generally taken the Liberal side in its discussions of English politics, which might embarrass Reid's relations with the Conservative Government then in power. The French mission, Blaine felt, would be equally satisfactory to the editor, and its acceptance would help still the whispers of Republican dissension which had arisen from Harrison's delay in bring Blaine into the Cabinet.

Other editor-ministers followed: Allen T. Richie, editor of the *North American Review,* to Russia; John A. Enander, editor of the Chicago *Hemlandet,* to Denmark; John Hicks, editor of the Oshkosh *Northwestern,* to Peru; and John New, editor of the Indianapolis *Journal,* consul general in London. At home there were other plums, among them, J. S. Clarkson, editor of the *Iowa State Register,* appointed to be first assistant postmaster general, and Ellis H. Roberts, editor of the Utica *Herald*, made assistant United States treasurer in New York.

These were only the major appointments. In fact, the number of news-papermen seeking patronage was so great that there were not enough jobs to satisfy even the most persistent, best-qualified applicants. Many of them had to be content with postmasterships. When he was a senator, Harrison had often criticized "the subsidized press," a phenomenon dating back to the beginning, as we have seen, but this kind of subsidy did not seem to bother Harrison the president. Godkin, in the *Nation* of May 2, 1889, unkindly reminded him that his grandfather, William Henry Harrison, had warned in his inaugural address against attempts to subsidize the press through executive patronage, and in fact against the spoils system in general. These admonitions, said Godkin, "have been strangely overlooked by his grandson and successor."

In making all these appointments the Republican Senate advised and consented without demur until it came to the nomination of Murat Halstead, editor of the Cincinnati *Commercial Gazette*, to be minister to Germany. The senators rejected him, remembering it was Halstead who had charged senatorial corruption when that body had refused to investigate, at the request of the Ohio legislature, the election of Sen. Henry B. Payne of Ohio.

Newspapers that had opposed Halstead's nomination as a part of their fight against patronage now turned and attacked the Senate for refusing one of their own, charging the senators with "striking one of the most desperate blows ever aimed at the liberty of the press," as one of those most carried away characterized it. The stentorian voice of Marse Henry Watterson was heard in the land: "The rejection of Mr. Halstead carries with it primarily a warning from the Senate to the press of the country to look to its utterances when dealing with that body or any of its members."

Among those "utterly opposed" to editors being given political positions was Theodore Roosevelt, but he unveiled this stricture privately. In public, he happily accepted an appointment from Harrison to the United States Civil Service Commission, which the president had pledged to use as an instrument for reforming the service. Meanwhile the president named his former law partner, William Henry Harrison Miller, to be attorney general and appointed six of his own relatives to government posts.

The elevation of Miller stirred Godkin to renewed wrath. "There are signs," he wrote in the *Nation* on May 30, 1889, that "even among the Republican organs which are already subsidized or hoping to be subsidized, of surprise or disgust at such a proposition." But what could be expected, he went on, since Harrison as a senator had "showed plainly that he regarded public office as a private benefit for his family and friends."

Nepotism reached an extreme, however, in the favoritism lavished on the president's grandson, Benjamin ("Baby") McKee, one of numerous members of his family who lived in the White House. Baby got so much attention from the press and from office seekers in the form of presents that Colonel Halford finally asked reporters to tone down their stories "lest people should come to believe the tales about this child's having more influence than the members of the Cabinet."

It was too late. An anonymous wit coined a political quatrain (such partisan chanting was a common diversion then) that linked Baby McKee with Vice-President Levi P. Morton, who also owned the Shoreham Hotel and Bar, and Postmaster General John Wanamaker, who reportedly taught the largest Sunday School class in the nation:

> The baby runs the White House
> Levi runs the bar;
> Wanny runs the Sunday School
> And, damn it, here we are.

This piece of doggerel swept the country.

On the other hand, the press was equally quick to report that the various Harrison ladies were charming, particularly the First Lady, Caroline Scott Harrison (called "Carrie"), and her vivacious daughter Mary, Baby McKee's mother; these were clever, tactful women who did much to make Harrison's life easier. Mrs. Harrison, it may be added, was not the first president's wife to complain about uncomfortable living conditions in the White House, but she *was* the first to suggest improvements designed to enhance the family's personal privacy.

This was a problem the Harrisons had inherited from the Clevelands. The new journalism had no more respect for one family than the other. Carrie Harrison shared her husband's feeling that they were being persecuted by the press, egged on by public curiosity, and, if there was one thing she had detested all her days, as she frequently said, it was being made a circus of. It did not soothe her to know that most of the publicity was favorable. Unfortunately in this case she was less than her usual tactful self, and an attitude she considered simply protective of her husband only helped to alienate the press from him further.

Carrie's complaints were not unfounded by any means. Just before the summer of 1890, Postmaster General Wanamaker and some of her Philadelphia friends had presented her with a handsome gift, a summer cottage at Cape May Point, New Jersey, which was a welcome retreat and a source of enjoyment for her. But even that small pleasure was marred by an editorial in the New York *Sun,* in Dana's most cynical style, which inquired: "Who are these generous individuals that have bestowed upon Mrs. Benjamin Harrison a cottage at Cape May Point, clear of encumbance [sic] and with floors swept clean for Baby McKee to creep over this summer? . . . The President who takes a bribe is a lost President." The *Sun* went on to urge that the names of the subscribers be made public and that the president return the gift.

Friendly papers argued that, even though the cottage had been built as a gift, it was no different a situation than the presenting of a house in Long Branch, New Jersey, to General Grant, and in this case Harrison himself had not accepted it. The president, seeking some resolution of the problem, wrote Wanamaker a gracious yet businesslike letter, enclosing a $10,000 check and asking him to be good enough to see to its correct disposition, which was a delicate way of buying the cottage. But the Democratic New York *Times* would have none of such subterfuge. It suggested that the president had paid for the summer place only after he had been subjected to criticism. In any case, there could be no proof of presidential ownership, since the title had been placed in the name of W. V. McKean, editor of the Philadelphia *Ledger,* who happened to be Wanamaker's close friend.

Even with the knowledgeable guidance of Colonel Halford, an old newspaperman himself, Harrison could not seem to make any substantial progress in his press relations, no matter what he did. Republican papers, led by the *Tribune,* continued to defend him loyally, and the White House clipped the pages of Reid's paper daily, pasting its friendly reports in huge scrapbooks. Meanwhile the Democratic press continued to denounce Harrison, and the independent journals appeared to consider him too insignificant and contemptible to be excited about.

Harrison seldom dealt with the press in a direct way, preferring to remain withdrawn and aloof as much as possible. When he was ready to deliver his first message to Congress, he went to extreme lengths to avoid any preliminary leaks which might be embarrassing. He sent a confidential White House clerk, Col. William H. Crook, to carry sealed copies by train to Baltimore, Philadelphia, and New York. These copies were given to trusted agents who were pledged not to release them to newspapers and press associations until the message was safely in the hands of Congress.

Moreover, the great white albatross of James Blaine continued to hang around the neck of Harrison, now in a tragic way. In the spring of 1891 the secretary fell ill with what was diagnosed as a nervous disorder, and for nearly six months the president had to take over his duties, while the Democratic press leaped to attack. James Gordon Bennett, Jr., whose own mental condition was not of the best, permitted his New York *Herald* to proclaim these sensational headlines: "Is BLAINE'S MIND GIVING WAY? Flashes of Intense Brain Activity Followed by Periods of Extreme Mental Depression . . . Diplomatic Business Suffers. Blaine Breaking Down, Though Friends Deny It. Continued Work Would Render Him Liable to Falling in the Harness." Inevitably, rumors spread that Blaine had died, and some papers were quick to report it, impelling Harrison to write sarcastically to a friend, "The over-readiness of the newspapers to kill off public men is one of the curious and discreditable phases of modern journalism."

But if the papers could not have Blaine dead, they would still savage him alive, again exploiting rumors that were no doubt started by his numerous enemies. It was said that there was bad feeling between the Harrisons and the Blaines because Mrs. Blaine had asked the president to promote a son-in-law in a stormy interview that ended when the secretary's wife assured the president that his denial "would cost him a renomination and that she would now have Mr. Blaine take the field against him."

By this time Blaine must have known that he would never be physically able to run again; lifelong hypochondria was now becoming a medical reality for him. But whether it was this reality or simply politics as usual that led Russell Harrison, the president's son, to let it be known that Blaine's condition was so bad it precluded his running again is hard to say. In any case, this alleged remark made to friends was quoted in the *World,* which stood by its story in spite of the expected White House denial, further straining not only the Harrison-Blaine relationship but the president's relations with the press. Four months before the convention of 1892, however, Blaine formally and finally withdrew his name from any consideration, thus ending the argument. Three days before the convention he resigned as secretary in a curt exchange of letters. Less than a year later he was dead.

"After Mr. Blaine, what?" Samuel Bowles, son of the former editor, inquired in his Springfield *Republican* on February 8, 1892. "Benjamin Harrison, now President of the United States, will have to be nominated for a second term. However little some of the prominent men of the Republican party may fancy this situation, it cannot be escaped."

Few were happy with the inevitable choice. The public had shown what it thought of the Harrison administration by dealing the Republicans a heavy blow in the midterm congressional elections, depriving the party of its majority in the House. There was national unrest in various quarters. Farmers and working people had cast bankers and monopolies as the villains who were creating hard times for them. They had organized in a variety of groups that were fighting big business, especially the predatory railroad barons. The result was a third party, the People's party, which was strong enough to win more than 8 percent of the votes in 1892.

As the conventions met, it was obvious that there would be a rematch of Cleveland and Harrison, since neither party had produced any rivals powerful enough to challenge them. Plaintive cries for Blaine were heard from diehard Republican delegates—"the ladies and the babies in the cradle want Blaine," one of them declared—but the dying Knight had put a firm stop to any nomination attempt.

By contrast with what had gone before, the campaign was limp and excessively dull—no torchlight parades, no chanting marches, no more outrageous personal attacks on the candidates, who themselves were unprecedentedly quiet. Cleveland sat on the front porch of his summer place at Buzzard's Bay, on Cape Cod, during much of the summer, suffering from gout. Harrison had no inclination to campaign after October 25 for a sadder reason; his beloved Carrie had died. Only Gen. James B. Weaver, the Populist candidate of the People's party, toured the country in the usual way. He spoke to large and enthusiastic crowds as a mood of social unrest gripped the nation.

The unrest boiled over during July in the notorious affair at the Carnegie steel plant in Homestead, Pennsylvania, where three hundred hired Pinkerton detectives fought a bloody battle with striking workers after a pay cut that appeared prompted more by management arrogance and determination to break the union than for any reason of economy. Negotiations had broken down, and the company had locked out its workers. The Pinkertons had been hired to protect the strikebreakers with whom Carnegie was attempting to resume operations. These detectives, armed to their badges, faced a small army of five thousand men, and the struggle went on for two days, ended only by the arrival of state militia, who succeeded in reopening the plant.

A fire storm of public outrage swept the country after this event, as Carnegie and his partner Henry Frick were denounced by all but the spokesmen for wealth and privilege. Nervous Republican leaders, fearing the worst, appealed to both these entrepreneurs for moderation and a resumption of negotiations, but the steel men were adamant. Cleveland took full advantage of the situation. He came out strongly in favor of the workers, terming Carnegie's union-busting tactics as "the tender mercy the workingman receives from those made selfish and sordid by unjust governmental favoritism." For once he had the majority of the press on his side. Editorial writers reminded the public that the company which now wanted to cut wages was run by the same men who had been arguing for the protection of high tariffs to *prevent* wage reductions. Certainly, said the papers, the Carnegie mills' substantial profits offered no rational reason for wage reductions. It was a field day for all those opposed to high tariffs.

Harrison proved to be the real victim of the Homestead battle. Cleveland won the election by 277 to 145 electoral votes (again failing to get a majority of the popular vote), in spite of the defection of many Democrats to the Populists in five of the Western states. The million votes polled by the Populists was a clear signal to both parties that it had better pay attention to the farmers, as Greeley had told them for decades. Godkin analyzed the election returns with his usual perception in the *Nation:*

> Mr. Cleveland's triumph today has been largely due to the young voters who have come on the stage since the reign of passion and prejudice came to an end, and the era of discussion has opened. If the past canvass has consisted largely of appeals to reason, to facts, to the lessons of human experience, it is to Mr. Cleveland, let us tell them, that they owe it. But they are indebted to him for something far more valuable than this—for an example of Roman constancy under defeat, and of patient reliance on the power of deliberation and persuasion of the American people. Nothing is more important, in these days of boodle, of cheap bellicose patriotism, than that this confidence in the might of common sense and sound doctrine and free speech should be kept alive.

It was a prematurely optimistic judgment.

Harrison was not ready to accept the verdict of party and public that he was responsible for the loss of Republican power so recently regained. If people were unhappy with the performance of Congress, and particularly with the McKinley Tariff, that could not be laid entirely at his door, as he saw it. The voters, he thought, simply had not understood. One reason they had not, he asserted, was the way the press had misrepresented him and "persecuted" both him and his family from the day they entered the White House. He could not accept the reasoned verdict of the New York *Times,* delivered in an editorial on March 4, 1893, his last day in office, accurate though it was:

> When Mr. Harrison took office four years ago there was an opportunity open to his party to establish itself again with considerable firmness in the confidence of the

American people. . . . Three important questions awaited party action—the tariff, the currency, civil service reform. Had the party been more moderate and just as to the tariff, firm and sound as to the currency, and honest and faithful to civil service reform, its candidate would, in all human probability, have been elected last year. Had Mr. Harrison led his party in these three matters he would, in all probability, have been its candidate, and would have been his own successor. It is with reference to these matters, and not with reference to any personal traits or minor questions, that his administration must be judged. Thus judged, it is obvious it cannot be said that the administration has been a success. It is well to remember . . . that Mr. Harrison's failure was not due to accident . . . it was due to his own course as to the three problems to which we have referred.

How Harrison felt about it emerged by chance on the same day this editorial appeared, when the New York *Sun*'s correspondent, Julian Ralph, one of the most accomplished newspapermen of his day, who had come down to cover the inauguration, called on the president. The illuminating story of what followed was told later by David S. Barry, a veteran Washington correspondent, who was with Ralph:

While waiting in an anteroom to be admitted into Harrison's private office, Mr. Ralph regaled me with tales of how he had been received by former Presidents when making his farewell call, and we both were somewhat eager to see Harrison unbend. When "Lige" Halford, Harrison's private secretary, suddenly opened the door and said, "Walk in, Gentlemen," we were still laughing over some anecdote of a former President, but the laughter froze on our lips when we came face to face with Harrison.

He was seated at a little desk writing notes of farewell on black-bordered paper to personal friends. Having finished one, he said, "Sit down, Gentlemen," and then in characteristic icy tones, "What can I do for you?" Ralph, who was a cheery, friendly soul not easily abashed, started in to tell the President of his innocent penchant for writing presidential valedictories, but was cut short by Mr. Harrison's abrupt condemnation of the newspaper press generally for what he described as their cruel, unfair, and discourteous references to himself and Mrs. Harrison since they had been living in the White House. He said the persecution had been persistent, and dwelt upon the subject at length, but specifically mentioned only one incident that seemed to justify his wholesale indictment. This was the alleged criticism of the newspaper press, led possibly by the New York *Sun,* of himself and Mrs. Harrison for having accepted from John Wanamaker, of Philadelphia, Postmaster-General in Harrison's cabinet, a gift of a summer cottage at Cape May Point.

It was true that newspaper comment had been severe, especially on the part of the *Sun,* but undoubtedly it had rankled in the bosom of the President more bitterly than the public had imagined. When Ralph had partly recovered his wits from the unexpected attack he attempted to apologize for the press. He said he thought it a mistake to say that they had ever criticized Mrs. Harrison and that perhaps their criticism of the President had been more caustic than the facts had warranted, or perhaps that the facts were not entirely understood. He failed, however, to punctuate the President's cuticle, and after a few pointless remarks back and forth, we were shown out.

Harrison mellowed somewhat in the few years remaining to him, no doubt the result of a late second marriage in 1896 to a niece of his wife's, and the birth soon after of a daughter. But he could not forgive the press and in his few public speeches never missed an opportunity to make sarcastic references to those "unfailing chroniclers of the truth." The chroniclers gave him the customary pious editorial tributes when he died in 1901.

Cleveland Redivivus

Grover Cleveland, as it turned out, had chosen the wrong moment in national history for his reprise in the White House. Businessmen had taken the unusual step of endorsing a Democrat because they believed, mistakenly, that he was on their side in the growing social wars.

In the four years since Harrison's election, Cleveland had enjoyed what he told friends were the best times of his life—fishing at Buzzards Bay, relaxing generally, and discovering that there were other things in life besides politics. Yet, like most politicians, he could not really separate himself from the battle. Even in this brief, forced retirement, Cleveland was writing letters to party leaders and newspapers, in one of which he roundly condemned the coinage of free silver, which horrified his fellow Democrats but greatly pleased Republican businessmen because it appeared to confirm the wisdom of their choice.

There were great hopes on both sides, then, that a strong hand would be at the helm once more when Cleveland took office in 1893, but forces he could not control were at work. Even as he took the oath, investors were reeling from the collapse of the Philadelphia and Reading Railroad, leaving debts of more than $125 million. Just after the inauguration, the National Cordage Company went bankrupt, precipitating a panic in Wall Street. Then another railroad scandal was exposed, by which the Atchison, Topeka & Santa Fe was shown to have removed $7 million from the public's pocket. Matters moved rapidly from bad to worse. Before the end of Cleveland's first year in office there were four million unemployed workers; 158 national banks had been liquidated; 15,000 businesses had failed; and, most ominously, the Treasury's gold reserve had dropped below $100 million, the line drawn between solid and doubtful currency.

In this situation Cleveland did what prudence demanded, but it was clear that, no matter what he did, powerful interests and large blocs of voters would be hurt. He called a special session of Congress and urged upon them repeal of the Silver Purchase Act, thereby offending a substantial number of Democrats who favored free coinage. It took the help of gold-standard Republicans to get the act repealed, further separating the president from his own party. So the Democrats were affronted and the Republicans pleased, but still there was such a scarcity of gold that the already staggering economy was struck new blows every day. Farmers suffered particularly. New alliances were formed, as the free-silver Democrats and the Populists joined forces, and within Cleveland's own party a kind of grassroots crusade was launched against his monetary policies.

In the midst of these problems there was a sudden crisis in the president's health. Early in May, Cleveland had complained of a burning sensation in his throat, and upon examination by the White House physician, Dr. Robert O'Reilly, a large ulcer on the roof of the left side of his mouth was discovered. A biopsy confirmed O'Reilly's suspicion that it was cancerous, and Cleveland was told that his life would be in danger if he did not have it removed.

Considering subsequent presidential illnesses, it is instructive to observe how Cleveland and his advisers handled their problem. The first step was to throw a net of secrecy over the situation and keep it from the press. Public relations was a profession still a decade away from its birth, but George Parker, the president's close friend and press adviser, who would be one of the midwives at that birth, knew (as any astute politician would have known) that in this moment of national difficulty it was important to preserve the president's image as a strong, healthy and confident leader, even though the possibility existed that he might be dying.

Image-making was an art scarcely in its infancy, but Parker understood what he had to do. The press was told that the president would take a short vacation trip on the yacht *Oneida*, owned by his friend, Commodore E. C. Benedict. He would board this ship in New York and, after a few days of cruising, land at Buzzards Bay for a stay of several days at the presidential cottage, Gray Gables. What the press was not told was that an operation would be performed on the yacht.

As the *Oneida* moved at half-speed down the East River, after leaving its moorings beside Bellevue Hospital, in New York, Cleveland lay back in a reclining chair in the saloon and the surgeons went to work. O'Reilly had assembled a distinguished team: Dr. W. W. Keen, a Philadelphia specialist; a noted dentist, Dr. Ferdinand Hasbrouck; a general physician, Dr. E. G. Janeway; and an assistant. As the president lay anesthetized, Dr. Hasbrouck took out two bicuspids from the upper left jaw, after which a newly designed cheek retractor was inserted so that the surgeons could remove a portion of the upper palate and part of the jaw to make the tumor accessible. It had been agreed in advance, along with an oath of secrecy, that the outside of the president's face would not be cut and that there would be no visible evidence of the surgery.

The operation, which took two and a half hours, was successful—and just in time. In another week the left eye would have been affected. But the president was unhappy because he had lost control, momentarily, of his big voice, and the doctors were a little glum because they believed it was the kind of cancer that might recur. Later, after the ship reached Buzzards Bay, a specialist in what was then a new field, prosthodontia, Dr. Kasson C. Gibson, inserted a prosthetic device that restored Cleveland's speech and pulled him out of a deep depression. When the president died fifteen years later, it was from internal problems not related to his cancer. In 1971 University of Pennsylvania pathologists, examining the preserved tumor, found it was a rare type of cancer that does not spread— a fact unknown at the time of the operation.

Through it all, the press was kept in darkness by Parker, and, amazingly, he got away with it. It would have been impossible today, of course, but in Cleveland's time the president was not followed by a corps of White House correspondents everywhere he went. Press and president had not yet slipped into that close embrace which George Bernard Shaw once viewed, in a different connection, as the "dreadful intimacy of marriage." Even so, it was impossible to conceal completely the biggest news story of the day. Two months later the Philadelphia *Press* carried a fairly thorough account of what happened by a correspondent, E. J. Edwards, who signed his dispatches "Holland," in the old style. There had been a leak, and it appeared to have been one of the dental surgeons who helped perform the operation.

The expected denial duly came from the White House, but, surprisingly, it was not needed. For a public accustomed to reading all kinds of fanciful stories about presidents, the tale of the operation seemed like just another rumor, probably originating with the Republicans, and it was generally disbelieved. Even Cleveland's good friend, L. Clarke Davis, editor of the Philadelphia *Public Ledger,* who had been nearby the Cape Cod cottage, vacationing, told his paper that there was no more truth to the story than a toothache. Indeed, Davis said, he had seen the president several times, finding him in the best of health. While this scarcely seems credible in the circumstances, there is no evidence to support the idea that Davis was part of the cover-up, although it appears likely that he was. When Cleveland got back to Washington, he wrote confidentially to Ambassador Thomas F. Bayard, admitting that there had been "a most astounding breach of professional duty on the part of a medical man" and noting that his policy had been to deny and discredit the story.

A later president might well have handled this incident differently, appealing to public sympathy and using the operation to divert attention from the sea of troubles in which he was trying to stay afloat. Certainly Cleveland had plenty of reason to take that course. He was not only being compelled to deal with the results of the panic of 1893, the surging unrest among workers and farmers, and the difficult question of whether or not to sell bonds to keep the country on the gold standard, but he was soon confronted with a crisis in foreign policy that brought down upon him the Jovian wrath of Godkin.

There had been a kind of honeymoon between Godkin and the president since the start of the second term, while Cleveland was being strongly attacked in the opposition papers, particularly the *World,* and under constant pressure from the others. Godkin had concentrated most of what little criticism he offered on Cleveland's diplomatic and consular appointments, of which he naturally, and with reason, did not approve—that is, until 1895. At that point he broke completely and dramatically with the administration on the question of England's long-running boundary dispute with Venezuela over how much Venezuelan territory was embraced by British Guiana.

This disagreement would not ordinarily have been viewed as any of America's business if the Monroe Doctrine had not been invoked, creating a wave of national jingoism that would not be satisfied short of war a few years later. The old notion that the Caribbean was an American lake had been firmly planted and was about to bear fruit. It did no good for the *Evening Post* to print and then distribute as a pamphlet an essay by John Bassett Moore entitled, *The Monroe Doctrine, Its Origin and Meaning,* intended to prove that the Doctrine had no bearing on the Venezuelan affair. Secretary of State Walter Q. Gresham, up to now admired by Godkin, had already written to the American minister in London that, if Britain persisted in her claims, the United States would be obliged to step in. He did not mention the Doctrine, but it was clear he meant to invoke it.

Nevertheless, a man as cautious as Gresham might not have pressed the point, but unfortunately he died two months after this warning, and his successor, Richard Olney, showed no such restraint. Instead he wrote a letter to Lord Salis-'bury, the British foreign minister, that came to be called the "twenty-inch gun" note, in which he asserted, "Today the United States is practically sovereign on this continent and its fiat is law upon the subjects to which it confines its inter-positions." Lord Salisbury did not choose to reply at once. Four months went by, during which a bellicose mood developed in Congress and the country, ex-pressed editorially by the Indianapolis *Journal* in its assertion: "When it comes to resisting British aggression, there will be no Republicans and no Democrats. We shall all be Americans, and if Grover Cleveland is President when the crisis comes we shall all be Cleveland men."

The reply from Lord Salisbury, when it finally arrived, was so supercilious that a new spasm of irritation jerked the American psyche. Cleveland responded by sending a special message to Congress on December 17, 1895, which in effect asserted that the United States should dispatch a commission to Venezuela, settle the boundary dispute itself, and presumably compel England to accept a *fait accompli*. It was exactly what the nation wanted to hear, and Cleveland immedi-ately regained a good deal of ground he had lost with the public. Jingoism was king, as the newspapers made abundantly clear. The *Tribune,* seldom a Cleve-land supporter, reported jubilantly that the president was no longer an idol in England, as he had been. Godkin's *Post* observed, without comment, that the two most popular generals in America, Lew Wallace (the author of *Ben Hur*) and O. O. Howard, were both "furious for war." The *World* and all the other sensa-tional papers were predictably ecstatic, overflowing with patriotic joy, but Cleveland was also supported by such sober journals as the New York *Times* and the Springfield *Republican*.

For some reason Godkin remained aloof. The *Post* and the *Nation* reported what was going on, but their comments were mild and brief. Then, on December 28, came the first thunderbolt. In the *Nation*'s usual summary, "The Week," a national reaction to the president's special message was disclosed that was quite unlike the paper's usual accurate observations. On Friday and Saturday after the message, said the *Nation,* Cleveland had been "overwhelmed with the execra-tions of business men; on Sunday he received the most unanimous and crushing rebuke that the pulpit of the country ever addressed to a President. He made his appeal to the conscience of the mob; he has now heard from the conscience of the God-fearing people, and their judgment upon him leaves him morally impeached of high crimes and misdeameanors."

This onslaught was accompanied by a scathing ten-thousand-word attack, oc-cupying seven pages of the paper, on Cleveland and the administration. "Was there ever such another case," Godkin demanded, in his best style of high moral indignation, "of a civilized man throwing away his clothes and joining the howl-ing savages? . . . Mr. Cleveland says now just what Debs said in the summer of 1894. Law or no law, Debs and his fellow anarchists gloried in being 'masters of the situation.' It is a melancholy thing to find the President who put them down with a firm hand, now displaying himself as the greatest international anarchist of modern times.''

If it is true, as some have argued, that Cleveland's dislike for the press has seldom been equaled among presidents (a statement that surely needs qualification), his hatred of it must have been doubled by the vitriolic blast from Godkin—the editor he had most trusted and who had upheld his policies with vigor until now. And it was soon followed by other blistering editorials, in which Congress did not escape either—that ''brutish body,'' as Godkin called it, ''a body of idle, ignorant, lazy and not very scrupulous men.''

Yet it was no great moral principle on which Godkin himself stood. He was primarily concerned with the effect the war would have on Wall Street, still shaking from the effects of 1893. It was all very well to talk about patriotism, he argued, but this sentiment should never be allowed to interfere with the nation's financial well-being. Indeed, said Godkin, the patriotism that had been ''diffused among the masses during the past thirty years, and even taught to the children in the schools, is a species of madness.''

In the end, as the saying goes, cooler heads prevailed. Angry editorial cries on both sides of the Atlantic were overridden by the voices of moderation, and Britain turned out to be the only loser. Cleveland was seen as the honest broker; the stock market shuddered but revived; and Venezuela got the territory in dispute. For Godkin, it was a triumph of sorts. On December 29, 1895, he boasted to his old friend, Charles Eliot Norton, with his unfortunate penchant for hyperbole, that the affair had not only been his greatest success but the greatest ever known in journalism, evidenced by an overwhelming number of congratulatory letters and, more important, a circulation rise of one thousand a day. In the same letter, however, and on the same subject, he told Norton, ''I am just now the great object of abuse, and the abuse is just what you would hear in a bar-room row.'' He did not appear to notice the paradox. The fact was that his blatantly pro-British stand in the matter cost him at least a part of his reputation for high-minded impartiality.

As for Cleveland, his popularity did not last long. Having tasted the juices of patriotic fervor, the interventionist press was now nourishing itself on the situation in Cuba, where insurgents had begun the guerrilla attacks on the colonial Spanish government that would end with full-scale war a few years later. In the United States the response was a dress rehearsal for the press's war with McKinley in the next administration.

The struggle during Cleveland's term was touched off by the president's action to prevent men and arms being shipped to help the insurgents in 1895. Cries of rage rose from the jingoist portion of the press, led by Pulitzer's *World* and the Indianapolis *Journal,* but also including the New York *Sun,* the Chicago *Tribune,* and other leading papers. When some prospective recruits and their munitions escaped a navy blockade and were captured by Spanish ships before they could reach Cuba, the outcry was even louder. Stories of Spanish atrocities began to fill the columns of these papers, a few of them real but most in the ''beastly Hun'' vein the country would become so agitated by in the First World

War. End "the slaughter of innocent women and children," the *World* demanded. Give the Spaniards a "sharp and stinging lesson," the *Sun* insisted. Yet Cleveland stood firm. When the House proposed recognizing Cuba's belligerency in 1896, he opposed it, and in his last annual message, in December 1896, he continued to counsel moderation, which only earned him a further editorial onslaught.

By this time, however, it hardly mattered for Cleveland. Whatever the press and public believed about him, his political career was over, buried beneath an accumulation of problems both foreign and domestic. Not only had the Venezuelan dispute and the crisis in Cuba made him unpopular, but the middle of his presidency, from July 1894 to July 1895, had been a nightmare. The financial condition of the country had been so perilous that it was necessary to arrange a loan from J. P. Morgan. Labor unrest reached a peak, resulting in the bloody Pullman strike in Chicago (only part of the 750,000 workers striking that year) and the famous march by Coxey's Army on Washington, that pathetic agitation by the social reformer Jacob Coxey who led about five hundred unemployed men to the capital, intending to petition Congress for relief, a journey that ended in absurd anticlimax when the leaders were arrested for walking on the Capitol lawn.

But there were other "armies" of the unemployed also marching on Washington during Cleveland's second administration, and everywhere they added to popular feeling against the president. Cleveland did not handle labor disputes or Congress well: "His Obstinacy," they called him. It did not matter that he always held steadfastly to his principles, nor did it help to have a hotheaded attorney general, Richard Olney, who swore in 3,400 deputies and helped to break the Pullman strike, overriding the courageous Gov. John Altgeld—the "Eagle of Illinois," as a later biographer, Harry Barnard, would call him—and putting the socialist leader Eugene Debs in jail, where he discovered Karl Marx and became a hero.

There are those who believe Cleveland was so completely middle class that he was frightened by both the rich and the poor, but, whatever the truth of this judgment, it is a certainty that he alienated those elements of the population while pursuing what he considered to be honest and honorable policies. Even worse, he alienated his fellow politicians, particularly Congress, which greeted his annual message in December 1895 with a humiliating, unprecedented near-silence, in which only four members could be heard applauding.

Oddly enough, it was none of the controversies just described that dominated the Democractic convention when it met in Chicago in 1896. The movement for free coinage of silver had been gaining momentum, and it was now reaching a climax, with thirty Southern and Western states already committed to it by formal resolutions, on the ground that staying with the gold standard would mean bankruptcy. It was a convention dominated by the free-silver men and by their hero William Jennings Bryan, who headed the Nebraska delegates after an earlier gold-standard delegation had been unseated.

As the monetary debate heated itself to a fever, Gov. Benjamin ("Pitchfork Ben") Tillman of South Carolina denounced the gold standard and its upholder, the president, as "a tool of Wall Street," going so far as to demand Cleveland's impeachment. It was a little late in the day for that, and in any case the delegates were waiting for Bryan, the "Silver-tongued Orator of the Plains," also sometimes known as the "Boy Orator of the Platte," who obliged them with his famed Cross of Gold speech, delivered in a rotund style not heard so tellingly since the days of Stephen Douglas and ending with his often quoted peroration: "Having behind us the producing masses of the nation and the world, supported by the commercial interests, the laboring interests, and the toilers everywhere, we will answer their [the opposition's] demand for a gold standard by saying to them: 'You shall not press down upon the brow of labor this crown of thorns, you shall not crucify mankind upon a cross of gold.'"

It was a historic moment, recalled vividly for years by those who heard it, when twenty thousand delegates and others attending the convention leaped to their feet, shrieking "Bryan! Bryan! Bryan!" in an echoing cadence that resulted a few hours later in the hero's nomination on the fifth ballot. Grover Cleveland was the forgotten man.

Three weeks earlier the Republicans had met in St. Louis, where an entirely different scene occurred. Here the convention was dominated from backstage by the celebrated millionaire politician from Cleveland, Mark Hanna, a hard-nosed, ruthless man who was said to run the Republican party from his back pocket, where his capacious wallet reposed. He was determined that his friend, Gov. William McKinley of Ohio, should get the nomination, and he was ready to do whatever had to be done to obtain it.

Hanna's personal campaign had begun long before the convention. For the first time in American history, a publicity agent, Hanna himself, had worked to get the nomination for a candidate. He sent McKinley around the country in a private railroad car, for which he paid, so that the governor could press the flesh of those who had never heard of him. Billboard advertising preceded and followed McKinley's arrival; on these hustings he was proclaimed as "the advance agent of prosperity," something the country badly needed. While McKinley traveled, Hanna worked even harder behind the scenes, doing what political action committees and party committeemen would do today—organizing, making local contacts, extolling his candidate, and, most important, reaching frequently into his back pocket and coming out with money—more than $100,000 of it.

Nothing like it had been seen before, and it was impressively effective. By the time McKinley got to the convention, he was greeted with demonstrations described as "spontaneous," and so they were at that point. The delegates also adopted a platform that came out for the gold standard and protectionist tariffs, which cost them thirty delegates from the Mountain States, who walked out. It did not matter. Mark Hanna and McKinley were riding high, and the former governor of Ohio was nominated on the first ballot.

The arguments resounding in both conventions boiled over into the campaign, which seemed much more like old times to those who had seen many of them. Big businessmen rallied to the Republicans with money and the slogan, "A full dinner pail," a promise that did not recommend them to those carrying the pails, who were advised in paycheck notes, according to custom, not to come back to work if Bryan was elected because the plant would be closed.

There were parades, rallies, and a few street battles over money (gold or silver), a subject close to everyone's heart. Bryan, the unexampled orator, swept through twenty-nine states, leaving samples of his simplistic rhetoric at every stop. Meanwhile McKinley had listened to the advice of his resident Svengali, Hanna, and conducted a front-porch campaign at his Canton, Ohio, home, meeting innumerable delegations brought in from everywhere on rails greased by Hanna money. He spoke and shook hands with such groups twenty times a day on occasion. Where was the press in this commotion? It was loud enough, but for some reason it did not seem to play a significant part in the campaign. It was divided along party lines, as one would expect, except for those papers, Republican and Democratic, which believed the only issue was gold or silver.

That was, indeed, the decisive issue. Money proved a stronger argument than Bryan's rhetoric or whatever the candidates might think about foreign policy—and they thought little enough about it, as did the voters, who for the moment were in no mood to think about Cuba. McKinley got more than 7,000,000 votes to Bryan's 6,509,051, in a record turnout. Bryan took the South, as expected, the Western states and Missouri, but he lost all the rest—a substantial victory for the effete East and Wall Street, where there was jubilation.

As for Cleveland, he joined the press, so to speak, as a magazine writer, contributing frequently to the *Saturday Evening Post,* which in 1897 embarked on the most influential phase of its long career under George Horace Lorimer's superlative editorship. The former president also contributed to such other magazines as *Collier's,* the *Atlantic,* the *Century* (whose editor, Richard Watson Gilder, was a close friend), the *Youth's Companion,* the *Independent, McClure's,* and *Ladies' Home Journal.* The last was the second of Cyrus H. K. Curtis's magazines, competing with its stablemate, the *Post,* under Edward Bok's direction. Thus Cleveland joined the commentators and political pundits. He was paid more than most of them, at a peak of $2,500 per article, and seemed quite as acerbic as many, in a dignified, ex-presidential way.

Cleveland was through with politics, but politics was not quite through with him. Late in 1903 he was urged to run again, now that many of his past transgressions had been forgiven and forgotten. But Cleveland, who had never really enjoyed the office and came to question why any sensible person would endure it, used the letters column of the Brooklyn *Eagle* to declare unequivocally that he would not run again under any circumstances. Even so, he had to repeat the denial several times.

In those years of his retirement, the press turned about, as it so often does, and joined in the growing public acclaim for Cleveland as a man who had been a courageous, principled leader, a phenomenon all too rare in politics. He was much in demand as a speaker, and some of his appearances produced ovations.

Just before his death in 1908, Cleveland summed up his view of the press and the presidency in a letter to his faithful press relations adviser George Parker. ''I simply could not and would not,'' he wrote, use these methods [any sacrifice of privacy] to ingratiate myself with the editors or owners of newspapers. I realize fully the fate I invited, but I looked upon my table or my parlor as my own, places reserved for my friends and for the congenial men whom they might send to me, and not proper mediums for bringing me support for public acts or policies. Merely because men were personally agreeable did not seem to me to constitute any reason for making myself familiar with them. I know that others in like positions pursue a different policy, but I notice that, in the end, they always suffer for it. Such methods grow by what they feed on.

Perhaps the root of Cleveland's troubles lay in a political schizophrenia well summarized by his friend Woodrow Wilson: "You may think Cleveland's administration was Democratic. It was not. Cleveland was a conservative Republican."

McKinley: A Reluctant Leader

In the history of America, there have been several major turning points, places in time where transition from one era to another was almost a visible thing. Just as the adoption of the Constitution marked the definite end of the colonial era and the beginning of the United States as a nation, so did the Civil War signal the end (or at least the forced resolution) of a deep political division and at the same time became the bridge between the agricultural America we had always known and the industrialization of the nation.

During the closing years of the nineteenth century America began to emerge as a world power, and with that change the nature of the presidency changed, too. William McKinley, the man who presided over this watershed, was not a herald of the future but a quiet undertaker of the past. After him the White House and its functioning would never be the same again, as Theodore Roosevelt began the presidential era in which we still live.

For the press the late 1890s were equally a transition point. An era that had begun with the first James Gordon Bennett was about to end, as the giants of the past quietly slipped away, never to be replaced in the same sense. Dana died in 1897, and while the *Sun* remained a superb product for many years after, the fire went out of its editorials when the man who wrote so many of them was no longer there. Godkin, his health broken, had to leave the *Evening Post* and the *Nation* in 1899; three years later he was dead.

James Gordon Bennett, Jr., had become more and more eccentric, to say the least. Self-exiled since 1877 after a scandalous incident in New York, he lived variously in Paris, his "lodge" in Versailles, his villa in Beaulieu, or on his yacht, the *Lysistrata,* with its hundred-man crew, and rarely came to New York, editing the *Herald* by remote control through a constant flow of cables, letters, and conferences with editors and writers whom he summoned across the Atlantic at the slightest whim. Consequently the paper's editorial page was no longer a major irritant to presidents, and it would not be again.

As for the New York *Times,* it was undergoing its own transition—in fact a near rescue from death. Since its sensational exposure of the Tweed Ring in 1871, it had been kept alive and fairly prosperous for a time by its astute business manager, George Jones, and an exceptional editor, Charles R. Miller, but after Jones's death in 1891 the paper lost ground rapidly. By 1896 its circulation was down to nine thousand; it was losing a thousand dollars every day, and would have died if it had not been bought by Adolph Ochs, the thirty-eight-year-old publisher of the Chattanooga *Times,* for $75,000. Ochs beat off unscrupulous advertisers and politicians, lowered the price of his paper to a penny in 1898, and in a year the circulation had tripled. The *Times* was never in trouble again.

That left only Joseph Pulitzer and a newcomer, William Randolph Hearst. Pulitzer was already ill with the strange nervous affliction which left him not only blind but so sensitive to noise that the slightest excess of sound would send him into a frenzy. He edited the *World* from his soundproofed apartment for a time, but his disease produced a restlessness that compelled him to travel constantly. Like Bennett, Jr., he went into voluntary exile, moving about constantly for nearly twenty years, much of the time on his yacht, editing the paper from wherever he happened to be. If he stopped at a hotel, he had to rent the rooms above and below and on both sides to ensure the quiet that was essential. Sometimes he crossed and recrossed the ocean without stopping. Yet, in spite of it all, he continued to edit the *World* closely, with incredible tenacity and intelligence, until his death in 1911. His curiosity never wavered for a moment.

Hearst was an entirely different kind of man, a unique figure among newspaper publishers. He was, to begin with, the first of the breed to arrive on the scene already rich. His predecessors had worked their way up from humble beginnings. Hearst began at the top, the fortunate result of having a father who was the first prospector to sink a pick into the Comstock Lode, the great silver mine in Nevada. Later George Hearst became a United States senator from California.

It has been said that Hearst was never interested in anything except money, but that was not the case, although it is easy to see why a young man at Harvard who preferred the philistine fleshpots of Boston to the company of such professors as George Santayana and William James could be suspected of an idle mind. He did have vaguely intellectual interests, however, derived from his beautiful, cultured mother Phoebe, who took him on the grand tour of Europe when he was only nine, awakening in him a lifelong appreciation of art that ultimately made him one of the world's great collectors.

During his Harvard years (he dropped out after two of them) Hearst also acquired a keen interest in contemporary journalism. He particularly admired Pulitzer's *World,* not so much for its editorials, which did not attract his attention, but for its flashy front page. Pulitzer, he believed, knew how to make newspapers, but Hearst thought he could do even better if he had the opportunity. That occurred when he persuaded his father to give him the San Francisco *Examiner,* which the senator had acquired as settlement for a political debt. He took over the paper when he was only twenty-four, thus beginning a career that became a legend.

Hearst made the *Examiner* into a more flamboyant and sensational *World,* employing ideas that were not particularly original but were more extensions and elaborations of what Bennett, Sr., had begun and Pulitzer was perfecting. In 1896, flushed with his San Francisco successes, Hearst arrived in New York, leaving the *Examiner* in competent hands, to start a new morning paper he called the *Journal,* with which he meant to challenge Pulitzer head on.

It was, indeed, a clash of journalistic giants, the last one of the nineteenth century and a battle that would not be equaled until the great Chicago circulation wars of the 1920s. This was a struggle that gave to the language that memorable and abused phrase, "yellow journalism," derived from Richard Outcault's stick-figure cartoon, "The Yellow Kid," which ran in the *Journal,* the first newspaper comic strip in an American paper and the first use of color in a daily. The Kid's costume was a rather ghastly yellow.

While they matched sensationalism in their news columns, the two publishers were quite unlike on the editorial page. Pulitzer's appeal was intellectual and high-minded; he meant to be an opinion-maker and to influence the president and other politicians. Hearst directed his editorials at the masses, writing them himself in a distinctive style, deliberately crafting them with short sentences, short paragraphs, and simple words. The ideas Hearst conveyed were essentially socialistic at that point in his career, although he had no real political convictions of his own, swinging the full circle through his long life from a kind of *ersatz* socialism to a radical conservatism. At the beginning, however, he wanted to appear as the champion of the exploited masses.

Ill health did not prevent Godkin in his final days from condemning both these journalistic houses. In the *Post* he growled disdainfully, "A yellow journal office is probably the nearest approach, in atmosphere, to hell existing in any Christian state, for in gambling houses, brothels, and even in brigands' caves there is a constant exhibition of fear of the police, which is in itself a sort of homage to morality or acknowledgement of its existence."

William McKinley was not a man or a president ideally suited to confront such powerful opponents as Pulitzer and Hearst. Historians today rank him among the "average" presidents, although slightly above Herbert Hoover, Gerald Ford, and Jimmy Carter. Yet he left office, the victim of an assassin's gun, the most widely loved president in memory up to that time, with the exceptions of Washington and Lincoln. George McClellan, Jr., said of him: "There have undoubtedly been greater and stronger Presidents than he was, but none was a more kindly nor a more courteous gentleman, and none has died more regretted by his countrymen, nor more beloved."

This old-fashioned man, reluctant to do anything except what he was certain the people wanted, another president with a profound distaste for personal publicity, faced a press that not only included the two strong men in New York but was growing rapidly as an industry, with a consequent ability to influence more voters. Newspapers were the media leaders in a great national debate that was beginning—over Cuba, over the trusts, over the general character of what America should be, at home and abroad. The wave of popular ten-cent magazines like *McClure's* and *Munsey's* had only just begun, and they had not assumed the national importance they would achieve after the turn of the century.

The nation itself was changing. It was predominantly a small-town and farm country; only 30 percent of the population lived in urban areas. Consequently most people depended heavily on newspapers for information and entertainment, which were supplied by the 14,000 weeklies and 1,900 dailies then extant. The national literacy rate was 88 percent, possibly higher, and newspaper readership had never been greater, equaling 25 percent of the population ten years old or older. In New York alone, fifteen dailies and more than twice as many weeklies drew a combined circulation of a million from a total population of three million; the competition there and in every city was intense. Even in a town as small as Emporia, Kansas, there were two dailies—one of them edited by William Allen White, whose campaign editorial, "What's the Matter with Kansas?" in the Emporia *Gazette*, had aroused Midwestern Republicans and projected White to the national stage.

In spite of growth and change, however, the relationship between president and press remained as parochial as it always had been. Newspapers did not consider the White House as a primary source of news, and so it was covered haphazardly. Editors seemed to prefer relying for news on the president's callers, cabinet officers, or members of Congress rather than the chief executive himself. That was McKinley's preference, too; he wanted to remain in the background as much as possible and had no sense whatever of how the press could be used to his advantage. It was the last time such a situation would exist in Washington.

There was something symbolic about the fact that McKinley was the last Civil War veteran to be elected president. In effect, although he did not realize it, he was in charge of shutting the door on the past, a past of which he was a true representative. He understood that the United States could no longer live in splendid isolation from the rest of the world, but somehow he failed to grasp the vast changes taking place under his nose at home.

His progress to the White House was in the American tradition. Born in Niles, Ohio, he was an intelligent, quiet, hardworking young man who thought about becoming a minister. He had to leave Allegheny College after his first term because of illness, and the family's financial problems prevented his return. He passed the time teaching school and clerking in a post office until the Civil War came. He enlisted, rose to be a major, fought with distinction in some of the most destructive battles, and had the ultimate satisfaction of having his commanding officer, who happened to be Rutherford B. Hayes, call him "one of the bravest and finest officers in the Army."

Still following the traditional pattern, McKinley studied law and became a lawyer after the war, in Canton, Ohio, where he quickly got into politics when his wartime friend, Hayes, ran for governor in 1867. That brought him into local prominence and led to his election as prosecuting attorney. It was entirely natural that he should marry the delicately beautiful and socially prominent Ida Saxton, a union that at first seemed ideal, with a daughter born to them a little less than a year later. But then a second daughter, born in another year or so, died after a few months. This event so shattered Ida's psyche that she sank into a mental and physical depression that led to a lifelong epileptic condition. Her descent into this emotional hell was accelerated by the death of her first daughter when the child was only four. Deprived of her children, wracked by depression and epileptic episodes, Ida developed an obsessive dependence on her husband, which followed him into the White House, but to which he responded with absolute devotion, although his own mental anguish was a daily matter.

For McKinley, politics was the escape route from his desolate private life, although it offered little relief from his financial worries resulting from doctors' bills and Ida's extravagant tastes. Elected to Congress in 1876, he took generally liberal stances on legislation, but he also found an absorbing interest, the tariff question, on which he became one of the leading advocates of protectionist policies, as he remained all his life. The McKinley Tariff he pushed through in 1890 was a ruinous piece of legislation, as noted earlier, but the controversy over it elevated him to national prominence and led to his association with Mark Hanna, the president-maker.

The springboard to Washington was the governorship of Ohio, to which he was elected in 1891 with the help of Hanna money and political organization. His life in the governor's mansion has been described by one historian:

Because he left the operation of the party machinery to Hanna, he had free time to spend with Ida, and she demanded all of it. Every day at exactly three o'clock, McKinley stepped to his office window and waved a handkerchief at his wife, who watched from their nearby home. Ida, who spent her time crocheting bedroom slippers (she reportedly made thousands of them), insisted on accompanying her husband to social affairs. He sat beside her at all functions and became adept at acting swiftly at the first sign of an epileptic attack. Quickly he would place a napkin or handkerchief over her convulsed face and retreat with her to another room. The painful scene was enacted countless times in front of embarrassed friends.

Men on their way to the White House had usually made both friends and enemies in the press, allying themselves with this editor or that, and in general positioning themselves politically with the leading editors and writers. McKinley's press relations, however, were just as haphazard while he was a congressman and governor as they were when he first ascended to the highest office. Yet he was always on good terms with the various proprietors of the Canton *Repository,* and when the editor of that paper came to him after his defeat for reelection to Congress in 1890, asking plaintively, "It's all over—what am I to say in the paper?" McKinley responded with a resounding platitude, "In the time of darkest defeat, victory may be nearest"—and agreed to write the editorial himself. He called his effort "History Repeats Itself." It was largely a defense of his tariff bill.

As a man who had always followed the classic pathway of rural virtue, McKinley should have been arguing what Bryan was preaching to the multitudes in 1896, but, instead, with a bow to Hanna, he wrapped himself in the mythology of the self-made man, offering the proposition that millionaires deserved to be in control because their roots were in poverty, which was the best school for turning out men of character and, of course, substance. This stance was greeted with

approval during the campaign by such Republican pillars as Whitelaw Reid and
Herman Kohlsaat.

McKinley also had the support of a preferred list of county newspapers across
the country, to which the Republican organizers thoughtfully supplied three and
a half columns of prepared material every week—again, an echo of the past. The
combined weekly circulation of these papers was 1,650,000. More important, in
New York he was supported by a solid phalanx of journalistic power, or at least
of vociferous advocacy, including the *World,* the *Sun,* the *Herald,* the *Evening
Post,* and the Brooklyn *Eagle,* all of them usually to be found in the Democratic
camp. It was only the gold standard that united them now with McKinley; they
would have none of Free-Silver Bryan, Democrat or not.

Another man might have cultivated these and other papers favorable to him as
insurance for the future, but McKinley simply treated their representatives pleas-
antly and with no particular favor. He held no press conferences, spoke informally with most of the reporters who cared to approach him, but said almost
nothing that was newsworthy and gave nothing that could be called an interview,
something he refused to grant as a tenet of his political religion.

If McKinley had one unremitting enemy among the publishers, it was young
Willie Hearst, at that moment the avowed savior of struggling humanity. The
Journal's superb cartoonist Homer Davenport depicted Hanna regularly as the
figure that inspired the cliché, "bloated plutocrat," a bulbous villain with dollar
signs covering his frock coat, wearing a silk top hat and pulling the strings of his
puppet McKinley. It was said, in a manifestation of urban snobbery, that farm
wives hid their children when his name was mentioned. Hanna, declared the
Journal, was the enemy of the workingman; for thirty years he had "torn at the
flanks of labor like a wolf." McKinley's mentor was irritated enough by this
treatment to contemplate a lawsuit, but thought better of it. Meanwhile Hearst
had become Bryan's most efficient fund raiser, matching contributions himself to
the amount of $40,901.20, the largest gift the candidate received.

In spite of his casual attitude toward the press and his carefully maintained
personal privacy, McKinley came to the White House on good terms with the
papers, even though he had given the reporters and editors nothing more than the
gold standard to warm themselves by. Moving in with his Ida and his large
family, he created a friendly, informal atmosphere, a considerable change from
the Cleveland regime.

Unfortunately McKinley chose for his first secretary—his buffer with the
press—a man named J. Addison Porter, who had organized the first "McKinley-
for-President" club but otherwise had no visible qualifications. Porter had
money and manners, but his pretentious demeanor and speech moved the correspondents to instant ridicule. The letters he wrote for McKinley were effusive
and patronizing. It was clear after a time that Porter would have to go, but
because McKinley could not bring himself to dismiss his man, George B. Cortelyou did the job while the secretary clung to his title until "over mental strain,"
as the announcement discreetly put it, compelled him to resign in 1900. Cortelyou then became the immediate ancestor of today's press secretary.

Political expedience had also governed McKinley's cabinet choices, and they, too, were unfortunate. Sen. John Sherman, who had been made secretary of state, came under particular attack because of his age (he was seventy-three) and because his elevation created a Senate seat for Hanna. McKinley had to defend him against the scorn of Joseph Medill, nearly at the end of his long career on the Chicago *Tribune*. The president wrote to Medill, diplomatically and optimistically: "I concur in your opinion that the stories regarding Senator Sherman's 'mental decay' are without foundation and the cheap invention of sensational writers or other evil-disposed or mistaken people. When I saw him last I was convinced both of his perfect health, physically and mentally, and that his prospects of life were remarkably good."

McKinley was either politically blind or producing an early example of modern cover-up, because Sherman's problems were not the "cheap invention of sensational writers." He began to exhibit distressing, and humiliating, evidences of senility (or perhaps Alzheimer's disease); important matters soon had to be taken out of his hands before his forced resignation occurred. Two years later he was dead. Ironically enough, Medill preceded him by two months, dying (so it was said) with the newspaperman's perennial inquiry on his lips, "What's the news?" Another nineteenth-century giant gone.

In spite of the difficulties with his appointees, however, McKinley continued to have a relatively good relationship with the press for a time. He was prompt to greet the correspondents in the East Room only three weeks after he took office, demonstrating a politician's memory for names and faces that could not help but please them. It was a welcome change from the Cleveland chill. A long table was set up on the second floor for the benefit of the White House reporters (the beginnings of a pressroom), and Porter appeared at noon and 4 P.M. nearly every day to speak with them—the first approach to a formal press conference.

Gratified by this attention, the correspondents invited McKinley to address them at the yearly Gridiron Club dinner, a ritual Harrison had begun, which in time would become an annual event. Cleveland had frostily declined to make an appearance. McKinley further improved relations three months later when he went on a short junket to visit Commodore Cornelius Vanderbilt's estate, from which underlings were about to exclude the press until the president announced that he would not enter if they were kept out. Still later in that first year, just after Christmas, newspaper correspondents were received socially at the White House for the first time in the history of the government at an official reception for them.

With such treatment the correspondents could forgive McKinley for not giving them interviews or permitting them to quote him directly. As the president's most recent biographer, Lewis L. Gould, observes, "Reporters had greater access to him as president than students of his press relations have realized. McKinley's deft handling of the journalists in his first year not only reestablished the White House as a significant source of news, it also was a large step in the enhancing of presidential power."

Yet there was a disquieting reserve beneath this smooth surface. It was true that the White House appeared much more open to the press than it had during the Cleveland administration, and it was also true that McKinley displayed unexpected tact in handling the correspondents. But there was a touch of monarchical remoteness in the unwritten rule that no newspaperman in the White House was to approach the president unless McKinley spoke first. News usually came from Cortelyou, who introduced the kind of routine that would soon become commonplace by giving releases first to the Associated Press so that they would reach the entire public faster. The reasoning, he said, was that pro- and antiadministration papers would thus get the same treatment and the public could be sure of rapid and impartial coverage. It was an eminently reasonable assumption that nevertheless invited violation by a highly competitive press and did not take into account the difference between morning and afternoon papers.

The correspondents were treated to the unusual spectacle of a president who wrote his own speeches, a lost art in our time, as well as his reports and messages to Congress, setting them all down on small slips of paper with a soft pencil in simple, declarative sentences—much the way he spoke in public. Reporters noted, too, that McKinley did not speak until he had something to say, another novelty, and when the correspondents verged on impertinence with the questions they were permitted to ask, he did not reprimand them.

A veteran correspondent, David S. Barry, described McKinley's initial press relations in the *Chautauquan* as follows:

> The President early set a good example by assigning a day for meeting all the representatives of the newspapers at the capital, by attending the dinner of the Gridiron Club, composed of forty Washington correspondents, and by letting it be known that the reporters are at liberty to call upon him and the members of his cabinet for information on public affairs. The officials of his administration have stated that they are at home to newspaper correspondents during business hours, and there are other signs that the era of friendliness between public men and newspaper reporters will be restored with the return of general prosperity of the country, unless, indeed, the good resolutions of the new cabinet officials are forgotten with the coming of the new year, as unfortunately, they are quite apt to be.

In this beginning climate of good will McKinley even permitted himself to pose for photographers on occasion, although ground rules were laid down, one of which banned pictures of him smoking. He told William Allen White that he did not think it was proper for "the young men of this country to see their President smoking."

On one occasion McKinley let down his guard long enough to give an interview, to Henry Loomis Nelson, a former editor of *Harper's Weekly*. Nelson tried to write with the extreme discretion he knew his privileged position demanded, producing a story without a single direct quotation. That pleased McKinley so much he granted a second interview to Nelson, but *Harper's,* which had printed the first one because it was delighted to have an exclusive, declined the second, having had enough of a discretion that was more soporific than illuminating. As any writer would have done, Nelson, reluctant to lose such material, rewrote his article "in a less intimate way," as he put it, and sold it to Pulitzer's *World.* This version mentioned how proud McKinley was of his recommendation that the

Puerto Ricans should have free access to American markets. The president, when he read it, was furious. He gave no more interviews for a time.

There was a reason for his anger. McKinley had changed his position on free trade for Puerto Rico and other American possessions because his party took the opposite view. When his friend Kohlsaat, who apparently did not know of the switch, wrote a scathing editorial in the Chicago *Times-Herald* referring to "the mysterious influence that has pushed the Republican party to the verge of a precipice over which lie dishonor, injustice, and disaster," McKinley wrote a letter mildly rebuking him—and then decided not to send it. But it was the end of his friendship with Kohlsaat. McKinley, however, had changed direction on this issue in such an indirect and passive way, cloaking the whole process in his usual silence, that when it became known to the press there were the inevitable charges that he was no more than Hanna's puppet.

Thus, on the issue of foreign policy, the early warm relationship with the press that McKinley had been able to establish began to unravel as the national argument over what to do about Cuba moved toward a patriotic explosion. As the historian Frank Freidel has pointed out, the possibility of war with Spain over Cuba had existed since the Spanish authorities and the Cuban revolutionaries first began their prolonged and bloody struggle in 1868. The initial phase ended ten years later, followed by an uneasy truce until 1895, when it was resumed again with greater fervor. Pulitzer hired young Winston Churchill to report what was going on in Cuba, and Churchill contributed some perceptive dispatches to the *World*. "My general conclusion," he wrote in one of them, "is that European methods of warfare are almost out of the question in a wild countryside," a hard truth the British regulars had learned more than a century before from the embattled farmers. Other correspondents were less perceptive as the war dragged on into 1898, and there was a good deal of inaccurate reporting, exaggerating the condition of the ravaged island, beset by hunger and disease. Nevertheless the situation seemed intolerable to many Americans, and public pressure began to build up on McKinley and Congress.

In the historiography of the Spanish-American War the role of the press has been both exaggerated and minimized. Popular history, at its most overblown, has depicted the jingoist press, led by Pulitzer and Hearst, as virtually forcing a reluctant McKinley to ask a willing Congress for a declaration of war. Part of the American mythology is that Hearst actually started the war by arranging for the battleship *Maine,* on a presumed "good will" visit, to be blown up in Havana Harbor—the act that precipitated the war. This fantasy is based on a cable of dubious authenticity supposed to have been sent by Hearst to Frederic Remington, who had asked to be relieved of his artist-correspondent assignment in Cuba. "Please remain," the publisher allegedly cabled. "You furnish the pictures and I'll furnish the war." Whatever Hearst may have meant by this grandiose claim, if he ever made it, he certainly did not plan to destroy an American battleship. He would as soon have blown up his mother.

Professional historians, on the other hand, scarcely mention either Hearst or Pulitzer in general histories of the United States, and in specific studies of the war they usually appear as no more than footnotes, when they are mentioned at all. While this may be a deserved scholarly corrective to popular history, it slights the considerable influence of the press in crystallizing an American opinion already inflamed by provocative news stories and editorials, not only in New York but all over the nation. While such influence cannot be measured quantitatively, a fact that makes the idea suspect to some historians, newspaper pressure was clearly a prime factor in the overwhelming public sentiment that made war inevitable.

Pulitzer was an earlier shaper of this movement than Hearst. Fifteen years before the *Maine* went down, the *World* was suggesting editorially that Cuba ought to be seized in the name of manifest destiny. But Pulitzer's mind could change quickly. On April 16, 1884, the *World* was advocating that the United States stay out of the Cuban problem and mind its own business. Next day it completely reversed itself, having heard a rumor that the consul general in Havana had resigned after being insulted by Spanish authorities for protesting the mistreatment of American citizens. "This feeble Republic has been insulted by the Spanish robbers in Cuba for about fifteen years and it is almost time to put a stop to it," Pulitzer proclaimed. Two months later the *World* declared war, after two stories it had run reporting negotiations for the sale of Cuba to the United States were reprinted in two Havana newspapers, which were promptly suspended by the authorities for twenty days: "It strikes us that when journals are not permitted to copy the *World*'s news with due credit it is time for a revolution. We are for Free Cuba from this time henceforth."

Jingoistic editorials, sometimes racist as well, became part of the *World*'s stock in trade. Mexico was advised, "If any Mexican greaser pulls down the American flag, beat him over the head with the flag-staff." When the State Department warned a Guatemalan dictator general not to carry out his plan to bring Honduras, Costa Rica, Nicaragua, and El Salvador into an alliance with his country by force if necessary, and fighting broke out in El Salvador, the *World* responded with patriotic pride that "our Government feels equal to a 'tussle' with the Guatemalan tyrant and . . . it will tolerate no nonsense at his hands." Pulitzer, along with some members of Congress, suspected that France, the Guatemalan general, and Panamanian rebels were in a conspiracy to obstruct the building of a canal across Panama.

Pulitzer himself was an unabashed jingoist, a xenophobe who believed sincerely that Americans would never go abroad as soon as they discovered how superior their country was to Europe. Yet he was also acutely conscious of mass emotions and tastes; it was this sensitivity that had made the *World* into the nation's most-read newspaper. Both Pulitzer and Hearst (in his own peculiar way) believed in the patriotic glorification of America and its deserved supremacy, but in pressing for war with Cuba they were only exploiting similar feelings they knew existed in the general public.

McKinley was not lacking in patriotism, but he was pacific by nature, a believer in negotiation and not inclined to rash statements of any kind. He could hardly ignore what was happening in Cuba, however, particularly when the level of violence escalated every day. There were also economic factors to be consid-

ered. The United States had at least $50 million invested in Cuban sugar planta-
tions, and, including total trade with the island, that figure could be doubled.
There was also the proposed Panama Canal to be taken into account. Conceivably it could matter whether Spain or the rebels were governing Cuba.

Having been elected on a platform advocating Cuban independence, Mc-
Kinley had hoped to achieve that goal by bringing diplomatic pressure to bear on
Spain. In his inaugural address he asserted that the country wanted "no wars of
conquest; we must avoid the temptation of territorial aggression." Further, he
had told Carl Schurz flatly that "there will be no jingo nonsense under my administration." But that was precisely what he was getting while he tried for more
than a year to find a diplomatic solution, even as the governor of Cuba, Gen.
Valeriano Weyler ("Butcher Weyler," as he was known to the jingo press),
herded Cubans into concentration camps and committed atrocities, some of them
real enough and others invented by Hearst's ingenious reporters, skillfully
matched by the Pulitzer minions.

Spain would not mediate, in spite of all McKinley's efforts, although Weyler
was called home and his policies on the island softened. The Spanish government
appeared willing at one point to grant the Cubans at least a degree of autonomy
and to give everyone in the Antilles the same rights as Spanish citizens, which
were not excessive. McKinley advised Congress that he believed Spain should be
given a chance to carry out its promises, but two events in quick succession
ended all further hope. The Spanish ambassador, Dupuy de Lôme, an able diplomat who had been dealing, as he hoped, successfully with the American government, had written an indiscreet letter to a Havana friend, a copy of which
somehow found its way into Hearstian hands in the Havana post office, by means
not unfamiliar to the *Journal*. Hearst had held this letter for nearly a year and a
half, waiting for the right moment to release it. Early in Feburary 1898 was the
right moment. The *Journal* published the text under a glaring headline, "The
Worst Insult to the United States in Its History."

It was hardly that, but it was enough. De Lôme complained to his friend about
the overheated political climate in Washington and, moving on to the president,
described him as "weak and a bidder for the admiration of the crowd, besides
being a would-be politician who tries to leave a door open behind himself while
keeping on good terms with the jingoes of his party." This estimate was not
entirely unfair, but it cost the ambassador his job and stirred the press to a new
frenzy. It was not Hearst's first venture into unofficial diplomacy. Earlier he had
sent one of his best reporters, James Creelman, to Madrid as an ambassador
without any portfolio except the publisher's instructions to make the Spanish
government see the light. Another reporter, Charles Michelson, had been dispatched to Cuba with somewhat similar instructions and was immediately im-
prisoned in Morro Castle. To show which side he was on, Hearst sent still
another reporter, Grover Flint, to present the insurgent general Antonio Maceo
with a jeweled sword. In New York, meanwhile, the *Journal* had to depend for
its news on Cuban propagandists, but that was not a handicap. The rewrite men
simply dressed up the latest rumors as dispatches, the copy desk put Havana
datelines on them, and the trouble of on-the-spot reporting was saved.

In the gathering storm McKinley could have reflected gloomily that he was not the first victim of press jingoism on the Cuban question. Cleveland, in his second term, had undergone the same kind of abuse for not being sufficiently alarmed and belligerent. Encouraged by the platform of 1896, the papers believed that McKinley would act where his predecessor had failed, but when it became clear that his views were not substantially different, the *Journal* and others accused him of being under Wall Street's (that is, Hanna's) influence and declared war on their own account.

McKinley and those around him were neither insensitive nor indifferent to the rising clamor for intervention. But they believed that some of the papers, in their vituperative criticism of the president, were verging on the excessive, and there was even a time when the cabinet seriously debated whether it was possible or advisable to have the editors of the New York *Evening Post* and the Springfield *Republican* (of all people) indicted for treason. (It should be noted that by this time Godkin was too ill to carry on. His earlier editorials, once so persuasive of other editors as well as the public, had been lost in the general commotion, and Rollo Ogden, now the *Evening Post*'s editor, was writing most of those that appeared in the paper.) But the de Lôme letter was only the penultimate push toward war. A few days later the *Maine* was sunk, and it was clear nothing could prevent a declaration. Even the pope's appeal for peace had been denounced in the headlines as "Papal Meddling," and every paper that had once preached moderation was now clamoring for war.

In the preoccupation with Pulitzer and Hearst, the most visible publishers, it is easily forgotten that not all the press was avid for conflict. Some of the most important papers had been skeptical. The *Times,* for example, had observed, "The most alarming Cuban revolutions have occurred in New York for many years—in speeches," and the *Tribune* had added, "It is doubtful whether any real attempt has been made to raise the standard of revolt in any quarter of the island. Revolutionists are most numerous and demonstrative in the cigar factories of New York or the cafés of Key West." Both the *Evening Post* and the *Herald* had been equally uncommitted.

The tide had begun to turn, however, by February 1895, when a steamer arriving in New York reported that it had been fired upon in the Windward Passage by a Spanish gunboat. In fact, the shots were blanks, and the Spaniards intended only to search the ship for contraband, but the jingo machine had been set in motion. "The next Spanish gunboat that molests an American vessel," the *Sun* proclaimed, "ought to be pursued and blown out of the water."

After the *Maine* there was no turning back. Never again, even in the hysteria of the First World War, would newspapers headline a story with such an imaginative description as the *Journal*'s "The War Ship Maine Was Split in Two by an Enemy's Secret Infernal Machine." The *World* was just as fanciful in its desperate struggle against Hearst for circulation. No wonder Godkin wrote in disgust, "Nothing so disgraceful as the behavior of these two newspapers . . . has ever been known in the history of journalism," a judgment not as exaggerated as it sounds.

McKinley could have resisted the clamor of the press if he had chosen to do so, but the pressures for war went far beyond the newspapers. Few advocates of moderation remained in Congress, and popular voices like those of Theodore Roosevelt, now the assistant secretary of the navy, were whipping up passions everywhere in the country. There was real political danger in resisting. The Democrats would seize joyfully upon such an issue and win with it.

A revealing picture of how the president suffered under these pressures has been given to us by George Cortelyou in his diary:

> The President does not look at all well. He is bearing up under the great strain, but his haggard face and anxious inquiry for any news which has in it a token of peace tell of the sense of tremendous responsibility and of his devotion to the welfare of the people of this country. The vile slanders uttered against him . . . have only tended to endear him to those of us who see him as he works here in the Executive Mansion, early and late. . . . The sensational newspapers publish daily accounts of conferences that never take place, of influences that are never felt, of purposes that are nothing but the products of the degenerate minds that spread them before a too-easily-led public.
>
> One of the most absurd of the lies that have found currency of late is the one to the effect that the President sees only the favorable side of the correspondence which comes to the Executive Mansion. . . . The President sees everything, whether in the shape of mail, telegrams, or newspapers, that can indicate the drift of public sentiment. . . . The ranters in Congress, the blatherskites who do the talking upon the street corners, and at public meetings, and the scavengers of the sensational press misrepresent public opinion when they assert that this country is for war except as a necessity and for the upholding of the national honor.

In the end McKinley succumbed to the fear that, if he did not go to war, he would lose his leadership of the party, and so he sent the decisive message to Congress in April 1898, after which the Foreign Affairs committees in both House and Senate authorized him to intervene in Cuba. House debate produced the Teller Amendment, in which the United States declared that it had no intention of exercising any kind of sovereignty over the island and promised to restore its government to the people. By the end of April the nation was at war with Spain.

The war itself is beyond the scope of this book, except to note a few relevant journalistic by-products. Often called the "Correspondents' War," it saw the rise of the foreign correspondent in the resplendent person of Richard Harding Davis, the apotheosis of the romantic daredevil with a pad and pencil, an image that lingered in the American imagination for many years. In one sense, it became a comic opera war when Hearst chartered a tramp steamer, filled it with a staff of reporters and photographers and a printing press in the hold, and steamed off to cover the conflict in person, appearing on the battlefield wearing a straw boater with a bright ribbon around it and taking notes from those still alive. Another, more talented correspondent was young Stephen Crane, sent by the *World,* who covered Colonel Roosevelt's charge up San Juan Hill with candor and considerable personal bravery. Some historians have called this storied event one of the great emotional expressions of the American people. For Roosevelt it was a personal triumph, leading his "improbable band of sportsmen, Texas Rangers, and other cronies," as they have been called, the First U.S. Volunteer Cavalry Regiment, better known as the "Rough Riders." Crane did not slight Roosevelt's own reckless heroism in leading the charge, nor did he neglect to mention how well black infantry and cavalry troops fought in the general action, but in describing the bloody death and destruction he somehow deeply ruffled the notorious Roosevelt temper. The colonel laid blame at the door of Pulitzer, but he would not forget what Crane wrote, with unexpected consequences a few years later.

As for Hearst and Pulitzer, the war was a turning point for both publishers. For the *World*'s owner it had been extremely costly, not only in the money he had been compelled to extract from his reserves in order to compete with the personal wealth Hearst lavished on his coverage, but his precarious health was left worse than ever. Both papers emerged with greatly increased circulations, and Hearst had established a solid base from which he would shortly spread a large umbrella of newspapers and magazines to become the first owner of a newspaper chain (which operators of similar aggregations later preferred to call "group ownership") and the proprietor of the first communications conglomerate, eventually involving all the media.

The war in Cuba was over quickly. American troops landed in late June, and after a few desultory battles pushed the Spaniards back into Santiago. In July the Spanish fleet was trapped in Santiago Bay and sunk. Two weeks later the city itself gave up, and in August, Spain agreed to a peace conference. McKinley wanted not only Cuba's independence but Puerto Rico's transference to the United States; the question of what do do about that other Spanish colony, the Philippines, was to be decided at the peace conference.

At the moment American expanionism was being extended westward. Hawaii had been annexed in July 1898, and now the American forces headed for the Philippines, gobbling up Wake Island and Guam, a Spanish island, on their way. But the Philippines were a different matter. Later, McKinley described how he made his decision about them: "I walked the floor of the White House night after night until midnight, and I am not ashamed to tell you . . . that I went down on my knees and prayed Almighty God for light and guidance more than one night. And one night later it came to me . . . that there was nothing left for us to do but to take them all, and to educate the Filipinos, and uplift them and civilize and Christianize them." No British diplomat of the nineteenth century could have phrased it better.

Not all the Filipinos were prepared to be Christianized and civilized. Some of them were possessed of the logical idea that freedom meant freedom from their liberators as well as the Spanish. Under an insurgent leader, Emilio Aguinaldo, they fought a savage little war for their independence until American forces finally defeated them and annexed the islands in 1901 by means of a civil commission to replace American military rule after the insurrection was put down.

McKinley did not live to see the outcome, but at the beginning of this struggle he felt the weight of press opposition from a new and unexpected quarter. A segment of the public, mostly confined to New England, opposed what was happening in the Philippines and their resistance resulted in what came to be known as the anti-imperialist movement. The revisionist historian, Daniel B. Schirmer, has described its origins:

> Writing a prospectus for his paper in the year 1900, Samuel Bowles, editor and owner of the Springfield *Republican*, recognized the war against the Philippine independence movement as a turning point in the national life, marked by the overbearing domestic influence of "incorporated and syndicated wealth," by "imperialism and militarism," by emulation of the policies and methods of European monarchies. All this represented to Bowles a significant break with our "traditional policies in government and foreign relations" which had been previously typified, as he saw it, by democracy and abstention from the militarism and long-standing rivalries of European states. In short, Bowles opposed the Philippine War as the expression of the new policies of imperialism and militarism which, in his view, corporate wealth was fastening on the country.
>
> Millions of his fellow citizens, in Massachusetts and the country at large, shared Bowles' feelings and beliefs. In consequence an organized movement of resistance arose of those Americans who opposed the foreign policies of the McKinley Administration and called themselves anti-imperialists.

In Cuba the small armies of Hearst and Pulitzer, attached to the legitimate troops, had charged about the landscape relatively unimpeded, participating in battles and suffering few conflicts with the military. In the Philippines, by contrast, the administration dealt harshly with the correspondents as part of a general effort to stifle dissent at home. It was the conviction of both the (by then) Roosevelt administration and the field commanders that the insurrectionists would not be able to function if it were not for the encouragement they were getting from those in America who opposed the war. News that reflected on either the military or the administration was censored in the field.

In a magazine called *The Verdict*, George Luks, later a prominent figure in the Ashcan school of painting, drew a cartoon captioned "The Way We Get the War News." It depicted a correspondent trying to write his copy while two generals with drawn swords surrounded him and a third held him by the arms. That was a radical exaggeration, of course, but the censorship was real enough. There were atrocities on both sides, and a few of the American troops went somewhat further, taking no prisoners, laying waste to villages, shooting down men, women, and children indiscriminately. As Frank Freidel has written, "On one notorious occasion, they shot up a wedding party. To elicit information from reluctant villagers they resorted to such Spanish techniques as the 'water cure.' . . . Others were hanged briefly to refresh their memories."

When all this began to emerge from soldiers' letters home, even though a few of the stories were later challenged and the American command went to extraordinary lengths to persuade some of the writers to repudiate themselves, there was a cry of protest from the portion of the press that had opposed McKinley and now was against Roosevelt. The public, however, remained apathetic. It was bathed in a warm glow of patriotism and war-induced prosperity. The voters were as ready to back Roosevelt as they had been McKinley when it came to questions of American supremacy. The anti-imperialists were thoroughly defeated.

When the Philippine Insurrection finally ended, more Americans had been killed than in Cuba, and an estimated two hundred thousand Filipinos had perished. Hearings were held on the allegations of army brutality, and a few convicted officers got off with perfunctory reprimands. The dissenters, led by a small portion of the press, had failed to do any more than stir briefly the conscience of the American people.

In their raucous defense of the public interest, which was largely synthetic except for Pulitzer's basic idealism, the role of the newspapers in the Spanish-American War, and in the McKinley administration generally, overshadowed some of the papers' real contributions to national life. Hearst had given pop culture the comic strip, with whatever its future implications might be. He and Pulitzer had also led the way in showing how newspapers could now cover a war and bring information to the public in a manner that had not been possible before. Unfortunately there was considerably less truth in what came out of Cuba than there had been in the Civil War. Some correspondents were instructed by Hearst and Pulitzer to show how cruel and inhuman the Spaniards were, and they faithfully obliged. That, of course, would not have been difficult in any war, since cruelty and inhumanity are the hallmarks of armed conflict between nations.

If there was a large element of irresponsibility in the war coverage, there was also a great financial drain, which took away whatever profits might have been achieved from high circulations. If the war had lasted two more years, Arthur Brisbane wrote later, every New York paper would have been bankrupt. There may have been nearly five hundred correspondents covering the struggle, some of them operating from whole fleets of press boats. Adm. W. I. Sampson's fleet barely outnumbered them.

The net result was no great credit to journalism. As Charles R. Brown has observed in *The Correspondents' War,* still the best account of the media's role in this conflict:

> Correspondents could have alerted the nation about the bungling of the War Department if they had told the truth about conditions at Tampa. They showed a reckless disregard for national security by writing about ship and troop movements early in the war and by their diatribes about the helplessness of the American army at Santiago during the truce negotiations. They puffed up minor naval and land engagements into stupendous feats of martial achievement. They were mixed up in their feelings about their role as reporters and patriots, interfering with military operations at times and leading or taking part in fighting that should have been left to the soldiers. But as [Richard Harding] Davis also wrote: "They kept the American people informed of what their countrymen—their brothers, fathers, and friends—were doing at the front. They cared for the soldiers when they were wounded, and, as Americans, helped Americans against a common enemy by reconnoitering, scouting, and fighting. They had no uniform to protect them; they were under sentence to be shot as spies if captured by the Spaniards; and they were bound, not by an oath as

were the soldiers, but merely by a sense of duty to a newspaper, and by a natural desire to be of service to their countrymen in any way that offered.''

If it demonstrated anything, the role of the media in the Spanish-American War was further proof that the press had the power to influence the masses on a large scale only if the masses were ready to be influenced. In 1898, they were ready.

The *Journal* had what could be called the last word. By exercising its customary methods of getting the news first—in this case, it was said, by bribing a Spanish diplomatic secretary—this Hearst paper was the first in the world to print terms of the peace treaty, crowing editorially that it was ''a journalistic achievement believed to be entirely without precedent. Such enterprise makes Senatorial secrecy an absurdity.''

Thus the war ended, as far as Hearst was concerned, with the Spaniards and McKinley confounded, the United States a world power, and he himself a hero to the Democrats and the Cubans. The island's first president Tomás Estrada Palma assured him: ''I do not believe that we would have secured our independence without the aid which you rendered.''

As for McKinley, he was in a melancholy mood. The party expected him to run again, although he protested that he had ''had enough'' of the White House. Ida McKinley's health and her obsessive need of him were a constant drain on his energies. Her ''good days'' were now much more infrequent, but she continued to insist on playing her role as White House hostess. As he had done when he was governor of Ohio, the president continued to protect her in the same way, removing her with handkerchief over mouth when she had seizures at state dinners and receptions, to the embarrassment of the guests.

At least the press respected his troubled private life, as it had not spared Cleveland's. Ida was never referred to except with the utmost discretion. The McKinleys did not make colorful newspaper copy, obviously, but reporters were compensated by the president's mother, who captivated them from the moment this indomitable eighty-seven-year-old lady walked out of the Washington station for the first time, her arms filled with roses she had gathered on the train. She was dignified yet sociable, completely unimpressed by her son's high office.

As has happened so often in presidential families, however, there were also troublesome relatives. There was McKinley's younger brother Abner, to begin with. His business transactions, which involved printing telegraph stock and selling worthless railroad bonds, brought pain to the president, and to the newspapers, particularly the anti-McKinley gazettes, a welcome flow of copy. Mrs. McKinley's only brother, George Saxton, also appeared on the front pages as the result of several sordid lawsuits involving romances that had led to legal actions rather than lasting relationships.

Those Americans not addicted to Hearst, Pulitzer, or the other ''new'' journalists got a somewhat different view of the president from the magazines. In the July 1898 issue of *McClure's,* for example, a rising young writer named Ida M. Tarbell provided a variant account of McKinley's press relations, one that was surprisingly uncritical for so accomplished a reporter. Miss Tarbell wrote:

A digest of the newspapers comes to him of course in conversation with his Secretary and friends, and in Cabinet meetings, where articles of special value and suggestions are frequently read and discussed; but his most intimate connection with the press comes from the peculiar relation which news-gatherers have to the White House. The President, as a matter of fact, has the newspaper man always with him. He is . . . a part of the White House personnel. . . . Accommodations are furnished him there, and his privileges are well-defined and generally recognized. Thus in the outer reception-room of the business part of the White House, a corner containing a well furnished table and plenty of chairs is set aside for reporters. Here representatives of half a dozen or more papers are always to be found, and during Cabinet meetings and at moments of grave importance the number increases many fold. Here they write, note the visitors who are admitted to the President, catch the secretaries as they come and go, and here every evening about 10 o'clock they gather around Secretary Porter for a kind of family talk, he discussing with them whatever of the events of the day he thinks it wise to discuss. . . .

It is part of the unwritten law of the White House that newspaper men shall never approach the President as he passes to and fro near their alcove or crosses the portico to his carriage, unless he himself stops and talks to them. This he occasionally does, for he knows all of the reporters by name and treats them with uniform kindness. If a man disappears, Mr. McKinley is sure to inquire soon what has become of him, and if one falls ill, he asks regularly after him.

While this idyllic picture is certainly exaggerated in several respects, it is instructive to note how far the president-press relationship had progressed in a short time, moving inevitably toward being institutionalized, at least to some extent. In the Cleveland administration Dan Lamont, the president's secretary, had come to understand after a time something that was fundamental about this always troubled relationship. If he was going to project the president onto the public consciousness in a way that would best support Cleveland's policies, Lamont realized, he would have to see to it that reporters got ordinary, everyday information on a regular basis. He must also be available as their first source when important news was breaking. Thus was the concept of the press secretary born.

Lamont made the idea work in its early, rudimentary form, and it was clear from the beginning that how well it worked would much depend on the personality and abilities of the secretary. O. O. Seeley, a veteran reporter in the McKinley era, said of Lamont that he "had tact, judgment, knew what to say and how to say it, and what to do and how to do it. He let the 'boys' do most of the talking and guessing, but never allowed them to leave the White House with a wrong impression, or without thinking that they had got about all there was in the story."

In McKinley's time, as we have seen, George Cortelyou carried on what Lamont had begun, giving the reporters advance copies of speeches and arranging conferences and interviews with the president for them, few though these might be, and even holding daily meetings with them—"briefings," as they would one day be ubiquitously known. The president himself knew how important it was to keep in touch with public opinion. He did it by frequent consultation with his cabinet members, with leaders in Congress from both parties, and with what we would now call "opinion-makers" everywhere in the nation—and also, if we can believe his editor friend Murat Halstead, "by reading the newspapers thoroughly."

Halstead understood well enough what a presidential secretary's attitude toward the press was certain to be, even though as a newspaperman he might find it inconvenient or even reprehensible on occasion. A secretary must "tell the newspaper correspondents what they should know without seeming to suppress information," Halstead said. Since Cortelyou performed that function superbly, the editor was quite right in calling him the most popular such functionary the White House had ever seen. The Chicagoan particularly approved of the fact that Cortelyou handed out copies of McKinley's speeches in plenty of time when the president was on a speaking tour.

With such help McKinley approached his second term with some confidence that he would have substantial newspaper support. There was little doubt that he would be renominated, just as there was no reason to believe the Democrats would find anyone likely to please them more than Bryan. Meeting in Philadelphia, the Republicans would have sat through an unprecedentedly dull convention if it had not been for the controversy over selecting a vice-president to replace Garret A. Hobart, who had died during McKinley's first term. This struggle would prove to be another turning point in history, as events proved. McKinley's choice was Sen. William B. Allison, but Mark Hanna wanted Cornelius N. Bliss, secretary of the interior, a man not likely to disturb the party machinery.

As it happened, most of the delegates had no enthusiasm for either of these prospects. Their choice was the hero of San Juan Hill, Col. Theodore Roosevelt, now the governor of New York. Hanna did not think Roosevelt was "safe," a judgment of extraordinary acuity. The contretemps led to an interior battle of bosses—Hanna against Thomas Platt, controller of the New York machine, and Matt Quay, centurion of the Pennsylvania legion. There was nothing high-minded about the motives of the latter two resident wizards. Platt wanted to get rid of Roosevelt as governor because he was not, as we would say now, a team player. The colonel's contempt for bosses was barely concealed. What Quay's motives may have been are obscure, but it is quite possible he simply yearned to cut Hanna down to size.

Roosevelt himself was not enchanted by what was happening. His eyes were already on the White House, and he was afraid that, if he were vice-president, he would simply fade into that comprehensive obscurity that seems to envelop the office. Consequently he told Hanna plainly that he did not want the job; he was quite happy to be governor of New York. Hanna was in fervent agreement. He thought Roosevelt had "dangerous" ideas that, if he could carry them out, would not be in the best interests of business, Hanna's primary concern. To McKinley, Hanna made a prophetic remark: "You know, a President sometimes dies, and where would we be if Roosevelt should come to the White House?" Where, indeed? It was not the only strange premonition of what was to come.

According to A. W. Dunn, McKinley had told Kohlsaat, "If it were not for Ida, I would prefer to go as Lincoln went." He had no enthusiasm for the campaign.

In Philadelphia, when Roosevelt made his seconding speech for McKinley, the ovation that followed it was so tremendous that the governor appeared flushed, dazed and (for him) nearly overcome. It was plain that the delegates were going to settle the war between the bosses. They wanted Teddy, and their tumultuous enthusiasm made it impossible for him to refuse. Hanna said to McKinley, recalling their previous conversation, "Now it's up to you to live."

When the Democrats met in Kansas City, there was no such subterranean maneuvering to enliven the scene. Bryan was nominated by acclamation, and Adlai E. Stevenson as his running mate injected that name into national politics for the second time; he had served as vice-president under Cleveland. In Bryan's first attempt, he had borne the Cross of Gold to defeat. Now he was asked to campaign on a theme of anti-imperialism, which was eminently worthy and wholly out of key with the mood of the nation, notwithstanding the rapturous tumult that broke out when a flag seventy feet long was unfurled over the heads of the perspiring delegates, bearing the inspirational legend: "The Flag of the Republic forever; of an Empire never!"

Once more McKinley conducted his campaign from the front porch in Canton, clinging to the abused and quickly receding tradition that it was undignified for a sitting president to canvass the country. Bryan, on the other hand, took to the stump as though it were a permanent dwelling place, making a total of six hundred speeches in twenty-four states. His oratory was magnificent, but its effects were minimal once again. When the balloting was over, McKinley had won by nearly a million votes, and Platt went to bed in the happy conviction that it was the end of Roosevelt's political career.

Six months after his inauguration, the president visited the Pan-American Exposition in Buffalo and on September 5, 1901, made his last speech to a receptive crowd, which received him warmly. Next day he gave a public reception in the Temple of Music on the exhibition grounds. Among those who crowded about to shake his hand was a young man whose right hand was bandaged, a circumstance that in a later day would have brought him to the immediate attention of the Secret Service. At that more innocent time, however, Leon Czolgosz, a twenty-eight-year-old anarchist, son of an immigrant Polish family, had no trouble approaching the president as though to join in the well wishing. He raised his bandaged hand, which concealed a pistol, and shot the president twice in the midsection.

It was one of those mindless acts with which history is replete, and from which great events have sometimes followed. Czolgosz had been a factory worker in Cleveland, but three years earlier had suffered a breakdown that was both mental and physical, as well as could be determined. Going home to the Ohio farm where his parents lived, he had been restless, disturbed, and despondent earlier in that summer of the great exposition and had drifted back to Buffalo, ostensibly to look for work. Quite probably he had read about McKinley as the symbol of big business and the bosses, the apotheosis of triumphant capitalism, because he told the police later, "I didn't believe one man should have so much service, and another man should have none."

McKinley was taken to the exposition's emergency infirmary (it would hardly be called a hospital), where the doctors operated hastily under inadequate lighting, which may have prevented them from locating and removing the second bullet, somewhere in the stomach walls. Then, with no more illumination than the dying rays of the afternoon sun and a reflecting mirror could provide, they sewed him up, neglecting to provide proper drainage, although presumably they did the best they could under extremely difficult conditions.

The president seemed to survive this ordeal at first, and his doctors were optimistic enough to do what physicians attending stricken presidents are likely to do. They issued a bulletin declaring to reporters and an anxious nation that "no serious symptoms have developed." But, in fact, the second bullet was festering inside, and gangrene set in. Early in the evening of September 14, the doctors had another bulletin for the press: "The President is dead."

A shock wave ran through the country, not alone because McKinley had died but because there was a deep need to blame someone or something for the awful event. The perennial whipping boy stood ready for punishment—the press—and there was circumstantial evidence to encourage the indictment. People recalled that Garfield's assassin had carried a marked copy of the New York *Herald* in his pocket. Now it was remembered that after the assassination of Gov. William Goebel of Kentucky, nearly two years earlier, Ambrose Bierce, who was no admirer of Hearst, had written a prophetic quatrain for the *Journal:*

> The bullet that pierced Goebel's breast
> Can not be found in all the West;
> Good reason: it is speeding here
> To stretch McKinley on his bier.

No wonder that Hearst, hearing the news of the assassination in the office of his Chicago *American,* is said to have remarked softly, "Things are going to be very bad."

In Buffalo the reporters sent out to cover the story were given access to Czolgosz and hammered away at him, trying to get him to admit he had been inspired by reading the Hearst papers and particularly one carrying the poem. The assassin was not much help. He told them he had never seen a Hearst paper and seemed to be uncertain just who Hearst was, which the publisher would not have found flattering. But his rivals were not discouraged. They published stories (recalling Garfield) that a copy of the *Journal* had been found stuffed in the assassin's coat pocket, a most unlikely circumstance. These rivals did not understand Hearst. His papers were sensational, but he himself was not a sensationalist. A cool and calculating man, he would no more have advocated shooting a president, even by inference, then blowing up the *Maine.* He did not want to shoot presidents, only to convert what they did into circulation.

Bierce himself wrote later of his damning poem:

The lines took no attention, naturally, but twenty months afterward the President was shot. Everyone remembers what happened then to Mr. Hearst and his newspapers. His political enemies and business competitors were alert to their opportunity. The verses, variously garbled but mostly made into an editorial, or a news dispatch with a Washington dateline but usually no date, were published all over the country as evidence of Mr. Hearst's complicity in the crime. As such they adorned the editorial columns of the New York *Sun* and blazed upon a billboard in front of Tammany Hall. . . . There was even an attempt made to induce Czolgosz to testify that he had been incited in his crime by reading them [the Hearst papers]—ten thousand dollars for his family to be his reward, but this cheerful scheme was blocked by the trial judge who had been informed of it. During all this carnival of sin I lay ill in Washington, unaware of it, and my name, although appended to all that I wrote, including the verses, was not, I am told, once mentioned. As to Mr. Hearst, I dare say he first saw the lines when all this hullabaloo directed his attention to them.

Bierce could not resist tempering this generous estimate with the thought that Hearst's newspapers had "always been so unjust that no injustice could be done to them, and had been incredibly rancorous toward McKinley, but no doubt it was my luckless prophecy that cost him tens of thousands of dollars and a growing political prestige."

As Bierce said, Hearst had indeed been "incredibly rancorous toward McKinley," particularly during the campaign, where the excuse was partisanship because the publisher was president of a national association that included several thousand Democratic clubs, which put him in the position of controlling a substantial bloc of political power. He had appeared for the first time as a public speaker before the national convention of this association in Indianapolis. The attacks he made on McKinley in his papers were characterized by an arrogance and virulence reminiscent of the worst excesses in the old days. Editorials by Arthur Brisbane and himself, supplemented by Homer Davenport's biting cartoons, were aimed at both McKinley and Hanna.

In Thomas Beer's memorable description of these assaults,

> Marcus Alonzo Hanna [was] revealed in all the newspapers owned by William Randolph Hearst as an amalgam of all sins. He was foulness compact. He was the red boss of Cleveland's city politics. The town council trembled when he sent minions to address it. He had stolen a theatre from poor John Ellsler, foreclosing a cruel mortgage and rejecting the man's plea for time. He ruled Cleveland from his office, terrorizing unions and running rival street railways. He sent poor sailors, forced on his ships by bestial labor masters, out to sea on the wintry lakes, cold and starving, unpaid and mutinous.

No doubt there were some elements of truth in these accusations, but considerably less in the depiction of McKinley as twice the monster Hanna was supposed to be. Even Hearst was somewhat taken aback by one editorial (probably written by Arthur McEwan, one of his more excitable editors) which suggested that, if shooting were the only way to get rid of bad men, then shooting might be justified.

All these attacks were revived in public memory by Hearst's rivals in politics and business in the wake of the president's death. Other publishers, echoed by Republican politicians, labeled Hearst as "a teacher of anarchists." He was hanged in effigy across the country, while his papers were banned from clubs, libraries, and newsstands. A gun lay always on his desk, and his mail was frisked for bombs. Nothing like it had been seen since Lincoln's assassination. It did him no good to point out, with some justice, that his papers had been far from the first, or even the worst among them, to attack presidents, including McKinley. The *Sun,* he recalled, had gone on vituperating against Grant and Garfield long after they were dead and buried. The *Evening Post,* which had taken a hostile view of Hearst from the beginning, had itself referred to McKinley as "a liar, a renegade, a traitor," the *Journal*'s publisher reminded his enemies, and during Cleveland's time had been among those to brand him as the father of an illegitimate child.

No one was listening. Hearst, in the end, departed from trying to reason and returned to his natural mode, defiance—unregenerate, unashamed, admitting nothing, denying everything. In an editorial he wrote: "All the enemies of the people, of the democratic people conscious and unconscious—all who reap where others have sown, all the rascals and their organs, and many fools caught by the malignant uproar, are yelling at the *Journal*. LET THEM YELL." Fortunately for Hearst, the explosive advent of Theodore Roosevelt made the public forget to be angry at him for the old reasons. There were always new ones, however, as time went on.

McKinley's death was as much the end of an era as the century that had just closed. Twentieth-century America was to be a different kind of country in nearly every way. As William Allen White pointed out later, McKinley was the last of the old order, "the last President to stand apart from the people, pedestaled, shielded from publicity." After him relations between press and president would never be what they had been. The imperial presidency was at hand.

PART FIVE

The Imperial Presidency

The First Roosevelt: Laying the Foundations

With the coming of Theodore Roosevelt, the foundations were well laid for what is popularly called "the imperial Presidency," a phrase that came into general currency with the publication of Arthur Schlesinger, Jr.'s book of the same name in 1973. It is important, however, to define it here in the context of this study. Schlesinger was concerned with the rising supremacy of the president in both foreign and domestic affairs, particularly his war-making powers, an issue we are still debating. Here we will be dealing with only one aspect of presidential imperialism—the ability that White House occupants have slowly acquired in this century to manipulate and control the media, with the intent of making them as much as possible an arm of government.

Admittedly, it is a thesis for which there is not a great deal of sympathy or agreement extant. Presidents believe that it is the media which hold the power and use it to distort and sabotage what the White House is trying to do; the adversary relationship that began with George Washington continues unabated. This position of hostility toward the media is also held predominantly by the business community, by much of the judiciary, and by an overwhelming majority of the general public, which ranks the press near the bottom of American institutions liked and trusted.

This is a view constantly reinforced by the media criticism industry, which now supports several magazines devoted to the purpose, provides jobs for people who are themselves working for the media, and is a source of promotions and higher pay among academics in journalism, political science, and sociology faculties who, often helped along by grants and other assistance, have created a vast literature of media studies, nearly all of it negative. The literature supporting or defending the media would not fill a ten-foot shelf. A corollary of all this is the Mea Culpa Syndrome prevalent among those media people who would rather be liked than right.

The president-press relationship is only one aspect of this phenomenon of our time, but it is a highly important one because presidents have learned how to use the massive power of the media, particularly television, to influence the way people think about not only themselves and their administrations but how the public views the media as well. It can be, and is, a dangerous use of presidential imperial power—dangerous in the sense of its threat to the functioning of a free press in a democratic society.

How did this situation come about? As we have seen, the nineteenth century was characterized by a general level of mediocrity among the presidents and a high degree of control of them by the major political parties. For the press it was a time when its manipulation by these parties slowly diminished, as strong publishers rose to challenge political leaders and assert their independence. It was a time, too, when the level of competence in the press began to rise toward the end of the century, and a degree of professionalism was introduced that resulted in a somewhat more accurate, more fair, and more responsible presentation of political and other news. There were, of course, setbacks occasioned by the sensationalism of Pulitzer and Hearst, and certainly the levels being attained by the major metropolitan papers at the end of the century were far from matched by the smaller dailies and weeklies. But it was these major papers that increasingly maintained correspondents in Washington and threatened presidents with their new independence and still rudimentary professionalism.

At the turn of the century, however, Washington coverage was a relatively small operation for both newspapers and magazines. True, the numbers had risen considerably from the time of James Madison, when there were only four correspondents in Washington. Press galleries had been established in the Senate and House in 1823, for the benefit of only a dozen reporters, but their number began to climb sharply after the Civil War. There were 58 correspondents in Washington in 1868, and 171 by 1900. Still, it continued to be a slow rise: 209 in 1920, 251 a decade later. The explosion occurred in more recent times, most of it since 1945, and it has been all but incredible. In 1982, as James Deakin pointed out in a recent perceptive memoir, using figures supplied by press gallery officials, there were 4,300 accredited members, and since there are a great many other free-lance journalists and writers who either do not qualify or have no need for accreditation, the estimate is that there are about 10,000 media people in Washington.

The breadth of this growth is remarkable in itself, as Deakin observes. Television has accounted for a large percentage of it, but the corresponding multiplying of specialized magazines (and some newspapers) in a variety of fields, all of them representing readerships with a substantial interest in what Washington does, has resulted in an astonishing proliferation of reporters assigned to the capital. Besides the original Senate and House press galleries, to which only newspaper and wire services may be accredited, there are now five others—those for radio and television, and for the periodical press, in both Senate and House, and the press photographers' gallery in the Senate. There were as many as 1,700 journalists with press passes to the White House in 1982, but only a small number of them covered the president regularly. The full-time White House correspondents are still a relatively small and select company.

Here is media power indeed, numerically speaking, as its enemies often assert, but even in the relatively much smaller world of Theodore Roosevelt, when the White House had comparatively no more than a corporal's guard to contend with, it was obvious to the president, and to at least some of his more immediate successors, that the press was much more of a force to be reckoned with than it had been in the previous century. Not only was there a continuing rise in independence and professionalism, but the media as a whole (newspapers, magazines, and book publishing) were proliferating at a rapid rate. A whole new category of periodical, the ten-cent magazine, had sprung up suddenly in the 1890s and had become a more potent force in investigative journalism than the newspapers. For the first time, too, it was possible for a book to sell more than a million hardcover copies. The twentieth century was here with a vengeance.

As for the newspaper press that the first Roosevelt dealt with so successfully, it was undergoing a radical change in its basic structure. In the nineteenth century it had been the product of individual entrepreneurs, financed at first largely through political contributions, but then more and more through circulation as James Gordon Bennett and the post–Civil War publishers found that a newspaper could live and prosper and make them rich from circulation alone, with only a minimum amount of advertising.

Then came a second discovery—that high circulations could attract advertising and thus make a newspaper even richer. It was not long before advertising became more important than circulation, as the first agencies were organized and as the continued rise of business and industry made more and more products available. Consequently newspapers, drawing their profits primarily from capitalist institutions, became business enterprises themselves in a way they had not been before. With that, the inevitable sharpening of competition for circulation occurred, and the consequent equally inevitable consolidation as weaker papers suffocated in this economic climate. It was the beginning of a slow shrinkage of the metropolitan press that has not yet ended, and also the rise of chain journalism, which Hearst had pioneered.

Correspondents in Washington during the Roosevelt administration were not representing some strong-minded publisher like Dana, or Greeley, or Bennett, Sr., men deeply involved in politics, using whatever influence they possessed for political ends. Pulitzer was still very much alive, of course, but so ill that control of the *World* was gradually passing into able but less spectacular hands. Otherwise publishers were already on the way to becoming businessmen who would soon, with a few exceptions, be as little known to the public as their nineteenth-century predecessors had been national figures. It was an ideal situation for a strong president like Roosevelt to exploit, and he took full advantage of it. Sometimes it seemed (to him as well as others) that only Pulitzer and the *World* stood in the way of his total domination of the press. What the daily newspapers were beginning to lose was their intellectual force and leadership, as Allan Nevins has reminded us, and these qualities were passing at least in part to the weekly opinion journals—William Jennings Bryan's *Commoner,* founded in 1900, almost alone at first, to be followed by *La Follette's Magazine, Solidarity,* and others, including the *Nation* and the *New Republic,* which became the leaders in the field.

As a result of the decline of major figures among publishers, and the consequent loss of leadership, the newspapers Roosevelt confronted were, by and large across the nation, lacking in aggressive opinion makers of the kind that had so dominated the scene in the nineteenth century. The remaining leaders stood out like lighthouses on the national landscape—the *World* in New York, the *Post-Dispatch* in St. Louis, the *World-Herald* in Omaha, the Fresno *Republican*, and Fremont Older's San Francisco *Bulletin,* not forgetting, in its own special category, the *Christian Science Monitor* in Boston. There were a few others, like the Louisville *Courier-Journal,* the Atlanta *Constitution,* the Hartford *Courant,* the Boston *Evening Transcript,* and the Providence *Journal,* but most of the press did not carry much political or intellectual weight in the early part of the new century.

Theodore Roosevelt came upon this scene like the proverbial thunderbolt, and in eight years he transformed the relationship between the press and the presidency. His possible coming had been feared by his political enemies, as we have seen, but not even they could have predicted the tremendous impact his overwhelming, ubiquitous personality would have on Washington and the national scene. He was such a complex man and his influence was so varied that scholars and popular historians alike are still analyzing and writing about him today with great interest.

The period of political and intellectual upheaval that Roosevelt and Woodrow Wilson presided over had long been labeled in the textbooks and elsewhere as the Progressive Era, but in the 1970s scholars fell out over what "progressivism" was or even if it actually existed, and today the attempt to track down and fully identify this elusive animal has fragmented, like so many other areas of historical study, into a dozen different pursuits. Nor is there complete agreement about Roosevelt's standing among the presidents. In four pollings of historians from 1948 to 1982 he is ranked once among the "great," although fourth after Lincoln, and among the "near great" in the other three, but yielding first place in that category to Jackson in one of them.

There is no doubt, however, about what Roosevelt did when he got to the White House. He consolidated and established the power and authority of the presidency as it had never been done before, and he manipulated the media with an unprecedented skill to promote himself and his causes. He became the first president to shape public opinion, and he did it with a master hand, using the newspapers like a poker player.

Several circumstances made it easier for him. For one, the Associated Press and the United Press Association (it became "Associations" in 1907) were distributing news on a national basis by this time, and, since they served both Republican and Democratic papers, their reports had to be politically neutral, providing ideal channels for Roosevelt's shrewd interpretations of neutrality and giving him access to a broad range of papers. Moreover the most partisan of the partisan publishers of the past were now all dead, except for Pulitzer, and their successors wanted the news from Washington to be reported more objectively. Again that fact provided additional protection for the president, and at the same time gave him another avenue for his cleverly contrived versions of "objectivity."

There were some compensating factors, however. Washington correspondents might be shamelessly and effectively manipulated, but at the same time they now had acquired some of the independence and power once concentrated in publishers. The adversary relationship was not completely eclipsed by the Roosevelt personality. But what a formidable opponent he was! As one modern Washington reporter, Richard Rovere, has summed it up, Roosevelt "enjoyed the company of poets, read Dante in Renaissance Italian, could rattle off long passages in French from the *Chanson de Roland,* made a special study of Rumanian literature, and, while President of the United States, was also honorary president of the Gaelic Literature Association."

Moreover Roosevelt was a far more accomplished writer than the correspondents who were covering him, with only a few possible exceptions. Before he died he wrote thirty-eight books, encompassing history, natural history, biography, political philosophy, and casual essays. Qualified historians of the time believed that his *Naval War of 1812* and four-volume *Winning of the West* were definitive, a verdict altered by time and further scholarly research. The British historian George Trevelyan even compared him, extravagantly, with Thomas Babington Macaulay.

Roosevelt was a prodigious reader of newspapers, magazines, and books, happily admitting that "reading with me is a disease." Like any ardent booklover, he read everywhere and anywhere—on the presidential yacht, no matter how foul the weather; on his campaign trips between stops; in bed at night; even while waiting for his carriage to be brought around. Busy as he might be, he got through at least one book every day. Owen Wister, the novelist, staying overnight at the White House for an evening's entertainment, gave the president a book just before the performance and, having breakfast with him the following morning, was astounded to hear Roosevelt give him a full review of it. As Wister wrote later, still amazed, "Somewhere between six one evening and eight-thirty next morning, besides his dressing and his dinner and his guests and his sleep, he read a volume of three-hundred-and-odd pages, and missed nothing of significance that it contained."

By contrast the Washington correspondents who greeted the new president in 1901 were, with such notable exceptions as Lincoln Steffens (not a regular) and a few others, not far removed from the police, city hall, or state legislative beats. They had learned about politicians the hard way and had no high opinion of their general integrity. About Roosevelt they could not fail to have opinions and convictions, good or bad, since his rise to power had been highly visible, marked along the way by a usage of the press that clearly foreshadowed what was to come. In those earlier years, too, Roosevelt had formed his own conception of the press, which was not much different from those of all the presidents who had preceded him and experienced the unbridled attacks of partisan newspapers.

In fact, Roosevelt's first appearance in the New York State Assembly in 1882 attracted the immediate attention of reporters, particularly those from the opposition Democratic papers. As David McCullough, one of his recent biographers, tells it:

> The new gold rimmed spectacles and their fluttering black ribbon, his gold watch fob, the part in his hair, the narrow cut of his clothes, made him known at once. For reporters for the *Sun,* the *World,* and other Democratic papers, he was the fairest kind of game and they went right after him. He was called a "Jane Dandy," "his Lordship," "weakling," "silly," "Oscar Wilde," "the exquisite Mr. Roosevelt," "little man," the fun always at his expense. The *World* reported that his trousers were cut so tight that when making his "gyration" before an audience, "he only bent the joints above the belt."

These ponderous estimates were about as far as possible from Roosevelt's real character and the image he would ultimately project, but they undoubtedly wounded him and began to condition his attitudes toward the press. Not all the reporters in Albany were so unperceptive, however. William Hudson of the Brooklyn *Eagle* saw through the outer appearance to the man inside, and even more so did George Spinney, legislative correspondent of the New York *Times,* who soon became a friend and one of his chief chroniclers. Others began to revise their initial opinions after they heard the new assemblyman deliver his first speech, which "made a very favorable impression," the New York *Evening Post* correspondent had to admit.

In a characteristic burst of whirlwind energy, Assemblyman Roosevelt then introduced four bills within forty-eight hours after his appointment to a committee, all of them aimed at privileges cherished by machine politicians. Almost overnight he created his own image, as the scourge of these entrenched bosses and their presumed overlords, the big-money Wall Street crowd, led by Jay Gould. That won Roosevelt applause and support from some of his fellow assemblymen, as well as from the press.

Soon after, Roosevelt endeared himself even to those reporters who had made fun of him by supporting a motion to kill a bill that would have amended the penal code by permitting publishers and editors to be sued for libel in any place in the state where their newspapers were circulated. "Taking it for granted that this is a bill for gagging the newspapers," he said, "I trust that the motion will prevail. I think that if there is one thing we ought to be careful about it is in regard to interfering with the liberty of the press. I think it is a great deal better to err a little bit on the side of having too much discussion and having too virulent language used by the press, rather than to err on the side of having them not say what they ought to say, especially with reference to public men and measures."

It was a noble Jeffersonian sentiment, and no doubt Roosevelt was sincere about it at the time, but nonetheless it was hardly consistent with the man who filed the most celebrated libel suit in presidential history and who did not hesitate to advocate suppression if he thought his own exalted ideas of patriotism were threatened. Roosevelt's outspoken condemnation of the penal code change, however, convinced his fellow legislators, who voted against the bill without a division, and quite naturally it pleased the press. (It may be noted that in 1984 the United States Supreme Court, in a jurisdictional decision, ruled that authors of alleged libelous statements could be sued in every state where a publication was circulated.)

Roosevelt's whirlwind progress through the Assembly was enough to establish him as a public figure. Already the press, and particularly the cartoonists, were making him well known and defining his public personality. As an earlier historian, Joseph B. Bishop, described their work:

> One of them represented him with a huge pair of scissors clipping the claws of the Tammany Tiger; another as Ajax defying the corrupt influences behind police corruption; another as a woodman cutting down a huge tree of municipal graft and rascality; another represented him garbed as a policeman, entitled "Our New Watchman, Roosevelt," in the act of dismissing the political bosses. When Grover Cleveland signed the Roosevelt bills, Nast published a cartoon, representing the Assemblyman standing with the bills before the Governor, who was seated at his desk, pen in hand, in the act of signing. This was captioned, "Reform Without Bloodshed."

Theodore Roosevelt had seized the historical moment, as so often happens in the flow of events. He came on stage when voters were increasingly suspicious of the Republican party, presumed to be in the hands of Jay Gould and his friends. Here now to fight these malefactors of great wealth was a new Champion of the People, incorruptible and passionate in defending the public against machine politicians, predatory big business, and corrupt judges. And he was a Republican, at that.

The headlines in the very papers that had initially maligned Roosevelt proclaimed his arrival. One of them, the pre-Pulitzer *World,* which Jay Gould had bought in 1879 as part of a highly questionable railroad deal, continued to lampoon the assemblyman at every opportunity, but the public in general applauded when Roosevelt denounced the paper as "a local, stock-jobbing sheet of limited circulation and versatile mendacity, owned by the arch thief of Wall Street and edited by a rancorous kleptomaniac with a penchant for trousers."

Already the most adroit of politicians, Roosevelt could thread his way through a minefield of controversy, as he demonstrated when Governor Cleveland vetoed the so-called five-cent bill, reducing the fare on the Manhattan Elevated Railroad (owned by Gould) from ten cents to five, a principled and courageous action described in an earlier chapter. Roosevelt had supported this popular bill, which swept through both branches of the legislature by large majorities, but, when Cleveland declared that it was unconstitutional and vetoed it, Assemblyman Roosevelt was the first to support him. He, too, questioned whether the bill was constitutional and won himself further applause from a portion of press and public with his assertion that "the State must not only be strictly just, but scrupulously fair," at the same time being careful to denounce once more the railway's owners as "common thieves. . . . They belong to that most dangerous of all classes, the wealthy criminal class."

It was a phrase that rolled across the front pages of the nation, sounding gratefully in the ears of millions victimized by the excesses of the new industrialism. It was one of the first Rooseveltian phrases to lodge itself in the national consciousness, an early demonstration of his ability to shape public opinion. Yet Roosevelt's speech supporting the veto, probably the best he ever made while he was in Albany, was lashed with bitter scorn by newspapers on both sides of the political fence—"weakling," "hoodlum," "bogus reformer," he was called— in the mistaken belief that the public cared more about having five cents knocked off the elevated fare than having honest politicians. But there were many voters who appreciated their favorite assemblyman's peroration: "We have heard a great deal about the people demanding the passage of this bill. Now anything the people demand that is *right* it is most clearly and most emphatically the duty of this legislature to do; but we should never yield to what they demand if it is wrong. . . . I would rather go out of politics having the feeling that I had done what was right than stay in with the approval of all men, knowing in my heart that I have acted as I ought not to."

Much of the press missed the point. The former Champion of the People was reduced to being an object of ridicule again in many papers, particularly the Democratic journals. One even intimated that, as a scion of wealth himself, Roosevelt might also be a member of that "wealthy criminal class." He was pictured as a slightly ridiculous snob, and in the *World,* which showed no gratitude for his help in preventing the owner's transit income from being reduced, he was attacked with a particularly low blow: "The friends who have so long deplored the untimely death of Theodore Roosevelt (Senior) cannot but be thankful that he has been spared the pain of a spectacle which would have wounded to the quick his gracious and honorable nature."

Roosevelt survived this wave of assaults easily. He knew the public thought better of him, and by the time he left Albany for the first time he had regained the respect, even admiration, of most newspapers. A prime factor in this conversion was his personal investigation of an incident involving Jay Gould and that financier's acquisition of the Manhattan Elevated Railraod, a deal presided over by Judge Westbrook. The New York *Times* had run a story about this event, questioning the court approval and accusing the financier of trying to depress the railroad's stock before he bought it. Roosevelt, aroused, went directly to the *Times,* talked to Henry Loewenthal, the city editor, and got permission to look at documents the paper had in its possession, after which he and Loewenthal went back to the Roosevelt house at 6 West Fifty-seventh Street and went over the papers meticulously until three o'clock in the morning. Particularly incriminating was a letter the judge had written to Gould, declaring, "I am willing to go to the very verge of judicial discretion to protect your vast interests." It appeared that Judge Westbrook had not gone only to the verge but slightly over it.

Returning to Albany, Roosevelt drafted a resolution calling for an inquiry, which was duly passed. The majority report of the investigators insisted that there had been no wrongdoing, but for Roosevelt it did not matter; his reputation had been made. In the New York *Evening Post* he was hailed as a man who had "accomplished more good than any man of his age and experience had accomplished in years,'' and later there was a dinner in his honor at Delmonico's, at which the triumphant assemblyman served up a plate of assorted bromides.

Roosevelt's immediate reward was to become minority leader in the Assembly, almost unprecedented for so young a politician. Only Democratic control of the Assembly prevented him from being Speaker. But it was a short-lived triumph. After the death of his mother and his wife—on the same day, February 14, 1884—Roosevelt declined to run for another term and went west for a while. In 1889 he accepted an appointment as civil service commissioner, a post in which he had ample opportunity to exercise his zeal for reform. It would have been too much to expect that he could wholly cleanse this corrupt body of bureaucrats, but Roosevelt was successful in making a solid start and pointing the Civil Service toward a more progressive future. In the process he toured the country, making speeches to gain public support, writing voluminous letters to newspapers and responding to attacks, with the result that he won a great many new friends among both press and public. Cleveland kept him on when he became president, but Roosevelt resigned in May 1895 to be a police commissioner of New York.

While Roosevelt was still on the Civil Service Commission, however, he was involved in a confrontation with a reporter that recalled the old days in journalism. Frank Hatton, a writer for the Washington *Post,* assailed him almost daily in terms more violent than he had yet encountered. On the morning after a particularly vicious Hatton article appeared, a friend discovered Roosevelt pacing up and down in front of the newspaper's office, in a state of grim rage. "What are you doing here?" the friend inquired apprehensively. "I'm looking for a [expletive deleted]," Roosevelt told him. "And I'm going to punch his head!" The friend succeeded in averting bloodshed.

Roosevelt transferred his ebullient enthusiasm intact from the Civil Service to the New York Police Department. His first day in the job as commissioner he fairly exploded on the scene, as Lincoln Steffens, then covering the police beat for the *Evening Post,* recalled in his autobiography. Steffens and Jacob Riis, who was the *Evening Sun's* man on the beat, heard the news of Roosevelt's arrival in the press room, and about an hour later Roosevelt came walking down the street with three other men. As Steffens tells it:

> I said that they walked. I mean that they came on foot; and three of them did walk, but T.R. ran. He came ahead down the street; he yelled, "Hello, Jake," to Riis, and running up the stairs to the front door of police headquarters, he waved us reporters to follow. We did. With the police officials standing around watching, the new board went up to the second story, where the old commissioners were waiting in their offices. T.R. seized Riis, who introduced me, and still running, he asked questions: "Where are our offices? Where is the board room? What do we do first?" Out of the half-heard answers he gathered the way to the board room, where the old commissioners waited, like three of the new commissioners, stiff, formal, and dignified. Not T.R. He introduced himself, his colleagues, with hand-shakes, then called a meeting of the new board; had himself elected president—this had been prearranged—and then adjourned to pull Riis and me with him into his office.
>
> "Now, then, what'll we do?"

It was all breathless and sudden, but Riis and I were soon describing the situation to him, telling him which higher officers to consult, which to ignore and punish, what the forms were, the customs, rules, methods. It was just as if we three were the police board, T.R., Riis, and I, and as we got T.R. calmed down we made him promise to go a bit slow, to consult with his colleagues also. Then we went out into the hall, and there stood the three other commissioners together, waiting for us to go so that they could see T.R.

Riis, at forty-six, was then one of the city's most notable reporters, whose greatest fame as a muckraker, like Steffens's, was still to come, although his subsequently famous *How the Other Half Lives* had been published five years earlier and had engaged Roosevelt's favorable attention. Steffens, at twenty-nine, was a newspaperman whose notable career as a muckraker also lay ahead, but already he was a "vain, arrogant, selfishly ambitious" young man, as one historian describes him, although it may be doubted that he had "the beady eye of a born investigative reporter," a genus whose eyes are often indistinguishable from those of rewrite men.

Roosevelt's impact on his department as police commissioner can be measured by these newspaper headlines during his first ten days in office:

REIGN OF TERROR AT POLICE HEADQUARTERS
Merit Wins Promotion Now—
Political Pulls Frowned Upon

*   *   *

RATTLED—THE DRY OLD POLICE BONES
Kick the Politicians; Lecture the Legislature
Snub the Roundsmen, Warn the Drunken Bluecoats
Abolish the Police Parades, & Stir Up Departmental Surgeons

*   *   *

ROOSEVELT AS JUDGE
The Reform Commissioner Tries Nearly 100 Policemen in One Day
"Pulls" Found Worthless Before the Inquisitor with Big Teeth and Rasping Voice

"A subhead in the *World*," Edmund Morris wrote, "summed up the new commissioner's policy in these words: Publicity, publicity, publicity. He seemed determined to expose to general scrutiny every aspect of his department's work, from transcripts of board meetings to dossiers on the moral fitness of officers for promotion. His habit of inviting reporters to spend the day in his big, bare office made it difficult for the representatives of political organizations to have private speech with him."

Later, in Albany as governor, Roosevelt established the same kind of easygoing relationship with the press—easygoing, that is, except for those who displeased him. Morris has given us a vivid account of how he dealt with the journalists there, foreshadowing the presidency:

Twice daily, without fail, when he was in Albany, he would summon reporters into his office for 15 minutes of questions and answers—mostly the latter, because his loquacity seemed untrammeled by any political scruples. Relaxed as a child, he would perch on the edge of his huge desk, often with a leg tucked under him, and pour forth confidences, anecdotes, jokes, and legislative gossip. When required to make a formal statement, he spoke with deliberate precision, punctuating every phrase with his own dentifical sound-effects; the performance was rather like that of an Edison cylinder played at slow speed and maximum volume. Relaxing again, he would confess the truth behind the statement, with such gleeful frankness that the reporters felt flattered to be included in his conspiracy. It was understood that none of these gubernatorial indiscretions were for publication, on pain of instant banishment from the Executive Office.

It was this kind of style that Roosevelt brought to his president-press relations, and clearly it was like nothing that had been seen before at that level. Veteran reporters were familiar with such relationships on the city hall beat, or with other public officials on the lower echelons, but to see it in the governor's mansion, and later in the White House, took some mental adjustments both to accommodate it and to restore a little normality.

Between the police commissioner's office and the White House there were only a few more stops, and at every one of them Roosevelt made the most of his opportunities to establish his unique relationship with the press, in one way or another. As assistant secretary of the navy he delivered an opening address at the War College that he wrote personally, as he always did, a novelty in itself. Published in full across the country, it sent forth a clarion Rooseveltian call that everyone recognized. Here was a unique voice, stirring and confident, lifting party politics out of the usual mire. Even papers like the New York *Sun,* which had never been much more than lukewarm toward Roosevelt, if that, praised his words, as did such an outright enemy as the Washington *Post.*

Roosevelt spent only a year as assistant secretary, but he took full advantage of the fact that Secretary John D. Long, an indifferent holder of the office who was often away from it, had delegated much authority to him. The energetic assistant not only argued the case for greater naval power in every possible forum but labored to prepare a battle fleet for the war with Spain he confidently expected, even hoped, would occur. Like a small boy Roosevelt wrote to a friend: "The Secretary is away, and I am having immense fun running the Navy."

Roosevelt found time to add another heavy editorial gun to his arsenal. Not yet thirty years old, William Allen White had leaped into the national spotlight suddenly in 1896 with his anti-Populist editorial, "What's the Matter with Kansas?" printed in his Emporia *Gazette,* thereby becoming a kind of Republican Bryan. Roosevelt shrewdly estimated that White would be an effective voice in Republican politics, as indeed he did become, and set out to annex him as a valuable salesman for Rooseveltian expansionism. It was an easier annexation than those others the new imperialism contemplated. After their first meeting White confessed later, "I was his man." The *Gazette* was a small-town paper, but it had a national following.

In the Spanish-American War, as we have seen, Roosevelt became a hero and an object of near-adoration in the press. There was only that nagging sour note at San Juan Hill, noted earlier—the story written by the *World*'s Stephen Crane, which gave credit where it was due but reported truthfully that Colonel Roosevelt's haphazard regiment of Rough Riders—who, after all, were an extemporaneous unit, and not regulars—momentarily panicked under fire. As we have noted, the furious colonel who read this story would not forget Joseph Pulitzer, the publisher who printed it.

After San Juan Hill the road to the governor's mansion in Albany was clear, and it was there that Roosevelt honed down and perfected the unique personal style he would bring to the presidency, into which McKinley's death abruptly catapulted him. It was only a question of time in any case; he was a man meant for the White House, if anyone ever was.

Thus, trailing clouds of glory, Theodore Roosevelt came to his natural destination, at forty-two the youngest president ever to achieve the office, the first ever to be a native-born big-city boy, and the first rich man's son since William Henry Harrison. David McCullough sums him up succinctly: "He was a well-to-do, aristocratic, big-city, Harvard-educated Republican with ancestral roots in the Deep South and a passionate following in the West, which taken all together made him something quite new under the sun."

Just *how* new, viewed against the background of all those who had preceded him, is evident in Lincoln Steffens's account of those first days in Washington:

> I went to Washington to see him; many reformers went there to see the first reformer president take charge. . . . And he understood, he shared, our joy. He was not yet living in the White House. He used the offices, which were then in the main building, upstairs on the second floor; he worked there by day, but he had to go home at night to his own residence till the McKinleys were moved out and the White House was made ready for Mrs. Roosevelt. His offices were crowded with people, mostly reformers, all day long, and the president did his work among them with little privacy and much rejoicing. He strode triumphant around among us, talking and shaking hands, dictating and signing letters, and laughing. Washington, the whole country, was in mourning, and no doubt the President felt that he should hold himself down; he didn't; he tried to, but his joy showed in every word and movement. I think that he thought he was suppressing his feelings and yearned for release, which he seized when he could.
>
> One evening after dusk, when it was time for him to go home, he grabbed William Allen White with one hand, me with the other, and saying, "Let's get out of this," he propelled us out of the White House into the streets, where, for an hour or more, he allowed his gladness to explode. With his feet, his fists, his face and with free words he laughed at his luck. He laughed at the rage of Boss Platt and at the tragic disappointment of Mark Hanna; these two had not only lost their President McKinley but had been given as a substitute the man they had thought to bury in the vice-presidency. T.R. helped at their downfall. And he laughed with glee at the power and place that had come to him.

Some historians have doubted this story because White neglected to mention it in *his* autobiography, but it has the ring of authenticity, and Steffens had no reason to enhance the tale, much less invent it, as his overpowering ego sometimes impelled him to do on other occasions. Curiously Roosevelt himself was much like Steffens in this respect. "He was not consciously a liar," Henry Pringle observes. "That he stated facts incorrectly is beyond refutation, but egoism and not mendacity was the motivation."

As he contemplated the coming exercise of his power, Roosevelt well understood the basic political axiom. A leader as strong as he meant to be must have the country solidly behind him. How to get that support had always been a problem. If there was not some national emergency to unite the country, people had to be persuaded to follow a president. Earlier presidents had used an administration paper as their chief vehicle of persuasion, and later they had been able to push for domestic reforms with the help of influential editors and their newspapers. Obviously the press was the vehicle he must use, but it was now rich and independent, a few of its owners having reached that level of predatory wealth upon which Roosevelt had heaped his reformist scorn. How could a president employ such papers and their publishers to advance his causes?

Roosevelt was as confident about his ability to do this as he was about everything else. Newspapers might be money institutions, and their political correspondents become news gatherers rather than the partisan advocates they had once been, but they were vitally interested in the news, as always, and in the people (especially presidents) who made the news. Washington and the White House were where all these demands came together, and Roosevelt meant to satisfy them as no other chief executive had done before him. If public relations is the art (or science, as some of its practitioners insist) of persuading public opinion, Roosevelt would soon qualify as the first public relations man, four years before Ivy Lee. What Roosevelt initiated is today a meticulously polished instrument that dominates the presidency, but most of its present practices were anticipated by Roosevelt, and, even without the help of television and radio, his use of the media was as skillfully effective as that of any subsequent president.

George Juergens, whose study of White House press relations in the so-called Progressive Era is the best detailed analysis we have, summarizes admirably the insights Theodore Roosevelt brought to his task:

> To begin with, he assumed that the news that appears in a daily paper, and the way it is presented, does far more to mold public opinion than editorials. If he could seize the headlines and influence the way reporters wrote about him, it would not matter a great deal what the press might have to say about him on its inside pages. From this followed the further insight that the definition of news as a daily chronicle of official activity was much too passive and limiting in its implications. With any sort of imagination a modern president could generate news on demand to insure continued domination of the front page. And the more he did so, monopolizing public attention, the more he established his credentials as national leader, which in turn made it easier to keep on generating news about himself. His final insight was that a strong president must not only make news, he must pay close attention to how the news is disseminated. There are different ways to release information to the press. Roosevelt understood that using the correct technique in different circumstances could have a major bearing on the amount and kind of coverage he received. Indeed, handled

adroitly, news could be his most telling weapon in the struggle for specific political goals.

The techniques Roosevelt used may seem elementary today, but they are still standard equipment in the White House, although refined to a remarkable degree. One was to create headlines where none had previously existed. Presidents today know how to do this superlatively, which partly explains their outrage when the headlines result from something they did *not* originate. Roosevelt also pioneered the familiar devices of releasing bad news on Friday afternoons, relying on the relatively low readership of Saturday papers, and securing extra attention and readership by putting out news on Sunday, usually a dull news day, which would be seized upon by editors to beef up their thin Monday papers.

Roosevelt's incessant moving about from one thing to another only served to reinforce his impact on press and public by virtue of sheer quantity and variety. As Mark Sullivan puts it: "To the headlines and news dispatches that he especially devised and timed for the direct purpose of promoting the matter he had in hand were added the dispatches that arose spontaneously from his multifarious collateral activities, the investigations he ordered, the indictments he incited, the prosecutions he pursued, the denunciations he uttered."

One of the president's chief assets in this new and extraordinary relationship was his knowledge of newspapers and newspapermen, built up through many contacts while he was rising to power. Other presidents, as we have seen, had made these connections, too, but never to the extent Roosevelt had achieved, largely by virtue of his personality and incredible energy. But he went much beyond even this valuable attribute because of his equally detailed knowledge of the magazine business, which was on the eve of becoming a potent political factor as he came into office. One historian, Elmer E. Cornwell, has summarized the extent of his knowledge:

> He made it a point to get acquainted with magazine staffs, knew traits and biases, and, it is said, even knew the ins and outs of office politics as he knew the internal frictions of party committees. He did not hesitate to both praise and disagree with things he read, or explain his policies in detail, by letters to the editor. Partly by inspiring articles by intimates, and partly through the sheer magnetic attraction of his personality and ideas, he kept the pages of the popular magazines glowing with support of his crusades.

While it was easy for Roosevelt to exploit the establishment magazines, the new genre that had suddenly appeared was a different matter, presenting him with some perplexing and ultimately embarrassing problems. These were the muckraking magazines. The coming of those ubiquitous ten-cent periodicals has been well described by Louis Filler, their chief chronicler:

> Suddenly there appeared in certain magazines a new, moral, radical type of writing by men and women who yesterday had been entirely unknown or had written less disturbingly. These writers savagely exposed grafting politicians, criminal police, tenement eyesores. They openly attacked the Church. They defended labor in dis-

putes which in no way concerned them personally, decried child exploitation, wrote
pro-suffragist articles, and described great businesses as soulless and anti-social.
These writers, using the most sordid details to make their points, shocked and bewildered the conservative reader.

They also stimulated and excited a wide mass audience, accustomed to reading
magazines (although the blue-collar class was a very small part of that readership) for entertainment or education. The muckrakers made business and politics, and the corruption in both, seem as exciting as a novel. These were
reformers who went far beyond Roosevelt.

Why, then, did the president, whose whole career had been based on his zeal
for reform as the Champion of the People, view this development with dismay as
time went on? Though several of the muckrakers, such as Steffens and Ray
Stannard Baker, were his friends, most of the industries they were attacking
happened to be run by those rich, well-placed, and politically generous Republicans who were the traditional financial, if not the moral, strength of the Republican party. Reform was one thing if it was Roosevelt attacking corporate or
political evil, as though every assault were a charge up San Juan Hill. It was
another matter if a muckraking writer exposed the appalling conditions in Chicago meat-packing plants that were owned and operated by friends of the president and his party—financial contributors all.

Roosevelt was soon placed in an impossible position, in which all his skill in
manipulating the press did not save him from the inevitable fate of presidents, as
Filler describes it:

> He was charged with every conceivable crime by gossip-mongers and the extreme
> reactionary press. He was so openly accused of being a drunkard that he felt con-
> strained to fight the allegations in the open himself. Throughout his campaigns
> against ''the malefactors of great wealth,'' as he called them, it was generally whis-
> pered, among the highest circles of righteousness, that he was insane. To certain
> influential persons he was an incendiary who was ruining America, and every
> weapon that might be used to discredit him was justifiable. For conservatives sensed
> revolution, or at least genuine reform—which was almost as bad—and Roosevelt,
> far from applying force to it, was trying to conciliate it. When contrasted [sic] with
> McKinley, in particular, Roosevelt appeared a prophet of doom to those who clung
> to the old economic traditions.

It was a situation redolent of paradox and irony. People tended to identify the
president with the muckrakers—after all, was he not intent on ''busting the
trusts,'' in his memorable phrase?—even though it was he himself who had
given the new journalists their name. Speaking at a dinner hosted by Speaker
Uncle Joe Cannon, at the Gridiron Club, Roosevelt strongly denounced ''the
man with the muckrake'' in both newspapers and magazines—those writers who
made scandalous attacks on men in public life and at the same time defended
labor leaders engaged in employing violence to fight those who were intent on
dissolving unions, as conservative Republicans wanted to do. ''The man with the
muckrake'' was picked up by newspapers everywhere, and the phrase quickly

became conveniently shortened by headline writers to "muckraker." Roosevelt was pleased with the word and the elaborate straddle he had concocted and decided to expand on the theme, using the single word this time, in a ceremony marking the laying of the cornerstone for a new House office building.

By this time, in his attempt to be all things to both sides, Roosevelt was beginning to sound like an old-school Mugwump. "One reason I want to make that address," he wrote to Ray Stannard Baker, who had become a muckraker only by degrees, "is because people so persistently misunderstood what I said that I wanted to have it reported in full. . . . I disapprove of the whitewash brush quite as much as of mud slinging, and it seems to me that the disapproval of one in no shape or way implies approval of the other. This I shall try to make clear." Even though Roosevelt failed to make it much clearer, his speech was carried in full by many newspapers, provoking widespread national comment and further controversy.

The truth was that Roosevelt wanted to have it both ways. He could not have made that more plain than when he declared:

> I do not dislike but I certainly have no especial respect or admiration for and no trust in the typical big money men of my country. I do not regard them as furnishing sound opinion as regards either foreign or domestic policies. Quite as little do I regard as furnishing such opinion the men who especially pride themselves on their cultivation—the men like many of those who graduated from my own college of Harvard, and who find their organs in the New York *Evening Post* and *Nation.* These papers are written especially for cultivated gentlefolk. They have many minor virtues, moral and intellectual; and yet during my twenty-five years in public life I have found them much more often wrong than right on the great and vital public issues.

Thus the early appearance of the Eastern elitist press.

Roosevelt's primary weapon in maintaining his often precarious supremacy, besides his overwhelming personality and general popularity, was his continuing courtship of the Washington correspondents, and his skillful use of them. In 1903, for example, he called in the reporters and, first warning them not to reveal the source of their information—they could only say "on high authority"—told them that six senators had received telegrams from John D. Rockefeller arguing against the enactment of antitrust legislation—a bill for which Roosevelt was pressing. The president said he did not know exactly how the telegrams had been worded, but the reporters did not stop to ferret out the details. Their stories produced a predictable uproar among the newspapers and led to passage of the bill, 251 to 10. "I got the bill through by publishing those telegrams and concentrating the public attention on the bill," Roosevelt observed later, with satisfaction.

Opposition papers demonstrated on occasion that they could be even more devious. The *World,* anticipating the era of checkbook journalism in the popular press, paid $150 to obtain letters that tended to show that the president was not above considerably distorting the truth to prove that he had never asked E. H. Harriman, the railroad baron, to raise money for him in the 1904 presidential campaign. That the president had sought help from one of the muckrakers' chief targets caused a wave of unease and distrust in the country, which some historians believe was a factor in bringing on the panic of 1907.

Instead of uniting the country behind a strong leader, as he had intended, Roosevelt emerged as the president of a divided electorate—those who were for or against him strictly on party lines, those who saw him as a mixed bag (mostly liberals and independents), and those who constituted what amounted to a cult following, seeing no evil in anything the Great Man did—not an uncommon phenomenon in American politics. The president regularly denounced the muckrakers even as the reforms they pressed for began to work their way into regulatory legislation, but several of them, notably Steffens and Jake Riis, his friends from police headquarters days, remained friendly; Riis, in fact, was a member of the cult. And to most of the voters Roosevelt was still a hero.

All this equivocation is not to imply that Roosevelt was without principles. As president he had the courage to take unpopular public stances, as he had done when he sat in Albany. In a country not much less racist than it had been before the Civil War, he had no hesitation in asking Booker T. Washington to be his dinner guest at the White House only a few months after he took office, causing a wave of anger to roll across the country in editorial columns and in public venues. But it was a Democratic paper, the *World,* no friend of the president, that, to its great credit, wrote: "An American named Washington, one of the most learned, most eloquent, most brilliant men of the day—the President of a college—is asked to dinner by President Roosevelt. And because the pigment of his skin is some shades darker than that of others a large part of the United States is convulsed with shame and rage. . . . Truly Liberty must smile at such broadminded logic, such enlightened tolerance. Or should she weep?" Yet it was the same president, only three years later, who refused to see Maxim Gorky, the visiting Russian novelist, joining a large company of other hypocrites. Roosevelt (and the others) might have tolerated Gorky's Marxism but not his mistress, who was traveling with him.

A primary reason that the president was able to maintain his close relationship with the reporters in Washington, no matter what might be happening in their executive offices, was his acute recognition that the time of the great editors was past and the focus was now on reporting. Newspapers were no longer the extensions of a publisher's ego, with only a few exceptions, and, while it still mattered to some extent whether a journal supported a president or not, what the public really wanted was the news. The upper classes turned more and more to magazines for opinion, a category in which there was now a great variety, while the workers and middle-class readers were more interested in news and features, an interest that could be summarized in one word—"people." In short, readers could be guaranteed to be fascinated by the multitude of things Roosevelt did, and they preferred, on the whole, to hear about those things rather than what he thought. That was in key with Roosevelt's general style. Since his Albany days he had demonstrated repeatedly that he could survive even his support of unpopular policies as long as the image was kept constantly burnished and thrust before the electorate. Along the way, he also hoped to convince people that he was eternally right.

In Washington, as in Albany and New York, Roosevelt's relationship with reporters was a close one, even intimate with some. He took them under his wing in the White House, psychologically and physically. McKinley had already taken the first step in that direction, as we have seen. But Roosevelt went further. When the West Wing was built on the White House in 1902, providing the office space the president desired and creating the Oval Room, Roosevelt designated an office next to his secretary's as a pressroom and moved the reporters into it from the welcome but cramped quarters McKinley had provided. Here they were also given telephones, eliminating at last the familiar sight of messenger and telegraph boys on their bicycles, lined up along Pennsylvania Avenue, waiting to bear dispatches.

There was symbolism involved, too, in the creation of this first real pressroom, as Juergens suggests. The reporters were no longer guests of the president but established as a recognized public function of government. There was altruism in this move, but not much. What Roosevelt wanted was a publicity machine ready at hand that he had only to crank up whenever he needed it. That basic idea has grown and grown until it has reached today's monstrous proportions, fed by a constantly growing White House publicity and public relations machine of outsize dimensions. Roosevelt meant to do the feeding all by himself, and he was more than able to do it.

The president built his machine quickly and carefully. McKinley was scarcely in the ground before he had summoned the three wire-service reporters—Charles Boynton of the Associated Press; David Barry of the Laffan Agency, owned by the New York *Sun*; and Ed Keen of the Scripps-McRae Press Association, forerunner of the United Press. (Hearst did not create his International News Service until 1909.) Since their stories reached newspapers everywhere in the country, Roosevelt knew they must be the major conduits for the flow of news and seeming news he was about to generate, and he let these reporters know that he would be accessible to them.

As for the others, the president organized them into two camps. In one were his favorites, meaning those who did not cross him or write unfavorable stories; he made them insiders to an extent never seen before, or even contemplated. The others remained outsiders, most hoping to get in. If any reporter wrote something Roosevelt believed was not true, or wished was untrue, the offender was invited to join the Ananias Club. Members of the Paradise group could be tossed into the Infernal camp if the president thought they had betrayed him or, worse, were left to languish in Purgatory. If a reporter wanted to get the news, he had to aspire to be in the Paradise group and be careful to stay in it. Small wonder, then, that the president's press reports were largely favorable.

Roosevelt kept his side of the unequal bargain. He did make himself accessible, and he did talk to the reporters with a candor that left the veterans flabbergasted. Sometimes they could scarcely believe that the president of the United States was speaking. The newsmen (or at least some of them) were particularly

enchanted by the president's custom of inviting a half-dozen or so of their number to watch him get shaved at one o'clock every afternoon, by the world's most
forbearing barber, who worked regularly as a Treasury Department messenger.
He stood by calmly whenever his distinguished customer, with typical exuber-
ance, jumped out of the chair excitedly to wave his arms and walk up and down,
illustrating a point. It was a series of miracles as the barber lifted his razor just in
time.

There were numerous other contacts as well. Some reporters Roosevelt saw
with more or less frequency on an individual basis, particularly his friend Oscar
King Davis, head of the New York *Times* Washington bureau, whom he called
by his nickname "OK." Although the *Times* criticized the president constantly
in its editorials, opposing many of his policies, Roosevelt had considerable respect, in the beginning at least, for the fairness and impartiality which Adolph
Ochs, the new owner, was continuing to maintain in its columns, and so he had
no hesitation in keeping Davis within the inner circle. In his memoirs Davis
recalled how their relationship worked:

> I was in the habit of seeing the President two or three times a week, for private
> talks, some of which had been rather extended. I had found that the evening hour,
> when he signed the day's mail, was by far the best time to see him. He would come
> back to the Executive offices directly from his exercise, clear up his desk, and then
> go over to "the big house" to dress for dinner. He had amazing facility for carrying
> on conversation while he was going over the mail. He would glance over a letter,
> make an addition or alteration with his pen, and sign his name at the same time that
> he was keeping up a steady fire of talk about whatever subject happened to be under
> discussion.

While Davis and a few others were singled out for these private discussions,
Roosevelt did not slight the other newspapermen. He was forever taking a few
moments from his busy day to give impromptu briefings, and on important matters he would summon the press to his office and talk with them, speaking with
astonishing frankness about even the most delicate matters. It was some time
before it began to occur to them that there was nothing haphazard about any of
this; it was calculated by the new master of public relations, who played upon the
correspondents as though they constituted a human typewriter. They were able to
ask questions only when they could find an infrequent opening. For the most part
the president carried on a rapid monologue and could not be interrupted until he
paused momentarily for breath or to switch subjects. The reporters learned to
watch for and take advantage of these breaks to get in their queries.

Although he would not have been averse to the idea in principle, the president
was never interviewed in the conventional sense. One question would touch him
off, and the answer might take up the next twenty minutes or more. The give-
and-take of the press conference in later administrations was not possible in this
one. The president was always in control, always in command of the situation.

Davis has given us a graphic picture of the Roosevelt "press conference" or
"interview" in operation: "You might have an hour with the President and talk

all around the horizon, politics, diplomatic affairs, military, naval or congressional situation, money, labor, undesirable citizens, or what not, and yet not get out of it all a word that you could write that day. Then, within a week, something might happen that would be trivial and unimportant to one who had not had such a talk with the President, but which furnished a good story to one who had.''

In this and other exchanges the press was deluding itself. True, there was much more and qualitatively better news coming out of the White House than the correspondents had been able to get before, but in the excitement of getting it in such an unprecedented way, and in such volume, most of the newsmen seemed to ignore the fact that what they were getting was the president's version of the news. It was not his intent to inform the public so much as to convince it that his policies were correct. For the moment, at least, the old adversarial, or at least critical, role of the press was seriously diluted. Reporters were made to feel part of the act, rather than critics sitting in the front row.

It was not entirely cold-blooded calculation, however. Roosevelt honestly liked most of the reporters, and he was deeply interested in journalism itself; he was, after all, an accomplished practitioner of the craft, more accomplished than most of those who covered him. Only someone with such knowledge would have waited to sign a Thanksgiving proclamation until the Associated Press photographer could get there to record the event. Roosevelt even interrupted a conference with the secretary of state until the camera could be set up and the picture taken. He knew that his image would be carried to every part of the country. Such ''photo opportunities,'' as we call them now, are overly common today, and presidents use them routinely as public relations devices, but they had been unknown until Roosevelt arrived.

The president had some publicity problems with his large and lively family, ranging all the way from three-year-old Quentin to Alice, seventeen when her father took office. They were as exuberant as the president himself, and an asset in the sense that they always made good copy and kept the Roosevelt name in the public eye even on the dullest news day. The president tried to shield them as much as possible, but they were usually not particularly shy about publicity, and Alice lived her free-ranging, unconventional life in a fashion remembered even today. When critics asserted that he should take a firmer hand with her, Roosevelt responded with words any father could understand: ''Listen, I can be President of the United States—or—I can attend to Alice.'' The press faithfully and happily recorded her escapades and the antics of the other Roosevelt children for a public that seemed unable to get enough of them.

In his use of the press, Roosevelt did not overlook any of the devices that have become standard equipment in our times. He was a master at floating the trial balloon, and he lofted frequent flights of them, treating the whole thing as a game between him and the reporters. They were more often fooled than not. He was also adroit in using the presidential power to make news and suffocate anyone opposing him by denying the other person the normal publicity he might expect to get. The president appeared in the front-page headlines, while his rival or opponent wound up on page sixteen.

The high-level leak was another of the White House weapons that Roosevelt developed. While it is not too difficult for knowledgeable readers, at least, to see through these planted stories today, there was no such sophistication in Roosevelt's time, and the reporters themselves could be trusted far more to conceal the source in ambiguity. The president supplemented this with frequent use of the background briefing, in which he was able to tell the public how he might feel about a certain issue when it would have been impolitic to make any kind of public declaration. In that way he conveyed his support for William Howard Taft as his successor without making a public statement that would have aroused instant opposition. After the backgrounder he gave reporters on this subject, their stories conveyed the necessary impression.

In carrying out his elaborate public relations campaign, Roosevelt had the help first of George Cortelyou, the secretary he had inherited from McKinley, and seventeen months later William Loeb, Jr. (who had worked with him in Albany), after Cortelyou became the first secretary of commerce and labor. They were not press secretaries in the modern sense, because media relationships, which today require large staffs, were only a part of their duties. As executive secretaries they not only took the president's dictation, as any secretary would, but were essentially office managers in the White House, taking care of the president's financial matters as well, making his appointments, and acting as confidential advisers on whatever matters the president desired. Nor was that all. Liaison work with Congress and other parts of the government, discreet fence mending with political leaders, and a thousand similar chores fell within the province of the presidential secretary. With the press, he was the one to whom reporters came with questions on those occasions when the president was too busy to see them or the questions themselves could be answered just as well by the secretary. It was a difficult, demanding job, completely absorbing the man who held it. Loeb proved equal to it, as Cortelyou had been.

The extent of Roosevelt's control over the press was noted ruefully by Archie Butt, who was Taft's secretary in the following term and the unfortunate handmaiden of an administration in which press relations became just the opposite of what they had been. "Mr. Roosevelt understood the necessity of guiding the press to suit one's own ends," Butt wrote candidly. "He saw the newspapermen freely, but they understood that they were only to print what he authorized them to use, and if they did anything else he would not allow them near the White House or office, and he has been known to have them dismissed from their papers. . . . Nothing went out from the White House except as the President wanted it."

Control, however, had its problems. Roosevelt's policy of making an inner circle out of those correspondents who did not offend him and gave him proper deference, casting into outer darkness those who broke his rules, produced a natural rivalry between the insiders and the outsiders. In the new climate of independent journalism, there were those who stubbornly refused to follow what the president implicitly demanded—that their stories be tailored to support him. They were willing enough to become part of the Washington establishment, a process the president was busily engaged in, but they had no intention of becoming presidential publicity men, however dangerous resistance might be. To them it was a clear choice between corruption and honesty. But these dissidents were few in number. It took courage and support from the front office to resist Roosevelt's bullying, to be named as candidates for the Ananias Club, and to be shut out as far as possible from covering the White House at all. As Juergens observes, "Roosevelt even banished people he knew were innocent, such as those he used to float trial balloons. Long after he left the White House the memory of suffering arbitrary punishment at his hands remained with Washington journalists. . . . Even into the next decade the memories rankled. 'There are correspondents still alive,' Herbert Corey wrote in the *Saturday Evening Post* in 1932, 'who are as full of umbrage as they were the day that President Roosevelt denied them.'"

Roosevelt not only resented any criticism of himself, as all presidents have, but he was angered by the new investigative reporting, by the uncovering of sin and corruption in a national life that he regarded as bully beyond compare. That attitude was difficult in a time of muckraking, when there was a great deal of muck to be raked, but it was made even harder because Roosevelt wanted newspapers to pay far more attention to good news, to be upbeat—in a word, to be more like himself. When they insisted perversely on doing what they had always done, he harbored a growing inner rage against them, regarding even the most respectacle journals as venal liars. "Papers like the New York *Times,* both in their editorials and in their correspondence," he wrote to John Allen Sleicher on February 25, 1906, "lie in response to the demands of the big corporations that the editors and correspondents shall lie; and lie those editors and correspondents like those of the New York *Times* do, because they make their bread and butter by so doing."

This kind of nonsense could only be justified by remembering that Roosevelt sincerely believed that those who did not agree with him, and who made statements with which he did not agree, must be lying. The truth, he was convinced, lay entirely with him. The president must have known that there was no more honest and conscientious publisher in the business than Adolph Ochs of the *Times,* a man whom he had entertained at Oyster Bay and to whose daughter Iphigene he had sent an autographed picture of himself. Yet the *Times* had opposed him on this issue or that, and so its writers and editors must be a pack of liars, in his distorted view. It was a thought process that led him finally, at the end of his two terms, to the kind of presidential invective so familiar among nineteenth-century presidents. Speaking of several leading editors and publishers of the time, Roosevelt on November 11, 1905, advised Richard Watson Gilder, editor of the *Century* magazine, that they represented "a lower type than the worst and most corrupt politicians, or than the worst and most corrupt financiers, and on the whole do more evil."

Thus the paradox of a president who understood the press and how it worked better than any of those who had preceded him, yet whose overblown ego and rigid self-righteousness prevented him from understanding its function in a democracy any better than his predecessors had done. He feared criticism of the American democracy itself, and of established institutions whether right or wrong, because such exposures might convince people that something must be done to change things. He had the true conservative's deep-rooted fear of change.

Not much more could be expected, his critics believed, from a man who thought (as he told S. S. McClure) that the "reformers" of the French Revolution brought on the Terror because they gave a one-sided view of the injustices being done to the poor, a thought quite unworthy of a Harvard man. Needless to say, such ideas of his did not become public; Roosevelt was too good a publicist to say anything so indiscreet. But by this logic he came to regard even an old friend like Steffens as only a cut above the other muckrakers he deplored.

When he attacked the muckrakers in public, Roosevelt could conceivably have been embarrassed (a lesser president would have) by the fact that the most applause came from those newspapers, like the *Sun,* which he had once roundly denounced as "organs of the criminal rich." But he was far too intellectually obtuse to be so burdened, and one may suppose that he felt more personal grief over the alienation of those like Steffens and Ray Stannard Baker, who had once been his friends and supporters. "I could never again give him my full confidence," Baker wrote later, "nor follow his leadership."

The paradox of Roosevelt reached its first flowering in the election of 1904. There were big businessmen who opposed him because they were alarmed and fearful as a result of the series of domestic reforms he had pushed through Congress, but the bigger fish in the financial pond—J. P. Morgan, Jay Gould, John D. Rockefeller, Edward Harriman—believed in his denunciation of the muckrakers and were confident he would keep reforms within safe channels until they could be undermined later, as in fact they were. Conservative newspapers that had railed against Roosevelt the Reformer now praised Roosevelt the Muckrakers' Enemy. Those in and out of Congress who had been outraged by the lawless, conscienceless grab that created the Panana Canal Zone were nevertheless afraid to oppose a move that so obviously strengthened the United States as a world power.

As far as the public was concerned, unmoved by what either Wall Street or the press might think, Roosevelt was a highly popular president, a man who told the people what they wanted to hear, colorful, exciting, omnipresent, a giant in a forest of political pygmies. They gloried in a president who walked softly and carried a big stick, which he shook threateningly over small Latin-American countries and big nations alike; they responded to the declaration that they were going to be given a Square Deal, although the deal they were actually getting had resulted in some of the worst labor unrest the country had seen. America slept in a bourgeois calm of peace and prosperity.

To no one's surprise Roosevelt was nominated unanimously when the Republicans met in convention, with an obscure senator from Indiana, Charles W. Fairbanks, named as vice-president, because, as the president himself put it with brutal candor, "Who in the name of heaven else is there?" Fairbanks would be the most invisible of vice-presidents. The Democrats, gloomily contemplating disaster, named Alton B. Parker, a conservative New York judge, in the vain hope that he would attract businessmen and other conservatives who might still be disgruntled by Roosevelt reforms. His running mate, an eighty-year-old millionaire from West Virginia, Henry G. Davis, was nominated in the even more forlorn hope that he would give the party a great deal of his money. It was astonishing that this combination could poll as many as five million votes against a popular president, who got at least two million more.

The campaign would have been a graveyard if Joseph Pulitzer had not erected a blazing light in the middle of it with an eight-column editorial in the *World* that raised a number of possibly embarrassing questions for the president. Why, Pulitzer wanted to know, had the new Bureau of Corporations done so little to justify its existence? Could it be that the campaign funds pouring into Republican coffers from the corporations the bureau was supposed to oversee constituted some kind of protection money? Was it not odd that the bureau's new head, George Cortelyou (replacing that old press villain, Mark Hanna), had been made Republican National Committee chairman? In his new job, had Cortelyou been the recipient of funds from the beef, paper, coal, and sugar trusts?

In a campaign speech the suggestion was made by Judge Parker not only that such funds had been paid but that they were in effect insurance money so that the Bureau of Corporations would not disclose damaging facts concerning them—in short, blackmail. Roosevelt, silent up to this point, indignantly denied the charge. But whether it was true or not, the voters were unimpressed. They did not want to be bothered with issues; they simply wanted to reelect a hero. The hero responded to his election by advising the country that he would not accept a third nomination under any circumstances, a promise he profoundly regretted in 1908.

Roosevelt's greatest satisfaction in 1904 was to be no longer an accidental president but a chief executive in his own right, and during the next four years the imperial circus continued in Washington with even more intensity than it had demonstrated before. But whatever he did, whether at home or abroad, the president was greeted with abuse by many of the Democratic papers and a smattering of still alienated Republican journals. Otherwise his press support was formidable. In the White House he continued to dominate the correspondents, and those who would not be dominated were cast out. It was an unprecedented situation, never to be repeated.

The one voice Roosevelt could neither outshout nor silence was Pulitzer's. The publisher's ego was as boundless as the president's, and, even though he was ill and blind, he continued to be a thorn in the Rooseveltian side—not politically dangerous, to be sure, but a constant public irritant, as he had been from the beginning of the president's public life. Pulitzer had never believed in Roosevelt the Reformer. When the young Republican had endorsed Blaine in 1884, the *World* had denounced his pretensions to reform as hypocrisy. Ten years later, when he was police commissioner, Roosevelt's strict enforcement of the Blue Laws drew Pulitzer's scorn because, as he wrote, this was a moralistic crusade being carried out while the real criminals went free—a common editorial complaint down the years. Then had come the probing questions of the 1904 campaign. Given the kind of man he was, Colonel Roosevelt no doubt still felt a rankling resentment of the *World*'s San Juan Hill coverage. Obviously a shoot-out at high noon between the president and Pulitzer was an ever-present possibility.

There were other journalistic villains in the Roosevelt pantheon, of course, and they appeared to constitute a large part of the New York City press. After the election in 1904 Roosevelt excoriated the "New York *Evening Post* crowd" for what he termed a hypocritical opposition to him. "They have loudly professed to demand just exactly the kind of government I have given, and yet they have done their futile best to defeat me," he wrote to Owen Wister.

It appeared that with the press, at least, Roosevelt could not overcome the contradiction of being a reform president who nevertheless found money and support among the financiers and industrialists he was supposed to be reforming, while they, in turn, continued unabashed many of the practices that the muck-rakers were still exposing, although with diminishing zeal. All this came to something of a crisis with the panic of 1907 and the predictable search for scapegoats. For his part, Roosevelt blamed the financial collapse not only on reckless speculation by the big-money Wall Street crowd but also on the news-papers and magazines that had been disclosing their rascality, thus precipitating a loss of public confidence and consequent panic among investors.

This curious line of reasoning was founded in the president's conviction, which he cherished, that much of the New York press was in the hands of these same rascally financiers, who manipulated the papers for their own purposes. His ideas were disclosed in a letter to a Buffalo friend, in which he once more as-serted that papers like the *Sun* and the *Times* and magazines like *Harper's Weekly* were not only read by "the financial classes" but "I believe financed by them also." Their object, he went on, was

> to attack me, continually and habitually, not merely misquote what I say, but deliber-ately invent statements which I have never uttered, and attribute to me an attitude which I have never held. They may have hurt me a little by this; but the people they have really damaged are the members of the business community whom they have persuaded to believe that I am attacking all wealth. . . . It is the so-called conser-vative press, the capitalist press that has misrepresented me.

By "the capitalist press" the president meant primarily the *Sun, Times, Evening Post, Harper's Weekly, Herald,* and the *World.* Among the major New York papers, that left only Whitelaw Reid's *Tribune,* which everyone else considered to be the apotheosis of capitalistic journalism. Roosevelt did not include it be-cause the *Tribune* was virtually undeviating in its support of Republicans and Republicanism. Of them all, the *Sun* and the *World,* although diametrically op-posed to each other, were considered his particular enemies.

The threatened shoot-out with Pulitzer finally took place in the last year of Roosevelt's second term. During the previous troubled year, when the president was already under fire because of the panic, the *World* had aggravated his prob-lems, as we saw earlier, by printing on its front page, under banks of glaring headlines, a letter from Harriman, in which the railroad magnate described his generous contributions to Roosevelt's reelection. The revelation did not have the impact that Pulitzer obviously hoped it would have because there was nothing particularly startling in it, but a certain uneasiness had been created. Pulitzer and the *World* stumbled into the ultimate confrontation, however, without prior intent.

On October 2, 1908, the paper's city editor got a tip that William Cromwell, junior partner in the rising young law firm of Sullivan and Cromwell, later to be one of the city's most prestigious, had gone to District Attorney William Travers Jerome with the complaint that he was being made the victim of a blackmail scheme in connection with the Panama Canal, then under construction. A *World* reporter was sent to look into the matter but came back empty handed; neither Jerome nor Cromwell would make any comment.

Later that night a former *World* reporter, Jonas Whitley, now a Cromwell press agent (or representative, as he preferred), came into the office and told Caleb Van Hamm, the managing editor, that he understood the paper was about to print an inaccurate story about Cromwell and he wanted to help get the facts straight. During the conversation he confirmed what the *World* had been trying unsuccessfully to pin down.

Invited to tell his (that is, Cromwell's) side of the affair, Whitley did so, and Van Hamm then wrote a story that was potentially highly scandalous and politically lethal. It reported that at a time when it was clear the United States was going to take over the rights of French bondholders in the De Lesseps Company, builders of the canal, Cromwell and a French speculator named Philippe Bunau-Varilla had formed a syndicate that bought $3.5 million of the stocks and bonds of the De Lesseps Company. Knowing that the United States Government was about to acquire the French property for $40 million, the syndicate was able to make a quick profit of $36.5 million, dividing it, as Van Hamm's story put it, "among the Government favorites in the world of politics and finance."

The political dynamite in this story lay in the names of those Americans who had allegedly joined the syndicate. Among others, they included Charles P. Taft, half-brother of William Howard Taft, who at that moment was in the midst of his campaign for the presidency, anointed for the task by Roosevelt; and Douglas Robinson, the president's brother-in-law. Cromwell, as it happened, was Taft's close friend and adviser.

All these allegations had been laid before District Attorney Jerome by W. J. Curtis, of Sullivan and Cromwell, who told the prosecutor that a "certain man" had come to Cromwell and told him the Democratic National Committee was in possession of a statement setting forth these charges and would presumably publish them unless the attorney used his "personal influence" to stop it. Not unnaturally, according to Curtis, Cromwell had construed this to mean that he was being blackmailed.

But then Van Hamm's story went on to quote Whitley as saying that the truth of the matter was that the American government's $40 million had in fact gone to France through the firm of J. P. Morgan & Co. and that the entire amount had been paid into the French courts. Whitley was further quoted as denying emphatically that any Cromwell syndicate had ever existed and that the United States

Government had acquired the De Lesseps Company bonds through regular channels, not through any intermediate holding company.

When Van Hamm finished writing this story, based on the statements Cromwell's press emissary had just given him, he showed it to Whitley, who had been waiting. Whitley read it carefully, changed the name of Charles P. Taft to Henry W. Taft, then changed it back, and announced: "The story as it now stands is accurate." An hour later the *World* was on the street with it, and the foundation had been laid for what would be one of the most incredible chapters in the entire history of the relationship between the press and the presidency.

Later editions of the paper that night carried an additional explicit denial by Cromwell himself that either he or anyone allied with him had ever made a penny out of any dealing in Panama stocks and bonds, nor had he ever received a single dollar of the $40 million. Next day's papers carried similar denials by Charles P. Taft and his half-brother Henry. Robinson, however, refused to talk to reporters.

Over the next several weeks the *World* followed up with other articles about the alleged canal deal, which were widely quoted by the Democratic press and completely ignored by the president, his party, and their journalistic supporters. It was a nonissue in the campaign, and presumably would not affect Taft's election.

The whole affair might have blown over, no doubt, if the Indianapolis *News* had not printed on November 2, the day before election, an editorial about the supposed deal, in which for the first time a question was raised that would rock the nation: "But who got the money?"—meaning, of course, the $40 million that the government had paid for the canal property. The story noted the denials by all hands but declared that the charges had not been answered, although the records were available in Washington; the public, however, would not be permitted to see them until after the election, if ever.

If this story had any political effect, it was minimal. Republicans lost the state ticket in Indiana but Taft took the electoral vote, so no real damage was done. But disturbing questions had been raised, and a friend of Roosevelt's, William Dudley Foulke, sent the president a clipping of the *News* editorial, which had been written by its editor, Delevan Smith, and asked simply, "What are the facts?" The president sent back a detailed reply, denouncing Smith as a liar, asserting that the $40 million had been paid directly to the French government, denying that either his brother-in-law or Charles Taft had been involved, or that any syndicate ever existed.

Again, the matter might have ended there, but the *World* was unwilling to let it drop. On December 8 it carried a blazing editorial that began: "In view of President Roosevelt's deliberate misstatements of fact in his scandalous personal attack upon Delevan Smith, editor of the Indianapolis *News*, the *World* calls upon the Congress of the United States to make immediately a full and impartial investigation of the entire Panama Canal scandal. . . . To the best of the *World*'s knowledge and belief, each and all of the statements made by Mr. Roosevelt are untrue, and Mr. Roosevelt must have known they were untrue when he made them.'' Under a subhead, ''Who Got The Money?'' the *World* amplified its charges and raised more questions.

James Wyman Barrett, the paper's last city editor, certainly not always an impartial observer but in this case one whose memory withstands investigation, notes here an incident that puts Pulitzer and his paper in a somewhat different light. At the time the editorial quoted above was appearing, the publisher was living on his new yacht, the *Liberty*, one of the largest private yachts ever built up to that time (it cost $1,500,000 to construct, $200,000 a year to operate)—launched, ironically, during the panic, in December 1907. Pulitzer had to live on this vessel to escape the noise that so profoundly affected his nervous system. After cruising in Mediterranean and European waters, the *Liberty* docked in Charleston on the day Roosevelt's letter to Foulke was published. The local papers were brought in, and the story was read to Pulitzer. One fact caught his attention immediately. ''When Delevan Smith says he got his information out of a New York paper, what does he mean?'' Pulitzer demanded. Told that Smith meant the *World*, the publisher exclaimed, ''I knew it! If there's any trouble, the *World* is sure to be in the middle of it.''

Arriving in New York a few days later, Pulitzer sent for Van Hamm and demanded at once, ''What proof have you that Douglas Robinson and Charles P. Taft are involved in this matter?'' ''None at all,'' Van Hamm said. ''My God!'' Pulitzer exclaimed. ''No proof? You print such stories without proof?'' Van Hamm explained that the two men had come into the case only because of Cromwell's complaint to the district attorney. Pulitzer was somewhat mollified, but he was apprehensive. ''Just remember,'' he told Van Hamm, ''Roosevelt is likely to make trouble. . . . If he does, I will fight him to the finish!''

So the gage was thrown down, and, as Pulitzer had predicted, the president was first to pick it up. A week after the *World*'s editorial appeared he sent a special message to Congress, informing its members that the stories needed no investigation but were simply ''a string of infamous libels''—libels, he added, not only on individuals but on the United States Government. Consequently, he went on to urge, Pulitzer himself should be prosecuted for libel by the government. Then he added a little of what could conceivably be called libel of his own, although privileged: ''It is a high national duty to bring to justice this vilifier of the American people, this man who wantonly and wickedly seeks to blacken the character and reputation of private citizens and to convict the Government of his own country in the eyes of the civilized world of wrong-doing of the basest and foulest kind.'' At the end he dropped his bomb: ''The Attorney General has under consideration the form in which the proceedings against Mr. Pulitzer shall be brought.''

No president had ever sent such a message to Congress, and no administration had prosecuted an editor for libel since the earliest days of the Republic. But ill as he was, Pulitzer was not the kind of man to be intimidated. His reply was a long editorial in the *World* on December 16, which was written by the paper's brilliant chief editorial writer, Frank I. Cobb, but whose essence was pure Pulitzer. It began, ''Mr. Roosevelt is mistaken. He cannot muzzle the *World*,'' and after a long recitation of denials and countercharges, with further attacks on the president, it ended: "So far as the *World* is concerned, its proprietor may go to jail, if Mr. Roosevelt succeeds, as he threatens, but even in jail the *World* will not cease to be a fearless champion of free speech, a free press and a free people. It cannot be muzzled!"

There was a brief interval while the president completed preparations to leave for an African safari as soon as he was out of office. According to Archie Butt, he was as confident as ever, telling George Sheldon, the National Republican Committee's chairman, and Douglas Robinson and his wife at a White House luncheon that "they will put Old Pulitzer in prison." Old Pulitzer, back on his yacht and steaming into warmer southern waters, was less confident than his brave words might have indicated. He was extremely nervous, Barrett notes, worrying about legal defenses and even making some apprehensive inquiries about federal prisons.

On February 17, 1909, the blow fell. A grand jury in the District of Columbia brought indictments against Pulitzer, Van Hamm, Robert Hunt Lyman (the *World's* night editor), and the Press Publishing Company, corporate owners of the paper, charging that they had criminally libeled Roosevelt, Morgan, Charles Taft, Robinson, Secretary of State Elihu Root, and Cromwell. There were additional indictments returned against Delevan Smith and Charles R. Williams of the Indianapolis *News*. Bench warrants were issued for those involved, and a summons for the Press Publishing Company.

It had taken an excessive straining of the law to bring such indictments; criminal libel itself is seldom invoked. In this case the government's lawyers had to go back to an ancient statute of 1662, based on English law, which unfortunately offered them no help in how to get the defendants into the District's jurisdiction for trial. It was going to be some time, obviously, before the case could begin. Meanwhile, as soon as Taft was safely inaugurated, Roosevelt went off to Africa, while Pulitzer remained aboard the *Liberty* in Charleston. All this meant a frustrating disappointment for Cromwell, who had expected that Taft would appoint him attorney general, which the new president now considered politically unwise in the circumstances, naming George W. Wickersham instead.

The case soon took a downturn for the government when it tried to extradite the two Indianapolis defendants and bring them to the District. United States Attorney Joseph H. Keating produced a sensation by resigning rather than undertake any such proceedings, declaring, "To drag these defendants from their homes to the seat of government while there is good and sufficient jurisdiction in the State courts . . . is very dangerous, striking at the very foundation of our form of government." To compound this setback, the federal judge in Indianapolis, Albert B. Anderson, not only dismissed the government's extradition writ but remarked that he, too, would like to know who got the money. That brought delayed Rooseveltian wrath on his head. Speaking at the Indianapolis Columbia Club a year later, the former President referred to Judge Anderson as "a jackass and a crook." The judge, accepting this as a compliment, did not sue for libel.

By this time it was clear that the government would have to move in a different direction; consequently Henry L. Stimson, then United States Attorney for the

Southern District of New York, filed a complaint with a federal grand jury in that jurisdiction, and on March 3 the Press Publishing Company and Van Hamm were duly indicted. Strangely, Pulitzer was not. The legal basis for this indictment was remote to say the least. It rested on a law dating back to the infamous Alien and Sedition Acts of 1798, which had been invoked only twice since, in 1825 and in 1898, when a jingoistic Congress had revived it as an antiespionage measure.

This obscure statute was called An Act to Protect the Harbor Defense from Malicious Injury, and for Other Purposes. To make it operable, the indictment had to contend that the *World* had circulated a "malicious, libelous, and untruthful article on government property at West Point, and in the New York City Post Office Building." That was true enough. The *World* routinely sent single copies of the paper to the post office, as required by law, to be inspected for unmailable matter. In this case, the indictment charged, the purpose was to "stir up disorder among the people." As for West Point, twenty-nine copies of the paper had been duly delivered there to subscribers.

Weak as this case might be, Pulitzer was well aware that the *World* was not standing on solid legal ground either. He was convinced that the paper had gone too far in printing the Cromwell story in the first place and should not have responded so sharply to Roosevelt's attack on Delevan Smith. Nor was he at all sure that Taft and Robinson should ever have been linked with the syndicate, if it indeed existed. The *World*'s best defense, he believed, was to insist that it was Cromwell, not the paper, who had made the original allegations. His lawyers assured him that this was not a defense. The *World* had, in fact, uttered the libel, if it were proved to be so.

Congress did conduct an investigation of the Panama affair, as the *World* had demanded, but the result brought no cheer to Pulitzer. Taft and Robinson were cleared of any involvement, and so was Roosevelt. The only question left unanswered in the hearings was the old one: who got the money? Nevertheless, Pulitzer was lucky that neither Taft nor Robinson elected to bring libel suits, which they would almost certainly have won.

In public, however, the *World* remained defiant. It frequently repeated the Great Question about the money, so no one would forget, and self-righteously proclaimed that the government was persecuting the *World* because it was the only Democratic paper in New York, a slight to some smaller, inferior journals. Meanwhile, in court, a Wall Street lawyer named De Lancey Nicoll was conducting a brilliant defense of the paper, aided by its reporters, who spent a good deal of time trying to dig up helpful evidence. Nicoll was chiefly opposing Henry A. Wise, who had succeeded Stimson.

The *World*'s busy investigators never found out who got the $40 million when it reached France, but they did establish (beyond reasonable doubt, Barrett believed, and subsequent study confirms it) that Cromwell was primarily responsible for engineering the so-called revolution in Panama that led to American acquisition of the Canal Zone and was the paymaster for this operation as well, an endeavor in which he had the full support and connivance of the Roosevelt administration, from the top down. Most of this information came from a copy of Cromwell's brief, a detailed account of everything the firm did for the government in the Panama affair. This brief was "obtained," as the saying goes, by the *World*'s investigative reporters. How a copy of it turned up on a desk in the paper's office remains unexplained.

At last District Judge Charles M. Hough reached a decision in the case, ruling on the legal point that the crime charged in the indictment could only be regarded as an offense against the United States if it was also an offense against the law of New York State, which it clearly was not. He ordered the indictment quashed. The *World* was triumphant in an editorial that declared:

> If there exists in Washington the shadow of a suspicion that a Federal libel suit can be created by construction or interpretation—if there still remains the likelihood that another Roosevelt will prostitute his powers . . . in order to prosecute newspapers that have offended him—if there be the ghost of a belief that the Federal Government has coordinate power with State governments in the prosecution of alleged libel, and that every American newspaper is at the mercy of the President—then the sooner there is a final decision of the Supreme Court of the United States the better.

The government was not anxious to appeal, but the *World* applied public pressure, so a writ of error was filed. On January 3, 1911, a unanimous opinion was handed down, written by Chief Justice Edward Douglass White, completely upholding the verdict of the lower court, and once more the *World* was able to proclaim: "The decision is so sweeping that no other President will be tempted to follow in the footsteps of Theodore Roosevelt, no matter how greedy he may be for power, no matter how resentful of opposition."

The *World* was overly optimistic on that point, as we know now, but it was nevertheless a victory, although the case had been decided on a legal technicality and none of the serious questions it raised had been answered. In the continuing struggle between press and president, the result was not an affirmation of principle but only a legal victory in a case that should never have been brought into court on such flimsy grounds.

Vindicated, and the District indictment against him dismissed at the request of the Department of Justice itself, Joseph Pulitzer died seven months later, the last of the nineteenth-century journalistic giants to go. He had won a small battle against the new imperial presidency, but the conduct of the *World* had not been above reproach, as he well knew. Moreover the entire press (as Barrett was to point out later) had been grossly negligent in its coverage of the entire Panama affair, in which the Cromwell case represented only one aspect of a story so large the papers let it get away. If ever there was a chapter in American political history that demanded investigation, Panama in all its ramifications was a prime subject.

As for Theodore Roosevelt, he emerged from the fray with his reputation relatively intact. He had acted toward the press in a high-handed way, but he had unquestionably been provoked. Although the courts had rebuked him, in a sense, their verdicts had done nothing at all to define either the prerogatives of a president or the responsibility of the press. These questions were left to the future.

Taft: A Step Backward

William Howard Taft was Theodore Roosevelt's mistake, as the president himself admitted. The initial mistake had been made in Roosevelt's decision to honor the no-third-term tradition and refuse a nomination that would surely have been his, but then it was compounded by his second decision, to handpick and support his secretary of war, considered to be a virtual assurance of nomination, if not election.

There was every reason for Roosevelt's confidence in his man. Taft was a close friend and, beyond that, appeared to be as well qualified as anyone could be. His father Alphonso had also been a secretary of war, a demanding parent who had great ambitions for his son. Second in his class at Yale, believed by at least one classmate to be the most admired and respected man in the college, young Taft read in his father's law office, studied at Cincinnati Law School, and earned pocket money as court reporter for the Cincinnati *Daily Commercial*. Not that he had any intention of following journalism as a career; he was interested in the job only because it gave him access to courtrooms, where he could study the workings of the law at first hand. He stayed with the paper for only a year.

Once Taft had his law degree in hand, progress was rapid—assistant county prosecutor, district collector of internal revenue, judge of the Ohio State Superior Court, United States solicitor general, Federal Appeals Court judge in the Sixth Circuit, first American civil governor of the Philippines, and finally the appointment to be secretary of war, made by the man who had been his good friend since his days as solicitor general. In their new relationship Taft found himself even closer to Roosevelt, advising, acting as roving ambassador, becoming on occasion a kind of assistant president.

In those days Taft was a popular man. His immense weight, varying from 340 to 350 pounds, made him the apotheosis of the jolly fat man. He exuded amiability, seemingly at ease with reporters, joking and laughing with them, always at least cordial and friendly. Nothing in his relations with either the president or the press gave the slightest foretaste of what was to come.

Those few historians who have made an attempt to rehabilitate or revise Taft's reputation (a task undertaken on behalf of all presidents by successive generations of revisionists) have tried to explain Taft's later behavior as president by asserting that there were really two men contained in that globular body—the Taft whose great love was the law and whose only ambition was to be on the Supreme Court and the Taft who was pushed into the presidency by an ambitious wife and brother. Perhaps that is the only reasonable explanation for the extraordinary reluctance Taft displayed when he found himself in the White House.

Paradoxically Taft could have realized his desire to be a Supreme Court justice long before. Roosevelt twice offered him the appointment, first while he was still governing the Philippines, but he felt compelled to refuse because of his conscientious desire to complete his work in the islands. Again, when he was secretary,

Roosevelt dangled the tempting prize before him once more, and this time he would have accepted if his family had not urged him so fervently to wait for the real prize that could be his—the presidency.

Yet, in spite of their close friendship, Taft was not Roosevelt's first choice to succeed him as president. He would rather have had Elihu Root, his secretary of state, follow him into the White House than any other man, as he let it be known, but Root was a pragmatist who knew that even with the president's help there would be a fight to obtain the nomination, and, if he won it, his election was unlikely. At his insistence, Roosevelt stopped considering him. Taft was the second choice.

Immediately after Root conveyed his decision through William Loeb, Jr., the president's secretary, Roosevelt dispatched Loeb to the War Department to inform Taft he was going to be the man. "I must go over and thank Theodore," Taft said, and did so. "Yes, Will," Roosevelt told him, "it's the thing to do." Thus, almost casually, the course of presidential history was determined for the next four years.

Taft was nominated on the first roll call; it would have been Republican blasphemy to oppose Roosevelt's wishes. It could not have been entirely comfortable for the nominee, however, on the day before his ascension, when a reference to Roosevelt in a speech by the permanent chairman, Henry Cabot Lodge, set off a demonstration on the convention floor that lasted forty-nine minutes and would have led to a stampede for the president if Lodge had not firmly admonished the delegates: "Anyone who attempts to use his name as a candidate for the Presidency impugns both his sincerity and his good faith." The faithful subsided, but they gave Taft only a twenty-nine-minute ovation.

William Jennings Bryan, the Democrats' nominee, did better than either of the Republicans, with eighty-seven minutes of hysteria occasioned by the fact that the Western free-silver Democrats were once more in the saddle and riding high in Denver, the convention city. Not many of the practical politicians, however, could have entertained any real hope for their resurrected hero, who had failed them twice before. The atmosphere was more like that surrounding a great diva making her absolutely final farewell tour.

The election results bore out this feeling. Taft polled over a million popular votes more than his rival and swept the electoral college by 321 to 162. Even so, there were some on Inauguration Day who could not help feeling that Roosevelt was the real winner; he dominated that event as he had every other. There had been a heavy, wet snowfall in Washington the night before, of near-record proportions, continuing into the day itself with sleet and rain so that the ceremony had to be held inside in the Senate Chamber rather than the usual Capitol portico. As Taft and Roosevelt left the White House, the incoming chief executive observed gloomily, "Even the elements do protest," to which Roosevelt responded with the characteristic, almost exultant remark, "I knew there would be a blizzard when I went out." Immediately after the ceremony Roosevelt departed the stage he had held for so long with a final dramatic gesture, hurrying to Union Station and boarding a train that would take him to New York and Oyster Bay. Taft was now alone, for the first time.

The press had no reason to believe that its relationship with the new occupant of the White House would be anything but cordial. As the chief Washington correspondent of the New York *Times,* Oscar King Davis (OK to TR) recalled in his memoirs, it had been "a favorite occupation for the correspondents to 'go Tafting'" when the jovial fat man was secretary of war. Nearly every afternoon a large group of them would convene in his office for a half-hour or so of relaxed conversation, which often produced news stories. King recalled that

Mr. Taft exerted himself to get, and keep, on good terms with the newspapermen. He talked frankly about affairs in his own department, was much more communicative, as a rule, than other Cabinet officers, and at times would even "take assignments" for the boys. When they had struck difficulties in other departments, it was by no means unusual to appeal to Mr. Taft, and not infrequently he dug out the desired information. He seemed to accept the argument which the correspondents at Washington are constantly advancing to Government officials, that the Government business is public business, knowledge of which in all but a few special cases, belongs of right to the public.

Davis had come gradually to be on intimate terms with Taft—so intimate that he performed services that would be considered highly unethical (and unheard of) today. Not only did he cover Taft's quick rise to power for the *Times,* but he helped with his campaign publicity, writing several magazine articles about him, some under his own byline and others ghostwritten, as well as a campaign biography. Davis asserts that other correspondents who were on friendly terms with Taft voluntarily on many occasions did not write stories that they thought would hurt their friend's chances and went out of their way to produce stories that might help him.

What happened after the election, then, was all the more stunning to these friends and allies. There was a premonitory shudder soon after Christmas 1908, when the president-elect and his wife came to Washington for the first time since his victory, as guests of a good friend, Mabel Boardman, who had been active with Taft in the Red Cross. Davis describes what followed:

One afternoon during this visit I went, with one or two other correspondents who had been very friendly to Mr. Taft, to call on him. Naturally, we wanted any news we could get, but our chief purpose was merely to pay our respects to the President-elect, and to offer again our congratulations on his election. In both respects the call was a good deal of a failure. We did see Mr. Taft for a few moments, but there was certainly no important news in what he told us, very little, indeed, that was worth sending, beyond the fact that he had received us and had nothing to say. And when we left the Boardman house every one of us had the same queer feeling that something had happened to "put us in bad" with the new President. The old cordiality and friendliness which had always marked his dealings with us . . . was wholly gone, and there was in its place a reserve that almost amounted to coldness. There was not one of those correspondents who had not done Mr. Taft substantial favors repeatedly, but there was nothing in his bearing that afternoon which would indicate the slightest realization of that fact on his part.

Several of these correspondents were among those who hoped to give their special congratulations to Taft after his inaugural. It had been a terribly difficult day for them. Getting out the biggest story of the moment had proved to be an extraordinary feat because the storm had buried Washington in a foot of snow and isolated it as telephone and telegraph wires came down. Davis pieced the inaugural story together from the work of his staff man and sent it in sections on every train that struggled out of Washington that day, passed along slowly up the snow-buried route by an army of signalmen. The object was to get the copy to Philadelphia, where it could be telegraphed to New York.

Late in the afternoon, enough order had been restored so that Davis and some other correspondents felt it was time, and safe enough, to trudge over to the White House through the still dismal weather and pay respects to their old friend. Again Davis relates the surprise that awaited them:

> There and then we got our first, emphatic demonstration that it was not only a new President in the White House, but, in fact, a new man, and not at all the pleasant, genial, helpful, good-natured man we had known as Secretary of War. If differentiation from Roosevelt was an essential principle of the new Administration, as some of us straightway came to believe, it received a practical reinforcement that afternoon. For the President declined to receive us. I think it was the most surprised group of Washington correspondents that I have ever seen, to whom Fred Carpenter, the new Secretary to the President, brought that message. This was a group of men who had hewed wood and carried water to help make Mr. Taft President, and to be told rather curtly by the new Secretary that the new President would not see them was not in the least what any of them had expected. Then, when Mr. Carpenter added that the President did not expect to see newspaper men as frequently as he had done when Secretary of War, but if and when he desired to see any one he would send for him, the climax was very fittingly capped.
>
> For a minute or two the boys stood around, first on one foot and then on the other, and not much of anything was said. Then somebody had the inspiration to suggest that we were really not after news, but only wanted to pay our respects to the new Chief Magistrate. That seemed to relieve Carpenter, who went again into the inside office. Presently he returned and said the President would see us, and at once Mr. Taft came out. He shook hands, graciously, all around, and some one said something at which he laughed.

The laughter was hollow on both sides. Obviously something had gone wrong with the relationship, but the correspondents were at a loss to know what it was. Nor did they ever find out. Was it because Taft believed that Roosevelt was such a hard act to follow that he had made up his mind not to follow it at all, as far as the press was concerned? Was he politically and intellectually lazy, as some believed? Or did he simply have a different conception of relationships between the president and the press, a conception that leapfrogged backward into the darker days of the nineteenth century?

No one could tell for certain. All that could be said definitely was that relations worsened rapidly. Only a month after Taft had entered the White House, reporters were warning Fred Carpenter that there was a good deal of anger among them because they believed the president was deliberately withholding information. They were told curtly that the press would have to adjust itself to new conditions, after which Taft drew still further into his shell. "I see very few news-papermen," he wrote in November of that first year. Baffled and cut off, the reporters retaliated with an increasing flow of critical stories. Not only was the president no help to them, but Carpenter had no more knowledge or understanding of the press than his employer. As Taft's former secretary, he had been promoted to a White House job he did not fully comprehend and was not well qualified to handle, a mistake the president made because he himself did not understand what the job of White House secretary had become.

Blocked from their usual sources of news, reporters had to turn elsewhere, and "elsewhere," as one historian, Robert C. Hilderbrand, has pointed out, included

> the camp of Taft's enemies, and anti-administration news soon occupied a more prominent position in the newspapers. With the White House refusing to provide advance information of its plans and policies, the press frequently heard executive news from Taft's detractors, re-creating the kind of situation the presidential press release had been designed to remedy in the first place. At the same time, news leaks began to emerge from the White House. Although many of these unauthorized sources doubtless believed themselves to be assisting a president needlessly alienating the press, others had personal—and sometimes vindictive—motives for confiding in reporters; in either case, their information usually did the administration more harm than good. Nevertheless, responsibility for such leaks must ultimately lodge with the president, whose nonchalance in press matters had resulted in lowered standards of confidentiality for White House personnel and whose unwillingness to provide journalists with information had sent them searching for less official sources. All in all, Taft's treatment of the press caused him to lose his grasp of the process of distributing White House news, placing control over the president's public relations in outside hands for the first time in a decade.

Much of the president's problem must be ascribed to his acute realization that he did not possess the skills and qualities his predecessor had employed so well in handling his press relations. He had no facility with words, whether written or spoken, in contrast to Roosevelt's extraordinary facility in both. Consequently Taft believed that he would never be able to use the press as his friend had done, and so, as he wrote to Roosevelt in 1909, there was no point in even trying. Taft was painfully aware, too, that his temperament was at the opposite pole from Roosevelt's and that he completely lacked the former president's understanding of news, of how to make it, and of the organizations that printed it. Moreover Taft was the first of what could be called the "lazy" presidents, that is, those who liked the glory of the job but hated the hard work that went with it. As the first president addicted to golf, he was happiest when he was traversing the back nine with his friends. No doubt his indolence was at least partly the result of his excessive weight, which also caused him to fall asleep in public on occasion. In the end Taft fell back on an aphorism that had been heard before in the White House. It would not be necessary to sell himself or his policies to the people, he believed. All he had to do was to "get things done," as he said, point to his accomplishments, and ultimately he would be vindicated by the "result of my labors." That notion had never been justified before, and it would not be now.

It was a situation, however, that was bound to change, at least to some extent. In 1910 Fred Carpenter departed, to be succeeded by Charles D. Norton, who had once been assistant secretary of the treasury, and an immediate improvement in press relations resulted. For the first time it became possible to get an appointment with the president, even on short notice, although these favors were not distributed indiscriminately or in quantity. Inspired, perhaps, by serious Republican losses in the midterm elections, Taft appeared to see the necessity of repairing some of the damage he had done, and he even sought publicity for the first time by granting two magazine interviews and making an effort to improve his speeches and his more frequent messages to Congress.

Norton had taken the trouble to talk with correspondents before he took the job and had learned something of what was needed from a White House secretary as far as the press was concerned. He saw that the best previous secretaries had really been assistants to the president, and this was the role he created for himself. He did it too well. Success resulted in more power, and power inevitably produced frictions with others in the administration. Balancing improved press relations against inner disruptions of White House life, Taft characteristically decided to avoid further trouble and asked for Norton's resignation.

For Norton's successor, the president unaccountably dipped again into the pool of Treasury assistants and came up with Charles D. Hilles, who was guaranteed not to be ambitious. But the correspondents observed that lessened secretarial power also meant less authority, and, although they liked Hilles personally and saw that he was trying to do a good job, he had little influence with them. Hilles resigned after a year, to be followed by Carmi Thompson, who appeared to be more successful than any of his predecessors but still failed to satisfy Taft—no doubt, as Hilderbrand observes, because Taft never fully comprehended the job himself.

Taft was not without friends and helpers in the press. Gus Karger of the Cincinnati *Times-Star* was as much a presidential confidant as he was a reporter, and he did his utmost to help the president improve his press relations. According to J. Frederick Essary, a veteran Washington reporter, Karger "had access to the Executive at all times, was permitted to examine the White House mail daily, and to know all that went on behind the scenes." Unselfishly, says Essary, Karger "gave to every newspaperman interested every line of news which he drew from the White House sources during the whole Taft period. He was an extremely valuable aid to Mr. Taft in getting the Taft viewpoint before the public."

An even more valuable help was Maj. Archie Butt, who had been Roosevelt's great friend and military aide and now, in the new administration, served Taft not only in his formal capacity but informally as intimate, adviser, and golfing companion. Butt spent more time with the president than anyone, and his "intimate letters," as they were called when published, have provided historians with insights into Taft's behavior. Butt, who was well acquainted with many reporters, tried to maintain some kind of relationship with them. A born publicist, he also maneuvered Taft into positions that might benefit his image, such as persuading him to attend a baseball game, then cajoling him into sitting in the bleachers with the average fans rather than in the boxes, which he preferred. No amount of image-making, however, could put much of a dent in Taft's appearance as a man who had little, if any, of Roosevelt's common touch.

In spite of all Butt's efforts, it was a pitifully small band of correspondents who remained friendly with Taft regardless of rebuffs. The president went so far as to visit with William Price of the Washington *Star* at his home, and occasionally he talked on a more intimate basis than usual with OK Davis, Richard Oulahan of the New York *Sun,* and Robert Small of the Associated Press. Of them all, however, it was only Karger whom the president trusted completely.

Taft's few attempts at meeting with the press, made as a result of Karger's urgings, were a failure and soon abandoned. The president insisted on seeing the correspondents in the cabinet room, so small it could accommodate only fifteen people, imposing a selectivity that could only cause more hard feelings. Taft was often late for these meetings, sometimes by as much as two hours or more, and, when he did arrive, he maintained the chilly reserve that had cloaked him since his arrival in the White House, making no effort to use these embryonic press conferences for the purpose of communicating with either press or public, as they were designed to do. Oddly enough, because Karger had been granted exceptional freedom in the White House, even to the extent of examining the president's morning mail, and because this popular correspondent shared everything he found out with his fellow reporters, he became as much a press secretary, in a sense, as though he had been appointed to the post, which many believed should have been the case.

Nothing that Karger or Butt could do, however, improved matters to any great extent. The frank but faithful major reports an occasion that sums up Taft's ambivalent and generally hostile attitude toward the press. After a dinner with his cabinet the president retired to the Green Room and excused himself for what the dinner guests believed would be a short time, since he had consented to be interviewed by the editor of the *Georgian,* who intended to advise him on how he could improve his relations with the press. Surprisingly, the interview lasted two hours, and, with even more astonishment, the waiting guests made conversation for still another hour while Taft talked with Oulahan of the *Sun.* Had the president reversed his well-known attitude? Was it the beginning of a new era in press relations? But then Taft rejoined the cabinet members and immediately, as Butt reported, threw a temper tantrum that disabused the cabinet members of any fear that he had gone soft on reporters.

> He at once sat down and began to damn the press, *Collier*'s in particular. He said that Seeley [the *Georgian*'s editor] had told him that [Norman] Hapgood and another of *Collier*'s editors wanted to come to see him, but he had told them that he would not see them; that he regarded them as murderers and thieves, and he would, if he had his way, condemn them all to hell and eternal damnation.
> After this burst of temper, which he laughed over himself, he fell asleep, and I

woke him once, but no one else liked to do so, so that it was after two o'clock when
he fully roused himself and begged our pardons and went to bed.

(Taft's animus against *Collier's* rose from the fact that under its brilliant editor,
Norman Hapgood, the magazine had become a late leader among the more fer-
vent muckrakers, and its liberalism was an offense to everything the conservative
Taft believed.)

Butt's comments about Taft's newspaper reading are equally revealing. Fuss-
ing over his recalcitrant friend, the major was perturbed by the president's preference for the *Sun,* as he wrote:

> I wish the President would not read the *Sun* so much. He always wants to see it
> first thing. He greatly enjoys its lampoons, especially those aimed at the Colonel
> [Roosevelt]. The Colonel never allowed it in the White House, and managed to get
> along without it. It did not do anything but abuse Grover Cleveland; and yet see what
> little harm it did to him. . . . I believe it would be better for it to abuse the President
> than to be continually praising him. The President is really affected by its editorials.
> He does not like to read disagreeable truths any more than he likes to hear them. He
> stopped taking the New York *Times* when it abused him and now reads it second to
> the *Sun,* since it had changed its policy toward him. He was once wont to read the
> Washington *Times,* but now never sees it and does not allow the clippings to be
> placed with the others in front of him because it criticizes him.

On vacation in Beverly, Massachusetts, in 1911, Butt recorded the following
colloquy between Taft and his wife about his predilection for the *Sun:*

> Last night after dinner, when he asked if the New York papers had come, Mrs.
> Taft handed him the New York *World.*
> "I don't want the *World,*" he said. "I have stopped reading it. It only makes me
> angry."
> "But you used to like it very much," said Mrs. Taft.
> "That was when it agreed with me, but it abuses me now, and so I don't want it."
> "You will never know what the other side is doing if you only read the *Sun* and
> *Tribune,*" said this wise woman.
> "I don't care what the other side is doing," he answered with some irritation.

Taft's entire administration, it appeared, was fated to be a tragedy—and not
simply his relationship with the press, which another kind of man might have
overcome. Roosevelt's return in 1910 from a long sojourn in Africa and Europe
was the signal for a break between these two politicians, so unlike each other,
which in turn symbolized the split between conservative Taft Republicans and
progressive Roosevelt Republicans. Roosevelt was not only disappointed in his
friend's conduct of the presidency but opposed him on most of the important
issues, particularly Taft's staunch advocacy of the Payne-Aldrich Tariff, another
of the ruinous protectionist measures that convervatives in the party had been
advancing since McKinley's day and before. The struggle between these factions, and between the two old friends, grew increasingly bitter until the friends

became outright enemies, and the progressives left the party to nominate Roosevelt on a third-party ticket.

Could any of this have been prevented if Taft had been able to build up a solid support from the public through a friendly and manipulated press, as Roosevelt would have done? Probably not, in the opinion of those few historians who have bothered to entertain the idea. But it is not unreasonable to assume that, if this scenario had been played out and Roosevelt and Taft had stood together, using their joint abilities to unite the party, with the press quite possibly serving both, Woodrow Wilson could conceivably have lost to a resurgent Roosevelt, running for a third term as a Republican, with historical consequences that can only be conjectured. It is, however, only another of those tantalizing "ifs" with which history is replete.

As matters stood, the last half of the Taft administration was a dismal winding down. To many then (and even to his most recent biographers) it seemed incredible that a man who everyone agreed was an outstanding public servant, who was unquestionably honest, incapable of the usual political flapdoodle, and with broad support from the public and the party in power—that such a man could let all this slip away until he mustered only eight electoral votes when he ran again.

One of those recent biographers, Donald F. Anderson, sees Roosevelt as the unwitting villain in this piece, as he no doubt was. "By working in the shadow of one of the most popular leaders in America who served as his mentor, press agent, and champion," Anderson writes, "Taft was never forced to develop the knowledge and skills of the professional politician concerned with winning and maintaining public support." Later, Anderson observes, "he was more willing to fight for a principle, a policy, or another person than for himself. . . . For most Americans, trust and confidence in the President as a person is their only link to the complex policies for which he stands. Taft's personal humility actually undermined public confidence in himself and his administration."

Fighting for a principle regardless of consequences, which usually strengthens a president's popularity, worked in just the opposite way for Taft. Most politicians would have considered it suicidal to advocate something that was absolutely certain to bring down the wrath of the entire media family (newspapers, magazines, and books in this case), but Taft did just that when he opposed lowering the tariff for paper and pulp in 1909. Since enactment of the protectionist Dingley Tariff of 1897, the tax on imported newsprint had risen to $6 per ton, and there had been joint agitation by both the Associated Press and the American Newspaper Publishers Association to get it lowered. In a stunningly brief message to Congress of only 324 words, Taft simply asked for "readjustment and revision of the import duties." It may well be that the president made this ambiguous approach in the interests of party harmony, but the result was predictable.

As tariff revision legislation moved through Congress, the House was ready to lower the rate on newsprint to $2, but the Senate's bill proposed $4, a figure that approximated what the ANPA had hoped to get. Nevertheless the prospect of a deeper cut led to severe press criticism of the Senate bill, which Taft defended while he attacked "deliberate misrepresentation" and "misconception of the facts'' in the newspapers. A compromise of $3.75 was reached in conference, but the president was not willing to let the matter go, declaring, ''I can not help attributing a great deal of bitterness of this controversy to the counting room of the newspapers which have been affected by the failure to reduce the tariff on print paper in a tariff bill.'' Anderson remarks that this action guaranteed the president would have ''an unsympathetic, almost hostile press when he needed it most . . . to build his own independent image as President.''

As though this were not a bad enough blunder, Taft used his annual message to Congress in December 1909 to call for a substantial increase in postal rates for magazines. While the rates for newspapers and magazines have been the subjects of periodic arguments since 1792, when Congress first established them on a broad basis, until the present moment, the howl that went up from the magazine business in the early months of 1910 was particularly anguished because the muckraking magazines were certain that it constituted an act of revenge.

This was a somewhat different tack than the usual terms of the argument—that, on the media's side, a *de facto* government subsidy is necessary because the alternative would be a limitation of the free flow of information and ideas in a democracy, and that, on the government side (especially in conservative administrations), special postal rates for the media constitute a subsidy that comes out of the taxpayer's pocket on behalf of a special interest. The fact that this particular special interest, unlike other government-subsidized interests, might well be hostile to any government, and an enemy of other special interests as well, only confirms the perennial opposition to such subsidies.

Taft stated his own case bluntly:

> The truth is that the present magazines are getting about fifty millions of dollars out of the Government that they are not entitled to, and I am going to fight that thing through. I do not care anything about them. They have shown themselves just exactly as selfish as the interests which they have attacked, and I propose to have justice done. If we wish to contribute a subsidy of fifty millions to the education of the country, I can find a good deal better method of doing it than by the circulation of *Collier's Weekly* and *Everybody's Magazine.*

He underestimated the opposition, however, and the stormy controversy that arose over his proposal dismayed even this obtuse man. To a member of the Senate Post Office Committee he complained, ''I never in all my knowledge of lobbies and of organized efforts to influence legislation have seen such flagrant misrepresentation and such bold defiant attempts by the payment of the heaviest advertisement bills to arouse the press of the country against the proposed legislation.'' Worse, he was compelled to accept a galling defeat. Forced to withdraw his proposal, he agreed to a face-saving appointment of a special commission to decide the matter. Composed as it was of three eminent conservatives—Supreme Court Justice Charles Evans Hughes; A. Lawrence Lowell, president of Harvard; and Harry A. Wheeler, president of the Chicago Association of Commerce—the commission recommended doubling second-class rates. Taft presented this to

Congress as a victory, but he knew it was not; in reality, it was an extremely modest increase compared with what he had wanted.

Taft was unrepentant. When the tariff and postal rates controversies were over, he wrote to Herman Kohlsaat, publisher of the Chicago *Record-Herald,* ''I have not been familiar myself with any situation politically where there has been so much hypocrisy, so much hysteria, so much misrepresentation by the press growing out of their own personal interest in legislation as within the last year, and this affects not only the newspapers but also the periodicals.''

Yet, in spite of everything, not every newspaper raised its hand against the president, and Taft himself appeared for a short time in the spring of 1910 to be establishing a bridge between himself and the press. Speaking to a group of editors and educators in New York, he demonstrated such a grasp of the issues and presented enough of his former genial personality that many of those present were convinced they had been wrong about him. Among the converts was Arthur Brisbane, Hearst's chief editor, who said afterward: ''The fact of the matter is, none of us has ever given the President a fair show as yet. We have all been judging him by the standards of his predecessor, and we have yielded to the public clamor for him to use the attacking methods of Roosevelt. We are beginning to see him rightly, and I think he will win out if this Roosevelt homecoming does not upset all plans and purposes of thoughtful men.''

But then the Roosevelt homecoming *did* occur in June, in a flash of teeth and glasses, and the result Brisbane had intimated might happen did take place. The papers were filled with the returning hero; a tumultuous welcome greeted him everywhere he went; and his opinions again occupied the headlines, among them his refusal to endorse Taft's record. Just at the moment of what might have been an important recovery from a bad start, Taft saw his ebullient friend snatch away all the publicity available, and with it the nation's attention. Overshadowed once more, he could only retreat.

At this point Taft seemed to give up any hope of changing the opinions of the press or the people in and out of his party who opposed him, including Roosevelt. His attitude toward both was hardening. When Kohlsaat wrote to him, advising that Republicans were apathetic about his administration, Taft replied on March 15, 1910: ''You describe the feeling among the Republicans as a 'don't care a damn' feeling. I have that myself. It is exactly that feeling that I have with reference to the views of the press and of those people who think that they are going to have a better government by defeating the Republican party, or are going to accomplish anything by doing so.''

New prospects for a change arose, however, during the lame-duck session of the Sixty-first Congress, when Taft moved to relieve some of the antagonism caused by the Payne-Aldrich bill's paper tariffs and the subsequent increase in second-class postage rates. In dealing with the issue of Canadian reciprocity, he proposed lower tariffs on print paper and wood pulp, which had been a continuing goal of the American Newspaper Publishers Association. A new agreement with Canada would constitute a revision of Payne-Aldrich and give the publishers even more than they had demanded in 1909. This was enough to swing the ANPA's lobby and many of its member papers around to support the president, and momentarily Taft found himself with a small army of unlikely allies.

The honeymoon was not lasting. Again Taft lost the opportunity through his puzzling nature. His occasional disparaging remarks about Canada in public were just what the Liberal government's opposition in that country needed in its efforts to kill the agreement. The president's references had the ring of colonialism and empire about them, although they were not as crude as the chauvinistic bellow that arose in the House when the Democratic leader, Champ Clark, in endorsing the agreement, declared that he hoped "to see the day when the American flag will float over every square foot of the British North American possession clear to the North Pole." When the agreement passed Congress, Taft may have sealed its fate in Canada by publicly praising the Hearst papers for "their earnest and useful effort to spread the gospel of reciprocity," seemingly unaware that these papers had also been conducting for some time a campaign advocating the annexation of Canada. Two months later the Liberal government fell over the reciprocity issue, and the opportunity was lost.

As the break between Taft and Roosevelt widened in 1911, and the former president became the leader of the insurgent Republican wing of the party, Taft could not bring himself to reply to the increasing barrage of criticism from his former friend. He was hurt and bewildered by what was happening. Muddled as ever about the press, he took some comfort in the fact that papers that had always opposed Roosevelt were now attacking him again. "I have not answered Roosevelt and his charges," he wrote to a friend. "I have ignored him and let the newspapers attend to him and they are doing it. He is now engaged in attacking the newspapers. They can be trusted to answer for themselves, both Democratic and Republican." One of the papers that came to Taft's defense was the Springfield *Republican,* which reviewed favorably everything he had done and concluded, "The like is not to be found in the whole seven years of Roosevelt's administration. . . . Even the hysterical, screaming 'Back-from-Elba' army [Roosevelt's progressive supporters] must now admit that as one who 'does things' the former President is being outclassed."

That was not the case, of course. In fact a reluctant Taft, pushed by Rooseveltian political tactics that would now be called showboating, was being dragged into an increasingly personal campaign against the man he had thought was his dearest friend. Taft even became the first president to go on the stump during the primaries. For his part, Roosevelt had tossed aside all his protestations and vows about not running again and had thrown himself into the nominating fray because he was convinced Taft could not be elected again and the Republicans would be out of power. "Based as it was upon personality rather than principle," says Paoela Coletta, one of Taft's recent biographers, "the Taft-Roosevelt contest became a sorry spectacle that approximated a national disgrace."

As usual, Taft was almost embarrassingly candid about his purpose. He told Charles W. Thompson, a New York *Times* reporter, "Whether I win or lose is not important, but I am in this fight to perform a great public duty—the duty of keeping Theodore Roosevelt out of the White House." Nevertheless the personal circumstances made it a cruel ordeal for the president. After a climactic defense of his policies in a Boston speech in April 1912, Louis Seibold, the New York *World*'s veteran correspondent, found Taft slumped over, head between his hands, weeping. Looking up, he blurted out despairingly, "Roosevelt was my closest friend!"

In his struggle Taft was doing what he had never done before—using the press to help him. He gave an exclusive interview to A. V. Pinci, of *Harper's Weekly,* which emerged as a defense of all his policies, foreign and domestic, with a note of gratitude to the American people for having elected him but neglecting to say anything at all about the campaign. Seibold, noting the omission, asked for an interview to talk about the issues and the relationship with Roosevelt. Taft granted it. Seibold wrote his story, then rode up to New York on the train with the president, who was on his way to attend General Sherman's funeral in Utica. During the trip Seibold gave the president his copy, inviting him to edit it as he wished. Taft did so and appeared disturbed about some of the statements he had made concerning Roosevelt, although he did not question their accuracy. He told Seibold that, before he released the story, he wanted to consult his lawyers, Root, Wickersham and Barnes, in New York. "I'm afraid that's too late," Seibold told him. "But Roosevelt was my closest friend," Taft reiterated, and would not release the interview. It was never printed. After the election Seibold asked Taft for a copy of it (the president had kept the manuscript), but Taft said it was gone and that he had ordered his secretary to burn his notes. In fact the manuscript did exist, and Henry Pringle found a transcript of it in the Library of Congress when he was doing research for his authorized but not official two-volume biography of Taft, published in 1939. There was no startling revelation. Taft had simply blamed his break with Roosevelt and the division of the party on the quarrel over the Payne-Aldrich Tariff. In any event, it had been Taft's last opportunity to tell his side of the story to a sympathetic reporter, and once more he had tossed it away.

As the conventions approached, wiser Republican heads were alarmed by the divisive quarrel between Taft and Roosevelt, and it was suggested that they both withdraw and a compromise candidate, possibly Charles Evans Hughes, be named. Roosevelt would have none of it. If there were to be a compromise candidate, he said defiantly but obscurely, "He'll be me." Thus the Republicans gathered for their suicide pact in Chicago, with Roosevelt himself on hand to direct the progressives' operations. But for once, he had made a serious mis-calculation. Taft had the party's bosses and their machines on his side, and they prevailed.

On the night before the balloting, sensing what was going to happen, Roose-velt made a speech in another hall before a large and enthusiastic audience. Even for him, it was an address full of spectacular bombast. "We fight in honorable fashion for the good of mankind," he told his sweating troops, "unheeding of our individual fates; with unflinching hearts and undimmed eyes, we stand at Armageddon, and we battle for the Lord."

But the Lord was not listening, as so often happens with politicians. The convention nominated Taft overwhelmingly, although the victory was tarnished by the fact that 344 Roosevelt delegates refused to vote. The progressives promptly organized themselves into a third party, met in Chicago, and nominated their hero, who told the cheering delegates that he felt "as strong as a bull moose," giving the new party its nickname. As for the Democrats, when they convened in Baltimore, they nominated a progressive, too, Woodrow Wilson of New Jersey, a man Taft later came to hate with a pure passion. At that, it took them forty-six ballots to do it, and they were not hopeful of beating the entrenched Republicans. The Socialists nominated Eugene V. Debs.

In the campaign it was often hard to tell the difference between Rooseveltian and Wilsonian progressivism ("the New Freedom," Wilson called it). A few weeks before the election, as Roosevelt left a Milwaukee hotel, he stood in the back seat of his seven-passenger touring car and turned to throw up his arms in a salute to the cheering crowd. A man in the front row whose hatred of a third term exceeded his better judgment suddenly raised a large revolver and shot Roosevelt in the chest. Staggered but not daunted, the colonel insisted on being driven to the auditorium, where he was to speak, instead of to the hospital. "It may be the last one I shall ever deliver," he told his anxious attendants, "but I am going to deliver this one."

Before he spoke, doctors examined the wound, about a half-inch under the right nipple; it was bleeding a little, but Roosevelt declared he felt no pain. He walked onto the stage as vigorously as ever, told the shocked audience he had just been shot and boasted, "But it takes more than that to kill a bull moose." When he drew out the manuscript of his speech, fifty thick sheets of heavy paper, he saw that it had probably saved his life, deflecting the bullet just enough so that it did not slip through his ribs into the heart but was stopped by the fifth rib.

After he had spoken for thirty-five minutes an attempt was made to stop him, but he refused angrily, even though he was obviously unsteady on his feet by this time. A little later he paused long enough to ask how long he had spoken. Told it was forty-five minutes, he declared he would go on for fifteen minutes more, but instead he continued for another forty-five. When he had thrown down the last page, he turned to the doctors and said, "Now I'm ready to go with you and do what you want." Surgeons soon removed the bullet, and in a day or two Roosevelt was as good as ever.

Thus, at the very end, the indomitable colonel had upstaged his onetime friend and present rival. It was a display of bravado that won him cheers but not the election. The result of the Republican split was apparent when Wilson took forty of the forty-eight states, and the former Princeton professor who few thought would win emerged as the next president of the United States.

Taft seemed greatly relieved as the smoke cleared away. Just before Wilson's inauguration he gave a farewell speech at the National Press Club in a manner approaching the humorous urbanity of his days as secretary of war, professing neither regret nor bitterness. "I have no occasion for kicking or squealing," he told his audience, few of whom could have believed he meant it.

In his role as former president, Taft was a much different man, teaching at Yale as Kent Professor of Law, writing an article for the *Saturday Evening Post* on "Personal Aspects of the Presidency" (in which he managed to be kind even to Wilson), writing a series of six articles about the trusts for the Sunday New York *Times,* lecturing everywhere in response to great demand, showing no trace of his former distate for the press—and, of course, serving at last as chief justice of the Supreme Court. If it is true that the presidency can make a man, as it has, it is equally true that it can unmake one, as it did in Taft's case.

There was a melancholy footnote to this rather odd episode in presidential history. Archie Butt, the close friend of both Roosevelt and Taft, had withdrawn from the unseemly struggle in the spring of 1912, when the cruelty was at its worst, and went to Europe in an effort to pull his anguished self together. The vessel on which he booked return passage was the *Titanic,* which, like Roosevelt, had been considered unsinkable. The major was spared the knowledge that it was the ship which went down first.

Wilson: A "Modern" President?

Thomas Woodrow Wilson has been called the first "modern" president, but it is difficult to fit so complex a man into a single category, even such a vague one. It is true that he was "modern" in the sense that he broke away from the political clichés of the nineteenth century. As the first intellectual in the White House since Jefferson and Madison, save perhaps for TR, he promised a new approach to the office, and it was at least his intent to begin a new era in press relations with something resembling the apparatus of today. Certainly, as a historian and political scientist, he well understood the necessity for a president to shape public opinion toward the realization of his policies.

There was a forecast of the future, too, in the emergence of radio during Wilson's two terms, although it was not yet ready to be the potent presidential weapon it would soon become. The first political broadcast to the public was a postelection analysis of the 1916 campaign, carried by an experimental New York State radio station, but the medium was not heard from again in this respect until the 1920 election results were broadcast by Station KDKA, Pittsburgh.

Between 1912 and 1920 the image of the president held by the public was still determined by the print media, underlining their importance in the shaping of public opinion. The president-press relationship was assuming an increasing importance not only because of the newspapers' economic strength and circulation growth but as a result of the rise of cheap weekly magazines to a position of influence. Under George Horace Lorimer's direction, for example, the *Saturday Evening Post*'s editorial page, carrying Lorimer's unsigned essays, was rapidly becoming a factor in Republican politics, as the 1920s would demonstrate further.

There were limitations. Taft had shown, once more, that a president hostile to the press could not simply stand on his record, self-righteously, and make no attempt to sell it to the electorate. On the other hand Theodore Roosevelt had proved, with equal clarity, that a popular president who was a master at manipulating the press could not rely either on his popularity or the media to ensure success if practical politics constituted the other half of the equation.

Other factors were involved as well. Economic considerations had their own profound influence in determining elections, regardless of what a president might say or the media report. In the making of foreign policy, Robert C. Hilderbrand argues, presidents from McKinley to Wilson were "not affected to any significant degree by considerations of public opinion," meaning that it "had little impact on the actual process of policy formulation." However, to call the role of public opinion a "myth," perpetuated by historians, presidents, and the press, all of whom want to believe in it for their own diverse purposes, is to overlook entirely the fact that while presidents may and often do formulate policy without regard for public opinion, they are usually compelled to sell it to Congress and the public if they want to implement it successfully, and in this process the media have always played a role, more significant at times than at others, as we have seen in this history, but one that has become far more important in the television era. It may be true, as Hilderbrand insists, that only executive officials have the authority to *make* decisions, but to conclude from this fact that "no real power has ever been given to the people" unaccountably excludes the role that public opinion, influenced at least to some extent by the press, unquestionably has had in the *carrying out* of those decisions, which after all is their most important aspect.

This was never more clear than in the case of Woodrow Wilson, who may well have been the most complicated man ever to sit in the White House. We know a great deal more about Wilson today than was known in his time or for years afterward, the result of what has been called the Wilson "industry," beginning but certainly not ending with Arthur S. Link's magisterial multivolume biography. Presidents with strong, many-faceted personalities naturally attract both historians and biographers, and Wilson continues to be a mine seemingly capable of endless exploration.

One of the more recent explorers, Edwin A. Weinstein, professor emeritus of neurology at Mount Sinai Medical School in New York City, conducted a medical and psychological safari into Wilson's anatomy and psyche, with results that, although disputed, may explain much about his behavior, including his complete about-face with the press, concerning which there have been several theories. Avoiding the Freudian booby traps of psychohistory, Weinstein gives us a portrait of Wilson that would have astounded his contemporaries. Here was a man with a lifelong obsession about his health, the son of a morbid and demanding mother who planted deep roots of dependency in him, a man who suffered (strangely, considering his later career) from what we would call dyslexia today. As so often happens, his parents blamed his impaired reading ability on laziness and laid upon him a heavy Presbyterian load of guilt and shame.

In 1896, Weinstein reports, Wilson suffered his first (or possibly a second) stroke, at the early age of forty. A decade later, while he was president of Princeton, he was stricken with another one, which cost him most of the sight in his left eye. He responded to these episodes, as he did to his other physical problems, with outbursts of energy, often creative, believing that the body must serve the spirit. Along with these positive evidences of malfunctioning, Wilson also was afflicted with respiratory problems that Weinstein believes were psychosomatic, and with intermittent mild depression.

Much worse was a slowly developing cerebral vascular disease that in time caused brain damage, and to this could be attributed Wilson's personality changes, the often puzzling decisions he made in both his private and public lives, even his peculiar speech patterns—and his changing, contradictory attitudes toward the press. The strokes continued. One came during his tenure as governor of New Jersey, at least one and possibly others while he was in the White House, and at last the one that disabled him completely. (It should be noted that Weinstein's diagnoses have been disputed by some scholars and physicians.) While it would be tempting to recapitulate the history of where Wilson's disturbed body and mind led him in private life—his ambiguous relationship with his aide Col. Edward M. House, and his extramarital affair with the fascinating Mrs. Mary Peck, for example—his complicated relationship with the press is not only the aspect of his life that is relevant here but quite enough in itself to consider.

Wilson, in fact, had family roots in the newspaper business. James Wilson, his Scotch-Irish grandfather, had taken over control of William Duane's *Aurora* (which he, in turn, had acquired from Benjamin Franklin Bache) in 1812, when he was twenty-five. He had come to America as an immigrant only five years before. Pushing on westward, he became proprietor of the Steubenville (Ohio) *Herald* in 1815, changing its name to the *Western Herald and Steubenville Gazette.* Following a familiar pathway, newspaper editing led to politics; James Wilson later became a member of the Ohio legislature and an associate judge of the Court of Common Pleas. His oldest son (one of seven), named William Duane Wilson, also went into the newspaper business, becoming one of Pittsburgh's leading publishers and later editor of the Chicago *Tribune,* in its pre-Medill days. Joseph Wilson, the youngest of James's sons and Woodrow's father, was also trained as a printer and founded a new triweekly, the *Pennsylvania Advocate,* in Pittsburgh in 1832, although he did not follow the trade, becoming a distinguished preacher and scholar.

With this kind of family background, it was only natural that young Woodrow Wilson should grow up believing in the press, and with at least a small understanding of it. As a scholar in his early years, his feelings about newspapers were Jeffersonian, convinced that government must be conducted in the open, without secrecy. It is the voice of a young, idealistic Wilson we hear in 1884, as he writes: "Light is the only thing that can sweeten our political atmosphere—light thrown upon every detail of administration in the departments; light diffused through every passage of policy; light blazed full upon every feature of legislation; light that can penetrate every recess or corner in which any intrigue might hide; light that will open to view the innermost chambers of government."

That idealism had not diminished twenty-five years later when Wilson was running for the presidency. "Government ought to be all outside and no inside," he declared then. "I, for my part, believe there ought to be no place where anything can be done that everybody does not know about. . . . Secrecy means impropriety." Or, in the ringing, familiar phrase he coined as president, "open covenants openly arrived at."

Even as he waited at Sea Girt, New Jersey, his summer home, to hear whether he had won the presidential nomination, Wilson was still inclined to talk freely with reporters, but it was there, too, that he found himself disillusioned with the press for the first time. It was a small episode in itself, but according to Ray Stannard Baker, who was there and knew him well, Wilson's attitude toward the correspondents began to change from that moment.

Killing time with the about-to-be candidate at Sea Girt, a reporter asked Wilson, almost idly, how he felt about the tidal wave of mail that was pouring in upon him. Wilson answered, just as casually, that in replying to all the letters he felt like the frog that had fallen into the well and "every time he jumped up one foot, he fell back two." Next morning a New York paper headlined this story, "Wilson Feels like a Frog." The candidate found that both disheartening and offensive, says Baker, confirming him

> in the strong dislike he had always felt for personal publicity. He felt that he could not be outspoken with men who could not understand, or with editors who permitted or required their writers to treat what he considered a solemn undertaking in a spirit so trivial, so personal. . . . From this time onward he was never quite free with groups of correspondents. He continued to receive them, then and afterwards, but they felt that he was on his guard, that he was "cold," that he gave them as little as he could. No man could have been franker than he with writers whom he came to know and to trust; he numbered among them many friends, several intimate friends; but he came more and more to shrink from miscellaneous interviewing.

There were other evidences, too, of a growing chilliness in Wilson's feelings about the press. One of the earliest editors (if not the first) to suggest Wilson as a candidate had been George Harvey, owner and editor of the *North American Review,* the most distinguished literary and opinion periodical of its time. But Wilson rewarded Harvey's support during the campaign by telling him bluntly that it might hurt his chances, particularly in the West. That action placed a permanent blight on their friendship. About the same time as Harvey, St. Clair McKelway, another highly esteemed journalist, editor of the Brooklyn *Eagle,* saw the presidential possibilities in Wilson and sent one of his best reporters down to Princeton to sound him out and offer him editorial support. The visit greatly disturbed Wilson, who sent McKelway a rather windy and overly modest protest.

Eventually Wilson accepted the support of the *Eagle* and a growing number of influential newspapers and periodicals, but he drew a firm line at having anything to do with the Hearst papers, which at the time were liberal Democratic, in keeping with their owner's political ambitions. Hearst invited Wilson to dinner, but the candidate declined even to meet him, much less dine with him, and refused to accept him on any terms. "I want the Democratic presidential nomination and I am going to do everything I can, legitimately, to get it," he declared, "but if I am to grovel at Hearst's feet, I will never have it!"

As time went on Hearst and his papers became Wilson's most implacable enemies, but according to Joseph Tumulty, Wilson's secretary for eleven years, Wilson

> never gave expression to any ill feeling or chagrin at the unfair attacks that were made upon him. I remember a little incident that shows the trend of his feelings in this regard, that occurred when we were discussing the critical Mexican situation. At this time the Hearst papers were engaged in a sensational propaganda campaign in behalf of intervention in Mexico. The President said to me, "I heard of a delightful remark that that fine old lady, Mrs. Phoebe Hearst, made with reference to what she called her 'big boy Willie.' You know, Mrs. Hearst does not favor intervention in Mexico, and it was reported to me that she chided her son for his flaming headlines urging intervention, and told him that unless he behaved better she would have to take him over her knee and spank him."

By that time, of course, Willie had long since stopped listening to his mother.

It was hardly surprising that Wilson's light-and-freedom approach to the presidency would not last long after Inauguration Day and quite predictable that, in its application to the press, it should end even sooner. His Scotch-Presbyterian character and his previous career as college professor and president, then governor, were not an adequate preparation for meeting what was by now a press corps whose ranks included, along with graduates of the police and city hall beats, a number of skilled, well-educated professionals. Experience had taught the veterans among them that politicians saw the press not as a means of conveying information but as a convenient machine for advancing their interests.

Personalities, too, made a substantial difference. Reporters had called Theodore Roosevelt "Teddy" among themselves, as Americans generally did, but no one would have thought of calling Wilson "Woody" during his presidency or at any other time, although he was not always as austere as he seemed and was even capable of occasional wit and humor in his exchanges with reporters. Newsmen who learned something of his private life found its pleasures difficult to reconcile with the reserve and wariness he constantly exhibited toward them and others in his public persona. They knew he was a man who liked limericks, popular novels, and vaudeville, who enjoyed gathering around the piano with people and singing along. His family life was relaxed and happy, though far from being as conventionally domestic as it appeared. Like Taft, however, he simply did not have the common touch in public.

George Juergens, in his study of press relations during the Progressive Era, points out that some of Wilson's friends in the press who wished him well went to see him during the 1912 campaign to help him understand and offset the image he was conveying. These reporters included Charles Thompson of the New York *Times,* Don Martin of the New York *Herald,* and James Doyle of the New York *Press.* Juergens describes their meeting:

> Pointing out how his aloofness was hurting him, they noted that other public figures, not least Roosevelt, came across in newspapers as full-blooded personalities, and had their programs adequately explained, because they opened up to reporters they

trusted and spoke informally with them on a non-attribution basis. If Wilson would take the three into his confidence they would try to do the same for him. According to Thompson, Wilson was moved by the offer but still had to reject it. "I appreciate this more than I can tell you," he replied. "Every word you say is true, and I know it. Don't you suppose I know my own handicaps? I'd do what you advise if I could. . . . But it's not my nature . . . *I can't make myself over.*" The reporters made a significant effort, and their failure forecast the much larger failure that was to come.

It was not entirely Wilson's rigidity that was at fault. He could not forget the shock of meeting the press for the first time as presidential nominee at his Sea Girt summer place, when some of the offhand remarks from reporters struck him as unforgivably boorish, as indeed they were. He was incapable of responding to them in the same offhand, good-natured manner. Such an encounter produced only shock and dismay in him and led him to further caution and a hardly concealed distaste in later meetings. Then, when it came to the way the press dealt with his family, his reaction was even stronger than the reactions of some of his predecessors—Cleveland, for example. There was a certain amount of hypocrisy in this. Having an affair with Mrs. Peck on the side, with his wife's indulgence, was one thing, but having the press intrude on his family's privacy was something else. Wilson's attitude was orthodox nineteenth century: one's own women were to be worshiped and protected as pure creatures; others were in a different category.

While Wilson expected that the reporters would come looking for human interest now that he was in the national spotlight, the idea of the human interest story repelled him. Nor did members of his family understand their situation any better. Eleanor, his daughter, wrote later about those tumultuous days at Sea Girt, after the convention:

> We had become accustomed to reporters, but now the human interest variety descended upon us in full force. Father had told us to be good sports and try to be as pleasant as possible, but even he sometimes withdrew into silence, after being subjected to hours of silly personal questions. We, who had been taught to be close-mouthed about our family affairs, found this prying into our lives strange and annoying. They did not hesitate to question us about any and every detail of our lives. What were our favorite colors, occupations, sports? Did we like to dance? Were we in love or engaged? Did we intend to marry and, if so, when?
>
> We never gave interviews, but that didn't interfere in the least with the literary efforts of the ladies and gentlemen of the press. They simply invented them. We were startled to read in one paper that we were three "high-brows," with our noses constantly buried in ponderous volumes, and in another that we were frivolous and gay, eager to reach the White House and liven up Washington society. Jessie, who abhorred slang and had great natural dignity, was quoted as saying, "Gee, Pop's a practical man."
>
> The numerous pictures they took of us, singly and in groups, were revelations of the power of the camera to misrepresent.

It was an old story. Obviously there could never be any real reconciliation between such sharply opposed attitudes and ways of living. The reporters and the Wilsons occupied different worlds.

Even with the evidence before him, Wilson could not accept what the proper kind of press support might do for him. William F. McCombs, who had studied under him at Princeton and was chairman of the Democratic National Committee in 1912, was unable to understand why his earnest and successful efforts with the press were spurned outright by the candidate. McCombs had suggested to S. S. McClure, publisher of the extremely popular *McClure's Magazine,* that an article on Wilson might be of interest, and McClure responded by assigning one of the best magazine writers of the time, Burton C. J. Kendrick. It was a flattering, helpful piece, and McCombs had more than a half-million copies of it printed up as a pamphlet and distributed throughout the country. Then, with the help of Walter Hines Page and his *World's Work* magazine, a widely read opinion periodical, McCombs arranged for Bayard Hale to write four articles on Wilson. But these and other efforts failed to impress the candidate, and he repudiated McCombs's help as he had George Harvey's and the work of many others who did their best to send him to the White House.

A basic problem in Wilson's relations with the press was certainly not a new one. He simply had no understanding of news. To him the word meant announcing a decision, or an action taken, that should be conveyed to the public without any interpretation or comment by the newspapers. As a corollary, such news should never be anticipated or speculated about, and, like so many presidents, he deplored the news leak, although he was not above doing it himself, then self-righteously denying he had done so.

Addressing a meeting of the Associated Press in April 1915, Wilson offered the astonished editors this proposition:

> There is news and news. There is what is called news from Turtle Bay that turns out to be falsehood, at any rate in what it is said to signify, but which, if you could get the Nation to believe it true, might disturb our equilibrium and our self-possession. We ought not to deal in stuff of that kind. We ought not to permit that sort of thing to use up the electrical energy of the wires, because its energy is malign, its energy is not of the truth, its energy is of mischief. . . . We cannot afford . . . to let the rumors of irresponsible persons and origins get into the atmosphere of the United States.

It was possible to sift the truth, Wilson told these editors, who spent a good deal of their working hours trying to do exactly that, and the way to accomplish it, he went on, was to go to the government official responsible for a statement or an action. Apparently it did not occur to Wilson that many of these editors, as reporters, had sought the truth in just this way and then been lied to over and over by these same responsible officials. In short, Wilson was advancing the idea that the truth always reposed in the hands of those who made the news and only they could certify it—a notion far from dead nearly seventy years later. Moreover he equated compliance with his belief with patriotism. If the reporters did not comply, he intimated, they would be endangering America in a time of world peril, since the First World War had begun.

The correspondents already had good reason to doubt Wilson's own veracity, on which he continued to insist with Victorian dignity. In the days between his election and the inauguration, when there was naturally an intense interest in who would be named for cabinet positions, there was much speculation about whether William Jennings Bryan would be made secretary of state. Wilson had, in fact, offered Bryan the post at a meeting with him late in December and had his immediate acceptance, but when reporters asked Wilson later whether he had made the appointment, he denied that the subject had even come up. When the newsmen persisted, Wilson flared at them: "You gentlemen must learn sooner or later that you must take me at my word. I have told you repeatedly that I have reached no decisions, and I object very much to questions which put my word in doubt." When the same questions were put to him at a later conference, he struck the desk with his fist and exploded: "I'm not here to amuse the newspapers. . . . If the newspapers expect me to do [so] . . . I'll be damned if I will." Then a moment later he apologized: "Pardon me for blowing up. These stories about Cabinet appointments are all false. I have told you men here in Trenton that I have made no selections for the Cabinet, and to keep on questioning me about it is to doubt my veracity."

The reporters continued to doubt his veracity, and with reason. Wilson misled them again a month before his inauguration, when he deliberately let them believe he was going to a dinner at the Hotel Astor in New York, where he assured them nothing whatever political would happen, and so they would be perfectly safe in writing advance stories for their papers and going home. Instead he went to Colonel House's apartment on East Thirty-fifth Street, where he intended to continue high-level discussions with important figures in the party about cabinet appointments.

Only the vigilance of two reporters, Charles Thompson of the *Times* and William Keohan of the *Tribune,* disclosed the deception. After having dinner together, they had made a final check at the Astor, just to be sure nothing was occurring, and discovered that Wilson had not even been invited to the banquet. Hurrying down by cab to the House apartment, they learned the truth—it could be sifted, as Wilson would advise them later—and were in time to revise their stories for the final edition. The other reporters were not so fortunate, and they were not inclined to forgive Wilson for deceiving them, although he appeared to be amused by his success.

It was not surprising, then, that Inauguration Day found the new president and the press in a state of disillusionment with each other. Nevertheless, the day got off to a promising start when Tumulty, exuding Irish charm, called the reporters into a press conference of his own. His appointment as secretary had seemed to be the most felicitous veteran reporters could remember. Tumulty not only understood his job in relation to the president, but he was an old hand in dealing with the press and understood its function and problems. He had been with Wilson since 1911, acting as his secretary in Trenton and also advising on such matters as public opinion—advice that Arthur Link, the most noted of Wilson historians, describes as sometimes "foolish." Tumulty was, however, just the kind of buffer against the press Wilson needed. At his March conference Tumulty told the assembled correspondents: "You boys are great personages in public affairs, and in Washington I will look after the publicity of this administration myself." They would have much better access to information than before, he assured them, and he himself would always be available.

The reporters listened with some skepticism. They had heard Wilson talk about his "open-door" policy as governor and had heard him orate with progressive fervor on the necessity of conducting government in the pitiless glare of public scrutiny. But it did not take much sophistication to perceive, even at such an early stage, that there was a considerable difference between Wilson the academic theorist steeped in political science and Wilson the political human being who had come into a practical reality for which theory had not prepared him. They had seen at first hand how he dealt with the press, and not all of Tumulty's charm could convince them that the secretary was truly going to be publicity director of the White House. Such direction came only from the top, as even the youngest reporter knew.

Nevertheless it appeared to be a significant step forward when the new president announced that he would hold regular press conferences, thus initiating the institution familiar to us today. What the correspondents did not understand at first was how Wilson conceived of these conferences, a conception quite consistent with his general view of both his office and the press. By meeting with the reporters regularly, he would be throwing that white light on public affairs that he advocated and he would answer questions from the press about matters that reflected the concerns of the public. But in the process of seeing the correspondents all together as a group, on a regular basis, he meant to avoid seeing them any other time, so far as possible. It was a notion that would have done credit to Taft.

From the first conference it was clear that the president's plan was not going to work. He met with 125 reporters in the Oval Office, eleven days after his inaugural, and, according to Edward Lowry, one of those present, it did not go well. "There was a pause, a cool silence, and presently someone volunteered a tentative question," Lowry recorded later. "It was answered crisply, politely, and in the fewest possible words. A pleasant time was not had by all."

A week later Wilson and the reporters tried again. This time nearly two hundred undismayed correspondents appeared, necessitating a move to the East Room to accommodate all of them. The president appeared and made a half-hearted apology for the crowding, and for the previous week's failure to accomplish much, pleading the fatigue he had felt that day. His bearing before them, however, had already discouraged his audience. One of them, Oliver P. Newman, no critic of Wilson, wrote later, on January 13, 1928, to Ray Stannard Baker about the scene:

> It was appalling. He came into the room suspicious, reserved, a little resentful—no thought of frankness and open door and cordiality and that sort of thing. In the first place, he was embarrassed. There were about two hundred of the correspondents and it was in the East Room of the White House. It was a silly thing to do. . . . He could not be as frank as he could have been with one; and he was embarrassed and had this

rankling feeling. . . . He utterly failed to get across to these men anything except that this was very distasteful to him, and they, on their part, resented it very, very seriously. They came out of that conference cursing, almost indignant.

One of the reasons for the reporters' anger was that Wilson insisted on lecturing to them (an academic habit) on their function as Washington correspondents. In this impromptu address he offered a preview of what he would tell the Associated Press editors two years later. With a preliminary request to keep his remarks confidential (''off the record'' had not yet been invented), Wilson said: ''I feel that a large part of the success of public affairs depends on the newspaper men— not so much on the editorial writers, because we can live down what they say, as upon the news writers, because the news is the atmosphere of public affairs.'' Presumably the reporters felt a little easier; none of them would have disputed that point. ''I sent for you, therefore,'' Wilson went on, ''to ask that you go into partnership with me, that you lend me your assistance as nobody else can. . . . I did want you to feel that I was depending upon you, and from what I can learn of you, I think I have a reason to depend with confidence on you . . . not for me, but for the United States, for the people of the United States, and so bring about a day which will be a little better than the days that have gone before us.'' In short, as the correspondents sensed beneath the rhetoric, the president was inviting them to join him in presenting the news that he saw fit to present, for the greater glory of the people and the American Republic. Nothing could have demonstrated more clearly Wilson's complete misunderstanding of the nature of news.

It was this difference that continued to widen the gap between the president and the press as time went on. The correspondents wanted to do their job and get the news, whatever it was, as accurately as possible. The president wanted to give them information and news of decisions he had already made. He would decide what the public should know, particularly in the area of foreign policy, about which he was especially sensitive. As he told the correspondents in a press conference on January 29, 1914:

> The foreign policy of the government is the one field in which, if you will permit me to say so, you ought not to speculate in public, because the minute the newspapers in any large number state a certain thing to be under consideration by the administration, that is of course telegraphed all over the world and makes a certain impression upon foreign governments, and may very easily render the things that we really intend to do impossible. . . . I feel the thing very keenly. I do not think that the newspapers of the country have the right to embarrass their own country in the settlement of matters which have to be handled with delicacy and candor.

It is not difficult to understand Wilson's point of view, given his background and training, but it is also easy to see why any kind of satisfactory relationship with the press would never be possible. Yet, as Hilderbrand reminds us, only a few months before, in 1913, there were some correspondents who had believed that the early press conferences were successful. Charles Thompson, for example, whose version of these events a decade or so later was much more critical, wrote in his paper of the first meetings: "As he went on talking, the big hit he was making with the crowd became evident. There was something so unaffected and honest about his way of talking, that it won everybody, despite the fact that many of the men there had come prejudiced against him." Richard Oulahan, another veteran, agreed: "Things at the White House are working out first rate. The semi-weekly talks with the President are now on a good working basis."

While it was true that Wilson grew more adept at fielding questions as time went on, there was never any real understanding between the two sides, which some historians have suggested; the transcripts of the press conferences (on microfilm at the Princeton University Library), as well as subsequent events, make this clear. Once Wilson threatened to discontinue the sessions entirely, angered by the action of a few newspapers in breaking the rule against quoting him. The general uneasiness had already resulted in the formation of a Standing Committee of Correspondents, and Oulahan, its chairman, was able to persuade the president to continue the conferences, with the understanding that the rules would be tightened. Even after that was done, Wilson's sessions with the press were more in the nature of duals than the give-and-take that came with later administrations.

Unfortunately Wilson continued to treat the correspondents as though they were students who were not very bright, and it was this barely concealed contempt for their intellectual qualities—as though a brilliant professor were being challenged by a group of presumptuous freshmen—that led to the ultimate discontinuation of the meetings. As Oswald Garrison Villard, a journalistic intellect of no mean accomplishments himself, wrote later, the press conferences were abandoned because "the President could not submit to being cross-questioned by men some of whom he did not respect and by an entire group he deemed his intellectual inferiors."

Wilson was not entirely wrong. The caliber of these reporters was not as high as it would be later, and the president often had reason to be impatient with them and to regard their questions as hardly above the level of an interview with a ward heeler. Among such reporters, too, some unfairness and distortion could be expected. Obviously there was fault on both sides, but the larger fault by far lay with Wilson, who concealed from the press, and consequently from the public, what should not have been concealed and, in the same manner, committed his own sins of distortion and falsity.

There was also the matter of family privacy, which rose to a boiling point in March 1914. As noted earlier, the family had been highly irritated from the beginning by speculation about the romances of his daughters. Jessie had removed herself somewhat from the spotlight by marrying Francis Sayre in November 1913, and Eleanor would be marrying Secretary of the Treasury William Gibbs McAdoo two months later, although the press had virtually forced her family to announce the engagement. But now the president's wife Ellen was seriously ill in bed, ostensibly from a bad fall but actually (although Wilson did not know it) suffering from a terminal kidney ailment; in five months she would be dead. It was entirely natural for the newspapers to write about her health, but no matter how sympathetic they might be about her, and about her husband's obvious anxiety, Wilson deeply resented this added intrusion on family privacy. Tumulty described him later as "fighting mad" when he opened his press conference of March 19 with this pained outburst:

> Gentlemen, I want to say something this afternoon. . . . I am a public character for the time being, but the ladies of my household are not servants of the Government and they are not public characters. I deeply resent the treatment they are receiving at the hands of the newspapers at this time. . . . It is a violation of my own impulses even to speak of these things, but my oldest daughter is constantly represented as being engaged to this, that, or the other man in different parts of the country, in some instances to men she has never even met in her life. It is a constant and intolerable annoyance. . . .
>
> Now, I feel this way, gentlemen: Ever since I can remember I have been taught that the deepest obligation that rested upon me was to defend the women of my household from annoyance. Now I intend to do it and the only way I can think of is this. It is a way which will impose the penalty in a certain sense upon those whom I believe to be innocent, but I do not see why I should permit representatives of papers who treat the ladies of my household in this way to have personal interviews with me. . . . My daughters have no brother whom they can depend upon. I am President of the United States; I cannot act altogether as an individual while I occupy this office. But I must do something. This thing is intolerable. . . .
>
> Now, if you have ever been in a position like this yourselves—and I hope to God you never will be—you know how I feel, and I must ask you gentlemen to make confidential representations to the several papers which you represent about this matter.

Whether the correspondents were frightened by the threat to deny them access and the display of presidential anger, as Eleanor believed, or whether they simply responded to his appeal, it was some time before there were any stories in the papers that provoked Wilson in the same way. But the incident was significant in another respect. It demonstrated how much newspapers had changed in two decades or less. One can only imagine how Bennett, or Pulitzer, or Dana would have responded to such a presidential declaration of war.

In any case, the idea of the press conference was slowly dying in this administration. During the first twenty-one months, conferences had occurred twice a week, taking place usually at 10 A.M. on Monday and Thursday mornings. They were cut back to once a week, on Tuesday mornings, beginning with December 1914, and after the sinking of the *Lusitania* in May 1915, which the president used as a convenient excuse, they stopped completely. Wilson did not see the press again until December 1916, after his reelection, but it appeared from the tone of that meeting that he intended to meet with them regularly again, on a weekly basis. Events overwhelmed him, however. The correspondents were to see him only three more times in a press conference, on February 14 and June 27, 1919, in Paris; and in Washington on July 10 of that year, when he was beginning his personal crusade for the League of Nations.

Wilson's definitive word on his press conferences came in a remark he made, during the Great War, to George Creel, head of the Committee on Public Information, which itself became a center of controversy. As Creel recalled it more than a decade later, the president declared:

> It [the press conference] is a waste of time. I came to Washington with the idea that close and cordial relations with the press would prove of the greatest aid. I prepared for the conferences as carefully as for any lecture, and talked freely and fully on all large questions of the moment. Some men of brilliant ability were in the group, but I soon discovered that the interest of the majority was in the personal and trivial rather than in principles and policies.

How best to convey "principles and policies"? For a time the president considered the creation of a national publicity bureau, as he conceived it, which bore a close resemblance to the "ministries of information" in authoritarian countries at a later date. Instead of suppressing opposition viewpoints, however, as they would do, Wilson seemed to believe in a bizarre coexistence—on the one hand a government bureau that would dispense "the truth" and on the other a press that would continue to interpret and "distort" the facts to suit itself. He explained his idea in a letter to Charles W. Eliot:

> We have several times considered the possibility of having a publicity bureau which would handle the real facts, so far as the government was aware of them, for all the departments. The real trouble is that the newspapers get the real facts but do not find them to their taste and do not use them as given them, and in some of the newspaper offices news is deliberately invented. Since I came here I have wondered how it ever happened that the public got a right impression regarding public affairs, particularly foreign affairs.

The notion of a publicity bureau, which Wilson conceived in 1914, was realized, at least in its general outlines, in 1917 with the creation of the Committee on Public Information, headed by George Creel. To make it more palatable, the cooperation of newspapers was solicited on the grounds of wartime necessity, but, as his private papers show, Wilson believed that such cooperation was impossible "because of the small but powerful lawless elements among them who observe no rules, regard no understanding as binding, and act always as they please." Creel wrote later, however, that he had been "surprised and gratified" by the results of the voluntary censorship undertaken by the press. "It is the best we can do, and it's really very good," he concluded.

There was more than a little official optimism in this estimate. Creel's Committee on Public Information came to be viewed as the propaganda organization it was, fully capable of completely misrepresenting the facts—so much so that "Creeling" was coined as a slang word to describe this kind of official chicanery. In that sense the committee was a serious Wilsonian mistake, leading to general distrust of anything the government said. But it had been a mutual distrust from the beginning, as Wilson made plain in a letter to a friend early in his administration. "Do not believe anything you read in the newspapers," he told her.

If you read the papers I see, they are utterly untrustworthy. They represent the obstacles as existing which they wish to have exist, whether they are actual or not. Read the editorial page and you will know what you will find in the news columns. For unless they are grossly careless the two always support one another. Their lying is senseless and colossal. . . . Power consists in one's capacity to link his will with the purpose of others, to lead by reason and a gift for cooperation. It is a multiple of combined brains.

Underlying hostility toward the press on the president's part was the basic reason for the end of the press conferences, but there were no doubt other reasons as well. When it seemed possible that the United States might be drawn into the Great War that had already begun, there was some speculation that Wilson might not want to discuss matters of foreign policy with reporters at all, because German journalists might relay significant pieces of information, and it would not be possible to bar them without also keeping out the British, which no one in the administration wanted to do. (There was already a problem with the Allies. During the first two years of the war so much pro-German sentiment existed in the United States that the British and French refused to accredit American correspondents. An enterprising journalist, Mary Roberts Rinehart, the well-known mystery-story writer whose work appeared in the *Saturday Evening Post*, enlisted with the Belgian Red Cross so she could get to the front and report for that magazine. Most of the other correspondents had to cover the war from Berlin.)

But even though the press conferences ended on such a disquieting note, the mere fact that they had been established, and would become a White House fixture after Wilson was gone, constituted a long step forward in the relationship between presidents and press. On occasion, too, they had served to show Wilson in a different light, trying to be humorous with the reporters by telling stories to illustrate his point (a common presidential device). They may not have been good stories (Wilson was no raconteur), but the correspondents appreciated seeing a side of the president that only a few of them recognized as characteristic of his private life. These bantering exchanges were also a relief from the customary tension and the president's hardly concealed irritation and contempt.

The ending of the conferences had another result. Unwillingly, Tumulty was thrust into the role of press secretary, without the title—the sole and not always certain link between the press and the White House. He played the part extremely well, as Hilderbrand tells us:

From his first days in office, the secretary met every morning with White House reporters, a task he described as ''delightful interludes in a busy day.'' He made public the routine comings and goings of White House business and presented news of the president's decisions on policies and appointments in a way that rarely failed to capture reporters' interest. He had a talent, according to David Lawrence, for ''revealing, bit by bit, and with an air of mystery, things which appeared to be great secrets, data which Tumulty, with all the arts known to the practiced publicity expert, divulged with an idea to headlines and conspicuous display.'' He also seemed to know what newsmen were after—and whether or not he ought to give it to them—and could be as coquettish or as straightforward as the situation required. For their part, Washington journalists were taken by his easy humor, and Tumulty became one of the most popular presidential secretaries.

The correspondents were also now in a better position to deal with their natural adversary in the White House. To bring order out of the disorganized mob they had been before, they had organized on February 25, 1914, as the White House Correspondents Association, which was not only a social organization but served as a board to hear complaints against or by the reporters and also to decide on who was eligible to attend press conferences. This was a second effort at self-regulation; the Standing Committee of Correspondents had been established earlier, but its task was to administer the congressional press galleries.

As the White House shepherd of this flock, Tumulty did his best to smooth relations with important editors and correspondents, often acting where Wilson would not. At the same time he kept a careful watch over the reporters to see that they did not violate their own rules and go unpunished. Although it was unrealistic of him, he even held the wire services accountable for the sins of their members and clients. Conversely, he came to the defense of correspondents (when he reasonably could) if they offended the president.

When Wilson sought (unconsciously, of course) to emulate Roosevelt and not only barred a New York *Herald* correspondent from the White House but tried to have him fired as well, Tumulty persuaded the president to withdraw the latter request and later saw to it that the offender returned unobtrusively to the secretary's morning meetings. Tumulty understood that, while Roosevelt had been able to get away with such high-handed treatment, the organized correspondents were genuinely shocked when the action came from Wilson, and a serious breach could have occurred.

Tumulty's hand could be seen everywhere—discreetly arranging for news leaks, promoting the president's ideas, or improving his image by setting up interviews with journalists who could help him. Edward G. Lowry, for instance, was called upon to aid Wilson's controversial Mexican policy, and the result was an article in *World's Work* entitled "What the President Is Trying To Do for Mexico." Samuel G. Blythe, for years the *Saturday Evening Post*'s Washington man, did a similar piece, based on an "exclusive" interview, which was made to seem even more exclusive through its title, "A Talk with the President."

It was much safer to channel such promotions into magazines rather than newspapers, thus avoiding competitive discord among the correspondents, and Tumulty managed these occasions adroitly. This device proved to be effective in the campaign of 1916, when articles by Ray Stannard Baker and Ida Tarbell for *Collier's* did much to humanize the president and place him in a flattering light, as seen through the eyes of two trusted and sympathetic friends who believed what they wrote and whose reputation with the educated reading public was high.

That was the kind of press Wilson wanted to see in Washington—one that would print what was given to it, presenting him in the most favorable way for the ultimate benefit of the Republic. For a political scientist he was astonishingly blind to the reasons why this was not possible in the American democracy. His secretary of state, William Jennings Bryan, was equally obtuse in the matter. It was the jointly held belief of the president and his secretary that no information about policy should be given to reporters until the president decided it was time to do so. Bryan sent a memo to State Department officials declaring that "the policy of this government on international questions, insofar as announcement is made from the Department, will be announced when the President thinks that the public interest will be promoted thereby. Until these announcements are made, questions concerning such policies will not be answered."

The press resisted any such arrangement, as officials less naïve than Wilson and Bryan could have predicted, and matters quickly reached a stalemate at both the White House and the State Department, with the reporters continuing to cross-examine on matters of foreign policy and the president and secretary refusing to answer. Bryan was furious with the resistance of the press. He suggested to Wilson in February 1915 that he was thinking of excluding reporters altogether from the State Department. In spite of his campaign pledge of "pitiless publicity," in which he did not truly believe for a minute, Wilson might have agreed to this politically unwise move if Tumulty had not succeeded in persuading him that it would be counterproductive, as later wizards of the White House would term it.

Nevertheless Wilson continued to pick his way through a semantic minefield where foreign policy was concerned, in a way that has become overly familiar in our own time. When the border raids of the Mexican guerrilla leader Pancho Villa resulted in American deaths in 1916, Wilson decided to send Gen. John J. Pershing with some troops to put down this annoyance in a neighboring state. He did not want a war with Mexico, particularly in an election year, but the problem was how to explain an invasion of another country, in which both foreign and American troops might well be killed, as something entirely different and indeed justified. That would require the help of the press, and the president used the oldest weapon, patriotism, to bludgeon it into support.

In a press release he asked the reporters to be "good enough to assist the administration in presenting this [his administration's] view of the [Mexican] expedition to the American people," so that everyone on both sides of the border would understand that this was only a punitive expedition against bandits. The press could avoid any other interpretation, he said, simply by agreeing "not to interpret news stories regarding the expedition as in any sense meaning war, to withhold stories of troop movements and preparations that might be given that interpretation, and to refrain from publishing rumors of unrest in Mexico." At the same time the State and War departments issued reassuring statements confirming the president's view.

It is a measure of the control that even then the power of the presidency was able to exert on the press that so many publishers acted against their better judgment and agreed to find other terms to describe this invasion and small war that the government insisted was neither in spite of what was obviously happening. Although troops were already across the border killing Mexicans, a new secretary of state, Robert Lansing, declared that Pershing's expedition did not constitute "invasion of any kind of the affairs of our sister Republic," a view not shared by many Mexicans. The semantic evasions went on until the expedition ended without a declared war, lost in the shadow of the far larger conflict that now loomed.

By this time Wilson had developed a much more effective, if circuitous, method of getting maximum publicity without the necessity of meeting the press. It was a brilliant political stroke on his part to begin delivering addresses to joint sessions of Congress, something that had not been done for 113 years, in John Adams's administration. Jefferson, a splendid writer but no orator, had sent his messages to be read by clerks in both chambers, and so it had been done ever since by successive presidents, with minimal dramatic effect. By the simple device of appearing before Congress to read speeches he had largely written himself (sometimes with Tumulty's help), he gained the attention of both Congress and the nation, at the same time guaranteeing that the press would give him maximum coverage. What reporters might say about the speeches next day in the editorial columns was less important. He relied on his oratorical skill and his practiced writing to make the impact he desired.

One admiring editorial writer, in the New York *Times,* saw the point at once. After Wilson's first such appearance in 1913, he wrote on April 9: "The wonder is that in seven years Theodore Roosevelt never thought of this way of stamping his personality upon his age." With the help of Tumulty and these personal appearances, Wilson survived his first term with a reasonably good press, in spite of his troubles with the press conference and his often open hostility toward the correspondents.

Toward the end of that period, however, the uneasy relationship began to show signs of unraveling. The key element was Tumulty. Wilson had no high opinion of his secretary, regarding him as hopelessly provincial, but he had the intelligence and integrity to scorn the complaints of assorted bigots who thought Tumulty should be dismissed (and never appointed in the first place) because he was a Catholic. Tumulty's more formidable opponents were Colonel House, the president's confidant and (so many believed) the *éminence grise* of the administration, and Edith Galt, Wilson's second wife, whom he had married following Ellen's death in August 1914.

The colonel's opposition may well have been simple—though unjustified— jealousy because of Tumulty's close relationship with the president. The colonel's was much closer, but almost from the beginning he laid before Wilson a running list of complaints about the secretary. He thought Tumulty talked too much and was indiscreet in what he said. House also found him lacking in such sterling character traits as "refinement," "discretion," and "broad vision," in contrast, of course, to his own character. As for the second Mrs. Wilson, she had begun by looking down on Tumulty as "uncouth and common," in Juergens's description, and wound up hating him after she discovered that Tumulty had advised Wilson not to marry her until the 1916 election was over—advice he rejected. It was no secret that the secretary had been close to Ellen Wilson and mourned her loss. A confrontation with her successor was avoided momentarily while the campaign of 1916 ran its course.

The president approached this second ordeal with some confidence. He could look back on a record of reforms that fulfilled many of his campaign promises.

The Payne-Aldrich Tariff's excesses had been reduced by the Underwood Tariff, which introduced the income tax to American life. Sectional banks had been set up under a Federal Reserve Board, and big business—the trusts TR had failed to bust—was now to be controlled (or so it was hoped) by the Clayton Anti-Trust Act and the Federal Trade Commission. Nor had labor's needs been neglected. Taft had created a Department of Labor, but Wilson had appointed its first secretary, and the national disgrace of exploitive child labor had been curbed by means of the Keating-Owen Child Labor Act, making fourteen the minimum working age in factories, considered by many employers as a step toward socialism, along with the attempts already begun to reduce the twelve-hour working day. Judge Elbert Gary was to denounce that a few years later as a prelude to communism. Moreover, under Wilson, agriculture had been helped with the first "dollar-matching" bill, and the Federal Highways Act had opened up an era of road building.

The war in Europe had also strengthened Wilson's position. It had meant prosperity for many American businesses involved with supplying the Allies. And even though the sinking of the *Lusitania* and the subsequent continuance of German submarine warfare had brought stern representations from Wilson, the president was presenting himself to the nation in 1916 as the man "who kept us out of war." More thoughtful citizens had only to look upon the preparations for conflict under way in the United States to realize the hollowness of this slogan, but the Democratic candidate was nonetheless offered to the voters as the ideal pacifist. His policies might not satisfy "the fire-eater or the swashbuckler," former Gov. Martin Glynn of New York told the delegates at the Democratic convention in St. Louis,

> but it does satisfy the mothers of the land at whose hearth and fireside no jingoistic war has placed an empty chair. It does satisfy the daughters of the land from whom bluster and brag have sent no loving brother to the dissolution of the grave. It does satisfy the fathers of this land and the sons of this land who will fight for our flag and die for our flag when Reason primes the rifle, when Honor draws the sword, when Justice breathes a blessing on the standards they uphold.

After they had wiped away their tears of gratitude, the delegates would have nominated Wilson by acclamation if a cynic from Illinois had not protested, leaving the final vote 1,092 to 1. This lone dissenter may have represented (pitifully enough) the feeling of disquiet among those hard-nosed politicians who did not want the party branded as the apostle of pacifism. They wanted to be sure that this and other convention bombast could be translated into another word, patriotism, because they were wise enough to see that substantial quantities of rhetoric might have to be swallowed in a short time.

There was no contest among the Republicans either. They had already settled on Charles Evans Hughes, associate justice of the Supreme Court and former governor of New York, because he was the one man on whom most Republicans could unite. Not the Progressives, however. They clung to their hero of 1912, Theodore Roosevelt, and nominated him. He responded to their devotion by first declining the nomination and then throwing his support to Hughes, thus ending the brief career of the Progressive party.

Wilson refused to go on the campaign trail, believing that the country wanted to see its president on the job in a time of national peril, but Hughes toured the country with vigor and little effect. He did not excite the voters. Even so, considering the depth of opposition to Wilson's liberal domestic program on the part of conservative voters, he might have won if he had not made a fatal mistake in California, where his advisers prevented him from meeting with the state's popular governor, Hiram W. Johnson. As a consequence Hughes lost California by a small margin, and with it the election. If he had carried that state, he would have won in the electoral college by a single vote. As in the Tilden-Hayes election, it was believed that Hughes had won until the results from California came in next day, silencing the Republicans who had spent the night celebrating. Wilson, carrying the South and West, had a popular majority of nearly six hundred thousand.

The peace Wilson had promised lasted five months, but not through any lack of effort on his part to end the war. His first act after the election was to ask both groups of belligerents what terms they could accept; their replies were wholly unsatisfactory. The president then turned to Congress and, proposing "peace without victory," offered his own plan for proposed negotiations. Germany, centering its hopes for victory on a blockade of England, responded by announcing unrestricted submarine warfare, directed against both Allied and neutral shipping. Diplomatic relations were broken off by the United States, and Wilson ordered the merchant fleet armed by invoking a statute of 1797 after the Senate filibustered and defeated his bid for an authorization to do so—"a little group of willful men," the president called the orators, giving future chief executives a useful phrase to apply to those who frustrated them.

Only a slight push was needed, and Germany supplied it. The assertion was circulated (by the State Department) that, if the Kaiser won, he had made a deal with Mexico to give it Texas, New Mexico, and Arizona in return for its support. While there might have been some poetic justice in this, considering how that territory had been acquired, the thought of losing the Alamo and its environs was enough to inspire a popular rage worthy of Roosevelt, who had been advocating war from the beginning. The sinking of three American merchant ships in March was the last straw. Wilson asked for a declaration of war from Congress and got it on April 6, 1917.

Meanwhile, back at the White House, other warlike events were occurring on a less cosmic scale. Mrs. Wilson and Colonel House brought pressure to bear on the president to fire Tumulty, asserting that he had been hurt in the close election by his employment of a Catholic in so confidential a position. Reluctantly Wilson gave in, but when he tried to dismiss his secretary painlessly by offering him another position on the Board of General Appraisers of the Customs, a pathetic and demeaning tug of war developed. Tumulty had been completely taken aback by Wilson's proposal. He did not want to go. While he hesitated day after day, in agonizing indecision, Edith and the colonel hammered away at the president, determined to have their way. It was nearly two weeks before Tumulty could bring himself to write an abject letter, almost pleading to stay but promising to go if there was no alternative, and proudly rejecting another position.

This move had shocked the correspondents, too. David Lawrence spent nearly an hour with Wilson, pointing out to him that the press would never understand this gross display of ingratitude to a faithful employee who had given him exceptional service. Not so much out of consideration for the press, but feeling guilty about the undeserved blow he was trying to deal Tumulty, Wilson relented and told his secretary he could stay. But as Juergens reminds us:

> No one really won in this power struggle. If the president demonstrated his affection for Tumulty in retaining him despite even Mrs. Wilson's wishes, the further fact is that the relationship between the two men could never be the same as before. They had both surrendered too much of self-respect, and perhaps even respect for the other; Tumulty in clinging to his job when he had been asked to leave, Wilson in bowing to a conspiracy against the secretary and then not making it stick.

This struggle was to have long-range consequences for the president in his press relations. For the moment, however, Tumulty continued his own cordial relationship with the reporters and might have done so indefinitely had America not entered the war. Eight days later the Committee on Public Information was established, and from then until the end of the struggle it became the intermediary between press and President. George Creel was now the salesman for administration policy, as well as the dispenser of wartime censorship. There was no longer any point in Tumulty's daily briefings, and he gave them up. The result was an isolation of the president from the public of a kind not seen since the days of Harrison and Cleveland. It was a withdrawal with extremely unfortunate results.

In appointing forty-one-year-old George Creel as head of the Committee on Public Information (meaning Propaganda and Publicity Bureau, an early example of Newspeak), Wilson had chosen a man with the proper credentials but possessed of hidden liabilities. Most important to the president, Creel was a trusted loyalist who gave him the same kind of unquestioning idolatry that Bernard Baruch brought to his new task as director of the Office of War Mobilization. Creel was, furthermore, an experienced journalist, who had begun with the Kansas City *World* and the New York *Journal;* founded and edited the *Independent,* a public affairs weekly magazine; free-lanced for various periodicals; and edited the *Rocky Mountain News* in Denver. He had an unblemished reputation as a liberal supporter of worthy causes.

What could possibly be wrong with such a man? Notably, his inability to see anything in terms other than black or white, right or wrong; there were no shades of gray in Creel's character. When he fought with Hearst's journalistic army in Cuba, he believed far more than the publisher that he was preserving honor and justice in the Western world. Nor did it help that his view of Wilson was so completely uncritical that he could never expect to deal with journalists who held a less exalted view of the president.

Creel's first efforts, however, seemed encouraging. He established a News

Division of the CPI, as it was acronymically called, which pumped out hard information on a twenty-four-hour basis in a virtual tidal wave of releases. No one could complain about a lack of facts, particularly those that could only come from reliable sources in the government—casualty figures among them. There was one gap. Secretary of State Lansing took an aloof position, regarding everyone outside his department as incapable of judging what should or should not be published and therefore unqualified to get any news. Not even the president could make him change his mind. That, of course, was an invitation to the reporters to obtain the news any way they could.

But at State, as elsewhere, reporters were frustrated by the government's complete control of the sources. Whatever they were given amounted to little more than handouts, and they saw themselves as becoming not much more than clerks delivering packaged products. Moreover it was extremely difficult to tell when the CPI was lying and when it was telling the truth. Because the press had voluntarily submitted to wartime censorship, the normal news-gathering function was all but stifled.

In its propagandistic zeal the CPI sometimes overreached itself, with dismaying results. When the first shiploads of American troops sailed for France, their arrival in St. Nazaire was announced by an AP European dispatch, never cleared with the CPI, but the agency could not attack this breach of the rules without disclosing that there was another group of ships still at sea, reportedly under U-boat assault. When word came they had reached St. Nazaire safely, Creel decided to make a propaganda circus out of their arrival, taking advantage of the coincidental July Fourth holiday to put out a release that went beyond the facts to describe their passage as a virtual running naval battle with a pack of U-boats, which were fiercely attacked and vanquished by escort vessels. The story was a natural. It was splashed over the front page of nearly every major daily, backed up by triumphant patriotic editorials.

It was two days later before the truth caught up. An AP reporter in England interviewed the naval escort's officers, who asserted that the heroic battle had never occurred; the glorious victory had been a product of Creel's imagination. Although this story contradicted the official communique, it went out on the wire without the benefit of comment from the Navy Department. When Secretary of the Navy Josephus Daniels read it, he delivered such an angry telephone rebuke to Melville Stone, the AP's general manager, that the wire service sent out a follow-up "kill" order—too late.

As the true story emerged eventually, it turned out that there had indeed been a minor skirmish, in which one U-boat might conceivably have been sunk. But in trying to explain how he had written his story from the commanding admiral's report, Creel used such devious language that his credibility was seriously impaired. The editors who had been taken in were indignant, and the New York *Times* called his appointment a blunder and demanded his dismissal.

No such egregious error occurred again. Creel resorted to much more subtle distortions of the news, with the understandable intent of doing what his job demanded, that is, to disseminate a flow of upbeat, patriotic propaganda in support of the war effort. If truth was sacrificed in the process, it was no worse than the suspension of civil liberties and the temporary abrogation of the First Amendment under the pressure of wartime hysteria. These repressive measures extended down the line to state and local governments. Few among the public questioned what was occurring, and those who did could expect ostracism at the least and much worse in some cases. The press went along not only because it had no economic choice but because the majority of its owners, editors, and writers believed in Creel's wartime propaganda and wanted to believe it even when they knew it was false. In any case vigilante groups could be depended upon to carry out a harsh enforcement. That represented the dominant mood of the country, not seen since the Civil War and not repeated in the Second World War. And once turned on, the propaganda of hate was not easily turned off, as the postwar Great Red Scare demonstrated, when "German spies" became "communist spies" and basic liberties were once more mangled by unreasoning hatred.

As for Wilson, he had at last the kind of press relations he wanted, especially when, on May 10, 1917, the CPI began to publish its daily *Official Bulletin,* with the declaration on its masthead that it was "Published Daily under Order of the President by the Committee on Public Information." Here was news, in the president's triumphant view, that could not be interpreted or rewritten or otherwise "distorted" from what he wanted to be published. The *Bulletin*'s circulation, however, was never more than 115,000, and it had little credibility with the press, which believed, correctly, that through it the president hoped to usurp their function. Better still from his standpoint, it removed the necessity for him to meet the correspondents.

The unification of the country under what amounted to an authoritarian command has been amply documented and need not be rehearsed here. It set the stage not only for postwar disillusionment but laid the groundwork for Wilson's later ruinous encounters with the press. With only a few minor exceptions, newspapers complied with wartime censorship, and still the president did not trust them. He wanted statutory censorship, too, and he got it in the Espionage Act, passed in June 1917, which at any other time would not have withstood a First Amendment test. A cry of outrage went up from the press. "Does the Administration really feel that this Prussian edict would be a proper return for the services the newspapers have rendered to the authorities in Washington?" the New York *Times* demanded on May 24, 1917. Similar editorials appeared in papers from Boston to Los Angeles. The most telling of them was the roll of thunder that sounded from the highly respectable New York *Tribune*—Republican, to be sure, and therefore anti-Wilson, but a strong supporter of the war from the first. It was the affronted patrician voice of Whitelaw Reid that spoke:

> Tyranny has always founded itself upon the press gag, and the press has always prevailed to the ruin of tyranny. . . . Why, then, has Mr. Wilson adopted the chief instrument of the Czar and the Kaiser as an essential and all-essential instrument in a war for democracy and against tyranny? . . . No President in our history ever made a greater mistake than Mr. Wilson has now made. If . . . he has his way, this power will not merely wreck his Administration, but it will hereafter awaken a revolt in

public opinion unknown in this country since our last King lost his American colonies by policies which Mr. Wilson would now imitate.

The *Tribune* greatly overestimated the public's devotion to the First Amendment, and, indeed, papers in Richmond, Baltimore, Indianapolis, and Nashville, as well as the otherwise blameless *World,* supported Wilson and the new legislation. Yet real damage had been inflicted to basic principles, as the paper charged, and it would have later results. Although the final version of the bill had been watered down, the result was dangerous ambiguity and a granting to the postmaster general of powers like those he had exercised in the Civil War, in obvious contempt of First Amendment rights. Further legislation—the Trading with the Enemy Act and the Sedition Act of May 1918—gave additional powers to the Justice Department and the Post Office, curtailing constitutional freedoms in ways that would never have been tolerated except for the mass madness of the moment.

In the end all dissent was effectively repressed, except for the largest papers, which had the strength to resist, among them the *Times* and the New York *Evening Post.* The left-wing newspapers and magazines, the small-town gazettes, the foreign-language publications, and little journals everywhere that were helpless to fight back—these were the chief objects of governmental attack. Censorship ended officially on November 27, 1918, but in practice it was kept alive by the first serious wave of American paranoia about Russia (it had existed since pre–Civil War days), and First Amendment freedoms were not restored until the Harding administration.

In the war's aftermath the events of the Versailles Peace Conference brought Wilson's relationship with the press to its predictable conclusion. Again the details have been well documented, but, viewed in the light of president-press relationships from the beginning, the results were striking and instructive.

The president had left Tumulty in Washington to keep him informed of public reaction to the conference's work and had taken Ray Stannard Baker to Paris as his liaison man with the correspondents. He also took along his deeply felt belief that the press could only do him harm, particularly where foreign relations were concerned; consequently it was his intention to give the five hundred or so reporters assembled in Paris as little as possible from the American side. It was a tragic mistake, and it was compounded by the early decision of the Council of Ten, to whom the real business of peacemaking was entrusted, to tell reporters nothing about their negotiations except for announcing decisions they had made, nor would they be available to the press at any time.

When news of what had happened to "open covenants openly arrived at" reached the United States, there was an explosion of protest from the press that generated a deep uneasiness in the public. It seemed to many to be a mockery of everything the war to end wars had been fought for. But Wilson's answer after Tumulty had reported this reaction, in near panic, only reflected once again his utter distrust of the press.

The objects of Wilson's scorn in Paris were not inconsiderable journalists. The war, and in fact the entire Progressive Era, had produced a generation of well-educated, informed, able reporters who were a distant cry from those of the nineteenth century. The reporters assembled at Versailles represented an impressive force, as Baker, who had to deal with them on a daily basis, was the first to recognize. He wrote later: "In many ways the most powerful and least considered group of men at Paris were the newspaper correspondents—we had one hundred and fifty of them from America alone. I heard them called 'ambassadors of public opinion.' Here they were with rich and powerful news associations or newspapers or magazines behind them, and with instant communication to every part of the world." To the newspaper correspondents, who numbered among them the best men from the major journals, were added the representatives of those magazines of opinion that had risen to positions of influence—Oswald Garrison Villard of the *Nation;* W. E. B. Du Bois of the *Crisis;* Norman Angell of the *New Republic;* Steffens, at the moment writing for *Everybody's;* Will Irwin of the *Saturday Evening Post;* Mark Sullivan of *Collier's;* and William Allen White, momentarily a feature writer for the Wheeler Syndicate. These were hardly people deserving of the president's contempt.

There was organized protest from the correspondents at the conference, and it was not limited to the Americans. British reporters drew up a protest petition to be presented to the British prime minister, David Lloyd George, while Herbert Bayard Swope of the New York *World,* president of the United States Press Delegation, prepared a similar protest for Wilson. Only France and Italy dissented; they came out strongly for secrecy, as could be expected from countries in which press freedom was not an embedded tradition. Nor was there complete unanimity in the British and American ranks; the two nations differed with each other on a few points, and there was some individual dissension in each camp. These differences came to a head when a committee appointed by the correspondents met to try to resolve the conflicts, and Arthur Krock of the Louisville *Courier-Journal,* later the noted Washington correspondent of the New York *Times,* made some disparaging remarks about the French press and was challenged to a duel by the marquis de St. Brice of *Le Journal.* No blood was spilled.

In the end the reporters won admittance to the plenary sessions, in which nothing of importance was discussed, and the quarrel raged on, poisoning the atmosphere, with a middle ground seemingly unobtainable. When the Council of Ten became the Council of Four, the cloak of secrecy was even more tightly drawn. Baker was in no position to keep the press even partially informed, since he knew so little himself of what was going on; Wilson gave him virtually nothing of consequence to report. Baker's news conferences became a bad joke, and the correspondents got little more at their daily briefings from the heads of the American delegation. That was because Wilson kept them in ignorance of the more serious deliberations.

Only Colonel House, who met reporters every evening at six o'clock at the Hotel Crillon, was able to maintain any kind of liaison with the press, and by that time he, too, was being distanced by Wilson. House even met briefly with individual reporters from time to time, and, as Juergens tells us, "Some of the major news beats to come out of the conference can be traced to these meetings with the cooperative commissioner. Herbert Bayard Swope's report on the amended text of the League of Nations covenant, which appeared in the New York *World* on April 2 and 3, is the shining example. . . . Even his colleagues conceded that Swope had scored the most impressive triumph in covering the conference.''

It is not easy to understand these dispensations of the colonel's. Surely he must have foreseen what would happen. The favored correspondents he met with quite naturally made him their favorite, but since he could not begin to see all the reporters, those who were necessarily deprived of his informal briefings were unhappy, at the very least. Furthermore House antagonized Secretary of State Lansing, who considered him a dangerous source of leaks, and, worse, he angered the president and widened the growing rift between them. To cap it all he further stimulated the enmity of Mrs. Wilson, who thought he was trying to take away the spotlight from her husband. These circumstances, and others, combined to bring about a breaking of the relationship between Wilson and House, whose more intimate details may still be concealed in the Wilson Papers. Before the peace conference ended the colonel's meetings with newsmen stopped abruptly. After he and Wilson returned to the United States, they never saw each other again.

That left the president as the only source of news once more, and he was as adamant as ever about disclosing little or nothing. He remained isolated from the reporters for the most part, but when they saw him, it was plain to many of them that the severe strain of the conference was affecting his health. He looked gray and tired. On the two occasions he did meet formally with the press, the results were unhappy. After the first, a backgrounder in which he was not to be quoted or have anything attributed to him, Truman Talley, chief correspondent of the New York *Herald*'s celebrated Paris edition, broke the rules and quoted the president directly even on the most sensitive subjects, causing him acute embarrassment, particularly when the story also appeared on the front page of the *Herald* in New York. Swope also quoted Wilson directly in the *World*. Talley was slapped on the wrist by the Correspondents' Executive Committees with a two-week suspension of privileges, revoked after six days; Swope escaped censure entirely. These issues only confirmed Wilson in his view that he had been right about the press all along.

The fault again, of course, was on both sides. As William Allen White summed it up: "The newspaper men, for the most part eager to support the American position, were not permitted to know even semiofficially what the American position was. It is not surprising that under this state of facts they began to lose confidence in American leadership." White's use of words illustrates the approach to political reporting that still existed—the newspapers were eager "to support" the American position, not just report what it was and let the editorial writers and columnists support it or not, as they chose.

Wilson's physical collapse on April 3, 1919, under the fatiguing strain of the conference, came in a dark hour when the Americans and French had reached an impasse over the terms of the treaty and the Continent itself was virtually in a state of anarchy. A drastic step was needed, and Wilson still had the courage to take it, using the much despised press as the medium—as he could have used it long since if he had wanted to make it his ally and his weapon. Adm. Cary

Travers Grayson, his doctor, was authorized to leak to the New York *Times* correspondent Richard Oulahan that the liner *George Washington,* which had brought him to Europe, had been called to take him home. Oulahan knew he was being used but pretended a little coyly that he did not. He wrote later:

> Now far be it from me to say President Wilson and Admiral Grayson knew that . . . a translation of my dispatch would be quickly communicated to the French Government. And further still be it far from me to say that President Wilson had a shrewd conviction that my dispatch would create the impression in the minds of the other members of the Big Four that he meant business in sending for the *George Washington.* But as things turned out there was modification of the proposed terms of peace to which he objected and President Wilson remained to sign the Versailles Peace Treaty in behalf of the United States.

So the peace conference ended, with a seeming bluff that worked (although Wilson was ready to leave in any case), and it was followed by further blunders of the same kind, and for the same reasons, that had attended the meeting from the beginning, as the powers tried to keep the full text of the treaty from the press before it could be ratified—an idea of truly impressive mindlessness. It was leaked in every direction, unloosing a storm of angry debate in the United States and elsewhere, particularly in the Senate, which would have to ratify it. The way had been witlessly paved for its ultimate rejection.

When the *George Washington* brought Wilson home, the hero's reception he was given when he landed in New York misled him into thinking that the country was going to support the treaty, and, even more important, the League of Nations that it envisioned. Certainly in the beginning the nation's newspapers appeared to support him; only 13 percent of 1,377 papers polled by the *Literary Digest* opposed the treaty. All the major dailies offered editorial support, across the country. However, if one combined the few who were against with those who wanted to impose certain conditions before approval, there was obvious trouble. When Wilson refused to make any concessions to dissenters, the balance shifted until he could count on reasonably solid editorial support only in the South.

If Wilson had possessed Roosevelt's skill with the press, using it as a medium of both instruction and persuasion, he might have been able to secure solid public support, but it would have been unreasonable to expect him to change his attitudes at such a late date, and as ill as he was. While it could be said that his rigidity had produced the very sins among the newspapermen that he condemned, at the same time their response to it, understandable though it might be, had not been the kind that would make him alter his opinions. The conduct of a few reporters only confirmed the president in his conviction that none could be trusted, and that none were honest.

The story of Wilson's valiant but futile attempt to reach the public himself through a speaking tour across the country has often been told. It was the act of a man who so believed in himself and his views that he was prepared to sacrifice anything to achieve what he wanted. He avoided Chicago on his trip because there the *Tribune* and the Hearst papers represented a solid wall of opposition unlikely to be cracked. Elsewhere, he hoped, things would be better.

Thirty correspondents went with him, including James Hagerty of the New York *Times,* whose namesake son would one day be considered the best press secretary of them all; Louis Seibold of the *World;* David Lawrence of the *Evening Post,* in time to become one of the most noted of Washington correspondents; Byron Price of the AP, who would be its general manager; Hugh Baillie of the United Press, who would head that agency; Jack Neville of Hearst's International News Service; and Jerome Williams of Universal News Service. This assemblage guaranteed the highest level of reporting the president could have hoped for.

During the early part of the trip Wilson was uncharacteristically affable with the reporters, visiting them in the press car and creating an unexpected atmosphere of good will, even giving off-the-record interviews, an almost unbelievable condescension on his part. Just as surprisingly, Mrs. Wilson joined, at least somewhat, in this unprecedented camaraderie, sending back to the press car, with her compliments, a part of the food gifts thrust upon the president by grateful voters whenever the train stopped.

Hugh Baillie described Wilson's astonishing sessions with the press, and to anyone who had watched the president's painful, angry progress with reporters from the beginning of his administration, it was a revelation of what could have been. These meetings in the press car were "surely the most informal of their kind ever held," Baillie recalled,

> more like bull sssions than press conferences. Wilson would sit somewhere around the middle of the car, with the reporters about him, and we would all gab and argue together—as though the President were one of the reporters himself. We'd ask him the questions that were most agitating the opposition. . . . [He] would answer without palavering or hemming and hawing. He'd reach over and tap you on the knee and say, "Now, look here," and argue nose-to-nose with any member of the press corps.

No one has offered a satisfactory explanation for this abrupt reversal. Perhaps it could be explained by the idealistic, crusading spirit dominating the president at that moment. He saw himself as a salesman, selling a magnificent idea to the American people, one that would change the world, and it may well have been that he also saw, at last, the correspondents as allies who could help him. On the other hand the change might have been caused by something as prosaic as the mood swings associated with his physical condition.

In any case it was a brief idyll, and it ended through no fault of the press. William C. Bullitt's inexplicable and indiscreet confession at a hearing before the Senate Foreign Relations Committee changed the president's mood completely once again, as well it might have done. Bullitt, who had been a member of the American peace delegation, told the senators that he had talked with Secretary of State Lansing and both had agreed that many provisions of the peace treaty were unacceptable and that the League of Nations, on which Wilson's hopes now rested, was "useless." Lansing's embarrassed acknowledgment that this conversation did, indeed, take place was the final thrust. For the president it was a cruel slap in the face, and from those he thought he could trust.

When reporters tried to question him about Bullitt's testimony, they found a changed man, one who had reverted to his tense, suspicious attitude toward them and had once more erected the wall of reserve. As the train moved on to the West Coast, Wilson's physical condition began to alarm Admiral Grayson. Neuritis, severe headaches, and loss of appetite were among the symptoms, as the doctor suspected (or already knew), of something more serious. Wilson's nervousness was further stimulated when one of the cars in his motorcade went out of control near Portland, Oregon, killing a reporter who had been one of those participating in the happy press car sessions and badly injuring another. This tragedy seemed to distance him still further from the reporters.

With unrelenting determination Wilson pressed on, his fragile health slipping away as the train carried him to one exhausting stop after another. He was traveling now on nerve alone; there were few reserves left in his tortured body. During the return swing across the continent, as the train neared Wichita, Kansas, the president collapsed at last one night with another stroke, and the remainder of the trip was canceled. Small wonder. The eight-thousand-mile expedition he had undertaken would have felled a younger and healthier man. As the train rolled back to Washington at full speed, stopping only to change engines, it was clear that Wilson was extremely ill.

Now—and not for the first time in the history of the president-press relationship—the correspondents were faced with the problem of how to deal with an incapacitated president, and this time the situation would be acute. The customary cover-up had already begun. Grayson, through Tumulty, was telling the press in a series of bulletins that there was nothing to worry about, the president had simply been working too hard and had a digestive upset. He was suffering from overwork, a second statement said, and the diagnosis was nervous exhaustion. When the train reached Union Station in Washington, Wilson made a tremendous effort and walked to his car, lifting his hat to acknowledge the cheers. He looked pale and his tall figure was bent a little, but it was not possible to see how ill he was. Ten of the reporters who had been on the trip were invited to the White House next day for tea, but Mrs. Wilson received them alone and told them the president was still resting.

Three days later Wilson suffered his final stroke, a massive cerebral thrombosis that paralyzed the left side of his body. There were later prostatic and digestive complications. He was near death for several weeks, while the press was given another series of soothing bulletins. The president was having a nervous breakdown, with some complications, the reporters were told, but as soon as he was completely rested he would be back at his desk, as well as ever. This good news was followed by other encouraging reports, so that the public got the impression it was all the doctors could do to restrain Wilson from leaping out of bed and resuming work. Nevertheless because all of these accounts were so vague, and since the president did not appear week after week, rumors began to circulate about his condition, ranging from speculation that he was insane to reports that he was in a coma, or even dead. It was a truism the White House never seemed to learn—that secrecy could only produce the kind of speculation and wild stories everyone presumably wanted to avoid.

It was four months after Wilson's stroke before the truth about his condition finally emerged. It took that long for his family to decide that it was better to give the public the facts. They chose a circuitous way to do it. One of the attending physicians, Dr. Hugh H. Young of Johns Hopkins, was authorized to issue a detailed account of the president's illness, which was released to the Baltimore *Sun,* giving it an exclusive for no particular reason.

Stricken as he was, Wilson stubbornly refused to compromise as ratification of the treaty was argued in the Senate, with his chief adversary, Sen. Henry Cabot Lodge, leading the opposition. When the treaty failed of the necessary two-thirds majority by seven votes, the full measure of the president's inability to understand the press was exacted. There were many other factors involved, certainly, but with the country half ready to be convinced of the treaty's worth and the league's value, a Rooseveltian kind of campaign through the press rather than the suicidal trip across the continent might have carried the day. With hindsight, historians have speculated that, if Wilson had only possessed the radio as his instrument of persuasion, he could have stayed in the White House and reached the whole country with what he did best—speaking quietly and persuasively in the voice of an accomplished speaker. Ironically, for his final speech in November 1923, three months before he died, he employed that medium, reluctantly. It was a pathetic plea for the league, badly delivered because he could barely see his script and carried by a network that projected his voice no farther away than Providence and Schenectady. But the transcontinental network was just around the corner, and with it would come the penultimate political weapon in the hands of a president.

Harding: Editor in the White House

What now can be said for Warren Gamaliel Harding, perennially cited as the worst of presidents by historians? While the reputations of so many others have been improved by latter-day examinations of accepted estimates, Harding's administration and career, deeply shadowed by the scandals of his personal life, have only been further blackened by disclosures of previously hidden evidence. When the rare attempt has been made to elevate him, the results have bordered on the bizarre. In a much admired recent book, *Modern Times,* the conservative revisionist historian Paul Johnson, former editor of the *New Statesman,* advanced the novel idea that the Harding and Coolidge administrations, rather than being absurd anomalies in American political history, were actually virtual ideal representations of the voting public—''a marriage between a democratic people and its government,'' as he put it.

If that were true, it would be a painful indictment of the electorate, which has quite enough to burden its collective soul. Few historians would accept Johnson's verdict, however. Most of them see Harding and Coolidge as products of a system that had reached a low point—Harding as the triumph of the most sordid kind of machine politics, Coolidge as another accidental president, a respectable nonentity who represented little more in the life of American voters than a need for peace and quiet while they were occupied with making money.

It is not impossible to view Harding sympathetically, as a man whose all-too-human failings led him to make a life that was, in the main, a tragic one in spite of the presidency's ultimate prestige. As for his press relationships, it was a bad joke on the media that, when one of their own finally reached the White House, for the first and probably the last time, his reflected glory failed to illuminate them. No one on either side could have asked for a cosier relationship; an old city hall reporter would have wanted nothing better. Yet, in spite of the camaraderie and a common language, Harding could not help but be an embarrassment to many of his fellow professionals, as he was to those who believed that a president was obligated to maintain somewhat higher standards than the benighted populace that elected him.

The election that brought Harding to power was an anomaly in itself, in which candidates of both major parties and of the independent Single Tax party were newspapermen. Harding was editor and publisher of the Marion (Ohio) *Star*. James Middleton Cox, the Democratic candidate, had been owner and publisher of the Dayton (Ohio) *Daily News* since 1898 and later acquired other newspapers. Robert C. Macauley, who bore the forlorn banner of the Single Taxers, was a reporter on the Philadelphia *Inquirer*. Such a remarkable coincidence had never occurred before, and mercifully has not occurred since.

Harding was the quintessence of the small-town editor of his day, fully aware that such journals live on the printed names of the town's citizens; Harding tried to print those of every man, woman, and child in the community at least once a year. But the *Star* was not entirely parochial, by any means; it also devoted space to national and foreign news. The editor was aware of what was happening in the world, even though it is doubtful whether he had more than a surface understanding of it. Moreover he was enterprising enough to start a Republican weekly, which greatly increased his circulation in the county. For the *Star* he soon obtained an AP franchise and dropped the boiler plate on the front page, which had made the paper look so uninspired.

Little more than nineteen years old, Harding in 1885 was the proprietor of a newspaper still struggling financially but always meeting its payroll. Deficits were sometimes made up by Harding's luck and skill at poker. But eventually his financial difficulties were overcome, and the *Star* began to make money. If the paper was accepted by the Marion populace, however, its publisher remained outside the pale of middle-class respectability. He appeared to these citizens as a young man of exactly the kind he was—friendly, easygoing, a poker player, an enthusiastic social drinker. Marionites, in common with many small-town people, looked on newspapermen as actors had been regarded in the previous century, that is, no better than they should be, in the old-fashioned phrase. Much worse, the whispering had already begun (supposedly started by a rival publisher) that he had black blood in his veins—"the shadow of Blooming Grove," as Francis Russell, a recent biographer, calls it, meaning his possibly mixed origins in the small Ohio village of his birth.

Harding began his climb to respectability by marrying Florence Kling De Wolfe, a rather plain woman, five years older, a divorcée with a son—and the daughter of one of the town's rich men, who had made his money in the traditional small-town way, real estate and banking. It was no love match, biographers have agreed. The advantages for Harding were obvious, but for Florence it may have been no more than the fact that twenty-five-year-old Warren was a handsome young man she thought she could dominate. Her aggressive nature led such earlier biographers of Harding as Samuel Hopkins Adams, William Allen White, and Norman Thomas (who once worked for the *Star* as a delivery boy) to conclude that in the fourteen years during which she helped her husband with the paper, she saved it from ruin. Later studies, however, show that this was not true.

The marriage was a bargain, of sorts, in the end. Harding got the respectability and wealth he wanted so badly, and Florence got what any girl in a little Ohio town would not have dreamed of, to be First Lady. There was a price, of course. Harding had to endure a nagging wife and a loveless marriage. Florence suffered with the knowledge that her husband had betrayed her twice, once with the wife of close family friends in Marion, a liaison that lasted for ten years, and again with a girl young enough to be his daughter, as the phrase goes, by whom he had an illegitimate child.

Aside from this more intimate background, Harding's rise to the presidency was accomplished through the efficacy of Ohio machine politics, an example of the most sordid kind of efficiency. It was a progress interspersed with mysterious visits over a dozen years to the Battle Creek Sanitarium in Michigan, an institution sponsored by the Seventh Day Adventists. In the manner of politicians, this was passed off first as treatment for "nervous indigestion," an ailment not found in the *Materia Medica,* but which Harding himself later referred to as a nervous breakdown, a diagnosis just as unlikely.

Harding's road to the top was paved in the traditional way. State senator, lieutenant-governor, an unsuccessful attempt to be governor, nominating Taft for a second term at the Republican convention, and then election as United States senator. Two factors eased his passage. One was his affability, in which charm, friendliness, and enthusiasm were mixed in the most soothing manner; and as history has shown us, such affability can carry an otherwise mediocre man to extraordinary heights. The other was the expert guidance of Harry M. Daugherty, the very model of a model machine politician and lobbyist, whom Harding had met early in his career and who was at his elbow the remainder of the way. It was Daugherty and Florence who persuaded Harding to run for senator at a time when he was ready to quit politics, and it was Daugherty alone who was first to see that the editor looked even more like a president than he did a senator.

These attributes carried Harding through an utterly undistinguished career as senator, which at the same time were the happiest years of his life—playing poker with cronies, traveling about with his wife, and occasionally running up to New York by himself, where he was seeing twenty-year-old Nan Britton, the precocious little girl who, at twelve, had delivered school news to him at the *Star* and had lingered in his office long enough to fall in love with him. After her father's death, she had moved to New York, where Harding found her a job and an apartment, in which, presumably, their daughter was conceived; she was born in October 1919.

In spite of these circumstances, which would surely have offended the moralists and ended his political career, the romance of Warren and Nan was a genuine love affair, as their letters so clearly show. It was the only real love and affection from a woman Harding ever enjoyed, and he was pathetically grateful for it. He knew that it was a relationship which could only mean extreme danger for him, but even as president he was so far from giving it up that he actually contrived to have Nan visit the White House and enjoyed her in an anteroom closet while the Secret Service prevented any intrusion. There was far more abject devotion than simple infatuation in this madness.

As the conventions of 1920 approached, the Republicans began to see Harding as a distinct possibility. He could scarcely look more presidential; he was wholeheartedly for business, an isolationist of the Lodge school, a man who had offended no one; best of all, he would be a president the party leaders knew they could control. If there was anyone who was not convinced, it was Harding himself. He believed, correctly, that he was not a big enough man for the job, and it took Daughterty and his wife to talk him into running for the nomination. Only a few days before the convention Harding told the president of Columbia University, Nicholas Murray Butler, that he was certain he would never be nominated, although at that moment Daugherty was assuring the New York *Times* that he would be.

Both conventions, as it proved, were historic, not so much for the presidential candidates nominated but (uniquely in American history) for those who were to run with them. In Chicago the Republicans found themselves deadlocked, and Daugherty's prediction that the managers would turn to Harding "at two o'clock in the morning in a smoke-filled room" (another memorable phrase given to political language) was realized. It was somehow consistent with the character of the candidate.

When the fifteen president-makers in that smoky room concluded that Harding would be their man, they first summoned him and asked him if he knew of anything that might embarrass him before the voters. Then this man who was an inveterate gambler, a somewhat more than social drinker, who had slept with his best friend's wife and had a mistress and an illegitimate child in New York, assured them solemnly that he could see no impediment. He conceived himself as no better or worse than most of the people he knew, and there was no reason to believe, in any case, that the voters would ever find out.

Next morning Harding became the candidate, as ordered. The wire-pullers had a candidate for vice-president, too, but the delegates, in a belated gesture of rebellion, turned to another safe, all-but-invisible candidate, Gov. Calvin

Coolidge of Massachusetts. H. L. Mencken, then a young reporter for the Baltimore *Sun,* wrote later that, after the delegates had done their work, he

> retired to the catacombs under the auditorium to soak my head and get a drink. On one of the passages, I encountered a colleague from one of the Boston papers, surrounded by a group of politicians, policemen and reporters. He was making a kind of speech. . . . To my astonishment I found he was offering to bet all comers that Harding, if elected, would be assassinated before he had served half his term. Some one in the crowd remonstrated gently, saying that any talk of assassination was unwise and might be misunderstood. . . . But the Bostonian refused to shut down. ''I don't give a damn,'' he bawled, ''what you say. I am simply telling you what I know. I know Cal Coolidge inside and out. He is the luckiest——in the whole world!''

But first there would be Warren Harding. He had no inclination to go on the stump, and his natural inertia (he and his friends called it, quaintly, ''bloviating'') was helped by the deathbed verdict of the old Republican boss, Boies Penrose, of Pennsylvania, who gave a final word of advice: ''Keep Warren at home. Don't let him make any speeches. If he goes out on a tour somebody's sure to ask him questions, and Warren's just the sort of damned fool that will try to answer them.''

Harding's opponent, James Cox, was not a formidable candidate to face. At the Democratic convention in San Francisco the party had little choice but to run on Wilson's record, yet at the same time the delegates (or their leaders) shrank from nominating the president's son-in-law, William Gibbs McAdoo, and, after pulling and hauling through forty-four ballots, they compromised on Cox, who was then governor of Ohio. On his recommendation the convention nominated as vice-president a man who already overshadowed the candidate, Assistant Secretary of the Navy Franklin D. Roosevelt.

Following Penrose's advice, the Republican leaders kept Harding at home in Marion for a front-porch campaign, much to his pleasure. Harding loved it, and so did the press, which had never been treated so well. The candidate had a three-room house built especially for the reporters, behind the dwelling of his next-door neighbor, George B. Christian. What went on there is described by one of Harding's old friends and fellow publisher, Sherman Cuneo:

> Once each day and not infrequently twice, the presidential candidate, bareheaded, visited the boys in what they called their ''shack.'' Usually he seated himself on the rail of the porch and after lighting a stogie or cigarette . . . or ''bumming'' a chew of fine cut, he'd say ''Shoot!'' Then in a jolly, intimate, confidential fashion, he answered without evasion any question that might be fired at him. Now and then, however, he would say, ''You may use that if you wish,'' but all else he trusted to the boys to keep in their bosoms inviolate, and to the credit of the newspaper profession be it said that in no instance was the trust violated.
>
> Those talks did not end with the election . . . the last thing he did on the train carrying him from Marion to Washington for inauguration, was to summon the cor-

respondents about him in his private car and unbosom himself in a most intimate fashion.

The reporters must have felt that they had died and gone to heaven. Nothing like this had ever been seen in presidential politics. Carried away, they gave Harding a private banquet at the end of the campaign and assured him, "There isn't a man here who is not impressed with your character. If you don't make a fine President, our judgment is no good and we are in the wrong trade." As it proved, they were.

Thus Warren Harding went to Washington, on the wings of a victory over Cox by seven million votes and with the voice of Florence in his ears: "Well, Warren Harding, I have got you the Presidency; what are you doing to do with it?" He did not have the slightest idea, but he did know what he was going to do with the White House: he threw it open to tourists and other visitors for the first time in years. And there was Florence inside, telling everyone that she and Warren were "just folks."

How could any self-respecting serpent enter this paradise with a hope of success? Harding was giving the public what he had promised them, "normalcy," a relief (to say the least) from Wilsonian idealism. Everyone was invited to relax and make money. The press, except for a few recalcitrant Democratic diehards, was behind him, and the assembled correspondents behaved as though they were in some exalted city room under the gaze of a benevolent editor. Yet the serpent was there, and it proved to be the same snake that had brought unwelcome wisdom to other, earlier presidents—the naming of cabinet members. Not that Harding simply gathered political cronies about him. Charles Evans Hughes was his secretary of state, and Herbert Hoover his secretary of commerce. Yet the cronies were there, too, in the persons of Harry Daugherty, the new attorney general, and former Sen. Albert B. Fall, a notorious anticonservationist who inexplicably, and fatally, became secretary of the interior. Along with them arrived a little group of gentlemen bandits from the political dregs who came to be known as the "Ohio Gang" and whose purpose, as it developed, was to use Harding's naïve good nature as a burglar's tool to get at the public treasury.

Much as it might love him, the press could hardly stomach the spectacle of Harry Daugherty as attorney general, and Harding's insistence on appointing him was the beginning of disillusionment, although in retrospect it is hard to see how anyone could have been surprised. Even before Inauguration Day, while the president-elect was recuperating from the campaign in Florida, and before Daugherty's appointment was announced, the mere rumor of it had brought a subdued roar from the press that Harding could not ignore. For the first time he reacted with anger, like any other president in the same situation. Meeting with the correspondents, he waved an irate finger at Louis Seibold, the New York *World*'s chief political reporter, and declared prematurely, "I am ready today to invite Mr. Daugherty into the cabinet as my Attorney General. When he is ready there will be an announcement. And you can set that up in a block on your first page!" At least he spoke the language, but what he said was all too familiar.

Nevertheless Harding quickly recovered his equanimity, and cordial relations were resumed as soon as he was in the White House. He talked intimately with the reporters he knew best, but he played no favorites and seemed to be on good terms with all of them. Conferences were held twice a week, and for the first time they were not only on a regular basis but it was promised the schedule would be maintained no matter what the circumstances. It was a promise kept but nearly broken.

With a newspaperman in the White House, the presidency was subjected to professional appraisal, and the general attitude was summarized by Robert T. Barry, Washington correspondent of *Editor & Publisher,* then as now the industry's leading trade journal. Barry wrote in the issue for March 12, 1923:

> It should not be hard for newspapermen generally to appreciate the novelty of the midnight interview on the south portico of the White House but the even greater innovation of a president discussing a cabinet meeting with the corps may lack something in impressiveness due to unfamiliarity with the mechanics of news gathering in the capital.
>
> Mr. Harding seems to have developed to a marked degree a happy faculty for regarding the persistence of the Washington correspondents in the light of what he, as publisher of the Marion *Star,* might expect of one of his men. To that he adds a very keen appreciation of the fact that newspaper men represent the public in Washington.
>
> The President has been more than cordial in his relations with the corps. He has done unusual things and all but the few chronic kickers are hailing him . . . The great majority of the correspondents have laid aside their axes and fine tooth combs and are ready to do their share toward making permanent the program of mutual helpfulness thus established by Mr. Harding.
>
> The President came into office without a flare of trumpets to herald his devotion to the cause of full publicity on all affairs of government. He had been decent to the men who were with him at Marion all summer, in Texas, and Panama and Florida, and he just kept on being that after he handed his hat to a White House valet. . . .
>
> Since he entered the White House the President has sought on several occasions to reach a working understanding with the correspondents. He has outlined to them some of his troubles and he has voiced a generous estimate of their problems. He asked for fair play. He has promised a square deal.

"Fair play" and "square deal"—how often those reassuring words had been heard before, and no less sincerely intentioned. Certainly no president, not even Roosevelt, had gotten off to a better start; one journalist described the atmosphere in Washington during those first heady days as a cross between Old Home Week and a college class reunion. It had been a very long time since correspondents had played poker with a president, and no one could remember when reporters had their hands shaken at the door of the press conference room and been greeted individually or referred to as "our newspaper family."

Small-town America had been transferred to Washington, but not many of the correspondents were acute enough to notice it. The values that town represented were already under attack by Sinclair Lewis and Sherwood Anderson, and H. L. Mencken was about to gallop off in full cry, pursuing the "booboisie," from

whose ranks Harding had presumably come. But if the correspondents were forbearing about the administration because they had been largely co-opted and
made a part of it, writers such as F. Scott Fitzgerald were not similarly inhibited;
his play *The Vegetable* was widely viewed as a satire on Harding's incompetence. Similarly the more sordid side of the presidency was on view in Samuel
Hopkins Adams's novel *Revelry*. Harding was proving the truth of the Great
American Dogma—that any man could be president.

At the White House, Harding had the help of an able staff, including George
B. Christian, his former neighbor and fellow newspaperman in Marion, who was
the secretary, and he also had a "political" secretary, Judson Welliver, whose
principal job appeared to be answering the hard questions the president was not
prepared to answer, which covered a rather broad range of topics. When Arthur
S. Draper, one of the New York *Tribune*'s most knowledgeable foreign correspondents, called on Harding and asked for his views on matters abroad, Welliver was hastily summoned, and Harding told Draper, "I don't know anything
about this European stuff. You and Jud get together and he can tell me later; he
handles these matters for me."

But neither Christian nor Welliver could protect Harding from such writers as
Mencken, who called the president's language "Gamalielese," a cruel blow to a
man who had always prided himself on his oratory. The phrases that had always
gone down well in Marion and on the campaign trail were joyously described by
Mencken as "a string of wet sponges." Harding was hurt, but not so injured as
to prevent him from asking Welliver to write most of his speeches from that time
on.

From the beginning reporters could see that Harding did not enjoy the work of
the presidency. "There is nothing in this job here," he told William Allen
White. What he liked was meeting people, as he confided to George Christian:
"It is the most pleasant thing I do; it is really the only fun I have." For the rest,
he played golf three times a week, went to poker parties in and out of the White
House, and gave stag breakfasts and dinners for his friends as often as possible.
His chief reading matter was a book of press clippings kept for him from day to
day, but he was also a reader of the Washington *Post* and Chicago *Tribune,* as
well as the Columbus (Ohio) *Dispatch*. Among the magazines, he liked and read
the *Saturday Evening Post* and the *Literary Digest*. More specifically, he enjoyed
comic strips and books by Mark Twain and Zane Grey. When he was photo-
graphed, it was often in the company of his dog Laddie Boy, but he was never
pictured in two of his most characteristic poses, raising a drink or a cigar to his
always receptive mouth.

Most of all Harding loved the daily reception between 12:30 P.M. and lunch-
time, when the public was invited to shake hands with him in a receiving line that
streamed out of the White House and down the drive through the open gates,
which had been closed since war was declared in 1917. Then he was at the peak
of his affability, obviously enjoying himself, a posture that could not help
provoking a warm response from nearly everyone. Even Wilson, who was the
president's polar opposite, said simply, "I really like him."

Florence Harding had also been transformed by success. She often stood in line with him, shaking hands and being as gracious as possible. At his "Poker Cabinet," the euphemistic name for his little parties with cronies, she was frequently to be found mixing drinks and chatting up the guests. Of the "Duchess," as the president called her, he observed, "Mrs. Harding wants to be the drum major in every band that passes."

Among the newspapermen who were regular attendants at the Poker Cabinet meetings was Ned McLean, owner of the Washington *Post,* a circumstance that led some critics to call his paper the "Court Journal." That was unkind, since the *Post* maintained a discreet balance in its coverage of Harding. But McLean did lend money to one of his poker-playing comrades, Secretary Albert Fall, who used it to promote the scandalous dealings that would be known as Teapot Dome.

So this small-town boy presided as president, using his "bungalow mind," as Wilson described it in a less charitable moment, as little as possible, telling the veteran correspondent David Lawrence: "Oftentimes as I sit here," pointing to his desk, "I don't seem to grasp that I am President," and writing later to a friend, "Frankly, being President is rather an unattractive business unless one relishes the exercise of power. That is a thing which has never greatly appealed to me."

In his dealings with the press Harding laid down the customary rules: when he spoke off the record, he was not to be quoted; unless permission was given specifically, he was never to be quoted directly. These rules were observed better than in any previous administration, with only an occasional leak from a journalist who was not a regular and had somehow slipped by the Standing Committee of Correspondents that did the accrediting.

Harding introduced something new when the Washington Conference on the Limitation of Armaments brought an international assemblage of diplomats to the capital. The foreign visitors, in the usual manner, asked for secrecy, but the president insisted on an open conference, refusing to make Wilson's mistake at Versailles. In the event, of course, it was not "open" in the way reporters would like to have the word defined, yet it was a notable improvement over what had gone before. Harding also saw to it that press facilities for covering the conference were ample. With such generosity, it was unfortunate that there was even one disturbing incident. At a press conference a correspondent asked a question that put the president in a bad light with the Japanese, but it was a minor matter. Nonetheless it alarmed Harding enough so that he revived the rule that questions must be submitted in writing, in advance; he did not intend to be caught off guard again.

Inevitably, however, in the normal course of Washington events there were breaches and abuses of the rules from time to time, and the generous editor began to act more like a president. It gave the veteran correspondents a strong sense of *déjà vu* to hear him begin to complain about and question the news judgment of those editors and correspondents who were not content with what came out of the press conferences and insisted on printing congressional criticism, particularly when the criticism was directed at the cabinet members and others in the administration who had brought the smoke-filled room to Washington with them and were already suspected of shady practices.

The sense of the past was even stronger when Harding implied, without actually saying so, that correspondents who lent one ear to Capitol Hill could not expect to find the other ear unimpeded in the White House. Here it came, once more: there was news the way the government (that is, the president) saw it, and that was legitimate news; then there was news from outside the circle that was unfavorable, which was either incorrect or distorted. If the president could not read good news in the press, furthermore, the press was given to understand that he would rather not read any at all.

It appeared that even a newspaperman like Harding could not learn from history. By letting this unwise attitude become generally known, he not only created an antagonism among the correspondents and their editors for the first time, but he encouraged his enemies in Congress to increase their attacks through a press that would probably now be more receptive. Again it was the newspapers' own organ, *Editor & Publisher*, that called the shot. Harding, it said in the issue for June 10, 1922, had

> cast aside the knowledge that came to him from years of experience on the Marion *Star* and attempted to tell the press of America what is and is not news from the Presidential standpoint.
>
> There were glorious days, not long ago, when the pen of Editor Harding carried some wormwood and gall that was not greatly relished by either the followers of the late Theodore Roosevelt or Woodrow Wilson and it is not difficult to state what his reply would have been had any newspaperman in those days attempted to tell him to curb his editorial opinion.
>
> President Harding seems to have forgotten those days, and his knowledge that democracies progress under militant criticism.

In another incident Harding behaved like the publisher he was in an action for which he was criticized, particularly by working newsmen, who had seen (as so many have since) the extent of an owner's devotion to his property. Harding was often heard to express his love for the *Star* and his yearning to return to it as soon as he could decently leave the White House. In 1923 he was offered a substantial sum for the paper, and in an emotional speech to the American Society of Newspaper Editors assured his listeners that he would rather be a newspaper publisher than anything else in the world and intended to be chief owner of the *Star* until his estate had to settle it. Only city room cynics were unsurprised to hear a month later that he had sold the paper to Louis H. Brush and Roy B. Moore, who were then beginning the group of journals known later as the Brush-Moore newspapers. Harding simply could not bring himself to turn down a half-million dollars, most of it clear profit, since he had bought the paper at a sheriff's sale for next to nothing. The new owners thought they were acquiring an asset in the president's agreement to remain a stockholder and to be a contributing editor for ten years. Six weeks later, however, he was dead.

It had been a long climb to the White House, but the fall was rapid. In spite of the camaraderie and the poker parties and the happy reception lines at noon and the ever-ready affability, circumstances were beginning to close in upon the administration. It was becoming a case of Grant all over again. How much did the president know about the chicanery that was going on among his subordinates?

At the time there were many ready to excuse him, not least the correspondents, who after the fall were quite ready to depict Harding as a man who had been betrayed by associates he thought he could trust but were carrying on scandalous activities under his nose without his knowledge. As in Grant's case, however, it is extremely difficult to believe that Harding did not know what was happening around him. What seems far more likely is that for some time he was not disturbed by it because the chicanery was so little different from what he had seen all his life in the backrooms of politics. As it would seem to later presidents, the flagrant dishonesty and lawbreaking appeared to Harding, at least for a time, as no more than the way political business was done.

If he had been wholly or even partially ignorant, there would have been no reason for the deep anxiety that was obviously disturbing him in 1923. Here was Harry Daugherty, the man to whom he owed everything, involved in graft to an extent that was causing widespread underground whispering. At the beginning of his administration Harding had approved the transfer of Western oil reserves from the Navy Department to the Department of the Interior, and now Secretary Fall was busy leasing this government oil illegally to Harry Sinclair and Edward L. Doheny, in the Teapot Dome scandal that erupted at last after Harding's death. These were only the most glaring examples. The administration was filled with minor officials who were stuffing their pockets with public funds, and the rich odor of political corruption was beginning to suffocate even the cigar smoke from the Poker Cabinet.

Whatever Harding may or may not have known, there is some evidence that he did not approve, else why would he have gone to the rear lawn of the White House one night, as Charles Forbes reported, and cried. Forbes was too occupied with his own fraudulent operations in the Veterans' Bureau to cry, but Charles Cramer, one of the lawyers who worked for him, shot himself to death, leaving a suicide note for Harding, which he refused to read. A little later one of Daugherty's oldest and closest Ohio associates, Jesse Smith, another Harding crony, was also found dead, but whether it was suicide or murder could not be determined. In the wake of this tragedy Fall suddenly resigned.

Mounting pressure produced a fight-or-flight response, and Harding chose flight. It was his misfortune, as it had been Wilson's, that he did not have a fully developed radio network to carry his case to the people and proclaim that he, at least, was not a crook. His inauguration had been the first ever to be described on the air, and he had twice used the medium to broadcast speeches, once at Fort McHenry, Baltimore, in June 1922, at the dedication of the Francis Scott Key Memorial, and again a year later, when his speech on the World Court at St. Louis was broadcast over stations there and in New York City. But the electronic voice was still feeble.

Sending Nan Britton off to Europe, Harding went with Florence on a transcontinental train trip, during which he hoped to improve his image with the voters, shake off the miasma of Washington, and restore his health, which had not been good. Again, in the shadow of Wilson, it proved to be a serious mistake. The rigors of travel only increased his physical problems, giving him a heart spasm, severe indigestion (perhaps, rather, another heart symptom), ptomaine poisoning, and a touch of pneumonia.

Hoover traveled with him on the trip, as did William Allen White and Frederick G. Bonfils, the extraordinary editor of that extraordinary paper the Denver *Post* (immortalized by Gene Fowler in *Timberline*), who had told George Christian a year earlier that the paper was investigating the various aspects of Teapot Dome and, as an expert in such matters, gave it as his opinion that it was ''an awful mess and a smear.'' There were other reporters in the party, and, as White reported later, Harding kept asking those he trusted most, and Secretary Hoover as well, what a president ought to do when his friends betrayed him. History does not record their answers.

Harding got as far as Alaska on his trip, which he called ''a voyage of understanding.'' It brought him only exhaustion, and as the return swing began, a coded message arrived from Washington (its contents were never disclosed) that must have convinced him that the house of cards was about to collapse. In San Francisco he went to bed, and his wife began to read to him an article in the current *Saturday Evening Post* by Samuel G. Blythe, its Washington correspondent, entitled ''A Calm View of a Calm Man.'' It was soothing music to the president's ears, and murmuring, ''That's good, go on,'' he turned his face to the wall. They were his last words.

The official diagnosis was a blood clot on the brain, and so it no doubt was, but a wave of uneasy speculation swept the country, particularly when Mrs. Harding refused to permit an autopsy. There were those who thought she had killed him, others that Daugherty had done it, still others who believed it was suicide. But as one historian, David Jacobs, has put it, perhaps he died ''because it was the best thing to do.''

Thus an administration that began with a promise of ''normalcy'' ended in shabby disgrace, not wholly deserved, perhaps, but still difficult to excuse. In the aftermath both Daugherty and Secretary of the Navy Edwin Denby resigned under fire, and a dozen other administration figures, including Fall, Forbes, and Col. T. W. Miller, the alien property custodian, went to jail.

In death the press treated Harding with the affection he had earned and the peculiar kind of sentimentality it is capable of. ''Warren Harding came home today,'' ran the often-quoted lead of a story filed by one reporter who covered the president's return to his home town for burial. It was the simple truth. Harding belonged to Marion, and he should not have left it, in the opinion of those few who knew him and had nothing to gain from his presidency.

Coolidge: A Quiet Interval

Not long after he entered the White House, Ronald Reagan undertook the task of revisionist historian. By his order the portrait of Thomas Jefferson that had hung in the White House cabinet room was removed and replaced by a picture of

Calvin Coolidge. For a president whose grasp of history seemed tenuous at best, this judgment was at least puzzling.

Reagan's expressed admiration for Harding's successor was easier to understand, since it appeared to be nothing more profound than the devotion of one fiscal conservative to another. Coolidge had been deeply alarmed by the size of the budget, the growth of the bureaucracy, and high taxes. So was Reagan. The man Americans came to know as "Silent Cal" also was a strong believer in voluntarism. "If all the folks in the United States would do a few, simple things they ought to do," he said, "most of our big problems would take care of themselves." That, too, became part of Reagan doctrine.

Cal and Ron, a most unlikely duo, were also firm believers in using the electronic media, although Coolidge had to limp along with radio, a medium just coming into its own. Even so, he not only arranged to have his inauguration broadcast, the first time for such an event, but during his administration he spoke on an average of once a month to the growing radio audience. For a man whose signature was brevity, Coolidge was a communicator when it mattered, and to the surprise of most observers he turned out to be the most adroit manipulator of the media since Theodore Roosevelt. Both Coolidge and Reagan were ardent believers in *laissez-faire* and the sanctity of the business community. And as a final fillip to the comparison, it should be noted that both were adept in the use of the one-liner, although Coolidge's lines were likely to be considerably shorter.

It is a thought that staggers the popular conception. Was this unobtrusive little lawyer from Vermont the Reagan of his time? Hardly. While they shared political views, whose common origins were primarily in the McKinley administration, they were obviously quite unlike personalities. In fact, Coolidge's arrival in the presidency marked him as something new and strange in political life—a completely self-effacing human being, yet one capable of surprising those who thought him without qualities. Before his sudden elevation to the White House, however, he was so little known or regarded by the people close to Harding, who were his complete antithesis, that when the president died, no one in the confused entourage thought of notifying him at once, either through Washington or at his father's house in Plymouth, Vermont, where he was vacationing at the moment.

The Associated Press was more vigilant. At the first indication Harding might be seriously ill, several days earlier, the AP dispatched its Boston night editor, W. E. Playfair, to Plymouth, there to await developments. He found two of his string correspondents already on the scene, planning for contingencies. There were no telephone or telegraph lines in this small village; Rutland, more than a dozen miles away, was the nearest leased wire point, and it was eleven miles to Bridgewater and Ludlow, where there were telephones.

When the news of Harding's death reached Playfair in Ludlow, by means of a telephone call from the AP's Boston bureau, he drove down dark and unfamiliar country roads to the Coolidge farm, where he found the unsuspecting new president in bed. Playfair's stringers arrived at about the same time, and the noise of all these cars in the rural night woke up Coolidge, who came downstairs. "Good morning, Mr. President," one of the reporters greeted him. Coolidge's reply was characteristic: "Is this information authentic?" he wanted to know.

Assured that it was, Coolidge issued an immediate official statement, characterizing Harding as "a great and good man," whatever his real opinion might have been, and he made the customary pledge to "carry out the policies which he has begun for the service of the American people," after which all the correspondents except one AP stringer departed to file their stories, and it was this man, Joseph Fountain, of Springfield, Vermont, who was the only witness to the actual swearing in by the light of a kerosene lamp at 2:43 A.M., with Coolidge's father, a justice of the peace, administering the oath.

Immediately after his return to Washington, Coolidge met the correspondents in his hotel suite, where he was staying until it was possible for him to move into the White House, and made the promises that by now had become familiar: "I am glad to meet you. I want you to know the executive offices always will be open as far as possible, so that you may get any information your readers may be interested to have. This is your government. You can be very helpful in the administration of it." He added that he intended to continue the twice-a-week conferences Harding had begun.

The reporters saw Coolidge next at the first of these regular meetings, which displayed the physical atmosphere of conferences for a long time to come, in the sense that reporters crowded into the office around his desk, four or five deep. But there was not yet the rapid interchange of questions and answers. The reporters had submitted their questions in advance, and they lay in a neat pile on the president's desk. He was wearing a dark blue double-breasted suit, with a mourning band for the dead Harding on one arm. The reporters noted that his desk was clear, in contrast to his predecessor's, which had been as messy as its occupant's mind.

Coolidge stood up and began by repeating his pledge to keep the doors of the executive office open to provide them with information. Then he picked up the written questions and gave a brief answer to each one. George McAdams gave a full account of this first press conference in the New York Sunday *Times,* immediately after.

> He was completely master of the situation, as if he had been replying to similar interrogations all his life, and even paused to tell an amusing story of something that had happened at the cabinet meeting. One of the old-timers who called for a cheer for the President had his suggestion vetoed by others who realized that such action would be in poor taste, with Mrs. Harding still in the White House. Coolidge, who overheard phases [sic] of the whispered debate, commented, "Seems to be opposition to my administration already." The applause did come later.

Coolidge never forgot that spontaneous burst of handclapping.

But the applause did not last long. As the conferences continued, a feeling of disquiet gripped the press corps. It was not that Coolidge failed to understand the importance of public relations to the presidency, as so many others had done, nor did he underestimate how helpful the press could be to him as a sounding board.

As always, it was simply a question of personality. He could not help being formal, and there was a certain chilliness in his meetings with the correspondents that he was helpless to avoid. He could only be what he was, a New England lawyer with a natural reserve and a laconic wit that made him seem more silent than he really was.

William Allen White wrote that Coolidge slipped into his meetings with the press "without a word, with scarcely a nod or a greeting. He looked bored, with a certain touch of discouragement to his boredom." As time went on, however, the correspondents adjusted to his personality in a way that brought sharp criticism from one of their own number, Frank R. Kent of the Baltimore *Sun,* then beginning to make his own reputation. Kent wrote of the press conferences:

> Mr. Coolidge does not smile. He utters no greeting, does not even nod his head. There is a dour, discouraged look about him. He seems not to be pleased. He puts on his horn-rimmed glasses, glances at the top question of the sheaf he holds in his hand, and passes it to the bottom. He silently reads a second question and passes that to the bottom, too. The reporters are respectfully expectant. Finally, he finds a question which he reads aloud and answers, then another and another. His voice corresponds to his appearance. What he says is mostly noncommittal, neutral, evasive. To many questions he replies that he has no exact information on the subject but expects to have it shortly, or that he is informed some department has the matter in hand and is handling it in a satisfactory manner. Even when his replies are defiant, which is rare, they are flat and meatless.

If the correspondents had known, however, Coolidge had his own frustrations, which they never saw and the public never heard of. Donald R. McCoy, another of his recent biographers, tells us that these accumulated tensions "would eventually be released in the White House in a storm of abuse and shouting, or in a long frost of silence and nasty looks. That was the price of the public reserve that made Coolidge appear to be the rock of stability."

Whatever restraints the newspapermen were beginning to feel in the conferences, however, it was not easy to find grounds for saying that they were badly treated. Coolidge worked at his press relations about as much as he worked at anything. It was true that he picked and chose from the written questions submitted to him, and never answered many of them, and that he was as prickly as his predecessors about being quoted directly, but on the other hand he did maintain the twice-a-week conferences, trying to mix propaganda with suitable enlightenment. When he chose to answer questions, the reporters were often surprised by his candor. If he did not know the answer, he admitted it with disarming frankness, and if there was real information he wanted to give them, it was given with uncharacteristic generosity. Seldom did he appear uninformed, and many of his comments were perceptive. "He also maintained considerable rapport with the newspapermen," McCoy tells us.

> On occasion he had them in as guests at social affairs. Once he felt free to ask the newsmen for nominations for the secretaryship of the navy and another time he earnestly advised them to wear rubbers to keep their feet dry in the heavy morning

dew. He was not one of the gang, like Harding, nor was he as open-mouthed, but he did give them much of what they wanted, and in return was treated kindly in the news. Indeed, Coolidge used the press more adroitly than it was able to use him, and he set a valuable precedent for the regularly scheduled press conference.

To those who were present, however, it did not appear that way. If he was treated kindly, said Kent, it was because what Coolidge gave them was so "pale and anemic" that they were compelled to put "their own vigor" into his words, with the result that the president's statements emerged as "the forceful and vigorous talk of a red-blooded, resolute, two-fisted, fighting executive, thoroughly aroused and determined." That was extremely helpful to Coolidge, Kent pointed out, but entirely misleading as far as the public was concerned. The reporters did not intend to mislead, he contended; it was largely unconscious,

> a twist that springs from the necessities of the situation. If anything at all is to be got out of these Presidential utterances it is necessary to inject enough strength into them to make them stand up. . . . The President's . . . views are never incorrectly presented. All that happens to them is that they are made vital, vigorous and fair to look upon. . . .
>
> Newspapermen who have regularly attended these Coolidge conferences from the start will tell you that they are the most uninspiring, uninteresting, deadly dull affairs of the kind ever known in Washington. . . . In the year that they have been held, twice every week, no one who has been in attendance can recall a single word from Mr. Coolidge that sparkled or glowed or indicated any force, feeling, grasp or spirit. . . . But that is not the picture the country gets. That cannot be written. It is not news.

Significantly, as a measure of how much times have changed, it would not only be considered news today, but it would be endlessly analyzed by columnists and the entire breed of media critics. Kent, however, was considered unorthodox, perhaps radical, in speaking out so openly.

Kent was not the only one to be disturbed by what was happening at the press conferences, although the underlying dissatisfactions did not spill over until late in Coolidge's first administration, in 1924, when several of the most experienced Washington correspondents unburdened themselves at a meeting of the Institute of Public Affairs in Charlottesville, Virginia. As *Editor & Publisher* summarized it in August, the burden of their complaints was that Coolidge was using them, giving them propaganda instead of news simply to advance his political aims. Ludwell Denny, then beginning his long career as correspondent for the Scripps-Howard newspapers, was the harshest critic. "President Coolidge's press conferences," he said, "are a vicious institution in American life, and should be abolished. They have been turned into propaganda agencies for the President and correspondents have to submit in order to protect themselves."

It is difficult to see, in retrospect, how the older reporters, at least, could have found Coolidge's use of the press so different from what had gone before, particularly in the Roosevelt and Wilson administrations, except that TR had done the same thing much more skillfully and the Princeton professor had accomplished it through rigid didacticism. There was nothing particularly vicious about it, as

Denny charged. It was simply the way that presidents had been coming to view
the press for some time, as a vehicle for their own purposes. There was little
substance, too, in the charge that Coolidge was inaccessible. He saw the reporters regularly, twice a week, which was more than the others had done, and if the
substance of these meetings was unsatisfactory, that was not solely the president's fault but also the reporters', for not only accepting what was given them
but making it seem more substantive than it was, as Kent had accused them of
doing.

The fact was that the institution of the presidency, even in the care of such a
retiring, unaggressive chief executive, was taking on a shape which would become the norm in time. Press conferences were held, but nothing much came
from them. Government handouts, some emanating from the White House, had
grown from being a bland trickle to a fairly respectable stream, and it would not
be long before they would resemble a paper Victoria Falls.

Few of the correspondents were prescient enough to understand something
else that was about to overtake them. When it was decided to broadcast
Coolidge's inaugural address, for the first time in history, the president had been
much concerned about whether he was doing the politically wise thing, but when
it turned out to be one of his most successful speeches (and he was no orator), he
was quick to see that when he could reach an estimated twenty-two million people over a network of twenty-five stations, a network just beginning to grow,
there was a great deal of political hay to be made. As William Allen White
appraised it, "He developed talent as a radio speaker. He spoke slowly, used
short sentences, discarded unusual words, was direct, forthright and unsophisticated in his utterances. And so, over the radio, he went straight to the popular
heart. His [1924] radio campaign helped greatly because it is one of the few
campaign mediums by which the President always appears with his best foot
forward."

Coolidge was the first president to understand this fundamental fact, and the
discovery was a fortunate one, since his campaign to be elected in his own right
in 1924 had been badly managed. It was doubly fortunate that by this time he was
also an extremely popular president as the country, recovering from a postwar
depression that had somewhat reduced the meaning of Harding's "normalcy,"
rose exuberantly on a surfing wave of prosperity. At the Republican convention
in Cleveland, Coolidge had been nominated on the first ballot, with a Chicago
banker, Charles G. Dawes (who also composed a salon piece played endlessly as
an encore by a generation of violinists), as his running mate.

The Democrats, in New York, were hopelessly divided into squabbling
camps, which appeared to polarize around the issue of the Ku Klux Klan. The
anti-Klan forces were led by Gov. Alfred E. Smith of New York, nominated by
Franklin D. Roosevelt, while the pro-Klan troops favored William Gibbs
McAdoo, who took pains to separate himself from most of what they advocated.
After a record 102 ballots the weary delegates nominated John W. Davis, a New
York liberal lawyer, as a compromise candidate. He ran with Gov. Charles W.
Bryan of Nebraska, whose chief qualification appeared to be that he was the
Great Commoner's brother.

Coolidge conducted a campaign as quiet as he was, staying out of sight as much as he could in Washington, relying on prosperity and the Republican slogan, "Keep cool with Coolidge," for reelection. What little was done for him, insiders like White believed, was wrong. "He was smocked and put to pitching hay in Vermont," the Kansas editor complained. "He was touted as the poor man's candidate. No more obvious, cynically conscious demagoguery ever was flaunted in the faces of the American people." An extreme statement, to say the least. But, said White, "Through it and over it, he appealed to something in the American heart." Yes, Democratic cynics agreed—money.

One of the factors in Coolidge's reelection that has been overlooked by most historians was the powerful support of the *Saturday Evening Post,* then at the peak of its influence under the editorship of George Horace Lorimer, whose wife was on the Republican National Committee and who himself was a potent behind-the-scenes mover in the party's affairs. The *Post* at this time was easily the most popular magazine in America, with a paid circulation of three million but reaching millions more as it was passed around. It spoke to middle-class America in a way that no other magazine has ever equaled, and its unsigned Lorimer editorials were known to make the *Post* as influential as any other publication in America.

As soon as Coolidge entered the White House, Garet Garrett, one of Lorimer's ablest political writers, wired the editor: "Here's a President nobody knows anything about; let's find out." The "Boss," as he was known on the magazine, told him that George Pattullo, another staff writer, had already examined Coolidge and reported, "There's nothing in this man." But Garrett was unconvinced. After spending an hour with the president he wired Lorimer again: "Let's have another look at this man," and the editor agreed.

The president and Lorimer met, liked each other, and became instant friends. Although they were completely unlike as personalities, they continued to meet frequently to exchange ideas, and the editor spent long hours on the presidential yacht, the *Mayflower.* But Garrett found Coolidge puzzling. At the end of a typed letter to Lorimer, reporting on a meeting with the president, he added a postscript in his own hand: "I can't make Coolidge out. He makes very keen sounds and no wrong ones. I could easily believe he has more strength than has been revealed. I overran my time and stopped. He said, 'Go on.' And that was all he said, except to ask me suddenly when I was born, until the end, which I have indicated. No. He said one other thing. He interrupted me to ask how I knew a certain thing to be so. I told him. He nodded and said again, 'Go on.'" Lorimer sometimes laughed about Coolidge's peculiarities and often refused to take him seriously, but as a Republican pragmatist, he supported what he considered to be the president's sound Republicanism; a convincing evidence of support was his payment to the former president in 1931 of a $10,000 fee for an article entitled "Party Loyalty and the Presidency."

While Coolidge presided in Washington, however, Lorimer was not nearly as optimistic about what he was doing for the country as his magazine, reflecting the general optimism and prosperity of the times, led people to believe. His private disquiet expressed the uneasiness of real conservatives, such as he was, who did not see Coolidge as a strong leader. In March 1927 he wrote his friend Corra Harris in words that have a reminiscent sound:

> Never in my experience has there been so much scrambled and uninformed opinion about everything. Led by the pinks, the preachers and the professors, we seem to be in danger of mob rule. I can't see that the preachers and the professors are doing their own job well enough to warrant us in believing that they can successfully run the country and dictate our foreign policies. They have swallowed the Mexican, the Nicaraguan, the Chinese, the French and English propaganda at one big gulp and when the real facts are presented to them they brush them aside rather impatiently. There is something almost ludicrous in the attitude of the church towards our army and navy. On the one hand they are preaching total disarmament and on the other they are using the navy and the marines to protect and save the lives of their missionaries in China. What happens to our other advance guards of civilization, the businessmen, seems to be a matter of small consequence to them. The elements who attack the presence of our marines in Nicaragua are the same as those that demanded warships from Secretary Hughes to protect their schools and colleges in Turkey when they were threatened.

Thus the state of the conservative mind at the height of Republican prosperity.

Little or none of Lorimer's doubts about Coolidge were to be seen in the *Saturday Evening Post* or in other Republican newspapers and magazines. Nor did the Democrats seem overly ready to proclaim that Coolidge was a menace to the country, if not to Western civilization. It was the Jazz Age, the Era of Wonderful Nonsense—nightclubs, gangsters, sinful college students, and the ubiquitous flapper on the one hand, and the massive presence of small-town America, as represented by Coolidge, on the other. The preoccupations of the nation appeared to be how to make more money in the stock market, and where to get a drink.

To the correspondents in Washington, who had to deal every day with what they sensed was a growing dichotomy in American life, trying to find out what Coolidge was doing, and why, continued to be frustrating. He was not an easy man to understand, this president who appeared to be not much interested in how he stood with Congress, or in how to discuss issues with the voters, or indeed in how to make any other use of his executive power. Still, he was undeniably popular. People liked the dry little one-liners that the papers loved to quote, and they especially liked the pictures for which he so willingly posed—as a cowboy, an honorary Sioux Indian, a Boy Scout, or anything at all that required some dressing up—and that to his critics made him appear absurd. He was the delight of the newsreel and press photographers, and Coolidge enjoyed the attention. When he once shouted to his elegant and reserved wife Grace, "Oh, Mammy, they're making a perfect fool of me," she and the spectators knew he did not mean a word of it.

Colonel Starling of the Secret Service once remarked that he thought Coolidge was enjoying a delayed boyhood, and that was a shrewd diagnosis. How else to explain Coolidge's sudden impulses to press all the buttons on his desk at once, just for the fun of it, amused by the confusion he created? As his friend White acknowledged, he could be sentimental, mischievous, inconsiderate, and cruel, as well as silent. These qualities angered the radical and left-wing press to such an extent that they led an otherwise temperate and perceptive correspondent, Oswald Garrison Villard, to say in the *Nation* that Coolidge was a "midget statesman" and to quote one of the president's journalistic acquaintances as remarking of him, "Never in years of political experience have I met a man in public life so despicable, so picayune, so false to his friends as Cal." Nor was it entirely the radical press that expressed such a low opinion, for here was White, one of the Republican's chief journalistic sentinels, in his Emporia *Gazette,* referring to the president as "this runty, aloof, little man, who quacks through his nose when he speaks."

In the end Coolidge proved to be perhaps his own best analyst when he told his friend Frank W. Stearns:

> Do you know, I've never really grown up? It's a hard thing for me to play this game. In politics, one must meet people, and that's not easy for me. . . . When I was a little fellow, as long ago as I can remember, I would go into a panic if I heard strange voices in the kitchen. I felt I just couldn't meet the people and shake hands with them. Most of the visitors would sit with Father and Mother in the kitchen, and the hardest thing in the world was to have to go through the kitchen door and give them a greeting. I was almost ten before I realized I couldn't go on that way. And by fighting hard I used to manage to go through that door. I'm all right with old friends, but every time I meet a stranger, I've got to go through the old kitchen door, back home, and it's not easy.

That would explain a number of things, including Mencken's observation that Coolidge's ideal day was "one on which nothing whatever happens." It explains, too, his silence, and what sometimes seemed to the correspondents as pure laziness. Coolidge had a deep emotional need to take things easy and not go through the kitchen door if he could help it, avoiding any kind of irritation if it were possible.

So well insulated was Coolidge from anything the correspondents might say that he found it hard to understand if others were more sensitive. When Herbert Hoover complained to him about attacks he was enduring from the magazine *Wallace's Farmer,* Coolidge asked in real surprise, "Do you mean to say that a man who has been in public life as long as you have bothers about attacks in the papers?" "Don't you?" Hoover asked, equally surprised, and he mentioned a recent attack on Coolidge by Frank Kent in Mencken's new magazine, the *American Mercury.* "You mean that one in the magazine with the green cover?" Coolidge inquired. "Well, I started to read it, but it was against me, and so I didn't finish it."

That green cover was often seen protruding from the pockets of newspapermen in the 1920s, particularly those who were young. The iconoclasm of Mencken's little periodical, co-edited with George Jean Nathan, appealed to the disillusionment and cynicism of the young in the postwar era, before the Depression leveled everyone to equality. Kent was not the only White House correspondent who

contributed to the *Mercury*. In a free-spending, hedonistic society, these reporters and many other people looked upon Coolidge, as the historian Donald Mc-
Coy remarks, much as jaded eighteenth-century aristocrats in France must have
regarded the homespun figure of Benjamin Franklin, although, in Franklin's
case, he was no doubt more sophisticated than any of his French contemporaries.

There was little change during Coolidge's presidency. He continued to confound the press on small matters, particularly about the nagging question of
quoting him directly. He suggested once that he be referred to as a "White House
spokesman," introducing that now-hoary cliché. But then, in a later conference,
he complained that the reporters were abusing this evasion, especially when the
"spokesman's" utterances were placed between quotation marks. He told the
reporters finally that he thought it would be a good idea to drop any such reference entirely from their reports of the conferences, since the device had been
used so much that everyone knew it was the president speaking. Use of the term
"spokesman," he added, had never been authorized by him in any case.

Coolidge also forbade the correspondents to take down anything he said in
shorthand, asserting it would interfere with his freedom of expression because it
would produce verbatim quotations from the "spokesman" that he might have
wanted put in different language. As for foreign affairs, he refused to talk much
about them. He could only say certain things, he protested, and to keep repeating
them would only irritate foreign governments. Part of this prohibition was directed at Charles Michaels of the New York *Times,* whose needling questions
had incurred the president's continuing dislike.

Yet Coolidge did try to be helpful much of the time—or rather, when it suited
him—and he was always obliging to the photographers and newsreel men, not
only because he liked the attention but because he understood the value of a good
picture, which could not be misquoted. Consequently he endured much more
from the picture takers than he would have from the reporters. One afternoon,
White recalled, when an impatient newsreel man called out to a presidential
party, "Look pleasant, and for heaven's sake, say something—anything—good
morning, or howdy do!" Coolidge replied, with his usual poker face, "That man
gets more conversation out of me than all Congress."

Coolidge was not, however, forthcoming about either his business or private
life, a secrecy he extended even to accomplishments he could easily have boasted
about—his ability to read Latin, for instance. There was not, in fact, much
private life for the reporters to discover. He enjoyed the company of his wife,
who was as reserved as he was but well liked by everyone who knew her, and he
was often accompanied by his large collie dog Laddie. Otherwise the president
had no recreational activities—wasters of time and energy. Thrift and caution
were his watchwords; he distrusted innovations and anything that was foreign.

The correspondents could at least be sure he would not do anything unexpected. They knew it was his rule to be in bed before ten o'clock at night, and it
was learned that he often went to the White House kitchen for what was to him a
late snack, just as he had done as a boy in Vermont. (John F. Kennedy, incidentally, had the same habit, frequently going down to the kitchen after a state
dinner featuring the French cuisine he did not care for and asking René Verdon,

the White House chef, if it was possible to produce a corned beef sandwich and a bottle of beer.) Coolidge was up fairly early in the morning, but he took a nap in the afternoon and, all told, slept about eleven hours out of the twenty-four. On the rare occasions when the president did do something unexpected, there was never any explanation, as when he refused to see Edward Elwell Whiting, editor of the Boston *Herald,* who had campaigned for him and written a favorable biography and had come to pay his respects.

Underneath the generally placid surface of the White House, a well-concealed resentment existed on both sides. As his final term drew to a close, it surfaced on Coolidge's part in a speech at the dedication of the National Press Club Building, when he offered his view of the press in terms that were obviously intended to be high-minded but instead disclosed that, along with many other presidents and a considerable part of the public, he believed that newspapers should not criticize either the government or the country and, in effect, should tell the good news, not the bad news. It was authoritarian conservatism, with the flag drawn around it. In this speech Coolidge deplored

> the constant criticism of all things that have to do with our country . . . and the attempt to foment class distinction and jealousies, weaken and disintegrate the necessary spirit of patriotism. There is always need for criticism, but there is likewise need for discrimination. There is a requirement for justice and truth. . . .
>
> Constantly to portray the failures and the delinquents is grossly to mislead the public. It breeds an unwarranted spirit of cynicism. Life is made up of the successful and the worthy. In any candid representation of current conditions they have the first claim to attention. In the effort of the press to destroy vice, it ought not to neglect virtue.

To editors who believed that life was made up of considerably more than "the successful and the worthy," particularly in politics, these words were the proverbial red flag. The New York *Telegram,* flagship of the Scripps-Howard papers, said editorially: "Mr. Coolidge has made a serious charge against American newspapers which do not continuously 'yes' the Government in all its foreign policies. In justice to the newspapers and in justice to the newspaper readers of this country, Mr. Coolidge should name names." The Baltimore *Sun* inquired sarcastically whether the president believed the motto of the press should be, "My country, right or wrong." In the New York *World* the president's "insinuations" were called yellow journalism. Only the professional patriots of the Hearst newspapers greeted Coolidge's remarks with enthusiasm, endorsing his "clarion call to patriotic journalism" and making its own charge that "foreign correspondents of certain American newspapers are more interested in furthering the interests of foreign governments than in furthering the interests of the United States. . . . The President wants to stop this business of foreign governments influencing American governmental policies by subtle control of the American press."

If he did not have a high opinion of the newspapers, except rhetorically, Coolidge did not disdain them either, as Taft had done. He read the New York

World, especially its outstanding editorial page edited by Walter Lippmann; the New York *Times,* which he liked for its foreign news; the Washington *Post,* for congressional and local news; the Baltimore *Sun,* particularly for Frank Kent's column; and a smattering of weekly magazines as well.

But after forty-eight months of relative peace and quiet in the White House between the president and the press, in spite of all that bubbled beneath the surface, the relationship reached a peculiar Coolidgean climax in the summer of 1927, when the president had set up his summer White House in Rapid City, South Dakota, in the Black Hills, convenient for his favorite and only sport, trout fishing. On the morning of August 2, the fourth anniversary of his presidency, he met the correspondents at nine o'clock, as usual, in the mathematics classroom of the local high school. The conference passed in its customary routine, almost listless fashion, but the president asked the reporters to come back at noon for a further statement, giving them no slightest indication of what might be forthcoming. When they returned, they found Coolidge holding in his hand a fistful of two-by-nine-inch slips of paper. Telling them, ''The line forms on the left,'' he began to pass them out. When the first reporter opened his, he ran for the telephone. It said, ''I do not choose to run for President in 1928.''

It was a typically Coolidge performance. He refused to make any further comment or explanation. Only his secretary, Everett Sanders, had known in advance; not even his wife, it was said, had been told; and Sen. Arthur Capper of Kansas, who happened to be there, was as surprised as anyone. Coolidge had cut up the statements into identical sizes himself, and he had timed the announcement to minimize its effect on the stock market, so it was said later (although it is difficult to see how that would be accomplished), and to serve both afternoon and morning papers, although again the afternoon dailies would certainly have had the story first.

There was an immediate uproar, but at his press conference next day and during those that came later he offered no further elaboration. Speculation has continued to this day, and veteran correspondents have offered various entertaining theories, but Coolidge was probably speaking the simple truth when he wrote in his autobiography: ''I had never wished to run in 1928 and had determined to make a public announcement at a sufficiently early date so that the party would have ample time to choose someone else. An appropriate occasion for the announcement seemed to be the fourth anniversary of my taking office.''

Thus Calvin Coolidge faded out of the Washington scene as unobtrusively as he had entered it. If the press had not particularly enjoyed the experience, Coolidge professed (and probably meant it) to have nothing but fond recollections. In his autobiography he wrote:

> One of my most pleasant memories will be the friendly relations which I have always had with the representatives of the press in Washington. I shall always remember that at the conclusion of the first regular conference I held with them at the White House they broke into hearty applause. I suppose that in answering their questions I had been fortunate enough to tell them what they wanted to know in such a way that they could make use of it.

>While there have been newspapers which supported me, of course there have been others which opposed me, but they have usually been fair. I shall always consider it the highest tribute to my administration that the opposition have based so little of their criticism on what I have really said and done.
>
>I have often said that there was no cause for feeling disturbed at being misrepresented in the press. It would be only when they began to say things detrimental to me which were true that I should feel alarm.
>
>Perhaps one of the reasons I have been a target for so little abuse is because I have tried to refrain from abusing other people.
>
>The words of the President have an enormous weight and ought not to be used indiscriminately.

The little barbs were there, to be sure, but on the whole it was a more generous assessment than most other presidents had seen fit to give.

If beating the reporters at their own game could be considered the best revenge, the president had this satisfaction, too. After he left the White House, writing became his chief source of income. There was, of course, his autobiography, for which he had begun compiling notes while he was still president; it was a masterpiece of dullness and told the public nothing it did not already know. But Coolidge was paid extremely well for it by the Hearst interests, which ran it serially in *Cosmopolitan* magazine and then issued it as a book through a publishing division, the Cosmopolitan Book Corporation.

But the writings of a former president, even one with as little to say as Coolidge, have their own market value, and he was paid the highest rates for articles in *Ladies' Home Journal, Collier's,* and the *Saturday Evening Post.* Then in 1930 he was signed to write a series of daily columns for the McClure Newspaper Syndicate, called "Thinking Things over with Calvin Coolidge," for which he got the highest price ever paid for feature articles. They were little essays of stupefying vapidity (to some readers it seemed that even Coolidge was bored by them), but in the single year they were syndicated to nearly a hundred newspapers they earned $203,045, most of which went to their author. He wrote them in rough drafts every evening, in pencil, then dictated them to his secretary next morning, after which they were revised, recopied, and sent by Western Union to the syndicate offices. Needless to say, he was never late.

Hoover: "He is not for this hour . . ."

In the person of Herbert Hoover, past and present meet. He is the pivot point on which not only the history of president-press relations turns but the history of the presidency as well. After him, nothing was ever the same again, either in the White House press room or the Oval Office. Hoover, it could well be said, was defeated by history, by forces and shifting social winds neither he nor anyone else had foreseen. Unfortunately, in spite of his acknowledged virtues, he was not the man to cope with them successfully.

The case for and against Hoover has been argued by scholars and a wide assortment of popular writers, with the controversy usually viewed (much less by scholars, of course) as a conflict between left-wing and right-wing ideology. It is a far more complicated matter, however, as recent studies have shown. Hoover appears to have been a victim of his own personality rather than a major casualty in the continuing social war between left and right. His presidency is also a striking example of how little politicians (not to mention many of those less exalted) seem able to learn from the past and of how they fail to understand that it is the future, not their present enemies, which is threatening them.

Hoover came to power at a time when the world was on the verge of great changes. The press, which had virtually created him, so to speak, and which would soon be an equally powerful factor in destroying him, had changed remarkably from the early years of the century. It was now a big business in its own right, and while its owners were, by and large, nowhere nearly as colorful and well known to the public as the nineteenth-century giants, they had an unprecedented influence in politics, local as well as national, and, with the arrival of radio and television, the media as a whole would create an entirely new political climate in America.

No president before Hoover had ever approached the presidency with so much help from the press, including this time not simply the Washington press corps but a collection of publishers and editors representing many millions in circulation. In the phrase of a later day, they could justifiably be called "opinion-makers." Hoover himself was well aware of what these friends could do for him, and he intended to make full use of their talents, so much so that at least one scholar has viewed him as a president who brought into full focus what stout Theodore Roosevelt had viewed with a wild surmise, far from silent on a peak in Oyster Bay, and then practiced in ways not seen before his time. "Given the large number of publicists surrounding Hoover's work," says Craig Lloyd, in a recent study, "it is understandable that several students of governmental publicity have looked upon him as instrumental in bringing the techniques of administrative publicity to maturity in American government. And when one adds to the outpourings of his press bureau his friendly and productive associations with influential journalists, it is easy to see why his activities provoked suspicion that he was bent on advertising himself."

The push to make Hoover president began before the election of 1920, and much of it centered in the newspaper and magazine community. The first major endorsement came from Walter Lippmann's editorial page in the New York *World,* a significant move in itself since the *World* was avowedly Democratic and fortified its endorsement with the declaration that it would support Hoover regardless of party. Ralph Pulitzer, the paper's owner, and Frank I. Cobb, its notable editor, had lunched with Hoover to discuss the possibility of his running. At that luncheon there was the gray but disgraced eminence, Colonel House (he was, in fact, the host), and Cyrus H. K. Curtis, publisher of the *Saturday Evening Post* and other periodicals.

In the New York *Times,* the Detroit *News,* and the Philadelphia *Public Ledger,* it had already been reported that Wilson himself favored Hoover, but there was little substance in this rumor. Later, in an uncharacteristically candid moment,

Hoover gave it as his opinion that Wilson had been a great man until he had gone insane and wanted to rule the world, while Wilson at about the same time was characterizing Hoover as a man who "would rather see a good cause fail than succeed if he were not the head of it," adding that he was "one of the most selfish people I have ever known."

For a time it seemed that Hoover, as Arthur Link has surmised, could have had the Democratic nomination in 1920, although such Republican stalwarts as Bernard Baruch, who idolized Wilson, thought differently. Hoover, Baruch protested, had "delusions of grandeur—he really believes all the wonderful things he has written about himself. . . . As a mining engineer he never had a success in his life." (The two remained friends in later years, however, although Baruch's opinion did not change substantially. In their old age they lunched occasionally in Hoover's suite at the Waldorf Towers. Baruch returned to his office from one of these meetings, settled back in his big desk chair, and observed with as much vehemence as though it were still 1920, "This man won't do!")* The general feeling about Hoover, as McAdoo believed, was that he was only using the Democrats in order to secure the Republican nomination.

While astute party men could see that Hoover was no Democrat, nor likely to be one, Republican enthusiasm for him did not diminish, in spite of his supposed flirtation with the enemy. One of these enthusiasts was George Lorimer, editor of the *Saturday Evening Post,* an early admirer who had approached Hoover with an initial skepticism even while respecting his work as food administrator in the Great War, but drew closer to him in the early 1920s, finding that they agreed on a good many conservative ideas, including the conviction that the Reds were about to take over America. In May 1923 Hoover spent the night with Lorimer in his country place, Wyncote, on Philadelphia's Main Line, discussing the state of the nation and the railroad strikes in particular, and their alliance appears to have been consolidated then.

Earlier, when the 1920 nomination approached, Lorimer and the *Saturday Evening Post* had joined what was by now an impressive array of newspapers and magazines supporting Hoover's candidacy, a movement orchestrated by the Hoover Publicity League, which was headed by Edward Eyer Hunt, cofounder with Walter Lippmann of the Harvard Socialist Club. As Mary Austin wrote, "Seven out of ten men who work with Hoover become his permanent press agents," and that list now included hundreds of devoted followers who turned out a steady stream of articles and feature stories. The *New Republic,* at that time intimately involved with Colonel House, mobilized the intellectuals, while Cyrus H. K. Curtis and his magazines—the *Saturday Evening Post,* the *Ladies' Home Journal,* and *Country Gentleman*—with a total circulation of more than five million, exhorted the middle class and the farmers. The Scripps-Howard newspapers were also prominent among the many journals supporting Hoover. These publications were reinforced by engineering societies, scientific management organizations, and university faculties (Harvard voted for Hoover, two to one, in a poll).

* Personal recollection of coauthor John Tebbel.

For the moment, however, it was all in vain. Hoover, preoccupied with the Children's Relief Fund and the Second Industrial Conference, would not even campaign for the 1920 nomination. Nevertheless, he placed fourth in total primary votes and showed impressive strength in the *Literary Digest* poll, so soon to vote itself out of existence. Consequently it was surprising, at the convention itself, when he won only ten and a half votes on the ballot that nominated Warren Harding.

Hoover's friends bided their time. They were not convinced it had come in 1924, but they were making plans for 1928. In 1925, for example, Lorimer and the *Saturday Evening Post* were so closely allied with Hoover that the editor discussed *Post* political articles with him, tailoring them if necessary to (as Lorimer put it in one case) "eliminate anything that seems ill advised in view of the present situation." A year before the convention of 1928 Lorimer had his scouts out listening for whispers in the wind, but what he heard at first was not encouraging. Sam Blythe reported from New York in a letter to Lorimer on January 12, 1927, "It is an extraordinary thing that most of the folks financially downtown think, firmly believe, that Coolidge will be nominated, that he expects to be and that he will accept."

Hoover himself appeared in no particular hurry to rally support for his nomination, at least publicly, but his private views were quite different, as Isaac Marcosson, a *Saturday Evening Post* writer who had virtually invented the magazine interview, reported to Lorimer in September 1927:

Hoover is very anxious that you know his position with regard to the presidency. He therefore talked to me on Saturday with great frankness. Hoover said that he would make no effort to get the nomination. He declared that, in his opinion, the scramble for delegates is "a degradation of the office." He further stated that most of the party leaders had been to see him, asking him to announce himself and enter the race. This he has so far declined to do. He maintained, however, that if the nomination were offered him he would accept it. Hoover made an interesting point which makes me believe that he is very keen for the nomination. He said that, with the exception of Dawes, every man mentioned would be past seventy years of age if he served a second term. He is the youngest of the lot. I therefore pass this on to you for what it is worth.

Meanwhile, and regardless of what he was telling Lorimer, Hoover was at last persuaded in the fall of 1927 to mobilize the vast public relations machine that he had created to advance and publicize his work in Belgium, then with the Food Administration, and finally with Commerce Department programs, setting it now at the task of selling him as a political candidate for the Republican nomination.

For that effort he had the ready help of such veteran editors and writers as William Allen White, Mark Sullivan, Will Irwin, and William Hard. They fired the first barrage of "Hoover-for-President" articles and campaign biographies, which were then syndicated by the press services and presented as happy gifts to the delegates at the Republican National Convention in Kansas City. They nominated him, overwhelmingly, on the first ballot. After the nomination this preliminary material was recycled by the National Committee for use in the campaign. Clearly, it was durable stuff. Old friends and associates were also called in to help, and, at the candidate's former offices in New York, past public statements that had been carefully cataloged over the years were now culled for pregnant statements that could be mailed out to influential editors and organizations. As might be expected, the Associated Business Editors joined in with a "Hoover-for-President" subcommittee, devoted to propagandizing business editors, who scarcely needed to be stroked.

Hoover also had valuable allies in the Republican press, particularly A. H. Kirchhofer, then editor of the Buffalo *Evening News* and a member of the board of the American Society of Newspaper Editors, who wrote Hoover publicity for the National Committee. Another helper was Bruce Barton, the New York advertising man who had put both the Bible and Jesus on the map with his two best sellers, *The Book Nobody Knows* and *The Man Nobody Knows*. In what was something of a comedown after that, he had written speeches for Coolidge, and now, smarting from Mencken's description of Hoover as "a fat Coolidge," he wrote a well-circulated rebuttal. Plump, perhaps, but not fat. And through Merle Thorpe, a friend of Barton's who was editor of *Nation's Business,* the adman was able, as Craig Lloyd tells us, to suggest "the spirit and much of the wording" of the emotional (for him) telegram that Hoover sent to the Republican convention, accepting the nomination.

This kind of coordinated support and advocacy was not overlooked by political commentators. The *Nation* believed that no other person "had a personal publicity machine as powerful and effective" as the one that elevated Hoover to the White House. Walter Lippmann noted that this elevation had been "planned with great care and assisted throughout by a high-powered propaganda of the very latest model." Lippmann considered him to be "the first American President whose whole public career has been presented through the machinery of modern publicity. The Hoover legend, the public stereotype of an ideal Hoover, was consciously contrived. By arousing certain expectations, the legend has established a standard by which the public judgment has estimated him. . . . For the ideal picture presents him as the master organizer, the irresistible engineer, the supreme economist." This was partisan talk, to be sure, but it was mainly the truth, although it discounted the intense sincerity behind what Hoover's friends wrote about him. They were true believers.

Yet their very skill embodied the seeds of disaster. Hoover had been oversold, and he was the first to know it. Even before his election he had told Ray T. Tucker, one of the reporters on the campaign train, that he hoped he could "live down his reputation as an engineer." Once in the White House his fears grew, and he complained to a friend that he had been "over-advertised." He was not a superman, he said, able to solve "the most difficult and complicated problems." People might well expect the impossible of him, he feared, and he predicted gloomily that, if he could not make the governmental machinery cope with the nation's problems, *he* would be the one to suffer. He did not mention the possible sufferings of the nation. Hoover knew, as others would soon discover, that there was a formidable gulf between the Hoover of Bruce Barton and the real man. Yet it was he who had permitted himself to be pictured as a master mind, a superman, an engineering genius. Barton and associates had advertised the product well, sold it, and the consumer was now about to test it, with memorable results.

When he had been finally persuaded to enter the race, Hoover's political naïveté dismayed Lorimer and the *Saturday Evening Post*'s political writers. The editor hastily sent Blythe to advise the reluctant candidate. Meanwhile he pursued the campaign in the *Post* with editorials and articles, some of them in direct consultation with Hoover about their contents. Will Rogers, another friend and writing ally of the editor's, pushed for Hoover on his lecture tours, taking polls of the audiences and finding them solidly for the candidate.

Yet Hoover did not seem to understand what an asset he had in such wide-ranging support as the *Saturday Evening Post* and its friends and writers gave him, not to mention the other far-flung parts of the campaign publicity apparatus. During the final weeks before the convention, and after his nomination as well, he followed his own inclinations about publicity, which irritated Lorimer, who at the same time liked to believe that he himself was independent of the broad battle he was waging from the editor's chair. He resented even the implication that he was hand-in-glove with Hoover, and, indeed, he would never have tolerated suggestions from either the candidate or his advisers. It was his conviction that undeviating support was legitimate as long as the ideas originated with him; consequently it did not seem inconsistent to him that the *Post* had become a Hoover propaganda organ. It was true that everything he had done was on his own initiative, but neither Hoover nor his managers could have done any better if they had owned the magazine and written the articles themselves. After Hoover's election, the new president sought to reward Lorimer by asking him (verbally) if there was some federal post or ambassadorship he might like. Lorimer declined politely, and when Hoover later asked him more specifically if he would like to succeed Charles G. Dawes as ambassador to the Court of St. James's, he replied bluntly that he did not want to leave the *Saturday Evening Post*.

Disillusion, in fact, had set in almost at once, and progressed rapidly after the Crash. By the end of November 1931, William Allen White, who had worked with Lorimer on the Hoover project from the beginning in 1920, was writing to Julian Street: ''He is a grand administrator but has no sense of public relations. He can press a button and call a man in and hire him or fire him wisely, but he can't hold a joint debate with him, and that is the trouble. He is all right. I am very fond of him. But is he not for this hour.'' Speaking of a speech Hoover had just made to the American Legion convention, White added: ''The sad and almost hopeless part of the situation is that the man thought he was just raising hell—talking short, ugly words with the bristling barbs! That was his idea of a sizzler. Which shows beautifully how little a man who works with *things* knows about the power of *words*.''

How could Hoover have fallen so far in the estimation of his friends and allies, let alone the press, in so short a time? The answer lay in his character and personality, and in his inability to cope with change. His relations with the press reflected the nineteenth-century attitudes that had characterized president-press relations for some time.

The extent of Hoover's fall can be understood when one remembers the support of newspapers and magazines from both right and left that he enjoyed at the beginning and the personal popularity with correspondents during his earlier career in the cabinet that no other president had enjoyed at a similar career point, except possibly for Taft. Paul Y. Anderson, who covered Washington for the *Nation* and soon became a celebrated reporter for the St. Louis *Post-Dispatch* as well, wrote of those glowing cabinet days in words strongly reminiscent of Taft in a similar position:

> Long before the death of Harding, it became the custom of a group of correspondents, including some of the ablest in the business, to gather several afternoons each week in Hoover's office. There he talked freely, not only about his department, but about the departments of his Cabinet colleagues and about the affairs of the Presidency. . . . He was the best "grapevine" in Washington, and a perfect gold mine of "graveyard stuff." He was able, moreover, invariably to convey the impression that he knew what he was talking about. Gradually . . . an impression pervaded the Washington press corps, just as it pervaded their editors and the American public, that Hoover knew more about the affairs of the government and the actual condition of the country and the world than any man in the administration.

It was an admiration that deteriorated even before the election. During the campaign reporters began to notice the same things about the candidate that had so irritated Lorimer. Hoover was reluctant to talk about important issues or refused outright to discuss them. Not only did he decline to answer pertinent questions, but it was clear that he resented the fact they were asked. He saw the press only infrequently, and these meetings were devoid of any real news, consisting mostly of reiterating campaign platitudes and avoiding questions. While he was still much admired as a world citizen and the rescuer of starving millions, he had provoked no human interest stories, no biographies that revealed, or even pretended to reveal, his personality. Worse, from the press's standpoint at least, he would not pose for pictures of the kind that are ordinarily meat and drink to campaigning politicians. Veteran reporters and photographers were astonished; they had never before seen a candidate so reluctant to display himself. And this from a man of whom, as secretary of commerce, the Washington *Evening Star* had written only a short time before, "Hoover certainly has got the whole town by the neck from a news standpoint—no one can get near enough to see the dust."

During the campaign the reporters (if not their editors and publishers) had generally favored Gov. Alfred E. Smith of New York, the Democratic candidate, not only because of their natural tendency to be liberals but because Smith was Hoover's antithesis. When he was nominated on the first ballot at the Houston convention (Ohio switching its vote to make that possible), Franklin Roosevelt's characterization of him in the nominating speech as the "Happy Warrior" had a sound that much of the press liked. The working press also heartily endorsed Smith's pledge to modify Prohibition, as against Hoover's stern demand for strict enforcement, and the more liberal among newspapers were appalled by the wave of bigotry that rippled over the country because Smith was a Catholic—something Hoover denounced as giving "violence to every instinct I possess." Few reporters shared the conviction of many Americans, backed up by millions of campaign dollars poured into a virulent propaganda barrage, that the pope would rule America if Smith sat in the White House. Because both sides had appealed to big business for support, total expenditures were the largest ever seen: nearly $9.5 million for the Republicans and $7 million for the Democrats.

In spite of Hoover's foot dragging, he won the election handily by a landslide, carrying forty states, including Smith's own New York, and putting a five-state dent in the Solid South. Thus he came into office on the wave of overwhelming popular approval, but with the suspicions of the press already aroused. That had occurred not only for the reasons already cited, but as a result of the censorship experienced by the eighteen reporters who accompanied the president-elect on his preinaugural tour of Latin America aboard the USS *Maryland*. For this journey Hoover had appointed George Barr Baker, a naval censor during the Great War, as his press aide and empowered him to screen the correspondents' dispatches before they were transmitted by radio from the ship. Bringing his training with him, Baker carefully removed anything he thought the president might not like, which both alarmed and angered the correspondents.

At Hoover's first press conference, however, the day after his inauguration, the correspondents momentarily thought themselves mistaken. The new president appeared about to begin a new era in president-press relations. As one correspondent described it:

> Smiling, cordial, expansive, he informed the 200 assembled correspondents that the worn-out Coolidge ghost, "the White House spokesman," had been abolished in favor of a more liberal system. Under the new rules the reporters would continue to submit written questions in advance, but the President's answers would be divided into three categories, as follows: (1) to be quoted directly in the first person; (2) to be attributed to the White House; and (3) to be used as information given by the correspondents upon their own authority, or as "background." The privilege of quotation was new and very desirable.

Speaking to the Gridiron Club for the first time, only a month later, Hoover offered further encouragement by declaring the obvious—that the press was the most important vehicle available to form public opinion, consequently it was his desire to give the reporters prompt, accurate, and authoritative information. "Absolute freedom of the press to discuss public questions is a foundation stone of American liberty," he told the assembled newsmen, who had never doubted it, any more than had Jefferson and Hamilton and Madison.

To help him inaugurate the new regime, Hoover asked the correspondents to form a committee that would establish guidelines, and he instructed George Akerson, his press secretary, to meet with the reporters twice every day. A rosy-fingered dawn appeared to be breaking over the White House, but within a few months the whole plan lay in ruins, and disillusionment was complete. By July 1929, only four months after inauguration, George Manning, Washington correspondent of *Editor & Publisher,* was reporting in a two-part article on the demise of "liberalization." It had become instead, he said, a "general tightening-up," and the cause was a very old one. Some unfavorable but true stories about the president had appeared, and Hoover, who soon proved himself to be one of the most thin-skinned of chief executives, was trying to punish the reporters who wrote them by attempting to get them fired—reverting to the days of Theodore Roosevelt.

That effort was only a part of Hoover's first attempts to muzzle his critics. Drew Pearson, already a controversial journalist, found himself threatened with being barred from every government office, Manning reported, although the White House had not yet carried out the threat. In spite of his usually easygoing ways as secretary of commerce, reporters now remembered, Hoover had made the same kind of threats when he was displeased in earlier days. Moreover, Manning wrote, the news conferences were becoming no more than a platform for disseminating handouts, in which the newspapermen became simply transmission belts for government propaganda. This feeling on the part of the correspondents was enhanced by Hoover's exclusion of them from following him to his retreat, Rapidan Camp, another predecessor of Camp David.

Nearly all the presidents before him had resented the press's invasion of their privacy, in varying degrees according to how private they had been as individuals before their rise to the White House. Even the most generous had insisted on some measure of seclusion from the public, and in the past most of the press had been willing to grant them that surcease. In the new era, however, there was much more public curiosity about the presidents, and the now highly competitive newspapers and magazines were eager to satisfy it.

It has been an intractable problem to this day, and every administration has been another battleground. But Hoover, for the first time, took stern measures to protect himself. He made the Secret Service responsible for carrying out his orders that the press was not to trail him to Rapidan Camp (the "pool" had not been invented), with the consequence that the reporters were made to feel like suspected terrorists. They might have been mollified if they could have been sure that the president was only resting and fishing, but then they found out that he was, on occasion, transacting important public business, as when he met with British Prime Minister Ramsay MacDonald.

Worse, from the correspondents' standpoint, Hoover did not exclude *every* reporter from his private retreat. He sometimes took one or more of his favorites with him—Mark Sullivan, for example, who had been a friend and adviser from the beginning; or William Hard, already a conservative reporter; or Roy Roberts of the Kansas City *Star.* It might have been possible for the reporters to forgive the presence of Richard V. Oulahan, now of the New York *Times,* who was considered the dean of the press corps (and who would die while Hoover was in office), but not the others, who were also the recipients of the president's occasional individual interviews. That kind of favoritism had been a recurring complaint for years.

Hoover was discovering what other presidents had learned so painfully—that real privacy was impossible in the presidency. If reporters could not follow him to Rapidan Camp, some of them at least would be busy picking up whatever human interest items they could find or whatever else might be available. Most of these stories were extremely small beer, indeed, measured against the hard news of the day. It was disclosed, for example, that Mrs. Hoover was concerned about her voice and was taking sound tests. When one of the president's several dogs bit a marine, the incident appeared on front pages. There were frequent stories about the Hoover family's predilection for driving cars at high rates of speed. Hoover was greatly irritated when comments appeared about the pace at which his motorcade traveled in whisking him away to Rapidan Camp, leaving pursuers far behind. When a reporter and his wife in a following car wrecked their vehicle and suffered serious injuries, it was seen as a reflection on the "flying cavalcade," although the pursuing correspondent had been uninvited.

The president liked to drive his sixteen-cylinder Cadillac himself after he left the White House, and in 1933, while he was making a transcontinental trip in it, he was stopped for speeding, after which his son Allan took the wheel and was soon tooling along at eighty-five. "What's holding you back?" his father inquired testily. As president, Hoover had been allowed no such excesses, but he apparently encouraged them in others. His wife Lou, who did drive during the presidency, was said to have terrified the wives of cabinet members unfortunate enough to be her passengers. Mrs. Hoover's driving alarmed her friends and amused the press, which duly recorded her adventures, along with reports of her system of hand signals and other esoteric devices she employed with secretaries, waiters, and ushers. Her reaction to these stories was so indignant that even her husband considered her "oversensitive."

Sometimes the printed tales about the Hoover family were not so trivial, as when the Baltimore *Sun* printed an erroneous rumor that Herbert Hoover, Jr., a radio engineer, had influenced an air mail contract. His father exploded, "I have not in my experience in Washington seen anything so rotten in an attitude of the press towards the President of the United States." He was to see far worse.

More serious was the action of the New York *World,* in a rare display of irresponsible checkbook journalism on the part of so distinguished a paper, paying $12,000 for a story made out of whole cloth by a disgruntled employee that charged corruption in Secretary of the Interior Ray L. Wilbur's office over the sale of worthless oil shale lands. The *World* believed it had another Teapot Dome scandal, in spite of the secretary's detailed denials, and kept the story alive long past the time when it was generally discredited.

As in the past, when the correspondents could not get news from the White House, they turned to Capitol Hill, where the president had a collection of enemies, not all of them Democrats. Out of this marriage of necessity came the well-publicized revolt of the Senate over the appointment to the Supreme Court of John J. Parker, who was rejected, and the similar but unsuccessful fight to prevent Charles Evans Hughes from becoming chief justice. The reporters were aided assiduously by Charles Michelson, the Democratic National Committee's talented publicist.

The president did not get much help from his press secretaries. George Akerson, who had been working with him since 1926, was a former Minneapolis

Tribune reporter, a Harvard graduate with a well-known fondness for alcoholic uplift. The correspondents liked him, and drank with him, but he committed a series of blunders, interlaced with entertaining but embarrassing displays of public drunkenness. He left for Hollywood late in 1930 to work for Paramount Pictures, to be succeeded by another newspaperman, Theodore Joslin, who had worked for the prestigious and deeply conservative Boston *Evening Transcript.* It was not a salutary change. Joslin's personality was so prickly that even Hoover thought him trying, and the correspondents viewed him with undisguised contempt. One termed his appointment ''the first known instance of a rat joining a sinking ship.'' Drew Pearson and Robert S. Allen, beginning their careers as political columnists, wrote that Hoover had chosen ''one of the most tractable, stodgy and partisan trained seals of the Washington press corps.'' They went on to describe him unsparingly as a man without political experience, of mediocre intelligence, ponderous, and pompous.

Joslin had been in office no more than six months before the tension over coverage of the president while he was at Rapidan Camp came to a sudden crisis. The correspondents had been compelled to stay twenty-five miles away from the camp in a town called Orange and were told they could join the presidential cavalcade, if it left Rapidan, at a nearby town called Criglersville. In July 1931 this was the arrangement one weekend when Hoover was at the camp and the press was alert for developments in the negotiations over the French war debt moratorium.

Such a development did occur, and a call from the White House summoned the president back to Washington so hurriedly that the Secret Service was unprepared and the press was not notified. Nevertheless the reporters saw the cavalcade roar by, and while there was no hope of catching it, the White House pressroom was informed, and by comparing the time the speeding cars swept by and the time they arrived at the White House, these ingenious correspondents figured that Hoover had embraced his old love for rapid travel and the entourage had been going more than fifty miles an hour, high speed for those times.

Next day the papers carried a story about the trip, including the speed calculation, but without any solid information concerning its purpose, which had not been forthcoming. Hoover was furious. He demanded to know how the story had leaked, and he was particularly incensed by the references to speed. Then he decreed, in a formal directive, that no more news would come from the White House except through him or Joslin. The correspondents raised cries of suppression and censorship.

It was a declaration of war, in effect. In *Editor & Publisher* for July 18, 1931, George Manning described the atmosphere:

> White House correspondents . . . continued their news-gathering activities as usual this week in the most strained atmosphere that has pervaded the White House press circle since the Congressional investigation of the Wilson regime. . . . The President, through Theodore G. Joslin . . . has ordained that no news of the White House or members of its household shall be published unless it is obtained from ''stated official sources,'' the sources being the President and Joslin. . . . Meanwhile, the White

House, for one reason or another, has seen fit to call off, at the last minute, most of the recent scheduled press conferences and neither has news from the "stated official sources" been forthcoming at the rate it might.

The editorial reaction in the papers was mixed, some supporting the reporters' charge of censorship, others simply observing that the president was short-sighted, because the news was going to be reported no matter what he thought. But three months later the situation between press and president had sunk to such a nadir that Paul Anderson wrote in the *Nation*, October 14, 1931, that relations had reached a stage of unpleasantness "without parallel during the present century. They are characterized by mutual dislike, unconcealed suspicion, and downright bitterness. This ugly condition has frequently been reflected in the utterances of the President and the conduct of his aides, and is bound to be reflected in some of the news dispatches, although to nothing like the extent of its actual existence." Anderson called the press conferences "a bitter joke," and another correspondent declared that Hoover had "scarcely a friend or defender among the hundreds of working newspapermen of Washington."

Matters, in fact, had been coming to a head since early in 1930, when Anderson had reported that "less reliable and printable information comes from the White House than at any time while Coolidge was president" and went on to summarize the situation:

Written questions have been so consistently ignored that few reporters any longer trouble to submit them. The direct quotation phase has degenerated into a system of Presidential "hand-outs," palpably propagandist in character and seldom responsive to any inquiry. . . . In addition, the practice of having "fair-haired boys" . . . has been resurrected, whereby the President gives private audiences to correspondents who have demonstrated their willingness and ability to publish stories that he particularly desires published.

It was an intolerable situation, and the correspondents were the first to try alleviating it by appointing a committee to meet with the president. At the session Hoover was full of complaints about the trivialities he saw in the press, but the correspondents ignored that and offered five suggestions for the coverage of White House news. These seemed reasonable enough. The reporters wanted to be sure their written questions actually reached the president; to be able to stop when they were accompanying the president on long trips so that they could file their stories; to get the release of radio speeches at the start of broadcasts; to make better arrangements at Rapidan; and to establish a system at the White House which would ensure that they knew of the family's movements and who was being entertained.

Hoover said he would take the suggestions under advisement, but he seemed upset, and no one was surprised when the latest "new era" ended two weeks later, over what seemed a trivial matter on the surface. The president was conducting secret negotiations with Canada concerning the St. Lawrence Waterway project, and Gov. Franklin Roosevelt of New York had written a letter to him about it—not a secret communication. Inexplicably, both the White House and the State Department denied any knowledge of the letter. Two days later Roosevelt said he would make the letter public unless Hoover did so, whereupon the White House admitted getting the letter and State admitted replying to it. After that, the White House denied making its first denial.

The Scripps-Howard papers led the assault on this deception, asserting that it was the president's duty "to protect the integrity of all future public confidence" and calling for clarification. It was not forthcoming. That impelled the ever-alert George Manning to report in *Editor & Publisher* on September 5, 1931, "Steadily, almost stealthily, there is growing up in Washington to plague the correspondents and to confound newspaper editors and readers 'back home' a wall of official silence on public questions, of evasion, misrepresentation, and sad to say in some cases, of downright lying by public officials."

There was a brief truce after this, but then Hoover gave an exclusive interview to Merryle S. Rukeyser, financial editor of International News Service, and the resulting explosion impelled Manning to report on October 16:

> Utterly disregarding editorial warnings . . . from coast to coast . . . President Hoover and a determined group of bureaucrats have literally thrown down the gauntlet to the Washington correspondents on the question of censorship. True, verbal denials persist, from the White House down, that there is any thought of censorship. It is stated and reiterated that the newspaper men are free to write what they will, but these declarations are accompanied by "suggestions" that it might be more discreet and consonant with public interest to write only what is handed out officially.

This was followed by a petition from members of the National Press Club deploring the tendency of some government officials and those under them "to become secretive regarding the conduct of the public business," protesting at the same time the "wall of silence" and denouncing the "evasion, misrepresentation, and downright lying" by officials. They vowed to fight against abridgment of "the rights of newspapers and of the public to know in detail what their government is doing."

This petition defined the battleground on which presidents and the press would be contesting for administrations to come, and it would be a steadily losing battle for the press as the imperial presidency became more imperial. In its barest terms it was a conflict with its basis in differing concepts that had their origins in the beginning of the Republic—the conviction of presidents that they had the right to conceal what they were doing if it was in the country's interest (and somehow it invariably was), and the press's equally strong conviction that Jefferson and Madison had designed the First Amendment to give the press freedom to report to the governed what the government was doing. No mention was made of the First, however, at this juncture. The Supreme Court had only begun to interpret it in 1919, and it would be some time before the press would invoke it.

From that point in 1931 when the final crisis erupted for Hoover, his relationship with the press continued to go steadily downhill. In the opinion of an insider—that other Hoover, Ike, major domo of the White House for forty years—the fault was on the president's side. "There is no doubt President Hoover has treated the newspaper men, especially those on duty at the White House, with scant consideration," he wrote in his memoirs. "He has seemed suspicious of them always. Other Presidents have had them eating out of their hands, as it were, and Hoover could have done so if he had taken the trouble . . . but when antagonism is experienced there is no end to the unfavorable criticism from the newspaper men."

As the campaign of 1932 approached, the president found himself with little support in the press, whether Republican or Democratic. The situation at the White House remained unchanged. Hoover gave out whatever news it pleased him to dispense, and the correspondents employed their alternate sources in Congress and elsewhere in the government. When the president sailed off on the official yacht, the *Sequoia,* to Chesapeake Bay for some fishing in the summer of 1932, the reporters were simply ignored and had to rent a pair of cabin cruisers to keep him in view. No press conferences were held between September 15 and Thanksgiving, and after Hoover's defeat, as Pollard notes, "all that remained of his press relations were the mimeographed handouts issued through the office."

During that period even these scraps trickled off, and in the final weeks there was no contact whatever between Hoover and the press, an unprecedented situation in the history of the relationship. Joslin released what little news emerged, and he would not elaborate on anything he gave out. During the campaign of 1932 no conferences were expected, but afterward the silence continued. No meetings were held between the election and the inauguration of Franklin Roosevelt. Veteran correspondents could not remember an administration that had ended on such a low note, with the president obviously blaming the press for much of his misfortune and the press feeling that it had run into a stone wall that was stronger than any previous president had been able to erect.

No doubt a primary reason for the estrangement was Hoover's profound irritation with those elements in the press, not all of them Democratic, which blamed him at least in part for the great Wall Street Crash of October 1929 and then grew more and more impatient with him as the subsequent Depression deepened in 1931 and 1932. The measures he took were considered inadequate, at the least, by a substantial part of the press, and as unemployment, hunger, and fears of a total economic collapse began to envelop the country, Hoover was increasingly angered by the swelling chorus of criticism in the newspapers and magazines.

Hoover left the White House labeled as a leader who, if he did not actually cause the Depression (and there were those who believed he did), had done little to curb its effects. In the popular mind he was viewed as a stiff-necked upper-class president, with a splendid humanitarian record for feeding the millions abroad but no talent, even as the Great Engineer, for coping with economic collapse at home. Democrats ran on that image of him for years.

Whatever failures can be charged to Hoover, the popular conception of him that historians are only now beginning to revise can be attributed largely to a massive "Smear Hoover" campaign, carried out chiefly through magazines and books. The Democrats considered it smart politics, and Hoover, understandably, thought it despicable, dwelling on it at length in his memoirs, a book with some degree of accuracy, considerably tempered by self-serving justifications.

The "smear" campaign originated with John J. Raskob, a Du Pont executive who had been chairman of the Democratic National Campaign Committee in the 1928 race. Raskob and others in the party, especially Catholics, had been outraged by the anti-Catholicism beneath the surface of the campaign, and, even though Hoover had had nothing to do with it, they could not wholly exonerate him. These partisans were also devoted to Al Smith, and they could not forgive the Republicans for defeating him.

Soon after the inauguration in 1929 Raskob brought in two new people to run the National Committee in Washington. One was Charles Michelson, an experienced correspondent for the New York *World* until he deserted the newspaper business for politics; he was a congenial, clever man, well liked by the press corps. The other was Jouett Shouse, a publicist of some reputation. Shouse would be executive director and Michelson publicity director. In his own memoirs Michelson admitted that Raskob told him he could have a million-dollar budget to carry out his assignment, but the committee's later sworn statements to Congress showed that, in fact, about $2.3 million was received in loans between 1928 and 1932. The heaviest contributors included not only Raskob himself but such Democratic stalwarts as Herbert H. Lehman, Bernard Baruch, Pierre du Pont, and Vincent Astor. These donors had also given substantially to Smith's candidacy in 1928.

The campaign that Michelson orchestrated was a masterpiece of its kind, even by today's standards, when such propaganda machinery has been raised to a fine art. Reams of press releases were the everyday production of the committee, many of which were planted in the *Congressional Record* by obliging Democrats to be quoted freely by the press. These operations also included the fabricated would-be Teapot Dome reprise in the New York *World,* and the story first propagated by Congressman John Garner that Hoover was involved with corruption in the sugar lobby, later repudiated by the Democrats themselves after a Senate investigation. There was also the insinuation by Sen. Kenneth McKellar that Hoover had profited by misappropriating funds from government relief during the Armistice, to the extent of $100 million. Although there was not even the possibility that this could have been true, it was widely believed by at least a part of the public for years.

Michelson also used the opinion magazines to carry on his campaign. It is impossible now to determine which stories were planted by his efforts and which were simply attacks by independent dissident writers; it is reasonable to assume that a significant part of the criticism that appeared constantly in these magazines was the result of his assiduous work. Criticism could be expected in any case from such liberal weeklies as the *Nation* and the *New Republic,* but it was also rampant in *Scribner's,* the *Atlantic, Current History, Harper's, Survey Graphic,* and the *North American Review,* among others.

It should be pointed out, however, that the combined circulations of all these journals did not begin to equal the mass coverage of those magazines which continued to beat the drums for Hoover and defend him throughout his administration; they would not, in fact, have begun to approach the circulation of even one of them, the *Saturday Evening Post,* and whether their influence was greater would be impossible to prove. Nor were the opinion magazines completely onesided. *Scribner's,* for example, exposed what was going on in the Michelson office as early as September 1930, in an article by Frank Kent. He wrote:

> The political agency in Washington that more than any other has helped to mold the public mind in regard to Mr. Hoover, magnifying his misfortunes, minimizing his achievements . . . [is] an illuminating illustration of the amazing power of unopposed propaganda in skillful hands. . . . The new Democratic publicity bureau . . . [under] Charley Michelson . . . was not in the least understood by the country as a whole. . . . [It is] the most elaborate, expensive, efficient and effective political propaganda machine ever operated in the country by any party, organization, association or league. . . . Mr. Raskob, Chairman of the Democratic National Committee . . . selected the astute, politically seasoned and personally popular Mr. Jouett Shouse of Kansas City to act as Executive Chairman . . . picked Mr. Michelson . . . a Democrat with a real capacity for mischief . . . [and] gave him a free hand. . . . The goal set for him was to "smear" Mr. Hoover and his administration. . . . It has been his pleasant task to minimize every Hoover asset [and] . . . to obscure every Hoover virtue and achievement. . . . His game is to "plant" interviews, statements, and speeches with Democratic members of the Senate and House of sufficient standing and prominence to make what they say news. . . . [It is] priceless personal publicity for such men. . . . Speeches, interviews, articles, statements, he has written for them . . . have appeared as their own. . . . Every move Mr. Hoover has made is followed by the firing of a Michelson publicity barrage. . . . Editorials and news items have streamed through the mails to small papers hitting Hoover . . . in a hundred different ways.

Kent, it must be remembered, was a Republican partisan of the president's, but there is not much exaggeration in his account.

The attack was also carried on through books written for a popular audience, but again it is impossible to determine which ones were the result of Michelson's efforts. Certainly there were some produced under shady auspices. The one that disturbed Hoover most was John Hamill's *Strange Career of Mr. Hoover under Two Flags,* published in 1931. In his memoirs Hoover calls Hamill "a down-and-out English literary beachcomber" who was, he asserted, hired by two Tammany Hall men named Kenny and O'Brien to write the book. It was published by Samuel Roth, a small but opportunistic publisher of erotica in New York, who later was sent to jail for a long term (there were also earlier convictions on the same charge), although books far more explicit were not prosecuted under pornography laws while he was still in prison. Roth's erotica would raise no one's blood pressure today, and evidently he saw in Hamill's book a chance to make quick money for a volume he was told the Democratic Committee would buy and distribute widely.

Instead a quarrel ensued among Roth, Hamill and O'Brien over payments to the author and profits that had been promised to Roth from five hundred thousand copies to be sold through the committee, a transaction that never took place.

When the argument went to court, the case was thrown out, but the resulting publicity attracted the attention of one of Hoover's lawyer friends who, under the implied threat of a criminal libel action, compelled Hamill to confess under oath and in writing that he had made up the whole thing.

Another of the volumes that greatly disturbed Hoover was one by Walter Liggett, whom he described as "a fellow traveler who was later murdered by gangsters in Minneapolis." In fact Liggett was a free-lance muckraker, whose *Rise of Herbert Hoover* in 1932, although no doubt inspired by personal animosity toward the president as a result of their differences on Russian relief, was only an incident in his career. His subsequent murder was the result of investigative reporting that annoyed the mob; it was not political. There were others as well: *The Great Mistake* (1930) by John Knox (probably a pseudonym), *Hoover's Millions and How He Made Them* (1932) by James J. O'Brien, and *Herbert Hoover, An American Tragedy* (1932) by Clement Wood, also published by Roth.

Only Hamill's book did well, reaching sixth place on Macy's list of best-selling nonfiction, but all of them were recommended by the *Nation,* and the *New Republic* believed in them enough to assert that they must be answered. Harry Elmer Barnes, the noted liberal historian who reviewed Hamill's volume, observed that it was "appalling if true and very likely true," and in 1932 during the campaign Sen. George Norris's secretary told correspondents they should read both Hamill and Knox. The National Committee, however, disavowed any connection with the books and, not without some dissent, adopted an extremely cautious policy in dealing with them as campaign material. The historian David Burner's assessment that the authors ranged from "honest radicals to dollar chasers" seems quite correct.

Although it was not Michelson's doing, press coverage of the historic Bonus March on Washington in 1932 was considered by Hoover to be so distorted as to have constituted a major factor in his defeat that election year. In his version of the event, the march was "in considerable part organized and promoted by the Communists and included a large number of hoodlums and ex-convicts determined to raise a public disturbance," who were frequently addressed by Democratic congressmen and financed by some publishers from "the sensational press" (he did not name them). Hoover contended in his memoirs that only five thousand participated in the march after six thousand bought tickets for home with money appropriated by Congress at the president's request, and that of this number a sampling of two thousand by "government agencies" (probably the Federal Bureau of Investigation) showed that fewer than a third were veterans and more than nine hundred were former convicts and communists.

About fifty marchers, said Hoover, were occupying "old buildings" on Pennsylvania Avenue and getting in the way of construction work, and, when ordered to move, they became the center of an attack on the police by a thousand marchers from outside, in which several were injured and two marchers were killed. At this juncture the president directed Gen. Douglas MacArthur to take charge, with Col. Dwight D. Eisenhower as second in command. "Without firing a shot or injuring a single person, they cleaned up the situation,'' Hoover wrote.

More objective historians have given us a somewhat different version. There are variations in details and opinion, but the ascertainable facts, fully reported without distortion in the news columns of most newspapers (however much the editorial writers and political columnists might differ), is that the Bonus March originated in Congress's failure to provide for immediate payment of a promised bonus to World War I veterans in the darkest earlier hours of the Depression. In 1931 Congress had passed, over the president's veto, a bill that permitted veterans to borrow on their certificates up to 50 percent, but a year later, when the recipients demanded the whole payment as the Depression worsened, the House passed a bill permitting it, but Hoover persuaded the Senate to reject it.

While this was taking place, unemployed veterans began drifting into Washington to lobby for the bill, and after Congress adjourned for the summer in early July without giving them anything at all, the "Bonus Expeditionary Force," as it called itself, simply squatted in a shanty village on the flats of the Anacostia River in Washington (one of many so-called Hoovervilles in the country) to await developments. Hoover had refused to talk to them. It was a disquieting and politically obnoxious spectacle, which Hoover attempted to deal with by paying the fare home for six thousand. Of the five thousand who remained, however, many were wives and children, and in spite of the "government agencies'" survey, they were far from being hoodlums, former convicts, and communists, although some of these ingredients may have been mixed in with this desolate "army" of ragged, often hungry men, women, and children.

As the humid, tropical Washington summer closed in on them, some of the veterans sought relief by sleeping at night in government buildings, which were made of stone and were therefore cool, or on the Mall. To Hoover this was an unsightly and unseemly spectacle. Against the tatterdemalion Bonus Expeditionary Force he deployed Gen. Douglas MacArthur, tastefully dressed as usual, at the head of a force consisting of four troops of cavalry, four of infantry, one machine-gun squadron, and six tanks. It was a miracle that only two members of the Bonus Army were killed. Afterward this American force burned down (although the government continued to deny it) the ragged village of shacks and tents in which the veterans had been living, in the process employing bayonets and tear gas to persuade the inhabitants to leave, injuring scores of them, including women and children. Referring to this scene during the 1932 campaign, Hoover was properly reverential. "Thank God," he said, "we still have a government that knows how to deal with a mob."

While editorial opinions differed politically on this episode, as they would on any other, the bald facts as related in the news columns (not to mention their sensationalizing in a few papers) did more, perhaps, to diminish Hoover's reputation and solidify his negative image than anything else while he was in office. The portrait of the Great Humanitarian was fading, like the reputation of the Great Engineer who could not, in the popular view, do anything visible to save the country from the profound disquiet and cruelty of the Depression. Unjust or not, it was that feeling for which Hoover blamed the press.

There were those in the newspaper business, however, who earnestly tried to save him from himself. They were the few privileged correspondents—William Hard, Sullivan, White, David Lawrence, and a few others, members of what came to be called the "Medicine Ball Cabinet"—who attempted to advise him but perhaps were too partisan to be of much real help. Karl A. Bickel, president of the United Press Associations, a Hoover supporter from the beginning, had warned the president that neither he nor anyone else could "control, mould, direct or shape the press in this country," but he was brushed off. A. H. Kirchhofer of the Buffalo *Evening News,* a publicity director and potent supporter of Hoover in the 1928 campaign and afterward, sent a fifteen-page single-spaced memorandum to the president, giving him the most detailed advice on how to mend his relationship with the press and preserve it, noting how important it was to his success. Hoover thanked him briefly for his "helpful remarks" and paid no attention to the advice.

Yet Hoover understood perfectly well that the press could be of the utmost importance to him in accomplishing what he was so strenuously trying to promote—that is, the creation of a feeling of unity in the nation that would be strong enough to enable it to surmount the terrible problems it confronted. Some historians have speculated that he might have been able to accomplish this if he had behaved differently toward the press from the beginning and in the crisis had it strongly behind him as an ally. And so it might have been, but, politically, such a thing would have been virtually impossible.

In any case Hoover was not inherently the kind of man who could inspire such unity. His idea of promoting "psychological confidence," as he called it, was to ask his few friends among the correspondents to cancel stories or even suppress them if he thought they endangered that mythical confidence. These men tried to persuade him to take his case to the public by means of that rapidly growing medium, radio, thus circumventing a largely hostile press and building on what Coolidge had done, but Hoover was simply not capable of making such a direct approach. He did not enjoy making speeches, and those who heard them shared his feelings. Hoover's recent biographer, Craig Lloyd, has summed up the president's failure succinctly:

In the lonely isolation of the White House, Hoover's lifelong fears of failure became reality; and ironically, the sense of this was heightened by the image of "master of emergencies" and "social engineer" that his public relations style had created for him. Under the warping pressures of a crisis-dominated presidency, moreover, the traits that had moulded this style and so terribly unsuited him for the times—his distaste, in other words, for public exposure, his inability to dramatize his leadership, his dogmatic individualism and antistatism, his sensitivity to criticism—were painfully revealed for all, even his closest friends, to see; and under the new set of circumstances, such characteristics only antagonized the press, confused and frustrated his aides, publicists, and advisers, and made him all the more unpopular. An effective publicizer of causes throughout his career, Hoover thus saw his own presidency become, paradoxically, a public relations disaster and the White House, truly, "a compound hell."

(The latter was Hoover's description.)

The defeat in the 1932 presidential election was a bitter humiliation. Hoover saw himself referred to in Henry Luce's bright new newsmagazine, *Time*, first of its kind, as "President Reject," as cruel as it was true. It was also symptomatic of a different kind of journalism creeping over the horizon, one that would cause further problems for presidents. When Congress met after the election for its lame-duck session, Congressman Louis McFadden introduced a measure to impeach Hoover, citing his declaration of the moratorium on debts as illegal and unconstitutional. There was an immediate motion to table, which was carried easily, but it was significant that eleven members of the House felt impelled to oppose it.

Hoover carried his emotions after the 1932 defeat into the grave, referring to himself many years later as the only president who had a depression named after him. In Franklin Roosevelt's administration the triumphant Democrats would not let die the untrue charges first made by the *World* in its attempt to resuscitate Teapot Dome, and the fact that not one of these allegations of fraud and corruption was ever proved was of small consolation to the former president. Whatever else he may have been, Hoover was honest, but only diehard Republicans appeared to believe it.

For the remainder of his life Hoover worked hard to rehabilitate his reputation, but it was not until after the Second World War that Harry Truman restored him to respectability by asking him to repeat his World War I success in feeding the hungry, which he did with distinction. He also served on commissions appointed by both Truman and Eisenhower to reorganize the government, a laudable cause that produced few results. As a cap to his restoration in the public eye, Eleanor Roosevelt pronounced him as not responsible for causing the Depression. At that moment anyone with a taste for irony would have relished the fact that some of the same bad Democratic jokes that had been made about Hoover were then being told by Republicans about Roosevelt. The stories circulated about FDR were, if possible, even more derogatory.

After Hoover's death in 1964, at ninety, the editorial writers searched in their bag of obituary tricks, designed to fit any dead politician regardless of what his life might have been, and came up with four words—courage, integrity, and humanitarian service—which they solemnly fashioned into suitable tributes. It was a testimony to Hoover's essential qualities that so few felt inclined to deny them.

PART SIX

The Presidency Triumphant

The Second Roosevelt: "Greatest Managing Editor"

With the exception of Theodore Roosevelt, the presidents beginning with McKinley who attempted to establish a species of imperialism in their relationships with the press failed for some time to make their efforts stick. These were failures of philosophy, tactics, or both, but there was a cumulative overall gain to offset them. In spite of their personal failings, the presidents had begun to learn how to use the power of their office to identify the news and control it, and they had discovered what a mighty engine of political influence the press could be if it were tamed and harnessed.

The terms of the traditional adversarial relationship were beginning to change as well. Throughout the nineteenth century "the press" had meant newspapers, with only a few magazine exceptions, directed by highly partisan individualistic editors and publishers, who considered themselves little kings in their own right and often the equals or superiors of presidents. Beginning with the turn of the century, however, magazines had come to play a much more important role, and in the 1920s radio opened another doorway to power. Starting with Eisenhower, a striking new dimension was added with the advent of commercial television, which would come to dominate the others.

Thus, in 1984, to speak of "the press" (or "the media," a more common catchword) one would have to include more than 1,700 daily newspapers, 8,000 or so weeklies, at least 22,000 periodicals and newsletters (there is no exact figure), some 850 television stations, 6,400 radio stations, and several thousand book publishers of various sizes, turning out about 40,000 titles a year, some of them potent political weapons. In our time, consequently, that handy phrase "the media" has come to have little substantial meaning. When people say "the media" do this or that—and most often they say it with disapproval—it usually means that the New York *Times*, or the Washington *Post*, or *Time*, or Dan Rather of CBS News, or some other highly visible publication or television figure has written or said something they don't like.

Conservatives are fond of saying that "the media" are prisoners of the liberals, but upon analysis this usually turns out to mean that these hostages constitute no more than a bare half-dozen news organizations. Liberals, on the other hand, tend to believe that the media are by and large a part of the military-industrial complex because they are, in themselves, big business. And it is true that they are unquestionably big business, and conservative viewpoints are in the large majority, but one of the glories of the media in this country is that they represent every conceivable point of view, although newspapers, radio, and television are less diversified than magazines and book publishing.

In the White House presidents look out upon this landscape with different eyes. They are "not like you and me," as F. Scott Fitzgerald once observed of the rich. Seasoned politicians, they are pragmatists. Beginning with Franklin Roosevelt, they began to reverse the conception of the press that had been held for a century, no longer seeing it in terms of individual correspondents to be cajoled or bullied, as TR had done, or ignored, as Hoover had tried to do. Publishers were no longer perceived as somewhat distant, if lesser rivals, like rulers of city-states, but as people who could be invited to the White House to stay overnight, to socialize with—in short, individuals with whom a president could share common interests and goals. Deeply partisan party feelings remained sharp at first, but after Eisenhower these began to decline somewhat, along with voter participation in the democracy, as the old lines became blurred. Today it is often difficult to distinguish between conservatives of both parties, or their liberal antitheses.

This has meant an evolutionary change in the press conference, which had become a staple of presidential press relations, initiated by the first Roosevelt. The second Roosevelt used radio to go over the heads of a largely hostile press to reach the people, and when Ronald Reagan came to power, he demonstrated that television, with some (to him) irritating limitations, could be used not only in that way but in several others.

Much less visible to the public, but perhaps even more effective, has been the growth of the president's personal public relations and publicity machine, operated by experts in every aspect of the media, from the simple handout, to the major television effort in campaigning, to the manipulation of news conferences. As a result the press conference itself, as we shall see, has lost much of its original meaning and usefulness and has become more a tool of presidential convenience than a means of getting the president to explain his policies and actions to the electorate. The design now is not to inform the voters but to sell them, through professional techniques developed in the advertising and public relations fields.

If the president has come to regard the press (or "the media," as one prefers) in a different light, and with different purposes, so has the press come to have a changed view of the presidency since the time Theodore Roosevelt first gathered the correspondents about him in his office. To begin with, government has grown to such a size that it takes a small army of reporters, representing all the media, to keep up with what is going on. Where the Oval Office and the floors of House and Senate were once the primary sources of news, the various departments, particularly State and Defense, now rank close to them. Within this vast governmental sprawl so many points of contact are possible and so much occurs that two paradoxical results have become apparent as far as the press is concerned. One is that, because there is so much to know, it becomes extremely difficult to put it together in a way comprehensible to the mass audience the media now serve, but, on the other hand, the possibilities for concealment are so great, ably assisted by presidents themselves, that it is equally difficult to be sure that what is being presented is the truth, or anywhere near it.

The public, always the third party in this relationship, has also changed. In a more manageable and more innocent era, people got their national political information from their favorite paper, and they were loyal to it as long as it represented their own political point of view. If not, they switched to another. Today information comes from such a bewildering variety of sources, print and electronic (much more impartial, by and large, than they have ever been in media history, in spite of the cherished convictions of the more rabid partisans), that it is often nearly impossible for the average citizen to arrive at settled conclusions—if, indeed, he is conscientious or curious enough to make the attempt to inform himself.

It is often said that Americans have access to more information than any other people on earth, and it is obviously true, but the very dimensions of this flood also preclude them from being any better informed than those in comparable cultures. Relatively few people have the time or inclination to absorb more than a highly selective part of what is available, and comparatively few have the knowledge and training necessary to analyze it properly. Newspapers, with a few exceptions, are increasingly read for local interest, and, as the polls show, most Americans get their news from television and from editorials and columnists in the newspapers, especially the latter. Quite naturally people tend to read only those columnists and newspapers they agree with politically, and to regard the others as liars. Most are unable to make any distinction between the news columns and the editorials and commentaries, or between individual television anchor people or correspondents and the general pattern of television news. As for books and magazines, they are often highly effective carriers of ideas and information in their own right, but they reach smaller, elite audiences.

Where once a trickle-down effect enabled the media to influence mass opinions, the trickle now comes up against the hard rock of mass indifference and the inability to comprehend—and stops. The audience has become too large and the issues too complex for mass comprehension. The public's view of the president is shaped primarily by television these days, and secondarily by other sources. Unfortunately readers and viewers are not good at identifying and evaluating sources involved with the presidency; that would require far more training and experience than the average citizen is likely to possess. A high rate of functional marginal illiteracy is also operative here, which throws an even greater burden on the electronic media.

The end result of this national confusion has been a dramatic rise in distrust of the media. Where it was once largely the whipping boy of politicians, it is now perceived by many, perhaps most, people as the prime source of our discontent, responsible for virtually everything that is wrong in society. Where the presidency is concerned, people see the president of their particular party as embattled, fighting against an always hostile and too inquisitive press. This situation is exacerbated by presidents themselves, who are clever enough to exploit these feelings to their own advantage, and indeed it would be hard for most politicians, given such power as the presidency endows them with, to resist the temptation.

How all these changes have succeeded in altering significantly the relationship between the presidency and the press is the subject of this concluding section.

II

Since the accession of Franklin Roosevelt, more has been written about the presidents than in all the country's previous history. The chief reason, of course, is the tremendous expansion of the media during that time, but it is also because the presidency has been a national battleground for much of that period. When one considers the amount of newspaper space and the number of books and magazine articles about the presidency and its problems produced from 1932 to the present, not to mention the quantities of radio and television time expended, the total is staggering.

Even in so restricted an area as the relationship between presidents and the press, the subject of concern here, there has been a comparable explosion, not only as the result of popular interest but as a consequence of mass communications studies in colleges and universities, which have produced an ever-flowing torrent of dissertations, monographs, and various kinds of critical studies, constituting a small industry in itself. The lives and times of presidents beginning with the second Roosevelt are now so twice familiar to most literate people that it would be idle to rehearse them again here. What we propose to do, then, is to pull together the historical strings that have been running through this narrative from Washington's time, in an effort to make more understandable the critical nature of the relationship between press and president, with the public as the pivot point, which may well change the nature of our system in important, perhaps ultimately fateful, respects.

Franklin Roosevelt makes an ideal beginning for such an inquiry and assessment. Embedded in his still controversial personality and presidency were the seeds of everything that was to follow. He was another bridge between past and future. As the Australian researcher Graham White reminds us, Roosevelt's view of the press was consistent during his unprecedented three terms: "The simple thesis which he propagated tirelessly throughout his Presidency was that the press opposed him; that its opposition was proprietor-based; and that he was confronted, as a result of such hostility, not merely with widespread editorial disapproval, but with tendentious and distorted news reports."

There was substantial truth in that thesis, but it needs qualification. There is no question that a majority of newspapers opposed Roosevelt, whether it was the 85 percent he customarily cited or some other figure—the ambiguous gradations of opposition being what they are. That this opposition was proprietor based is equally incontestable, since the owners' reactions to his policies, once they had recovered from the fear and confusion gripping everyone when he took office, were what one could expect from a body of businessmen who were essentially conservative and the proprietors of large enterprises. The widespread editorial disapproval is also easily documented, but the "tendentious and distorted news reports" are another matter.

Such reports certainly existed, but they were confined to a rather small number of papers, including first and foremost the trio often called the "McCormick-Patterson Axis"—that is, the Chicago *Tribune,* the New York *Daily News,* and, secondarily, the Washington *Times-Herald;* the Hearst newspapers; and, a little later than the others, the Scripps-Howard chain. The worst of this opposition occurred between 1935 and 1940, when the more sweeping domestic reforms, such as Social Security, were being pushed through Congress, and the struggle between isolationists and interventionists reached its peak.

On the president's side were an overwhelming majority of the Washington press corps. There were some among them, typified by Walter Trohan, the Chicago *Tribune*'s correspondent, who were as bitterly opposed to him as the most rabid Roosevelt haters among the Republicans as a whole. But most were captivated by the president's personality from the day of his first conference, and their consequent willingness to go along with him whatever he did led to those familiar encomiums citing Roosevelt as "the greatest managing editor of all time" and "the best newspaperman who has ever been President of the United States."

In certain respects Roosevelt did not understand the news process any better than other presidents, but he did understand how to manipulate the press, and he did it superbly, far better than any of his predecessors, even the other Roosevelt, and he would not be equaled until Ronald Reagan, whose approach was utterly different. Few reporters could be said to "love" Reagan, but Roosevelt commanded the genuine love, affection, and admiration of most of the correspondents who crowded into the Oval Office, or gathered around his car, or besieged him wherever he appeared. His jauntiness, cockiness, and self-confidence inspired the same kind of frustrated rage among Republicans that Reagan's similar attributes provoked later in Democratic ranks.

For the correspondents the difference was not only the warm personal link that Roosevelt established with them but their realization that his grasp of both domestic and foreign affairs was of the first order. They respected his intelligence, even when he exasperated them. It is true that most presidents have regarded themselves as intellectually superior to the reporters, an opinion that has so often led to irritation and contempt. Sometimes this feeling has not been justified, but, in the case of both Roosevelts, it was. Having the support of the correspondents made FDR's task easier, and, unlike his predecessors, he could overcome the resistance of the publishers' majority, and that of the Republicans who fought him, by going over their heads to the people, where his support was solid, through the medium of radio.

All this is not to say that Roosevelt's press relations were a long unalloyed honeymoon. He shared the erroneous belief of most presidents that the function of the press in government is to serve as a channel through which "facts" are transmitted to the governed. Like the others, his interpretation of "facts" was sometimes indistinguishable from propaganda and at other times was designed to cover up political embarrassments. The protests of reporters, and their attempts to get at the truth, led as always to restrictions on coverage, but in general the correspondents accepted them because of the way they were imposed.

The press conferences, consequently, followed a standard pattern. Correspondents tried to find out what they wanted to know, and the president gave them what he wanted the public to know. Recognizing the discrepancy, Roosevelt did what no other president before him had done, providing long, off-the-record background discussions. Sometimes he saw that more help was necessary. In 1933, when it was proposed that the United States go off the gold standard, the correspondents found themselves unable to explain this complicated subject adequately, having little or no background in economics themselves, and so they appealed to the White House. The president sent them a government economist to explain the nuts-and-bolts of the matter. In such an atmosphere it was difficult to maintain the traditional adversary relationship.

Richard L. Strout, the *Christian Science Monitor*'s White House reporter for several decades, recalled recently the atmosphere of the early press conferences:

> Roosevelt started off having two press conferences a week. He continued until the war came, then he had one press conference a week. Altogether, I think he had a thousand press conferences. I was present at practically all of them. One press conference was held in the morning for the afternoon papers, one in the afternoon for the morning papers the next day. We'd gather outside and there'd be anywhere from fifty or more reporters. At big times, 200 reporters might be there. We'd go in and stand around his desk. It was covered with dolls, totems, and knick-knacks. It was like a meeting of a club. . . .
>
> We might not have agreed with his politics, but we had a symbiotic relationship. He got everything he could from us and we got everything we could from him. We nearly always got a good story. He would sit behind the desk with his long cigarette holder and his glasses. He had one curious trick which I haven't seen reported before. He would bring his right hand around and scratch his left eye while he was dangling his glasses on his cigarette holder in the left hand. He talked to us informally and unconventionally. He had little jokes.

For those who had suffered with Coolidge and Hoover, the change must have been startling.

As Kenneth Crawford, another veteran of those days, recalls, the correspondents were divided into two echelons when Roosevelt arrived: "There were the old-timers, who had by that time been there for twenty-five years or more, a group who wore spats and who did not think of stepping out without their canes. The great majority were youngsters, usually from the sticks like me." Before Roosevelt's death the old-timers with their spats and canes would have all but vanished, and some, at least, of the hungry young men from the sticks would have established themselves as among the best correspondents the press corps had ever seen.

It was a new generation of reporters come upon the stage, just as Roosevelt represented a change in the form of government, moving control from big business and Wall Street to Washington as zealously as Reagan was intent on reversing the process in the 1980s. Nothing could have symbolized the change in atmosphere more than the campaign of 1936, when those reporters who had begun in the 1920s, with the green covers of the *American Mercury* protruding from coat pockets, witnessed with disbelief the spectacle of H. L. Mencken, their idol, the onetime scourge of the "booboisie," riding on Alf Landon's campaign train with a large sunflower in his buttonhole, proclaiming Republican gospel as though he were the apotheosis of Kansas respectability instead of the Sage of Baltimore. It took some time for the faithful to realize that Mencken had always been a conservative, in spite of the radical sounds he appeared to be making.

Another innovation in the Washington press corps was the appearance of an increasing number of women. The most notable was the First Lady herself. Eleanor Roosevelt's column "My Day" was syndicated through hundreds of newspapers, which made her, technically at least, a member of the working press. Although she made no attempt to intrude on the work of the correspondents, she did attend meetings of the Washington chapter of the newly organized American Newspaper Guild, sitting in the front row, knitting, as Crawford recalls. She also did her best to help the women journalists who were beginning to invade the hitherto virtually all-male Washington sanctuary, holding her own press conferences with them—some five hundred in all—and helping them over the roadblocks in their way. It was Mrs. Roosevelt who saw to it that toilets for women were installed in the Capitol's press galleries, where they had never been thought of before. Women who traveled with the other reporters into male strongholds outside the capital were similarly provided for. Before Eleanor, no other First Lady had met the press regularly, and none has since her time.

The way was smoothed for *all* reporters, in fact. As Crawford remembered it:

> The atmosphere was very free and easy in Washington. We could descend on any Cabinet officer. Almost all of them had regular press conferences, and between press conferences you could walk in and talk with them. The conferences were successful because the New Deal had a great deal to sell to the public. The press was a go-between between the government and the governed. We could get at Senators very easily too. We also worked in the Capitol, sending pages onto the floor and calling members of the floor to what was the "President's room."

What is most remarkable about Roosevelt's press relations is their consistency. Until the end, he controlled and used the correspondents along the lines he had laid down at his first press conference, and, although he may have alienated some reporters in the process, they were in the minority. At that first conference, taking command at a time when the country was on its knees, and needing the press, as he did, to do what Hoover had failed to do—that is, inspire the nation with confidence and a feeling of unity—he nevertheless laid down the rules with firmness:

> I am told that what I am about to do will become impossible, but I am going to try it. We are not going to have any more written questions; and, of course, while I cannot answer seventy-five or a hundred questions simply because I haven't got the

time, I see no reason why I should not talk to you ladies and gentlemen off the record in just the way that I have been doing in Albany and in the way I used to do in the Navy Department down here. . . . There will be a great many questions, of course, that I won't answer . . . because they are "if" questions—and I never answer them. . . .

And the others, of course, are the questions which for various reasons I do not want to discuss, or I am not ready to discuss, or I do not know anything about. There will be a great many questions you will ask that I do not know enough about to answer.

Then, in regard to news announcements, Steve [Press Secretary Stephen T. Early] and I thought it would be best that straight news for use from this office should always be without direct quotation. In other words, I do not want to be directly quoted unless direct quotations are given out by Steve in writing. That makes that perfectly clear.

Then there are two other matters we will talk about. The first is "background information," which means material which can be used by all of you on your own authority and responsibility, not to be attributed to the White House, because I do not want to have to revive the Ananias Club.

Then the second thing is off-the-record information, which means, of course, confidential information which is given only to those who attend the conference.

Again, the change from predecessors was remarkable to the assembled reporters, who could not help wondering how long these clear and apparently sensible rules would be observed. For the moment, however, they put aside their doubts, and, when Roosevelt had finished, they gave him the first standing ovation any president had ever been accorded by the White House press corps. It did not occur to them until the euphoria had passed that what had happened was a laying down of rules which would guarantee, if followed, that the president would control the dissemination of news at his pleasure. And they learned, as time went on, that his control was sophisticated. There were significant blind spots in his understanding, but Roosevelt had a better knowledge of the news process than any of his predecessors except Harding.

That first conference was greeted by one reporter as "the most amazing performance the White House has ever seen," an opinion generally shared by most of the others. There were those who could scarcely believe that such effusiveness was coming from the lips of hard-bitten veterans who had been disillusioned by previous incumbents. The aura of cooperation and friendship was so well established at the beginning that it lasted virtually unimpaired for nearly two years. More than a year after the inaugural, in June 1934, Raymond Clapper wrote in a *Review of Reviews* article: "Mr. Roosevelt . . . came to Washington. The correspondents saw him and were conquered. He won them and he has still a larger proportion of them personally sympathetic than any of his recent predecessors."

One reason for the correspondents' continuing delight was the constant flow of hard news from the press conferences, much of it worthy of front-page display. That was not surprising, since a great deal of what Roosevelt was doing in those early years was revolutionary, laying out a broad pattern of social progress designed not only to attack the Depression but to set the country on a different social track. It was just these innovations, of course, that began to swing the publishers over one by one into the notorious "85 percent opposition," bringing with them a substantial body of readers.

The correspondents, however, with notable exceptions, remained loyal, and not simply because so many of them agreed personally with what Roosevelt was doing. They were getting a steady flow of solid news; the president had shown himself willing to discuss confidential policies informally; and he saw to it that they were well treated, not only in the White House but when he traveled from it. They were overjoyed, too, when he gave up the written questions format and took on responsibility for his answers himself. Besides all that, the president was a man of formidable, almost overwhelming, charm—a man only a Republican could hate—and they also deeply respected his superb news sense.

The inevitable result of such a relationship, as the correspondents themselves realized by the end of 1934, was that they were writing stories that were largely uncritical. Editors back in the office wanted to know if their reporters in Washington were so hypnotized that they were losing their objectivity. As another year went by it seemed to some who were not completely under the president's spell that the press had become nothing more than a propaganda transmission belt, an opinion heartily endorsed by Republicans.

Still, the general character of the relationship remained relatively unchanged, in spite of the rise of a virulent opposition, through all three terms. It weathered several storms along the way that would have sunk a less well-constructed vessel. Whatever the tempests that raged in the country, as conservatives fought the reformers and later on as the coming war divided the nation, the geniality, warmth, and civilized character of the relations between president and press seemed to be impervious to any kind of assault from without. In a sense it was a paradoxical relationship. The reporters understood that they were being used by a master hand, but at the same time they knew that the president's obvious affection for them was sincere and deeply felt, and they could not help responding to it. For the first time in the history of this relationship, both sides looked forward to the press conferences, a phenomenon not to be repeated until the arrival of John F. Kennedy.

In such an atmosphere it was not difficult for the reporters to overlook the president's faults. If he chastised them, singly or collectively, if he deliberately put obstacles in their way or displayed a momentary anger or petulance, the coolness was only momentary, like a family quarrel, and did not lead to the distancing that had characterized relations under similar circumstances before Roosevelt.

The feeling of the correspondents was summed up admirably by Walter Davenport, a reporter who had served under four presidents, in an article he wrote for *Collier's* just before Roosevelt's death in 1945: "With Roosevelt, this is the only time that I had the feeling I was as important here as a member of the Cabinet or of Congress—even more important. I think you'll find that feeling general . . . here, at Hyde Park and on his special trains, we're not only welcome but we have the distinct feeling—for the first time—that we belong there, that he's *our* President. Ours. See?"

With that kind of relationship, a press secretary was scarcely necessary, in the usual sense, but here, too, the president was fortunate in having Stephen T. Early to serve him. Early was a former Associated Press reporter who had also worked for the Paramount newsreel company (another medium that would become important to Roosevelt), and he had been the president's friend since Roosevelt's years as assistant secretary of the navy, becoming part of a group that also included Marvin McIntyre and Louis Howe, who in time were White House secretaries.

Early proved to be an extremely valuable adjunct to the president's smoothly functioning machine. Not only was he well liked by the correspondents and respected for his professional knowledge of their work, but he was always at the president's elbow, suggesting many of the nuances in his treatment of the press that proved to be so effective. He was always accessible, and if there was something he did not know, he never hesitated to find out and relay what he had learned. At the press conferences it was Early who made sure that the president had newsworthy announcements to make, helped him to anticipate questions, and briefed him on replies.

Most of all, as many of the correspondents believed later, Early was responsible for the policy of impartiality with which Roosevelt treated the press. The day of the fair-haired boy was nearly completely gone, unlamented. There were a few lapses, but they were relatively minor and mostly involved columnists rather than reporters. The most significant of these lapses centered on the unusual direct access the president frequently gave to Arthur Krock, chief Washington correspondent and columnist for the New York *Times,* a man of impressive ego who sometimes appeared to believe that he was Roosevelt's personal spokesman. On two occasions Krock used his privilege to obtain exclusives, one of which won him a Pulitzer Prize and momentarily angered the other correspondents. Such incidents would have blossomed into alienation in the past, but under the Roosevelt spell most of the reporters got over their anger.

As Graham White points out, Roosevelt was able to keep secret a much more flagrant violation of his evenhanded treatment policy—his close association with George Creel, which had begun during the Great War. Creel's articles, appearing in *Collier's* and other magazines, often contained paragraphs dictated by the president. Some were trial balloons to test public opinion, others were simply propaganda, at which Creel was an expert, as we have seen. Oddly the press did not appear to grasp the connection, although the closeness of Creel and the president was no secret. In fact the newspapers displayed an amazing disinterest in these articles and gave most of them no further publicity.

An irony of Roosevelt's press relations was the struggle of black reporters to gain admission to the Great Liberal's press conferences. They began petitioning as soon as the president took office, but it was not until January 1944 that they were admitted. In refusing, Early had cited several technicalities, among them that the conferences were only for representatives of daily papers and most of the Negro press was weekly. But then the black news organizations found that twenty-five correspondents from weekly trade journals had been admitted, and that gave them the loophole they sought. Early, in fact, had already made exceptions for such nonregular journalists as the gossip columnist Walter Winchell, an ardent Roosevelt supporter, who was given permission to attend any time he pleased.

With the press conferences, the preferential treatment given to a few correspondents, and the magazine articles of Creel and others, Roosevelt contrived to use the press as a transmission belt for stories, nearly always favorable, that appeared on front pages everywhere in the country and, as he understood, served to overwhelm the adverse editorials in most of the same papers. Roosevelt ideas and policies dominated the front pages day after day, to the exasperation of his many enemies.

The only outlet the president could not control was the equally steady flow of criticism and speculation that emanated from the political columnists, a specialty that had been growing steadily since the turn of the century, attracting many readers who spent little time with the editorials or, for that matter, the hard news. Roosevelt was utterly contemptuous of the columnists, denouncing them in and out of the press conferences. He looked upon them as the lowest form of journalistic enterprise. They represented an opposition that was caustic, often unfair, and sometimes abusively vitriolic, and they could be neither disregarded nor controlled. Since many were syndicated, their presumed influence was national rather than local. The chief opponents included such well-known figures as Frank Kent, Westbrook Pegler, Paul Mallon, David Lawrence, Mark Sullivan, Hugh Johnson, and (in his much more restrained way) Walter Lippmann. Pegler and Kent were the worst offenderss; the other Roosevelt would have sued them for libel. There was a good deal of partisan lunacy in nearly all these columns, but since the public could not be expected to distinguish between slander and truth, Roosevelt had to console himself with the belief that the columnists were preaching to the already converted.

Opposition to the president in the press did not begin in earnest until near the end of his first term, when the introduction of the Social Security Act in 1935, capping a long series of other reform measures, pushed conservative publishers and editors to a point of no return and they began to defect from their earlier support in large numbers. Social Security was attacked by some of them as a communist plot, and it was widely believed by the more rabid that Roosevelt was in league with the Kremlin, a charge actually made repeatedly through all three of Roosevelt's terms.

The opposition was led by Col. Rutherford R. McCormick and his Chicago *Tribune,* joined by its other Axis members, the New York *Daily News,* whose publisher was Capt. Joseph Patterson, McCormick's cousin, and the Washington *Times-Herald,* formerly a Hearst paper, owned by Eleanor Medill ("Cissy") Patterson, Joseph's sister. McCormick, an eccentric congenital right-winger (Cissy called him her "Bourbon cousin") fought Roosevelt and the New Deal almost from the beginning. Patterson, who had fancied himself as a socialist earlier in his career, began as a Roosevelt supporter and was invited with his wife to the White House from time to time, but he gradually fell away; after the first term, his paper was nearly as virulent a critic as the *Tribune.* Cissy, an old friend and admirer of Hearst, had bought the *Herald* from him soon after she joined it as editor in 1930, later merging it with the *Times*. She supported Roosevelt in 1932, even defended him editorially against the "whispers" that the Republicans were already whispering, and she called Mrs. Roosevelt "the noblest woman I have ever known." Cissy did not defect until the 1936 election, but after 1940 she repeated the worst canards of the Roosevelt-hating press and invented a few of her own.

Aside from these papers, the defections among Roosevelt's early supporters that began about 1934 included Roy Howard, publisher of the Scripps-Howard newspapers; the Los Angeles *Times,* always a conservative organ; and the Hearst papers. Roosevelt thought the hatred expressed by these and other papers was as illogical as it was cruel, and by late 1935, it had begun to arouse him to a response in kind. As his biographer James MacGregor Burns relates:

> In August 1935, the President somehow got hold of a message from a Hearst executive to Hearst editors and to its news service: "The Chief instructs that the phrase Soak the Successful be used in all references to the Administration's tax program instead of the phrase Soak the Thrifty hitherto used, also he wants the words Raw Deal used instead of New Deal." Roosevelt was indignant. He even had a press release prepared—"The President believes that it is only fair to the American people to apprise them of certain information which has come to him. . . ." But more prudent counsel prevailed and the release was not issued. The editorial lions roared louder and louder. Early in 1936 the Chicago *Tribune* was already running as its "platform" the slogan "Turn the rascals out," with the admonition "Only 201 (or 101, or 17) days in which to save your country. What are you doing to save it?"

All of Roosevelt's outbursts, Burns observes, were directed against the press, and he quotes a letter the president wrote to Ambassador Claude G. Bowers in Spain: "As you know, all the fat-cat newspapers—85% of the whole—have been utterly opposed to everything the Administration is seeking, and the best way to describe the situation is that the campaign of the spring, summer and autumn of 1936 is continuing actively throughout the year 1937. However, the voters are with us today just as they were last fall."

That was the saving truth. The voters were indeed still with him, as they had been and would be, in spite of everything the Hearst and McCormick-Patterson newspapers could say about him—and they encompassed the vocabulary of virulence. What they said often irritated and upset Roosevelt (as much as he ever permitted himself to be), but it was the political columnists who had been his *bêtes noirs* from the beginning. The simmering antagonism he felt toward them, carefully kept below the surface most of the time, had boiled over a few months before the 1936 election, at the annual Gridiron Club dinner in April, which presidents traditionally attend.

Harold Ickes, Roosevelt's irascible secretary of the interior, relates the details of the encounter in his so-called secret diary, and although it is a partisan's story, other accounts confirm it. As Ickes notes, the custom is to have two speeches at the dinner, one by a leader of the opposing party and the last by the president himself, giving him a chance to respond to the more or less good-natured ribbing that has preceded it. At this dinner, however, Frank Kent gave the first speech, and in it, as Ickes reports,

> he was pretty savage in his onslaught on the New Deal. It was the most outspoken attack I have listened to yet in the presence of the President. He was like a little bantam cock fighting a big rooster. He said he knew that the President's extensive research staff had looked up everything which he had ever said or done and intimated that he was prepared for the worst. He plainly thought that he was offering himself as a martyr to the cause. In somewhat plaintive terms he referred to the fact that the President would speak last and that he would have no chance to reply. He took some terrific slaps at the Republican party, but he devoted his main efforts to an attack on the New Deal—all that it had done and stood for. He also expressed his personal disapproval of the leaders of the New Deal.
>
> I kept wondering how the President would answer Kent because to have answered him would have been to descend to personalities. Shortly after he began to speak, I came to the conclusion that he wasn't even going to mention Kent or refer to what he had said. About halfway through, the President began to pay sarcastic respects to certain columnists and Washington correspondents and then I wondered whether he would include Kent. However, he did not. There was no slightest intimation that he had ever heard of Kent or that Kent had made a speech preceding his own. It must have been a sore trial to Kent to mount the funeral pyre, prepared bravely to suffer martyrdom, and then find that his posturing had escaped the attention of the man who was to apply the match to the faggots.
>
> The President's speech was well done but very sarcastic. What he said about some of the political commentators must have made them writhe. He had a lot of fun with the Republican candidates for President, as well as with the newspaper correspondents. I think the President acquitted himself pretty well, although his sarcasm in some places was so subtle that I do not doubt that it was over the heads of a good many of his auditors.

This was typical of the way Roosevelt handled those he knew hated him, both in the press and outside it. He was a master of sarcasm, but that was as far as he would go; indignant denunciation was not his style, as it had been with so many of his predecessors. He remained in control because of his immense popular support, but inevitably some of the bloom had gone off the rose by the spring of 1938, when Hugh Johnson, who was one of the most acid of his columnar enemies, wrote gleefully that "the old Roosevelt magic has lost its kick." That was the consensus among conservatives, and some others joined in. There had been a "Roosevelt recession," which cooled off a certain portion of his supporters, and he was losing his ability to dominate Congress as this second term wound down.

Yet Roosevelt continued to control the hearts and minds of most voters, and radio was the medium he used to do it, establishing an invisible link with his listeners by the sheer magnetism of his voice—a paradox in itself, since he spoke to the people in cultured Eastern accents that were far from being the *lingua franca* of the country at large. The popular belief is that Roosevelt invented the device of the "fireside chat," as these broadcasts were called, after he became president, but, as Burns has long since noted, he began them during his first term as governor of New York, directing his appeal toward upstate voters who otherwise got their political ideas from a heavily Republican press. Reception was still uncertain in those days, particularly at night, and James Farley, the Democratic boss, had to inquire anxiously from local party politicians how the governor's voice had been received in their particular part of the state. Roosevelt described these gubernatorial broadcasts as nonpartisan reports, but of course they were unalloyed party propaganda from the beginning. To supplement them he set up a press bureau in Albany (at Henry Morgenthau, Jr.'s suggestion) that churned out Democratic "news" releases to upstate rural papers.

As president, Roosevelt turned the fireside chats into a valuable political weapon. Burns has described their remarkable effect:

> Read in cold newspaper print the next day, these talks seemed somewhat stilted and banal. Heard in the parlor, they were fresh, intimate, direct, moving. The radio chats were effective largely because Roosevelt threw himself into the role of a father talking with his great family. He made a conscious effort to visualize the people he was talking to. He forgot the microphone; as he talked, "his head would nod and his hands would move in simple, natural, comfortable gestures," Miss [Frances] Perkins noted. "His face would smile and light up as though he were actually sitting on the front porch or in the parlor with them." And his listeners would nod and smile and laugh with him.

On the radio, Roosevelt was at his best as a manipulator of public opinion, and in his daily contact with the press he was still the chief entrepreneur of that medium. In spite of the general hostility of the newspapers, although not from most of their representatives in the White House, he rarely lost his touch. Extreme pressure could make him falter, however, as it did after the failure of his "court-packing" campaign—his attempt to increase the number of justices in the Supreme Court to counter the conservative majority—which he had attempted to sell to the public as necessary judicial reform. It was a defeat that appeared to wound him more deeply than any other, and in the closing days of the struggle the correspondents saw for the first time a Roosevelt who momentarily lost his poise.

Roosevelt berated the faithful Steve Early for releasing a statement on the court fight that he declared had been garbled by the papers. At a press conference he lashed out again over a story most of the press had carried about a social call the New York Democratic boss Edward Flynn had paid on him, which had been interpreted by the reporters as intervention by the president in the New York mayoralty race. For most of the forty minutes consumed by that conference Roosevelt berated the reporters for their handling of the Flynn visit, directing his fire particularly at Ernest K. Lindley, who was also his biographer and friend and had worked closely with him on some of his most important speeches. He read from Lindley's story, branding as lies one statement after another and repeatedly demanding that Lindley apologize.

There was also the matter of his interview with Hugh Johnson, who had once worked for him as head of the National Recovery Administration but who had written a column accusing Roosevelt of party treachery. Invoking the spirit of

Speaker Joe Cannon, the president told Johnson that this noted loyalist would have called Johnson "a liar, a coward, and a cad," and he repeated the charge, slowly, with such effect that Johnson broke into sobs of contrition, according to Roosevelt.

Not much in the press escaped the president's attention. He worked his way quickly through a dozen newspapers every morning, focusing his attention on any stories that had emanated from the White House and sampling the editorials. His staff people also assiduously clipped a broad sampling of the nation's newspapers each day and kept a scrapbook that gave the president and those around him a sense of what the press, if not the country, was thinking.

Aside from the fireside chats, it was the reporters who wrote the stories he read every morning who Roosevelt understood must be his chief concern. So complete had been his capturing of them at the beginning, aside from the hard-shell conservatives, that it seemed impossible the magic would ever fade. Some of the correspondents had come closer to him than any had ever done with previous presidents—or ever would again. Lindley, as noted, had helped him with important speeches, and so had James M. Kieran of the New York *Times,* who is credited with inventing the term "Brains Trust" to describe the first Roosevelt cabinet and its attendant advisers. Roosevelt had known both of these men since his days in Albany, where Lindley had been correspondent for the *Herald Tribune,* as Kieran was for the *Times.*

These extremely able reporters represented the elevation in quality that had occurred in the Washington press corps since the turn of the century. Leo Rosten, taking a sample of 127 correspondents in 1936, which included 186 leading dailies, the wire services, and the leading columnists, found them a superior group measured by previous standards. Nearly three-fourths of them had gone to college, and more than half had graduated. They were seasoned reporters, having spent an average of nearly nineteen years in the business and nearly ten of them in Washington. Three-quarters of the correspondents had chosen journalism as a career deliberately, which could not have been said of their nineteenth-century counterparts.

With such a group Roosevelt's style had its perils as well as its obvious great advantages. At the beginning the correspondents had been thoroughly seduced by it, but as time went on certain doubts began to arise. For one thing, as White observes, "such a competent, dedicated, and professionally self-conscious group were not always willing to accept with passivity and equanimity lectures on their professional shortcomings by a man whose credentials as a press expert they suspected, whose conception of their role seemed unrealistically circumscribed, and whose depiction of their motives was often, in their view, grotesque." In short, the mixture as before.

The outburst against Lindley and the others over the Flynn visit, described earlier, was perhaps the worst disruption of the relationship, but there were others. At the core of them was Roosevelt's conviction that the reporters' output was controlled, both in quantity and content, by the newspaper owners, and secondarily by the editors. Stories that were not consistent with the president's version of the facts he condemned as "interpretative" at best, "lies" at the worst.

During the argument over the Flynn story, the president had told the reporters at the conference: "I understand. You fellows are placed in such a position very often. . . . We can talk about it in the family and off the record. I can appreciate what you are told to write. . . . It does not take away, in any way, from my affection for the group of you. . . . That is why the newspapers are losing the influence they had ten years ago . . . because of interpretative stories that do not hold water."

Similarly, when Roosevelt attacked the correspondents again at a press conference on February 3, 1939, over a story that reported the president as telling the Senate Military Affairs Committee that America's European frontier was the Rhine, he told them it was the newspaper owners, as well as certain senators, who were behind what he termed the "misrepresentation." With an unusual display of anger he pointed to several newspapers lying on his desk and charged that their stories and headlines were giving a false impression and that the readers of these accounts were beginning to realize that what they were consuming in the press was "pure bunk," echoing Henry Ford's verdict on history. Roosevelt called the Rhine frontier story a deliberate lie, but it was plain the correspondents did not believe him and resented the accusation. Even Arthur Krock, long a Roosevelt favorite, defended his sources for the Rhine story and charged that the president's wrath had domestic political roots.

This incident was the "first wide-open break with the White House," *Editor & Publisher* reported, and it was a clear signal that the inevitable clash between president and press had occurred in this administration as it had in all the others, despite the relationship's magical beginnings. The Greatest Managing Editor had alienated his reportorial staff by giving its members something of the treatment a tough city editor might impose on a cub. In the city room that would have to be tolerated, but in the White House pressroom it was viewed as dogmatic, gratuitous, and wrong. A father figure who derided them, ridiculed some of the "family's" most respected members, and insulted the writers who displeased him most could hardly expect continued love and devotion from his children. Most of all, perhaps, the reporters resented Roosevelt's often-repeated belief that they were mere lackeys who wrote what their papers' owners and editors told them to write—a profound misconception on Roosevelt's part, also believed by a large segment of the public.

The outbreak of war only provoked new tensions. While the troublesome problem of wartime censorship was handled with a smoothness never seen before, under the direction of Byron Price, an able and trusted Associated Press executive, the correspondents who covered the president found themselves subjected to what they considered unreasonable restrictions as Roosevelt tried to keep his movements as secret as possible. He seemed to treat the correspondents with a kind of amused contempt, as when he toured the country for two weeks, inspecting defense plants and clearly visible to large crowds in the cities he visited but not permitting the reporters to file their stories until the tour was over. That led to a formal protest by thirty-five correspondents and another stormy press conference.

When the president met with wartime leaders of other countries the secrecy was again excessive. Roosevelt undertook an elaborate maneuver in which he was advertised as being on a fishing trip aboard the *Potomac,* anchored off the Massachusetts coast, from which daily meaningless bulletins were issued. All the time, of course, he was meeting with Churchill on a warship in the North Atlantic, where the Atlantic Charter was drawn up. This news reached the world first from two British newspapermen who had somehow become part of Churchill's party on the ship. It was, as Paul Mallon put it, "a shabby deal" for the press.

The correspondents fared no better at the president's overseas conferences. Barbed wire held them back at Cairo, and, when this meeting was transferred to Teheran, they were prevented from leaving Cairo by military order. The British papers, again, broke the news, although they had agreed not to, as they had at the Atlantic Conference. At Casablanca, Roosevelt arranged to have a former White House correspondent for the International News Service, now a captain in the Air Transport Corps, smuggled in as a baggage officer, but it was not until Yalta, the last act, that he permitted reporters to become members of his official party. Meanwhile, at home, the same kind of secrecy was being enforced, with far less excuse.

Much of this censorship was incredibly petty, and a great deal more of it was absurd. The worst example, and the one that angered the press more than any other, was the freedom correspondents were given while Roosevelt was running for a fourth term in 1944, when virtually all the former restrictions were lifted— only to be clamped down again immediately after the election, when coverage of the president was no longer useful to him. Only two months before Roosevelt's death the resentment over such treatment had grown so deep that Byron Price warned the White House, through Early, that this kind of arbitrary censorship in the name of security was placing the voluntary censorship system in considerable danger.

Again and again during the war Roosevelt's underlying distaste and disdain for the press came to the surface, adding to the disaffection of even those correspondents who had begun by loving him and enjoying his company, which included most of them. Now they heard their president not only impugning their integrity, which he had been doing more frequently ever since the second term began, but casting doubt on their patriotism, calling some of their number "sixth columnists" and making a mock award of the Nazi Iron Cross to John O'Donnell, a *Daily News* reporter. That seemed like a low blow to his fellow correspondents, even those who considered O'Donnell's reporting as a little above gutter level.

Nothing shook the president's certainty that there were only two kinds of news, the "facts" and "interpretation," the latter including whatever he, as sole arbiter, saw as contrary to the "facts" as he determined them. To the professionals who heard this bogus philosophy repeated again and again, it seemed incongruous that it should come from a man of such great talents and intelligence. The fact that Roosevelt was obviously sincere about it did not mitigate the offense. It never occurred to him that when he told the assembled correspondents, "If I were writing this story, this is how I would write it," he was doing exactly what he was accusing *them* of doing. Nor did it seem to dawn on him that when he used the reporters as a club to beat the newspaper owners, whom he regarded as the real villains, he was implying that the correspondents were only stooges who could do nothing about their unfortunate condition. He was sharply challenged on that point repeatedly during numerous news conferences but it was as though he never heard them.

On the other hand, some of Roosevelt's suspicions about the owners were real enough in the case of several of the most powerful. The paranoid excesses of the McCormick-Patterson alliance have been well documented. The more subtle hostility of Henry Luce's publications was a little less obvious but nonetheless represented the philosophy of a man who was wrong on most of the public issues of his time and did not hesitate to use his magazines as political weapons, sometimes with as little regard for the facts as though he had been a politician himself.

Roosevelt could, and did, maintain at least friendly relations with some of these owners if they were (as he himself would never have put it) of his class. One of them was Helen Rogers Reid, of the New York *Herald Tribune,* co-owner of the paper with her husband Ogden. When the paper ran a cartoon in 1942 depicting Roosevelt as a president who neglected conducting the war for the sake of his own domestic political interests, he wrote a "Dear Helen" letter to Mrs. Reid, marked "personal, confidential, and 'off the record,' " which began, "As you know, I have, during a long course of years, acquired, of necessity, the skin of a rhinoceros—but there are occasions—in fact, very rare instances—where I speak to real friends of mine in regard to matters which 'just are not true.' " He went on to chide her gently about the cartoon, but there was an edge in the chiding, as when he observed, "And because the good old *Herald Tribune* has on the whole a decent respect for veracity, I think a cartoon which is based on the opposite of veracity is something that you and Ogden and Mr. Parsons [Geoffrey Parsons, the chief editorial writer] ought, for your own sakes, to take up." He continued with a detailed defense of himself, branded the cartoon again as "based on a false statement," urged the paper to make "what, in the old days, we used to call the 'Amende Honorable,' " and concluded, "Don't for a moment imagine I am sore about this, but I have always thought that the *Herald Tribune* was big enough to know when it had printed something when it was not true." In this letter Roosevelt referred to "the very nice visit with you I had the other day," a testimony to the social relations he continued to have with a few publishers, even those who opposed him. Ickes, too, saw a good deal of Cissy Patterson and apparently discussed politics with her in a more equable way than the *Times-Herald* did.

All these amenities, however, did not change Roosevelt's basic view of the press, and of its owners. He disregarded any evidence that might contradict it. Nevertheless he tried to maintain friendly relations, at least on the surface, with the most important publishers. McCormick was written off at the beginning as irreconcilable, but Patterson was a frequent White House visitor until he broke completely with the president in 1936. With Roy Howard, Roosevelt maintained a friendly but fluctuating relationship during his time in office. His relations with Adolph Ochs of the New York *Times* and his successor Arthur Hays Sulzberger were cordial for the most part, although Roosevelt did not hesitate to instruct them in the ways of journalistic virtue. He was friendly with Eugene Meyer of the Washington *Post.*

If there was one publisher and editor who merited the president's unwavering high regard, it was William Allen White of the Emporia *Gazette,* who had turned his back on the Republicans in 1932, possibly because of his disappointment with Hoover. Roosevelt sometimes called him to the White House to get "a few helpful thoughts from the philosopher of Emporia," as he called him. A lesser but stronger and unwavering alliance was maintained with J. David Stern, owner of the Philadelphia *Record,* the Camden (N. J.) *Courier,* and briefly the New York *Post,* from 1933 to 1939. Still another ally was Marshall Field III, owner of the newspaper *PM* and the Chicago *Sun,* both of which strongly supported the president.

Against this list of friends could be placed the implacable enemies—McCormick and the Pattersons, and, most of all, William Randolph Hearst. The others in the "85 percent opposition" group were simply unreconciled Republicans whose papers would have upheld the party regardless of what Democrat sat in the White House. Graham White believes that the support of Roosevelt's powerful friends offset the opposition, the size of which he is convinced the president grossly exaggerated. Whether or not this is true, however, the lesson to be drawn from the Roosevelt administration is that a popular president who can communicate with the voters will find an opposition press, whatever its size, irrelevant to political success.

Whether the "famous 85 percent," as Roosevelt called it, actually existed or was a false conception, as White believes, remains a matter of controversy. What newspapers declare themselves to be politically, as well as the infinite gradations of both opposition and support, are such elusive factors that it is extremely difficult to compile convincing evidence either way. It may be the voices of opposition were so strident that they overshadowed the voices of support, making it appear that the Roosevelt haters were in the majority. In the end, however, much as this opposition may have irritated the president, it did him minimal damage.

Aside from his obsession with the publishers, his use of the reporters to flay them, and the deviations described earlier, Roosevelt's relations with the press over more than a dozen years were a study in mastery. As Merriman Smith, the United Press's veteran White House correspondent, summed it up: "Mr. Roosevelt was good and he knew it. He was superbly confident that he was the best political strategist known in American history. He knew for a fact that he could outguess and outmaneuver his opponents. And he did, time and again." That was precisely what he did with the correspondents. Whether they loved him or not, they could never escape his powerful presence. Outside the ranks of the working press he also won the ardent support of such liberal writers as the poets Carl Sandburg and Stephen Vincent Benet, and the playwright Robert Sherwood, who joined his staff.

One scholar, Alfred Haworth Jones, has concluded that Roosevelt used these ideological and personal allies to build an image of himself as a modern Lincoln, to advance his political career. However that may be, and there is reason to doubt that there was any such deliberate attempt, Roosevelt did not need any image projection of this or any other kind. He was a monumental figure in American political life, capturing the imagination of both press and public. Most people believed in him so much that the flood tide of words pouring from the media, pro and con, had no more effect on them than the washing of waves on a deserted beach. Some erosion could be expected, but the landscape remained substantially unchanged through twelve of the most fateful years in the history of America.

Truman: Friend and Enemy

As sharp as the change had been from Hoover to Roosevelt, the transition from Roosevelt to Harry Truman was even more drastic. While they had a few characteristics in common, these two men employed entirely different styles and could hardly have been more unlike. The temptation at the beginning was to think of Truman as only another accidental president, although it was clear to many observers who watched Roosevelt struggle through the campaign of 1944 that the tremendous strain of the war had accelerated the deterioration of his body (his mind, too, said his enemies) and that he was old and ill. The revealing photographs of the war leaders at Yalta confirmed the fact, and when Roosevelt for the first time made a speech sitting down after his return from the conference, there was renewed speculation about his health. Still, it was a shock of national surprise when he died on April 12, 1945.

No doubt there were those who could not, for just a moment, remember who would step into those giant shoes. But for the more politically conscious, the memory of the Democratic convention of 1944 was still green. It had been another of those occasions when the delegates clearly wanted one man, Vice-President Henry A. Wallace, to keep his job, and the bosses, augmented by conservatives and Southern reactionaries, just as plainly wanted someone else. Roosevelt's endorsement of Wallace had been mild and equivocal. Truman was only one of several possible alternates, but the fight narrowed down to him and Wallace, and once again, as in the past, the bosses maneuvered behind the scenes to get their way. Truman won on the second ballot, and cynics pointed out that this was no more than the expected outcome, since Truman himself was a product of Boss Tom Pendergast's fragrant Kansas City political machine.

After the convention Truman was promptly forgotten. The approaching end of the war, Thomas E. Dewey's ignominious defeat in November, and the Yalta conference overshadowed everything else—except for those who looked at the photos of a wraithlike Roosevelt, shockingly changed from only a few months before—and wondered. In the wake of a national outpouring of grief not approached since the death of Lincoln, Americans awoke on the morning of April 13 to see a new face in command, a hitherto all-but-forgotten man who would soon be memorable in his own right.

No president ever approached the task with more humility. On the morning after his inauguration, on the way to have lunch with some of those he had formerly served with in the Senate, Truman turned to the reporters who surrounded him, men and women he would now have to approach on a far different basis, and said earnestly, "I feel as though the moon and all the stars and all the planets have fallen upon me. Please, boys, give me your prayers. I need them very much."

Thus, at once, Truman began to establish the image of himself that he believed in—a man who represented the epitome of the American Dream, of the country boy who works hard, makes friends, stays out of trouble, climbs the ladder, and winds up being president. As Robert Griffith summarizes the views of Truman's early biographers, the president was "a direct and uncomplicated man, an honest and plain-spoken son of the middle border who rose from common origins to become president of the United States." This image, Griffith points out, was further reinforced by Truman's own memoirs and by dozens of books and articles. Historians, of course, could not accept such an appraisal. Griffith has summarized their more recent conclusions:

> He was indeed a complicated, not a simple, man; a man at times both diffident and aggressive, capable of both humility and arrogance; a man who could leap to decisions quickly, and perhaps impulsively, but who could also be vacillating and indecisive; a man who always seemed to know his own mind, yet who appears in retrospect to have been highly dependent on those who advised him; a man who valued honesty and plain speaking, but who was also capable of contradiction and deception, including and perhaps especially, self-deception; a man whose instincts sometimes led him in contradictory directions as he struggled, often unsuccessfully, to master the complex forces which were shaping a new political age.

Truman's image of himself has passed into popular mythology, but the more complicated man the historians have seen is the president the correspondents saw at the White House and elsewhere. The veterans among them who had watched strong personalities succeeded by seemingly frailer ones could sympathize with the Truman they first encountered. One of them, Jonathan Daniels, proprietor of the Raleigh (N. D.) *News and Observer,* a friend and admiring biographer, wrote of Truman's first days in the White House that, even though Roosevelt's effects had been meticulously cleaned out of the Oval Office, "it seemed still to be Roosevelt's desk and Roosevelt's room. It seemed to me, indeed, almost Roosevelt's sun which came in the wide south windows and touched Truman's thick glasses. . . . I remember [that] he swung around in the President's chair as if he were testing it, more uncertain than ever I was about its size."

Understandably, Truman was deeply resentful when reporters or political columnists made invidious comparisons between him and Roosevelt, but he made no complaint in public, saving his anger for the private papers he kept. He had no high opinion of FDR or the men around him, whom he called the "Palace Guard." As for the former president's supporters, he considered them "crackpots" and "professional liberals" and in his diary gave it as his private opinion that "I don't believe the U.S.A. wants any more fakers. Teddy and Franklin are enough."

With such a personality, whose complexities were not visible on the surface, it is not surprising that the usual tensions between president and press began to develop almost at once. At the beginning it was evident that most of the corre-spondents liked this plain, bluff man from Missouri, but many of their publishers did not, whether the proportion was 85 percent, inherited from Roosevelt, or another figure. The owners had no way of knowing that the new president was privately thinking some of their own thoughts about Roosevelt; all they knew was that another Democrat, presumably with further ideas of social reform, sat in the White House, and they were prepared to oppose him. Obviously hard times in the pressroom lay ahead.

As his buffer, Truman was fortunate in having three extremely able press aides during his terms, beginning with Charles Ross, followed by Joseph Short, and finally Roger Tubby. These men had to work with a press corps that was itself becoming a complicated matter. By this time there was a hard core of anywhere from ten to twenty correspondents whose sole job was to cover the president, wherever he was. They represented the (then) three national wire services, the major Eastern dailies, and two of the radio-television networks. Television, in Truman's second term, would at last be coming into its own.

These full-time White House reporters were not regarded as entirely top drawer by the press secretaries, particularly Tubby, who considered them not all equally competent or reliable, and in the bargain "quarrelsome, querulous, bored with themselves, often dissatisfied, and always there." The secretaries felt themselves perpetually harassed by these reporters for whom they were supposed to be at once nursemaid, friend, and protector, while at the same time protecting the president from them. In short, the concept of the permanent White House correspondent corps was being born, and neither side felt comfortable with the arrangement.

Secretaries complained too about the frenetic tempo of wire-service reporting, with its heavy emphasis on spot news, which made both the president and his press aides feel that the press conferences were being run at wire-service speed to satisfy the services' particular requirements, leading to "bear baiting" of the president. This atmosphere, it was believed, also put the reporters who worked at a different speed and with different aims at a disadvantage.

As a result of these factors, Truman and his staff assumed a defensive stance toward all the permanent White House correspondents—a stiffening that was intended to put some space between the reporters and the president. It was a policy that only led to more trouble for both sides. One of the worst results was to make it harder for the best reporters, who wrote reflective, analytical pieces at a slower tempo, to get the kind of material they had been used to obtaining from informal and confidential briefings. Naturally they resented it.

The secretaries were also aware that their duties were often of no more than a technical nature, since speeches, the presidential calendar, and advisory func-tions were in other hands. Only a man with a strong personality could make himself felt in the internal organization. Short, one of Tubby's two assistants, was such a personality. He had been a White House correspondent himself, much respected, and although he was considered a "taut, tense, 'ulcer-type,' " he was also "sharpminded, persistent, and passionately loyal," as Francis Heller

tells us in his analysis of the Truman administration. But these admirable qualities, says Heller, only

> contributed to the disaffection of his former colleagues in the press corps. They saw
> him as impatient, overly protective, and lacking in appreciation of their special need
> for background information to guide their interpretations. Short closed off, as nearly
> as might be, all avenues to the staff save through the press office. But having done
> so, he then tended—as reporters were fond of complaining—to act less like a press-
> relations expert than as a confidential policy adviser (which, of course, he did be-
> come), more concerned with minimizing the momentary harm the press could do
> than with maximizing the ''breaks'' that it might give in response to the right timing
> and conditioning.

(It is worth noting that Short's wife Beth was named to be correspondence secretary, and thus Truman became the first president ever to appoint a woman to a top
staff position.)

The strain of the press secretary's job in the modern imperial presidency was
evident in its fatal effect on some of the men who held it. As Tubby pointed out,
Early, Ross, and Short all died on the job, and Irving Perlmeter, Tubby's associate, suffered a heart attack. Other secretaries did better (James Hagerty served
eight calm years under Eisenhower), apparently adapting to the pace, or more
likely as a result of having more help.

Short was the first to see that help was necessary. After his appointment he
moved across the hall from the pressroom, where he had spent the previous two
decades covering the White House for the AP and the Baltimore *Sun,* and with
his extensive knowledge of presidential operations immediately asked for two
assistants instead of one, on the ground that the presidency was now such a large
affair he could not know everything that was going on. That was how Tubby
came to the job, since Short wanted the experience in foreign affairs he had
gained in working for the State Department. Similarly he hired Perlmeter because of the knowledge of domestic affairs he had acquired through his work
with the AP and for the Treasury Department.

Tubby had a particularly clear-eyed view of his job. ''There is an adversary
relationship that exists between the president and the press, or between his press
secretaries and the press,'' he said later,

> which is inherent and natural and often quite healthy. With President Truman there
> was . . . an openness and a candor in the morning staff meetings which gave all those
> present a feeling of what the others were up to and what the president was interested
> in having done. The press secretary's role then was not simply to be a transmission
> belt from the president to the press, merely passing on whatever it was that should be
> passed on to the press; the job was a two-way street.
>
> President Truman was very anxious to know, not only through us in the press
> office but through others on the staff, through the cabinet, and through people on the
> Hill, what the people out in the country were interested in and what they wanted. For
> our part, we would brief him not only on what had been in the papers or on the

radio—TV was very new in those days—but on what some of our friends in the press corps were saying about things. . . .

In preparing for the president's own press conferences, the press staff would try to guess what questions might be asked and then offer recommended answers and provide background material in each category for each question and answer. This we usually did on Mondays, coming up with fifty or sixty possible questions. We then referred them to the various departments and asked for recommended responses. When these came in, we would go over them, maybe check back, and put the material into a black looseleaf notebook for the president. He would take it with him the night before he was to meet the press and go over it. Then on the following morning we would get together, update that material, and check with the staff on whether we ought to recommend some changes.

This was the modern system introduced by Tubby that was passed on to Hagerty and used through the Eisenhower years, and with modifications, amplifications, and other trimmings is still in use today.

But in spite of the excellent work of his press staff, Truman's relations with the press were strained and sometimes hostile from the start. It was not that the correspondents disliked him personally, as in the case of Coolidge and Hoover. Truman's outspoken honesty and bluff readiness to talk with them, the common touch that he provided as the ultimate common man, could not help but please them. Some appreciated his grasp of American history (and world history, too), the result of more reading in the field than any other modern president with the exception of Theodore Roosevelt. Truman was always conscious of his own historical position, for which he had the greatest reverence.

Reporters (and the public as well) were amused and entertained by some of Truman's habits, especially the early morning prebreakfast walks, which he took wherever he might happen to be. He was always accompanied by at least one and usually several reporters, trying to keep up with his 120 paces a minute; television cameramen learned to be rapid backward walkers. But what seemed like a splendid opportunity for informal interviewing was considerably hampered by the fact that it was impossible to take notes, and the president's avoidance of serious questions. He preferred light banter, in between responding amiably to the cries from early morning pedestrians of "Hi, Harry," "Give 'em hell, Harry," and other demonstrations of public appreciation. The reporters were often groggy from early risings, but Truman had been up since six o'clock, looked through three or four newspapers, and tossed off a letter or two or a memo before he appeared for his constitutional.

Not all the correspondents appreciated Truman's folksiness and down-home ways. Joseph Alsop, the syndicated columnist who was also a Roosevelt cousin, paid a visit to the Truman White House and viewed it with patrician disdain from the lofty altitude he customarily occupied. In a letter to Eleanor Roosevelt he observed that the White House under her husband had been a source of power, but under Truman it was like "the lounge of the Lions Club of Independence, Missouri, where one is conscious chiefly of the odor of ten-cent cigars and the easy laughter evoked by the new smoking room story."

Whatever the correspondents thought of him, however, was irrelevant, as it had been with Roosevelt. It was Truman's view of *them,* and of their employers, which determined the course of the relationship, and unfortunately the view was his predecessor's attitude toward the publishers, carried to the nth power, with embellishments that were peculiarly Truman's. Of the 348 reporters who crowded into his office (in Rooseveltian style) for his first fifteen-minute press conference, and who heard his crisp, decisive answers, there was probably no one who sensed that, deep down, he hated the press with a corrosive passion exceeding any of those who preceded him.

The correspondents could see it begin to emerge in later conferences, which were moved to the Indian Treaty Room on the fourth floor of the old State-War-Navy Building, across the street from the West Wing. The move was made, Charlie Ross said, because "more than two hundred reporters often showed up and they were stacked like hard macaroni. There was also an accident one time when the reporters broke for the telephones and one poor guy had his arm broken in the crush. But the final straw was when a reporter spilled ink on the President's rug." In these less crowded surroundings, Truman stood behind a desk, taking an occasional sip of water, and pressing on the desk top with his fingertips. "Between questions," Alfred Steinberg tells us in his biography, "he twisted a heavy gold ring on the little finger of his left hand, and while a question was asked, he turned from the waist to the reporter and listened, squinting, to his words."

There was trouble at the conferences from the beginning. Truman made the mistake of recognizing everyone, unlike Franklin Roosevelt and other presidents after Truman who learned to be selective and avoid trouble, if possible. He also felt obliged to give an answer of some kind to every question; slippery evasion was not a part of his nature. Besides, he genuinely wanted to be obliging, but at the same time, his extremely low boiling point and lack of reticence in expressing his opinions made him vulnerable to adroit questioning. His press secretaries were always worried about his habit of giving quick answers; it was too easy to make a mistake that might have political consequences. It was not until Tubby brought the conferences under control with the system described earlier that Truman was able to master these confrontations.

Away from the meetings, the president's attitudes toward the press began to emerge almost at once. Robert Donovan, the *Herald Tribune*'s correspondent who became Truman's friend and biographer, noted that he had been in office only a month before he referred to newspapers as "those damned sheets," and before the first year was over Truman had discussed press relations with Budget Director Harold D. Smith, who wrote in his diary: "After a press conference, he told me that press conferences were getting rather touchy, and they tended to put him on edge. He commented that some of the questions were close to being impertinent, though he felt that the questioners did not intend them to be so. They were sometimes difficult to answer off-the-cuff because of the tendency to put a wrong interpretation on quick answers."

In describing Truman's lively and continuing animus toward the press, Donovan makes it clear that he easily matched the most indignant outbursts of the past and, in doing so, disclosed the same kind of vision of how newspapers operate that had so blinded his predecessors. To Sen. J. William Fulbright, for example, he wrote: "It is a policy of the press, of course, to create a breach or a misunderstanding between members of the same party, particularly under conditions such as exist now [1947]. I have had too much experience to allow it to affect me so don't worry about it." It did affect him, however, as it does every president, and increasingly so as time went on.

Before the election in 1948, when he was particularly concerned about proving that he could be president in his own right and at the same time was combatting the liberals in his own party who were attempting to push him into early retirement, he referred to Hearst in a letter to his sister as "the old beast" who was pushing General MacArthur for the presidency, and to Sen. Joseph C. O'Mahoney he wrote:

> *Time* and *Life* and the scandal press, represented by Hearst and the McCormick-Patterson Axis, have been spending most of their time belittling the President. The last issue of *Time* spends three or four pages telling how people of brains are kept from the White House. The Emergency Fund was used to bring brains to the White House. . . . There seems to be a set pattern of belittling the President and his Cabinet and of using every effort possible to prevent the Executive Branch of the Government from obtaining the information necessary on which to base decisions.

Unlike other presidents, Truman found time to read history even while he was in the White House, and by early 1948 he had discovered that every chief executive before him had believed he was the victim of persecution by the press. Truman not only sympathized, but he considered them everlastingly right—in spades, doubled and redoubled, as he wrote to his sister:

> I've been reading a couple of books, one about the presidents and the press [it was probably James Pollard's *Presidents and the Press,* cited earlier in this volume, which had been published the year before] and another called *This Was Normalcy* [about Harding's administration]. It seems that every man in the White House was tortured and bedevilled by the so-called free press. They were lied about, misrepresented and actually libelled, and they have to take it. [Truman had an antique and often incorrect taste in spelling, as the double "lls" show.]
>
> The old SOB who owned and edited the St. Louis *Post-Dispatch* and New York *World* [he meant Joseph Pulitzer] was in my opinion the meanest character assassin in the whole history of liars who have controlled the newspapers—that includes old man Hearst and Bertie McCormick.
>
> Some day I hope a mucker will come along and dig up the facts on the distorters of news and facts. . . .
>
> When I am finished here, maybe I'll do it myself, I'll make a bet, however, that hell has become almost untenable for the devil since Old Pulitzer, Horace Greeley, Chas. Dana and the old Copperhead, Bill Nelson [founder of the Kansas City *Star*] and William Allen White arrived.

One can only imagine, with intense spasms of regret, what Pulitzer, Greeley, and Dana would have replied if they had been alive to read those words. As accomplished a conveyer of invective as he was, Truman was not in the same league with those dead giants of the past century; the McCormicks. Hearsts, and similar publishers of his time were mild extollers of conservative virtue by comparison.

Although Bess Truman scolded him for public lapses, the president frequently got carried away in defending himself and others from the press. During one speech he referred to the columnist Drew Pearson as a son-of-a-bitch, using the abbreviated SOB, as he usually did. No doubt he was delighted to watch the newspapers try to explain in a family journal what had been said—as always, oblivious to the fact that scarcely one among their readers would not know.

Truman lumped *Time, Life,* and *Fortune* together as the "Loose" publications, placing them in the same category with *Look, Newsweek, Collier's,* the *Saturday Evening Post,* and most metropolitan papers as part of a vast conspiracy to "misrepresent and belittle the President." The "Loose" magazines were "just too damn big anyway," he believed, and they had "too much power over people and what they think." The big publishers, he added, "have always been against me," and he had always been against them, with an exception made for his son-in-law (Clifton Daniel of the New York *Times*), "just the nicest boy he can be."

Personal confrontations with the enemy were rare, but Truman told Merle Miller, with considerable relish, of an encounter with Henry Luce, whom he considered among the worst of the lot, that occurred at a party given by the publisher to celebrate the acquisition for first serial publication in *Life* of Truman's memoirs.

> "Luce and I were introduced," Truman said, "and he said he was very glad to meet me. I said, 'Mr. Luce, a man like you must have trouble sleeping at night. Because your job is to inform people, but what you do is misinform them.'
>
> "Well, old Luce got red in the face, and Sam Rosenman came up to me—he was Roosevelt's friend and mine and he was one of the lawyers in charge of drawing up the papers—and he came up to me and said, 'Harry, be careful. We haven't signed all the papers yet. If you make him mad, maybe he won't sign up.' I said that wasn't true, that Luce needed us a hell of a lot more than we needed him, and in the end it turned out that was true.
>
> "I talked to Luce once more the same night. A little later, maybe when I was leaving, I don't remember. He came over, and he said that he thought if he and I just had the time to talk things over, we'd find we agreed on most things.
>
> "I told him I doubted that very much, and I did, and I still do."

A much more celebrated instance of the president's frontal attacks on press people who did not qualify as fact givers, which included most of them, occurred when Paul Hume, music critic of the Washington *Post,* covered the debut recital of Margaret Truman, the president's daughter, at a time when she hoped for a singing career. (Her true métier, it turned out later, was writing mystery stories.) Hume wrote that Miss Truman was "flat a good deal of the time. . . . She cannot sing with anything approaching professional finish. . . . She communicates almost nothing of the music she presents."

The president read that review on a morning when he was in the midst of his fight with General MacArthur and had seen on the front page of the *Post* a story quoting the general as saying the Korean War should be expanded to China. Then he read Hume's review. He was primed to explode in two directions, but there was no question of priorities. He took a piece of White House stationery and wrote to the critic: "I have just read your lousy review buried in the back pages. You sound like a frustrated old man who never made a success, an eight-ulcer man on a four-ulcer job and all four ulcers working. I never met you, but if I do you'll need a new nose and a supporter below. Westbrook Pegler, a guttersnipe, is a gentleman compared to you. You can take that as more of an insult than a reflection on your ancestry."

With that, Truman put his own stamp on the letter, scorning his franking privilege, took it with him on his morning walk, and dropped it into the nearest mailbox. When Hume received it, he found it hard to believe it came from the president. He showed it to the Washington *Star*'s music critic (according to Truman), who recognized the handwriting but cannily told Hume it must be a practical joke, then went back to the office and neatly scooped his colleague by writing the story—or so the president liked to believe.

Truman gave a slightly different version of his letter when he talked with Miller. Describing Hume as a man who did not know "a damn thing. Not a goddamn thing" about music, he recalled that in his letter he wrote "that if I could get my hands on him I'd bust him in the jaw and kick his nuts out." (He chuckled at the thought.) Memory may have improved on the original, as it so often does. No wonder that Mary McGrory, the *Post*'s columnist, wrote after the president retired: "Since Harry Truman left town almost nobody has spoken his mind. Mr. Truman took the tradition of plain speaking back to Missouri with him."

Along with Franklin Roosevelt and some earlier presidents, Truman clung stubbornly to the conviction that the press was bought and paid for. When he was preparing his inaugural address in 1949 he included a paragraph that he was prevailed upon to take out, but as Donovan says, "the words of the draft reveal the President's attitude": "Now, I have no bitterness in my heart against anyone, not even the bitter opposition press and its henchmen, the paid columnists and managing editors and the bought and paid for commentators. Never in the history of the country did a President need the honest help and cooperation of the Congress, press and the people as I have needed them since September 1945."

Only the people had stood by him, he implied. And surely there was deep resentment in his heart and mind. He wrote in his diary for March 26, 1949: "Pearson's no good. He, Fulton Lewis & Walter Winchell (Winchellski) are pathological liars par excellance [sic]." Truman often called Winchell "Winchellski" in private conversation; Donovan saw "real bias" in it. Again he wrote to Frank Kent: "I'm really surprised [by the columnist's attack on his budget] because I've always thought you intellectually honest. From David Lawrence, Pegler, Pearson, Winchell, I'd expect just such statements as you made—but you know that they are all liars and intellectually dishonest."

Lies, lies, lies. That was the burden of Truman's complaint, repeated over and over, as he declared that "people no longer in this great country can be fooled by people who write for money"—as though they should write for nothing. But it was who paid them, the paranoidal "they," that burned in him. Only history could console him: "When I read what the lousy press of the days of Washington, Jefferson, Jackson, Lincoln, Grover Cleveland, and Woodrow Wilson had to say about those men, I'm comforted, for I've had it easy by comparison." Again there was that fundamental error nearly all the presidents had made in their concept of the press's function in a free society, as Truman wrote to Thomas L. Stokes, the liberal columnist: "A free press is a free press because it is supposed to freely publish the facts on both sides of every question." That was not what Jefferson and Madison had in mind, as the president should have known from his reading of history, if prejudice had not blinded him.

Truman was the first president since Theodore Roosevelt to be angry enough at a newspaper to institute a libel action—or, more accurately, to suggest to his attorney general, J. Howard McGrath, that one be filed. When the Chicago *Tribune* called him a crook, he wrote to McGrath instructing him to "proceed with whatever action is necessary to get the right result," declaring that the slur was not only libel but criminal libel—TR's complaint about Pulitzer, in much the same kind of circumstance. Fortunately for the president, McGrath did not agree.

The president's correspondence, as well as his spoken comments and many of his speeches, are filled with tirades against the press. The wire services are out to discredit everything his administration does. The newspapers are making too big a thing of Sen. Joseph McCarthy. The "press people . . . are just as guilty of sabotaging the news as Pravda and Izvestia in Russia . . . and, before this thing is ended, you and I [he is writing to Sen. William Benton] are going to teach them a lesson." The Scripps-Howard Washington *News* is "the snotty little *News*." The Washington *Times-Herald* is a "sabotage sheet," along with most other papers. The Scripps-Howard chain and the Knight papers are merely imitators of Hearst, although not quite up to his dirtiest techniques. On the radio are "the lying air commentators" and in the papers, "the columnists whose business it is to prostitute the minds of the voters." At the climax of his second term, on December 6, 1952, he writes in his diary about the "lice" that infest the press and adds: "To hell with them. When history is written they will be the sons-of-bitches, not I. Look at old Medill, Horace Greeley et al. in Lincoln's time, Biddle in Jackson's and old man Pulitzer in Cleveland's. It isn't Jackson, Lincoln, and Cleveland who were wrong!"

Donovan, observing that Truman was no different from any other politician he had known in his attitude toward the press, thought the president simply did "what a lot of people do. After a long day he went home and downed a few bourbons, then he wrote this fiery stuff about the press." (On occasion, something could also be said of newspaper owners. Cissy Patterson once told William Bradford Huie, who was both investigative reporter and novelist: "I get up in the morning and look in the mirror and see that I'm never going to be young and pretty again, then I go down to the office and give Roosevelt hell.")

The problem is much more complex, of course, but at the same time personalities are more often than not the determining factors and serve to exaggerate views in ways that the sober analysis of historical evidence usually overlooks. In Truman's case, as Donovan says, his outbursts were not unique, but neither were those of the opposition press. As these pages have shown, the line runs historically true in both cases. Truman was a liberal Democrat who fought "the interests," in the traditional manner. He considered the Big Press to be among the interests and reacted accordingly. If he was unbalanced in his view, no less so were the Scripps-Howard, McCormick-Patterson, and Hearst papers, his chief enemies—and it was as enemies that each treated the other.

Few presidents have been so vulnerable to press attack as Truman was in his second term. There was the Hiss case, the victory of the communists in China, the rise of McCarthy, the war in Korea, the struggle with MacArthur, the cold war, the seizure of the steel mills under a strike threat, civil rights issues, scandals in the administration itself—an endless and dismaying list. Yet Truman faced the often unfriendly correspondents 347 times during his administration, fifty of them during the worst period of the second term, and he unflinchingly answered questions, sticking firmly to what he believed as a Midwestern progressive. Most of the correspondents could not help admiring his courage and integrity, even when they were personally doubtful about what he was doing. And most retained at least some measure of admiration and affection for him, in spite of his scarcely concealed low opinion of their profession, and often of them. His surprising elction victory of 1948 considerably enhanced their respect.

As those who were present recall, the press conferences were, in Donovan's words, "full of zip, full of humor, full of news," however deficient in substance they might sometimes be. Their major fault was a reprise of other presidential failures—Truman did not understand how to use the conference as a means of educating the public about his policies and practices, thus his sessions with the press became more exercises in defense than a means of persuasion and education. But nevertheless the president seemed to enjoy jousting with the reporters much of the time. They aroused his keen competitive spirit. The net effect, however, was to make the tone of the conferences more formal as time went on, as the president withdrew himself from the correspondents more and more.

In the most recent assessment of Truman's presidency, Griffith brings the president's relationship with the press into focus by inference in his general summation. It explains indirectly what lay at the core of his media problems. Griffith writes:

> It was this central tension between the local and the national, the traditional and the modern, the provincial and the metropolitan—and not just the conflict of liberal and conservative, Democrat and Republican, northerner and southerner, or president and Congress—which defined the Truman presidency. It was a tension which Truman himself never fully mastered. On the one hand his personal insecurities were reinforced by the received culture of modern America, which counseled deference to the values of education, status and hierarchical authority. On the other hand his personal resentments were sustained by the commonsensical and anti-modernist val ues of an older and very different America.

Harry Truman was still another transitional figure in the history of the presidency, but he did not change the press relationship in any significant way. The problems and tensions of the past were simply repeated. No new ground was broken.

Eisenhower: How Hidden Was the Hand?

In an America becoming inured, if not accustomed, to rapid change, the advent of Dwight D. Eisenhower was like the dawning of peace, a Rousseau-like interlude between the turmoil of the Truman years and the chaos of the 1960s and early 1970s. The voters who shouted joyously ''I like Ike'' during the campaign of 1952 continued to like him, even love him, during his two terms and for years afterward. But historians, political scientists, and the press took a different view for some time. For them, as Mary S. McAuliffe describes it, he was

> the dull leader of a complacent and uninteresting era. He was unintelligent, inarticulate, bland, passive and captive to the influence of corporate executives, who used him for their own ends.
>
> The American people . . . loved Ike for his war record and his grin. They elected him president as a kind of security blanket, so they could forget the troubles and pressures at home and abroad. The Eisenhower years, one critic [William V. Shannon] devastatingly pointed out, were the years of the ''great postponement.''

In the late 1960s, continuing through the 1970s and up to the present, a growing tide of revisionism has challenged this conception until now the idea of Eisenhower's ''hidden-hand'' presidency has become a cliché in itself. The thrust of these new appraisals has been to picture the general as a man who kept his great abilities as a leader and astute politician well hidden but nevertheless used them effectively in ways that were not apparent until the revisionists began their work—thus bringing the professionals around to the more generalized viewpoint held in happy ignorance all along by the amateurs, who never for a moment thought of Eisenhower as a weak and passive leader who permitted others to run the presidency.

The revisionists have already fallen out among themselves, however, and we now have several variations on the central theme. More recently the revisers of the revisionists have begun to publish their books and monographs, and now we can only be certain that Eisenhower was not the ''weak, bumbling, and disinterested'' president he was thought to be. The current aim is to reassess his administration and the quality of his effectiveness, with the ultimate goal of measuring his ''greatness''—if, indeed, he was ''great.'' Was he really a man of peace, or did he start us down the disastrous road that led to Vietnam? On this point, and others, there is not yet the beginning of a consensus.

There is a broad belief, however, that Eisenhower is to be admired rather than pitied or ignored and that he may be seen eventually as one of the century's most important presidents. That consensus is more convincing to the historians and political scientists than it is to the correspondents who covered him, some of them from the war years straight through the presidency. Their verdicts are somewhat sharper, as one would expect.

Eisenhower's relationship with the press had begun in 1942, when as supreme commander of Allied Expeditionary Forces in Western Europe he became the primary source of authoritative news about a war that was the best reported in the history of journalism. Eisenhower had few problems with the correspondents in those years. They saw him not so much as a great military leader—it was commonly understood that the general's function was not to devise grand strategy—but as a figure of military authority who could also be a master of public relations and coordinate the efforts of the disparate leaders of the Allied war machine, keeping such dissidents as Field Marshal Sir Bernard Montgomery and Gen. George S. Patton under control. Not without difficult episodes, he did that job superbly, and the correspondents who watched him doing it admired and liked him for the most part. In the interests of patriotism, not a word was printed of the wartime romance with his driver Kay Summersby, although it was an ill-kept secret. The supreme commander was compelled then to live in the same kind of goldfish bowl he would occupy when he came to the White House, where he would be a model of clean living.

After the war there was the brief, uncomfortable period during which Eisenhower was president of Columbia University, where he polished his skills as a billiard player in the handsome official residence on Morningside Heights while the Republican leaders dreamed and schemed to make him president. Reporters who saw him in those days found him grumpy and impatient. Academia was not his scene. He was greatly relieved in 1950 when he was recalled to the army to create the military organization of the North Atlantic Treaty Organization.

The war in Korea gave Eisenhower the opportunity to present himself, although his political ambitions were ambivalent, as a man who could and would end that conflict and give Americans the security they thought they had achieved by defeating the Nazis. His overwhelming victory in the 1952 presidential election was the beginning of a long triumphal procession. In that first election, as in 1956, the working press favored Adlai Stevenson, a gracious and highly literate man.

Something of Eisenhower's ambiguity can be seen in the beginings of his press relations. Although he had high regard for working correspondents as a result of his war experiences, he approached the institution of the press conference with distaste. Emmet John Hughes, in his political memoir of the Eisenhower years, tells us, ''For weeks before and after his first Inauguration, he grumbled and argued against even the necessity of press conferences, deploring their establishment by Roosevelt [not historically true] as a fixed form of presidential communication, and it required the persistent persuasion of [James] Hagerty to have him hold his first such conference, almost to a month after he took office.''

Eisenhower's version of how the press conferences began illustrates the ennobling view political figures take of themselves. ''One early decision of a relatively personal and yet official nature,'' he wrote in his memoirs, ''involved my conduct of periodic press conferences. These devices for informing the public had been handled differently by each President since the practice began. I determined to hold them weekly, depending on the amount of news, my location, and my involvement with official matters.''

In choosing Gov. Thomas E. Dewey's former press secretary to take over the same role for him, Eisenhower made the best choice possible. James G. Hagerty is generally regarded today as the most able press secretary since the institution began. Not only did he organize the modern system of news dissemination from the White House, but he stood at the president's elbow and steered him safely through hundreds of potentially damaging encounters—although it is hard to imagine that anything could have really tarnished Eisenhower's image. From the standpoint of historians, Hagerty performed another valued service by keeping a comprehensive diary, which unfortunately covers only a little more than a year. It has provided unusual insights, however, into the efficient operation he created.

Hagerty brought a solid background to his job. His father had been a political writer on the New York *Times* for years, and he himself served the *Times* in the same way as Albany correspondent before Dewey persuaded him to leave journalism for government service. He was the governor's press aide until he left to work for Eisenhower in the 1952 campaign, and after the election he served the entire eight years of the general's administration.

There had been other former working journalists in his job, bringing needed expertise about the press, but Hagerty possessed all the other attributes—a personality that made him well liked and much respected by the correspondents, a mind oriented toward organization as much as the general's, and, from the reporters' standpoint most essential of all, a closeness to the president. That would be a primary measure by which future press secretaries would be judged— whether or not they were so much in the president's confidence that they truly knew what was going on, or whether they were merely messenger boys and buffers.

A comprehensive summary of Hagerty's character and importance has been given us by Patrick Anderson, in his study of the men around Eisenhower. Hagerty's ''toughness, imagination, and zeal,'' Anderson writes,

> would soon make him the most effective—and historically, the most important—of all the presidential Press Secretaries. Truman's Charlie Ross and Kennedy's Pierre Salinger were better liked, Roosevelt's Steve Early and Johnson's Bill Moyers had fuller understanding of public issues, but it was the tough-talking Irishman Jim Hagerty who would have the biggest impact on the delicate relationship between the President and the press.
>
> He was the first presidential Press Secretary to be, both by instinct and experience, more of a professional public-relations man than a newspaperman. The homely, stocky, chain-smoking, hard-drinking Hagerty looked and talked like a character out of *The Front Page,* but his instincts toward news manipulation and techniques of mass psychology were as smooth and sophisticated as any Madison Avenue executive. . . .
>
> It was Hagerty's achievement . . . to manage the news in an unprecedented degree, and still maintain the confidence and good will of the regular White House

correspondents. The primary reason he was able to do this was his unsurpassed mastery of detail.

The fine touch of Hagerty was evident from the first. After the inauguration he was aware that the correspondents were speculating whether Eisenhower would hold any news conferences at all, or no more than irregularly, and if they took place, whether the unconsciously imperial manner of the supreme commander would prevail. Hagerty was able to persuade the president that it was necessary for him to continue the institution, and to do it regularly. When Eisenhower faced the press for the first time on February 17, 1953, he made the usual conciliatory overtures, going so far as to say that he knew of no individual who had been treated "more fairly and squarely" by the press. "Through the war years and ever since I have found nothing but a desire to dig at the truth, so far as I was concerned," he declared, "and be open-handed and forthright about it. That is the kind of relationship I hope we can continue." He closed with "Goodbye, I'll see you again," apparently not understanding the tradition of having the senior correspondent (in this case, Merriman Smith) end the session with "Thank you, Mr. President."

The conferences continued regularly, on the average of two or three a month, through both terms, held normally at 10:30 on Wednesday mornings in the Indian Treaty Room, following Truman's lead. How Hagerty moved these sessions away from the past into a new dimension has been described by Ray Scherer, the NBC White House correspondent who later became a vice-president of RCA:

> He [Eisenhower] prepared for news conferences by sitting down with News Secretary Hagerty, and, on occasion, selected cabinet officials. Hagerty would meet with a few of the press regulars before the news conference and tell them what was on the President's mind and they . . . would say what was on our minds, so Hagerty generally had some idea of what was going to come up so he could brief Eisenhower.
>
> Ike and Hagerty took the news conference into several new dimensions which made it a larger and more meaningful institution. For one thing, they authorized the use of a transcript. Reporters were allowed to hire an outside transcript service to come in and set up transcribing machines and then issue an authorized transcript of the news conference, so therefore you read Eisenhower in the New York *Times* and other papers the next day in direct quotes. This, of course, made the reporting of the press conferences much more vivid. He was the first president who went from indirect discourse to direct quotes. Another innovation was the use of radio recordings. Truman's news conferences were recorded, but only rarely was an excerpt given out and that was generated by the fact that somebody would ask, "Mr. Truman, may we have that in direct quotes?" He would use a particularly vivid phrase and he would say, "Yes, you may!"

But even though the transcripts contained the direct quotes, which were also heard on the radio, there was a small catch. Hagerty reserved the right to edit them, but in time the permissions became almost routine and the editing inconsequential. Hagerty would not permit live radio or television, fearing that

Eisenhower's often tangled syntax would result in what are still euphemistically called "misunderstandings." When television cameras were finally permitted, they were on tape and not live—and, as Scherer says, were really film cameras. They joined the newsreel cameras (about sixteen of both, all told) at the back of the room.

For the first time, as a result, a president was heard to speak not only on the nightly radio news shows but on the fifteen-minute television news shows as well. Before the second term was ended, NBC was able, also for the first time, to show the president in color. With the coaching help of Robert Montgomery, the screen actor, Eisenhower and Hagerty also devised evening television "specials" in which the president discussed his policies and projects with various cabinet members.

Another innovation were the informal dinners Eisenhower gave in the White House for the fifteen or so "regular" correspondents, those reporters representing the major media (newspapers, newsmagazines, and broadcasting networks). Sitting with them around a large table, as Scherer describes it, "he would hold forth in a very unrestrained kind of way. Then we would have drinks and he would sit next to the piano and hold forth at further length. Then we would all go to a hotel room and try to recapitulate what he had said. . . . He did this a number of times. These were good sounding boards for him, and he was wonderfully cordial at these occasions."

Eisenhower did not give exclusive interviews, but some reporters were able to get the equivalent by adroit work. The president had his favorites in the press. The *Herald Tribune,* chief Republican organ in the nation, was his favorite paper, and its general manager William Robinson was a good friend, as were Henry and Clare Boothe Luce, whose *Time* and *Life* usually gave him cordial support. He gave little attention to opposition papers, and it was believed he stopped reading the Washington *Post* at some point. As for the correspondents themselves, there were those he liked better than others but he kept even them at a little distance and in general exhibited a minimum of discrimination. There was always the sense that he was the general and the others were only privates.

Hagerty was ubiquitous, briefing the reporters on every detail of a forthcoming trip, paying attention to the needs of all the media, and smoothing the way for everyone in a fashion not seen before in the history of press relations. Whatever attempts in this direction had been made previously were far overshadowed by Hagerty's superb grasp of detail.

Eisenhower (with Hagerty's help) was a shrewd manager of the news, although an amateur by comparison with those who followed him, and his primary weapon was the press conference. He saw it as other presidents had conceived it, as a platform by which he could address the electorate, but he had no great expectations for it, any more than he did for the evening television shows that he was always reluctant to do, saying plaintively to his advisers, "I keep telling you fellows I don't like to do this sort of thing." He believed that the viewing public would not be intrigued by seeing him on their television screens for a half hour, but in that he was probably mistaken. The public continued to adore him through eight years of sailing on the Sea of Tranquillity that they believed he had personally created. There was little need to manipulate the media—with important exceptions, as we will see—since they generally supported him, too.

If there was a nagging flaw in this serene landscape, it was Eisenhower's awareness of the belief, fostered principally by some of the political columnists, that he was a man of inferior intellect, a conclusion based on the tangled sentences that emerged from the press conference transcriptions, even after editing. In time these reached the level of a national joke, not appreciated by Eisenhower or Republicans in general. They became the subject of parody, in a language christened "Eisenhowerese." The Gettysburg Address and other splendid documents were rendered in this arcane tongue by the humorists.

Elmo Richardson, one of the president's most recent biographers, offers this explanation of the phenomenon:

> The president . . . took great care not to reply impulsively. Precision, not style, was his concern. A perfectionist with the written word, he also tried to edit as he spoke. The resulting tangle of qualifiers and mid-sentence changes in person and antecedents sometimes resembled a literal translation from a foreign language. These responses were easily ridiculed, but none of his critics noted that the questions themselves were often poorly expressed, nor did they understand that the president frequently had to be wary of references to national security or other administratively confidential matters.

Eisenhower himself had an even more plausible explanation. "A word-for-word transcript . . . seldom reads like a polished text," he wrote in his memoirs.

> I soon learned that ungrammatical sentences in the transcripts caused many to believe that I was incapable of using good English; indeed, several people who have examined my private papers, many in my own handwriting, have expressed outright astonishment that in my writings syntax and grammatical structure were at least adequate. By consistently focusing on ideas rather than on phrasing, I was able to avoid causing the nation a serious setback through anything I said in many hours, over eight years, of intensive questioning.

(It could be added, too, that Eisenhower's language in the transcripts was no worse than can be seen in similar transcriptions of press conferences or interviews by most public figures.)

However, it is no denigration of Eisenhower to say that "at least adequate" describes his original writing, not all of which is as original as it seems. Like other public figures whose speeches are ghostwritten, Eisenhower came to believe that he really wrote the books and speeches issued in his name because he dictated the notes, or first drafts, on which the ultimate structure was built. He remained convinced, for example, that he had written *Crusade in Europe*, although in fact the actual writing was done by Kevin McCann, one of his aides, by Joseph Barnes of the *Herald Tribune*, and by assorted other assisting experts. All this, of course, is irrelevant, even trivial, in the perspective of Eisenhower's whole career; it simply illustrates one variety of self-deception that afflicts those in public life, especially presidents.

In the press conferences Eisenhower's concern for what was said extended from the original spoken words to the transcripts because the president, a cautious man in any case, was particularly aware of "the earth-shaking impact that a carelessly chosen presidential word or phrase might have," as another of his biographers, Arthur Larson, puts it. Larson emphasizes that this was why the president spent so much time preparing for the conferences, conscientiously going over every subject that might come up. The effort paid off. It is true, as Eisenhower declared in the memoirs, that in eight years he never once uttered a careless word possibly damaging to American interests or adding unnecessary fuel to controversies—a record not even approached by other presidents. (He did, of course, lie about the U-2 spy plane.) He would rather have sentenced himself to a year in the brig than to toss off a casual aside like Truman's, "Well, I never really did like Franco, anyway," in response to a question about Spain.

After taking such pains to get his ideas across without misunderstanding, it is not surprising that Eisenhower was irritated, in various degrees from growling to staff sergeant tirades, by reporters whose dispatches seemed to have lost something in the translation. Nor did he take kindly to anything that could be regarded as "interpretation," a favorite word of presidents. In his view the press should not even report on what he called "family matters," meaning events in the White House, on the ground that since quarters had been provided for correspondents and photographers in the White House, that was the same as extending its hospitality to the press. They were guests, he implied, and should behave like guests.

Such a breach of Eisenhowerian etiquette may well have been the reason he abandoned the Washington *Post* to its own evil devices after the paper reported on the rehearsal for the first of his evening television "specials." These preparations, said the *Post,* were conducted "amid strict secrecy precautions." An executive of Batten, Barton, Durstine & Osborne, the New York advertising firm, had come down to coach the president and his fellow participants, Oveta Culp Hobby, Herbert Brownell, and Ezra Taft Benson. The *Post* described his rehearsal:

> The White House itself took on something of a Radio City appearance. Television technicians and advertising agency officials scurried through the lobby in a bustle of preparations. . . . White House reporters were barred from the conference room, which has been transformed into a TV studio. . . . Although the White House had indicated the program would be "spontaneous and unrehearsed," as the television trade calls it, "cue cards" containing the first few words of each participant's remarks were set up out of camera range.

While this seems commonplace enough, even primitive, to those of us surviving thirty years later, it was vaguely shocking to many Americans who read about it at the time in the *Post* and elsewhere. These may have been among the first premonitions of the pervasive uneasiness that in time stirred beneath the surface of American life as people came to realize how thoroughly they were subjected to the images projected on the shiny tubes in their living rooms.

It was publication of this story that led the president to remark sourly on the presumed status of correspondents as guests in the White House. His reaction was mild, however, compared with the vehemence he displayed when he read in the Washington *Evening Star* a front-page headline, ''Hobby Note Flouts Segregation Order, Powell Charges.'' The story was based on a telegram to the president from Congressman Adam Clayton Powell, Jr., a New York Democrat from a district in Harlem, charging that the president was enforcing desegregation in some federal institutions but was silently permitting officials in the army, navy, Veterans Administration, and new Department of Health, Education and Welfare to practice segregation in the institutions and installations under their control. Mrs. Hobby figured in the story because of Powell's accusation that she had ''virtually countermanded'' the president's orders in schools on army posts. Eisenhower was greatly upset over both the charges and the fact that the *Evening Star* had printed them—all the more so when his advisers told him that Powell had a legitimate case. The administration had been caught off base, and, while the matter was smoothed over eventually, it was not easy for the president to forgive either Powell or the newspaper.

The major crisis—if it could be called that—in the Eisenhower administration's press relations came in the months before the second term, when such a term seemed most unlikely both to the president and others. It provided Hagerty with an opportunity to employ his maximum skill in managing the press, and it provided still another unlovely insight into the realities of political life.

In August 1955, as the St. Louis *Post-Dispatch* correspondent James Deakin has reconstructed the story, Eisenhower and his wife Mamie went to Colorado for a vacation. The president was giving every indication to the public of bouncing health. He went up to Fraser, high in the Rockies, on a fishing trip, standing in icy water and casting for hours. It was there he got word that the Soviet premier, Nikolai A. Bulganin, had sent a reply to his ''open skies'' proposal for aerial surveillance of the United States and the Soviet Union. Deciding that he must read this letter, Eisenhower raced with his motorcade down the mountain to Denver at speeds sometimes approaching eighty miles an hour—shades of Herbert Hoover!—covering the eighty-two miles in less than two hours, descending in altitude meanwhile from 8,700 feet to 3,400—foolhardly, indeed, for a man with a bad heart. Then, to compound this medical indiscretion, he worked three hours in his office at Lowry Field and went off to play eighteen holes of golf at the country club—followed, incredibly, by nine more. In between, he had lunch: a double hamburger decorated with large slices of onion. Interspersed, too, was a mixup in which he made two frustrating trips from golf course to clubhouse trying to take a telephone call from Secretary of State John Foster Dulles, inspiring a display of the famous Eisenhower temper.

The predictable result that night, after a heavy dinner and a round or two of billiards, were the chest pains that woke him at 1:30 A.M.—symptoms of coronary thrombosis, diagnosed as such by the White House physician two hours or so later. In the morning he would be transferred to a nearby army hospital. Meanwhile it was announced to the reporters at an 8 A.M. briefing that the president had ''suffered a digestive upset in the night.'' That was the beginning of the first major deception of its kind since Woodrow Wilson's stroke.

It was 2:30 in the afternoon before it was admitted that Eisenhower had suffered a heart attack. The delay, explained Dr. Howard McC. Snyder, was because he wanted the president to have a sedated rest that night, protected from any tension and anxiety, and to spare Mamie and her mother from sudden shock. The reporters accepted this explanation at first, but then, as Deakin reports, they began "to sort things out" and "the customary journalistic doubts arose as to where judgment and discretion had left off and secrecy had commenced."

There was a brief confrontation with Hagerty. Why wasn't an ambulance called? Why was Eisenhower permitted to walk downstairs from his second-floor bedroom, instead of using a stretcher, and then taken to the hospital by car? Obviously, the chosen procedure was safer and more orderly, but it was also a cover-up—a small one, to be sure and in the end not important, but, as Deakin points out, it brought into focus the whole president-press relationship as it had developed at that point. "All these tensions," Deakin writes,

> —the difference in perception between the news media and the government, the chronic dispute over secrecy, the multiplicity of facts and explanations, the question of what can and cannot be justified in the name of prudence, safety or order— underlay the brief confrontation over the ambulance that was not summoned and the stretcher that was not used. To understand those few moments in the pressroom at Lowry—why the government said what it said and why the reporters said what they said—is to understand an entire mechanism. The same tensions, the same unresolved conflicts, make themselves felt at every presidential press conference, every briefing by the White House press secretary, every face-off between journalists and officials. They underlie the entire relationship between the press media and the government. As a matter of fact, they *are* the relationship.

These tensions and conflicts, slowly accumulating since Theodore Roosevelt's day, were in essence the result of an eroding confidence in the truth of anything a president or his men might say, and that in turn was a direct product of growing presidential expertise in manipulating the media. They were trends that would reach a climax with Richard Nixon. The disturbing paradox was that the media's growing distrust of the president was matched by the public's growing distrust of the media.

The seven weeks in the Denver hospital were followed by five more at the farm in Gettysburg, Pennsylvania, where Eisenhower suffered the depression that often accompanies recovery from heart attacks.

The chief political question was simple—not *should* he run again, but *could* he? Eisenhower wanted to believe he could. The Republican managers wanted to believe it, too, because they were convinced that other possible candidates, particularly Vice-President Richard M. Nixon, could not be certain of victory. In any case, Eisenhower had never trusted Nixon since the famous Checkers speech of 1952, in which Nixon successfully defended himself on television against accusations about a private political fund.

Eisenhower decided (intimates said it was Mrs. Eisenhower's decision) that he would indeed run again, and that was announced on February 29. The president returned to Washington, and on the night of June 7 he retired after the annual dinner of the White House Photographers Association only to wake up after midnight with stomach pains that were diagnosed at 2 A.M. as an intestinal blockage—ileitis.

Now Denver was reprised. At 8:30 next morning Hagerty told the press that Eisenhower had an "upset stomach and headache. . . . There is nothing wrong with his heart." At 10:30 he assured them again that it was the kind of stomach upset anyone could have. At 12:25 he called the correspondents to his office and told them the truth, adding that the president was being taken to Walter Reed Hospital. The cover-up had been much briefer this time.

On June 9 a team of army surgeons performed an ileo-transverse colostomy on the president, bypassing ten inches of the ileum, part of the small intestine. After the surgery Hagerty assured the reporters that the president looked "very good and in good spirits." Then he set about the task of using the press to convince the voters that, whatever might be said to the contrary, the president could run for reelection.

In Hagerty the president had a press secretary with a newspaperman's knowledge that told him what to do about this particular problem, even if he was not especially concerned about the broad issues involved. His response was to give the reporters so much information that they had no way of knowing whether they were getting too much or too little. Medical bulletins were issued four times a day. Questions were answered promptly and sometimes in excessive detail, including the entire recipe for a vegetable soup the president's valet had made for him.

For seven weeks there were four briefings a day. The total statistics disclosed what a massive operation coverage of the president had become: two and a quarter million words filed to newspapers, wire services, and magazines by the correspondents assigned to Eisenhower's seven-week stay in the hospital—a contingent numbering more than a hundred reporters, photographers, and cameramen. To those who cite these figures as the beginning of what would be called overkill today, it may be answered that they reflected the tremendous growth of the media since the close of the war, to which television was a prime contributor, although it was still in its relative infancy.

This coverage reached its ultimate absurdity in the press conference held by Dr. Paul Dudley White, who headed the team of doctors treating the president, in which he reported the medically significant fact that the president had been able to have a normal bowel movement. Since it was still considered indelicate to speak of such functions in family journals, how to handle this news caused crises in some newspapers, and particularly at the Associated Press, whose numerous clients were bound to be of diverse sensibilities. In some papers the art of circumlocution enjoyed its finest hour, but the reporters themselves, as Deakin tells us, were rudely overjoyed by this event, and a Boston journalist, remembering Emerson and the bridge at Concord, paraphrased the sage of Cambridge in irreverent but memorable verse:

O'er this rude pan that arched the bed
His ass to autumn's breeze unfurled,
Our embattled prexy sat,
And fired the shit heard round the world.

Such *lèse majesté*, of course, never reached the correspondents' newspapers even in a milder and printable form. Eisenhower was much admired by the majority of newspaper publishers, most of whom were Republicans, and consequently editors kept a careful rein on the news from Washington, so that the general climate of newspaper coverage became as bland as the administration itself. This made Hagerty's job much easier.

At the same time the reporters did not entirely overlook political overtones, so that when White was describing the president's bowel movement, they were also aware of the scarcely hidden political message that Hagerty was conveying to them elsewhere in the briefing. White's pronouncement declaring Eisenhower's chances for a complete recovery were "reasonably good" meant he would be able to run again for a second term.

As time went on, Hagerty continued to feed the reporters with stories of the decisions the president was making from his convalescent bed. As he knew it would, the fact of the decisions made the headlines and the front pages, while the additional fact, pried out from a reluctant Hagerty, that Eisenhower was not strong enough to devote more than a few minutes to decision-making and was not completely in charge of his job by any means, remained buried in the story, as the secretary also knew and intended it to be. The reporters understood what was really occurring, but there was no way of reporting it without charging something they could not prove.

Hagerty continued to give the impression that the president was recovering rapidly and conducting the nation's business ably from his hospital room. Nevertheless, Eisenhower had to go back to his Gettysburg farm, where it took him five more weeks to recover from the operation, the second major medical crisis the sixty-five-year-old general had survived in less than a year. But the imperatives of political power wait for no man. He ran again, was reelected, and, ten months after he was sworn in, had a stroke.

This time Hagerty was in Paris, and Anne Wheaton, his associate, had to handle the press. Although the cerebral occlusion was diagnosed almost immediately, it was twenty-four hours before the press and the country learned the truth; "nothing serious" had been the first pronouncement. During that time the utmost confusion prevailed in the West Wing, where the correspondents were trying to find out what was happening. When Wheaton gave them a statement at last, its language was obscure and reporters could not be certain the president had suffered a stroke, although they were fairly certain that was the case. Under a storm of persistent questioning as the correspondents tried to pin her down, the beleaguered associate secretary at last admitted that the president had suffered a "form of heart attack," but when someone pointed out that the medical bulletin had used the word "cerebral," she admitted further that it might have something to do with the head. Having had it both ways, the United Press made its own diagnosis. Eisenhower, it said, had suffered ''a heart attack of the brain,'' thus writing a new chapter in medical history. It was never officially admitted that Eisenhower had been felled by a stroke.

In fact, as soon as Hagerty returned, the comforting news was soon pouring out about the president's rapid recovery, how he was working while he sat up in an easy chair, joking about the ''slight difficulty'' he had in pronouncing words. The storm was a small one. Eisenhower was back in his office a week later, the papers reported the cover-up without making an issue of it, and the matter quickly faded away. In the current context the event was unimportant, but in a larger context it was an ominous forerunner of what would soon be common practice in the conduct of the presidency. During Eisenhower's years in the White House, Hagerty stood between him and the press at every point of contact, sitting behind him at the press conferences, accompanying him constantly. The president displayed his dependency openly, often checking with the secretary before he answered a question, at other times telling the reporters that Hagerty would explain something to them later, which they took to mean that he would translate what the president had said. Hagerty did not even hesitate to appear swiftly at Eisenhower's side while he was answering questions, saving him from bear traps.

No amount of rhetoric by revisionist historians, consequently, will convince reporters who were there that Eisenhower was deliberately obfuscatory in his language, that he used battered syntax to conceal what he was doing, and that he always *knew* what he was doing. If he did conceal his real actions and used language as a weapon in that process, he was, as Deakin and others have pointed out, lying. If he did not, the fact that so many different interpretations could be placed on what he said would testify to a certain fogginess of perception and knowledge. Self-preservation may be a better description of the Eisenhower process with the press than Machiavellian control.

The president had another weakness where the press was concerned. He could not accustom himself to its persistence in trying to get the news, something he had not experienced as supreme commander, and he did not know how to deal with it. His first reaction was bewilderment, after which came anger. He tried to curb the importunities of the correspondents as much as possible by confining his contacts with the press to the conferences, where he and Hagerty could exert some control. Consequently he had 193 press conferences in his eight years, an average of two a month, but he seldom met reporters anywhere else. Occasionally he invited a few elder statesmen of the press, men known to be friendly, to stag dinners at the White House—such correspondents as David Lawrence of *U.S. News & World Report,* Roscoe Drummond of the *Christian Science Monitor,* and Richard Wilson of the conservative Cowles publications. Walter Lippmann, one of the administration's most perceptive critics, was never invited.

Whatever else he may have been, Eisenhower was shrewd enough to understand his position in the president-press relationship. He knew that the correspondents were the enemy and that a general gets the last word, especially if he happens to be president. He also sensed the mounting public hostility toward the press, and at the Republican convention of 1964, which nominated Barry Goldwater in a paroxysm of mistaken conservative fervor, he deliberately touched that raw nerve when he told the delegates to pay no attention to "sensation-seeking columnists and commentators, because, my friends, I assure you that these are people who couldn't care less about the good of our party." The media people present were appalled by the reaction to these words. As Deakin recalls it, "the convention exploded in a pandemonium of rage against the news media. The delegates stood on their chairs, shouting, raving, shaking their fists and cursing the reporters in the press section."

The net result of Eisenhower's dependence on Hagerty to conduct his press relations, orchestrating them every step of the way, was to make the secretary a part of the decision-making process, which he was not reluctant to undertake, although he was neither ambitious nor egotistical enough to overreach himself. But he was also acutely conscious of the public relations function, to keep the president's image brightly polished, and, in doing so, he shaped the pattern which subsequent secretaries have followed, that is, always to be sure that the image comes first in the list of priorities. The correspondents understand that the secretary might have a responsibility to them, but the president must always come first. Everything that is done must put him in the best possible light, regardless of the truth or any other consideration. Thus the adversary relationship is institutionalized.

Yet the occasional confrontations between Eisenhower and the press during the conferences, when the telltale crimson flush began to suffuse the president's neck and face, seldom spilled over into the news stories. Somehow that much derided quality, objectivity, prevailed. In spite of the correspondents' increasing skepticism about everything that came out of the White House—indeed, out of any part of the government—there was still a respect for the presidency itself; that further loss was still to come. Besides, however skeptical the reporters might be, there was no disposition on the part of either them or their editors to permit much of this to seep into the news columns, especially where a president so popular was concerned, who survived the usual scandals of his administration because no criticism would stick to his exterior or dent his general public image. Eisenhower was the Ronald Reagan of his time. When the lies of his administration were exposed by the press, the truth was not believed by the public, which in any case did not *want* to believe it. An imposing structure was rising on the earlier foundations of the imperial presidency.

Kennedy: The Refinement of Manipulation

Was it Camelot or the beginning of a nightmare? That question haunts the historians as well as the public when the brief presidency of John F. Kennedy comes into view. Now that the blurred vision of the stricken car in Dallas, the indelible image of assassin Lee Harvey Oswald's anguished grimace as he clutched his stomach after he was shot, and the heartbreaking sound of muffled drums in the funeral cortege have all faded into memory—already ancient history to a new generation of students—we have come to grips with the hard questions. Americans had not experienced such hope and adoration since Franklin Roosevelt's advent, nor such grief at his passing, made the worse by its shocking nature. The conception of the martyred president who, for one glorious moment, visioned the American Camelot dies hard, yet it appears to be dying nonetheless. The revisionists are at work, but a great deal needs to be done before Kennedy can be seen with some measure of unemotional objectivity. And since he is inseparable from his volatile, controversial family, the task becomes even harder.

An examination of Kennedy's press relations may not shed much light on these unresolved questions, but it does offer further testimony as to how the imperial presidency continued to develop and how the persisting efforts by the White House to harness the press in the interests of the government—making it "part of the team"—were carried out by a man likely to have been recognized as a master of the art if he had lived.

Kennedy had the necessary equipment to become that master. As a former newspaperman himself, who could have made a career of it, he understood the mechanism of the press, if not its overall purposes; he had an acute sensitivity to public relations and how to use the media; and he had the kind of attractive personality that drew media people to like and admire him, in the same way he affected so many others. The reporters joined the public in liking Ike, but they found Kennedy much more congenial. He was more like them.

It was not love at first sight, however. Only 16 percent of the press backed Kennedy in 1960, but that represented the disaffection of the publishers; he was, after all, a liberal Democrat. The working press traveling with him during the campaign had come to love him, warts and all. The warts were already visible.

Given this situation, Kennedy came to the same conclusion several of his predecessors had reached: he would use the correspondents to appeal to the people over the heads of the publishers, an unusual misjudgment for so knowledgeable a politician who was also possessed of more than ordinary intelligence. He had, it seemed, learned a great deal about the political process but not much about media history.

The model, of course, was Franklin Roosevelt, as well as the first Roosevelt and Woodrow Wilson, all of whom had mounted the "bully pulpit" with more or less success. Kennedy worked assiduously to surpass them all, and, in sheer numbers, he did so. During his three years he gave nine television reports to the nation from the White House. Moreover he made many more public speeches in his brief time than Wilson or either of the Roosevelts, and he was equally prolific in his meetings at the White House with every kind of opinion-maker. He used the press with great skill, and he showed the way to others in his use of the new medium, television.

To his followers in the press, however, and even to some of those close to him, it was not considered to be enough, at least in the beginning. Arthur M. Schlesinger, Jr., the eminent historian who became resident White House intellectual, notes that as early as March 16, 1961, he had written in a memo to the president: "There is increasing concern among our friends in the press about the alleged failure of the Administration to do as effective a job of public information and instruction as it should and must. Lippmann had a column about this last week. Joe Alsop has been haranguing me about this over the telephone and plans to do some columns about it soon. Lester Markel is going to do a long piece about it in the *Times Magazine*."

Markel, the prickly Sunday editor of the New York *Times,* had come directly to the president with his complaint, Schlesinger recalls, apparently under the impression that FDR and the others had used the "bully pulpit" much more than was actually the case, in comparison with what Kennedy was already doing. The president knew better. "Lester has been in here saying that I ought to go to the people more often," Schlesinger remembers Kennedy telling him. "He seems to think that Roosevelt gave a fireside chat every week." (The correct figure for FDR was thirty chats in twelve years.)

For some reason never sufficiently explained, Kennedy was often reluctant to hold press conferences, even though he proved to be more skillful at it than any president since FDR. His average was only twenty-one a year, lower than either Eisenhower or Franklin Roosevelt. However, the conferences marked still another step forward (if that is the correct phrase) in the development of the institution. For the first time many of them were on live television and proved to be mass exercises in confrontation on a scale not seen before, making his success in handling them all the more remarkable.

To help him in and out of the conferences, Kennedy had the valuable services of Pierre Salinger, who came upon the White House stage saddled with the fresh memory of Hagerty, the hardest kind of act to follow. Salinger succeeded on his own terms. He had come from a family much interested in politics, although not politicians themselves, to whom the Great American Game was prime table conversation. When he got out of the navy in 1946, it was natural that he would want to get into the game himself, beginning with working in the San Francisco mayoralty campaign, later in Adlai Stevenson's 1956 run for the presidency. He also became a working journalist, with fourteen years on the San Francisco *Chronicle* and as a writer for *Collier's.* In September 1959 he went to work for the Kennedy campaign, and, by the time it had ended, he had proved to the successful candidate that he could handle as many as five hundred reporters—the number gathered in Hyannis on Election Day.

As press secretary, Salinger demonstrated a professional competence that equaled Hagerty's in many respects, operating with an insouciance much like the president's own style and some distance removed from his predecessor's more old-fashioned approach. It helped, too, that Salinger's heart was firmly with the media; after the assassination, he returned to journalism and ultimately to broadcasting for ABC in Paris. Salinger had no illusions about his relationship with the president. He realized that Kennedy could have been his own press secretary, given the time to do it, but he deftly took whatever part of the load it was necessary to bear, and, at the same time, he made some bold steps forward in advancing the technology of the job.

The major advance was to take the carefully edited press conferences of the Eisenhower regime into the hazardous glare of the televised live press conference. There were those who grumbled that it was theater, not news, and there was some truth in the complaint, but with an actor like Kennedy on the stage, it was a move that did more to promote his image than any number of the old conferences could have done. Kennedy usually had the facts ready in his agile brain, he was blessed with quick recall, and the inspiring personality that had won him the election made a vivid impression on the national audience.

Kennedy was the first president who understood how to use television, at a time when television was at last ready to be used, in ways that would soon begin to alarm both politicians and critics of the political process, who sensed in it an overwhelming presence that was capable of rendering the past obsolete. The president understood its possibilities and some of its dangers as well. For instance, he could see that television might be too much of a good thing, and for that reason he limited his exposure through the press conferences. But the networks were now lengthening their fifteen-minute evening news broadcasts to a half-hour, and Kennedy was first to recognize that a president could appear on them as a news-maker even when there was no real news to make. He became such a television virtuoso, in fact, that admiring and envious congressmen came over from the Hill to the State Department's new auditorium, in that district of Washington known aptly as Foggy Bottom, to observe the conferences and see how he did it.

To prepare for the conferences, Salinger refined the briefing book techniques in use for some time, which had been carried several steps forward by Hagerty. Besides giving the president a briefing before the conferences, Salinger instituted the two-a-day briefing for correspondents, which he or one of his deputies presided over. At these sessions the correspondents could expect the release of routine news, but they were also given the opportunity to clarify previous information given to them. After the Kennedy era these sessions drifted into an irregular one-a-day pattern.

Salinger was responsible for two other innovations. As associate press secretary, he brought in Andrew Hatcher, a journalist he had known in San Francisco, who was the first black to hold such an office. Later he created the post of assistant press secretary in charge of the foreign press. Jay Gildner, brought over from the United States Information Agency, held the job for a time, to be succeeded by Malcolm Kilduff, who came from the State Department. There were only five other people in the office, a token staff by comparison with the vast Reagan operation.

The correspondents had confidence in Salinger because he passed their primary test: he was close to the president, seeing him five or six times a day, able to walk into his office without permission—access the White House calls "on a need basis." Salinger remarked, long after he left his post, that he believed there was little negative reaction on the part of the press toward Kennedy because the president thought the relationship "should be as open and direct as possible. . . . He got angry with the press from time to time, but I think any President has some problem with the press. But he took a keen interest in what was said about him, as I think any President does. He was very accessible, and he would see newspapermen on an individual basis, perhaps several a day at the White House."

It was not only the print media reporters Kennedy saw. The television correspondents were making their presence felt for the first time, and soon they would be the stars of the show. They had not been included in pools on presidential trips before, but now Kennedy gave them the power base from which their stature grew. Still, print continued to dominate the White House press hierarchy. As always, the wire services stood at the top because they reached the most people. Then came the leading newspapers, beginning with the New York *Times,* and after them the major newsmagazines. For the moment, television ran last.

From the standpoint of the inner circle, the press conferences showed the president at his best, as Schlesinger recalls, offering "a showcase for a number of his most characteristic qualities—the intellectual speed and vivacity, the remarkable master of the data of government, the terse, self-mocking wit, the exhilarating personal command. Afterward he liked to relax, watch himself in action on the evening news and chat about the curious habits of the press."

As a newspaper reader, Kennedy equaled or surpassed FDR, but, unlike Roosevelt, he expected his staff to be equally well informed about what the press was saying. Like any other president, he was annoyed by stories that attacked him, particularly those that were the result of leaks—the obsession of every president, in varying degree. Once he canceled the White House subscription to the *Herald Tribune* because he objected to its "biased" coverage of concurrent investigations into scandals of his own and Eisenhower's administrations.

If there was one conflict with the press during his brief term that surpassed the others and made them seem trivial, it was the still-debated circumstances of the Cuban missile incident, the major crisis of his administration. After Sen. Kenneth Keating, an upstate New York Republican, charged that the Soviets were building missile bases in Cuba, there was growing public pressure to do something about it; some Republicans were even calling for invasion. Kennedy's response was to try to smother the movement by laying down a barrage of press conferences and speeches designed to play down the surge of jingoistic (and partisan) fervor. In spite of strong press support from many papers, principally the New York *Times* and the Washington *Post,* this strategy proved to be unconvincing, as the polls showed. Because Kennedy at the moment had no other strategy to answer increasing public concern, he saw that it would do no good to use his new weapon, television. As a result, in the subsequent battle for page one the administration lost out to its Republican opponents within a few short weeks between late August and early September 1962. A few distractions helped them momentarily. By means of strategic leaks and background briefings, the public was given to understand that a new crisis might be pending in Berlin. That reduced Republican access to the headlines for the time being.

But then, with dramatic force and suddenness, Kennedy appeared on television on October 22 to confirm that Soviet missiles were indeed in Cuba and announced a naval blockade. With that, the critics disappeared from page one. Then came the president's prime-time ultimatum to the Soviet Union, demanding removal of its missiles, and the showdown with Premier Nikita Khrushchev. This and subsequent events lay within the framework of modern presidential management of the news, particularly in crisis situations, which began with Kennedy.

As a president in good standing with the press, Kennedy could seek its cooperation and get it, as he did with the New York *Times* in particular and a few other leading publishers, convincing them on grounds of national security to withhold publishing what they knew about the crisis until he delivered his ultimatum. Afterward he instituted a systematic control of the flow of information to the press, and thence to the public, until the crisis was over. Control, in blunt terms, meant lying, and the implications of this practice rose to the surface when Assistant Defense Secretary Arthur Sylvester, the Pentagon's chief information officer and a former newspaper editor, called news part of "the arsenal of weaponry" in the cold war and asserted "the inherent right of the government to lie . . . to save itself when faced with nuclear disaster."

The resulting heated controversy was unilluminating. True, Sylvester had spoken inprudently, but what he said was actually a question of semantics. If he had declared that the government was justified in lying to save itself in such a circumstance (although the country was not faced with nuclear disaster in this case, unless self-inflicted), that would have been at least debatable. "Inherent right" was another matter, and most of Sylvester's and the government's critics centered their attacks on this extremely dubious, if not outright fallacious, proposition.

A recent study by Montague Kern, Patricia W. Levering, and Ralph B. Levering of Kennedy's methods in handling the press during the several foreign crises of his administration (Laos, in 1961; Berlin, in the same year; Cuba, in 1962; Vietnam, in 1963) aptly summarizes Kennedy's press management in the Cuban crisis:

> During the time between Soviet Premier Nikita Khruschchev's capitulation on 29 October 1962 and the mid-term congressional elections nine days later, Kennedy combined a stated policy of seeing no reporters and allowing no members of the Executive Committee (EXCOM), which had managed the crisis, to talk to the press with an actual policy of allowing selected members like McGeorge Bundy to see selected reporters. The result was a series of approving "now-it-can-be-told" articles in favored large-circulation magazines and newspapers. Kennedy himself was soon on the phone talking with journalists about Cuba and politics.

As these researchers point out, Kennedy worked hard at his press relations. He prepared carefully for his press conferences, used them skillfully to promote his policies, and developed more contacts with editors, publishers, and reporters than any of his predecessors. It was well understood by the correspondents that those who wrote favorable stories would be thrown some delicacies from the inside news table, while those who persisted in being critical would not be likely to get much extra help in their White House labors. In this the entire Kennedy clan was united, especially the president's brother and attorney general Robert F., who was much more sensitive to criticism. The Kennedys wanted to make the "good" reporters feel like honorary members of the family. Bernard Eismann, then a CBS correspondent, recalls that when he was reproached by Ethel Kennedy for a story he had put on the air, he asked her if it was wrong, and she replied, "No, Bernie, but palship counts for something, doesn't it?" * Reporters who demonstrated suitable palship were suitably rewarded.

Kennedy's method of broadening his press contacts was unique. He gave luncheons from state to state for editors of papers that had circulations of twenty-five thousand or less—a direct means of getting to the grassroots and possibly to help dispel the impression that he was a child of the Eastern Establishment, which no one could doubt. He knew personally most of the editors of the large papers, and he charmed them all except for the ironbound Republicans. It was a method, taken in context with his other manipulations, that was calculated to alienate as well as attract, since the less favored or ignored were inclined to be skeptical and even those who were being wooed were not insensitive to the fact that they could be thrown into the Camelot moat if an offense against the court were committed. In November 1962, after a year of Kennedy charm, William V. Shannon wrote in the New York *Post* that the president was devoting "such a considerable portion of his attention to leaking news, planting rumors, and playing off one reporter against another, that it sometimes seems his dream job is not being Chief Executive of the nation but Managing Editor of a hypothetical newspaper."

By about mid-1962, as Schlesinger notes, the guerrilla war between press and government in the Kennedy administration had reached a point where both sides considered the other hypersensitive to criticism. The reporters complained about the stick-and-carrot approach, while the Kennedy people protested that, if they dared to disagree with the story, they were immediately charged with managing the news. *Look* magazine had been one of the recipients of favors in terms of planted, more or less exclusive stories, but when it printed a catalog of Kennedy offenses against the press, the president laughed, according to Schlesinger, and observed, "This is the best example of paranoia I have seen from those fellows yet."

While he might show flashes of anger over a particular story, Kennedy almost never displayed the kind of outrage so many of his predecessors gave voice to when they were pushed beyond their particular level of tolerance. Asked at a press conference in the spring of 1962 what he thought of the press, he replied:

Well, I am reading it more and enjoying it less—[laughter]—and so on, but I have not complained nor do I plan to make any general complaints. I read and talk to myself about it, but I don't plan to issue any general statement on the press. I think that they are doing their task, as a critical branch, the fourth estate. And I am attempting to do mine. And we are going to live together for a period, and then go our separate ways [laughter].

It was lucky for Kennedy that he enjoyed the fondness and admiration of the press corps, by and large, because his private life, notably his sexual activities, was an open secret to many, if not most, of the reporters. While these amorous interludes were the subject of Washington gossip and spoken of freely in private by the correspondents, the general public knew nothing of them. Even the most critical columnists did not hint at this situation, and it was some time after Ken-

---

*Bernard Eismann to authors, July 18, 1984.

nedy's death before it was discussed more or less openly, and even then in an indulgent tone by most. At the time, however, it could have been a political disaster if any of the details had reached an electorate that likes to think of itself as moral.

But they did not. Camelot's towers were unsullied. Reporters who came up from Washington on weekends when the president was spending happy evenings at the Hotel Carlyle simply took a night or two off in New York, knowing where he was and making only cursory checks to see that he had not slipped off somewhere else, which would not have been impossible. It may have occurred to them later that if, by some bizarre mischance, the Dallas assassin had been at the hotel instead, they would have been left in the cold on a story much larger than the interludes they chose to ignore.

That was only one of the Washington stories that did not reach the press in this or any other administration. A New York *Times* managing editor, on a brief inspection tour of the Washington bureau, once sank back in his chair at the National Press Club after a day in which he had talked to several staff members, hearing a large quantity of information everyone knew, and asked plaintively: "Why don't I see any of these stories in the New York *Times?*" Those were the realities of politics he was talking about, which never reach the public for several reasons having nothing to do with the suppression of news—and if they did, they would not be believed by readers, who would accuse the press of slandering good men.

Kennedy escaped a great deal of censure and much more possibly damaging exposure of sins (which were, after all, irrelevant) because he was, more than any other president has been, where the reporters were concerned, one of the boys. He could talk shop with them, knew many of them socially, and enjoyed being with them. He was as much at home with them as he was with politicians. Yet, as his good friend and speech writer Theodore G. Sorenson observed,

There remained a curious dichotomy in his [Kennedy's] attitude toward the press. He regarded newsmen as his natural friends and newspapers as his natural enemies. He was more concerned about a news column read by thousands than a newscast viewed by millions. He both assisted and resented the press corps as they dogged his every footstep. He had an inexhaustible capacity to take displeasure from what he read, particularly in the first half of his term, and an equally inexhaustible capacity to keep on reading more than anyone else in Washington. He always expected certain writers and publications to be inconsistent and inaccurate, but was always indignant when they were. While he fortunately grew insensitive to old critics, he remained unfortunately too sensitive to new ones. He could find and fret over one paragraph of criticism deep in ten paragraphs of praise. He dispensed few favors to his journalistic friends [Sorenson was extremely charitable here] but ardently wooed his journalistic foes. He had an abhorrence of public relations gimmicks, but was always acutely aware of what impression he was making.

Few, if any, Presidents could have been more objective about their own faults or objected more to seeing them in print. Few, if any, Presidents could have been so utterly frank and realistic in their private conversations with reporters and so uncommonly candid in public—but few, on the other hand, could have been so skillful in evading or even misleading the press whenever secrecy was required. Finally few, if any, Presidents could have been more accessible and less guarded with individual reporters and editors—or more outraged when anyone else "leaked" a story.

More than any other president, Kennedy understood the press. He once told Sorenson, "Always remember that their interests and ours ultimately conflict." But he realized the importance of a free press in a free society, as he demonstrated in observing that "the totalitarian system has many advantages such as being able to move in secret . . .[but] there is a terrific disadvantage in not having the abrasive quality of the press applied to you daily. . . . Even though we never like it, and even though we wish they didn't write it, and even though we disapprove, there isn't any doubt that we could not do the job at all in a free society without a very, very active press." He had never told a reporter friend what to write, he once said, so he could hardly start telling him what *not* to write.

As the foremost newspaper reader among presidents, Kennedy not only looked through a large sampling of the domestic press, including the social, sports, and financial news (even some of the gossip columnists), but he was equally fascinated with periodicals, absorbing a broad range of them (at least sixteen) from *The New Yorker* to *Sports Illustrated*. Besides all these he sampled the foreign press as well—several British papers and journals and *Le Monde*. Of the newsmagazines, he was a constant reader of *Time* and *Newsweek* but disdained *U.S. News & World Report*. In the case of *Time,* he read it and despaired. As Sorenson says, he regarded it as "consistently slanted, unfair and inaccurate in its treatment of the Presidency, highly readable but highly misleading." That feeling was particularly difficult for him because Henry Luce was an old friend of the Kennedy family, and Hugh Sidey, *Time*'s White House correspondent, was a man whom he "continually befriended, chastised and sought to enlighten," in Sorenson's words.

Sidey's public view of Kennedy, apart from his magazine, was not unfriendly, but neither was it uncritical. In his memoir of the president, published the year of the assassination, he wrote:

> Reporters are an adaptable breed, and they can get used to almost any conditions. But what would remain most unsettling to them was Kennedy's awareness of every word printed about him. Personal references bothered him much more than did attacks on policy.
>
> So often—for years—correspondents who wrote about the president had felt they might be writing in a vacuum for all the reaction their words provoked. But Kennedy changed all this. Every word, every phrase was absorbed, tested for its friendliness, dissected and analyzed with scientific precision, to detect the degree of approval or disapproval. Even at moments of crisis he would not ignore words about himself. When he was asked why he concerned himself with what was written, he asked simply, "Would you rather I didn't read it?" . . . For all of Kennedy's cunning about public relations and his profound knowledge of reporters and the American news business, there was trouble ahead for him in his relations with the press.

In retrospect, Kennedy's relationship with the press remains as complicated as his personality. An immediate affinity was established as the candidate traveled about the country in the campaign of 1960, and liking turned to respect and admiration when his television debates with Nixon, the first of their kind, appeared to be a turning point. There were four of these hour-long "Great Debates," as they were called, carried by all three networks, in which a youthful, confident Kennedy offered a vivid contrast to the dark-jowled, almost receding Nixon personality.

The debates were a landmark event in the history of television's relationship to presidential politics, now a question of considerable magnitude, and they produced a torrent of studies from the wizards of opinion and attitude research, more than any other single public event had evoked. They were viewed as a triumph for television as much as for Kennedy, yet their actual effect on the campaign remains a matter of controversy. Kennedy won the election by a margin so narrow that it alarmed and amazed his managers, and later there were unsubstantiated reports that irregular vote counting in Democratic Chicago, a perennial phenomenon in that unregenerate city, had given the new president his narrow, decisive edge.

But if the debates were an uncertain triumph for television, Kennedy certainly made a major contribution to the new medium when his first press conference was televised live from Washington, on January 25, 1961, only five days after he took the oath of office. There were 418 reporters, a record crowd, jammed into the room, blinking in the bright television lights, aware that sixty million people were about to see what was taking place. Shrewdly, the broadcast was scheduled for the dinner hour. It was a thirty-nine-minute virtuoso performance, and, as Charles Roberts, of *Newsweek,* who was there, recalled: "I sensed from the moment the President walked onstage that the presidential news conference would never be the same again. It had not only become 'show business'—confirming the dire predictions of recalcitrant writing reporters—it had also, as *Newsweek* noted in its next issue, opened 'a new era in political communication.'"

Live cameras transformed the press conference, making it a "bully pulpit" more powerful than anything Theodore Roosevelt could have dreamed of and giving the president a platform, as Roberts puts it, "from which he could speak, literally, over the heads of reporters and editors, anchormen and commentators . . . directly to the voters on any issue at almost any time." It was a historic and major breakthrough. Audiences leveled off, after the novelty had worn away, to a mere six million, but Kennedy and his men knew they had in their hands an instrument of power no president had ever before possessed.

But if Kennedy was able to go over the heads of the press, at the same time he made it possible for the reporters to go where Eisenhower had forbidden. Except for Sherman Adams, the White House staff had been off limits to the press in the general's administration, but Kennedy permitted the correspondents to talk freely with key members of his team, either in their offices or at lunch. That made it somewhat easier for them to accept the dazzling way in which the president exploited television, particularly the "specials," which were such a success. For a print reporter, it could have been unendurable to see Mrs. Kennedy taking millions of viewers on an hour-long tour of the White House in 1962, into places where neither the public nor the press had been permitted to go.

As time went on, it was clear to the reporters that even when all the unprecedented positive aspects of the relationship had been added up, the one grinding negative factor remaining was that what Kennedy really wanted from the press was cheerleading, not criticism, and in that respect he was just as old-fashioned as those who had come before him. They saw him become hypersensitive and petulant toward many of their number, and a certain disenchantment set in, although a *Look* survey showed that the correspondents were about evenly divided over the administration's knuckle rapping. The critical reception of Kennedy's blackout of the news during the Cuban missile crisis seemed to give him pause and some concern, but there was worse to come.

The "worse" was Vietnam. Here, during his administration, were laid down the lamentable foundations for the structure that brought Lyndon Johnson to ruin and confounded Richard Nixon. In Saigon, far from the Washington scene and the semibenevolent Kennedy touch, correspondents were experiencing their first difficulties in getting information from American officials. These were respected figures in the business—Homer Bigart and Keyes Beech, among others—and they complained. Kennedy responded by sending an envoy to Saigon with instructions to clear away some of the obstacles. That was done, silencing the complaints for a few months.

As a result of this liberalization, Kennedy and his advisers expected to see more stories coming out of Vietnam that they would rather not read, but they were not prepared for what emerged when the spigot of truth was turned on—or distortion, as it was immediately labeled. For the first time Americans learned from these stories how heavily the United States was becoming involved, with some loss of American lives. Obviously the war in Southeast Asia was widening, an impression Kennedy did not want to give to the electorate. Consequently, against Salinger's advice, he withdrew part of the carrot and ordered rules enforced that would make it difficult for correspondents to observe field operations themselves. He had been particularly angered by a story reporting the shooting down of eight American helicopters. Why he believed the fact that there were only five was a better as well as a more accurate way to look at it became a part of the ghastly fabric of deceit and stubborn wrongheadedness being woven by the American government.

With such initial actions, the greatest confrontation between presidents and the press in American history began, stretching over three administrations. The pattern was clear from the beginning. Presidents wanted to downplay the war that was never declared and pursue their policies in Vietnam no matter how much they were opposed at home. The press, and particularly the reporters on the scene, wanted to report fully and expose what would become a national tragedy. Compromise was immpossible, although Salinger and a few others around Kennedy believed they could find a middle ground. In the end the Vietnam War had a great many damaging and enduring effects on American life, as most people now understand, but among the worst were the government's accelerated loss of credibility, which it has never regained, and the creation of a vast reservoir of public hostility toward the press as the messenger bearing the bad news it did not want to hear.

The driving of the wedge between press and government in the Vietnam War began in the closing months of Kennedy's time in the White House, starting in late 1962, when the mutual hatred between President Ngo Dinh Diem, his brother Ngo Dinh Nhu, and Nhu's wife and the American correspondents erupted into a battle in which Kennedy backed the Vietnamese. The Diem family succeeded in getting Francois Sully, Saigon correspondent of *Newsweek,* and James Robinson of NBC expelled from the country, but it was not as easy to rid themselves of the three correspondents they particularly despised: David Halberstam of the New York *Times,* Neil Sheehan of UPI, and Malcolm Browne of the Associated Press. These three men were not only officially opposed by the United States mission in Saigon, but Kennedy suggested to Arthur Hays Sulzberger, who had just become publisher of the *Times,* that Halberstam be given another assignment. In his Kennedy memoir of 1966 Salinger argues that, although the three reporters did their job well and faithfully from a military standpoint in reporting the war, their accounts of the Saigon government's crisis in 1963 reflected their hatred and bias against the Diem family. In the light of subsequent events, however, their stories seem models of restraint, and these correspondents went on to be considered among the best.

What was developing in the Kennedy administration with the coming of the Vietnam affair was the extension and modernization of an old doctrine—that it was unpatriotic to report anything that put the government in a bad light and that self-censorship by the press was necessary in the interests of national security. The government, of course, would always determine what was national security. Kennedy developed this idea as a result of the Bay of Pigs fiasco in 1961, in which he had tried to intimidate the New York *Times* through pressure on its publisher, persuading it to suppress its accurate advance story of the event. This attempt succeeded only because of cold feet on the part of the *Times*'s management; its news executives had already locked it in place as the lead page-one story. A vague, truncated story was substituted.

Ten days after the Central Intelligence Agency led its troops to ignominious defeat in Cuba, Kennedy spoke to the American Newspaper Publishers Association, in New York for their annual meeting, and advised the owners that the news media must come to grips with their responsibilities "in the face of a common danger: the totality of the Communist challenge to our survival and to our security"—a warning we are still hearing today, twenty-five years later, and in the same sense Kennedy used it, directed at the same audience. Continuing his call to arms, Kennedy asserted: "If the press is awaiting a declaration of war before it imposes the self-discipline of combat conditions, then I can only say that no war ever posed a greater threat to our security. If you are awaiting a finding of 'clear and present danger,' then I can only say that the danger has never been more clear. . . . [I ask] every publisher, every editor and every newsman in the nation to re-examine his own standards, and to recognize the nature of our country's peril." They were almost the same words, in the same context, that President Reagan was intoning a quarter century later.

In his speech Kennedy raised the specter of how "this nation's foes" were getting information from the newspapers that they would otherwise have been compelled to obtain by spying, including "details of . . . covert preparations to counter the enemy's covert operations." His elaboration of this theme made it appear that the nation's press, witting or unwitting, had become an arm of the Kremlin. How to end this subversion? Easy. Kennedy invited the newspapers to ask themselves with respect to every story not whether it was news but whether it was in the interests of national security. He added that, if the press would voluntarily set up the machinery to enforce this self-censorship, it would be assured of the wholehearted cooperation of his administration. No one could doubt it.

The media responded with an indignant refusal to embark on any kind of censorship program, to go on a war footing in peacetime, or to define national security every day, or even accept the president's (any president's) definition of it. What was astonishing was the reaction of such astute professionals as Kennedy and Salinger. They were surprised and disappointed, they said, by this "violent" media reaction, and a little indignant, too, on their own account.

Deakin points out, and others have confirmed it, that Kennedy made this speech because at the time, humiliated by the outcome at the Bay of Pigs, he blamed the media for his failure, declaring they should not have printed anything about it. When he had recovered, he completely reversed himself and asserted the *Times* should have printed more, not less, of its invasion story. It was one of the first major nails in the coffin of credibility.

Nor did the president learn anything from this episode. In October 1962, as the Cuban missile crisis developed, Kennedy issued a memorandum to the news media listing twelve categories of information the government believed was vital to national security and therefore publication would be "contrary to the public interest." This was a bald attempt at official censorship in peacetime, as no war or national emergency had been declared. At the same time State Department and Defense Department officials were forbidden to talk to reporters unless a third person was present or details given afterward to the information office. The State Department rescinded this rule when the crisis was over; Defense did not, for many months.

Thus the way was paved for later confrontations in the Vietnam era and an intensification of these doctrines when Ronald Reagan came to power. For the time being, however, Kennedy emerged after his martyr's death as a hero. His feet of clay took some time to expose, and, even now, two decades after his death, historians and media people who knew him well are not agreed whether the clay or the bulk of the statue represents the real man. There appears to be a consensus that no president ever enjoyed a better relationship with the media, making his administration an island in a historically turbulent sea.

But there are dissenters here as well. For example, Harrison Salisbury, the noted New York *Times* correspondent and its former assistant managing editor, has asserted: "The greatest con game in the world was done by Kennedy so that many people thought that he just loved the press. I knew Jack Kennedy very well, and I know he hated the press. It's very normal for a president to have that attitude. I don't think there is any other way for a president to be, but I often smile—a sweet sad smile—when I listen to some of my colleagues who regarded themselves close to Jack.'' Deakin, however, sums up the majority opinion succinctly: ''Kennedy's dealings with the media were normal; a mixture of seduction and hostility. It was the last 'normal' situation for ten and a half years.''

Johnson: A Struggle to the Death

Suddenly Kennedy was gone, and, in the aftermath of the nation's shock and horror, there stood Lyndon Johnson in the White House. No greater change ever took place in the presidency. Shelves of books, thousands of articles, endless newspaper columns, uncounted numbers of doctoral dissertations, and a vast array of other forms of pontification have tried to explain what happened in the next five years. These labors have been mighty and not in vain. Those who have worked through even a fraction of this outpouring now understand Johnson far better than they did while he was in office. Yet he is still difficult to grasp or explain in his entirety, and it may be that the psychohistorians will have the last word.

Assessment is complicated, of course, by the shattering events that took place during Johnson's administration. There was the coming to grips at last with the question of black civil rights and Johnson's response to these and other domestic social concerns by his attempted creation of the Great Society, with both the conflicts and positive good that action generated. Then, overriding everything else, there was the reaping of the whirlwind Kennedy had sown—the Vietnam War, which divided the country as nothing had done since the Civil War (and before that, one might add, the American Revolution). The resulting civil strife over both these issues tore the nation apart beyond Johnson's power to repair it. He became the victim of his own policies, good and bad.

If Johnson's relationship with the press was only one aspect of these major events, as it would be in any presidency, nevertheless in his case it is a relationship that tells us a great deal about the man. It goes beyond the relatively narrow scope it implies, because the president's conduct contributed heavily to the continuing loss of credibility in what the government says and does—or says it does. This gap has, in turn, increased widespread distrust of the presidency except among devoted partisans, the uninformed, and the apathetic. At the same time it has also further lowered public confidence in the press, as noted before.

The sum of all that has been written about Johnson is that he was one of a kind. No man even remotely like him has ever occupied the White House, and, while that might also be said of Richard Nixon and Ronald Reagan, Johnson outranks them as a unique figure in American politics. His relationship with the press combined all the worst elements of what had gone before, leaving scarcely one redeeming feature to permit a charitable conclusion. And the press responded by fighting him as it had not fought anyone since Lincoln.

The shape of things to come could be seen from the beginning. Marianne Means, of the Hearst papers, one of a slowly growing number of women correspondents, recalls that Johnson's first conference was ''the usual nervous kind of a hullabaloo,'' which might have been understandable in the circumstances. But then,

> by his second press conference he was really a very changed man. You could tell the difference between his first press conference with the nervous laughter and the jokes written out in advance and the second when he did pretty well. So I wrote a comparison between the first and the second press conference saying how much better he was. He was in command, you know, he seemed more like a president. So the next time I see him, what does he say? ''You didn't like my first press conference? What was wrong with it?''

Aside from Johnson's complex personality, there were additional reasons why his press relations could not have been other than disastrous. As majority leader of the Senate, he had long been accustomed to having a small group of reporters whom he could bully into submission, or, if not, seduce with favors. Since that had worked so well, he assumed it would be just as effective with the White House correspondents—a major mistake. He favored seduction because he believed it had been Kennedy's highly effective technique.

In the tangle of his love-hate feelings about the dead president, Johnson admired Kennedy's ability to charm the press but at the same time hated him for the qualities which made that possible. Johnson could never get over the feeling that this Harvard man, this intellectual, this representative of the elite Eastern Establishment had cast a shadow on him that he could never emerge from as a man who was the antithesis of everything the former president represented. It was much worse than the shadow that Blooming Grove had cast on Warren Harding.

But if seduction was to be the name of the game, Johnson decided, he would play it in his own style, which meant outsize and excessive. Consequently he removed the boundaries that still existed for the reporters and invited them, in essence, to become a part of his family, giving them free access to virtually every part of the White House except the bedrooms, and including the Oval Office. He openly courted such *pooh-bahs* of the press as James Reston and Walter Lippmann, inviting them to his office and asking their advice, which of course he had no intention of taking. At his first Christmas as president in 1963, he sent his own plane to bring Reston and his wife from Phoenix to the Texas ranch.

Nor did he mean to ignore the foot soldiers for the elite. He gave them private interviews, sometimes over lunch, and when he went down to the ranch to relax, he did not disappear from view for the most part, as previous presidents had done. On that first Christmas he invited three correspondents who were standing by in Austin, fifty miles away, to come over to the ranch for a fish fry, where he gave them what came to be known as ''The Treatment,'' talking for hours with complete freedom about policy matters. On other occasions reporters were subject to chats that gave the appearance of being confidential, conducted wherever Johnson happened to be—on the front porch, rocketing around the ranch at high speed in his car, at parties on his motor launch, or even in his bedroom, and on one or two celebrated occasions, in his bathroom.

It was, as the columnists Rowland Evans and Robert Novak pointed out in one of the first assessments of Johnson, in 1966, a conflict between the private and the public person. In the Senate the reporters had been relied upon not to disclose too much about Johnson's private person, since they were then presumed to be part of the senator's entourage. In the White House the correspondents were certain to print as much about the private person as they could, and he gave them ample opportunity. This situation was complicated by the fact that Johnson had acquired a typically presidential view of the press—that the reporters wrote only what their employers ordered—consequently he treated them with suspicion and a certain contempt. He saw every story in a newspaper, or article in a magazine, as something that was either inspired by a political adversary or ordered by a publisher. Further, he made the serious mistake of trying to deal with fifty or more White House correspondents in the same way he had dealt with the dozen or so regular reporters he had had to contend with in the Senate.

One of Johnson's most difficult psychological problems was his underlying lack of confidence in himself, despite the surface appearance of overwhelming bravado. Seeking always to divorce himself from any comparison with Kennedy, he refused at first to undertake the televised press conferences that his predecessor had instituted in the more spacious arena of the State Department auditorium. He had serious, and justified, doubts about himself as a television performer. He preferred to return to the days of FDR's regime and meet the White House regulars only in the Oval Office, but he gave in to the pressure from his advisers for more exposure and made himself available to the television cameras at Kennedy's former site in April 1965. Having made the point, and proved that he could do it, he retreated again to his office for subsequent conferences.

As George Reedy, who became his press secretary, put it, Johnson had the press "eating out of his hand" during the first six months he was in office,

> but he kicked that away himself. He'd get mad at them for some reason, and they couldn't understand it. Everything was overdeveloped in Johnson. He simply could not understand why it was he could buy a reporter a drink and take him out to the Ranch, show him a good time, and that reporter would write a story he didn't like. Again, I think that's because Johnson had so little respect for the integrity of words. I think he thought words were just something you used as weapons. He himself really didn't know what a good story was. He thought a good story was something that began, "Lyndon Baines Johnson is a calm, collected statesman who is the finest representative of the American dream."

Hugh Sidey of *Time,* in an assessment of Johnson at the end of his term, believed that the president scorned the press as he did the intellectuals, ranking them in the same class. When he said "the press," he usually meant "the columnists," a conception prevalent among the public today. It was hard for him to understand their world since it was so alien to the one he had always known. In his world, as Sidey says, if you made a deal and gave something, you got something back. Consequently he considered it bad manners when a reporter, after getting "The Treatment," wrote something he thought was adverse. "Why, I had that man at my table and then he went out and did that," Johnson complained in one such instance. "His idea of great flattery to a correspondent," Sidey writes,

> was to take the man under his arm, wine him and dine him and entertain him, treat him to a few innocuous secrets, and then suggest a story line. If it came out as Johnson wanted it to, he invited the fellow back for more intimate moments. And that time there was apt to be a call from the President himself to the publisher or editor of the man's paper and a spirited Johnson tribute over the phone. How little Johnson understood the responsible press was evident when, with the reporter listening, he passed out his most lavish praise. He would tell the publisher or editor that this correspondent was the best in the White House press corps because he had written that story just the way the President of the United States wanted it written. Any self-respecting editor, of course, made a mental note to consider shifting such a reporter from the White House beat. Any self-respecting reporter tried to avoid such suffocating embraces in the future. Unfortunately, too many editors and reporters liked to get those telephone calls and liked to hear that kind of tribute.

A press secretary as powerful as Hagerty might have been able to save Johnson from some of his worst mistakes with the press, but none of the four who served the president in a little more than five years was able to control him to any extent, although in George Reedy he was fortunate enough to have one of the best. Even for Hagerty, however, the job could well have been impossible.

Coming to the White House at a moment of crisis, Johnson did not want to upset the existing machinery for the time being, and so he accepted Pierre Salinger as an inheritance. He immediately ran through that inheritance in a succession of incidents, notably his idea that Salinger should take position papers prepared by Jack Valenti and Horace Busby, the president's Texas aides, and plant them with selected reporters. Then he asked Salinger to complain—in his own name, not the president's—to reporters who wrote unfavorable stories, in at least one case excommunicating a correspondent who had angered him. In vain Salinger tried to convince Johnson that, if he did good things, he would get good publicity, which otherwise could not be manufactured by any process known to him. He also took pains to point out that Johnson really had nothing to complain about from the press in these difficult transition days, when the media were willing to give him the benefit of every doubt.

It was no use. The president simply could not understand. It was typical of him that a man like Salinger at whose house Johnson had been entertained in December 1963 could no longer stand living with him by March 1964. Salinger, who at the time had political ambitions of his own, resigned on March 18 to run for the Senate from California.

There was no question in the president's mind where he would turn. He called George E. Reedy, who had been on his staff for thirteen years before the assassination of Kennedy. Reedy had been a wire-service reporter in earlier years, inspired to a newspaper career, no doubt, by his father, George E. Reedy, Sr., who had been a crime reporter for the Chicago *Tribune* in the *Front Page* era. The younger Reedy could have pursued virtually any career he chose, however, because he had an IQ that made him a child prodigy, and in his college career at the

University of Chicago had majored in sociology, emerging as an intellectual who might have been expected to undertake more scholarly pursuits.

Instead Reedy went to work in the Washington bureau of UPI, and, after a wartime interval in the Pacific as an air force intelligence officer, he went back to the same job, which led him into the embrace of Senator Johnson. Reedy was not unaware of the senator's faults but believed the man could get useful things done and was convinced he would one day be president. Resigning from UPI in 1951, he went to work full time for Johnson and became perhaps the most brilliant man to occupy the press secretary's chair—and the most besieged.

When the president called him in his hour of sudden need, Reedy was in Doctors Hospital, not far from the White House, trying to lose some of the 295 pounds that had accumulated on his six-foot-two-inch frame. He was also catching up on his book reading. Eric Goldman, who remained for a time as the resident intellectual in the White House until it became clear that the president thought intellectualism might be subversive, asserts that Reedy "had a swift, powerful mind, a delight in books and talking about them, an instinct for philosophical quandrums, and a quiet, subtle religious faith."

Reedy also knew, as a result of long experience, what Lyndon Johnson wanted, and he understood that the president's relations with the press were already beginning to deteriorate before they had barely begun. There was, first of all, the Bobby Baker scandal, in which the Senate was investigating the fast-track operations of a man who had been Johnson's friend and (although he denied it) protégé. Then had come that celebrated first Easter holiday as president, when Johnson, by now feeling himself firmly in the White House saddle and coming out from under the Kennedy shadow, celebrated by cramming six reporters, including three women, into his cream-colored Lincoln Continental and taking them on a whirlwind tour of the LBJ spread at ninety miles an hour, balancing a paper cup of beer on the dashboard and drinking from it intermittently. When a woman reporter in the back seat called out a terrified protest over the speed, the presidential driver simply put his Texas Stetson over the speedometer. Reporters and photographers, following in five other cars, watched the president's erratic progress with delighted fascination.

Naturally the story was widely told in the press, with comment ranging from sober (and often horrified) concern for the president's life to *Time*'s description of him as "a cross between a teen-age Grand Prix driver and a back-to-nature Thoreau in cowboy boots." When he read these accounts, Johnson was enraged, and he was annoyed enough by *Time*'s story to call its Washington and New York editors. In fact, the image projected by all the media accounts alarmed the entire staff for its political implications, and these fears were confirmed by the indignant editorials pouring from clean-living moralists. Most of all, Johnson could not understand how these guests of his, whom he had treated to such a good time, could betray him.

Bobby Baker and high life on the ranch were not all of Reedy's immediate problems, by any means. He had to deal with a president who did not want set press conferences in the traditional way, for which everyone could prepare on both sides, but much preferred suddenly called briefings in his office or walks around the White House grounds, where he could "look my questioners in the eye," as he phrased it. When he traveled, the arrangements were also dismayingly haphazard. Worst of all, the reporters were becoming increasingly unlikely to believe what the president told them. The credibility gap was beginning to open wider. Johnson made statements that turned out to be wrong and denied rumors that proved to be true.

Reedy did his best to repair the damage, but it was a losing struggle. His conception, as he said later, was that the president had political problems, not press problems, but in fact they were inextricably mingled. Reedy was further handicapped by the fact that the correspondents were soon aware he did not have the full confidence of his boss—not that anyone else could have merited it. At the beginning they had supposed him to be close to the president as the result of their long association, but then it turned out that the president had a loudspeaker connection with the room where Reedy held his own meetings with the press and listened to the proceedings. When something disturbed him, according to Marquis W. Childs, he rushed out of his office and into Reedy's, bearing corrections and his own comments. (Reedy denied that this ever happened except on one occasion.)

Another complication was Reedy's conception of his job. He did not mean to be Johnson's public relations man but a conveyer of all the information that could be reasonably expected from the president, relying on the press thereafter for fair treatment. That was not, as we have seen, Johnson's notion, and inevitably there were differences of opinion. Reedy was not the kind of man to be pushed around, although some correspondents believed he was. He said later:

> I regarded the press staff as primarily a service institution and thought that razzle-dazzle public relations would actually be harmful to the Presidency. LBJ, on the other hand, thought that the purpose of the office was to get his name in the newspapers. He had grossly exaggerated views of what Michelson had done for Roosevelt, Hagerty for Eisenhower, and Salinger for Kennedy. We reached a complete stalemate and it is true that information was withheld from me because he wanted to save it and redesign it for "public relations." I also developed some strong reservations about the war in Vietnam and about some of his Great Society programs (which I believed were raising expectations that could not be fulfilled as long as the war was going on and therefore would breed cynicism). My private expression of views served to increase the gulf between us.

Lady Bird Johnson was not on the secretary's side at this point, and it was at her urging, according to most accounts, that Reedy gave in to the pressure and resigned early in July 1965, needing surgery for a painful foot problem and at odds with the president over his Vietnam decisions. Both Johnsons wanted William Moyers as Reedy's successor, and he agreed to add the press secretary's job to his other responsibilities on Johnson's staff. Moyers, another Texan, who had worked for LBJ's radio and television stations in Austin and later on his Senate staff, was also an ordained minister. At the time of Kennedy's assassination, he was deputy director of the Peace Corps.

Arriving in the hornet's nest of the Press Office at the age of twenty-nine, Moyers proved to be an entirely different sort of individual. He appeared to regard Johnson with a kind of amused tolerance, which the president found baffling, according to Alfred Steinberg, who quotes the president as telling a visitor: "That boy has a bleeding ulcer. He works for me like a dog, and is just as faithful. He never asks for anything—but for more work. He won't go home with that bleeding ulcer until nine or ten o'clock. I don't know what I'd do without him." Theodore White saw Moyers as "shy . . . witty, thoughtful, of definitely superior quality, he was, however, difficult to get to and so dedicated to the President's privacy that one could only vaguely guess where, in his all-embracing functions, was the main thrust of his influence."

Moyers, too, did his dedicated best for eighteen months before he resigned in 1966, a departure that appeared to reflect, as in Reedy's case, his differences with the president over Vietnam and his feeling that Johnson was inflexible. His departure brought on George Christian, a man who had something of Hagerty's background, having been press secretary to two Texas governors, Price Daniel and John Connally, before he came to Washington in 1966 as W. W. Rostow's aide in National Security.

The correspondents, in general, viewed Christian as a technician, and many thought he served Johnson better than the others because of his belief that the press secretary's job was simply to give the president's views to reporters as accurately as possible. The White House press corps, for the most part, agreed that he did just that and, further, that he possessed the other all-important ingredient—the president's confidence. His lot was made somewhat easier, too, by the fact that, in the last year or so of Johnson's presidency, the president was not behaving like a man who expected to succeed himself. In the first place, there was the matter of the Tet offensive in 1968, when a Viet Cong enemy portrayed previously by both Johnson and the military as on the brink of defeat suddenly launched a coordinated, massive attack on more than a hundred South Vietnamese towns and cities, of such ferocity that it reached the grounds of the American Embassy in Saigon. At home, during the month this conflict raged, viewers of American television got another bloody firsthand look at the realities of the war, and it marked a turning point in the public's view of both the war and Lyndon Johnson. The Tet offensive remains a matter of controversy, kept alive by those still trying to justify the Vietnam tragedy, but at the time it was a stunning blow to the president.

Through it all, and through succeeding crises, George Christian exhibited the same unwavering loyalty and integrity that had appealed to the president and impressed the reporters, even though the credibility of Johnson and his military leaders was slipping rapidly. Reedy and Moyers had possessed these qualities in abundance, but somehow it had not worked out quite the same way. It was logical that Christian should go on to a successful public relations career after he left the White House.

The celebrated "credibility gap" was probably the most explosive and significant element in the history of Johnson's press relations. Some scholars have characterized it as a myth, but the facts appear to be otherwise. If that makes the gap between scholars and correspondents on the scene appear to be even wider than usual, it may be because academic researchers, by training, examine every piece of available evidence, consider all the alternatives, and inevitably come to conclusions that can only be open to further questions. If they marshal their evidence to prove a thesis, other scholars selectively assemble evidence from the same sources (and sometimes others) to prove them wrong.

In the case of Lyndon Johnson this kind of methodology was offered particularly rich supplies of source materials because of the president's highly ambiguous nature, in which he was often apparently unable to distinguish between what was true and what was not, handling the facts in whatever way would serve him best. Some biographers have attempted to explain this by picturing him as a true product of the American frontier, a Texan who exemplified the tendency of the pioneer culture to create instant myths—the tall tale, the exaggeration for the sake of humor or emphasis, the larger-than-life approach to everything.

While this theory may be convenient enough to satisfy the psychohistorians, the reality that the reporters who covered Johnson every day had to face was the dense, tangled web of lies, half-truths, evasions, and image-making about Vietnam, begun in the Kennedy administration but reaching its full flowering under Johnson. In his speech of March 31, 1968, during which he proclaimed a partial pause in the bombing of North Vietnam and at the same time announced he would not run for the presidency again, it was significant that neither statement was believed by much of the press, or by many other Americans in and out of government. It was soon clear that the first statement was another mishandling of the truth; it took time to prove him correct on the second.

When the bombing "pause" was attacked, Sen. Mike Mansfield defended the president by asserting that he "did not lie. Technically he is correct." That was exactly the point, as Deakin has observed: "Technically he was correct. That is the story of so much of the credibility gap—the half-truth, the manipulation, the distortion."

It is worth remembering that the credibility gap between the president and the press initially, then the public, began in August 1964 with the Tonkin Gulf Resolution. This was the result of a claim that the destroyer *Maddox,* along with other naval units, had been fired on by North Vietnamese torpedo patrol boats. The clash, if it actually occurred, took place outside the three-mile limit recognized by the United States but inside the twelve-mile limit claimed by Hanoi. A second encounter, of more dubious validity, occurred the next day. What actually occurred in the Gulf of Tonkin is still a matter of dispute, but there is no doubt about what happened in Washington. The president asked for a congressional resolution that would give him the authority to take "all necessary measures to repel armed attack," and although there was great uneasiness and controversy in Congress, he got it on August 7. It gave Johnson what he wanted: a blank check for the president to make war. An incident whose authenticity was challenged almost at once by some portions of the press became the starting point for America's real entry into the Vietnam quagmire.

In the campaign of 1964 the Republican candidate, Sen. Barry Goldwater, was portrayed by the Democrats as a dangerous hawk, while *their* candidate, the accidental president, was cited as a man who, in his own words, would never send American boys to fight a war that should be fought by the young men of Asia. Within months of the election, however, Johnson was at work escalating the war, substantially increasing the American commitment, and the press began to learn a great deal more about his credibility.

It took much longer for the public to learn about it, so skillfully was the lying done, and because of the reluctance of so many people to believe what their government was doing. Presidents did not lie. Military leaders in the field did not lie. That was the national mythology. For a long time, until the overwhelming rush of events proved otherwise—events that television made appallingly plain—the public generally believed it was the media that were lying. Everyone knew the press did not tell the truth, as presidents had always reminded them. Millions still embrace this doctrine, in spite of all evidence to the contrary.

Johnson was obsessed with secrecy, as his successor proved to be. He concealed facts not only from the press but from his own staff, even from cabinet members. Some had to read the newspapers to find out what was happening to them. The regular White House correspondents were the first to understand that such obsessive secrecy, with its consequent evasions and outright lies, was Johnson's disease. Day by day, incident by incident, this relatively small group of newsmen watched the disease spread like a rapid cancer. But when they tried to tell the public about it, their efforts often not only antagonized the president but sometimes threatened their own credibility as well.

Gradually, and grudgingly, the truth emerged in bits and pieces, leading to the miasma of alienation, withdrawal, suspicion, cynicism, the revolt of the young, the disquiet of the parents, the polarization of America—all the agonizing elements that characterized the Vietnam era. The public reluctantly came to understand the difference between Johnson's public and private personae. What they saw was so ugly they did not want to believe it, but the words and pictures they were confronted with could hardly be denied, although strenuous efforts were made to do so.

Most alienated of all, perhaps, was the press. Whatever the president's virtues might be, and whatever the faults of the correspondents, they could not help but react strongly to Johnson's dark side because they saw it constantly, and just as constantly heard themselves lumped in with his numerous enemies. Deakin summarized their feelings succinctly:

> White House reporters groan inwardly when they see one of Johnson's humility fits coming, for they have glimpsed the hard man beneath the mush: Johnson slicing up a reporter for asking a ''chicken-shit'' question; Johnson impugning another newsman's patriotism for daring to inquire critically about the Dominican intervention; Johnson bludgeoning Senator Frank Church for his reservations about the Vietnam war (''Okay, Frank, next time you need a dam in Idaho, ask Walter Lippmann for one''); Johnson excoriating another Vietnam critic as ''that (obscenity) Hartke''; Johnson neutralizing a diplomat's career with a stroke of his pen across a promotion list because the man once disagreed with him; Johnson blasting a team of magazine reporters (''Someone ought to do an article on you and your damn profession, your

First Amendment''); Johnson warning the Republicans via the grapevine that if they press him too hard on Bobby Baker, some G.O.P. tax returns will be audited; Johnson in a bloody undercover war to the death with Bobby Kennedy, no holds barred, no quarter asked or given.

As Doris Kearns, one of his associates, observed, "It was the contrast between this earthy man and the image of the pious preacher he projected that did Johnson in."

The president was a man obsessed with television as well as secrecy, yet television constantly betrayed him with its merciless, revealing eye trained upon him, and its devastating reporting of the Vietnam War, while secrecy resulted only in more exposure. Kearns recalled later:

Television and radio were his constant companions. Hugging a transistor radio to his ear as he walked through the fields of his ranch or around the grounds of the White House, Johnson was a presidential teenager, listening not for music but for news. The transistor gave Johnson an exclusive beat, allowing him to play newscaster, dispensing bits and pieces of the latest news to his staff and guests. Since he liked to watch the evening news on all three networks at once, Johnson had the famous three-screen console built into the cabinet beside his desk in the Oval Office, and a duplicate installed in his bedroom. He had it equipped with an automatic control so he could tune in the sound of whichever network was, at that particular moment, commenting on him or his activities. To the left of the console stood the wire tickers— AP, UP, and Reuters—the keys steadily imprinting the bulletins across the unrolling paper. "Those tickers," Johnson later said, "were like friends tapping at my door for attention. I loved having them around. They kept me in touch with the outside world. They made me feel that I was truly in the center of things. I could sit beside the ticker for hours on end and never get lonely."

Although his own television appearances were dismal, since he was so afraid the profane, ungrammatical, impulsive Johnson would slip through before he could stop it, the president embraced the rapidly developing medium and its accompanying technology. He read his set pieces (offering an image of "feigned propriety, dullness, and dishonesty," as Kearns says) surrounded by the sheltering arms of the bulky podium the reporters called "Mother" because it seemed to embrace him with its arms containing microphones, the teleprompter visibly rising from its top. It was Johnson's security blanket; he took it with him everywhere he had to speak, and without it he was in a panic.

"Mother" could not save him from the press, and it was Johnson's final conviction that it was the press which sabotaged him. He believed he was loved by the people, but that when the papers were constantly telling them that he gave uninspired speeches and that the war against Vietnam was a bloody mess, they gradually stopped coming to hear him and began to think he was wrong about the war.

In the president's mental state, the world had become black and white (if he ever thought it was any other way), and in this fantasy world it was easy enough for him to identify heroes and villains. To confront it, he organized the White

House like an imperial court in which, as George Reedy described it, there was "one purpose and one purpose only—to serve the material needs and the desires of a single man." The imperial presidency was in full flower. In this atmosphere of yea-sayers and sycophants, the irreverence, disbelief, and often hostility of the correspondents were a galling contrast.

But it was television that proved to be the real villain. More than the papers, it was television's images of the war in Vietnam that ended Johnson's presidency. Those images daily contradicted his view of the conflict and helped to alienate the public from both it and him. Combined with the continuing exemplification of these images in the press, and the rolling barrage of opposition to the war from campuses across the nation, making headlines and more images, the net result could only be political extinction. Television brought to millions of people an image of the president that may have only suggested what the reporters saw, but was enough in itself, coupled with the Vietnam images, to unseat him. As Hugh Sidey summarized it:

> Rather than making it possible for a President to build any image he pleased, as some political experts at first feared, the persistent exposure on TV clearly stripped away the make-believe. The real man stood exposed as no one in history had ever been. While Johnson could carefully regulate the cameras in the White House, he could do nothing about those which greeted him in every city in the country, and just about wherever he went in Washington beyond the Mansion gates there was a camera crew to record his words and his actions.

If he could not control television, Johnson did, for a time, have hopes of exerting some kind of control on the press. He was convinced that people believed what they read in the papers, and consequently it seemed logical to him that the way to deal with this situation was to change what the papers printed. If it was not safe to trust people with the facts, then he would create facts they would believe. But the "facts" which he and his aides concocted were so obviously not facts at all that the battle he fought against his steadily slipping credibility was a losing one almost from the start.

In the beginning, at least, Johnson's relations with the press improved or deteriorated in rough cycles, coinciding with his unpredictable moods. Sometimes he was in a state of euphoria after making a hard decision, inclined to be generous and to tell the reporters he gave them an A-minus. Then something would go wrong, the reporters would convey it to the public, and he would tell "your cruel little press" how contemptible he thought the bearers of bad news were. At the start he had tried to woo the media, to take them into camp by sheer force of his personality—"make big men" of those who consented to be taken—and when this tactic failed miserably, he fell into a state of disillusionment and bitterness from which he never recovered.

It was perhaps the most turbulent presidency in American history, one in which historians are still trying to weigh the substantial benefits of Johnson's domestic program against his conduct of the war in Vietnam. One negates the other, but in what degree it will take future revisionists to assess. There is little doubt, however, about Lyndon Johnson's legacy in the president-press relationship. His personality and his actions went beyond the normal tug-of-war between the press and the president, leaving an indelible mark on what followed and creating an atmosphere by no means dissipated today.

The atmosphere Johnson created with the press, and in time with the public, was one of distrust and suspicion. The press saw itself struggling against manipulation by a president who, with the rise of television, had a new and powerful instrument thrust in his hands, although he did not understand how to use it. Most of all, it was the development of the image-making concept and of the means by which a president could project a picture of himself that was contrary to the facts. Johnson failed abjectly in that respect. The images of the war he created were flatly contradicted by the reality reporters gave the public from the field, in words and pictures. The image of the man was similarly destroyed. Yet the mechanism was there, to be used in behalf of a president who might not be so outsize, so flamboyant, so delusional and obsessive that he could discern the true shape of neither himself nor the world.

Nixon: Imperialism Rebuked

Not much can be said of Richard M. Nixon, Johnson's successor, beyond what he himself and thousands of others have said in voluminous detail. We are close enough to the event so that we are speaking now of a man alive and able to defend himself, at length, and whose persistent campaign to rehabilitate his reputation has not been unsuccessful, which tells us a great deal about the American people and their presidents.

The details of Nixon's rise and fall are thrice familiar. Not only is there the small mountain of printed detail, but television has brought the dramatic collapse of his presidency directly into the homes of most citizens, and the rehabilitation process appears on their screens by the courtesy, and money, of the very networks that Nixon, as president, tried to control if he could not destroy. His similar attitudes toward the press have been rewarded in this latter-day atmosphere of Christian forbearance and cheek turning by applause from the same publishers who were once the objects of his deepest contempt. When he appeared in May 1984 at the annual meeting of the American Society of Newspaper Editors in New York, the former president was greeted with nearly a minute of enthusiastic applause from some of the same people who had once regarded him with deep, justifiable suspicion and hostility. Yet the man himself had not changed, admitting nothing except errors of judgment, defiantly unrepentant.

"I have no enemies in the press whatsoever," he told them blandly, projecting the image of the new Nixon, the latest of several to emerge from this multiphasic personality during a long political life. If that assertion was true, it was a confession of moral failure on the part of the press and a shortness of memory more typical of senility. At his last appearance before such such a group, the Associated Press Managing Editors convention in Orlando, Florida, in November 1973, he had told them, "I am not a crook." Few in the audience could have believed him then; in 1984, when the ASNE editors confronted the same man, there appeared to be none ready to accuse him of crookedness or anything else. The essential hypocrisy and unreality of politics were never better illustrated.

Nixon's method of dealing with press and television had been on display long before he came to the White House. These incidents had certainly conditioned his attitude toward the media and shown him the way they could be used to seize power and influence voters. He discovered the power of the press to set events in motion when his part in the unlikely discovery of the incriminating "pumpkin papers" led to the trial of Alger Hiss. Here was a real discovery. A young and relatively obscure congressman could become a national figure overnight simply by having his name associated with a major event. As vice-presidential candidate on the Eisenhower ticket, and more accomplished by this time, Nixon had employed basic emotional appeals in the famous Checkers speech, as noted earlier, to vindicate himself when he was first charged with deception. Later, as vice-president, there would be the Kitchen Debate with Premier Nikita Khrushchev, where the image of confrontation, not what was said or done, would be used to create a positive public reaction. But Nixon rehearsed much of what was to follow when he confronted the assembled reporters after the race for the governorship of California and told them, like a defiant child, "You won't have Dick Nixon to kick around any more," expressing both his masochism and paranoia toward the press in blaming it for his defeat.

Thus Nixon entered the White House with press relationships already determined not only by virtue of his personality (which continues to be dissected as though it were a perpetual cadaver) but by those attitudes toward the press that he had long since made clear. Battle lines had been drawn, as they had not been in any previous administration. In the subsequent struggle a large portion of the public continued to believe, as it does today, that Nixon was victimized by a hostile, Eastern Establishment press, full of liberals and quite possibly dictated to by the Kremlin. Part of this continuing trust in Nixon was a result of the deep division over Vietnam, but a significant portion arose from the increasing public unwillingness, beginning with Kennedy and Johnson, to believe that presidents could and did lie and manipulated the public through the media.

Unlike Johnson, Nixon well understood these attitudes, and in time he developed the means to exploit them, with the intention of further discrediting a press he had given up trying to control. He also developed numerous protective devices to conceal what he and his closest associates were doing, meanwhile, as we know now, also paradoxically creating the means to disclose everything, or nearly everything. If the Johnson White House had been Byzantine in its operations, it had remained within the context of American politics; with Nixon, it came close to being clinically institutional.

Before total amnesia overtakes both press and public, it may be worthwhile here to review briefly exactly what it was that Nixon did which produced his epic battle with the "elitist" newspapers and with those who, as he thought, conspired to bring about his downfall. It is a catalog much too lengthy to be given in detail, but the outlines will suffice.

Watergate still stands as the symbol of Nixon's disgrace, yet that was only one episode, although the critical one, in his plan to exalt the presidency, and himself with it, to an imperialistic eminence not previously envisioned by anyone. It was to be, in the end, a concentration of power in the executive branch that would make Congress and even the courts subservient. Nixon expected opposition and some measure of exposure from the press, but he meant to counter that by the customary evasions and falsifications, and, where those familiar techniques failed, he intended to employ threats and intimidation if necessary to silence the media as far as possible, meanwhile employing his stalking horse, Vice-President Spiro T. Agnew, to conduct a campaign against the press through speeches and other public statements that would exploit underlying public hostility. It was a grand design that might have succeeded if it had not been for the inept bungling of the Watergate burglars, those amateurs whose relatively trivial operation eventually destroyed the careful work of the professionals.

Nixon was a politician who held grudges, who wanted to get even with and punish those who opposed him or did him wrong. He could not forget how, in the 1960 campaign, as we have seen earlier, television had relentlessly exposed his dark jowls as looking unshaven and his general manner as that of an earnest high-school debater, in contrast to Kennedy's handsome, confident appearance. In his memoirs, recalling that period, he noted "the substantial and influential power that the emergence of television as the primary news medium gave the reporters, commentators, and producers. It was largely they who decided what the public would hear and see of the campaign." Nixon had already identified television as his principal enemy in the media, but he had long been convinced of the press's enmity, and the campaign against Kennedy had only reinforced that conviction. "Another new political phenomenon," he wrote, "was the way so many reporters in 1960 became caught up in the excitement of Kennedy's campaign and infected with his personal sense of mission. This bred an unusual mutuality of interests that replaced the more traditional skepticism of the press toward politicians."

Seven years later, as he considered announcing his candidacy again, Nixon, even in his memoirs, dropped such a relatively temperate approach to the subject and admitted that he was "bored by the charade of trying to romance the media. They were being relatively courteous at this period, but I knew the majority opposed my views and would strongly oppose my candidacy." Then, in these pages, his lifelong anger overcame him, and he wrote frankly:

After the press treatment I received during the Hiss case and the fund episode, and after the flagrant media favoritism for Kennedy in 1960, I considered the influential majority of the news media to be part of my political opposition. Whatever the reasons—institutional, ideological, or simply those based on personality—my relationship with them was somehow different even from that of other political figures whom they disliked or with whom they disagreed. I knew that I must expect no generosity, even for mistakes: I knew that my conduct and that of my family would be held up to the most severe scrutiny, and I felt that if anything ever went seriously wrong, the media would jump in and give me a fight for my political life.

I was prepared to have to do combat with the media in order to get my views and

my programs to the people, and despite all the power and public visibility I would
enjoy as President, I did not believe that this combat would be between equals. The
media are far more powerful than the President in creating public awareness and
shaping public opinion, for the simple reason that the media always have the last
word.

Immediately after his initial election, on December 11, 1968, Nixon met with
the cabinet members he had selected, and their wives, for the first time, and in a
sense "went public" with his view of the media. He wanted to warn his associates of what to expect. "Always remember," he told them,

the men and women of the news media approach this as an adversary relationship.
The time will come when they will run lies about you, when the columnists and
editorial writers will make you seem to be scoundrels or fools or both, and the
cartoonists will depict you as ogres. Some of you wives will get up in the morning
and look at the papers and start to cry. Now, don't let that get you down—don't let it
defeat you. And don't try to adjust your actions to what you think will please them.
Do what you believe is the right thing to do, and let the criticism roll off your back.
Don't think the criticism you see or hear in one or two places is all that is getting
through to the public.

Who were these enemies waiting outside the gates? Nixon knew. He might use
the words "media" and "the press" as loosely as the public, but he knew the
difference between friends and enemies, and the former outnumbered the latter,
beginning with the 80 percent of newspapers that had supported him in the campaign. Among them were such journals as the Los Angeles *Times,* the New York
Herald Tribune (whose chief editorial writer, Raymond K. Price, became his
chief speech writer), the New York *Daily News,* the Chicago *Tribune,* the *Christian Science Monitor,* the Washington *Star,* and the St. Louis *Globe-Democrat,*
one of whose editorial writers, Patrick Buchanan, became another speech writer.
Among the magazines he favored such conservative publications as *Fortune* and
U.S. News & World Report. He also had a few individual friends in the press: C.
L. Sulzberger of the New York *Times;* Richard L. Wilson of the Cowles publications; William F. Buckley, already the darling of the conservatives; and Joseph
Alsop, the syndicated columnist.

The enemies, it turned out, numbered chiefly only four among the newspapers:
the New York *Times,* always the target of conservative paranoia; the Washington
Post, even more calculated to provoke frothing at the mouth; the Boston *Globe;*
and the St. Louis *Post-Dispatch,* in which the ghost of Joseph Pulitzer lived on.
Time and *Newsweek,* although they might support Nixon on some issues and
ideas, were the principal magazine enemies. Among the columnists, it was hard
to choose, but Nixon particularly hated Tom Wicker, Marquis W. Childs, and
Jack Anderson. Always, however, he did not forget that television was foremost
on his enemies list, which in time took concrete written form, the media constituting only one of seven categories. He welcomed the support of such rare
conservative correspondents as Howard K. Smith of ABC, but he hated, collec-

tively, the news departments of CBS and NBC and the executives who controlled them.

Nevertheless Nixon made unusual preparations to deal with friend and enemy alike. As he noted in his memoirs, one of his first acts was to ask for a daily summary of ideas and opinions contained in a cross-section of news reports, editorials, columns, and articles appearing in fifty newspapers, thirty magazines, and the two major wire services, AP and UPI. Then he created a special office to serve the executive branch, naming the first communications director, Herbert Klein, a former reporter and editor for the conservative San Diego *Union,* who had been his press spokesman in 1960 and 1962. As press secretary Nixon named Ronald Ziegler, who had been his campaign press assistant, and who was only twenty-nine.

Ziegler was singularly unqualified for his job. His working background was confined to serving as a press agent for Disneyland, and five years as an account executive at J. Walter Thompson, where he had been the protégé of Bob Haldeman, who would become Nixon's presidential assistant. A handsome and arrogant young man who apparently knew little about the press, Ziegler antagonized the reporters so thoroughly that before the end of the first term his press conferences had degenerated to the point of "macabre sadism and black humor," in Theodore White's words, and the correspondents had turned more and more to Ziegler's deputy Gerald Warren. Even the president had shown displeasure toward Ziegler by giving him a public shove in the back, and Melvin Laird and John Connally had both demanded his dismissal, while a National Press Club committee had asserted that he "misled the public and affronted the professional standards of the Washington press corps."

It was no surprise, then, that when Klein left the White House at the end of Nixon's first term, Ziegler was appointed to the job, where he faithfully carried on, following the president into his voluntary retirement and staying with him until 1979 at San Clemente. Warren, who succeeded Ziegler as press secretary, had been a reporter. He conducted a brief holding operation until Nixon's resignation. Before Ziegler was sent to replace Klein, the job of communications director was held by Ken Clawson, a former Toledo *Blade* reporter, but he soon had to depart for reasons of health, leaving the door open as a haven for Ziegler.

Convincing defenses have been made of Ziegler, some by newsmen. It is pointed out that he reflected what Nixon was thinking, as far as anyone could tell what the president thought, and that he had more to conceal than others. No one would deny that he worked hard at his job and that he was a good organizer who did valuable work in that aspect of his position. But he was always severely limited by both the president and Haldeman, and he was seldom on good terms with his own staff, which resented his martinetlike approach.

At the beginning, however, in spite of apprehensions, relations between press and president appeared better than anyone could have expected. The first press conference was held nine days after Nixon took office, and in the subsequent five months he held five others—not nearly as many as either Johnson or Kennedy, but the correspondents considered themselves lucky, knowing Nixon.

Moreover, to their astonishment, Nixon appeared to be looking after their material comfort. One Sunday in 1969, a few months after he entered the White House, the president left his office, where he had been working, and walked into the pressroom—a place he had never entered before. Curiosity was only a part of his motivation. He had been told how overcrowded and cramped it was, and he had come to see for himself. There was no doubt that he had been told the truth. The room had been deteriorating steadily since Theodore Roosevelt had established it, and there was distaste in Nixon's voice when he asked Helen Thomas of the UPI, "Is this where you have to work?"

As a result of his visit, the President ordained that a new pressroom be constructed in the West Terrace, an enclosed corridor connecting the White House and the West Wing, then occupied by a sauna, two massage rooms, a flower room, and kennels for the presidential dogs. These were all relocated and the reporters were duly installed in an unaccustomed elegance, which Nixon designated as the West Terrace Press Center.

The elegance had one disadvantage. Correspondents discovered they no longer had a firsthand view of the president's visitors arriving and departing but were now separated from the reception room by a network of offices between pressroom and lobby, housing the president's vast press and publicity department, which continued to grow under Nixon. In the first Roosevelt's day reporters had been compelled to stand outside and wait to identify visitors. That was why TR had brought them inside out of the cold and wet, as described earlier. Now, nearly seventy years later, they were back out in the weather, outside the West Wing, the only differences being that they were a hundred feet farther up the driveway.

Nevertheless the correspondents moved into their new home in the spring of 1970, having no other choice, and found themselves installed in a decor that Deakin calls "Orange County Dental." The pressroom was equipped with a podium, concealed behind a curtain and recessed in the wall. For press briefings the curtains were drawn, the podium lowered, and a lectern set on it; if the president was to appear, someone placed the presidential seal on the lectern. Another curtain, at the opposite end of the room, concealed television cameras on a platform, placed there permanently. Deakin notes that in time the pretense of the curtain was dropped, and the podium and lectern, as well as the cameras, were left exposed. Moreover the reporters, ignoring signs forbidding food and drink, soon transformed the room into something much more familiar, resembling a city hall pressroom.

Such cosmetic reforms could not save Nixon's press relations. At this early stage the correspondents appeared wary but willing to make a new start with a president whose history of press hatred was so well known as to be a cliché. It was a short honeymoon, however, as the reporters learned that Nixon did not intend to give them any news. Hard information was nearly totally absent from the first six press conferences. While there was a great deal happening, particularly in Vietnam, Ziegler's briefings were bland denials that anything at all was occurring. With the invasion of Laos by South Vietnam, Ziegler was soon confronting a roomful of frustrated, irate reporters who could not get beyond his stock answer, "I really have no information to provide you."

The press was delinquent, as it has always been, in not reporting exactly what was happening, since this early stonewalling could be considered legitimate news. But the correspondents followed common practice in not reporting it, and the public did not know that the president was telling them nothing about the scarcely secret war he was conducting. Again they had to rely on the bits and pieces that emerged from foreign correspondents for both print media and television and the speculations provided by columnists and magazine writers. Since most of the public was not equipped to do any such investigating, even if it had the inclination, its resulting ignorance was of considerable help to a president who wanted the electorate to know as little as possible about what he was doing.

Nixon's battle plan to maintain this situation was well thought out. It began with Ziegler's noninformational briefings, for which he, not the president, would be compelled to take the heat. It continued with the functioning of the communications director, whose task it was to carry administration propaganda over the heads of Washington reporters to editors and opinion-makers in the form of press releases, none of which contained any real or accurate information. Nixon's own press conferences were part of the plan. The idea was to limit them as much as possible, but at the same time to achieve maximum television coverage by making speeches or announcements after which there would be no questioning. Another part of this strategy was for the president virtually to disappear from view for long periods, followed by a sudden, dramatic announcement. Interviews were given infrequently, and then only to trusted conservative writers or individuals of sufficient importance that some weight would be attached to their reports of the conversation. Otherwise the president remained largely out of sight. Reporters, and the public, had no solid information about what he thought of the pressing issues of the day or what he intended to do about them.

Another major part of Nixon's strategy was to attack the media by hammering away at their mistakes, not to correct the record but to prove that they were all involved in a sinister conspiracy to distort the news—a thesis many people were prepared to believe, knowing even less about the news process than Nixon himself. Deakin has cataloged some of the phrases used by the White House propagandists: "A small little group of men who . . . enjoy a right of instant rebuttal to every presidential [speech]"; "a tiny small and un-elected elite." These subversive people lived and worked in the suspect areas of New York and Washington, and they "read the same newspapers and draw their political and social views from the same sources," and worse, "the views of this fraternity do not represent the views of America." The average, honest, God-fearing American knew "practically nothing" of these sinister people.

It was this message that was carried to the people by Agnew, in speeches written by Pat Buchanan, of which Nixon remarked, "That really flicks the scab off, doesn't it?" The speeches also conveyed a sense of cold outrage that such chicanery should be practiced on the American people. A similar outrage was experienced by at least some Americans when, a little later, they learned their vice-president had been accused of particularly shabby malfeasance and misfeasance in public office in Baltimore County, which led to his resignation. No doubt it was particularly galling to Agnew that it was newspapers, particularly the work of a young reporter for the Washington *Post,* Richard Cohen, which led to his personal disgrace. Agnew slipped into oblivion; Cohen became a respected syndicated columnist for the *Post.*

At the time, however, Agnew's attacks on the press served the purpose Nixon knew they would, encouraging the feelings of hostility toward the press already held by many citizens. They were particularly effective among those who favored the war in Vietnam and believed the newspapers were deliberately trying to discredit both the war and the president who was directing it. When Nixon went on the air to defend his policies, the network commentators appeared after the broadcast to analyze what he had said in terms that could be objected to only by dedicated partisans. But the partisans and the president did object strongly because in their analyses the network commentators had not only repeated what Nixon said but had dared to articulate the opposing viewpoints that were dividing the nation. For Nixon and his partisans, there was no such thing as a diversity of views in this diverse republic. There were only Nixon's "facts," and the rest was bias, the work of traitors. Haldeman put it plainly in an NBC interview on the "Today" show: "The only conclusion you can draw is that the critics [of Nixon's Vietnam policy] are consciously aiding and abetting the enemy of the United States."

Nixon understood, however, that it was not enough to denounce his enemies in the media or even to attempt to discredit them. If he was going to be an imperial president, he would have to use the powers of intimidation implicit in his office, although never used before for this particular purpose. Theodore Roosevelt and a few others had complained directly to publishers in an effort to get offending reporters fired or transferred, but Nixon had something else in mind to deal with the far more formidable foe represented by television.

The road to what he now undertook had its origins in a memo of October 1969, written by Jeb Magruder, a Haldeman aide who specialized in press relations without any visible qualification for the job. Magruder's memo was titled "The Shotgun versus the Rifle," in which he argued that it was ineffective to pepper the press with shotgun blasts from several White House sources directed to many papers and voicing complaints about coverage. He wanted to "get to this unfair coverage" in such a way that "the networks, newspapers and Congress will react to and begin to look at things somewhat differently." In short, legitimate persuasion—the art of public relations. Or was it? These were his persuasive suggestions:

1. Begin an official monitoring system [of network television news and commentary] through the FCC as soon as Dean Burch is officially on board as Chairman. . . . If the monitoring system proves our point, we have then legitimate and legal rights to go to the networks, etc. and make official complaints from the FCC. This will have much more effect than a phone call from Herb Klein or Pat Buchanan.

2. Utilize the anti-trust division to investigate various media relating to anti-trust violations. Even the possible threat of anti-trust action I think would be effective in changing their views in the above matter.

3. Utilizing the Internal Revenue Service as a method to look into the various

organizations that we are most concerned about. Just a threat of an IRS investigation
will probably turn their approach.
    4. Begin to show favorites with the media.
    5. Utilize Republican National Committee for major letter-writing efforts.

These ideas were quickly implemented. In the aftermath of a speech by Nixon
in which he rejected demands for a "precipitate withdrawal" of American forces
from Vietnam and called on the public to support his own unspecified timetable,
Dean Burch, the chairman of the Federal Communications Commission, called
the presidents of all three networks and asked for transcripts of their news analyses made after the address. This was followed by an Agnew speech that surpassed in ferocity and sinister mindlessness anything he had said before. The
networks, he asserted, enjoyed a monopoly sanctioned and licensed by government, therefore, he suggested, they should be "made more responsive to the
views of the nation." "Made" was a new word in the vocabulary of the presidency where the media were concerned; it had the chilling sound of authoritarian
governments everywhere. Meanwhile Agnew urged the public to write to the
networks and protest their news coverage.
    The result showed that Nixon had known how to tap the deep public resent-
ment of the press on his behalf. Within a few days after the Agnew speech, CBS
affiliates in seven different cities registered sixteen thousand telephone calls from
viewers who wanted to talk about it. Nine thousand of them supported Agnew,
rather less than what might have been expected. The media, print and electronic,
seemed to be oblivious to what was being done. Agnew's speech was duly reported, but there was little response to the idea that the media were going to be
"made" to do something by government. The spirits of Jefferson and Madison
were not once invoked.
    Response to the Agnew speech through letters to the editor were also heavy,
but it was difficult to tell how much of it was genuine because it represented
another part of Nixon's plan, unknown either to press or public, in which letters
written by White House aides were channeled through ordinary citizens across
the country, Nixon partisans, who signed them. These responses continued as
Agnew broadened the attack to include every conservative's favorite whipping
boys, the New York *Times* and the Washington *Post*.
    At the same time Nixon's men moved on another front. The Justice Depart-
ment subpoenaed unused portions of a CBS film about the Black Panther party
and, soon after, the materials used in its production as well. That was followed
by a similar seizure by a federal grand jury of reporters' notes on a riot in Chicago by the radical group called the Weathermen. This involved correspondents
for *Time, Life,* and *Newsweek,* and a New York *Times* reporter. Unused photographs were subpoenaed as well.
    Having tasted success, Magruder enthusiastically pursued his "rifle" attack,
with the approval and help of Haldeman and the president, who had added his
own touches to the speeches Buchanan wrote for Agnew. He urged the "mobilization of the Silent Majority" (Agnew's mythical creation) to carry on a letter-
writing campaign as a counter to the attack on Vietnam policy. Buchanan joined

in with a memo to Nixon suggesting that a dummy institute be set up whose product would be "studies" urging a reform in network news operations.

The White House war against the media was a full-blown operation by the summer of 1970. One of its objectives was Chet Huntley, co-anchorman with David Brinkley of the NBC evening news. In a particularly candid, and indiscreet, moment Lawrence M. Higby, Haldeman's principal assistant, wrote to Magruder that the point of the action against Huntley was not directed against the man personally, since he was about to retire from the network anyway, but "what we are trying to do is to tear down the institution." One of the ways that could be done was to use the White House propaganda machine to make objectivity itself the subject of a national debate. It would surely be inconclusive, but it could also be damaging to the networks and the press.

Another rifle shot at the networks occurred just before the 1970 off-year elections. Charles Colson, later convicted in the Watergate trials and sent to prison, where he found God, held what were euphemistically called off-the-record meetings with the executives of the three networks about their "slanted" news coverage and analyses of presidential speeches. During these talks Colson insinuated the idea that there might be government intervention in television news, and, as he reported to Haldeman later: "The networks are terribly nervous over the uncertain state of the law—i.e., the recent FCC decisions and the pressures to grant Congress access to TV. . . . There was unanimous agreement that the President's right of access to TV should in no way be restrained."

Meanwhile the campaign continued, with its rigged letters and telephone calls attacking the press and praising the president. It was needed because opposition to the Vietnam War was steadily rising. There was now beginning a long, deadly battle between press and president in which Nixon and his aides, civil and military, sought to cover up what was going on in Vietnam and Cambodia, and what the administration was doing domestically to silence its enemies and critics, on a scale never seen before. To counter these moves the media continued to dig deeper and deeper into this unsavory situation until the ultimate revelations occurred that brought down the president.

It is a dismal record to contemplate, surely the most shameful in the history of the presidency, and it has been rehearsed nearly to exhaustion, but a few highlights will serve to recall the pattern of deception and attempted repression. There was, for example, the case of the My Lai massacre, which William Manchester has called the American Lidice, recalling the 1942 Nazi killing of 190 men who lived in that Czechoslovakian village; the women and children were sent to concentration camps, where few survived. An American platoon under the command of Lt. William L. Calley, Jr., was more efficient when it seized the village of My Lai in Vietnam and killed 567 old men, women, and children. The army succeeded in covering up the massacre for a month, but the news began to seep out and it was forced to conduct an investigation, as a result of which Calley was convicted of murder and sentenced to life imprisonment. In the moral climate of the time, that verdict was greeted with anger by many Americans, who seemed to believe that Calley was either innocent or a scapegoat. Still another reason to hate the press, which had disclosed the shocking story. Nixon, sensing political capital, ordered Calley removed from the stockade and placed under house arrest, asserting he would review the case himself. Although Nixon later changed his mind, he was charged with playing politics with a war crime.

Then, in 1973, came the event that the London *Sunday Times* declared later "tipped the Nixon Administration over the edge." In its Sunday edition of June 13, the New York *Times* carried a front-page headline: "Vietnam Archive: Pentagon Study Traces 3 Decades of Growing U.S. Involvement." The story continued inside with six columns of type. These were what came to be known as the Pentagon Papers, originally commissioned by Secretary of Defense Robert S. McNamara, the work of thirty-five scholars who had laid out in forty-seven volumes of typescript a massively detailed account of how America had gotten into the Vietnam morass. Although it was officially secret, there was nothing in it involving military security, and indeed nothing involving Nixon, who did not even know of its existence.

Nevertheless, when the second installment appeared on Monday, Nixon agreed to Attorney General John Mitchell's urging that the *Times* be warned that if it printed any more, it would be prosecuted under the espionage law. The paper carried Mitchell's letter on the front page, beside the third installment. The government implemented its threat by going into federal court and getting a temporary restraining order pending an injunction. It was the first time in American postconstitutional history that an administration had attempted to exercise prior restraint of publication, which the First Amendment had been designed to prevent. The *Times* stopped publication but resumed again after the Washington *Post* began running its own summary of the Pentagon Papers, followed by the Boston *Globe* four days later. Meanwhile, the Associated Press began to circulate the story worldwide, a version printed by the *Times*.

Later that month the source of the documents was disclosed when Daniel Ellsberg, a former Pentagon official who had become a strong antiwar ideologue, appeared on television and admitted he had stolen the documents. At that point Nixon compounded his initial mistake and, issuing orders that "came right out of the Oval Office," according to later testimony, set up a "plumbers" group (as they came to be called; in reality the White House Special Investigations Unit), in a basement office, next door to the White House. Its job was to find out how the Pentagon Papers had been leaked. The method employed was to burgle the office of Ellsworth's psychiatrist, thinking to label Ellsworth as a Soviet spy, an act of such magnificent stupidity that it is hardly credible. Not only did the burglars find nothing but their act was discovered, and in any case the frame-up could only have endangered relations with the Soviets if it had been successful, besides the obvious fact that nothing in the psychiatrist's files could have offset forty-seven volumes of incriminating papers.

In a landmark decision the Supreme Court ultimately upheld the right of the newspapers to print the Pentagon Papers and the principle of no prior restraint was vindicated, but a large segment of the public supporting the war in Vietnam was enraged by the decision. These same voters applauded another decision by the court in 1972, which ruled five to four (Nixon's four appointees were among the majority) that newspapermen could be required by courts and grand juries to disclose matters given to them in confidence. "In a relatively short time," the American Civil Liberties Union declared, "the press in the United States has moved from what many considered a position of extreme security to one of extreme vulnerability."

Both Nixon and a hostile public had further reason to hate the press when the Washington *Post* began to disclose in October 1972 what it called "a massive campaign of political spying and sabotage . . . directed by officials of the White House and the Committee for the Reelection of the President." This was the result of the notorious Watergate burglary, in which seven men were caught trying to steal papers from the files of the Democratic National Committee in a Washington apartment building. The developing story, which the *Post* began to carry, was the work of two young reporters, Bob Woodward and Carl Bernstein, whose superb job of investigative reporting made them national heroes (at least in some eyes) when the truth of their work was proved. At the time, however, a Gallup poll showed that only half of the American people could even identify the Watergate affair.

Other papers, notably the New York *Times,* joined the *Post* in trying to ferret out what Nixon and his men were up to, an endeavor that led in time, with this kind of pressure, to the appointment of a congressional committee, under the chairmanship of an old-school North Carolina politician, Sen. Samuel J. Ervin, Jr. Witnesses from all quarters of the administration were called, and slowly, while a fascinated nation watched the proceedings on television, the whole pattern of Nixonian chicanery, suppression, cover-up, and general lawlessness began to emerge. When John Dean, the president's counsel, decided in effect to confess, the administration was doomed, and when another witness disclosed the existence of tapes that had recorded conversations in the Oval Office since 1971, the end was in sight. The tapes documented what had been charged, and the end result was the institution of impeachment proceedings against Nixon, during which he resigned, and the conviction and sentencing of Haldeman, John Ehrlichman, Mitchell, Dean, Charles Colson, and other members of the White House staff.

While this unprecedented story was unfolding, the media gave it equally unprecedented coverage, but the result of this exposure of governmental corruption, which was far worse even than the Grant administration had produced, was not universal admiration for the press, as might have been expected. Instead those who had defended Lieutenant Calley were among a considerable segment of the public which believed that the papers and the television networks had unfairly "hounded down" Nixon and his men. They saw nothing wrong, for instance, in the disclosure that Patrick Buchanan, the president's speech writer, had suggested in a memo to Attorney General Mitchell that a "Fair Coverage Committee" be created for the campaign of 1972 to "clock" the media's coverage of both presidential and vice-presidential candidates, or in the threats against papers and networks and the attempt to suppress or injure them that the tapes disclosed.

Among the damaging disclosures was the story of the open threat Colson had made against CBS, then as now the *bête noire* of conservatives, after it had broadcast a two-part report on the Watergate break-in during the evening news. Although he denied it, Colson had charged that the network was showing antiadministration bias by devoting so much time to the two-part documentary and had told Frank Stanton, the network's president, "We'll bring you to your knees in Wall Street."

As though this were not enough, when the licenses of two television stations— CBS affiliates owned by the Washington *Post,* therefore placing them in double jeopardy—came up for renewal, it suddenly developed that there were competing applications for their frequencies. It was no surprise that the applicants turned out to be businessmen friendly to Nixon. Public television, of course, was even more vulnerable. In June 1972 Nixon vetoed the public broadcasting bill, which would have funded public television at $155 million over a period of two years. Twelve years later Reagan was still vetoing PBS funding bills under the pretext of budget cutting.

Another expansion in the White House propaganda machinery had been the creation of the Office of Telecommunications Policy, whose director, Clay Whitehead, proposed that a broadcasting license bill be prepared that would extend the licensing period for a station only if, among other more standard criteria, the broadcasters' success in "meeting their responsibility" were measured. Nothing the administration had done until then so alarmed the networks. Its executives well knew that the affiliates were overwhelmingly conservative Nixon supporters, who hated liberals as much as Agnew did, and a threat to their licenses could endanger the whole structure of network broadcasting. Fortunately some measure of justice caught up to the Nixon crew before this blatant power grab could be carried out.

Ironically, even as Nixon carried on his crusade against the networks, trying to intimidate them into submission, he was using the medium to go over the heads of the media, including television itself, and make his case for support from the public. There was no way the networks could prevent this, since a president can command air time, or invent excuses to use it, in ways no other citizen can. They were in a dangerous and beleaguered situation, as became obvious near the end of 1973, when Dean Burch proposed that the FCC consider an examination of whether the existing ownership of affiliates was in the public interest, implying that the networks might be compelled to divest themselves of these stations that were their lifeblood. Their lawyers were already having to contend with an antitrust suit filed against them in April 1972 by the Department of Justice, obviously at Nixon's instigation.

The White House correspondents of the networks were caught in the middle of this war, since they were on the firing line. At the press conference of October 26, 1973, Nixon heard a reporter's question about the effect that a long succession of shocking events might have had on the country and took the opportunity to lash out: "I have never heard or seen such outrageous, vicious, distorted reporting in twenty-seven years of public life. I'm not blaming anybody for that. Perhaps what happened is that what we did brought it about, and therefore the media decided that they would have to take that particular line. But when people are pounded night after night with that kind of frantic, hysterical reporting, it naturally shakes their confidence.''

This outburst had all the appearance of being spontaneous, but in fact Nixon had told Sid Feders, a CBS producer, just before the conference began, ''Cronkite's not going to like this tonight, I hope.'' It was at this conference, too, near the end, that Robert Pierpoint of NBC, a particular Nixon nemesis, asked his much quoted question, ''What is it about the television coverage in these past weeks and months that has so aroused your anger?'' and got the equally quoted reply: ''Don't get the impression that you arouse my anger. . . . You see, one can only be angry with those he respects.''

Nixon had particular enemies among the correspondents whom he pursued. Daniel Schorr of CBS was considered a prime suspect, and the administration ordered a full investigation of him, including interviewing his friends and acquaintances, on the pretense that he was being considered for a job in the administration, which brought howls of derision from his friends and some pain to the subject. Dan Rather, also of CBS News, was another object of Nixon's wrath. In an interview with Richard Salant, president of that department, on the CBS morning news, presidential aide John Ehrlichman asked only half-jocularly whether Rather could not be reassigned to a remote CBS bureau. Later Rather was called to a meeting at the White House with Ehrlichman and Haldeman, both of whom directly accused him of biased reporting.

No one in the Nixon camp, however, went further than Clay Whitehead in attacking the media, particularly television. After the first day of the bombing of North Vietnam, he assailed the networks' coverage of that event in the same chilling language he had used before. The administration would propose legislation, he said, that would require the affiliates to be held responsible at license renewal time not only for the content of the network news they carried but for all the other network programming as well. That would constitute about 60 percent of their air time. He hoped by this brutal (and unconstitutional) means to make the stations put pressures on the networks to revise their news policies and eliminate what he was pleased to call ''ideological plugola'' and ''elitist gossip in the guise of news analysis.''

The operations summarized above do not begin to cover the entire range of the Nixon gang's operations against the media. They do not include the illegal wiretapping of reporters' telephones, the actions taken against those on the ''enemies'' list, and dozens of others that could all come under the head of what the historian Christopher Lasch once called ''the techniques of a sophisticated police state.'' It was Lasch who summarized the legacy Nixon left behind him, in a New York *Times* review of *Nightmare: The Underside of the Nixon Years,* by J. Anthony Lukas, a *Times* reporter who covered those years. ''Ever since the New Frontier,'' he wrote, ''large-scale lying has been part of the normal operations of Government. The Cuban missile crisis, the American involvement in Vietnam and the secrecy surrounding the assassination of President Kennedy are only the most obvious examples of official deception. Nixon was not the first President to resort to the big lie, nor will he be the last. Lying has become an official reflex—

a practice to which the President and his advisers instinctively resort in any emergency.'' These words were written in 1976, at a time of national confusion and despondency, but unfortunately nothing has occurred in the nearly ten years since then to challenge their validity.

In revisiting the scene of the Nixon political (and other) crimes, one is struck again by the president's seemingly infinite capacity for self-delusion. It was particularly apparent in the case of the press. Talking to the conservative novelist, Allen Drury, a sympathetic listener, on March 30, 1971, Nixon answered a question about the press with these words, which seem almost incredible in retrospect:

> The press? . . . I probably follow the press more closely and am less affected by it than any other president. I have a very cool detachment about it. I read it basically to find out what other people are reading, so that I'll know what is being given the country and what I have to deal with when I talk to the country and try to influence people [to support] my program. . . .
>
> I'm not like Lyndon [Johnson]. . . . The press was like a magnet to him. He'd read every single thing that was critical, he'd watch the news on TV all the time, and then he'd get mad. I never get mad. I expect I have one of the most hostile and unfair presses that any president has ever had, but I've developed a philosophical attitude about it. I developed it early. I have won all my political battles with 80 to 90 percent of the press against me. [It was exactly the opposite.] How have I done it? I ignored the press and went to the people.
>
> I have never called a publisher, never called an editor, never called a reporter, on the carpet. I don't care. And you know? . . . that's what makes 'em mad. That's what infuriates 'em. I just don't care. I just don't raise the roof with 'em. And that gets 'em. . . .
>
> I respect the individual members of the press—some of them, particularly the older ones—who have some standards of objectivity and fairness. And the individual competence of many of the younger ones. I respect that too, though nowadays they don't care about fairness, it's the in thing to forget objectivity and let your prejudices show. You can see it in my press conferences all the time. You read the Kennedy press conference[s] and see how soft and gentle they were with him, and then you read mine. I never get any easy questions—and I don't want any. I am quite aware that ideologically the Washington press corps doesn't agree with me. I expect it. I think the people can judge for themselves when they watch one of my press conferences. It's all there. I can tell you this . . . as long as I am in this office, the press will never irritate me, never affect me.

Was this mere camouflage, or did Nixon really believe it? Unfortunately, there is no convincing documentation either way, in spite of earnest attempts to find some. All we truly know is that the mighty have fallen from their positions of power, served their terms in jail, and returned to obscure civilian lives. Except for the master, who was pardoned although never convicted, and walks among us today, getting richer, hearing applause from the same people he tried to destroy, and seeing on every hand the evidence that the seeds he and Spiro Agnew planted have blossomed and created more distrust of the press than ever, while the White House machinery he devised thrives and improves in the hands of far more able operators who are not hampered by the particular madness that characterized the Nixon administration. And who has helped the Great Media Hater to so thoroughly rehabilitate himself? Of course—the media.

Ford: A Tainted Nice Guy

The temptation is to dismiss the presidencies of Gerald Ford and Jimmy Carter as a protracted yawn between Nixon and Reagan—afterthought presidents, in the words of Ronnie Dugger. Yet even in this desert of mediocrity there is something to be learned about the president-press relationship.

There is, first of all, a certain sympathy for these presidents, both of whom inherited a nation suffering from the worst traumas since the Depression and confronted with new and terrifying prospects in the nuclear arms race and the explosion of the Middle East. As another accidental president, who had not even been elected vice-president, Ford had little opportunity to be anything more than a caretaker, nor did he seem to want to be anything more. Carter found himself forced into impossible situations that could be guaranteed to give him political trouble no matter which path he took. Since indecision can be as fatal as making the wrong decisions, Carter found himself pilloried for the presumed stain on national honor deriving from the Iranian hostage situation, which he solved, too late, in the only reasonable way. People forgot that his negotiations through Algeria were successful and that the Iranian government, out of simple hatred of Carter, meanly withheld the actual release of the hostages until the moment of Reagan's ascension to power. The voters wanted to punish someone for four years of failure to solve problems for which no politician of any party could have devised better solutions, notwithstanding that some of them originated in the White House.

Gerald Ford's relations with the press began on a troubled note, but there was no subsequent rancor or alienation. Reporters found it impossible to dislike him, and while they might give him a respect deriving more from his office than his actions, and even make him the subject of running jokes, they could not help having an affection for him. He was, as has been frequently said, a nice guy who was trying to do his best in a job for which he was eminently unqualified, and the press appreciated his position.

Ford was the first president since Coolidge whom people could feel comfortable joking about. Even past presidents had joined in the fun. There was Lyndon Johnson's remark that Ford had played football so long at Michigan that it had made him ''so dumb he can't walk and chew gum at the same time''—a cleaned-up version of the original obscene observation. Before he had some reason to be grateful to his successor, Nixon asked rhetorically, ''Can you imagine Jerry Ford sitting in this chair?''

When he abruptly became president, Ford took the humor at his expense with his customary good nature, having already experienced the barbs as interim vice-president. If he knew that Nixon, still in the White House, had mocked him (and he must have), he remained steadfastly loyal, traveling one hundred thousand miles around the country, giving five hundred speeches in forty states, in all of which he defended the beleaguered president. Over and over he told his audiences: "He's been my friend for twenty-five years. He is my friend. I believe he is innocent of any charges." In his memoirs Ford was also forgiving about the attitude of the press toward him as vice-president: "The White House press corps doesn't take members of Congress very seriously. To many of those reporters, my Vice Presidency had seemed disorganized, so they harbored a natural skepticism about my talents and skills. Finally, I had no mandate from the people and the Congress understood that."

Certainly, as vice-president, Ford did not withhold himself from the press in any way. During the eight months he served in that office, he had fifty-two press conferences, gave eighty-five formal interviews, and spoke dozens of times with reporters informally. In an effort to show his good will, he walked over to the pressroom soon after he was sworn in as president and introduced his new press secretary, Jerald F. terHorst, of the Detroit *News,* an old Grand Rapids ally. As president, Ford went on, he still considered the reporters as friends, as indeed many of them were.

For terHorst, it was a somewhat dizzying switch. One week he had been among the reporters himself, and here, within a few days, he was taking their questions in the pressroom. He fielded whatever was thrown at him, but he must have shuddered inwardly near the end as one reporter reminded him that when Ford, as the House minority leader, had appeared before a Senate committee about to confirm him as vice-president, in anticipation of the president's forced departure, he had said, "I do not think the public would stand for it" when he was asked about a possible pardon for Nixon. Did Ford still think so? TerHorst dodged that one, but it was plain this was going to be a difficult issue.

Twenty days after he took office, Ford held his first press conference, on national television, an occasion for which he had spent ten hours of careful preparation, including dress rehearsals with staff members who spared him even less than the reporters were expected to. His advisers even thought of a splendid public relations touch. Instead of appearing before Nixon's presidential blue drapes, such unpleasant reminders of the most imperial of presidencies could be avoided by having Ford speak before an open door in the East Room. Some of the press swallowed this bait. *Time* magazine's headline read: "Plain Words before an Open Door."

As terHorst and the Ford staff had anticipated, the conference got around to the pardon with the first question, asked by Helen Thomas of UPI, who as senior wire-service correspondent had the privilege of the initial thrust. "Mr. President," she said, "do you agree with Governor Rockefeller that former President Nixon should have immunity from prosecution? And specifically, would you use your pardon authority if necessary?" The president gave her the evasive answer that might have been expected, providing no indication that only eleven days later he would grant "a full, free and absolute pardon unto Richard Nixon for all offenses against the United States which he . . . has . . . or may have committed."

It was the major mistake of Ford's brief presidency, and whether it was done out of unabashed party and personal loyalty, from inner conviction, or whether it was the result of a prior deal with the former president, has never been unequivocally established, although a strong case for the latter has been made. In any event the immediate effect was to reverse what *Time* had called the "mood of good feeling and even exhilaration in Washington that the city had not experienced for many years." The effect on public and press opinion was even more dramatic. Overnight the Gallup poll showed that the president's public approval rating had dropped from 70 percent to 50 percent, while press approval, which had been nearly unanimous, plummeted to near zero.

The move also cost Ford the services of terHorst, who resigned his post. It was a more serious loss than it appeared to be at the time, and not simply because this former reporter had been the president's trusted friend for twenty-five years. TerHorst's advice would have been helpful as a result of his reporting experience in Europe, Asia, and the Middle East, areas about which the new president had only the most elementary notions. As a syndicated Washington columnist, terHorst also had an intimate knowledge of the political scene and of the country itself, besides enjoying the respect of his colleagues.

TerHorst's extraordinary departure was a costly one in every respect, but again Ford was unfailingly loyal. Responding to Nixon partisans who were angry at terHorst because he had resigned as a matter of principle, implying (accurately) that the president did not share those principles, Ford told them, according to John Osborne, the *New Republic*'s correspondent, "You just don't understand these evangelical Michigan Dutchmen." Ford, as an old Grand Rapids boy, understood them well enough. He understood principles, too, but he valued loyal Republicanism more.

For a time, until a new press secretary could be found, Ford employed Jack Hushen, who had enjoyed the unenviable task of speaking for Attorney General John Mitchell, by that time better known to Americans as the "Big Enchilada" as a result of the Watergate hearings. It was Hushen who took the press conference podium the day after the pardon and told the fascinated reporters that Ford had authorized him to say that the White House was studying pardons for forty of Nixon's men, all defendants in court actions. After twenty-four hours of anguished silence, punctuated by no comments, Hushen explained lamely that he had really meant that it was the entire federal pardon policy which was being studied. To the reporters, it seemed that not much had changed since Nixon's departure. Was this the same Ford who had told them, immediately after his swearing-in, "I expect to follow my instincts of openness and candor?"

But the president had twenty-five years of experience behind him, and he had other assets—a well of good will among the reporters that he could always tap and his natural friendliness, a presidential attribute to which they were not accustomed. Deliberately Ford used these assets to mend the damage caused by the pardon, inviting such influential writers as David Broder of the Washington *Post* and James Reston of the New York *Times* to come to the White House for luncheon, where he asked their advice about the state of the nation instead of allowing them to conduct a standard interview.

At the same time Ford made some improvements in the White House propa-

ganda machine, already costing the taxpayers at least $400 million a year—
which, as Richard Reeves has pointed out, was

> more than double the combined news budgets of the three television networks, Asso-
> ciated Press, United Press International and the country's ten largest newspapers.
> Within 100 days in the White House, Ford expanded the Nixon public relations staff
> so that one out of five of the 250 men and women reporting to the President and his
> senior staff were working on public relations. Not only did Ford have a personal
> television director, Robert Mead (who used to be Dan Rather's White House pro-
> ducer for CBS), he had a $40,000-a-year joke writer, Bob Orben (who used to work
> for Jack Paar and Red Skelton).

Then Ford made another mistake with the press. To replace Hushen, he named
Ron Nessen, who had until then been a broadcast correspondent for NBC News
but had twenty years as a journalist behind him, although he was only forty. Ford
introduced Nessen to the correspondents, as he had terHorst, but this time with
obvious embarrassment. In the briefing session that followed, Nessen told the
correspondents, "It's a Ford White House now and it's not a Nixon White
House"—half-truth in itself—after which he went through what was now becoming a ritual for press secretaries, promising that he would never knowingly
lie to the reporters or mislead them. By this time even the youngest correspondent should have learned that if Nessen, or any other press secretary, carried out
that promise literally, he would be removed. Secretaries say what presidents
want them to say, and presidents knowingly lie to and mislead the press, and
through them the public, on the ground that the end justifies the means.

But had the reporters really learned this fundamental truth, proven to them
over and over again? Not exactly. John Osborne remarked that

> the numerous reporters and commentators, including some of the best in the busi-
> ness, who went practically "ape" over the "open" Ford White House that they
> thought terHorst bespoke and personified forgot that the controlling function of
> White House press secretaries and other official spokesmen is not to tell the truth. It
> is to put the best possible appearance upon what their principals do and say and, if
> necessary in the course of their endeavor, to conceal the truth. What my brethren in
> the White House press room were really celebrating, during the halcyon interlude
> that ended with the pardon of Richard Nixon, was the departure of Mr. Nixon and the
> quaint illusion that concealment and deception departed with him.

Ford did make an honest effort to raise the level of president-press relations
from the abysmal depths of the Nixon days. His press conferences—often in the
East Room, which he preferred—were conducted in a different spirit by far from
Nixon's, although they were not much more informative. Ford also removed the
White House some distance from Nixonian secrecy, inviting the author John
Hersey to compile material there for a book that described a typical day in the
president's life. There were, in addition, small group interviews with cor-
respondents.

The problem was Ron Nessen. A thin-skinned young man who dreamed of being a novelist (and became one after he left the White House), Nessen was given unusual access to information, more than most of his predecessors had enjoyed. The president had asked him a question: if he knew everything that was going on, and at his briefings was asked about a sensitive issue, would he be embarrassed or feel compromised before his former colleagues? Put another way, if he knew everything, would he be willing and able to say nothing, to evade, to mislead, even to lie—all those things that he had deplored as a reporter just the other day? It would be no problem, Nessen assured the president, who then advised him that he would have direct access to all staff members and be permitted to sit in on all staff meetings, unless they were private talks or secret sessions of the National Security Council. Thus Nessen was permitted to know much more about matters than he would often be allowed to discuss.

Nessen was delighted with the transition from being the asker to the asked, as he tells us in his memoirs, *It Sure Looks Different from the Inside*. It looked different on his first day, when William Casselman, one of the White House lawyers, called to say he hoped Nessen would not have to give the reporters any information about jewelry that appeared to be missing from 1,100 boxes of gifts to Nixon; they had been impounded. "It's not my job to tell them if they don't ask," he replied, admitting, as he says, that he was "surprised by how quickly I was shifting my loyalties and my attitudes" and going on to report that he asked his assistants for ideas to make White House press coverage more open, "or at least to give the appearance of being more open."

Not everything Nessen was called upon to stonewall or lie about was the result of legitimate inquiry. Betty Ford's frank comments about morality and other matters in interviews alarmed Ford's advisers, although not the president, but, rather than exciting the adverse press reaction that had been feared, her remarks only endeared her to all but the most conservative. When she spoke, the seldom-sniffed scent of honesty was in the air. Then there was the matter of the president's seeming lack of balance, first observed when he tumbled down the ramp from *Air Force One* in Salzburg on his way to a meeting with the Egyptian president, Anwar Sadat. On subsequent occasions Ford stumbled, bumped his head, and fell while skiing (hardly an unusual occurrence), and each time the reporters were full of questions. Were they simply accidents? Was there anything medically wrong with him? Privately it was speculated that Ford might have had one too many martinis on occasion or, more generously, that he was just getting older and losing his coordination, although he was an active skier and golfer. In any case, it seemed to be reportorial overkill, and it was damaging to Ford, who saw himself being given a public image as a stumbling, bumbling president. It was not funny, he said, although he laughed obligingly at the jokes made about him by Johnny Carson on television.

It was a continuing series of these minor mishaps, however, that led to open confrontation between the press and Nessen, who finally, with some reason, was exasperated by the continuing barrage of questions. Nessen found it difficult to convince the older correspondents in this matter; they had been lied to before about the medical condition of presidents, a hoary tradition in the relationship by this time. Nor was Nessen always given the complete access to information he had been promised. The Ford administration was marked by half-hidden infighting between Alexander Haig and other Nixon stalwarts who had not been caught up in the Watergate net and who now meant to retain power, as against those who wanted, like Ford, to lead the Republicans into much safer waters. When reporters asked questions about these squabbles, Nessen was often honest in telling them he had no information, but since it was well known that he had unusual access, his credibility suffered and was gradually eroded. It was, as he said, ''an unending struggle.''

But what virtually destroyed Nessen's credibility with the press corps, ending in the all too familiar rancor, was his tendency to magnify everything the president did in a way that sounded like aggressive press agentry. It reached a climax in his statement that Ford's agreement with the Soviets at Vladivostok was ''one of the most significant agreements since World War II. Richard Nixon could not achieve this in five years. President Ford achieved it in three months.'' It was the kind of grandiose puffery that pleased no one, particularly the correspondents, who knew better. Nessen knew better, too, on second thought. He invited fifteen or so reporters to his office, gave them drinks and peanuts, and admitted that he had ''messed up a little bit.'' It was too late. As he writes: ''The trip ended whatever honeymoon I had with the press. After that I was never able to recover fully the lost opportunity to build a relationship of mutual respect and friendship with the White House press corps.''

Nessen was not the first to admit his failings, by any means, but he was candid enough about them in his memoirs, in which he imagined a final press conference concerning his book in which a reporter asks, ''In this book you seem to display the same pomposity, pettiness, vindictiveness and ill temper that you had in the White House?'' To which he answers that he did, indeed, have a short temper, was not a good administrator, and had at least a reputation as a constant intriguer against the reporters—what one of them, Anthony Lukas, called his snide gibes and one-upmanship.

On the other hand, some forward steps were taken. Ford ordered the virtual dismantling of Clay Whitehead's Office of Telecommunications. He permitted follow-up questions at news conferences, something the press had long been pleading for, and he gave interviews to local reporters and anchormen who otherwise would have had no such opportunity. He also invited reporters to White House social events as guests, treating them as friends, an unaccustomed role. The problem was not that Ford did not try to have good relations with the press but that he was too much of a politician to try hard enough. He told correspondents he would be open and candid, but in the end he was closed and self-serving, as political realities dictated.

Nessen did not help him, but it is far from clear how much Ford could have been helped. Summarizing the press secretary's troubles with the correspondents, Deakin says:

> There were personality conflicts. There were credibility problems. Respect was lacking. Nessen accused the reporters of ''blind, mindless, irrational suspicion and cynicism and distrust.'' He said in effect that they were still operating as if Nixon

were president. He threatened to discontinue his daily briefings unless the press shaped up. . . . The White House press operation under Nessen remained blandly secretive and deceptive. Nessen was responsible for more of the journalistic "suspicion and cynicism and distrust" than Ford.

All these factors involving both the president and his press secretary made Ford's run for the presidency in 1976 a foredoomed affair. There was the public image of the president playing golf in Palm Springs while Danang, in Vietnam, fell in blood and terror, both events appearing on the same nightly news. There was Agriculture Secretary Earl Butz's tasteless jokes about blacks that, too late, cost him his job and Ford's acknowledgment that while he was in Congress he had accepted free golf holidays from corporate friends. Ex-Nixon aide John Dean chimed in with the accusation that the Nixon White House had recruited Ford to suppress an early congressional investigation of Watergate. In the public mind, the nice guy was still nice but tainted, and they turned to the honest farmer from Georgia who wanted to be called "Jimmy" and promised to exorcise the devil from the White House and government in general.

It was not a choice every voter wanted to make, which accounted for the halfhearted turnout, but the Carter promise, after years of turmoil and deception, was too much to resist. Still another new era of honesty in government was about to dawn—or so it was said.

Carter: The Unanswered Question

There were more practical reasons for Carter's election, of course—grassroots organization and campaigning, saying the right things at the right time, the ability to formulate populist ideas, among others. Still, it was a political miracle that an unknown figure from the Deep South could jump to the White House in one leap, bringing with him an entirely new cast of characters, so unknown themselves and so remote from those who had inhabited Washington for nearly twenty years that their advent was hailed with premature hosannahs. Here was a man of obvious intelligence, with an attractive family, an avowed determination to bring back at least some degree of honesty into government, possessed of an excellent sense of timing, and with other qualities, presumably shared by his staff, that promised a new day in national politics.

In the most recent analysis by an outsider of the Carter administration, Laurence H. Shoup argues that a small group of wealthy and powerful people—members of the corporate upper class—shaped the 1976 presidential selection process, helped a relatively obscure former governor of Georgia to gain power, and then molded his administration. To aid them, he says, they employed the "elite media," as part of the ruling class, whose interpretation of political events, even which events they consider newsworthy, could be decisive.

This argument depends on the validity of the idea, widely believed by academics, that such a thing as an "elite press" exists and that its selection of events it considers newsworthy and its interpretation of them are somehow different from that of other elements in the media. It is an attractive idea that fits neatly into a sociological view of the press, but there are few elements of reality in it, as the history of Carter's press relations testifies.

Hamilton Jordan, Carter's campaign manager, accepted the mythology of the "Eastern/liberal newspaper Establishment," meaning the New York *Times* and the Washington *Post*, and its importance as early as November 1972, when he wrote a memo to Carter which declared that this monolith "has tremendous influence. The views of this small group of opinion-makers in the papers they represent are noted and imitated by other columnists and newspapers throughout the country and the world. Their recognition and acceptance of your candidacy as a viable force with some chance of success could establish you as a serious contender worthy of financial support of major party contributors."

Jordan believed that the press could help Carter overcome his chief obstacle to nomination—his lack of "name recognition," in the jargon of the trade—and "give some depth to his new national image." But Carter's rise to prominence was due much less to the "Eastern Establishment press," which comparatively few voters actually read and whose trickled-down views were not nearly as influential as Jordan believed, than to the exposure he got on national television, which showed the public a kind of presidential candidate they had not seen before.

On the tube Carter developed the ability to change positions as rapidly as the images themselves changed, in the view of Peter Meyer, one of his early biographers. Television, said Meyer, showed voters the man as he was, rather than what he was about. Moreover, after he became president, his shifting from one position to another was even more evident on the televised press conferences. In September, Carter remembered the exact date when his old friend and director of the Office of Management and Budget Bert Lance advised him that he (Lance) was the subject of a Justice Department investigation about his previous dealings with Georgia banks; little more than a month later Carter could not recall ever hearing of the incident.

Television was at once friend and enemy to Carter in the 1976 campaign. It made his face and voice familiar to millions of voters who had never heard of him, and it established his image as a man of the people, coming as a born-again Christian to rescue them from the Washington devils. On the other hand, the televised debates Carter held with President Ford not only caught Ford in his memorable gaffe—"There is no Soviet domination of Eastern Europe"—which some reporters thought cost him the election, but there was also the moment at their first encounter when the sound went dead for twenty-seven minutes, leaving viewers with the feeling that they were looking at creatures of the medium, not its masters. Carter's stiffness and lack of informality were painfully evident in that embarrassing interval.

The correspondents who traveled with Carter during the campaign learned something about him the public did not know, as is frequently the case. In a book written not long after the 1976 election, James Wooten of the New York *Times* recalled that, during the New Hampshire primaries, Carter made some statement to a reporter with whom he was having lunch and got what would ordinarily have been an innocuous response: "That's hard to believe." But Carter, Wooten wrote, stared at the reporter, and "his voice was almost a whisper. 'Listen,' he hissed, 'I'm not a liar. You get that into your head. I'm not a liar.' He stalked away from the table and out of the restaurant, still hungry and mad as hell."

Meanwhile Carter was selling himself, and being sold, on television, for which Republicans and Democrats were spending about half the $21.8 million allotted to each candidate by federal subsidy. Most of the press was friendly to him, especially *Time* magazine, but also including such unlikely supporters as *Rolling Stone,* in its own fashion. If none of the media really succeeded in accurately describing him, it is not surprising, because they have been trying to unravel and explain his complex personality ever since, with only moderate success.

Following Jordan's early advice Carter made a conscious, serious effort to woo the press, particularly the feared Eastern elite monster, with the help of Gerald Rafshoon, a charter member of the new breed known as media consultants. If there was an obstacle to the salesmanship, it lay in an ineradicable and far from hidden part of Carter's personality, his devout religious beliefs, from which stemmed his excessive morality (or so it seemed to many people) and his equally excessive self-righteousness. That was why he had been so angry with the reporter in New Hampshire; he sincerely believed that he would never lie, an extraordinary piece of self-deception coming from a man who had been in political life for so long.

As Carter had convinced the electorate of his superior morality, the shock to some of the people was all the greater when the notorious interview with him appeared in *Playboy,* in which he confessed that he had lusted in his heart after women and employed such otherwise common words as "screw" and "shack up." Fellow moralists were horrified, others were highly amused, and some hardly knew whether to laugh or cry at the prospect of such a man in the White House. In the end opinion remained divided whether religion had plagued him all the way to Washington and afterward or whether it was religion that had been responsible for his being there at all. Certainly it was Richard Reeves's article, "Carter's Secret," in *New York* magazine during mid-March 1976, that precipitated religion into the campaign and led Carter to assert his "intimate relationship" with Jesus.

After fifteen months of the new administration, however, the Carter dilemma had become plain, and James Reston summed it up in the New York *Times:* "There has always been this puzzle about Jimmy Carter—whether the smile on his face or the chip on his shoulder would prevail. He has been trying to play the game both ways, being very moral on one hand, and very clever and political on the other. . . . [Carter] is discovering that there is a fundamental difference between how to win an election and how to govern after you win."

Nine months into office Carter was already in deep trouble, which once again Reston had summed up astutely in the *Times:* "Washington wants a clear sharp line from President Carter between high property taxes and adequate public services, between inflation and unemployment, the Israelis and the Arabs, the Soviets and the Chinese, but there are no clear lines, and Mr. Carter refuses to choose up sides. His latest press conference illustrates the point. Confronted with a series of complicated and ambiguous questions, he simply refused to give simple answers.''

Both the sharp line and the simple answers may have been unreasonable to expect, but it was true that Carter was failing to make his case either in the press conferences or the briefings, although it was no more the press secretary's fault than it had been Nessen's or Ziegler's. Indeed, Joseph Lester Powell, Jr., or ''Jody,'' as everyone knew him, was regarded as a valuable asset in the beginning, even though he was only thirty-three and was one of the few press secretaries without professional qualifications for the job. Like his boss, he was another good old boy from Georgia, who had worked for an insurance company, studied for a Ph.D. in political science at Emory University, and had been his press secretary since Carter became governor of Georgia in 1970. Powell was intelligent, extremely personable, with a quick sense of humor that made even his frequent stonewalling sessions with the press a little more palatable than otherwise. His primary qualification, of course, was that he was closer to Carter than any press secretary had been to a president since Jim Hagerty. That gave him unusual credibility with the correspondents.

Powell was another secretary afflicted by the belief that the press is all-powerful. In a David Brinkley documentary for NBC in 1979 he said of media influence: ''It is an awesome power in this country. In fact, there are probably few institutions in our nation that exercise as much power on a day to day continuing basis as does the press that covers the White House. And, of course, network television, because of the literally tens of millions of people that you reach every night, has a power for good or ill that probably has never been equalled at any other time in history.''

Politicians eagerly embrace this concept because, if the media puts too much pressure on them in an effort to make them accountable, it is then easy to blame the press for abusing its great power and, as some do, to argue that it should be curbed, meanwhile protesting a belief in its freedom. It is a concept that also leads to the paradoxical fear of and contempt for the press so often seen in public life. In the same Brinkley documentary Powell was shown talking to correspondents in his office and telling them: ''I certainly am not going to give an interview with the President on a particular subject to a reporter that I know doesn't have any idea on God's earth about what's involved in the subject. So I think that's legitimate. You don't cast your pearls before the swine, so to speak. But I don't consider that managing the news. I just consider that common sense.'' So to speak.

In fact Powell, for all his virtues, remained as naïve about the press when he left the White House as he was when he came to it, and it was exactly this failing that made Carter's press relations so difficult, since it was a naïveté shared by the president. If the swine could not be expected to understand the pearls they chose to cast, it was even more evident that this White House did not understand the news process any better than previous administrations, and probably not as well. At least the reporters could be reasonably sure that, on the infrequent occasions when Powell gave them any real information, it reflected what the president thought, not what the secretary believed he thought. Of course it was also true that, when Powell stonewalled, he reflected the president's unwillingness to commit himself.

Carter's self-righteousness and extreme sensitivity to criticism conditioned his view of the press, which was not unlike that of many of his predecessors. He considered the media as superficial and sensational, always out for a story without regard for the truth, and so there was no point in discussing serious issues with them. He, naturally, would define what the serious issues were. To circumvent the press, he embraced the delusion that had caused so many others to fail: he would go over the correspondents' heads to the people, who in their wisdom would understand what he was doing.

Sometimes, however, sheer rage against a particular paper would lead Carter to take a more direct route. While he had the good sense not to call the New York *Times* superficial and sensational, he did abhor its White House correspondent James Wooten because of his candid analyses of White House activities. On April 25, 1977, Wooten wrote:

The President tends to cling to his power, to intimidate subordinates and to be ill at ease with strong-minded assistants who dissent. . . . The effect of such an approach in the White House seems to have touched even such long-time aides as Jody Powell and Hamilton Jordan, ... More and more the president seems to be retreating into the sanctuary of his little study, emerging to speak "to the people" . . . but stepping further and further away from the people he gathered together to help him govern. . . . Mr. Carter has shown a mounting jealousy about his power and his responsibilities.

There was nothing particularly new in this estimate, which was shared by other reporters, but it infuriated both Carter and Powell, who attempted to prove that Wooten had never interviewed staff members, calling him the Erica Jong of reporters, a reference some of Wooten's colleagues who had read Jong's novels found obscure. But then the White House took a more effective action; it simply refused to give Wooten any interviews and ignored him. The *Times* responded by taking Wooten off the beat, on the grounds, as the evicted man put it, that he was now not as effective as someone else would be. The *Times* did not cave in to the White House, said Wooten; the White House just locked the door, leaving the paper no choice. It was as brutal as it was wrong.

Although they later came to revise their opinion, the network people at the beginning thought they had a natural—"a sensational performer," as one of them termed it—in Carter, and the president took full advantage of it. Barry Jagoda, who had worked for both CBS and NBC, was Carter's television adviser until early 1979, when Gerald Rafshoon was appointed to head the White House communications propaganda machine. Carter's great asset was to project himself as being natural, Jagoda said, and he was very good at it, instinctively doing the right things. Toward the end of his term that quality was wearing thin, and Rafshoon was unable to overcome growing public disillusionment and hostility. By that time Carter looked altogether too natural.

Network news executives and correspondents generally considered the Carter White House to be more clever in its handling of television than earlier administrations. Bob Schieffer, the CBS correspondent, remarked, "They know when it's to their advantage to be helpful to us. Like the joint swearing in of an antiwar guy [Sam Brown, director of ACTION] and a disabled Vietnam veteran [Max Cleland, head of the Veterans Administration]. You know you're being had, but you do it exactly the way they want it done because they're right, it's good television."

While Carter well understood what television could do for him and used the medium shrewdly, he was also aware it had its limitations when it came to communicating in-depth information about his actions and ideas; consequently in July 1979 he turned to the print media. In any case he and his staff believed they had just about exhausted television's possibilities for them; they could not come up with enough ideas to satisfy the insatiable cameras. In his press conference of July 25, 1979, Carter announced that he would no longer commit himself to two televised press conferences a month but instead would have more regional meetings with the press. Not that he considered himself no longer effective on television; he only meant to extend his range.

The idea of these regional press meetings, which translated into a series of private dinners, was Rosalynn Carter's according to some sources. She had always believed that the media did not fully understand her husband or reflect his ideas. Others gave credit for the move to Rafshoon, who had just joined the staff, entrusted with doing something about the president's public approval rating, which had dropped from a high of 70 percent to 28 percent. Nothing was spared. Carter involved him in every major substantive decision, so much so that a new word was added to the Washington vocabulary, "rafshooned," meaning being victimized by a media blitz engineered by the resident White House wizard. Rafshoon overdid it somewhat, becoming a controversial figure himself, but in any case he was too late, although he did succeed in elevating the President's popularity to a more respectable figure, for which he modestly took no credit.

As for Powell, he continued to be generally liked by most of the correspondents, in spite of the fact that he had become surly and combative with some of them and collectively meanspirited at his briefings. He was still able to defuse some intense situations with his down-home wit and just-one-of-the-boys attitude, but he cared to do so less frequently. He continued to maintain, with justice, that Carter was more personally accessible to the press than any recent president, but it was also clear that he was more accessible to some than to others. *Time,* for example, was more welcome than *Newsweek,* which was owned by the hated Washington *Post.* ABC felt itself less favored than its two rivals, and reporters such as Jack Nelson of the Los Angeles *Times,* who had known the Georgians in the White House for a long time, also seemed to have more access.

Carter overturned some cherished White House press traditions. He was inclined to depart for somewhere without the customary pool of newspaper, network, and wire-service reporters accompanying him. He was also in the habit of appearing suddenly, without announcement, at cultural events in the Kennedy

Center. Unlike his predecessors, however, he did not travel to distant spas in Florida, California, or elsewhere; he went back home to small-town Plains, Georgia.

In the end it was Carter's personality that ultimately did him in, both with press and public. As Deakin sums it up: "Carter was not Nixon. He did not abominate the news process so intensely that he tried to destroy it. But he disliked it deeply. 'He detested the process,' wrote James Wooten. He 'positively loathed it—all those questions about his motives and his positions.' . . . The vein in his right temple began to throb at every press conference. . . . So there was the self-righteousness problem as well. . . . All those questions! Who gave them the *right?*"

That was Powell's view, too, and his intense loyalty to Carter was no less than the president's loyalty to his friends. Under attack by the press or other critics, the Georgia boys rallied around each other. When Hamilton Jordan, the president's chief aide from the beginning, got into the headlines for alleged conduct unbecoming a Southern gentleman in a bar and at a party, as well as unverified charges that he indulged in what the law optimistically calls controlled substances, a tight ring was drawn around him and the accusers were counterattacked *en masse.*

Not all friends could be defended, however, as Carter had discovered early on in the case of Bert Lance, the Georgia banker who became his first director of the Office of Management and Budget. The administration itself brought on the Lance embarrassment, when in July 1977 it asked the Senate Governmental Affairs Committee to exempt him from the new moral rule laid down by Carter that top officials must sell their stocks and bonds within a year of holding office. Instead the commmittee called upon Lance to explain a $3.4 million Chicago bank loan. The investigation was dropped, but the press began looking into Lance's other banking activities, involving overdrafts by him and his friends, collateral for large loans, and additional matters. There were further Senate hearings, during which Powell attempted to discredit Sen. Charles Percy and Carter faithfully stood by his friend. When nothing indictable was discovered, the president exulted, "Bert, I'm proud of you." The report from the comptroller of the currency, however, had contained other information raising serious questions about whether some of Lance's banking practices had been improper or illegal, and although the president did his best to divert attention from his besieged friend, the press continued to pursue him, with the result that Carter suffered a sharp drop in the public approval polls. It was too much. For the good of the cause, Lance resigned under pressure, and the president accepted the resignation with personal if not political regret.

Nor did the president turn his back on William Alton ("Billy") Carter, his brother, whose jovial, wisecracking, beer-drinking, life-loving personality was the antithesis of the sober, God-fearing, intensely serious image the president presented. The media found Billy a welcome relief from the austerity of the Carter regime, and Billy found the media a welcome vehicle for his own good-natured aggrandizement of his family position.

Soon after his brother's election, Billy himself ran for office as mayor of

Plains, campaigning from the typical small-town gas station he owned, often filled with his drinking buddies, a place redolent of beer cans and grease. "Roll out the Barrel" was said to be his campaign song. The magic did not rub off, however, and Billy was defeated a month after his brother's victory.

Undismayed, Billy took full advantage of his new status in the nation. Compelled by the pressure of tourists and sightseers to abandon his gas station and his Plains home, he moved down the road a piece to a new house and soon began to be a show business figure. Americans, amused or horrified, who thought him no more than a red-neck swinger, a source of embarrassment to his quiet brother, revised their opinion when they saw him interviewed on television talk shows and heard him give his down-home view of the president and Carter family life from hundreds of lecture platforms, where he was so much in demand that he could get $5,000 for an appearance. Billy milked this cow until she ran dry, as they said in Plains.

The climax of his short career in the public eye came when the Falls City Brewing Company took advantage of his reputation as the nation's foremost beer drinker by launching a line of suds called Billy Beer, which touched off another round of celebrity as the younger Carter toured the country and appeared on radio and television to launch the brew. Carter partisans may have been embarrassed by all this, and the president's political enemies made as much hay as possible from the unexpected rural crop, but Carter simply shrugged it off. He could do no more about Billy than Theodore Roosevelt could about Alice, farfetched though the comparison might be.

In any case Carter had a great deal more to worry about than Billy. Of his many problems at home in 1979, the worst was the energy crisis created by the sharp reduction of oil from the Middle East. The country expected him to do something about it, and indeed he had a highly controversial energy bill he hoped to get through Congress, but the public had heard little from him and it was becoming irritable and impatient. The oil shortage had produced rising inflation, with long lines at the gasoline pumps as well as higher supermarket bills.

Late in June, Carter gave up a Hawaii vacation and retreated to Camp David, where he had already made history by bringing the Israeli and Egyptian leaders together in a compact known as the Camp David agreements, optimistically intended to achieve lasting peace in the Middle East. Now Carter meant to come up with a speech on energy that would get vital public support behind his program. He looked at several drafts, heard conflicting advice from his advisers, and then, only twenty-four hours before his scheduled appearance on television to address the nation, he abruptly canceled the speech.

Rumors spread rapidly. It was said that Carter was ailing from a variety of supposed diseases. The dollar plunged so rapidly that in order to stop it Carter had to announce he would give the wire services a general statement promising that he would act decisively on the energy problem. Political advisers were rushed up to Camp David by helicopter, and it was decided to call in leaders in politics, the media, business, unions, ethnic groups, religious and civil rights organizations for a ten-day national summit conference on the crisis. These guests represented a cross-section of people who had been close to Carter's or earlier Democratic administrations, and among the 134 people invited were twenty governors, ten professors, a sprinkling of congressmen, and others representing special interest groups.

The president ate with his visitors three times a day, presenting to them an unruffled facade that seemed quite out of keeping with the emergency nature of the meeting. He had consulted only his wife Rosalynn before the earlier cancellation, he told them, and then he verged onto new (for his listeners) puzzling territory. He had decided that it was useless to make any more speeches on energy, he said, because he had already spoken on the same subject to decreasing television audiences. No one was listening, he believed, and he was becoming convinced that the electorate was not ready to make the necessary sacrifices. He talked about spiritual exhaustion and his need to exert moral leadership in the country. In that case, some of his listeners suggested, he should fire Jordan, Powell, and James Schlesinger, the secretary of energy. It was all, as one historian had suggested, "high theater." David Broder, in his syndicated column, spoke of the strength it took for a man to learn from his own problems and correct his course.

Like Moses, Carter came down from the mountain eventually, but without exactly having talked to God, and delivered a speech written for him that presumably embodied what he had learned from the conference. He had rehearsed it several times beforehand, even to practicing clenching a visible fist as a symbol of determined leadership. In thirty-two minutes he made a bold and typical attempt to separate himself from responsibility for the crisis, laying it at the door of "government" caught in "paralysis . . . stagnation, and drift"—anticipating Ronald Reagan, who succeeded far better in separating the business from the boss. He had resolved to go back to the people, he said, and be their moral leader, after which he laid out a specific new energy policy for them to support.

Somehow, in the press, what emerged most memorably was the president's remark about these same people whose support he sought, whose man he had claimed to be from the beginning. He confessed that they had been disappointing him. A malaise had appeared in the land, bringing with it too much self-interest, even despair—no doubt deepest among those at the end of the gas pump lines.

If there was despair, it would soon be directed at him. On November 4 that year, militant Iranian students, fanatic followers of the Ayatollah Khomeini, seized the American Embassy in Teheran and began to hold ninety people, sixty-three of them Americans, as hostages in protest against Carter's admission of the ailing shah of Iran to the United States for a cancer operation. Thus began a 442-day ordeal for the captives, while America wallowed in anger, pity, and frustration. It extended into an election year, and national honor—"that terrible encumbrance," as Edmund Burke called it—was at stake. The result for Carter was increasingly certain as the days ticked away, marked on many front pages and on television news shows by a daily countdown, while the home screen showed from time to time humiliating pictures of the Embassy surrounded by chanting mobs, burning the American flag and denouncing America, the "Great Satan." There were also pitiful views of the captives themselves from time to time, receiving Christmas gifts and visitors, conveying the grimness of their situation.

The president of the United States was expected to do something, to restore national honor and bring the captives home. But what? Carter took the only rational course, which was to begin the slow and difficult business of negotiation through a mediator, Algeria. Impatient American partisans cited the Israeli rescue of similar hostages from the Entebbe airport in Uganda, but it did no good to point out that Teheran was not Entebbe. At last, in desperation, the president agreed to a harebrained military plan to rescue the hostages by means of a small force, equipped with helicopters, launched from a battleship. It was a ghastly failure, an aborted effort in which eight Americans were killed. Carter's ruin was complete, well before the votes were counted in 1980. His negotiations finally succeeded, but meanly the Iranians clouded his victory by keeping the released hostages on the ground at the Teheran airport until the moment Ronald Reagan was sworn in as President.

During the last four months in office the embittered president had held no press conferences. By this time he blamed the media for his approaching downfall. In those final days both Carter and Powell believed that the press was not dealing with substantive issues, focusing instead on personalities, but it was these same issues, covered by the press in depth, which led to Carter's defeat. He would never believe it, but the media had also given him equally extensive coverage of his undoubted successes—the Camp David summit meeting between Menachem Begin and Anwar Sadat, the Panama Canal treaties, the human rights campaign, among others. It was argued later that the press gave excessive coverage to the hostage crisis, but it is hard to imagine how such a story, which gripped the American public for so long as nothing else had done since Vietnam, could have been covered any differently.

When Powell had addressed the annual dinner of the White House Correspondents Association in July 1978, his remarks had been in the half-jocular spririt of the occasion, but few of those present thought he was entirely joking when he told them: "President Carter wanted to be here tonight. After all, he seldom has the occasion to dine with an institution [that is] held in lower esteem. . . . He, of course, wanted me to express his regrets. Unfortunately, time does not permit me to say all that is regrettable about the White House correspondents."

That time did come to Powell, as it does to all men, after he left the White House and had the leisure to write his memoirs, titled *The Other Side of the Story.* They were not like those written by earlier secretaries, even Nessen, but consisted of an ill-tempered attack on the media, which was wide ranging and venomous. It appeared that Powell hated the scandal-mongering *National Enquirer,* with reason, but he also hated the New York *Times,* the Washington *Post, Newsweek, Time,* the Boston *Globe,* Jack Anderson, Joseph Kraft, Rowland Evans and Robert Novak, and the networks. It was predictable that the Los Angeles *Times* and the Dallas *Times Herald* would emerge unscathed, as friends of the management. From this broadside it appeared that the media were fallible, occasionally made mistakes, and sometimes failed to live up to their own principles. That was hardly news, especially to the media. But there was also in Powell's book the same tone of self-righteousness that had characterized the Carter administration. Truth and virtue lay on the side of the anointed, and the others were living in outer darkness. Having said as much, Powell joined the enemy by becoming a columnist for the Los Angeles *Times* Syndicate and a commentator for ABC, where one presumes he could be counted upon never to deviate from the highest standards of accuracy and fairness.

Reviewing this book in the New York *Times Book Review*, Lester Bernstein, former editor of *Newsweek,* observed: "The fact is that Jimmy Carter as a national figure was almost invented by the media. He owed more to the engines of publicity for his emergence from obscurity to a Presidential nomination than any politician since Wendell Willkie in 1940. If Mr. Powell takes that as a norm, small wonder that he has felt shortchanged ever since."

Carter was not grateful. While he rarely attacked the press as president, once out of office the rage emerged, and in an interview with *Parade*, the Sunday magazine newspaper supplement, he rehearsed the familiar litany of presidents before him. The press is superficial and inaccurate. The papers publish stories they know are lies and treat rumors as facts without checking. They do not want to check because they do not want to see a good story killed. They never apologize for an inaccurate story. These were the same charges made by Powell, who selectively documented them with individual instances (many of them debatable) and from these extrapolated to include the entire media. Powell's descriptions of how newspapers operate were so far from reality that it was difficult to visualize him in his new role as a newsman. But then columnists and television commentators are not necessarily newsmen.

As these postmortem observations of the president and his men amply demonstrate, both Carter and Jordan lived in a fantasy world that blew up in the face of reality. The reality was Ronald Reagan.

Reagan: The Image Triumphant

The voters wanted someone who could make them forget about Carter, and Ford, and Nixon, and Johnson, all the way back to Kennedy. They got him in the person of the man who has been called, thousands of times, the "Great Communicator." Standing in virtual awe of his acknowledged communications skills, both press and public often tended to forget what he was communicating.

Whatever one's opinion of Reagan might be, there is no question that his path to the White House was unlike that of any other president, as the preceding pages of this volume testify. Although his political philosophy was deeply rooted in the McKinley era, at the same time he was peculiarly a man of his own period— paradoxically an antiquarian relic of the past and at the same moment a product of the American era that began with the Depression. Although his life and times have already acquired a substantial bibliography, it may be worth summarizing the salient points of his unusual career if we are to understand his relationship with the press, which was also like no other president's.

Growing up in the small town of Dixon, Illinois—population 8,191—Reagan acquired at an early date the attitudes that Sinclair Lewis so deftly harpooned in *Main Street,* a novel that appeared in 1920, the year Reagan came to this typical Midwestern community. It was the year, too, that the voters placed in the White House another small-town boy, Warren Harding. The two men shared many of the same convictions—traditional, unthinking patriotism; the feeling that only lazy no-goods accepted any kind of public welfare; the belief that woman's place was in the kitchen and the bedroom; the seldom acknowledged (at least by politicians) racism characteristic of all-white populations in which the only minority is the poor; and the macho conception of what a man should be and do. Young Ronald wanted to be called by his nickname "Dutch"; he thought "Ronald" was sissy.

It was true that both the elder Reagans were Democrats, and Jack, the father, was a Catholic, but Ronald never demonstrated, then or later, any passionate political or religious convictions. He was a Democrat when it suited him, a Republican when it suited him better; a man who later allied himself with Protestant fundamentalists but who told Catholics and Jews whatever they wanted to hear and seldom appeared in any church for devotional reasons. If he inherited anything from his father, who was a hard-drinking but not unsuccessful shoe salesman, it was an Irish gift for storytelling. Both Jack and his wife Nelle ran against the small-town grain not only as Democrats in a solid Republican community but in their disgust with racial and religious prejudice.

Those who observed the older Ronald Reagan in his first term, with his short attention span and obvious distaste for anything remotely intellectual, found it hard to believe that as a high school boy he was an avid reader of books. He favored the comics and sports pages in newspapers (as he still does), in stereotypical male fashion, and although he was too nearsighted to play baseball, he loved football and played it well. As a young man Reagan was pleasant and cheerful, at ease in his manner but at the same time keeping a little distance. He had that Midwestern small-town attribute of perennial optimism, the deeply felt conviction that people are essentially good and will be good to you unless crossed. It was a feeling that never left him.

The Depression struck Reagan while he was a student at nearby Eureka College, and he had to do what so many others did, taking on a part-time job so he could continue and at the same time send money home to his mother; his father had been fired. He always spoke of the profound impression the Depression made on him, but there is nothing in accounts of the period to indicate that it was a lasting one or even that he understood what was happening. These accounts show him as one of the few optimists to survive the collapse. No doubt it was this quality that made a Democrat of him, responding to Franklin Roosevelt, a man he much admired, who gave Americans hope.

Graduating in 1932, at the depth of the national misery, Reagan did odd jobs and served as a lifeguard but dreamed of getting into radio, and some day into acting. The Great Communicator was about to be born. Doggedly making the rounds of small-town radio stations in the Middle West, he at last got a job as a sports announcer at WOC (it stood for the World of Chiropractic, for its chiropractor founder, B. J. Palmer) in Davenport, Iowa. Reagan's manner and his

voice, particularly his voice, led to success. Without realizing it, he was already
an actor. He had presence as well, on or off the air. When WOC was merged
with WHO, a larger station in Des Moines, Reagan went with the deal and
became a successful sports announcer, as well as doing interviews. But he was
looking beyond Des Moines to Hollywood.

That opportunity came in 1937, when his job brought him to California, following the fortunes of the Chicago Cubs, where Joy Hodges, a singer and actress
Reagan met on a blind date, introduced him to her agent, who sold him to
Warner Bros. With that, Dutch Reagan the broadcaster became Ronald Reagan
the actor. He was sensitive about his acting career after he became a politician, as
one would expect from a man who spent thirty years of his life before the cameras or as a representative of other actors.

In his perceptive biography, *Reagan,* Lou Cannon, White House correspondent of the Washington *Post,* observes that until he became governor of California in 1967, Reagan was "Hollywood's child, citizen, spokesman and
defender." He was a successful actor in generally mediocre movies who somehow never became a star, although his performances were often better than the
pictures. Except for *Bedtime for Bonzo,* in which he costarred with an ape, Reagan the actor is remembered by older Americans for his portrayal of George
Gipp, the Notre Dame football player who died of pneumonia, in *Knute
Rockne—All American.* "Win one for the Gipper," the immortal Rockne plea,
was employed as a campaign exhortation in 1984, screamed lustily by young
voters to whom Gipp and Rockne were as remote and unidentifiable as Agamem-
non and Hector.

In the Second World War, Reagan was too nearsighted for combat, but he was
called up and spent the time making training films for the First Motion Picture
Unit of the U.S. Army Air Corps. After the war, divorced from a former leading
lady, Jane Wyman, in 1948, and remarried to another leading lady, Nancy
Davis, four years later, his screen career began to wind down in disputes with the
studio and as a result of his position as head of the Screen Actors Guild. But his
status as a celebrity in a celebrity-mad country was not seriously impaired, and
he parlayed his minor fame in films into a new career as politician, at fifty-five,
when he was elected governor of California. The professionals in office did not
welcome him, disbelieving in anyone who had not come up through the ranks in
the usual way, but Reagan proved to be a natural politician, with the same kind
of dubious talents they possessed.

In the 1950s Reagan had begun to become a conservative Republican, a rather
uneasy transition considerably helped by his new job as host for a television
series sponsored by General Electric, at the (then) high salary of $125,000 a
year, soon raised to $150,000. Reagan introduced the dramas in the series, and
played in some of them, also traveling the country for ten weeks every year to
promote GE products and hobnob with company personnel. Thus he was drawn
into the corporate mentality and the proximity to corporate wealth that would be
so helpful later.

He also, in the process, became an eloquent advocate of conservative causes
and acquired such a reputation as a speaker that he was sought out by the Na-

tional Association of Manufacturers, among others, to spread the gospel of *laissez-faire* capitalism. But he was annoyed when anyone called him a right-winger; in his simplistic way, he considered himself to be a standard, patriotic, plain American, committed to the ideals, if they could be called that, of those who were responsible for his income, which was getting progressively larger. In 1952 he switched his voter registration and became a loyal California Republican.

Reagan began his term as governor of California as a complete amateur, without a program, without any but the scantiest knowledge of how government worked. He learned, slowly and at the taxpayers' expense, and in the process he acquired a hatred of the press, particularly columnists. He freely lied to reporters for what he considered good reasons, in the manner of presidents. He was, as he himself jokingly admitted, playing the role of a governor, just as he had played movie roles, and as he would play his greatest starring role as president.

The ferment of the 1960s was beginning, and California, particularly the University of California campus at Berkeley, was in the forefront of the small revolution, focusing on Vietnam, that was sweeping the country. Reagan, riding on the crest of a conservative backlash, fought the Berkeley aspect of the national revolt, once by calling out the National Guard to enforce what amounted to martial law on the campus for seventeen days. Otherwise, in state affairs, the governor who would become a living symbol of opposition to high taxes was responsible for a tax bill far higher than what was needed, levied mostly against his chief supporters—corporations and upper-income people. Cannon, his biographer, calls this a combination of "shrewdness and ignorance."

By 1968 Reagan was already being promoted for president, and an oil millionaire named Tom Reed spent a good deal of time and money in the promotion, but Reagan did not believe the time was right. He continued to be a governor who learned on the job and who was a sworn enemy of the great Republican bugbear, "big government." A loyal defender of Nixon and Agnew, he left office in 1975 stamped as one of the few Republican leaders who believed the party had an immediate future. It was clear to him, if not to others, that he was headed for the White House, although it appeared to many politicians that he was remarkably unable to understand Watergate and what it meant. Reagan remained a Nixon defender to the end, but that loyalty had no effect whatever on Reagan's popularity.

Still, Reagan approached Washington reluctantly, deciding in 1974 not to run for the Senate. He continued to preach Republican dogma, attacking welfare costs, food stamps, and government spending in general. The encouraging response to these speeches led to his unofficial campaign for the nomination in opposition to Gerald Ford, many of whose ideas he did not approve. More and more Reagan was becoming the darling of the conservatives—popular at right-wing banquets, a constant reader of the *Reader's Digest, Human Events,* and the *National Review,* whose publisher, William Rusher, sought to encourage him and others in the formation of a third party.

The press took notice of Reagan's slow advance, but his calls for a New Federalism seemed not to excite them or anyone else but the right wing. Nevertheless Reagan announced his presidential candidacy in November of 1975. In the subsequent campaign he learned that the attention given such a candidate by the press is not the same scrutiny a governor attracts. His political ideas were picked apart and shown to be as simplistic as they were, and in his encounters with reporters he demonstrated a lamentable lack of background knowledge. Confident to the end, he lost the New Hampshire primary, and from then on, although he scored victories in some states, a discouraging failure was inevitable.

There was no doubt that Reagan would try again, however, and in November 1979 the process was under way once more, in accordance with the rules of the quadrennial national charade, beginning rather badly with a stumbling announcement speech. But he soon began to project the image of himself as an ordinary man who was really no politician, pulling out old chestnuts and homilies from past speeches, exhibiting at times his lack of knowledge about both domestic and world affairs, trying to cover up his hearing loss and advertising himself as young and vigorous, and somehow surviving with ease every blunder he made. It was then that his skills as an actor and his sure political instincts joined to convince those who watched him on television that he was what they wanted—a leader who would bring back the past, when, as they fondly believed, there were no hard questions to answer because no one dared to question the rightness and superiority of Americans.

Only such a candidate could have survived the blunders of that 1980 campaign—announcing his intention to establish official relations with Taiwan while George Bush was on his way to China; telling a fundamentalist Christian rally in Dallas (avoided by the born-again Carter) that he thought creationism should be taught in the schools; implying unintentionally in a Michigan speech that Carter was linked to the Ku Klux Klan. Since all these mistakes occurred in the first seventeen days of the campaign, the press was beginning to hover over him in anticipation of the next startling disclosure.

The polls gave Reagan new confidence, however, and he gained a great deal more ground in the television debates arranged by the League of Women Voters, in which his relaxed "aw-shucks," "there-you-go-again" style was in sharp contrast to Carter, who was better prepared but appeared stiff and nervous. "There you go again" was the clincher, a phrase uttered by Reagan in the sorrowfully reproving tones of a wise and benevolent uncle addressing an inadequate nephew. Coupled with the one-liners in which he was a practiced master, it added up to a kind of armor, capable of deflecting every assault and concealing his often astonishing weakness. Typically, his final campaign speech was a stirring evocation of America's mythical past, replete with images well removed from reality and full of reassurance that, far from suffering a national malaise, as Carter had said, Americans were past, present, and future heroes.

From this background, then, and by these means, Ronald Reagan became the fortieth president of the United States. As the first actor ever to occupy the White House, he found himself in command of a formidable propaganda machine that had been building steadily since the Kennedy administration and, with each advance in technology, had become a still more powerful instrument in the hands of a president who knew how to use it. To it Reagan brought the fundamental skills peculiar to the actor's craft, particularly the ability to suspend disbelief, as in the theater, and make illusion seem like reality. Since the vast panoply of the White House had been designed to do just that, the joining of the two was an epic conjunction—an actor working in a studio dwarfing in power if not in size the sound stages of Hollywood, and whose audience was an entire nation.

To manipulate this machine and make it work effectively, Reagan possessed an ideal combination of qualities. He was highly popular, as both the Roosevelts and Eisenhower had been, and he had the acquired ability, which no previous president had enjoyed, to create a character the whole country could enjoy— amiable, wisecracking, pointedly nonintellectual, embodying the virtues Carter talked about without agonizing over them. Nor did he have the negative qualities that had destroyed other presidents. He was not a tortured, introspective, compli- cated sufferer, as Johnson, Nixon, and Carter had been, but, as he sincerely believed, a plain, simple, eternally optimistic man of the people (albeit rich himself and living in the world of the rich and privileged) of a sort the Democrats had always talked about being. Such a man had never before emerged as a Republican.

The press found itself almost completely unable to deal with Reagan in the usual way. His mock humility, his seemingly total amiability, and his appear- ance as the big, rich, smiling daddy for whom the voters had yearned so long obliterated the fact that he meant to take the country back to the nineteenth century, if possible, and to impose on the most diverse nation in the world a uniformity of thought and belief that belonged to a nostalgic past where it had never actually existed.

Entering the White House, Reagan and his staff of intimates, several of them old California associates, began to bring the great presidential propaganda ma- chine up to date, oiling its gears the better to manipulate the media. When it was announced early in 1981 that the briefing room was to be remodeled once more, the reporters assumed it was being done for their greater comfort and efficiency. In fact it was Hollywood set building carried into politics. Permanent seats were installed in rows, and for the first time correspondents were assigned to these seats for the press conferences. It was not a permanent arrangement, it was ex- plained, except for the fact that the wire-service people and the television corre- spondents would always occupy the front row, where the cameras could be trained on the latter, and with the president also in view, so that Reagan could, in effect, carry on a direct dialogue with the television audience, for whom the conferences were primarily designed. That took care of the front seats.

The seats in the following rows went to news organizations in what the admin- istration considered roughly the order of their importance, that is, the Wash- ington *Post* in the second row and the New York *Times* in the third. As time went on, a reporter might find himself assigned to the front row for a single session and a single handpicked question, or be mysteriously relegated to a seat farther back, presumably by way of punishment. This renovation cost the taxpayers $166,000, but the Reagan people believed it was worth it, particularly when another Hollywood touch was added early in 1984. While the television cameras zeroed in from the back of the auditorium, the doors behind the podium, guarded by a marine in full-dress uniform, swung open at the end of the conferences to reveal a long, broad corridor leading to the executive offices. With the last question answered, or evaded, the president moved to the door as it swung open and the camera watched his broad back receding slowly down the long corridor until it disappeared. Fade-out.

There were other innovations. To emphasize the formality that the conferences now took on, as opposed to the old, informal days when such a thing as creeping disrespect might occur, the reporters were told to stay in their assigned seats and raise their hands if they wanted to ask a question. The idea, it was said, was to bring order into the conference, but it obviously enabled the president to be completely selective about whom he called on.

The press conferences, however, were only a relatively small part of the machine that had grown so explosively since Nixon's day. Ford had a press office staff of only 45 people, about seven times more than in 1960; most of the increase had taken place under Nixon, and it constituted about 10 percent of the entire White House staff of 500 people. Reagan's staff numbered about 600 people, possibly more, of whom 150, at a minimum, and nearly 500 at a more reasonable maximum, were devoting most of their time and talents to exalting the president and burnishing his image by every device known to publicity and public relations. In 1978 the Office of Media Liaison had been averaging 35,551 press release items each month, sending them to 6,500 news organizations, ethnic groups, and individuals. The figure under Reagan swelled to even larger proportions.

But the real power did not lie with this intricate, growing apparatus. It lay in the president's ability to make news and define it, at which Reagan showed himself to be a supreme master. A president can distract public attention from embarrassing episodes by creating an event that will put himself in a more favorable light. He can make "photo opportunities" that are calculated to portray him as he wants to be portrayed. He can look presidential for political purposes in a variety of ways. He selects the questions he wants to answer at a press conference and chooses the reporters whose questions he wants to hear.

Since everything the president does is news, and has been for a hundred years or more, the press has no alternative but to print or record it. It retains its independent right, however, to exercise its own judgment and define news from a professional, not a political standpoint, and that is what frustrates presidents. When their own definition of news and their own notions of the relative importance of individual items are contradicted by the press, they cry bias and distortion and sometimes unpatriotic opposition to what the government thinks is good for us. It was this difference that Reagan and the propaganda machine at his disposal exploited cleverly, playing on public attitudes to the administration's great advantage.

As Laurence I. Barrett, chief White House correspondent for *Time*, observes in a recent book, *Gambling with History*, Reagan was "the most overtly ideological President in the nation's history," a man who followed his instincts regardless of the facts. Representing such a president as press secretary was obviously going to be a problem, and when the White House staff managers James Baker and Michael Deaver sought to find one, they discovered they had a dilemma on their hands. The first three men they approached refused outright. James Brady, an intelligent, experienced newsman, had been transition spokesman and obviously wanted the job, but the Reagan aides had doubts about him. David Gergen was a possibility, but the conservative Reaganauts believed he was not conservative enough, and he was further tainted by his Eastern Establishment connections, having attended Yale and Harvard Law School.

In the end Brady got the job, but he was the last of the important staff appointments to be made, and it was done reluctantly. He was well liked by the correspondents, but they also knew that he was not close to Reagan, as Powell had been with Carter, and consequently his credibility suffered. Kerna Small was named as his deputy, a token appointment of a woman that incidentally humiliated Larry Speakes, Brady's assistant, but she lasted only six months. Gergen then became assistant to the president and staff director, thus outranking Brady, who did his best but was always aware that the reporters were going over his head for information. He might have overcome his problem if he had not been the chief victim of the assassination attempt on Reagan.

That event, on March 30, 1981, after Reagan had been in office only two months and ten days, had a strengthening effect on an administration already knee deep in controversy over both foreign and domestic policy. The would-be assassin was not an agent of the Kremlin or even a terrorist but the disturbed son of an upper-class Denver family, John Hinckley, Jr., twenty-five years old. His obvious mental condition canceled out any political considerations and enabled the public to focus on the personal heroism of the president. Brady lay on the sidewalk with a bullet in his brain after the shooting outside a Washington hotel, and two others lay injured, but Reagan was thrown into the car that he had been about to enter and a few minutes later walked into the emergency room of George Washington University Hospital, falling to one knee as he did so. The surgeons removed a bullet lodged only an inch from his heart.

Television, replaying the scene over and over and following the hospital story hour by hour, produced an outpouring of sympathy from a public still not recovered wholly from the shock of the guns that had killed John and Robert Kennedy and Martin Luther King. Both television and the print press faithfully recorded, in the days that followed, Reagan's ready supply of one-liners about his condition, his undoubted courage, his concern for the others involved, and the human qualities he displayed. As a survivor instead of a victim, he could not help enlisting the sympathy and support of most people.

After Reagan recovered, Gergen was made director of communications, while Speakes was named principal deputy press secretary, a division that made no one happy and created tension. Speakes, who eventually emerged as press secretary in his own right, had worked for small-town papers in his native Mississippi, later became an aide to the ultraconservative Sen. James Eastland, and then held minor jobs in the Nixon and Ford administrations. While Carter was president, he had retired from Washington briefly to be vice-president of Hill & Knowlton, the New York public relations firm. He was forty-one when he came to power at last, but looked younger, and he was considered less intense than his predecessors.

Press relations had started on the usual soothing note. The president declared: "I think that most of the time the overwhelming majority of them [the reporters] do a fine job, and as a former reporter, columnist and commentator myself, I know just how tough their job can be." Some eyebrows were raised at this assertion; Reagan had never held any of these jobs in a news organization and nothing in his entire career would lead anyone to believe he was a writer. But the correspondents let it pass, as they did so many other of the meaningless, genial things the president said.

Reagan and his men were determined not to give the impression that the new chief would be like Nixon, considering the press as his natural enemy and evading or attacking it at will, or like Carter, taking a moral attitude toward it. Yet the outcome was as it has always been. As Barrett summarizes it:

> It is one of journalism's jobs to underscore the mistakes of a government. It is one of the rights of incumbents to defend themselves vigorously. By the end of Reagan's first year this traditional adversary relationship was in full play. Each side occasionally was guilty of minor excess, but neither seemed eager to return to the kind of bitter combat that had raged intermittently since Lyndon Johnson's final agony. Reagan's second year brought more severe tests in the form of worsening economic problems and new alarms abroad. Commentators inevitably pointed out the White House's responsibility and examined more carefully Reagan's personal failings. Only a saint in the Oval Room could resist totally the temptation to blame the press for some of his problems. Still, the exchanges were conducted within certain bounds of civility; in this matter, as in some others, Reagan helped restore a piece of the past.

There were other correspondents who were not as optimistic. Reagan held only three press conferences during his first eight months in office, fewer than any president in that period for the past fifty years. In the scarce private interviews he gave, he demonstrated a distinct talent for elusiveness, avoiding follow-up questions, making pronouncements in his easygoing way, but carefully blocking the kind of questions that might compel him to explain or justify himself. A significant flaw in his performance was his inability to grasp or understand world history or single events. Without the help of a script, and therefore virtually helpless, and answering questions that were impossible to dismiss with one-liners, Reagan made misstatements and egregious errors at press conferences that grew to be so numerous that they attracted public attention and some controversy—even a collection of them in book form. Hastily, his managers restricted the conferences and stage-managed his appearances to avoid these embarrassing lapses.

As Barrett has pointed out, the president "was profoundly uneasy with the journalistic process," even when he got favorable coverage. Like all the others, he was angry when something was published that he wanted to see buried, and he echoed earlier presidents in his belief that it was disloyal to leak information and irresponsible to print what was leaked. He distrusted the press, even though he had gotten along well enough with reporters as governor of California, for the most part. Having spent much of his life in show business, he understood how important it was to get good publicity and to get along with the press. But by the time he arrived in Washington, getting along with the media had become entirely different from anything in his experience. After Vietnam, Agnew, Watergate, the pardon, and other events, presidential credibility was at its lowest point, and public relations was firmly in the saddle, with the White House publicity machine in control. In this climate early coverage of the Reagan presidency was surprisingly fair, as he acknowledged.

But then the leaks began, as they always do, and Reagan was as irate as his predecessors had been. At first it appeared to be his policy to punish, if he could (or at least chastise), those who had printed information he wanted suppressed, rather than the leakers. But then, in 1982, he issued an order forbidding speaking to reporters on a background basis by everyone in the White House, with a half-dozen exceptions, including his closest advisers and Gergen and Speakes. Baker and Deaver were alarmed by this edict, fearing correctly that it would lead to a direct confrontation with the press. They talked Reagan into a compromise, but by that time many of those in the lower echelons were intimidated and coverage was not as easy as it had been, especially in the Defense and State departments.

At the upper level of the White House, however, one leak occurred in a most unexpected way in November 1982, when the *Atlantic* appeared on the newsstands with an article titled "The Education of David Stockman," in which the thirty-five-year-old director of the budget admitted that he had deployed his figures so that they would not appear as the "voodoo economics" Vice-President George Bush had once described them before he was elevated to the sainthood. Stockman's blasphemy outraged the supply-siders who were the philosophers of the Reagan budget; they could scarcely believe the budget director's candid and devastating words about their economic liturgy.

Nor could the article have come at a worse moment. Only a few weeks earlier the national debt had soared beyond a trillion dollars, meaning $100 billion annually in interest payments; simultaneously unemployment had reached its highest point since 1975. How to pay for the deficit and the grandiose plans for military spending without raising taxes was at that juncture a dilemma that the president had no idea how to solve except by means which would be politically difficult and dangerous.

And the leaks, of course, continued. They roused the president's indignation again, and he responded with another directive designed to control conversations at the White House level and prevent background discussions. Reagan had, in fact, made a systematic effort to suppress and control the flow of information from such government agencies as the Justice Department, the Pentagon, and the Central Intelligence Agency. It was not altogether successful but it was enough to throw roadblocks in the way of journalists and historians who had been taking advantage of the Freedom of Information Act, which the administration sought to cripple. The result could only be increasingly abrasive relations between the press and the president, in spite of White House distaste for casting Reagan as an enemy of the media.

But the president was beginning to understand that in several important ways he did not need the media any longer, except as a convenient public relations outlet. Until recently, the White House had taken the public pulse by carefully scanning and analyzing what was printed and broadcast by the media. Reagan, however, now made use of the sophisticated new polling techniques available to him. Using funds from the Republican National Committee, he hired a firm called Decision Making Information, directed by an eminent polltaker named Richard Wirthlin, to carry out the most comprehensive (and expensive) poll taking on a continuous basis ever done for a president. What Wirthlin's figures showed became an important part of White House political strategy and sometimes influenced the president's decisions. Gergen was valuable in these operations because he, too, had been a successful polltaker, founder and editor of *Public Opinion,* a periodical devoted to that arcane art.

There were those who believed that some of this was wasted motion. Barrett, for example, considered it a myth that Wirthlin's figures gave Reagan an extraordinary power to shape public perceptions. If that were true, he pointed out, Reagan should have been relatively free from criticism, which was far from the case, and the process should also have insulated him from the political effects of bad news, which was also not the case. What helped the president more was not statistics but his amazing popularity. No matter how bad the news might be, none of it stuck to the presidential image—the "Teflon President," as his critics called him. The public simply refused to associate Reagan with the results of his policies, unless those results were good. That did not stop the White House, however, from continuing to use the most advanced techniques employed by media consultants to manipulate the media, and through them the public, still further.

Meanwhile the president accumulated an impressive record of actions, covert and otherwise, that not only tended to suppress information but attacked the press for the same reasons Nixon had attacked it, but using less confrontational methods, with some exceptions, than his predecessor had employed. By mid-1984 this massive campaign had compiled a record of considerable proportions, one that some historians and many observers of First Amendment freedoms and government-press relationships found deeply disturbing. Considerable damage to both the freedom and the relationship had already been done, these observers believed, and the prospect would be much bleaker if another four years of a Reagan administration occurred.

While most aspects of this campaign have been discussed, or at least noted, by the media, it may be instructive to summarize some of the more important phases of the Reagan record in this respect. At a time in the spring of 1982, when the country was gripped by a severe recession with its attendant human suffering, Reagan gave an interview to the *Daily Oklahoman,* of Oklahoma City, intended to reach the grassroots with the message that the situation had been greatly exaggerated by television news. Complaining about the "constant drumbeat," the president delivered the query that haunted him for some time: "Is it news that some fellow out in South Succotash someplace has just been laid off, that he should be interviewed nationwide, or someone's complaint that the budget cuts are going to hurt their present program?'' The ''downbeat,'' he added, could contribute psychologically to slowing down recovery. During the same week, Reagan had given another interview, published in *TV Guide,* owned by Walter Annenberg, a close friend of Nixon and the Republican party, complaining about the unauthorized disclosure of information, which was echoed in a speech at the same time by Edwin Meese, the White House counselor.

By early 1983 the president and his advisers had raised the manipulation of television news, begun in the Kennedy administration, to a fine art. These new efforts included the ten-minute daytime mini-news conferences, the making of public appearances with high-technology executives and auto workers, an intense multiplication of ''photo opportunities'' (really high-level press agentry), the briefing (that is, propagandizing) of local television news anchors and news directors; plus the usual news conferences. As Sam Donaldson, the ABC White House correspondent, observed, ''They want the impression of a President who frequently meets the press, but they are using every device to control it.''

When the president was due to give a speech whose success might be determined by the way it was treated in the media, reporters were briefed twice before it was given, once by a collection of top officials whose off-the-record and therefore anonymous views could be quoted next day, then by a five-page summary of the presidential remarks, prepared by the White House staff. Producing such fact sheets and background material had become a cottage industry. For the most important speeches, special briefings for network anchors were given. Sometimes as many as fifteen columnists were asked to the White House for specialized treatment, and foreign journalists were similarly invited. Government officials were also deployed in advance to appear on various television talk shows.

Reagan's supreme confidence in himself, and his equally abundant contempt for law, national or international, and for the press as well, was never better illustrated than in the Great War Against Grenada, when on October 25, 1983, the United States invaded this tiny dot in the Caribbean chain of islands, in clear violation of both American and international law, the United Nations charter, and the charter of the Organization of American States. The invasion—a year later Reagan was still calling it a ''rescue mission''—was carried out by a force of more than six thousand men, opposing some eight hundred Cubans, not all of them armed, and a Grenadian ''army'' that was little more than a police force. The pretext was that the Cubans were building an airport with a nine-thousand-foot runway from which it was presumed they intended to conquer the neighboring islands and possibly the United States. A corollary excuse was that the United States was rescuing some five hundred or so American students at the St. George's University School of Medicine before they could be killed or, what was worse from the Reagan viewpoint, be held as hostages like those in Iran.

It was not the most glorious day in the history of our armed forces. There was considerable confusion, some helicopters were wrecked and eighteen servicemen were killed, at least a few of whom had come under what the military euphemistically calls ''friendly fire.'' Most of these facts, however, did not emerge at once, some not until a year later, because the Reagan administration (although

Reagan stoutly denied he had anything to do with the decision) had taken the historically unprecedented action of barring the press from covering the invasion until three days after it was over. Even some conservatives were alarmed by this blatant violation of the First Amendment, in which reporters were treated as though they were spies. For a few hours the country had been in the grip of an authoritarian power—its own government.

In the wake of the invasion, whether what the public was permitted to know had any elements of truth in it came under scrutiny at last. As the New York *Times* summarized the result on November 6, 1983, "It has become clear that the Reagan Administration officials and military authorities disseminated much inaccurate information and many unproved assertions. They did so while withholding significant facts and impeding efforts by the journalists to verify official statements."

Reagan, however, had read the public mind as accurately as Nixon and Agnew had done. Instead of reacting angrily to this contemptuous treatment of press freedom, people in general not only applauded the invasion, which appeared to some to have wiped out the shame of Vietnam, but thought the meddling press had been given no more than it deserved. The people seemed to be agreeing that they had a right to know some things but not others, the decisions to be made by the government. No authoritarian, right or left, would have disputed it.

In the face of this renewed evidence of public hostility, media owners withdrew cautiously after making official representations of protest. A year later they compounded this mistake by consenting to negotiate with the Defense Department over the role of the press in future war situations, declared or undeclared, and agreeing to weasel-worded terms on matters that should never have been negotiated at all. The press did not stand up to the government, for fear of its customers, and the government came away with restrictions it had never been able to impose before.

As for the results of the invasion, on the first anniversary of the event debate continued about whether the medical students had ever been in any danger. Since it was thirty hours before American troops reached the bulk of them, they could easily have been massacred if that had been the intent of the Revolutionary Military Council, the left-wing group that had just seized the island from a possibly slightly less radical government. There was not the slightest evidence that any such action had ever been intended.

The airport, it turned out, had been under study since the mid-1960s, but not by the Cubans, and its purpose was to rescue the island's faltering economy by making it possible for tourists to come in large numbers by jet. Cubans had done largely "earthwork" at the airport, while most of the other construction had been in the hands of a Fort Lauderdale, Florida, company under contract to the leftist government, assisted by a consortium of American companies who supplied asphalt for the runway and even designed the extensive fuel storage tanks that the Reagan administration had asserted constituted proof of Cuban military intentions.

By spending $19 million of its own taxpayers' money, the American government finished the job and got the runway open at least on the anniversary of the invasion, so that Reagan, as a candidate for reelection, could demonstrate that something had been accomplished, even though the aiport opening was so hastened to meet this deadline that two-thirds of the installation was still uncompleted. The Grenadians were grateful. They said it was now possible that jet aircraft would bring the tourists who could save the island's economy—which, of course, had been the original intention in the 1960s. Reagan supporters denounced these reports when they appeared in the press a week before the election of 1984 as further proof that the unpatriotic media were trying to denigrate America and blacken the reputation of the greatest president since John Wayne—or was it Jimmy Stewart?

The president succeeded in laying much of the blame for his foreign policy failures at the door of the press, at the same time accusing it of being unpatriotic. Using *TV Guide* once again as his mouthpiece in 1982, he had said: "Suppose . . . I could say to the press, 'Look, I will trust you by telling you what we are trying to accomplish. If you use that story it will result in harm to our nation, and probably make it impossible to do what we're trying to do.' But they just go on with the story—and we read it." One analyst, Dan Hallin, remarked of this statement: "The President was nostalgic for an era when the media were indeed much more deferential toward political authority, above all in foreign affairs. And in that nostalgia he is not alone. Ever since Spiro Agnew directed his barbs—more precisely, barbs honed by Nixon speechwriters—at the 'nattering nabobs of negativism,' a growing chorus of critics has laid the failings of contemporary American politics at the door of the 'adversary' press."

The enemy, it appeared, was not the Soviet Union but the press. Gen. Maxwell D. Taylor, in his 1972 memoirs, *Swords and Ploughshares,* had said as much in his expressed belief that the United States could have won the war in Vietnam if only the media had been kept away from it. The press, Taylor added, had carried on a "campaign of defamation against the Presidency, the Congress, the courts, the church and business." Secretary of State George P. Shultz, a decade later, was saying, in defense of the Grenada censorship, that reporters had accompanied the troops in World War II because in those days they were on "our side."

At a subsequent press conference Reagan not only backed the secretary but complained that, beginning with the Korean War and continuing through Vietnam, "there was more criticizing of our forces and what we were trying to do, to the point that it didn't seem that there was much criticism being leveled at the enemy." But the president, as usual, had a primitive idea of history. In fact most of the criticism of the war in Korea had come from the Republican party, and during the Vietnam conflict a large part of the American press and even some correspondents in the field supported the war. Nor was there the slightest evidence to show that American forces were ever endangered by reporting in the press.

Employing his persuasive "aw-shucks" style, the president expressed the pious hope that "we could get together in what is of importance to our national security . . . what is endangering our forces and what is helping them in their mission." Here he was reiterating the belief of presidents that "national security'' is what they say it is and that, once defined, the press is morally obligated to give it unquestioning support. In the press conference, asked to identify who were the ''us'' that reporters were presumed to be against, he said it was ''our side, militarily—in other words, all of America,'' thus exemplifying another presidential belief, that his policy must be all the people's policy as well. Lincoln could have told him differently. It is typical of the ironies of our time that the president, in the same week, delivered a radio sermon to Cuba on the virtues of a free press.

Meanwhile the administration, in 1983, carried on what Dan Rather, anchorman of the CBS evening news, called ''unrelenting criticism'' of the network's news operations. There was pressure before the news went on the air, he said, and criticism after it was broadcast, but the White House denied it was instituting a campaign against the network, as Nixon had done, although David Gergen admitted that some of the president's right-wing supporters were urging him to do so. Rather declared that the Reagan administration's sophisticated approach made it more difficult to deal with the continuing pressure than it had been with Nixon. They were ''slicker and smarter and therefore more dangerous and more effective,'' he said.

After the president had made several statements bordering on absurdity at his press conferences, as noted earlier—misinformation, hopelessly twisted history, even worse syntax, and plain misstatements—tighter controls were exerted, and the president was aided by restraints that would prevent him from putting his foot in his mouth. The chief move to save him from himself was to change the press conference from the original afternoon sessions, which the networks could edit later for the evening news shows, to prime time in the evening, which they could not.

It was soon apparent in the Reagan White House that best results could be achieved by giving information to reporters whose relaxed ethical standards guaranteed that they would write favorable stories. A correspondent, consequently, could either be a sycophant or run the risk of attack. Those who ran the risk developed inside sources, a test of their professional ingenuity, which resulted in good reporting and constantly irritated the president and his aides. Even so, many reporters believed that a great amount of news that was in the public interest was being skillfully concealed.

One way to prevent embarrassing questions was to ban reporters from ''photo opportunities,'' so that nothing political could be shouted over the clicking of the shutters, particularly when the representative of a foreign government was in the picture. Some of these shouts were still heard over the roar of helicopters as the president journeyed to and from Camp David, or to *Air Force One*, but when these questions were disquieting in other locations—an airport during arrival on a speaking trip, for instance—a quick command from Speakes or another aide sent the Secret Service to move the reporters to a more inaudible distance.

Speakes's briefings tended to be long and tiresome, with a minimum of information. Veteran correspondents, after being subject to this kind of thing for so many years, began to question whether the briefings and the formal press conferences had ceased to have any real value. The former had become almost perfunctory, and the latter had been so skillfully designed to sell the president to a national television audience that the reporters had become little more than props. At least it could be said that the Reagan staff did not permit itself to be cut off from the press, as Hamilton Jordan had done during the Carter administration. Baker instructed his men not to carry grudges against the newsmen, but human nature made some alterations in these hopeful instructions, and the best that could be said was that the White House learned quickly how to cut its losses.

John Herbers, who had covered the White House for the New York *Times* during the Nixon and Ford administrations, observed in that paper's *Magazine,* ''Many students of the modern Presidency believe that people are less influenced by what the press has to say about the President than by their own perceptions of his performance.'' The truth of that observation, written in 1982, was proved in subsequent months when the president's public approval rating, which had sunk to a historic low during the worst of the recession, coinciding with crises abroad, rose to 53 percent by the summer of 1984, regardless of events or what the media thought about the president's handling of them.

This argues that at least some of the administration's carefully thought-out plans to prevent a bad press were wasted motion. A case in point was its 1984 Supreme Court brief, filed on a Friday afternoon (the best time to minimize or conceal stories), saying that tax breaks would no longer be denied to private schools discriminating on the basis of race. Ann Dore McLaughlin, the Treasury Department's public affairs officer assigned to carry out this strategy, asserted in a memo:

> Release of your statement at 4 P.M. insures that the first wire stories out—and thus the most widely used, especially by the broadcast media—will contain our rationale. An earlier release would give the media more time to conduct interviews with interest groups and thus politicize the story. A later release—one too late for the evening TV news—might cause the networks to hold the story until the next day, which would result in the same kind of expanded political story.

This, McLaughlin added, in a separate memo to the White House, was ''a relatively low-key strategy with maximum control of the story's content.''

The public remained unaware of this kind of planning, designed to influence them. When news of the decision finally reached their eyes and ears, people reacted to it along partisan and ideological lines. The net result was a public relations loss for the administration in the resulting backfire, which went on for weeks. But still the White House was more interested in cause than effect. Gergen had no thoughts on the morality, if any, that was involved, remarking only that ''some of the storm was caused by the way it was put out.'' The flaw, in short, was in the technique, not the idea.

One of the most unabashed efforts to throw out the First Amendment rights of individuals who happened to work for the federal establishment was the presidential order late in 1983 ordering government workers to sign agreements that would ensure censorship of their books, articles, and speeches for the remainder of their lives. The resulting outcry was so great that Congress voted a bill on

November 7 that it thought would stop implementation of the order. Yet, as 1984 began, the National Security Council was ordering fifty agency heads to get four million employees' signatures on the censorship forms, and the administration was moving to avoid the will of Congress in the matter and establish prepublication review as a going institution, regardless of what anyone might think.

It was a logical outcome of the move toward such censorship that began in 1972, with the Central Intelligence Agency's successful censoring of a book by one of its former operatives, Victor Marchetti, in which for the first time in American publishing history a book appeared with blank spaces marking deletions by the government censor—a significant and courageous act on the part of the publisher Alfred A. Knopf. Five years later came the case of Frank Snepp, the CIA's former station man in Saigon, and his book disclosing how the agency had abandoned its friends in the Vietnamese capital. The CIA wanted to apply the same treatment, although there was nothing in the book remotely affecting national security. Snepp resisted, and in 1980 the Burger Court upheld the government, as one would expect. The book was published, but the government took Snepp's royalties and he was required to submit anything he wrote in the future, even novels, to the CIA Publication Review Board.

So much for prior restraint, which the First Amendment had been intended expressly to forbid—violated again, as it had been earlier, by the rising authoritarianism of the imperial presidency. It was exactly this kind of censorship that the Reagan administration was intent on perpetuating in the form of commitments from its workers, forcibly procured on threat of dismissal.

Nicaragua and El Salvador, and Central American policy in general, offered a striking example of how Reagan and his men manipulated information to their own advantage, with little regard for the truth, meanwhile steadily impugning the motives and even the patriotism of the press. One sample, among hundreds, will suffice.

Sometime in 1983 the White House set up what it called the White House Outreach Working Group on Central America, an elaborate name for a propaganda mill. Its task was to provide information of every kind about Central America, all of it reflecting administration policy, to the president's supporters and to provide lists of speakers from which these people could choose proselytizers who might appear in local forums and affect public opinion. Regular meetings were held on Wednesdays for these partisans, but were closed to the press for nearly a year. The operation was under the control of the White House Office of Public Liaison, whose director, a conservative activist named Faith R. Whittlesey, expressed her belief that the American press lacked "fairness or equality" when it talked about human rights in El Salvador, for example.

The intellectual caliber of the Outreach meetings was illustrated by a speech at one of them in June 1984 given by H. Eugene Douglas, ambassador at large and coordinator of refugee affairs, who defended the administration's anticommunist hard line by declaring it would be continued even though "some people, beginning with the East Coast and the media, begin to uncomfortably squirm and stare at their shoes—which are likely manufactured abroad." The ghosts of Nixon and Agnew fluttered over his approving audience. With Reagan, as with Nixon, it was the East Coast, the media, particularly those deadly twins, the New York *Times* and the Washington *Post,* that constituted the perennial enemy, matched or exceeded by the television networks, which were loved and hated in almost equal degree. Nothing had changed.

Television, however, had become an ally of the president as it had never been before, and the actor in the White House used it with great effectiveness in a variety of ways. There was little the networks could do to offset presidential exploitation, and when even a small effort was made to do so, the public response was as swift as it was alarming. In the campaign of 1984, the networks tried to show what went on behind the scenes when the president was about to speak, demonstrating how expert professionals staged these appearances for television, as though they were theater shows. In no time the switchboards of the networks in New York and their affiliates elsewhere lit up as indignant viewers excoriated the broadcasters for attacking the president. Do not confuse me with the facts, they seemed to be saying.

The Reagan media people flooded the country with television images of the president. Not only was he seen looking presidential in the White House rose garden or in other settings at home, but he could also be seen picnicking with an Alabama family, talking to assembly-line workers in Michigan (later advising union leaders to go easy on the automakers who had just reported record years), and putting on a Smokey the Bear hat in Kentucky to proclaim himself as an environmentalist. Reagan and his men were without shame in these endeavors. Just before the election of 1984 the president appeared in a Long Island synagogue wearing a red-white-and-blue yarmulke as he addressed the congregation, thus insulting all religions simultaneously, including a great many offended Jews.

The images were designed to have subliminal effects. If viewers saw the president on Chesapeake Bay, on a Potomac River island, or in Mammoth Cave, Kentucky, they were invited to conclude that he was sincerely working for the environment, in spite of overwhelming evidence to the contrary. Further, in his public utterances, there was always the inference or the outright claim that he had not been given the credit he deserved for these and other accomplishments. The clear implication was that the media had kept the truth from the public.

There was little the media could do to counter these images. Since the days of Vietnam it had been abundantly clear that people did not want to hear the facts if they constituted bad news, unless there was no escape. It was much easier for them to believe the big, confident man whose smiling face they saw so often on television and whose one-liners passed into the national jokebook. If the press persisted in doing its job of probing, searching, trying to find the truth, and reporting it, the public would only think it was biased, unfair, and probably subversive; Reagan and his people constantly encouraged this viewpoint, both explicitly and by innuendo. Even the most able and distinguished reporter, not even the sainted Walter Cronkite, could begin to compete with the presidential image. That was what the president-press relationship had come to at the end of 1984.

The situation was summed up succinctly by Steven R. Weisman, chief White

House correspondent of the New York *Times,* who wrote in that paper's *Magazine:*

> As the campaign of 1984 enters its final weeks, it is increasingly evident that something extraordinary has happened to the relationship between President Reagan and the press. It is not simply that the level of friction is high, for that is typical of an election year. What is now clear is that Mr. Reagan has ignored some of the unstated ground rules under which reporters have traditionally covered the Presidency. As a consequence, he has dramatically altered the kind of information the public receives about him and his administration.
>
> . . . He and his aides have . . . achieved a new level of control over the mechanics of modern communication—the staging of news events for maximum press coverage, the timing of announcements to hit the largest television audiences. Moreover, the President has displayed his news media artistry at a time when television has become the dominant means by which the public gets its news. From the beginning of his Presidency, Mr. Reagan and his aides have understood and exploited what they acknowledge to be the built-in tendency of television to emphasize appearances and impressions more than information.
>
> Central to the President's overall strategy has been his unusual ability to deal with television and print reporters on his own terms—to decide when, where and how he will engage them. In short, the art of controlled access.

Given the emphasis on television in the Reagan media strategy, the question has been raised as to whether it has made the print media irrelevant. But if that is true, no president in recent memory, including Reagan, has believed it, otherwise so much time, money, and effort would not have been spent in creating an elaborate presidential propaganda apparatus designed to circumvent the print journalists. Presidents, in fact, need the print media because television, by its nature and the limitations imposed on it, cannot begin to tell the whole story of what a president is doing—and as every president knows, it can betray and destroy as well as persuade. That was why Nixon and Reagan were so apprehensive about permitting network news departments to have any measure of the same freedom the print media enjoy. Nixon made a serious effort to intimidate and control them. Reagan believed that his personality and general mastery of the news, coupled with his limited-access policy, would obviate anything adverse that television might be doing. Nevertheless he repeatedly demonstrated his hostility to some of its correspondents and news executives.

If a president should accept the notion that he no longer needs the print media, it would be the equivalent of saying that he would no longer be held accountable, since television is not able, particularly when it is a political instrument controlled by the president, to carry out the vital function that the First Amendment first entrusted to the press. To argue that the voters enforce accountability is to say that they would have to rely for their information almost solely on television. The home screen may now be dominant in that sense, but the print media are still demonstrably the prime agents in the forming of public opinion, and because of their great diversity, they can operate at every level, providing the opportunity for everyone to be heard. They are the critical element in making democracy work, as those in undemocratic societies understand all too well.

Taken together, the media unquestionably constitute the only way by which the voters can find out how their elected officials are conducting the nation's business—*their* business—and it would be only logical to believe that they would be deeply concerned that the relationship be improved and kept in good working order. As the events of the past quarter century have shown, however, and with increasing intensity, this is not the case. The campaign of 1984 was a devastating example of how the Reagan media philosophy of limited access for print journalists and maximum exploitation of television could not only succeed but overwhelm, even discredit, any attempts by the media themselves to counterbalance what was being sold to a willing public. The reporters (print and electronic) could be seen shouting their questions to a president who was always just about to disappear into an airplane, a helicopter, or an open doorway. The answers were too trivial or misleading to be recorded. While both sides spent staggering sums on television advertising, it could not have been as effective as the president's appearances in every conceivable kind of favorable situation before audiences guaranteed in advance to be enthusiastic.

When the League of Women Voters attempted to provide some perspective by another edition of the quadrennial television debates, the results only underscored the futility of trying to focus public attention on issues when the viewing public wanted entertainment—something like a national game show. The first debate, in which the president was caught for once without a script and the elaborate electronic means of delivering it, displayed him as the fumbler and bumbler he had been in the early press conferences, before his advisers stopped this kind of political hemorrhaging. In the second debate, reverting to his more comfortable freewheeling style, he was able to offer the customary mixture of half-truths, misinformation, and platitudes, but, much more important, he was perceived to have "won" because he managed to insert a one-liner about his age that got the only laugh in an otherwise drab night. Less partisan voters emerged from these events with the feeling that the debates had proved that neither candidate was qualified to face the issues confronting the nation and the world. And once again the Teflon factor was paramount. Polls showed that Reagan's approval rating did not change and, if anything, increased.

As for the nation's newspapers—whose correspondents in Washington and reporters elsewhere on the campaign trail were evaded, lied to, even scorned and frequently derided by the Reagan machine—whatever the working press may have thought about it, their managements failed to resent this ominous kind of treatment. And not only failed, but according to *Editor & Publisher*'s quadrennial survey, 58 percent of them supported the president, and a mere 9 percent declared for Walter F. Mondale. The minority included most of the best newspapers in the country, and it is true that some of the others (even the Chicago *Tribune*) gave rather grudging support to Reagan, but the message was clear and discouraging in the light of two centuries of press history.

Thus the campaign came down to the moment of truth on November 6, 1984, with the voters apparently oblivious to what was appearing in the news columns.

Within a few days in late October the president seemed to invite soldiers of fortune—mercenaries, that is—to join him in the illegal and undeclared war in Nicaragua; the secretary of state argued that the way to combat terrorism was through undeclared small wars, regardless of consequences; twenty-two ambassadors in the American foreign service took the unprecedented step of endorsing the reelection of a right-wing United States senator, Jesse Helms; and a Supreme Court justice made an ill-disguised political speech for the president, to the shock of many of his colleagues in the bar.

It made no difference. Voters saw and heard Reagan on television telling them that it was their destiny to be proud, strong, prosperous, and peaceful, and only his leadership could ensure it. James Reston, the elder statesman of political columnists, observed in the New York *Times* that Woodrow Wilson had remarked that "once a President had won the admiration and confidence of the country and rightly interpreted the national thought and boldly insisted upon it, he was irresistible." As we have seen, Wilson was cruelly disappointed in that aspiration. Reagan, however, had what Wilson did not have—television and the White House propaganda machine The difference alarmingly illustrated the new era into which America had entered. By means of new technology and new techniques, the president had not only interpreted correctly the national mood of "self-indulgence and acquisitiveness," as Reston put it, but had been able to help create it. It was the ultimate triumph of the image.

How complete a triumph it was became clear in the aftermath of the Reagan landslide of November 1984, when the president's Democratic rival Walter F. Mondale succeeded in carrying only his home state of Minnesota and the District of Columbia. In recent years Richard Nixon alone had been able to achieve such a victory.

While there were other factors involved, most notably the currently buoyant state of the economy, it appeared obvious to many observers, both Democratic and Republican, that the primary element in the voters' overwhelming approval was their perception of Reagan as a strong, confident leader and their response to his personality. Both these factors had been skillfully projected through television, not only in the best-designed political commercials seen since the medium was invented but in the endless ways Reagan was presented to the public as president, meanwhile carefully shielding him from anything but minimal questioning by the press. The projected images had been selected with the utmost care, so that the president was always seen surrounded by smiling faces, flags, familiar scenes, and obviously prospering people.

As Tom Wicker observed in his New York *Times* column, television had become "the new reality of American politics, the eye through which voters now see most of what they know about a Presidential campaign." Or, one might add, a president. Television had not only emerged as the most powerful political instrument ever invented but it was now in the hands of the most able manipulators of the medium yet seen on the political stage. Professionals of both parties could only admire the methods and techniques used. Alvin Hampel, chairman of the New York advertising firm of D'Arcy MacManus Masius, was quoted by Phillip H. Daugherty, advertising columnist of the *Times,* as saying: "It's the kind of advertising we've seen for products. Pure imagery by and large, it surrounds him with beautiful pictures of America. A lot of products tie in to America. It's big, uplifting. It's the kind of advertising that is usually used for a parity product. If you took some of the Reagan footage and put in some other voiceover and sound tracks, you could have the commercial for another product, and vice versa." This advertising was largely the work of an ad hoc volunteer group from the business called the Tuesday Team, most of them experts in selling consumer goods, particularly with commercials employing emotional approaches.

No one was more aware of how great a role television had played in his defeat than Walter Mondale. He told a postelection news conference: "Modern politics requires television. I think you know I've never really warmed up to television, and in fairness to television, it's never really warmed up to me. I don't believe it's possible anymore to run for President without the capacity to build confidence and communications every night. It's got to be done that way."

The significance of what the Reagan team had done was summed up by Raymond Strother, the Washington media consultant who had advised Sen. Gary Hart in the earlier campaigning during the Democratic primaries. "As long as the media, the press, can be manipulated like that," Strother said, "the politician who's going to be supreme is the person who can best manipulate the press." Reagan and the "hidden hands" behind him had proved in the campaign that they were the master manipulators, using not only the commercials to do it but the news itself, so that in the end they exhibited more control over the political content of the evening news reports than the networks' own news organizations.

What could the media expect from Reagan in his second term? It was made chillingly clear in his postelection news conference when a reporter asked if this president who had held fewer press conferences than any other in recent history expected to relax that policy—in short, did he plan to make himself more accessible to the press and therefore more accountable to the voters who had elected him? The president eyed his questioner for a moment with a kind of quizzical contempt, seeming to restrain himself from saying what he might have liked to say. "Look," he told the assembled reporters, "I *won*. I don't have to subject myself to. . . ." He stopped, but the unspoken message was plain. A nervous ripple of laughter greeted this obituary.

After that, the president climbed into his helicopter, whose motors no longer had to be revved up so reporters' shouted questions could not be heard, and prepared to leave for Santa Barbara. He turned and gave the familiar wave with one hand. The other hand clutched a book just given him by James Baker, one of the White House fabricators of the Reagan dream. It was a book called *The Real War*, and the author was Richard M. Nixon. The reporters watched until this precious cargo disappeared in the smog.

On Larry Speakes's desk there was a sign that said, "You don't tell us how to stage the news, and we don't tell you how to cover it." No more candid admission had yet come from the White House that its object was to "stage" the news, no matter what medium it was using to do it. It was an idea that epitomized the

New Age, an epitaph for presidential credibility, which had virtually expired in 1984 as far as the media were concerned.

Thomas Jefferson had an observation on this subject. ''Here,'' he said, meaning the University of Virginia, which he had done so much to create, ''we are not afraid to follow the truth wherever it may lead, nor to tolerate any error so long as reason is left free to combat it.'' The university succeeded in fulfilling that belief. The presidency shows no signs of it after nearly two centuries.

In the end, of course, the president *did* submit himself to press conferences as the second term began because he understood their value as a means of selling his program to the public. There were more conferences, in fact, than there had been before in the hard selling that ensued. Little information and a great deal of propaganda emerged from them. The president also acquired what his conservative supporters viewed as a valuable ally, when Patrick Buchanan was returned to the White House and quickly assumed a close advisory role as director of communications. Buchanan was a former Nixon press aide who had gone on to media riches, as his former employer had done, by means of a right-wing political column and tours of duty as a television commentator. He brought a hardline direction to his new job. To cap these second-term maneuvers, the White House propaganda machine created its own news service—''unfiltered,'' it was said— the first attempt by any President to establish a controlled new organization. It was ominously clear what lay ahead.

Perhaps Nikolai Lenin, a man who believed the press should be an auxiliary of government, should have the last word. Speaking in Moscow in 1920, he inquired: ''Why should a government which believes it is doing what is right allow itself to be criticized? It would not allow opposition by lethal weapons. Ideas are much more fatal things than guns.''

Sources

General

American Heritage Pictorial History of the Presidents of the United States. New York: American Heritage, 1968.

Barrett, James Wyman. *Joseph Pulitzer and His World.* New York: Vanguard Press, 1941.

Carlson, Oliver. *The Man Who Made News.* New York: Duell, Sloan & Pearce, 1942. A biography of James Gordon Bennett, Sr.

Deakin, James. *Straight Stuff: The Reporters, the White House, and the Truth.* New York: William Morrow, 1984.

Dunn, Arthur Wallace. *From Harrison to Harding: A Personal Narrative of a Third of a Century, 1888–1921.* New York: G. P. Putnam's Sons, 1922. Reprint. Port Washington, N.Y.: Kennikat Press, 1971.

Hudson, Frederic. *Journalism in the United States from 1690 to 1872.* New York: Harper & Bros., 1873. Reprint. New York: Harper & Row, 1969.

Kutter, Stanley I., and Stanley N. Katz, eds. ''The Promise of American History: Progress and Prospects.'' *Reviews in American History* 10, no. 4 (December 1982). Includes essays on recent historiography by Eric Foner, Daniel T. Rodgers, and Sean Wilentz.

Lorant, Stefan. *The Presidency.* New York: Macmillan, 1951.

Mott, Frank Luther. *American Journalism.* 3d ed. New York: Macmillan, 1962.

Nevins, Allan, ed. *American Press Opinion: Washington to Coolidge.* Boston: D.C. Heath, 1928.

Pollard, James E. *The Presidents and the Press.* New York: Macmillan, 1947. Supplement. New York: Macmillan, 1972.

Poore, Benjamin Perley. *Perley's Reminiscences of Sixty Years in the National Metropolis.* Philadelphia: Hubbard Bros., 1886.

Seitz, Don C. *The James Gordon Bennetts.* Indianapolis: Bobbs-Merrill, 1928.

Tebbel, John. *A Compact History of the American Newspaper.* New York: Hawthorn Books, 1963.

———. *The Media in America.* New York: Thomas Y. Crowell, 1974.

PART ONE: Foundations

Adams, John. *The Life and Works of John Adams.* Edited by Charles Francis Adams. Boston: Little, Brown, 1856.

Adams, John Quincy. *The Diary of John Quincy Adams.* Edited by Allan Nevins. New York: Longmans, Green, 1928.

———. *Memoirs of John Quincy Adams.* Edited by Charles Francis Adams. 1874–77. Reprint. Freeport, N.Y.: Books for Libraries Press, 1969.

———. *Writings of John Quincy Adams.* Edited by W. C. Ford. 1913–17. Reprint. New York: Greenwood Press, 1968.

Annals of Congress.

Beirne, Francis. *The War of 1812.* New York: E. P. Dutton, 1949.

Bemis, Samuel Flagg. *John Quincy Adams and the Foundations of American Foreign Policy.* New York: Alfred A. Knopf, 1949.

———. *John Quincy Adams and the Union.* New York: Alfred A. Knopf, 1956.

Bowers, Claude G. *Jefferson and Hamilton.* Boston: Houghton Mifflin, 1925.

———. *Jefferson in Power.* Boston: Houghton Mifflin, 1936. Includes passages from Margaret Bayard Smith's *First Forty Years of Washington Society,* a valuable source for the period.

Buell, Richard, Jr. "Freedom of the Press in Revolutionary America." In *The Press and the American Revolution,* edited by Bernard Bailyn and John Hench. American Antiquarian Society, 1980.

Cresson, W. P. *James Monroe.* Chapel Hill: University of North Carolina Press, 1946.

Dangerfield, George. *The Era of Good Feelings.* New York: Harcourt Brace, 1952.

Decatur, Stephen, Jr. *The Private Affairs of George Washington. Documents Relating to the Colonial History of the State of New York.* Vol. 3. Albany, 1953.

Ford, Paul L. *The True George Washington.* Philadelphia: J. B. Lippincott, 1897.

Freeman, Douglas Southall. *George Washington.* Vol. 6, *Patriot and President.* New York: Charles Scribner's Sons, 1954.

Jefferson, Thomas. *Letters and Addresses of Thomas Jefferson.* Edited by William B. Parker and Jonas Vilas. New York: West, 1905.

———. *The Portable Thomas Jefferson.* Edited by Merrill D. Peterson. New York: Viking Press, 1975.

———. *Writings of Thomas Jefferson.* Edited by Paul Leicester Ford. New York: G. P. Putnam's Sons, 1892–99.

Ketcham, Ralph. *James Madison.* New York: Macmillan, 1971.

Lee, A. M. "Dunlap and Claypoole: Printers and News-Merchants of the Revolution." *Journalism Quarterly.* Vol. 11, no. 2, pp. 160–78.

Lipsky, George A. *John Quincy Adams: His Theory and Ideas.* New York: Thomas Y. Crowell, 1950.

Lodge, H. C. *George Washington.* Boston: Houghton Mifflin, 1889.

Madison, James. *The Writings of James Madison.* Edited by Gaillard Hunt. New York: G. P. Putnam's Sons, 1900.

Malone, Dumas. *Jefferson the President: First Term.* Boston: Little, Brown, 1970.

———. *Jefferson and the Rights of Man.* Boston: Little, Brown, 1951.

May, Ernest R. *The Making of the Monroe Doctrine.* Cambridge: Harvard University Press, 1975.

Miller, John C. *Alexander Hamilton: Portrait in Paradox.* New York: Harper & Bros., 1959.

Monroe, James. *The Writings of James Monroe.* Edited by Stanislaus Murray Hamilton. New York, 1969.

Morse, John T. *John Quincy Adams.* New York: Chelsea House, 1980. Includes details on the story of Adams and the "beautiful American girl."

Mott, Frank Luther. *Jefferson and the Press.* Baton Rouge: Louisiana State University Press, 1943.

————, ed. *Oldtime Comments on Journalism*. Vol. 1, no. 5. Columbia, Mo.: Press of the Crippled Turtle, 1955.

Perkins, Bradford. *Castlereagh and Adams: England and the United States*. Berkeley: University of California Press, 1964.

Perkins, Dexter. *The Monroe Doctrine*. Cambridge: Harvard University Press, 1932.

Smith, Abbot Emerson. *James Madison, Builder*. New York: Wilson-Ericsson, 1937.

Smith, James Morton. *Freedom's Fetters*. Ithaca: Cornell University Press, 1956. Reprint. Ithaca: Cornell University Paperback, 1966. The best individual study of the Alien and Sedition Acts.

————, and Paul L. Murphy, eds. *Liberty and Justice: American Constitutional Development to 1869*. New York, 1965.

Smith, Page. *John Adams*. Garden City: Doubleday, 1962.

Washington, George. *Writings of George Washington*. Boston: Russell, Odiorne and Metcalf, 1838.

Wilmerding, Lucius, Jr. *James Monroe, Public Claimant*. New Brunswick: Rutgers University Press, 1960.

PART TWO: The Rise of Manipulation

Bassett, John Spencer. *The Life of Andrew Jackson*. New York: Macmillan, 1925.

Bowers, Claude G. *The Party Battles of the Jackson Period*. New York: Octagon Books, 1965.

Chitwood, Oliver Perry. *John Tyler*. New York: Russell and Russell, 1939.

Crockett, David. *Life of Martin Van Buren*. Philadelphia: R. Wright, 1837.

Dangerfield, George. *The Era of Good Feelings*. New York: Harcourt Brace, 1952.

Fraser, Hugh Russell. *Democracy in the Making: The Jackson-Tyler Era*. New York: Bobbs-Merrill, 1938.

Holmes, Alexander. *The American Tallyrand*. New York: Harper & Bros., 1935. A treatment of Martin Van Buren that includes discussion of his manipulative abilities.

Parton, James. *Life of Andrew Jackson*. Boston: Houghton Mifflin, 1888.

Remini, Robert V. *Andrew Jackson and the Course of American Freedom, 1822–1832*. New York: Harper & Row, 1983.

————. *Martin Van Buren and the Making of the Democratic Party*. New York: Columbia University Press, 1951.

————. *The Revolutionary Age of Andrew Jackson*. New York: Harper & Row, 1976.

Richardson, James D., ed. *Messages and Papers of the Presidents*.

Ritchie, Thomas. "Unpublished Letters of Thomas Ritchie." Edited by Charles H. Ambler. *John P. Branch Historical Papers* 3 (June 1911).

Schiller, Dan. *Objectivity in the News: The Public and the Rise of Commercial Journalism*. Philadelphia: University of Pennsylvania Press, 1981. An examination of the "great man" concept of journalism's rise versus the contributions of the penny press and a review of relevant scholarship.

Schlesinger, Arthur M., Jr. *The Age of Jackson*. Boston: Little, Brown, 1946.

Seager, Robert, II. *And Tyler Too*. New York: McGraw-Hill, 1963.

Smith, Culver Haygood. "The Washington Press in the Jacksonian Period." Ph.D. diss., New York University. A detailed view of the Jacksonian press.

Smith, William E. *The Francis Preston Blair Family in Politics*. New York: Da Capo Press, 1969.

Tyler, John. *The Letters and Times of the Tylers*. Edited by L. G. Tyler. New York: Da Capo Press, 1970.

Van Buren, Martin. *Autobiography of Martin Van Buren*. Washington, D.C.: Government Printing Office, 1920.

Van Deusen, Glyndon G. *The Jacksonian Era*. New York: Harper & Bros., 1959.

Webster, Daniel. *Letters of Daniel Webster*. Edited by C. H. Van Tyne. 1902.

PART THREE: The Power of the Presidency

Andrews, J. Cutler. *The North Reports the Civil War*. Pittsburgh: University of Pittsburgh Press, 1955.

Barnes, Thurlow Weed. *Memoir of Thurlow Weed*. Boston: Houghton Mifflin, 1884.

Bauer, K. Jack. *The Mexican War, 1846–1848*. New York: Macmillan, 1974. The best account of the war available to the general reader.

Brooks, Noah. *Washington in Lincoln's Time*. Edited by Herbert Mitgang. Chicago: Quadrangle Books, 1971.

Crozier, Emmet. *Yankee Reporters, 1861–65*. New York: Oxford University Press, 1956.

Curtis, George Ticknor. *Life of James Buchanan*. New York: Harper & Bros., 1883.

Dyer, Brainerd. *Zachary Taylor*. New York: Barnes & Noble, 1946.

Fillmore, Millard. *Millard Fillmore Papers*. Edited by Frank H. Severance. Buffalo: Buffalo Historical Society, 1907.

Greeley, Horace. *Recollections of a Busy Life*. New York: J. B. Ford, 1868.

Hale, William Harlan. *Horace Greeley: Voice of the People*. New York: Harper & Bros., 1950.

Hamilton, Holman. *Zachary Taylor: Soldier of the Republic*. 1941–51. Reprint. Hamden, Conn.: Archon Books, 1966.

Harper, Robert S. *Lincoln and the Press*, New York: McGraw-Hill, 1951.

Hawthorne, Nathaniel. *Life of Franklin Pierce*. Papers of the People, no. 2. New York, 1852.

Herndon, William H., and Jesse William Wilk. *Herndon's Lincoln: The True Story of a Great Life*. Chicago: Belford, Clark, 1889.

Horner, Harlan Hoyt. *Lincoln and Greeley*. Urbana: University of Illinois Press, 1953.

Ireland, John R. *History of the Life, Administration and Times of Zachary Taylor*. Chicago: Fairbanks and Palmer, 1888.

Klein, Philip Shriver. *President James Buchanan: A Biography*. University Park: Pennsylvania State University Press, 1926.

McCormac, Eugene Irving. *James K. Polk*. New York: Russell and Russell, 1965.

Marszalek, John F. *Sherman's Other War: The General and the Civil War Press*. Memphis: Memphis State University Press, 1981.

Mitgang. Herbert. *Abraham Lincoln: A Press Portrait*. Chicago: Quadrangle Books, 1971.

Nevins, Allan. *The Emergence of Lincoln*. New York: Charles Scribner's Sons, 1950.

Nichols, Roy F. *Franklin Pierce: Young Hickory of the Granite Hills*. Philadelphia: University of Pennsylvania Press, 1958.

Polk, James K. *Polk: The Diary of a President, 1845–1849*. Edited by Allan Nevins. New York: Longmans, Green, 1952. The complete diary was published in four volumes in 1910 by A. C. McClurg, of Chicago, for the Chicago Historical Society, but the edition was only five hundred copies. The manuscript is in the society's collection.

Rayback, Robert J. *Millard Fillmore*. Buffalo: Henry Stewart, 1959.

Reynolds, Donald E. *Editors Make War: Southern Newspapers in the Secession Crisis*. Nashville: Vanderbilt University Press, 1966.

Sandburg, Carl. *Abraham Lincoln: The Prairie Years*. New York: Harcourt Brace, 1926.
————. *Abraham Lincoln: The War Years*. New York: Harcourt Brace, 1939.
Schlesinger, Arthur M., Jr. *The Imperial Presidency*. Boston: Houghton Mifflin, 1973.
Schroeder, John H. *Mr. Polk's War: American Opposition and Dissent*. Madison: University of Wisconsin Press, 1973.
Sellers, Charles Grier, Jr. *James K. Polk*. Princeton: Princeton University Press, 1957.
Smith, Elbert B. *The Presidency of James Buchanan*. Lawrence: University Press of Kansas, 1975.
Tebbel, John. *An American Dynasty*. New York: Doubleday, 1947.
Townsend, George Alfred. *Washington Outside and Inside*. Hartford: James Betts, 1873.
Weisberger, Bernard A. *Reporters for the Union*. Boston: Little, Brown, 1953.

PART FOUR: The Aftermath of Power

Armstrong, William M. *E. L. Godkin and American Foreign Policy, 1865–1900*. New York: Bookman Associates, 1957.
Baer, Harry. *The New York Tribune since the Civil War*. New York: Octagon Books, 1972.
Barry, David S. *Forty Years in Washington*. Boston: Little, Brown, 1924.
————. "News-Gathering at the Capital." *Chatauquan*, December 1897, pp. 282–86.
Bishop, Joseph Bucklin. "Newspaper Espionage." *Forum*. Vol. 1, pp. 528–37.
Bowers, Claude G. *The Tragic Era*. Cambridge: Riverside Press, 1929.
Caldwell, Robert Granville. *James A. Garfield, Party Chieftain*. 1931. Reprint. Hamden, Conn.: Archon Books, 1965.
Castel, Albert. *The Presidency of Andrew Johnson*. Lawrence: University Press of Kansas, 1979.
Cleveland, Grover. *Letters of Grover Cleveland*. Edited by Allan Nevins. Boston: Houghton Mifflin, 1933.
Davison, Kenneth C. *The Presidency of Rutherford B. Hayes*. Westport, Conn.: Greenwood Press, 1972.
Doenecke, Justin D. *The Presidencies of James A. Garfield and Chester A. Arthur*. Lawrence: Regents Press of Kansas, 1981. The most recent assessment of Garfield's presidency.
Garfield, James A. *The Diary of James A. Garfield*. Edited by Harry James Brown and Frederick D. Williams. East Lansing: Michigan State University Press, 1967.
————. *Works of James Abram Garfield*. Edited by Burke Aaron Hinsdale. Boston: J. R. Osgood, 1882.
Glad, Paul W. *McKinley, Bryan, and the People*. Philadelphia: J. B. Lippincott, 1964.
Glasser, Theodore L. "Objectivity Precludes Responsibility." *Quill*, February 1984, pp. 13ff.
Gould, Lewis L. *The Presidency of William McKinley*. Lawrence: Regents Press of Kansas.
Green, Horace. "Grant's Last Stand." *Harper's Weekly*, January 6, 1887, p. 315.
Grossman, Michael Baruch, and Martha Joynt Kumar. *Portraying the President: The White House and the News Media*. Baltimore: Johns Hopkins University Press, 1981.
Hayes, Rutherford B. *Diary and Letters of Rutherford B. Hayes*. Edited by C. R. Williams. Ohio Archaeological and Historical Society, 1922–26.
————. *Hayes: The Diary of a President*. Edited by T. Harry Williams. New York: David McKay, 1963.

Howe, George Frederick. *Chester A. Arthur: A Quarter Century of Machine Politics.* New York: Frederick Ungar, 1935.

Howells, William Dean. *Sketch of the Life and Character of Rutherford B. Hayes.* New York: Hurd and Houghton, 1876.

Juergens, George. *Joseph Pulitzer and the New York World.* Princeton: Princeton University Press, 1966.

Leech, Margaret. *In the Time of McKinley.* New York: Harper & Bros., 1959.

Lynch, Denis Tilden. *Grover Cleveland: A Man Four-Square.* New York: Horace Liveright, 1932.

McFeeley, William S. *Grant.* New York: W. W. Norton, 1981. A much-praised biography that includes detailed account of Jay Gould's attempt to corner the gold market and Black Friday.

Merrill, Horace Samuel. *Bourbon Leader: Grover Cleveland and the Democratic Party.* Boston: Little, Brown, 1957.

Milton, George F. *The Age of Hate.* New York: Coward McCann, 1930.

Mitchell, Edward P. *Memoirs of an Editor.* New York: Charles Scribner's Sons, 1924.

Morgan, H. Wayne. *William McKinley and His America.* Syracuse: Syracuse University Press, 1963.

Murray, Robert K., and Tim H. Blessing. "The Presidential Performance Study: A Progress Report." *Journal of American History.* Vol. 70, no. 3.

Nevins, Allan. *Grover Cleveland: A Study in Courage.* New York: Dodd, Mead, 1933.

Olcott, Charles A. *William McKinley.* Boston: Houghton Mifflin, 1916.

Peskin, Allan. *Garfield.* Kent: Kent State University Press, 1978.

Reeves, Thomas C. *Gentleman Boss: The Life of Chester Alan Arthur.* New York: Alfred A. Knopf, 1975.

Schirmer, Daniel B. *Republic or Empire: American Resistance to the Philippine War.* Cambridge: Schenkman, 1972.

Sievers, Harry J. *Benjamin Harrison.* Indianapolis: Bobbs-Merrill, 1968.

Smith, Theodore Clarke. *The Life and Letters of James Abram Garfield.* 1925. Reprint. Hamden, Conn.: Archon Books, 1968.

Stryker, Lloyd Paul. *Andrew Johnson.* New York: Macmillan, 1929.

Tarbell, Ida M. "President McKinley in War Times." *McClure's Magazine,* July 1898, pp. 2080–86.

Tebbel, John. *The Life and Good Times of William Randolph Hearst.* New York: E. P. Dutton, 1952.

Thomas, Lately. *The First President Johnson.* New York: William Morrow, 1968.

Tugwell, Rexford G. *Grover Cleveland.* New York: Macmillan, 1968.

Welles, Gideon. *Diary of Gideon Welles.* Boston: Houghton Mifflin, 1911.

White, William Allen. *Masks in a Pageant.* New York: Macmillan, 1928.

PART FIVE: The Imperial Presidency

Anderson, Donald F. *William Howard Taft: A Conservative's Perception of the Presidency.* Ithaca: Cornell University Press.

Anderson, Paul Y. "Hoover and the Press." *Nation,* October 14, 1931.

Baillie, Hugh. *High Tension.* New York: Harper & Bros., 1959.

Baker, Ray Stannard. *Woodrow Wilson: Youth.* Garden City: Doubleday, Page, 1927.

———. *Woodrow Wilson and World Settlement.* 1922.

Barry, Robert T. Article in *Editor & Publisher,* March 12, 1923.

Bishop, Joseph B. *Theodore Roosevelt and His Times: Shown in His Own Letters.* New York: Charles Scribner's Sons, 1920.

Borck, Oscar Theodore, Jr., and Manfred Blake Nelson. *Since 1900: A History of the United States in Our Times.* New York: Macmillan, 1947. Includes an account of the Bonus March.

Burner, David. *Herbert Hoover: A Public Life.* New York: Alfred A. Knopf, 1979.

Butt, Archibald W., ed. *Taft and Roosevelt: The Intimate Letters of Archie Butt, Military Aide.* Garden City: Doubleday, Doran, 1930.

Coletta, Paoela E. *The Presidency of William Howard Taft.* Lawrence: University Press of Kansas, 1973.

Coolidge, Calvin. *Autobiography of Calvin Coolidge.* New York: Cosmopolitan Book Corporation, 1929.

Cornwell, Elmer E., Jr. *Presidential Leadership of Public Opinion.* Bloomington: Indiana University Press, 1965.

Cuneo, Sherman. *From Printer to President.* Philadelphia: Dorrance, 1922.

Davis, Oscar King. *Released for Publication.* Boston: Houghton Mifflin, 1925.

Filler, Louis. *The Muckrakers: Crusaders for American Liberalism.* 1939. Paperback ed. Chicago: Henry Regnery, 1968. A classic in its field since it was first published.

Fuess, Claude M. *Calvin Coolidge: The Man from Vermont.* 1940. Reprint. Hamden, Conn.: Archon Books, 1965.

Gramling, Oliver. *AP: The Story of News.* New York: Farrar and Rinehart, 1940.

Hilderbrand, Robert C. *Power and the People: Executive Management of Public Opinion in Foreign Affairs, 1897–1921.* Chapel Hill: University of North Carolina Press, 1981.

Hoover, Herbert. *Memoirs.* 1951–52.

Hoover, Ike. *Forty Years in the White House.* Boston: Houghton Mifflin, 1934.

Johnson, Paul. *Modern Times: The World from the Twenties to the Eighties.* New York: Harper & Row, 1983.

Juergens, George. *News from the White House: The Presidential-Press Relationship in the Progressive Era.* Chicago: University of Chicago Press, 1981.

Link, Arthur S. *Wilson: The New Freedom.* Princeton: Princeton University Press, 1956.

Lloyd, Craig. *Aggressive Introvert: A Study of Herbert Hoover and Public Relations Management, 1912–1932.* Columbus: Ohio State University Press, 1972.

Lowry, Edward. *Washington Close-ups: Intimate Views of Some Public Figures.* Boston: Houghton Mifflin, 1921.

McAdoo, Eleanor Wilson. *The Woodrow Wilsons.* New York: Macmillan, 1937.

McCoombs, William F. *Making Woodrow Wilson President.* New York: Fairview, 1921.

McCoy, Donald R. *Calvin Coolidge: The Quiet President.* New York: Macmillan, 1967.

McCullough, David. *Mornings on Horseback.* New York: Simon and Schuster, 1981. A study of Theodore Roosevelt.

Manning, George. Articles in *Editor & Publisher,* July 18, September 5, and October 16, 1931.

Morris, Edmund. *The Rise of Theodore Roosevelt.* New York: Coward, McCann & Geoghegan, 1979.

Oulahan, Richard. "Capitol Corps Praised." *Editor & Publisher,* April 25, 1931.

Pringle, Henry F. *Theodore Roosevelt.* New York: Harcourt Brace & World, 1931.

Romasco, Albert U. *The Poverty of Abundance: Hoover, the Nation, and the Depression.* New York: Oxford University Press, 1965.

Rovere, Richard. *Final Reports.* New York: Doubleday, 1984.

Russell, Francis. *The Shadow of Blooming Grove.* New York: McGraw-Hill, 1968.

Steffens, Lincoln. *The Autobiography of Lincoln Steffens.* New York: Harcourt Brace, 1931. Paperback ed. 1958.

Sullivan, Mark. *Our Times.* Vol. 3, *Pre-War America.* New York: Charles Scribner's Sons, 1930.

Tebbel, John. *George Horace Lorimer and the Saturday Evening Post.* New York: Doubleday, 1948. Coolidge material in this book is from Lorimer's private papers, now in the collections of the Pennsylvania Historical Society, Philadelphia, and from interviews by the author with Garet Garrett and other *Post* writers.

Tumulty, Joseph P. *Woodrow Wilson as I Knew Him.* Garden City: Doubleday, Page, 1924.

Villard, Oswald Garrison. ''The Press and the President.'' *Century Magazine,* December 1925.

Weinstein, Edwin A. *Woodrow Wilson: A Medical and Psychological Biography.* Princeton: Princeton University Press, 1981.

Westrate, John Lee. *The Presidency: Political Leadership and Public Relations.*

White, William Allen. *Calvin Coolidge.* New York: Macmillan, 1925.

———. *Woodrow Wilson.* Boston: Houghton Mifflin, 1924.

Wilson, Woodrow. ''Committee or Cabinet Government.'' *Overland Monthly,* January 1884. In *The Woodrow Wilson Papers.* Edited by Arthur S. Link. Vol. 2, p. 629. Princeton: Princeton University Press, 1966.

———. *The New Freedom.* 1913. Reprint ed. Englewood Cliffs, N.J.: Prentice-Hall, 1961.

———. Press conferences on microfilm at Princeton University Library.

———. *The Public Papers of Woodrow Wilson.* Edited by Ray Stannard Baker and William C. Dodd. New York: Harper & Bros., 1926.

PART SIX: The Presidency Triumphant

Barrett, Laurence I. *Gambling with History: Ronald Reagan in the White House.* New York: Doubleday, 1983.

Bernstein, Lester. Review of *The Other Side of the Story,* by Jody Powell. New York *Times Book Review,* April 1, 1984, p. 7.

Burns, James MacGregor. *Roosevelt: The Lion and the Fox.* New York: Harcourt Brace & World, 1956.

Deakin, James. *Johnson's Credibility Gap.* Washington, D.C.: Public Affairs Press, 1968.

Donavan, Robert J. *Eisenhower: The Inside Story.* New York: Harper & Bros., 1956.

Eisenhower, Dwight D. *The White House Years: Mandate for Change, 1953–1956.* New York: Doubleday, 1966.

Evans, Rowland, and Robert Novak. *Lyndon B. Johnson: The Exercise of Power.* New York: New American Library, 1966.

Ford, Gerald R. *A Time to Heal.* New York: Harper & Row and Reader's Digest Association, 1979.

Goldman, Eric. *The Tragedy of Lyndon Johnson.* New York: Alfred A. Knopf, 1969.

Gosnell, Harold F. *Champion Campaigner: Franklin D. Roosevelt.* New York: Macmillan, 1952.

Griffith, Robert. Article in *Reviews in American History,* September 1981.

Hallin, Dan. ''The Myth of the Adversary Press.'' *Quill,* November 1983, pp. 31ff.

Heller, Francis H. *The Truman White House: The Administration of the Presidency, 1945–1953.* Lawrence: Regents Press of Kansas, 1980.

Herbers, John. "The Press and the Press Corps." New York *Times Magazine,* May 9, 1982.

Hughes, Emmet John. *The Ordeal of Power: A Political Memoir of the Eisenhower Years.* New York: Atheneum Press, 1963.

Ickes, Harold. *The Secret Diary of Harold L. Ickes.* Vol. 1, *The First Thousand Days, 1933–36.* New York: Simon and Schuster, 1953.

Jones, Alfred Haworth. *Roosevelt's Image Brokers: Poets, Playwrights, and the Use of the Lincoln Symbol.* Reprint. Port Washington, N.Y.: National University Publications, Kennikat Press, 1974.

Kearns, Doris. *Lyndon Johnson and the American Dream.* New York: Harper & Row, 1976.

Keogh, James. *President Nixon and the Press.* New York: Funk & Wagnalls, 1972.

Kern, Montague, Patricia W. Levering, and Ralph B. Levering. *The Kennedy Crisis: The Press, the Presidency, and Foreign Policy.* Chapel Hill: University of North Carolina Press, 1983.

Larson, Arthur. *Eisenhower: The President Nobody Knows.* New York: Charles Scribner's Sons, 1968.

Lasch, Christopher. Review of *Nightmare: The Underside of the Nixon Years,* by J. Anthony Lukas. New York *Times Book Review,* January 23, 1976, p. 24.

Louchheim, Katie, ed. *The Making of the New Deal: The Insiders Speak.* Cambridge: Harvard University Press, 1983.

Lukas, J. Anthony. "The White House Press 'Club.'" New York *Times Magazine,* May 15, 1977, pp. 67–68.

McAuliffe, Mary S. "Eisenhower the President." *Journal of American History,* December 1981.

McKenzie, Angus. "The Big Chill." *Quill,* March 1984. A detailed analysis of the Reagan administration's moves toward censorship.

Maglish, Bruce, and Edwin Diamond. *Jimmy Carter: A Character Portrait.* New York: Simon and Schuster, 1979.

Meyer, Peter. *James Earl Carter: The Man and the Myth.* Kansas City: Sheed, Andrews and McMeel, 1978.

Miller, Merle. *Lyndon: An Oral Biography.* New York: G. P. Putnam's Sons, 1980.

———. *Plain Speaking: An Oral Biography of Harry Truman.* New York: Berkley, 1973.

Nessen, Ron. *It Sure Looks Different from the Inside.* New York: Playboy Press, 1978.

Nixon, Richard M. *Memoirs of Richard Nixon.* New York: Grosset & Dunlap, 1978.

Osborne, John. *White House Watch: The Ford Years.* Washington, D.C.: New Republic Books, 1977.

Reeves, Richard. *A Ford, Not a Lincoln.* New York: Harcourt Brace Jovanovich, 1975.

———. "The Prime-Time President." New York *Times Magazine,* May 15, 1977, p. 18.

Richardson, Elmo. *The Presidency of Dwight D. Eisenhower.* Lawrence: Regents Press of Kansas, 1979.

Rivers, William L. *The Other Government: Power and the Washington Media.* New York: Universe Books, 1982.

Salinger, Pierre. *With Kennedy.* New York: Doubleday, 1966. Includes a full explanation of Salinger's viewpoint on reporting of the Vietnam government's crisis in 1963.

Schell, Jonathan. *The Time of Illusion.* New York: Alfred A. Knopf, 1976.

Schlesinger, Arthur M., Jr. *A Thousand Days: John F. Kennedy in the White House.* Boston: Houghton Mifflin, 1965.

Shoup, Laurence H. *The Carter Presidency and Beyond*. Palo Alto, Calif.: Ramparts Press, 1980.

Sidey, Hugh. *John F. Kennedy, President*. New York: Atheneum Press, 1963.

————. *Lyndon Johnson*. New York: Atheneum Press, 1968.

Smith, Merriman. *Thank You, Mr. President: A White House Notebook*. New York: Harper & Bros., 1946.

Sorenson, Theodore G. *Kennedy*. New York: Harper & Row, 1965.

Spragens, William C., and Carole Ann Terwoord. *From Spokesman to Press Secretary: White House Media Operations*. Washinton, D.C.: University Press of America, 1980.

Steinberg, Alfred. *The Man from Missouri: The Life and Times of Harry Truman*. New York: G. P. Putnam's Sons, 1962.

Thompson, Kenneth W., ed. *Ten Presidents and the Press*. Washington, D.C.: University Press of America, 1980.

Truman, Harry S. *The Autobiography of Harry S Truman*. Edited by Robert H. Ferrell. Boulder, Colo.: Associated University Press, 1980.

Weisman, Steven H. "The President and the Press: The Art of Controlled Access." New York *Times Magazine,* October 14, 1984.

White, Graham, J. *FDR and the Press*. Chicago: University of Chicago Press, 1979.

White, Theodore H. *The Making of the President, 1964*. New York: Signet Books, 1966.

Whiteside, Thomas. "Annals of Television." *The New Yorker,* March 17, 1975, pp. 42ff. Includes an analysis of Nixon's attack on the media.

Newspapers and Periodicals

Albany *Argus*
Cincinnati *Gazette*
Editor & Publisher
Gazette of the United States. Includes House debates.
Huntress
Louisville *Courier-Journal*
Madisonian
Nation
National Intelligencer
National Journal
New York *Evening Post*
New York *Herald*
New-York Journal
New York *Sun*
New York *Times*
New York *Tribune*
New York *World*
Niles' Register
Philadelphia *Aurora*
Richmond *Enquirer*
Springfield *Republican*
Washington *Globe*
Washington *Republic*
Washington *Union*

Index

National Review, 534
National security, 48, 487, 488
National Union movement, 210
Nelson, Bill, 459
Nelson, Henry Loomis, 302
Nesselrode, Karl Robert, 158
Nessen, Ron, 518–21
Neville, Jack, 389
Nevins, Allan, 10, 45, 112, 148, 149, 167–69, 256, 320
New, John, 280
New England
  opposition to War of 1812, 47, 49, 50
  opposition to war with Mexico, 123–24
New Hampshire Patriot, 64, 72, 78, 88, 150
New Haven *Herald,* 54
New Haven *Journal,* 78
Newman, Oliver P., 371
New Orleans *Delta,* 127
New Orleans *Picayune,* 128, 131, 133
New Republic, 320, 386, 416, 428, 430
Newspapers, 334, 436
  chains, 308. *See also specific chain*
  destruction, in Civil War, 194
  early twentieth century, 320
  free subscriptions to presidents, 56
  increase in, between 1810, and 1828, 75
  influence
    in Madison's time, 45–46
    in McKinley's administration, 298
  Jefferson on, 39–40
  in Jefferson's administration, 30
  Jefferson's collection of, 40
  official, 27, 208. *See also specific paper*
  opposing FDR, 437, 438, 452
  partisan. *See* Press, partisan
  in post-Revolutionary America, 8–9
  in 1780s to 1800, 7
Newsreel, 443
Newsweek, 485, 503, 508, 526, 530
New York *Advertiser,* 60
New York *Age,* 254
New York *American,* 64, 93
New York *Argus,* 15
New York *Aurora,* 107
New York *Commercial Advertiser,* 189
New York *Courier and Enquirer,* 86, 87, 92, 93, 128, 131, 133, 218
New York *Daily Graphic,* 235, 238, 239
New York *Daily News,* 191, 192, 438, 444, 503
New York *Day-Book,* 191
New York *Enquirer,* 64, 70, 78, 86
New York *Evening Journal,* 115, 142, 145, 297, 300, 305, 306, 315, 317, 382

New York *Evening Post,* 35–36, 46, 88, 96, 103, 115, 124, 129, 148, 155, 166, 169, 174, 185, 189, 190, 202, 203, 207, 211, 224, 261, 262, 274, 289, 290, 295, 297, 300, 306, 317, 323, 325, 326, 342, 385, 389, 452
New York *Evening Sun,* 326
New York *Express,* 144
New York *Gazetteer,* 5, 8
New York *Globe,* 87, 92, 135
New York *Herald,* 9, 75, 79, 87, 92, 95, 96, 98, 106–10, 115, 119, 121, 124, 127–29, 144, 147, 149, 154–55, 161, 162, 165, 168, 173, 176, 178, 181–83, 187–89, 196, 202, 205, 207, 209, 212, 215, 218–21, 226, 227, 241, 246, 255, 262, 272, 283, 295, 300, 306, 342, 367, 377, 387
New York *Herald Tribune,* 448, 452, 458, 468, 503
New York *Independent,* 170, 206, 235, 294, 382
New-York Journal, 13–14
New York *Journal of Commerce,* 123, 166
New York *Mail and Express,* 280
New York *National Advocate,* 62
New York *Plebeian,* 107
New York *Press,* 367
New York State Register, 142, 143
New York *Sun,* 125–26, 189, 203, 218, 221, 222, 226, 227, 231, 234, 245, 246, 248, 261, 263, 276, 282, 286, 291–92, 295, 300, 306, 316, 317, 328, 340, 342, 355, 356
New York *Telegram,* 412
New York *Times,* 57, 146–48, 169, 174, 175, 178, 180, 181, 185, 189, 190, 202, 205–7, 212–15, 218, 219, 221, 224, 228, 229, 231, 237, 238, 243, 249, 253, 254, 262, 267, 273, 275, 283, 285–86, 290, 296, 306, 323, 325, 336, 339, 342, 351, 356, 360, 363, 367, 370, 379, 383–86, 388, 389, 394, 411, 413, 415, 422, 443, 448, 451, 466, 478, 480, 481, 483, 487, 503, 508, 510, 511, 513, 522, 525, 530, 548, 551
New York *Tribune,* 99, 110, 119, 124, 131, 132, 141, 148, 149, 154, 155, 165–67, 174, 189, 194, 202, 205, 207, 211, 212, 214, 222, 224, 225, 236, 238, 241–43, 245, 249, 254, 255, 266, 267, 273, 274, 280, 283, 290, 306, 342, 370, 384–85, 389, 398
New York *Truth,* 245